The Golden Age of

Top 40 Music

(1955 - 1973)

On Compact Disc

by Pat Downey

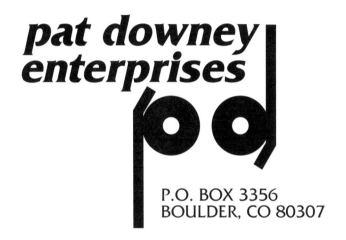

**pat downey
enterprises**

P.O. BOX 3356
BOULDER, CO 80307

Library of Congress catalog card number: 92-90455
ISBN 0-9633718-1-9

Printed in the United States of America and published independently by
Pat Downey Enterprises, P.O. Box 3356, Boulder, CO 80307.

TABLE OF CONTENTS

THE GOLDEN AGE OF TOP 40 MUSIC (1955-1973) ON COMPACT DISC

INTRODUCTION

The popularity of the compact disc format in the music industry has prompted record labels to remaster original analog tape recordings for release on compact disc. As consumers have discovered, sometimes at great expense, this renaissance has been completed with varying degrees of success. I have written this book to qualitatively look at the thousands of compact discs that have been released featuring the Top 40 hits of yesteryear.

When I first set out to write this book, I quickly discovered that a number of difficult decisions needed to be addressed such as what compact discs should be included in this effort and how should I develop a database of Top 40 hits. The latter was the easiest to resolve as I elected to use chart data taken from the respected music industry publication, *Cash Box*. The *Cash Box* chart data is used with permission from *Cash Box* and is taken from a previously released book, *THE CASH BOX SINGLES CHARTS 1950-1981* published by Frank Hoffmann in 1983. Frank elected to use the *Cash Box* "Nation's Top Juke Box Tunes" charts through July 28, 1956 and starting August 4, 1956 the "Best Selling Records" charts were used.

The first section, known as the ARTIST section, is an alphabetical listing of all artists who scored a hit on *Cash Box* magazine's pop singles charts which peaked in popularity from 1955 to 1973. Listed below each artist you will find a chronological listing of each song that particular artist placed in the national Top 40. The year of peak popularity and the highest chart position attained on the *Cash Box* charts is included for each song title, followed by any pertinent data peculiar to each compact disc appearance of that song. Please note that some of the compact discs referenced in this book may not be currently in print. Your local compact disc store or reputable mail order dealer such as DISCOLLECTOR (303-841-3000) should be able to advise you as to current availability. If a compact disc is out of print, I would recommend that you search for that compact disc at a store specializing in used compact discs.

If you recognize a song by its title and not the artist, then the second section known as the SONG TITLE section, will cross reference you to all the artists that have had a Top 40 hit with a specific song.

In preparing this book I have elected not to reference the following compact discs:

1) import compact discs

2) mail order compact discs

3) domestic compact discs whose content does not live up to the sound quality expected on compact disc

4) compact discs which contain obviously live recordings such as James Brown's "Live At The Apollo"

5) compact discs that are not readily available for retail stores to order, such as "Special Products" divisions of many major compact disc labels

6) 3" compact discs

7) special promotional only samplers that were never available for retail sale

The decision as to which domestic compact discs to include in this book was entirely made at the author's discretionary judgement.

Every reasonable effort has been made to assure the accuracy of the data included in this book but due to the size of the publication, some errors will unfortunately occur.

I must give special thanks and acknowledgment to Mike Hawkinson for his valuable insight and encouragement in the development of this book.

Pat Downey

EXPLANATION OF SYMBOLS AND TERMINOLOGY

SYMBOLS:

(M)   MONOPHONIC, with no separation in sound from left to right channel.

(S)   STEREOPHONIC, with a separation in sound from left to right channel.

(E)   ELECTRONIC, indicating some form of processing used to make a mono recording sound like it has separation from left to right channel. An example would be taking a mono recording and adding a slight time delay to one channel in an attempt to trick the ear into believing a song is really stereo. Another example of electronic processing would be emphasizing the high frequencies on one channel while emphasizing the low frequencies on the other. Remember that processing of this nature must be done after the session tape has been recorded so that you may be assured of not getting a first generation transfer from analog tape to digital when you see the (E) symbol. Electronic "doctoring" almost always results in a degradation of sound quality.

O.S.T.   ORIGINAL SOUND TRACK.

cd   COMPACT DISC.

LP   LONG PLAY, which is the nomenclature originally used for the record album.

45   45 RPM 7" RECORD, also known as a "single".

(X:XX)   TIME in minutes and seconds. This is the exact playing time of the song; not necessarily the time printed on the cd jacket, the cd itself, or the cd packaging. Even the time encoded on the cd and displayed on your cd player can be inaccurate if there is some "dead air" placed at the beginning or end of a selection.

dj   DISC JOCKEY.

►   This symbol is used exclusively in the title section to designate that a title is available on compact disc.

TERMINOLOGY:

alternate take	Not the version used for the original hit recording but another very similar sounding take probably recorded at the same recording session as the hit version.
cold	No fadeout.
countoff	Brief counting of numbers such as one, two, three that musicians use to synchronize all members of the recording session to the start of a song.
dropout	A temporary loss of signal.
intro	Introduction
length (45 or LP)	An indication that the time differs from the 45 to the LP format and that the difference in time is not due to new lyrics or instrumentation but simply an extension of the song before it fades out.
overdub	A vocal, instrumental or sound effect addition to what was on the original recording session tape. This is always done as an afterthought to try and strengthen the sound of a song. Since these overdubs are add on's, they do not exist on the session master tape and are often over-looked when master tapes are resurrected for release on compact disc.
remixed	Either the instrumentation or vocals have been tampered with resulting in a sound that differs slightly from the original version.
rerecording	Not the original hit recording but a version recorded at a completely different recording session, usually a long period of time after the hit recording session.
segue	To continue without break into the next selection.
truncated fade	An abrupt end to a song that is in the process of fading out.
version (45 or LP)	An indication that the song in question had more than one form. This term is used to denote a difference in lyrics, vocal take, instrumentation, sound effects or editing involving more than the length of fade at the end of a song.

FINDING YOUR WAY AROUND THE ARTIST SECTION

This section has hundreds of pages jam-packed with information. Below is a breakdown of what you'll find on these pages. For descriptions of the abbreviations, please refer to page *vii*.

Bold artist name   Song title

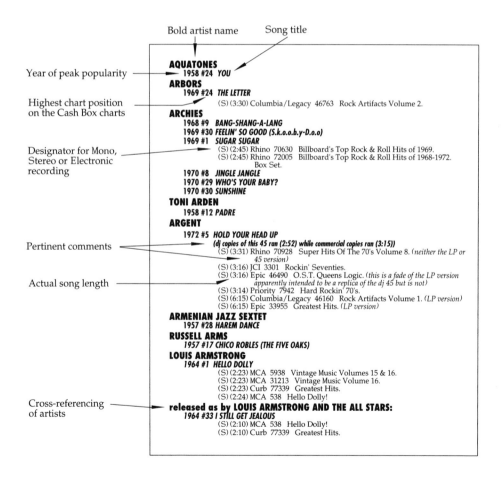

Year of peak popularity

Highest chart position on the Cash Box charts

Designator for Mono, Stereo or Electronic recording

Pertinent comments

Actual song length

Cross-referencing of artists

AQUATONES
1958 #24 *YOU*
ARBORS
1969 #24 *THE LETTER*
    (S) (3:30) Columbia/Legacy 46763 Rock Artifacts Volume 2.
ARCHIES
1968 #9 *BANG-SHANG-A-LANG*
1969 #30 *FEELIN' SO GOOD (S.k.o.o.b.y-D.o.o)*
1969 #1 *SUGAR SUGAR*
    (S) (2:45) Rhino 70630 Billboard's Top Rock & Roll Hits of 1969.
    (S) (2:45) Rhino 72005 Billboard's Top Rock & Roll Hits of 1968-1972. Box Set.
1970 #8 *JINGLE JANGLE*
1970 #29 *WHO'S YOUR BABY?*
1970 #30 *SUNSHINE*
TONI ARDEN
1958 #12 *PADRE*
ARGENT
1972 #5 *HOLD YOUR HEAD UP*
    (dj copies of this 45 ran (2:52) while commercial copies ran (3:15))
    (S) (3:31) Rhino 70928 Super Hits Of The 70's Volume 8. *(neither the LP or 45 version)*
    (S) (3:16) JCI 3301 Rockin' Seventies.
    (S) (3:16) Epic 46490 O.S.T. Queens Logic. *(this is a fade of the LP version apparently intended to be a replica of the dj 45 but is not)*
    (S) (3:14) Priority 7942 Hard Rockin' 70's.
    (S) (6:15) Columbia/Legacy 46160 Rock Artifacts Volume 1. *(LP version)*
    (S) (6:15) Epic 33955 Greatest Hits. *(LP version)*
ARMENIAN JAZZ SEXTET
1957 #28 *HAREM DANCE*
RUSSELL ARMS
1957 #17 *CHICO ROBLES (THE FIVE OAKS)*
LOUIS ARMSTRONG
1964 #1 *HELLO DOLLY*
    (S) (2:23) MCA 5938 Vintage Music Volumes 15 & 16.
    (S) (2:23) MCA 31213 Vintage Music Volume 16.
    (S) (2:23) Curb 77339 Greatest Hits.
    (S) (2:24) MCA 538 Hello Dolly!
released as by LOUIS ARMSTRONG AND THE ALL STARS:
1964 #33 *I STILL GET JEALOUS*
    (S) (2:10) MCA 538 Hello Dolly!
    (S) (2:10) Curb 77339 Greatest Hits.

JOHNNY ACE
1955 #7 *PLEDGING MY LOVE*
    (M) (2:29) Rhino 70641   Billboard's Top R&B Hits Of 1955.
    (M) (2:28) MCA 31200   Vintage Music Volume 3.
    (M) (2:28) MCA 5778   Vintage Music Volumes 3 & 4.
    (M) (2:26) Sire 26617   Music From The Film A Rage In Harlem.
    (M) (2:27) MCA 31183   Johnny Ace Memorial Album.

BARBARA ACKLIN
1968 #16 *LOVE MAKES A WOMAN*
    (S) (2:56) Rhino 75770   Soul Shots Volume 2.

BARBARA ACKLIN & GENE CHANDLER
1968 #40 *FROM THE TEACHER TO THE PREACHER*

JOHNNY ADAMS
1969 #18 *RECONSIDER ME*

CANNONBALL ADDERLY
1967 #18 *MERCY, MERCY, MERCY*
    (S) (5:09) Curb 77399   Best Of. (*LP version*)
    (S) (5:07) Capitol 95482   Best Of - The Capitol Years. (*LP version*)

ADDRISI BROTHERS
1972 #15 *WE'VE GOT TO GET IT ON AGAIN*
    (S) (2:46) Rhino 70928   Super Hits Of The 70's Volume 8.
    (S) (2:44) Columbia/Legacy 46763   Rock Artifacts Volume 2.

AD LIBS
1965 #10 *BOY FROM NEW YORK CITY*
    (M) (2:59) Rhino 75891   Wonder Women.
    (M) (2:58) Rhino 70988   Best Of The Girl Groups Volume 1.
    (M) (2:58) Garland 011   Footstompin' Oldies.

JEWEL AKENS
1965 #2 *THE BIRDS AND THE BEES*

WILLY ALBERTI
1959 #12 *MARINA*

ARTHUR ALEXANDER
1962 #27 *YOU BETTER MOVE ON*
    (S) (2:42) MCA 31202   Vintage Music Volume 5. (*45 version but missing a guitar overdub*)
    (S) (2:42) MCA 5804   Vintage Music Volumes 5 & 6. (*45 version but missing a guitar overdub*)

ALIVE & KICKING
1970 #5 *TIGHTER, TIGHTER*
    (S) (2:42) Rhino 70923   Super Hits Of The 70's Volume 3.
    (S) (2:42) Rhino 72009   Super Hits Of The 70's Volumes 1-4 Box Set.

DAVIE ALLAN & THE ARROWS
1967 #33 *BLUES THEME*
(M) (2:09) K-Tel 713 Battle Of The Bands.
(M) (2:09) Curb 77402 All-Time Great Instrumental Hits Volume 2.

REX ALLEN
1962 #25 *DON'T GO NEAR THE INDIANS*
(S) (3:02) Rhino 70683 Billboard's Top Country Hits Of 1962.

ALLMAN BROTHERS BAND
1973 #1 *RAMBLIN' MAN*
(S) (4:54) Rhino 70634 Billboard's Top Rock & Roll Hits Of 1973.
(S) (4:46) Polydor 839426 Dreams.
(S) (4:45) Priority 7995 Country's Greatest Hits Volume 2.
(S) (4:46) Sandstone 33002 Reelin' In The Years Volume 3.
(S) (4:42) Polydor 825092 A Decade Of Hits 1969 - 1979.
(S) (4:46) Polydor 825092 Brothers And Sisters.
(S) (4:51) JCI 3304 Mellow Seventies.
(S) (4:46) Capitol 96647 Hearts Of Gold - The Classic Rock Collection.

HERB ALPERT
1968 #1 *THIS GUY'S IN LOVE WITH YOU*
(S) (3:57) A&M 2501 Classics Volume 1.
(S) (3:57) A&M 3269 Greatest Hits Volume 2.
(S) (3:58) A&M 6011 Foursider.
(S) (3:58) A&M 3268 Solid Brass.
(S) (3:57) A&M 3266 Beat Of The Brass.

1968 #39 *TO WAIT FOR LOVE*
1969 #38 *WITHOUT HER*
(S) (3:21) A&M 3268 Solid Brass.
(S) (3:22) A&M 6011 Foursider.

HERB ALPERT & THE TIJUANA BRASS
1962 #6 *THE LONELY BULL*
(S) (2:14) A&M 3101 The Lonely Bull.
(S) (2:14) A&M 6011 Foursider.
(S) (2:14) A&M 3267 Greatest Hits.
(S) (2:14) A&M 2501 Classics Volume 1.

1965 #1 *A TASTE OF HONEY*
(S) (2:42) A&M 3157 Whipped Cream & Other Delights.
(S) (2:42) A&M 6011 Foursider.
(S) (2:42) A&M 3267 Greatest Hits.
(S) (2:42) A&M 2501 Classics Volume 1.

1966 #8 *ZORBA THE GREEK*
(S) (4:22) A&M 6011 Foursider. *(LP version)*
(S) (4:23) A&M 3267 Greatest Hits. *(LP version)*
(S) (4:22) A&M 2501 Classics Volume 1. *(LP version)*
(S) (4:23) A&M 3264 Going Places. *(LP version)*

1966 #27 *WHAT NOW MY LOVE*
(S) (2:14) A&M 6011 Foursider.
(S) (2:14) A&M 3269 Greatest Hits Volume 2.
(S) (2:14) A&M 2501 Classics Volume 1.
(S) (2:14) A&M 3268 Solid Brass.
(S) (2:14) A&M 3265 What Now My Love.

1966 #21 *SPANISH FLEA*
(S) (2:06) A&M 3267 Greatest Hits.
(S) (2:05) A&M 2501 Classics Volume 1.
(S) (2:06) A&M 3264 Going Places.

HERB ALPERT & THE TIJUANA BRASS (Continued)

1966 #20 WORK SONG
        (S)   (2:09) A&M 3269   Greatest Hits Volume 2.
        (S)   (2:06) A&M 2501   Classics Volume 1.
        (S)   (2:10) A&M 3268   Solid Brass.

1966 #24 *FLAMINGO*
        (S)   (2:24) A&M 3269   Greatest Hits Volume 2.
        (S)   (2:24) A&M 3268   Solid Brass.

1966 #17 *MAME*
        (S)   (2:07) A&M 6011   Foursider.
        (S)   (2:07) A&M 2501   Classics Volume 1.

1967 #22 *CASINO ROYALE*
        (S)   (2:35) A&M 6011   Foursider.
        (S)   (2:34) A&M 2501   Classics Volume 1.
        (S)   (2:35) A&M 3268   Solid Brass.
        (S)   (2:35) Varese 5265   O.S.T. Casino Royale.

1967 #36 *THE HAPPENING*
1967 #32 *A BANDA*
        (S)   (2:09) A&M 3269   Greatest Hits Volume 2.
        (S)   (2:10) A&M 2501   Classics Volume 1.
        (S)   (2:10) A&M 3268   Solid Brass.

1969 #35 *MY FAVORITE THINGS*
        (S)   (3:02) A&M 3113   Christmas Album.

AMBOY DUKES

1968 #20 *JOURNEY TO THE CENTER OF THE MIND*
        (S)   (3:32) Rhino 75892   Nuggets. *(bad dropout from (2:25) - (2:28) and numerous other points later in the song)*

AMERICA

1972 #1 *HORSE WITH NO NAME*
        (S)   (4:10) Rhino 70633   Billboard's Top Rock & Roll Hits Of 1972.
        (S)   (4:10) Rhino 72005   Billboard's Top Rock & Roll Hits 1968-1972 Box Set.
        (S)   (4:07) Warner Brothers 3110   History/America's Greatest Hits. *(tracks into next selection)*
        (S)   (4:10) Warner Brothers 2576   America.
        (S)   (4:06) Priority 7066   #1 Groups/70's Greatest Rock Hits Volume 12.

1972 #8 *I NEED YOU*
        (S)   (3:05) Warner Brothers 3110   History/America's Greatest Hits. *(previous selection tracks over intro; tracks into next selection)*
        (S)   (3:04) Warner Brothers 2576   America.
        (S)   (2:58) JCI 3303   Love Seventies.

1972 #8 *VENTURA HIGHWAY*
        (S)   (3:22) Warner Brothers 3110   History/America's Greatest Hits. *(previous selection tracks over intro; tracks into next selection; LP version)*
        (S)   (3:21) Priority 8667   FM Hits/70's Greatest Rock Hits Volume 6. *(LP version)*

1973 #20 *DON'T CROSS THE RIVER*
        (S)   (2:30) Warner Brothers 3110   History/America's Greatest Hits. *(previous selection tracks over intro)*

1973 #33 *MUSKRAT LOVE*
        (S)   (3:05) Warner Brothers 3110   History/America's Greatest Hits.

AMERICAN BREED
1967 #29 *STEP OUT OF YOUR MIND*
1968 #3 *BEND ME SHAPE ME*
      (S) (2:12) K-Tel 686 Battle Of The Bands Volume 4.
      (S) (2:14) MCA 31204 Vintage Music Volume 7.
      (S) (2:14) MCA 5805 Vintage Music Volumes 7 & 8.
1968 #30 *GREEN LIGHT*

ED AMES
1967 #8 *MY CUP RUNNETH OVER*
      (S) (2:45) RCA 8475 Nipper's Greatest Hits Of The 60's Volume 2.
1968 #14 *WHO WILL ANSWER*

AMES BROTHERS
1955 #2 *THE NAUGHTY LADY OF SHADY LANE*
      (M) (2:48) Pair 1215 Best Of.
      (M) (2:48) RCA 8467 Nipper's Greatest Hits Of The 50's Volume 2.
1956 #22 *IT ONLY HURTS FOR A LITTLE WHILE*
      (M) (2:40) Pair 1215 Best Of.
1957 #10 *TAMMY*
      (M) (2:22) Pair 1215 Best Of.
1957 #7 *MELODIE D'AMOUR*
      (M) (2:36) Pair 1215 Best Of.
      (S) (2:37) RCA 8466 Nipper's Greatest Hits Of The 50's Volume 1.
1958 #36 *PUSSY CAT*
1958 #34 *NO ONE BUT YOU*
1959 #33 *RED RIVER ROSE*

BILL ANDERSON
1962 #31 *MAMA SANG A SONG*
      (S) (3:26) Curb 77436 Best Of.
1963 #7 *STILL*
      (S) (2:46) Rhino 70684 Billboard's Top Country Hits Of 1963.
      (M) (2:46) Curb 77436 Best Of.

LYNN ANDERSON
1971 #1 *ROSE GARDEN*
      (S) (2:47) Rhino 70924 Super Hits Of The 70's Volume 4.
      (S) (2:47) Rhino 72009 Super Hits Of The 70's Volumes 1-4 Box Set.
      (S) (2:47) Columbia 45047 Pop Classics Of The 70's.
      (S) (2:52) Columbia 46032 Columbia Country Classics Volume 4.

LEE ANDREWS & THE HEARTS
1957 #33 *LONG LONELY NIGHTS*
      (M) (2:52) MCA 31200 Vintage Music Volume 3.
      (M) (2:52) MCA 5778 Vintage Music Volumes 3 & 4.
      (M) (2:52) Chess 9282 Best Of Chess Vocal Groups Volume 1.
      (S) (2:52) Garland 012 Remember When. *(rerecording)*
      (M) (2:50) Collectables 2508 History Of Rock - The Doo Wop Era Part 2.
      (M) (2:52) Collectables 5028 Biggest Hits.
      (M) (2:48) Collectables 5003 Gotham Recording Sessions.
1957 #25 *TEAR DROPS*
      (M) (2:21) Rhino 75763 Best Of Doo Wop Ballads.
      (M) (2:20) Chess 31320 Best Of Chess Rock & Roll Volume 2.
      (M) (2:19) Collectables 5028 Biggest Hits.
1958 #38 *TRY THE IMPOSSIBLE*
      (M) (3:02) Collectables 5028 Biggest Hits. *(mastered from vinyl)*
      (M) (3:04) Collectables 5003 Gotham Recording Sessions.

ANGELS

1961 #16 'TIL

1962 #35 CRY BABY CRY

1963 #1 MY BOYFRIEND'S BACK

(S) (2:35) Rhino 70624 Billboard's Top Rock & Roll Hits Of 1963. *(stereo LP version)*

(S) (2:35) Rhino 72007 Billboard's Top Rock & Roll Hits 1962-1966 Box Set. *(stereo LP version)*

(M) (2:13) Mercury 826448 Oldies Golden Million Sellers. *(45 and mono LP version)*

(S) (2:35) Mercury 816555 45's On CD Volume 2. *(stereo LP version)*

(S) (2:35) Rhino 70989 Best Of The Girl Groups Volume 2. *(stereo LP version)*

(S) (2:37) JCI 3110 Sock Hoppin' Sixties. *(stereo LP version)*

(S) (2:35) Warner Brothers 3359 O.S.T. The Wanderers. *(stereo LP version)*

(S) (2:35) Motown 5322 and 9087 Girl Groups: The Story Of A Sound. *(stereo LP version)*

1963 #23 I ADORE HIM

ANIMALS (and ERIC BURDON & THE ANIMALS)

1964 #1 THE HOUSE OF THE RISING SUN

(the original U.S. LP and 45 version both ran (2:58); the (4:26) version first appeared on the Animals "Greatest Hits" vinyl LP)

(M) (4:26) Abkco 4324 Best Of.

1964 #17 I'M CRYING

(M) (2:43) Abkco 4324 Best Of.

1965 #35 BOOM BOOM

(M) (3:00) Abkco 4324 Best Of.

1965 #17 DON'T LET ME BE MISUNDERSTOOD

(M) (2:25) Abkco 4324 Best Of.

1965 #32 BRING IT ON HOME TO ME

(M) (2:34) Abkco 4324 Best Of.

1965 #14 WE GOTTA GET OUT OF THIS PLACE

(M) (3:12) Abkco 4324 Best Of. *(alternate take)*

1966 #20 IT'S MY LIFE

(M) (3:10) Abkco 4324 Best Of.

1966 #34 INSIDE-LOOKING OUT

(M) (3:44) Polydor 849388 Best Of Eric Burdon & The Animals.

1966 #11 DON'T BRING ME DOWN

(S) (3:13) Polydor 849388 Best Of Eric Burdon & The Animals.

(M) (3:11) Mercury 816555 45's On CD Volume 2.

released as by ERIC BURDON & THE ANIMALS:

1966 #12 SEE SEE RIDER

(S) (3:59) Polydor 849388 Best Of. *(LP version)*

(M) (2:47) Rhino 70325 History Of British Rock Volume 7.

(M) (2:47) Rhino 72022 History Of British Rock Box Set.

1967 #33 HELP ME GIRL

(S) (2:37) Polydor 849388 Best Of.

1967 #19 WHEN I WAS YOUNG

(M) (2:59) Polydor 849388 Best Of.

(M) (3:00) Polydor 837362 O.S.T. 1969.

(M) (2:59) Rhino 70326 History Of British Rock Volume 8.

(M) (2:59) Rhino 72022 History Of British Rock Box Set.

1967 #8 SAN FRANCISCAN NIGHTS
>   (S) (3:19) Polydor 849388 Best Of.
>   (S) (3:18) Mercury 834216 45's On CD Volume 3.
>   (S) (3:19) Rhino 70326 History Of British Rock Volume 8.
>   (S) (3:19) Rhino 72022 History Of British Rock Box Set.

1968 #10 MONTEREY
>   **(dj copies of this song ran (3:29) and (4:14))**
>   (S) (4:14) Polydor 849388 Best Of.

1968 #16 SKY PILOT (PARTS 1 & 2)
>   **(the LP version tracked Parts 1 & 2 together; the 45 version did not)**
>   (S) (7:29) Polydor 849388 Best Of. *(LP version)*
>   (S) (7:24) Rhino 70734 Songs Of Protest. *(LP version)*
>   (M) (2:57) Rhino 70327 History Of British Rock Volume 9. *(Part 1)*
>   (M) (2:57) Rhino 72022 History Of British Rock Box Set. *(Part 1)*

PAUL ANKA

1957 #2 DIANA
>   (M) (2:25) Rhino 71489 30th Anniversary Collection.
>   (E) (2:25) Rhino 70618 Billboard's Top Rock & Roll Hits Of 1957.
>   (E) (2:25) Rhino 72004 Billboard's Top Rock & Roll Hits 1957-1961 Box Set.
>   (M) (2:25) Curb 77467 Five Decades Greatest Hits.
>   (M) (2:23) Curb 77525 Greatest Hits Of Rock 'N' Roll Volume 2.
>   (S) (2:18) RCA 3808 21 Golden Hits. *(rerecorded)*
>   (M) (2:25) Curb 77557 Sings His Big 10 Volume 1.
>   (M) (2:25) Curb 77558 Sings His Big 10 Volume 2.

1958 #9 YOU ARE MY DESTINY
>   (M) (2:44) Rhino 71489 30th Anniversary Collection.
>   (M) (2:45) Curb 77467 Five Decades Greatest Hits.
>   (S) (2:26) RCA 3808 21 Golden Hits. *(rerecorded)*
>   (M) (2:45) Curb 77557 Sings His Big 10 Volume 1.

1958 #36 CRAZY LOVE
>   (S) (2:26) Rhino 71489 30th Anniversary Collection.
>   (S) (2:25) RCA 3808 21 Golden Hits. *(rerecorded)*
>   (M) (2:24) Curb 77557 Sings His Big 10 Volume 1.

1958 #24 LET THE BELLS KEEP RINGING
>   (M) (1:57) Rhino 71489 30th Anniversary Collection.
>   (M) (1:59) Rhino 70588 Rockin' & Rollin' Wedding Songs Volume 1.
>   (M) (2:02) Curb 77557 Sings His Big 10 Volume 1.

1958 #28 JUST YOUNG

1959 #12 (ALL OF A SUDDEN) MY HEART SINGS
>   (S) (3:01) Rhino 71489 30th Anniversary Collection.
>   (M) (3:01) Curb 77467 Five Decades Greatest Hits.
>   (S) (3:01) Curb 77558 Sings His Big 10 Volume 2.

1959 #29 I MISS YOU SO
>   (M) (2:20) Curb 77558 Sings His Big 10 Volume 2.

1959 #1 LONELY BOY
>   (M) (2:34) Rhino 71489 30th Anniversary Collection.
>   (E) (2:32) Rhino 70620 Billboard's Top Rock & Roll Hits Of 1959.
>   (E) (2:32) Rhino 72004 Billboard's Top Rock & Roll Hits 1957-1961 Box Set.
>   (M) (2:32) Curb 77467 Five Decades Greatest Hits.
>   (S) (2:22) RCA 3808 21 Golden Hits. *(rerecorded)*
>   (M) (2:32) Curb 77558 Sings His Big 10 Volume 2.

PAUL ANKA (Continued)

1959 #2 PUT YOUR HEAD ON MY SHOULDER
      (S) (2:37) Rhino 71489 30th Anniversary Collection.
      (S) (2:36) Curb 77467 Five Decades Greatest Hits.
      (S) (2:33) RCA 3808 21 Golden Hits. *(rerecorded)*
      (E) (2:37) Curb 77557 Sings His Big 10 Volume 1.

1960 #6 IT'S TIME TO CRY
      (M) (2:24) Rhino 71489 30th Anniversary Collection.
      (E) (2:22) Curb 77467 Five Decades Greatest Hits.
      (S) (2:28) RCA 3808 21 Golden Hits. *(rerecorded)*
      (E) (2:22) Curb 77557 Sings His Big 10 Volume 1.

1960 #2 PUPPY LOVE
      (S) (2:39) Rhino 71489 30th Anniversary Collection.
      (M) (2:39) Curb 77467 Five Decades Greatest Hits.
      (S) (2:43) RCA 3808 21 Golden Hits. *(rerecorded)*
      (M) (2:39) Curb 77558 Sings His Big 10 Volume 2.

1960 #8 MY HOME TOWN
      (S) (2:28) Rhino 71489 30th Anniversary Collection.
      (S) (2:04) RCA 3808 21 Golden Hits. *(rerecorded)*
      (S) (2:27) Curb 77558 Sings His Big 10 Volume 2.

1960 #24 HELLO YOUNG LOVERS

1960 #23 SUMMER'S GONE
      (S) (2:41) Rhino 71489 30th Anniversary Collection.
      (S) (2:22) RCA 3808 21 Golden Hits. *(rerecorded)*
      (S) (2:41) Curb 77558 Sings His Big 10 Volume 2.

1961 #23 THE STORY OF MY LOVE

1961 #11 TONIGHT MY LOVE, TONIGHT
      (S) (2:06) Rhino 71489 30th Anniversary Collection.
      (S) (2:04) RCA 3808 21 Golden Hits. *(rerecorded)*

1961 #12 DANCE ON LITTLE GIRL
      (S) (2:17) Rhino 71489 30th Anniversary Collection.
      (S) (1:50) RCA 3808 21 Golden Hits. *(rerecorded)*
      (S) (2:17) Curb 77558 Sings His Big 10 Volume 2.

1961 #32 KISSIN' ON THE PHONE

1962 #12 LOVE ME WARM AND TENDER
      (S) (2:16) Rhino 71489 30th Anniversary Collection.
      (S) (2:17) RCA 8474 Nipper's Greatest Hits Of The 60's Volume 1.

1962 #22 A STEEL GUITAR AND A GLASS OF WINE
      (S) (2:09) RCA 8475 Nipper's Greatest Hits Of The 60's Volume 2.

1962 #24 ESO BESO (THAT KISS!)
      (S) (2:24) Rhino 71489 30th Anniversary Collection. *(:10 longer introduction than 45 or LP)*

1963 #30 LOVE (MAKES THE WORLD GO 'ROUND)

1963 #35 REMEMBER DIANA

1969 #26 GOODNIGHT MY LOVE
      (S) (3:13) Rhino 71489 30th Anniversary Collection.

1971 #38 DO I LOVE YOU
      (S) (3:09) Pair 1204 Best Of.

ANNETTE

1959 #18 TALL PAUL

1960 #16 FIRST NAME INITIAL

1960 #13 O DIO MIO

1960 #15 PINEAPPLE PRINCESS

ANN-MARGRET
1961 #15 *I JUST DON'T UNDERSTAND*
    (S) (2:35) RCA 8474 Nipper's Greatest Hits Of The 60's Volume 1.

RAY ANTHONY
1959 #7 *PETER GUNN*
    (S) (1:51) Curb 77403 All-Time Great Instrumental Hits Volume 1.
    (rerecorded)
    (S) (1:51) Curb 77402 All-Time Great Instrumental Hits Volume 2.
    (rerecorded)
    (M) (1:48) Capitol 94079 Capitol Collector's Series.
    (M) (1:49) Capitol 98670 Memories Are Made Of This.

APOLLO 100
1972 #6 *JOY*
    (the actual 45 time is (2:45) not (3:10) as stated on the record label)
    (S) (2:44) Rhino 70927 Super Hits Of The 70's Volume 7.

APPLEJACKS
1958 #26 *MEXICAN HAT ROCK*
1959 #31 *ROCKA-CONGA*

APRIL WINE
1972 #27 *YOU COULD HAVE BEEN A LADY*

AQUATONES
1958 #24 *YOU*

ARBORS
1969 #24 *THE LETTER*
    (S) (3:30) Columbia/Legacy 46763 Rock Artifacts Volume 2.

ARCHIES
1968 #9 *BANG-SHANG-A-LANG*
1969 #30 *FEELIN' SO GOOD (S.k.o.o.b.y-D.o.o.)*
1969 #1 *SUGAR SUGAR*
    (S) (2:45) Rhino 70630 Billboard's Top Rock & Roll Hits Of 1969.
    (S) (2:45) Rhino 72005 Billboard's Top Rock & Roll Hits 1968-1972 Box Set.
1970 #8 *JINGLE JANGLE*
1970 #29 *WHO'S YOUR BABY?*
1970 #30 *SUNSHINE*

TONI ARDEN
1958 #12 *PADRE*

ARGENT
1972 #5 *HOLD YOUR HEAD UP*
    (dj copies of this 45 ran (2:52) while commercial copies ran (3:15))
    (S) (3:31) Rhino 70928 Super Hits Of The 70's Volume 8. *(neither the LP or 45 version)*
    (S) (3:16) JCI 3301 Rockin' Seventies.
    (S) (2:53) Epic 46490 O.S.T. Queens Logic. *(this is a fade of the LP version apparantly intended to be a replica of the dj 45 but it is not)*
    (S) (3:14) Priority 7942 Hard Rockin' 70's.
    (S) (6:15) Columbia/Legacy 46160 Rock Artifacts Volume 1. *(LP version)*
    (S) (6:15) Epic 33955 Greatest Hits. *(LP version)*

ARMENIAN JAZZ SEXTET
1957 #28 *HAREM DANCE*

RUSSELL ARMS
1957 #17 *CINCO ROBLES (THE FIVE OAKS)*

LOUIS ARMSTRONG
1964 #1 *HELLO DOLLY*
    (S)   (2:23) MCA 5938 Vintage Music Volumes 15 & 16.
    (S)   (2:23) MCA 31213 Vintage Music Volume 16.
    (S)   (2:23) Curb 77339 Greatest Hits.
    (S)   (2:24) MCA 538 Hello Dolly!

released as by LOUIS ARMSTRONG AND THE ALL STARS:
1964 #33 *I STILL GET JEALOUS*
    (S)   (2:10) MCA 538 Hello Dolly!
    (S)   (2:10) Curb 77339 Greatest Hits.

EDDY ARNOLD
1966 #12 *MAKE THE WORLD GO AWAY*
    (S)   (2:38) RCA 3675 Best Of.
    (S)   (2:37) RCA 8474 Nipper's Greatest Hits Of The 60's Volume 1.
    (S)   (2:36) Curb 77416 Best Of.
    (S)   (2:38) RCA 58398 Pure Gold.
1966 #36 *I WANT TO GO WITH YOU*
    (S)   (2:35) RCA 3675 Best Of.
1966 #37 *THE LAST WORD IN LONESOME IS ME*
    (S)   (2:12) RCA 3675 Best Of.
1966 #38 *THE TIP OF MY FINGERS*

EDDY ARNOLD & JAYE P. MORGAN
1956 #24 *MUTUAL ADMIRATION SOCIETY*

ASHTON, GARDNER & DYKE
1971 #37 *RESURRECTION SHUFFLE*

ASSEMBLED MULTITUDE
1970 #16 *OVERTURE FROM TOMMY (A ROCK OPERA)*

ASSOCIATION
1966 #9 *ALONG COMES MARY*
    (S)   (2:47) Rhino 70906 American Bandstand Greatest Hits Collection.
    (S)   (2:48) Warner Brothers 1767 Greatest Hits.
    (S)   (2:47) Pair 2701 Songs That Made Them Famous.
1966 #1 *CHERISH*
    (S)   (3:25) Warner Brothers 1767 Greatest Hits.
    (S)   (3:24) Pair 2701 Songs That Made Them Famous.
1966 #26 *PANDORA'S GOLDEN HEEBIE JEEBIES*
1967 #1 *WINDY*
    (S)   (2:54) Warner Brothers 1767 Greatest Hits. *(truncated fade)*
    (S)   (2:52) Rhino 70628 Billboard's Top Rock & Roll Hits Of 1967.
    (S)   (2:53) Pair 2701 Songs That Made Them Famous.
1967 #1 *NEVER MY LOVE*
    (S)   (3:08) Warner Brothers 1767 Greatest Hits. *(LP version; truncated fade)*
    (S)   (3:08) JCI 3104 Mellow Sixties. *(LP version; truncated fade)*
    (S)   (3:07) Pair 2701 Songs That Made Them Famous. *(truncated fade)*
1968 #11 *EVERYTHING THAT TOUCHES YOU*
    (S)   (3:17) Warner Brothers 1767 Greatest Hits. *(truncated fade)*
1968 #23 *TIME FOR LIVIN'*
    (S)   (2:44) Warner Brothers 1767 Greatest Hits. *(truncated fade)*
1968 #29 *SIX MAN BAND*
    (S)   (2:12) Warner Special Products 27607 Highs Of The 60's.
    (S)   (2:12) Warner Brothers 1767 Greatest Hits.

SIL AUSTIN
1956 #12 *SLOW WALK*
      (M) (2:38) Mercury 832041 45's On CD Volume 1.

FRANKIE AVALON
1958 #11 *DEDE DINAH*
1958 #17 *GINGER BREAD*
1958 #25 *I'LL WAIT FOR YOU*
1959 #1 *VENUS*
      (S) (2:19) Rhino 75893 Jukebox Classics Volume 1.
      (S) (2:19) Rhino 70620 Billboard's Top Rock & Roll Hits Of 1959.
      (S) (2:19) Rhino 72004 Billboard's Top Rock & Roll Hits 1957-1961 Box Set.
      (S) (2:20) JCI 3203 Lovin' Fifties.
      (S) (2:18) Garland 012 Remember When.
      (S) (2:20) MCA 6340 O.S.T. Born On The Fourth Of July.
1959 #7 *BOBBY SOX TO STOCKINGS*
1959 #17 *A BOY WITHOUT A GIRL*
1959 #10 *JUST ASK YOUR HEART*
1960 #1 *WHY*
1960 #19 *DON'T THROW AWAY ALL THOSE TEARDROPS*
1960 #25 *WHERE ARE YOU*
1960 #26 *TOGETHERNESS*
1962 #36 *YOU ARE MINE*

AVANT-GARDE
1968 #35 *NATURALLY STONED*
      (M) (2:11) Columbia/Legacy 46983 Rock Artifacts Volume 3.

BACHELORS
1964 #10 *DIANE*
      (M) (2:29) Rhino 70323 History Of British Rock Volume 5.
      (M) (2:29) Rhino 72022 History Of British Rock Box Set.
1964 #34 *I BELIEVE*
1965 #27 *NO ARMS CAN EVER HOLD YOU*
1965 #16 *MARIE*
      (S) (2:17) Rhino 70324 History Of British Rock Volume 6.
      (S) (2:17) Rhino 72022 History Of British Rock Box Set.
1965 #40 *CHAPEL IN THE MOONLIGHT*
1966 #37 *CAN I TRUST YOU?*

JIM BACKUS & FRIEND
1958 #36 *DELICIOUS*
      (M) (3:05) Rhino 70743 Dr. Demento 20th Anniversary Collection.

BADFINGER
1970 #6 *COME AND GET IT*
      (S) (2:20) Capitol 97579 Magic Christian Music.

BADFINGER (Continued)
1970 #6 **NO MATTER WHAT**
    (S) (2:58) Capitol 98698 No Dice.
1972 #3 **DAY AFTER DAY**
1972 #9 **BABY BLUE**

JOAN BAEZ
1965 #31 **THERE BUT FOR FORTUNE**
    (S) (3:13) Vanguard 79332 Hits/Greatest & Others.
    (S) (3:12) Vanguard 6560/1 The First Ten Years.
    (S) (3:12) Vanguard 79160 Joan Baez 5.
1971 #3 **THE NIGHT THEY DROVE OLD DIXIE DOWN**
    (S) (3:23) Vanguard 79332 Hits/Greatest & Others.

GEORGE BAKER SELECTION
1970 #16 **LITTLE GREEN BAG**
    (S) (3:15) Rhino 70922 Super Hits Of The 70's Volume 2. *(neither the LP or 45 version)*
    (S) (3:15) Rhino 72009 Super Hits Of The 70's Volumes 1-4 Box Set. *(neither the LP or 45 version)*
    (S) (3:15) JCI 3115 Groovin' Sixties. *(neither the LP or 45 version)*

LAVERN BAKER
1955 #3 **TWEEDLEE DEE**
    (M) (3:07) Rhino 70598 Billboard's Top Rock & Roll Hits Of 1955.
    (M) (3:07) Atlantic 81294 Atlantic Rhythm & Blues Volume 2.
    (M) (3:08) Atlantic 82311 Soul On Fire.
    (M) (3:02) JCI 3552 Best Of.
    (M) (3:08) Atlantic 82305 Atlantic Rhythm And Blues 1947-1974 Box Set.
1956 #37 **I CAN'T LOVE YOU ENOUGH**
    (M) (2:36) Atlantic 82311 Soul On Fire.
1957 #15 **JIM DANDY**
    (M) (2:10) JCI 3204 Heart & Soul Fifties.
    (M) (2:11) Atlantic 81295 Atlantic Rhythm & Blues Volume 3.
    (M) (2:11) Atlantic 81769 O.S.T. Big Town.
    (M) (2:11) Atlantic 82311 Soul On Fire.
    (M) (2:11) JCI 3552 Best Of.
    (M) (2:11) Atlantic 82305 Atlantic Rhythm And Blues 1947-1974 Box Set.
1959 #10 **I CRIED A TEAR**
    (S) (2:34) Rhino 70645 Billboard's Top R&B Hits Of 1959.
    (S) (2:35) Atlantic 81296 Atlantic Rhythm & Blues Volume 4.
    (M) (2:33) Atlantic 82311 Soul On Fire.
    (M) (2:33) JCI 3552 Best Of.
    (M) (2:33) Atlantic 82305 Atlantic Rhythm And Blues 1947-1974 Box Set.
1961 #36 **BUMBLE BEE**
1963 #37 **SEE SEE RIDER**
    (M) (2:30) Atlantic 81297 Atlantic Rhythm & Blues Volume 5.
    (S) (2:27) Atlantic 82311 Soul On Fire.
    (M) (2:29) JCI 3552 Best Of.
    (S) (2:27) Atlantic 82305 Atlantic Rhythm And Blues 1947-1974 Box Set.

KENNY BALL
1962 #2 **MIDNIGHT IN MOSKOW**

HANK BALLARD & THE MIDNIGHTERS
1960 #6 **FINGER POPPIN' TIME**
1960 #7 **LET'S GO, LET'S GO, LET'S GO**

HANK BALLARD & THE MIDNIGHTERS (Continued)
1961 #14 *THE HOOCHI COOCHI COO*
1961 #24 *THE CONTINENTAL WALK*

BAND
1969 #26 *UP ON CRIPPLE CREEK*
     (S) (4:27) Capitol 46070 Best Of. *(LP version)*
     (S) (4:29) Capitol 46493 The Band. *(LP version)*
     (S) (4:29) Capitol 48419 Anthology Volume 1. *(LP version)*
     (S) (4:31) Capitol 92170 To Kingdom Come. *(LP version)*
1972 #23 *DON'T DO IT*
     (S) (4:33) Capitol 46070 Best Of. *(LP version but with 1:38 introduction removed)*
     (S) (4:40) Capitol 92170 To Kingdom Come. *(LP version but with 1:38 introduction removed)*
     (S) (6:05) Capitol 93595 Rock Of Ages. *(LP version)*

DARRELL BANKS
1966 #24 *OPEN THE DOOR TO YOUR HEART*

CHRIS BARBER'S JAZZ BAND
1959 #4 *PETITE FLEUR*

KEITH BARBOUR
1969 #33 *ECHO PARK*
     (S) (3:42) Columbia/Legacy 46160 Rock Artifacts Volume 1.

BOBBY BARE
1962 #29 *SHAME ON ME*
1963 #13 *DETROIT CITY*
     (S) (2:46) RCA 8475 Nipper's Greatest Hits Of The 60's Volume 2.
1963 #15 *500 MILES AWAY FROM HOME*
     (S) (2:40) RCA 8474 Nipper's Greatest Hits Of The 60'S Volume 1.

BAR-KAYS
1967 #17 *SOUL FINGER*
     (M) (2:18) Atlantic Group 88218 Complete Stax/Volt Singles.
     (M) (2:18) Warner Special Products 27609 Memphis Soul Classics.
     (M) (2:18) JCI 3105 Soul Sixties.
     (M) (2:18) Stax 88008 Top Of The Stax Volume 2.
     (S) (2:19) Atlantic 82305 Atlantic Rhythm And Blues 1947-1974 Box Set. *(truncated fade)*
     (S) (2:19) Rhino 70298 Soul Finger. *(truncated fade)*

RAY BARRETTO
1963 #18 *EL WATUSI*

JOE BARRY
1961 #19 *I'M A FOOL TO CARE*

LEN BARRY
1965 #1 *1-2-3*
     (S) (2:21) Rhino 70626 Billboard's Top Rock & Roll Hits Of 1965.
     (S) (2:21) Rhino 72007 Billboard's Top Rock & Roll Hits 1962-1966 Box Set.
     (S) (2:25) MCA 31204 Vintage Music Volume 7. *(with countoff)*
     (S) (2:25) MCA 5805 Vintage Music Volumes 7 & 8. *(with countoff)*
1966 #13 *LIKE A BABY*
1966 #17 *SOMEWHERE*

BARRY & THE TAMERLANES
1963 #25 *I WONDER WHAT SHE'S DOING TONIGHT*
    (M) (1:50) Rhino 70995 One Hit Wonders Of The 60's Volume 1.

CHRIS BARTLEY
1967 #35 *THE SWEETEST THING THIS SIDE OF HEAVEN*

FONTELLA BASS
1965 #3 *RESCUE ME*
    (S) (2:54) Rhino 75774 Soul Shots.
    (S) (2:50) Rhino 70651 Billboard's Top R&B Hits Of 1965.
    (S) (2:50) Rhino 72006 Billboard's Top R&B Hits 1965-1969 Box Set.
    (S) (2:54) MCA 31206 Vintage Music Volume 9.
    (S) (2:54) MCA 5806 Vintage Music Volumes 9 & 10.
    (S) (2:50) JCI 3100 Dance Sixties.
    (S) (2:53) Chess 31318 Best Of Chess Rhythm & Blues Volume 2.
    (S) (2:53) MCA 6467 O.S.T. Air America.
    (S) (2:52) Chess 9335 Rescued: The Best Of.
1966 #38 *RECOVERY*
    (S) (2:28) Chess 9335 Rescued: The Best Of.

FONTELLA BASS & BOBBY MCCLURE
1965 #29 *DON'T MESS UP A GOOD THING*
    (M) (2:51) Chess 9335 Rescued: The Best Of.

SHIRLEY BASSEY
1965 #7 *GOLDFINGER*
    (S) (2:48) EMI 46079 James Bond 13 Original Themes.
    (S) (2:47) EMI 95345 O.S.T. Goldfinger.
    (S) (3:19) Pair 1057 Sassy Bassey. *(live)*

LES BAXTER
1955 #1 *UNCHAINED MELODY*
    (M) (2:31) Curb 77403 All Time Great Instrumental Hits Volume 1.
    (M) (2:31) Capitol 91218 Baxter's Best.
    (M) (2:31) Capitol 98670 Memories Are Made Of This.
1955 #7 *WAKE THE TOWN AND TELL THE PEOPLE*
    (M) (2:31) Capitol 91218 Baxter's Best.
1956 #1 *THE POOR PEOPLE OF PARIS*
    (M) (2:23) Capitol 91218 Baxter's Best.
    (E) (2:23) Capitol 90592 Memories Are Made Of This.
    (M) (2:23) Curb 77403 All-Time Great Instrumental Hits Volume 1.
    (M) (2:23) Capitol 98670 Memories Are Made Of This.

B. BUMBLE & THE STINGERS
1961 #21 *BUMBLE BOOGIE*
1962 #25 *NUT ROCKER*

BEACH BOYS
1962 #10 *SURFIN' SAFARI*
    (M) (2:04) Capitol 46467 Endless Summer.
    (M) (2:04) Capitol 46324 Made In The U.S.A.
    (M) (2:04) Capitol 93691 Surfin' Safari/Surfin' U.S.A.
    (M) (2:03) Rhino 70089 Surfin' Hits.
    (M) (2:04) Capitol 96861 Monster Summer Hits - Wild Surf.
    (M) (2:04) Capitol 96795 Absolute Best Volume 1.
1963 #1 *SURFIN' U.S.A.*
    (M) (2:26) Capitol 91318 Best Of.
    (M) (2:26) Capitol 46467 Endless Summer.
    (M) (2:26) Capitol 46324 Made In The U.S.A.

BEACH BOYS (Continued)

(S) (2:27) Capitol 93691 Surfin' Safari/Surfin' U.S.A.
(S) (2:27) Rhino 70089 Surfin' Hits.
(S) (2:27) Rhino 70624 Billboard's Top Rock & Roll Hits Of 1963.
(S) (2:27) Rhino 72007 Billboard's Top Rock & Roll Hits 1962-1966 Box Set.
(S) (2:27) Capitol 96861 Monster Summer Hits - Wild Surf.
(S) (2:27) Capitol 96795 Absolute Best Volume 1.
(S) (2:27) EMI 90604 Beach Party Blasts.
(S) (2:28) MFSL 521 Surfin' U.S.A./Surfer Girl. *(first :03 of song are silent)*

1963 #25 SHUT DOWN

(M) (1:48) Capitol 46467 Endless Summer.
(S) (1:49) Capitol 93691 Surfin' Safari/Surfin' U.S.A.
(M) (1:50) Capitol 96862 Monster Summer Hits - Drag City.
(S) (1:48) Capitol 93693 Little Deuce Coupe/All Summer Long.
(S) (1:49) Capitol 96795 Absolute Best Volume 1.
(S) (1:49) MFSL 521 Surfin' U.S.A./Surfer Girl.

1963 #5 SURFER GIRL

(M) (2:24) Capitol 91318 Best Of.
(S) (2:24) Capitol 46467 Endless Summer.
(M) (2:22) Capitol 46324 Made In The U.S.A.
(S) (2:25) Capitol 93692 Surfer Girl/Shut Down Volume 2.
(S) (2:25) Capitol 96861 Monster Summer Hits - Wild Surf.
(S) (2:25) Capitol 96795 Absolute Best Volume 1.
(S) (2:25) MFSL 521 Surfin' U.S.A./Surfer Girl.

1963 #19 LITTLE DEUCE COUPE

(M) (1:49) Capitol 91318 Best Of. *(:11 longer fade than LP or 45)*
(S) (1:38) Capitol 46467 Endless Summer.
(S) (1:38) Capitol 93692 Surfer Girl/Shut Down Volume 2.
(S) (1:37) Capitol 96862 Monster Summer Hits - Drag City.
(S) (1:37) Capitol 93693 Little Deuce Coupe/All Summer Long.
(S) (1:37) Capitol 96795 Absolute Best Volume 1.
(S) (1:38) MFSL 521 Surfin' U.S.A./Surfer Girl.

1963 #8 BE TRUE TO YOUR SCHOOL

(S) (2:05) Capitol 46467 Endless Summer. *(LP version)*
(M) (2:06) Capitol 46324 Made In The U.S.A. *(45 version)*
(S) (2:04) Capitol 93693 Little Deuce Coupe/All Summer Long. *(LP version)*
(M) (2:06) Capitol 93693 Little Deuce Coupe/All Summer Long. *(45 version)*
(S) (2:04) Capitol 96795 Absolute Best Volume 1. *(LP version)*

1963 #34 IN MY ROOM

(M) (2:12) Capitol 91318 Best Of.
(S) (2:11) Capitol 46467 Endless Summer.
(S) (2:11) Capitol 93692 Surfer Girl/Shut Down Volume 2.
(S) (2:11) Capitol 96795 Absolute Best Volume 1.
(S) (2:12) MFSL 521 Surfin' U.S.A./Surfer Girl.

1964 #6 FUN FUN FUN

(M) (2:17) Capitol 91318 Best Of. *(45 version; truncated fade)*
(S) (2:02) Capitol 46467 Endless Summer. *(LP version)*
(S) (2:02) Capitol 93692 Surfer Girl/Shut Down Volume 2. *(LP version)*
(M) (2:18) Capitol 93692 Surfer Girl/Shut Down Volume 2. *(45 version)*
(M) (2:15) Capitol 46324 Made In The U.S.A. *(45 version)*
(S) (2:02) Capitol 96862 Monster Summer Hits - Drag City. *(LP version)*
(M) (2:18) Capitol 96795 Absolute Best Volume 1. *(45 version)*
(M) (2:18) Capitol 98138 Spring Break Volume 1. *(45 version)*

1964 #1   *I GET AROUND*
        (M) (2:10) Capitol 92639 Still Crusin'.
        (M) (2:11) Capitol 46467 Endless Summer.
        (M) (2:10) Capitol 46324 Made In The U.S.A.
        (M) (2:12) Rhino 70625 Billboard's Top Rock & Roll Hits Of 1964.
        (M) (2:12) Rhino 72007 Billboard's Top Rock & Roll Hits 1962-1966 Box Set.
        (E) (2:13) EMI 90604 Beach Party Blasts.
        (M) (2:09) Capitol 48993 Spuds Mackenzie's Party Faves.
        (M) (2:08) A&M 3913 O.S.T. Good Morning Vietnam.
        (M) (2:12) Rhino 70794 KFOG Presents M. Dung's Idiot Show.
        (M) (2:12) Capitol 93693 Little Deuce Coupe/All Summer Long.
        (M) (2:11) Capitol 96795 Absolute Best Volume 1.
        (M) (2:11) Capitol 98138 Spring Break Volume 1.
        (M) (2:10) Capitol 98665 When AM Was King.

1964 #26 *DON'T WORRY BABY*
        (S) (2:46) Capitol 46467 Endless Summer.
        (M) (2:40) Capitol 46324 Made In The U.S.A.
        (S) (2:46) Capitol 93692 Surfer Girl/Shut Down Volume 2.
        (S) (2:47) EMI 90604 Beach Party Blasts.
        (S) (2:46) Capitol 96795 Absolute Best Volume 1.

1964 #7   *WHEN I GROW UP TO BE A MAN*
        (M) (1:58) Capitol 46618 Spirit of America.
        (M) (1:59) Capitol 46324 Made In The U.S.A.
        (M) (1:59) Capitol 96795 Absolute Best Volume 1.

1964 #10 *DANCE DANCE DANCE*
        (M) (1:58) Capitol 46618 Spirit of America.
        (M) (1:58) Capitol 46324 Made In The U.S.A.
        (M) (1:58) Capitol 93694 Today/Summer Days & Summer Nights.
        (S) (1:58) Capitol 93694 Today/Summer Days & Summer Nights.
                     (alternate take)
        (M) (1:58) Capitol 96795 Absolute Best Volume 1.

1965 #13 *DO YOU WANNA DANCE?*
        (M) (2:16) Capitol 46618 Spirit Of America.
        (M) (2:17) Capitol 93694 Today/Summer Days & Summer Nights.
        (M) (2:16) Capitol 96795 Absolute Best Volume 1.

1965 #1   *HELP ME RHONDA*
        (M) (3:06) Capitol 46467 Endless Summer. *(LP version)*
        (M) (2:44) Capitol 46324 Made In The U.S.A. *(45 version)*
        (M) (2:45) Capitol 93694 Today/Summer Days & Summer Nights. *(45 version)*
        (M) (3:07) Capitol 93694 Today/Summer Days & Summer Nights. *(LP version)*
        (M) (2:45) Rhino 70626 Billboard's Top Rock & Roll Hits Of 1965. *(45 version)*
        (M) (2:45) Rhino 72007 Billboard's Top Rock & Roll Hits 1962-1966 Box Set. *(45 version)*
        (M) (2:45) Curb 77355 60's Hits Volume 1. *(45 version)*
        (M) (2:44) Capitol 48046 California Girls. *(45 version)*
        (M) (3:07) Capitol 96795 Absolute Best Volume 1. *(LP version)*

1965 #3   *CALIFORNIA GIRLS*
        (M) (2:36) Capitol 92639 Still Crusin'.
        (E) (2:36) Capitol 46467 Endless Summer.
        (M) (2:36) Capitol 46324 Made In The U.S.A.
        (M) (2:36) Capitol 93694 Today/Summer Days & Summer Nights.

BEACH BOYS (Continued)

       (M) (2:36) Capitol 48046 California Girls.
       (M) (2:35) Capitol 96796 Absolute Best Volume 2.

1965 #15 *THE LITTLE GIRL I ONCE KNEW*

       (M) (2:35) Capitol 46618 Spirit Of America.
       (M) (2:34) Capitol 96796 Absolute Best Volume 2.
       (M) (2:35) Capitol 93694 Today/Summer Days & Summer Nights.

1966 #1 *BARBARA ANN*

       (M) (2:05) Capitol 46618 Spirit Of America. *(45 version)*
       (M) (2:04) Capitol 46324 Made In The U.S.A. *(45 version)*
       (M) (3:05) Capitol 93698 Party/Stack-O-Tracks. *(LP version)*
       (M) (2:05) Rhino 75778 Frat Rock. *(45 version)*
       (M) (2:02) Capitol 96796 Absolute Best Volume 2. *(45 version)*

1966 #5 *SLOOP JOHN B*

       (M) (2:56) Capitol 48421 Pet Sounds.
       (M) (2:54) Capitol 46324 Made In The U.S.A.
       (M) (2:55) Capitol 96796 Absolute Best Volume 2.

1966 #7 *WOULDN'T IT BE NICE*

       (M) (2:21) Capitol 92639 Still Crusin'.
       (M) (2:23) Capitol 48421 Pet Sounds.
       (M) (2:21) Capitol 46324 Made In The U.S.A.
       (M) (2:21) Capitol 96796 Absolute Best Volume 2.
       (M) (2:22) Rhino 70588 Rockin' & Rollin' Wedding Songs Volume 1.
       (M) (2:21) Motown 6094 More Songs From The Original Soundtrack Of The "Big Chill".

1966 #38 *GOD ONLY KNOWS*

       (M) (2:49) Capitol 48421 Pet Sounds.
       (M) (2:47) Capitol 46324 Made In The U.S.A.
       (M) (2:49) Capitol 96796 Absolute Best Volume 2.

1966 #1 *GOOD VIBRATIONS*

       (M) (3:35) Capitol 46467 Endless Summer.
       (M) (3:34) Capitol 46324 Made In The U.S.A.
       (M) (3:35) Rhino 70627 Billboard's Top Rock & Roll Hits Of 1966.
       (M) (3:35) Rhino 72007 Billboard's Top Rock & Roll Hits 1962-1966 Box Set.
       (M) (3:34) Capitol 93696 Smiley Smile/Wild Honey.
       (M) (6:52) Capitol 93696 Smiley Smile/Wild Honey. *(several alternate takes strung together)*
       (M) (2:59) Capitol 93696 Smiley Smile/Wild Honey. *(alternate take)*
       (M) (3:35) Capitol 96796 Absolute Best Volume 2.

1967 #8 *HEROES AND VILLAINS*

       (M) (3:35) Capitol 46324 Made In The U.S.A.
       (M) (3:37) Capitol 93696 Smiley Smile/Wild Honey.
       (M) (2:56) Capitol 93696 Smiley Smile/Wild Honey. *(alternate take)*
       (M) (3:35) Capitol 96796 Absolute Best Volume 2.

1967 #22 *WILD HONEY*

       (M) (2:36) Capitol 93696 Smiley Smile/Wild Honey.
       (M) (2:36) Capitol 96796 Absolute Best Volume 2.

1968 #10 *DARLIN'*

       (M) (2:10) Capitol 93696 Smiley Smile/Wild Honey.
       (M) (2:11) Capitol 96796 Absolute Best Volume 2.

1968 #37 *FRIENDS*

       (S) (2:29) Capitol 93697 Friends/20-20.

BEACH BOYS (Continued)

1968 #8 DO IT AGAIN
    (M) (2:17) Capitol 46324 Made In The U.S.A. *(45 version)*
    (E) (2:24) Capitol 93697 Friends/20-20. *(LP version)*
    (E) (2:24) Capitol 96796 Absolute Best Volume 2. *(LP version)*

1969 #20 I CAN HEAR MUSIC
    (S) (2:37) Capitol 93697 Friends/20-20.

1969 #38 BREAK AWAY
    (S) (2:52) Capitol 93697 Friends/20-20.
    (M) (2:54) Capitol 46618 Spirit Of America.

BEATLES

1964 #1 I WANT TO HOLD YOUR HAND
    (S) (2:24) Parlophone 90043 Past Masters Volume 1.
    (S) (2:24) Parlophone 91302 Box Set.
    (M) (2:23) Parlophone 15852 Compact Disc EP Collection.

1964 #1 SHE LOVES YOU
    (M) (2:19) Parlophone 90043 Past Masters Volume 1.
    (M) (2:19) Parlophone 91302 Box Set.
    (M) (2:19) Parlophone 15852 Compact Disc EP Collection.

1964 #3 PLEASE PLEASE ME
    (M) (1:59) Parlophone 46435 Please Please Me. *(45 version)*
    (M) (1:59) Parlophone 91302 Box Set. *(45 version)*
    (M) (1:59) Parlophone 15852 Compact Disc EP Collection. *(45 version)*

1964 #29 MY BONNIE
(first released as by Tony Sheridan and the Beat Brothers and then after the Beatles scored big in the U.S., it was rereleased with credit given to The Beatles with Tony Sheridan)
    (S) (2:41) Polydor 823701 Early Tapes Of The Beatles.
    (M) (2:04) Rhino 70323 History Of British Rock Volume 5. *(this was the U.S. 45 version)*
    (M) (2:04) Rhino 72022 History Of British Rock Box Set. *(this was the U.S. 45 version)*

1964 #1 TWIST AND SHOUT
    (M) (2:32) Parlophone 46435 Please Please Me.
    (M) (2:32) Parlophone 91302 Box Set.
    (M) (2:32) Capitol 90803 Music From The Original Motion Picture Imagine.
    (M) (2:32) Parlophone 15852 Compact Disc EP Collection.

1964 #31 ALL MY LOVING
    (M) (2:05) Parlophone 46436 With The Beatles.
    (M) (2:05) Parlophone 91302 Box Set.
    (M) (2:05) Parlophone 15852 Compact Disc EP Collection.

1964 #30 ROLL OVER BEETHOVEN
    (M) (2:43) Parlophone 46436 With The Beatles.
    (M) (2:43) Parlophone 91302 Box Set.

1964 #1 CAN'T BUY ME LOVE
    (M) (2:10) Parlophone 46437 A Hard Day's Night.
    (M) (2:10) Parlophone 91302 Box Set.
    (M) (2:11) Parlophone 15852 Compact Disc EP Collection.

1964 #3 DO YOU WANT TO KNOW A SECRET
    (M) (1:55) Parlophone 46435 Please Please Me.
    (M) (1:55) Parlophone 91302 Box Set.
    (M) (1:54) Parlophone 15852 Compact Disc EP Collection.

1964 #38 THANK YOU GIRL
    (M) (2:01) Parlophone 90043 Past Masters Volume 1. *(45 version)*
    (M) (2:01) Parlophone 91302 Box Set. *(45 version)*
    (M) (2:01) Parlophone 15852 Compact Disc EP Collection. *(45 version)*

BEATLES (Continued)

1964 #1 LOVE ME DO
    (M) (2:18) Parlophone 46435 Please Please Me. *(U.S. 45 and LP version with Andy White on drums)*
    (M) (2:18) Parlophone 91302 Box Set. *(U.S. 45 and LP version with Andy White on drums)*
    (M) (2:21) Parlophone 90043 Past Masters Volume 1. *(Ringo Starr on drums but this was not the U.S. hit version)*
    (M) (2:21) Parlophone 91302 Box Set. *(Ringo Starr on drums but this was not the U.S. hit version)*
    (M) (2:18) Parlophone 15852 Compact Disc EP Collection. *(U.S. 45 and LP version with Andy White on drums)*

1964 #10 P.S. I LOVE YOU
    (M) (2:01) Parlophone 46435 Please Please Me.
    (M) (2:01) Parlophone 91302 Box Set.
    (M) (2:01) Parlophone 15852 Compact Disc EP Collection.

1964 #1 A HARD DAY'S NIGHT
    (M) (2:28) Parlophone 46437 A Hard Day's Night.
    (M) (2:28) Parlophone 91302 Box Set.

1964 #14 AIN'T SHE SWEET
    (M) (2:12) Polydor 823701 Early Tapes Of The Beatles.
    (M) (2:10) Rhino 70323 History Of British Rock Volume 5.
    (M) (2:10) Rhino 72022 History Of British Rock Box Set.

1964 #14 AND I LOVE HER
    (M) (2:27) Parlophone 46437 A Hard Day's Night. *(this was not the U.S. 45 or LP version as Paul's voice is double tracked on this version)*
    (M) (2:27) Parlophone 91302 Box Set. *(same comments as for Parlophone 46437)*
    (M) (2:27) Parlophone 15852 Compact Disc EP Collection. *(same comments as for Parlophone 46437)*

1964 #22 I'LL CRY INSTEAD
    (M) (1:43) Parlophone 46437 A Hard Day's Night.
    (M) (1:43) Parlophone 91302 Box Set.
    (M) (1:43) Parlophone 15852 Compact Disc EP Collection.

1964 #17 MATCHBOX
    (S) (1:56) Parlophone 90043 Past Masters Volume 1.
    (S) (1:56) Parlophone 91302 Box Set.
    (M) (1:56) Parlophone 15852 Compact Disc EP Collection.

1964 #34 SLOW DOWN
    (S) (2:54) Parlophone 90043 Past Masters Volume 1. *(LP version)*
    (S) (2:54) Parlophone 91302 Box Set. *(LP version)*
    (M) (2:54) Parlophone 15852 Compact Disc EP Collection. *(45 version)*

1964 #1 I FEEL FINE
    (S) (2:17) Parlophone 90043 Past Masters Volume 1.
    (S) (2:17) Parlophone 91302 Box Set.
    (M) (2:21) Parlophone 15852 Compact Disc EP Collection.

1964 #8 SHE'S A WOMAN
    (S) (3:00) Parlophone 90043 Past Masters Volume 1.
    (S) (3:00) Parlophone 91302 Box Set.
    (S) (3:01) Parlophone 15852 Compact Disc EP Collection. *(with countoff)*

1965 #1 EIGHT DAYS A WEEK
    (M) (2:41) Parlophone 46438 Beatles For Sale.
    (M) (2:41) Parlophone 91302 Box Set.
    (M) (2:42) Parlophone 15852 Compact Disc EP Collection.

BEATLES (Continued)

1965 #1 *TICKET TO RIDE*
    (S) (3:08) Parlophone 46439 Help!
    (S) (3:08) Parlophone 91302 Box Set.

1965 #1 *HELP*
    (S) (2:17) Parlophone 46439 Help!
    (S) (2:17) Parlophone 91302 Box Set.
    (S) (2:16) Capitol 90803 Music From The Original Motion Picture Imagine.

1965 #1 *YESTERDAY*
    (S) (2:03) Parlophone 46439 Help!
    (S) (2:03) Parlophone 91302 Box Set.
    (M) (2:03) Parlophone 15852 Compact Disc EP Collection.

1965 #28 *ACT NATURALLY*
    (S) (2:28) Parlophone 46439 Help!
    (S) (2:28) Parlophone 91302 Box Set.
    (M) (2:27) Parlophone 15852 Compact Disc EP Collection.

1966 #1 *WE CAN WORK IT OUT*
    (S) (2:13) Parlophone 90044 Past Masters Volume 2.
    (S) (2:13) Parlophone 91302 Box Set.

1966 #10 *DAY TRIPPER*
    (S) (2:47) Parlophone 90044 Past Masters Volume 2. *(truncated fade)*
    (S) (2:47) Parlophone 91302 Box Set. *(truncated fade)*

1966 #2 *NOWHERE MAN*
    (S) (2:41) Parlophone 46440 Rubber Soul.
    (S) (2:41) Parlophone 91302 Box Set.
    (M) (2:40) Parlophone 15852 Compact Disc EP Collection.

1966 #1 *PAPERBACK WRITER*
    (S) (2:16) Parlophone 90044 Past Masters Volume 2.
    (S) (2:16) Parlophone 91302 Box Set.

1966 #31 *RAIN*
    (S) (2:59) Parlophone 90044 Past Masters Volume 2.
    (S) (2:59) Parlophone 91302 Box Set.

1966 #1 *YELLOW SUBMARINE*
    (S) (2:36) Parlophone 46441 Revolver. *(LP version)*
    (S) (2:37) Parlophone 46445 Yellow Submarine. *(LP version)*
    (S) (2:36) Parlophone 91302 Box Set. *(LP version)*

1966 #12 *ELEANOR RIGBY*
    (S) (2:03) Parlophone 46441 Revolver.
    (S) (2:03) Parlophone 91302 Box Set.

1967 #1 *PENNY LANE*
    (radio stations were serviced with a special 45 version of this song which featured trumpets on the ending)
    (S) (2:58) Parlophone 48062 Magical Mystery Tour.
    (S) (2:58) Parlophone 91302 Box Set.

1967 #10 *STRAWBERRY FIELDS FOREVER*
    (S) (4:05) Parlophone 48062 Magical Mystery Tour.
    (S) (4:05) Parlophone 91302 Box Set.
    (S) (4:05) Capitol 90803 Music From The Original Motion Picture Imagine.

1967 #1 *ALL YOU NEED IS LOVE*
    (S) (3:46) Parlophone 48062 Magical Mystery Tour.
    (S) (3:46) Parlophone 46445 Yellow Submarine.
    (S) (3:46) Parlophone 91302 Box Set.

1967 #1 *HELLO GOODBYE*
    (S) (3:27) Parlophone 48062 Magical Mystery Tour.
    (S) (3:27) Parlophone 91302 Box Set.

BEATLES (Continued)

1968 #2 LADY MADONNA
(S) (2:15) Parlophone 90044 Past Masters Volume 2. *(truncated fade)*
(S) (2:15) Parlophone 91302 Box Set. *(truncated fade)*

1968 #1 HEY JUDE
(S) (7:06) Parlophone 90044 Past Masters Volume 2.
(S) (7:06) Parlophone 91302 Box Set.

1968 #11 REVOLUTION
(S) (4:13) Parlophone 46444 The Beatles. *(LP version which is technically titled "REVOLUTION 1")*
(S) (4:13) Parlophone 91302 Box Set. *(LP version which is technically titled "REVOLUTION 1")*
(S) (3:22) Parlophone 90044 Past Masters Volume 2. *(45 version)*
(S) (3:22) Parlophone 91302 Box Set. *(45 version)*
(S) (3:22) Capitol 90803 Music From The Original Motion Picture Imagine. *(45 version)*

1969 #1 GET BACK
(S) (3:05) Parlophone 46447 Let It Be. *(LP version)*
(S) (3:05) Parlophone 91302 Box Set. *(LP version)*
(S) (3:11) Parlophone 90044 Past Masters Volume 2. *(45 version)*
(S) (3:11) Parlophone 91302 Box Set. *(45 version)*

1969 #10 BALLAD OF JOHN AND YOKO
(S) (2:57) Parlophone 90044 Past Masters Volume 2.
(S) (2:57) Parlophone 91302 Box Set.
(S) (2:57) Capitol 90803 Music From The Original Motion Picture Imagine.

1969 #1 COME TOGETHER
(S) (4:16) Parlophone 46446 Abbey Road.
(S) (4:16) Parlophone 91302 Box Set.

1969 #2 SOMETHING
(S) (2:59) Parlophone 46446 Abbey Road.
(S) (2:59) Parlophone 91302 Box Set.
(S) (2:59) Capitol 46682 Best Of George Harrison.

1970 #1 LET IT BE
(S) (4:01) Parlophone 46447 Let It Be. *(LP version)*
(S) (4:01) Parlophone 91302 Box Set. *(LP version)*
(S) (3:48) Parlophone 90044 Past Masters Volume 2. *(45 version)*
(S) (3:48) Parlophone 91302 Box Set. *(45 version)*

1970 #1 THE LONG AND WINDING ROAD
(S) (3:36) Parlophone 46447 Let It Be.
(S) (3:36) Parlophone 91302 Box Set.

E.C. BEATTY

1959 #40 SKI KING

BEAU BRUMMELS

1965 #17 LAUGH LAUGH
(original 45 and LP versions of this song faded out)
(S) (3:01) K-Tel 686 Battle Of The Bands Volume 4. *(ends cold)*
(S) (3:02) Rhino 75892 Nuggets. *(ends cold)*
(S) (3:01) Rhino 70906 American Bandstand Greatest Hits Collection. *(ends cold)*
(S) (2:51) Garland 012 Remember When. *(ending fades)*
(M) (2:52) Rhino 70536 San Francisco Nights. *(ending fades)*
(S) (3:01) Warner Special Products 27607 Highs Of The 60's. *(ends cold)*
(S) (3:01) Rhino 75779 Best Of. *(ends cold)*

BEAU BRUMMELS (Continued)
1965 #7 JUST A LITTLE
        (S) (2:23) Rhino 75892 Nuggets.
        (S) (2:23) Garland 012 Remember When.
        (M) (2:22) Rhino 70536 San Francisco Nights.
        (S) (2:23) Rhino 75779 Best Of.

1965 #36 YOU TELL ME WHY
        (S) (3:03) Rhino 75779 Best Of.

BEAU-MARKS
1960 #40 CLAP YOUR HANDS

BOB BECKHAM
1960 #38 CRAZY ARMS

BEE GEES
1967 #17 NEW YORK MINING DISASTER 1941
        (S) (2:08) Polydor 843911 Tales From The Brothers Gibb. *(LP version)*
        (S) (2:08) Polydor 831594 Best Of. *(LP version)*
        (S) (2:08) Polydor 825220 Bee Gees' 1st. *(LP version)*
        (M) (2:08) Rhino 70326 History Of British Rock Volume 8. *(45 version)*
        (M) (2:08) Rhino 72022 History Of British Rock Box Set. *(45 version)*

1967 #24 TO LOVE SOMEBODY
        (S) (2:59) Polydor 843911 Tales From The Brothers Gibb.
        (S) (2:59) Polydor 825220 Bee Gees' 1st.
        (S) (2:59) Polydor 831594 Best Of.
        (S) (2:59) Rhino 70325 History Of British Rock Volume 7.
        (S) (2:59) Rhino 72022 History Of British Rock Box Set.

1967 #12 HOLIDAY
        (S) (2:52) Polydor 843911 Tales From The Brothers Gibb.
        (S) (2:52) Polydor 825220 Bee Gees' 1st.
        (S) (2:52) Polydor 831594 Best Of.

1967 #14 (THE LIGHTS WENT OUT IN) MASSACHUSETTS
        (S) (2:21) Polydor 843911 Tales From The Brothers Gibb.
        (S) (2:23) Polydor 833659 Horizontal.
        (S) (2:22) Polydor 831594 Best Of.

1968 #19 WORDS
        (S) (3:13) Polydor 843911 Tales From The Brothers Gibb.
        (S) (3:14) Polydor 831594 Best Of.
        (M) (3:16) Rhino 70327 History Of British Rock Volume 9.
        (M) (3:16) Rhino 72022 History Of British Rock Box Set.

1968 #40 JUMBO
        (S) (2:08) Polydor 843911 Tales From The Brothers Gibb.

1968 #3 I'VE GOTTA GET A MESSAGE TO YOU
        (S) (3:05) Polydor 843911 Tales From The Brothers Gibb. *(45 pitch but slightly longer than the 45 version which ran (2:59))*
        (S) (2:55) Polydor 831594 Best Of. *(LP length and speed which is slower than the 45)*
        (S) (2:55) Polydor 833660 Idea. *(LP length and speed which is slower than the 45)*
        (S) (3:04) Rhino 70327 History Of British Rock Volume 9. *(45 pitch but slightly longer than the 45 version which ran (2:59))*
        (S) (3:04) Rhino 72022 History Of British Rock Box Set. *(45 pitch but slightly longer than the 45 version which ran (2:59))*

1969 #6 I STARTED A JOKE
        (S) (3:05) Polydor 843911 Tales From The Brothers Gibb.
        (S) (3:06) Polydor 831594 Best Of.
        (S) (3:07) Polydor 833660 Idea.

BEE GEES (Continued)
1969 #18 FIRST OF MAY
(S) (2:46) Polydor 843911 Tales From The Brothers Gibb.
(S) (2:46) Polydor 825451 Odessa.
(S) (2:46) Polydor 831594 Best Of.
1969 #32 TOMORROW TOMORROW
(M) (3:55) Polydor 831594 Best Of.
(S) (4:05) Polydor 843911 Tales From The Brothers Gibb. *(with countoff)*
1971 #1 LONELY DAYS
(S) (3:44) Polydor 843911 Tales From The Brothers Gibb.
(S) (3:44) Polydor 833785 2 Years On.
(S) (3:44) Polydor 831960 Best Of Volume 2.
1971 #1 HOW CAN YOU MEND A BROKEN HEART
(S) (3:55) Polydor 843911 Tales From The Brothers Gibb.
(S) (3:55) Polydor 831960 Best Of Volume 2.
(S) (3:56) Polydor 833786 Trafalgar.
1971 #39 DON'T WANNA LIVE INSIDE MYSELF
(S) (5:24) Polydor 833786 Trafalgar.
(S) (5:23) Polydor 831960 Best Of Volume 2.
(S) (5:23) Polydor 843911 Tales From The Brothers Gibb.
1972 #15 MY WORLD
(S) (4:18) Polydor 843911 Tales From The Brothers Gibb.
(S) (4:19) Polydor 831960 Best Of Volume 2.
1972 #11 RUN TO ME
(S) (3:04) Polydor 843911 Tales From The Brothers Gibb.
(S) (3:07) Polydor 831960 Best Of Volume 2.
(S) (3:10) Polydor 833787 To Whom It May Concern.
1972 #26 ALIVE
(S) (4:01) Polydor 843911 Tales From The Brothers Gibb.
(S) (3:58) Polydor 831960 Best Of Volume 2.
(S) (4:02) Polydor 833787 To Whom It May Concern.

BEGINNING OF THE END
1971 #10 FUNKY NASSAU (PART 1)
(S) (3:11) Atlantic 81299 Atlantic Rhythm & Blues Volume 7.
(S) (3:09) Rhino 70785 Soul Hits Of The 70's Volume 5.
(S) (5:10) Atlantic 82305 Atlantic Rhythm And Blues 1947-1974 Box Set.
     (Parts 1 & 2)

HARRY BELAFONTE
1957 #17 JAMAICA FAREWELL
(M) (3:03) RCA 6877 All Time Greatest Hits Volume 1.
(M) (3:02) RCA 53860 Pure Gold.
(M) (3:04) Pair 1060 The Belafonte Songbook.
(M) (3:02) RCA 53801 Calypso.
(M) (3:02) RCA 52469 A Legendary Performer.
1957 #25 MARY'S BOY CHILD
(M) (2:56) RCA 6877 All Time Greatest Hits Volume 1.
(M) (2:59) Rhino 70636 Billboard's Greatest Christmas Hits (1955-Present).
(E) (4:21) RCA 9859 Nipper's Greatest Christmas Hits.
(E) (4:22) RCA 2626 To Wish You A Merry Christmas.
1957 #4 BANANA BOAT (DAY-O)
(M) (3:02) RCA 6877 All Time Greatest Hits Volume 1.
(M) (3:02) RCA 8466 Nipper's Greatest Hits Of The 50's Volume 1.
(M) (3:01) RCA 53860 Pure Gold.
(M) (3:01) RCA 52082 Day-O & Other Hits.

HARRY BELAFONTE (Continued)
>   (E)   (3:01)   RCA 61144   The RCA Records Label: The First Note In Black
>   Music.
>   (M)   (3:01)   RCA 53801   Calypso.
>   (M)   (3:01)   RCA 52469   A Legendary Performer.

1957 #9 *MAMA LOOK AT BUBU*
>   (M)   (2:53)   RCA 6877   All Time Greatest Hits Volume 1.
>   (S)   (3:05)   RCA 8467   Nipper's Greates Hits Of The 50's Volume 2.
>   (S)   (5:10)   RCA 52469   A Legendary Performer. *(live)*

1957 #32 *ISLAND IN THE SUN*
>   (M)   (3:06)   RCA 6877   All Time Greatest Hits Volume 1.
>   (M)   (3:06)   RCA 52082   Day-O & Other Hits.

1957 #35 *COCOANUT WOMAN*
>   (M)   (2:57)   RCA 6877   All Time Greatest Hits Volume 1.

ARCHIE BELL & THE DRELLS
1968 #1 *TIGHTEN UP*
>   (S)   (3:10)   Warner Special Products 27601   Atlantic Soul Classics.
>   (S)   (3:10)   JCI 3100   Dance Sixties.
>   (S)   (3:09)   Atlantic 81298   Atlantic Rhythm & Blues Volume 6.
>   (S)   (3:10)   Atlantic 82305   Atlantic Rhythm And Blues 1947-1974 Box Set.

1968 #15 *I CAN'T STOP DANCING*
1969 #20 *THERE'S GONNA BE A SHOWDOWN*
>   (S)   (2:41)   Rhino 70277   Rare Soul: Beach Music Classics Volume 1.

MADELINE BELL
1968 #36 *I'M GONNA MAKE YOU LOVE ME*

VINCENT BELL
1970 #27 *AIRPORT LOVE THEME*

WILLIAM BELL
1969 #36 *I FORGOT TO BE YOUR LOVER*
>   (S)   (2:39)   Stax 88005   Top Of The Stax.
>   (S)   (2:18)   Stax 8541   Best Of.

BELL NOTES
1959 #8 *I'VE HAD IT*

BELLS
1971 #4 *STAY AWHILE*
>   (S)   (3:21)   Rhino 70924   Super Hits Of The 70's Volume 4.
>   (S)   (3:21)   Rhino 72009   Super Hits Of The 70's Volumes 1-4 Box Set.

BELMONTS
1961 #22 *TELL ME WHY*
>   (M)   (2:34)   Arista 8206   Dion: 24 Original Classics 1958-1978.
>   (M)   (2:33)   Collectables 2508   History Of Rock - The Doo Wop Era Part 2.

1962 #26 *COME ON LITTLE ANGEL*

JESSE BELVIN
1957 #23 *GOODNIGHT MY LOVE*
>   (M)   (3:04)   Atlantic 81769   O.S.T. Big Town.

1959 #28 *GUESS WHO*
>   (S)   (2:51)   RCA 8466   Nipper's Greatest Hits Of The 50's Volume 1.

BOYD BENNETT
1955 #3 *SEVENTEEN*

JOE BENNETT & THE SPARKLETONES
1957 #19 *BLACK SLACKS*
    (M) (2:03) MCA 5938 Vintage Music Volumes 15 & 16.
    (M) (2:03) MCA 31213 Vintage Music Volume 16.

TONY BENNETT
1956 #34 *FROM THE CANDY STORE ON THE CORNER TO THE CHAPEL ON THE HILL*
1956 #30 *HAPPINESS STREET (CORNER SUNSHINE SQUARE)*
1956 #38 *JUST IN TIME*
    (M) (2:33) Columbia 40215 16 Most Requested Songs.
    (M) (2:33) Columbia/Legacy 46884 Forty Years:The Artistry Of.
1957 #32 *ONE FOR MY BABY*
1957 #8 *IN THE MIDDLE OF AN ISLAND*
1957 #35 *I AM*
1958 #31 *YOUNG AND WARM AND WONDERFUL*
1958 #20 *FIREFLY*
    (S) (1:36) Columbia/Legacy 46843 Forty Years: The Artistry Of.
1962 #22 *I LEFT MY HEART IN SAN FRANCISCO*
    (S) (2:50) Columbia 45019 Pop Classics Of The 60's.
    (S) (2:50) Columbia/Legacy 46843 Forty Years: The Artistry Of.
    (S) (2:51) Columbia 8669 I Left My Heart In San Francisco.
    (S) (2:50) Columbia 40215 16 Most Requested Songs.
1963 #15 *I WANNA BE AROUND*
    (S) (2:09) Columbia/Legacy 46843 Forty Years: The Artistry Of.
    (S) (2:09) Columbia 40215 16 Most Requested Songs.
1963 #25 *THE GOOD LIFE*
    (S) (2:13) Columbia/Legacy 46843 Forty Years: The Artistry Of.
    (S) (2:14) Columbia 40215 16 Most Requested Songs.
1964 #38 *WHO CAN I TURN TO (WHEN NOBODY NEEDS ME)*
    (S) (2:55) Columbia/Legacy 46843 Forty Years: The Artistry Of.
    (S) (2:55) Columbia 40215 16 Most Requested Songs.

BROOK BENTON
1959 #2 *IT'S JUST A MATTER OF TIME*
    (M) (2:25) Mercury 832041 45's On CD Volume 1.
    (M) (2:25) Rhino 70645 Billboard's Top R&B Hits Of 1959.
    (M) (2:25) Mercury 830772 Best Of.
    (M) (2:25) Mercury 836755 Forty Greatest Hits.
1959 #11 *ENDLESSLY*
    (S) (2:19) Mercury 830772 Best Of.
    (S) (2:19) Mercury 836755 Forty Greatest Hits.
    (S) (2:18) Curb 77445 Best Of.
1959 #10 *THANK YOU PRETTY BABY*
    (S) (2:29) Mercury 830772 Best Of.
    (S) (2:28) Mercury 836755 Forty Greatest Hits.
1959 #3 *SO MANY WAYS*
    (S) (2:29) Mercury 830772 Best Of.
    (S) (2:29) Mercury 836755 Forty Greatest Hits.
    (S) (2:29) Curb 77445 Best Of.
1960 #23 *THE TIES THAT BIND*
    (S) (2:49) Mercury 836755 Forty Greatest Hits.
1960 #3 *KIDDIO*
    (S) (2:37) Rhino 70646 Billboard's Top R&B Hits Of 1960.
    (S) (2:36) Mercury 830772 Best Of.
    (S) (2:37) Mercury 836755 Forty Greatest Hits.

BROOK BENTON (Continued)

1960 #16 THE SAME ONE
      (S) (2:29) Mercury 830772 Best Of.
      (S) (2:28) Mercury 836755 Forty Greatest Hits.

1960 #15 FOOLS RUSH IN
      (M) (2:26) Mercury 830772 Best Of.
      (M) (2:25) Mercury 836755 Forty Greatest Hits.

1961 #7 THINK TWICE
      (S) (2:32) Mercury 830772 Best Of.
      (S) (2:31) Mercury 836755 Forty Greatest Hits.

1961 #24 FOR MY BABY
      (M) (2:39) Mercury 836755 Forty Greatest Hits.

1961 #2 THE BOLL WEEVIL SONG
      (S) (2:37) Mercury 830772 Best Of.
      (S) (2:36) Mercury 836755 Forty Greatest Hits.
      (S) (2:36) Curb 77445 Best Of.

1961 #16 FRANKIE AND JOHNNY
      (S) (2:26) Mercury 830772 Best Of.
      (S) (2:27) Mercury 836755 Forty Greatest Hits.

1962 #16 REVENGE
      (S) (2:35) Mercury 836755 Forty Greatest Hits.

1962 #29 SHADRACK
      (S) (2:21) Mercury 836755 Forty Greatest Hits.

1962 #36 HIT RECORD
      (S) (2:35) Mercury 836755 Forty Greatest Hits.

1962 #10 LIE TO ME
      (S) (2:15) Mercury 830772 Best Of.
      (M) (2:13) Mercury 836755 Forty Greatest Hits.

1963 #6 HOTEL HAPPINESS
      (S) (2:40) Mercury 830772 Best Of.
      (S) (2:40) Mercury 836755 Forty Greatest Hits.

1963 #22 I GOT WHAT I WANTED
      (M) (2:34) Mercury 836755 Forty Greatest Hits.

1963 #29 MY TRUE CONFESSION
      (S) (2:20) Mercury 836755 Forty Greatest Hits.

1963 #30 TWO TICKETS TO PARADISE
      (S) (2:36) Mercury 836755 Forty Greatest Hits.

1964 #30 GOING GOING GONE
      (S) (2:47) Mercury 836755 Forty Greatest Hits.

1964 #40 ANOTHER CUP OF COFFEE
      (S) (2:48) Mercury 830772 Best Of.
      (M) (2:49) Mercury 836755 Forty Greatest Hits.

1964 #38 TOO LATE TO TURN BACK NOW
      (S) (3:26) Mercury 836755 Forty Greatest Hits.

1970 #2 RAINY NIGHT IN GEORGIA
      (S) (3:49) Mercury 836755 Forty Greatest Hits.
      (S) (3:49) Rhino 70658 Billboard's Top R&B Hits Of 1970.
      (S) (3:49) Rhino 70781 Soul Hits Of The 70's Volume 1.
      (S) (3:49) Atlantic 81911 Golden Age Of Black Music (1960-1970).
      (S) (3:49) Atlantic 81298 Atlantic Rhythm & Blues Volume 6.
      (S) (3:49) Curb 77445 Best Of.
      (S) (3:47) JCI 3303 Love Seventies.
      (S) (3:49) Atlantic 82305 Atlantic Rhythm And Blues 1947-1974 Box Set.

BROOK BENTON & DINAH WASHINGTON
1960 #2 *BABY (YOU GOT WHAT IT TAKES)*
    (S) (2:44) Mercury 816555 45's On CD Volume 2.
    (S) (2:44) Mercury 836755 Forty Greatest Hits.
    (S) (2:43) Rhino 70646 Billboard's Top R&B Hits Of 1960.
    (S) (2:44) Mercury 838956 Complete Dinah Washington On Mercury Volume 6.

1960 #5 *A ROCKIN' GOOD WAY (TO MESS AROUND AND FALL IN LOVE)*
    (S) (2:25) Rhino 70646 Billboard's Top R&B Hits Of 1960.
    (S) (2:25) Mercury 836755 Forty Greatest Hits.
    (S) (2:25) Curb 77445 Best Of Brook Benton.
    (S) (2:25) Mercury 838956 Complete Dinah Washington On Mercury Volume 6.

POLLY BERGEN
1958 #24 *COME PRIMA*

ROD BERNARD
1959 #17 *THIS SHOULD GO ON FOREVER*

CHUCK BERRY
1955 #5 *MAYBELLENE*
    (M) (2:19) Rhino 70598 Billboard's Top Rock & Roll Hits Of 1955.
    (M) (2:18) MCA 31198 Vintage Music Volume 1.
    (M) (2:18) MCA 5777 Vintage Music Volumes 1 & 2.
    (M) (2:20) JCI 3202 Rockin' Fifties.
    (M) (2:18) Chess 31319 Best of Chess Rock 'n' Roll Volume 1.
    (M) (2:16) RCA 5463 Rock & Roll - The Early Days.
    (M) (2:19) Rhino 70719 Legends Of Guitar - Rock: The 50's.
    (M) (2:18) Chess 31260 Berry Is On Top.
    (M) (2:20) Chess 92500 The Great Twenty Eight.
    (M) (2:19) Chess 80001 The Chess Box.
    (M) (2:19) Chess 31270 From the Motion Picture "Rock, Rock, Rock".
    (M) (2:19) Telstar 1002 Duckwalkin' Volume 1.
    (S) (2:37) MCA 6217 O.S.T. Hail! Hail! Rock 'N' Roll. *(live)*
    (S) (2:33) Mercury 826256 Golden Hits. *(all selections on this cd are rerecorded)*

1957 #3 *SCHOOL DAY*
    (M) (2:40) Rhino 70618 Billboard's Top Rock & Roll Hits Of 1957.
    (M) (2:40) Rhino 72004 Billboard's Top Rock & Roll Hits 1957-1961 Box Set.
    (M) (2:41) MCA 31200 Vintage Music Volume 3.
    (M) (2:41) MCA 5778 Vintage Music Volumes 3 & 4.
    (M) (2:39) Chess 92500 The Great Twenty Eight.
    (M) (2:39) Chess 80001 The Chess Box.
    (M) (2:39) Chess 9284 After School Session.
    (M) (2:42) Sire 6070 Rock 'N' Roll High School.
    (M) (2:39) Atlantic 82155 O.S.T. Book Of Love.
    (S) (2:34) Mercury 826256 Golden Hits. *(all selections on this cd are rerecorded)*

1957 #14 *ROCK & ROLL MUSIC*
    (M) (2:31) MCA 31203 Vintage Music Volume 6.
    (M) (2:31) MCA 5804 Vintage Music Volumes 5 & 6.
    (M) (2:30) Chess 92500 The Great Twenty Eight.
    (M) (2:30) Chess 80001 The Chess Box.
    (M) (2:24) Chess 92521 Rock N Roll Rarities. *(alternate take)*

CHUCK BERRY (Continued)

       (M)   (2:30) Telstar 1002 Duckwalkin' Volume 1.

       (S)   (2:31) Mercury 826256 Golden Hits. *(all selections on this cd are rerecorded)*

1958 #2 SWEET LITTLE SIXTEEN

       (M)   (3:10) MCA 31202 Vintage Music Volume 5. *(original recording speed)*

       (M)   (3:10) MCA 5804 Vintage Music Volumes 5 & 6. *(original recording speed)*

       (M)   (2:59) Chess 92500 The Great Twenty Eight. *(speed of 45 and LP, both of which were sped up considerably over the original recording speed)*

       (M)   (3:09) Chess 80001 The Chess Box. *(original recording speed)*

       (M)   (2:59) Curb 77323 All Time Greatest Hits Of Rock 'N' Roll. *(speed of 45 and LP, both of which were sped up considerably over the original recording speed)*

       (M)   (3:10) Chess 92521 Rock N Roll Rarities. *(alternate take with false start)*

       (S)   (2:38) MCA 6217 O.S.T. Hail! Hail! Rock 'N' Roll. *(live)*

       (S)   (2:12) Mercury 826256 Golden Hits. *(all selections on this cd are rerecorded)*

1958 #11 JOHNNY B. GOODE

       (M)   (2:37) MCA 31201 Vintage Music Volume 4.

       (M)   (2:37) MCA 5778 Vintage Music Volumes 3 & 4.

       (M)   (2:38) JCI 3201 Party Time Fifties.

       (M)   (2:37) MCA 31274 Classic Rock Volume 2.

       (M)   (2:37) Rhino 70732 Grandson Of Frat Rock.

       (M)   (2:37) Chess 31319 Best Of Chess Rock 'n' Roll Volume 1.

       (M)   (2:38) Capitol 48993 Spuds Mackenzie's Party Faves.

       (M)   (2:37) Chess 31260 Berry Is On Top.

       (M)   (2:37) Chess 92500 The Great Twenty Eight.

       (M)   (2:37) Chess 80001 The Chess Box.

       (M)   (3:08) Chess 92521 Rock N Roll Rarities. *(alternate take with false start)*

       (S)   (2:42) Mercury 826256 Golden Hits. *(all selections on this cd are rerecorded)*

1958 #31 CAROL

       (M)   (2:45) MCA 5936 Vintage Music Volumes 11 & 12.

       (M)   (2:45) MCA 31208 Vintage Music Volume 11.

       (M)   (2:44) Rhino 70561 Legends Of Guitar - Rock: The 50's Volume 2.

       (M)   (2:44) Chess 31260 Berry Is On Top.

       (M)   (2:45) Chess 92500 The Great Twenty Eight.

       (M)   (2:46) Chess 80001 The Chess Box.

       (M)   (2:46) Telstar 1002 Duckwalkin' Volume 1.

       (S)   (2:23) Mercury 826256 Golden Hits. *(all selections on this cd are rerecorded)*

1959 #31 ALMOST GROWN

       (M)   (2:18) Chess 31260 Berry Is On Top.

       (M)   (2:18) Chess 92500 The Great Twenty Eight.

       (M)   (2:18) Chess 80001 The Chess Box.

       (M)   (2:18) Telstar 1002 Duckwalkin' Volume 1.

1964 #32 NADINE (IS IT YOU?)

       (M)   (2:33) MCA 5939 Vintage Music Volumes 17 & 18.

       (M)   (2:33) MCA 31215 Vintage Music Volume 18.

       (S)   (2:46) Chess 92521 Rock N Roll Rarities. *(:13 longer fade than 45 or LP)*

       (M)   (2:32) Chess 92500 The Great Twenty Eight.

       (S)   (2:34) Chess 80001 The Chess Box.

       (M)   (2:32) Telstar 1002 Duckwalkin' Volume 1.

CHUCK BERRY (Continued)
1964 #9 *NO PARTICULAR PLACE TO GO*
(S) (2:41) Chess 31320 Best of Chess Rock 'n' Roll Volume 2.
(S) (2:41) MCA 31204 Vintage Music Volume 7.
(S) (2:41) MCA 5805 Vintage Music Volumes 7 & 8.
(S) (2:41) Chess 92521 Rock N Roll Rarities.
(M) (2:40) Chess 92500 The Great Twenty Eight.
(S) (2:41) Chess 80001 The Chess Box.
(S) (2:41) Chess 31261 St. Louis To Liverpool.
(M) (2:40) Telstar 1002 Duckwalkin' Volume 1.

1964 #15 *YOU NEVER CAN TELL*
(S) (2:40) MCA 31205 Vintage Music Volume 8.
(S) (2:40) MCA 5805 Vintage Music Volumes 7 & 8.
(S) (2:42) Chess 92521 Rock N Roll Rarities.
(S) (2:41) Chess 80001 The Chess Box.
(S) (2:41) Chess 31261 St. Louis To Liverpool.

1965 #35 *PROMISED LAND*
(S) (2:21) Chess 80001 The Chess Box.
(S) (2:21) Chess 31261 St. Louis To Liverpool.
(S) (2:28) Chess 92521 Rock N Roll Rarities. *(remixed)*

1972 #1 *MY DING-A-LING*
(M) (4:20) Rhino 70633 Billboard's Top Rock & Roll Hits Of 1972. *(a very close approximation to the 45 version but an extra line appears in the introduction)*
(M) (4:20) Rhino 72005 Billboard's Top Rock & Roll Hits 1968-1972 Box Set. *(same comments as for Rhino 70633)*
(S) (4:21) Chess 80001 The Chess Box. *(same comments as for Rhino 70633)*
(S) (11:32) Chess 9295 London Chuck Berry Sessions. *(LP version)*
(E) (4:13) Telstar 1002 Duckwalkin' Volume 1. *(45 version)*

1973 #30 *REELIN' AND ROCKIN'*
(S) (6:58) Rhino 75778 Frat Rock. *(live 1973 LP version)*
(S) (7:06) Chess 9295 London Chuck Berry Sessions. *(live 1973 LP version)*
(S) (7:06) Chess 80001 The Chess Box. *(live 1973 LP version)*
(M) (3:14) MCA 5940 Vintage Music Volumes 19 & 20. *(1958 studio version)*
(M) (3:14) MCA 31217 Vintage Music Volume 20. *(1958 studio version)*
(M) (3:14) Chess 80001 The Chess Box. *(1958 studio version)*
(M) (3:36) Chess 92521 Rock N Roll Rarities (1958 studio version; alternate take)
(M) (3:13) Chess 92500 The Great Twenty Eight. *(1958 studio version)*
(S) (4:14) Mercury 826256 Golden Hits. *(all selections on this cd are rerecorded; 1958 lyrics)*

BEVERLY SISTERS
1957 #31 *GREENSLEEVES*

BIG BOPPER
1958 #4 *CHANTILLY LACE*
(M) (2:20) Rhino 70164 Hellooo Baby! The Best Of.
(M) (2:21) Mercury 832041 45's On CD Volume 1.
(M) (2:22) Mercury 826448 Oldies Golden Million Sellers.
(M) (2:21) JCI 3202 Rockin' Fifties.

1958 #39 *BIG BOPPER'S WEDDING*
(M) (2:07) Rhino 70164 Hellooo Baby! The Best Of.
(M) (2:07) Rhino 70794 KFOG Presents M. Dung's Idiot Show.
(M) (2:07) Rhino 70589 Rockin' & Rollin' Wedding Songs Volume 2.

BIG BROTHER & THE HOLDING COMPANY
1968 #14 *PIECE OF MY HEART*
    (S) (4:13) Columbia 32168 Janis Joplin's Greatest Hits.
    (S) (4:12) Columbia 45018 Rock Classics Of The 60's.
    (S) (4:13) SBK 93744 China Beach - Music & Memories.
    (S) (4:13) Columbia 9700 Cheap Thrills.

MR. ACKER BILK
1962 #1 *STRANGER ON THE SHORE*

BILLY & LILLIE
1958 #4 *LA DEE DAH*
1959 #27 *LUCKY LADYBUG*

BILLY JOE & THE CHECKMATES
1962 #20 *PERCOLATOR (TWIST)*

BILL BLACK'S COMBO
1960 #13 *SMOKIE (PART 2)*
    (M) (2:06) MCA 25226 History Of Hi Records Rhythm & Blues Volume 1.
1960 #4 *WHITE SILVER SANDS*
1960 #9 *JOSEPHINE*
1960 #7 *DON'T BE CRUEL*
    (M) (1:55) MCA 25226 History Of Hi Records Rhythm & Blues Volume 1.
1960 #17 *BLUE TANGO*
1961 #17 *HEARTS OF STONE*
1961 #23 *OLE BUTTERMILK SKY*
1961 #39 *MOVIN'*
1962 #37 *TWIST-HER*

CILLA BLACK
1964 #38 *YOU'RE MY WORLD*
    (S) (2:57) Rhino 70320 History Of British Rock Volume 2.
    (S) (2:57) Rhino 72022 History Of British Rock Box Set.
    (S) (2:57) Rhino 72008 History Of British Rock Volumes 1-4 Box Set.

JEANNE BLACK
1960 #5 *HE'LL HAVE TO STAY*
    (S) (2:39) Rhino 70681 Billboard's Top Country Hits Of 1960.

JACK BLANCHARD & MISTY MORGAN
1970 #14 *TENNESSEE BIRD WALK*

BILLY BLAND
1960 #10 *LET THE LITTLE GIRL DANCE*

BOBBY BLAND
1962 #27 *TURN ON YOUR LOVE LIGHT*
    (M) (2:28) MCA 31219 Best Of.
    (S) (2:36) Rhino 70647 Billboard's Top R&B Hits Of 1961.
    (S) (2:34) MCA 31202 Vintage Music Volume 5. *(alternate take)*
    (S) (2:34) MCA 5804 Vintage Music Volumes 5 & 6. *(alternate take)*
    (E) (2:33) JCI 3204 Heart & Soul Fifties. *(alternate take)*
1963 #29 *CALL ON ME*
    (M) (2:36) MCA 31219 Best Of.
1963 #30 *THAT'S THE WAY LOVE IS*
1964 #16 *AIN'T NOTHING YOU CAN DO*
    (M) (2:37) MCA 31219 Best Of.
1964 #30 *AIN'T DOING TOO BAD (PART 1)*

MARCIE BLANE
1962 #2 *BOBBY'S GIRL*

BLOOD, SWEAT & TEARS
1969 #2 *YOU'VE MADE ME SO VERY HAPPY*

(S) (4:15) Columbia 31170 Blood, Sweat & Tears Greatest Hits. (*LP version*)
(S) (4:13) Columbia 45019 Pop Classics Of The 60's. (*LP version*)
(S) (4:15) Columbia 9720 Blood, Sweat And Tears. (*LP version; truncated fade*)
(S) (4:15) MFSL 559 Blood, Sweat And Tears. (*LP version*)

1969 #3 *SPINNING WHEEL*

(S) (4:05) JCI 3101 Rockin' Sixties. (*LP version*)
(S) (4:03) Columbia 45018 Rock Classics Of The 60's. (*LP version*)
(S) (4:04) Columbia 31170 Blood, Sweat & Tears Greatest Hits. (*LP version*)
(S) (4:04) Columbia 9720 Blood, Sweat And Tears. (LP version)
(S) (4:05) MFSL 559 Blood, Sweat And Tears. (*LP version*)

1969 #1 *AND WHEN I DIE*

(S) (4:01) Columbia 31170 Blood, Sweat & Tears Greatest Hits. (*LP version*)
(S) (4:00) Priority 8670 Hitchin A Ride/70's Greatest Rock Hits Volume 10. (*LP version*)
(S) (4:01) Columbia 9720 Blood, Sweat And Tears. (*LP version*)
(S) (4:02) MFSL 559 Blood, Sweat And Tears. (*LP version*)

1970 #9 *HI-DE-HO*

(S) (4:23) Columbia 31170 Blood, Sweat & Tears Greatest Hits. (*LP version*)
(S) (4:23) Columbia 30090 Blood, Sweat & Tears 3. (*LP version*)

1970 #17 *LUCRETIA MAC EVIL*

(S) (5:27) Columbia 31170 Blood, Sweat & Tears Greatest Hits. (*includes "LUCRETIA MAC EVIL" and "LUCRETIA'S REPRISE" which run together as one track.*)
(S) (3:03) Columbia 30090 Blood, Sweat & Tears 3. (*as with the original vinyl LP, "LUCRETIA MAC EVIL" is ever so slightly separated from "LUCRETIA'S REPRISE"*)

1971 #21 *GO DOWN GAMBLIN'*

(S) (4:12) Columbia 31170 Blood, Sweat & Tears Greatest Hits. (*LP version*)

BLOODROCK
1971 #36 *D.O.A.*

(S) (8:26) Capitol 91622 Bloodrock 'N' Roll. (*LP version*)
(S) (4:33) Rhino 70986 Heavy Metal Memories. (*45 version*)

BLOODSTONE
1973 #5 *NATURAL HIGH*

(S) (4:07) Rhino 70551 Soul Hits Of The 70's Volume 11.

1973 #35 *NEVER LET YOU GO*

BOBBY BLOOM
1970 #6 *MONTEGO BAY*

(the actual 45 time is (2:24) not (2:53) as the record label states)

(S) (2:55) Rhino 70923 Super Hits Of The 70's Volume 3. (*LP version*)
(S) (2:55) Rhino 72009 Super Hits Of The 70's Volumes 1-4 Box Set. (*LP version*)

BLUE-BELLES
1962 #16 *I SOLD MY HEART TO THE JUNKMAN*

BLUE CHEER
1968 #9 *SUMMERTIME BLUES*
    (S) (3:44) Mercury 834030 Good Times Are So Hard To Find.
    (S) (3:44) Warner Special Products 27607 Highs Of The 60's.
    (S) (3:44) Mercury 834216 45's On CD Volume 3.
    (S) (3:45) Rhino 70536 San Francisco Nights.

BLUE HAZE
1973 #21 *SMOKE GETS IN YOUR EYES*
    (S) (3:16) A&M 6015 Reggae Spectacular.

BLUE JAYS
1961 #26 *LOVER'S ISLAND*
    (M) (2:17) Rhino 75763 Best Of Doo Wop Ballads.

BLUE RIDGE RANGERS
1973 #10 *JAMBALAYA (ON THE BAYOU)*
    (S) (3:14) Fantasy 4502 The Blue Ridge Rangers.
1973 #33 *HEARTS OF STONE*
    (S) (2:10) Fantasy 4502 The Blue Ridge Rangers.

BLUES IMAGE
1970 #5 *RIDE CAPTAIN RIDE*
    (S) (3:41) JCI 3301 Rockin' Seventies. *(LP length)*
    (S) (3:41) Atlantic 81909 Hit Singles 1958-1977. *(LP length)*

BLUES MAGOOS
1967 #6 *(WE AIN'T GOT) NOTHIN' YET*
    (S) (2:14) K-Tel 713 Battle Of The Bands.
    (S) (2:14) Rhino 75777 More Nuggets.
    (S) (2:14) Mercury 834216 45's On CD Volume 3.
    (S) (2:15) Mercury 314512313 Kaleidescopic Compendium: The Best Of.

BOB & EARL
1964 #36 *HARLEM SHUFFLE*
    (the actual 45 time is (2:50) not (2:30) as stated on the record label)
    (M) (2:51) Rhino 70992 Groove 'N' Grind.
    (S) (2:28) Motown 6215 Hits From The Legendary Vee-Jay Records.
        (rerecording)

BOBBETTES
1957 #6 *MR. LEE*
    (M) (2:13) Rhino 70643 Billboard's Top R&B Hits Of 1957.
    (M) (2:13) Atlantic 81677 O.S.T. Stand By Me.
    (M) (2:12) Atlantic 81295 Atlantic Rhythm & Blues Volume 3.
    (M) (2:13) Warner Special Products 27602 20 Party Classics.
    (M) (2:12) Atlantic 82305 Atlantic Rhythm And Blues 1947-1974 Box Set.

BOB B. SOXX & THE BLUE JEANS
1963 #9 *ZIP-A-DEE-DOO-DAH*
    (M) (2:48) Abkco 7118 Phil Spector/Back To Mono (1958-1969).
1963 #30 *WHY DO LOVERS BREAK EACH OTHER'S HEART?*
    (M) (2:47) Abkco 7118 Phil Spector/Back To Mono (1958-1969).

JOHNNY BOND
1960 #25 *HOT ROD LINCOLN*
1965 #34 *10 LITTLE BOTTLES*

GARY U.S. BONDS
1960 #5 *NEW ORLEANS*
        (M) (2:49) Legrand 17001 Greatest Hits.
        (M) (2:49) Rhino 70971 Best Of.
1961 #1 *QUARTER TO THREE*
        (M) (2:27) Rhino 70971 Best Of.
        (M) (2:28) Rhino 75772 Son Of Frat Rock.
        (M) (2:27) Rhino 70622 Billboard's Top Rock & Roll Hits Of 1961.
        (M) (2:27) Rhino 72004 Billboard's Top Rock & Roll Hits 1957-1961 Box Set.
        (M) (2:32) Legrand 17001 Greatest Hits.
1961 #2 *SCHOOL IS OUT*
        (S) (2:26) Rhino 70971 Best Of.
        (S) (2:27) Legrand 17001 Greatest Hits.
1961 #32 *SCHOOL IS IN*
        (M) (2:05) Legrand 17001 Greatest Hits.
        (M) (2:05) Rhino 70971 Best Of.
1962 #6 *DEAR LADY TWIST*
        (S) (2:29) Rhino 70971 Best Of. *(:06 longer than 45 or LP)*
        (S) (2:38) Legrand 17001 Greatest Hits. *(:13 longer than 45 or LP)*
1962 #12 *TWIST, TWIST SENORA*
        (M) (2:38) Legrand 17001 Greatest Hits.
        (M) (2:34) Rhino 70971 Best Of.

BONNIE LOU
1956 #10 *DADDY-O*

JAMES BOOKER
1960 #27 *GONZO*

BOOKER T & THE MG'S
1962 #3 *GREEN ONIONS*
        (M) (2:51) Atlantic 81281 Best Of.
        (M) (2:51) Atlantic Group 88218 Complete Stax/Volt Singles 1959 - 1968. *(truncated fade)*
        (E) (2:48) Stax 88005 Top Of The Stax. *(intro fades in)*
        (M) (2:51) Rhino 70648 Billboard's Top R&B Hits Of 1962.
        (E) (2:50) Warner Special Products 27601 Atlantic Soul Classics. *(intro fades in)*
        (M) (2:50) Atlantic 81296 Atlantic Rhythm & Blues Volume 4.
        (M) (2:51) Atlantic 82305 Atlantic Rhythm And Blues 1947-1974 Box Set.
1967 #36 *HIP HUG-HER*
        (S) (2:24) Atlantic 81281 Best Of.
        (M) (2:22) Atlantic Group 88218 Complete Stax/Volt Singles 1959 - 1968.
        (M) (2:26) Warner Special Products 27602 20 Party Classics.
        (M) (2:22) Atlantic 82305 Atlantic Rhythm And Blues 1947-1974 Box Set.
1967 #24 *GROOVIN'*
        (S) (2:40) Atlantic 81281 Best Of.
        (M) (2:41) Atlantic Group 88218 Complete Stax/Volt Singles 1959 - 1968.
1968 #9 *SOUL LIMBO*
        (S) (2:21) Stax 60-004 Best Of.
        (S) (2:20) Stax 88008 Top Of The Stax Volume 2.
        (S) (2:21) Stax 4113 Soul Limbo.
1969 #14 *HANG 'EM HIGH*
        (S) (3:55) Stax 60-004 Best Of.

BOOKER T & THE MG'S (Continued)

    (S) (3:54) CBS Special Products 46808 Rock Goes To The Movies Volume 5.

    (S) (3:55) Stax 4113 Soul Limbo.

1969 #8 *TIME IS TIGHT*

    (S) (4:55) Stax 60-004 Best Of. *(LP version)*

    (S) (3:15) Warner Special Products 27609 Memphis Soul Classics. *(45 version)*

    (S) (3:16) Rhino 75770 Soul Shots Volume 2. *(45 version)*

    (S) (4:55) Stax 8562 O.S.T. Uptight. *(LP version)*

1969 #26 *MRS. ROBINSON*

    (S) (3:41) Stax 60004 Best Of.

    (S) (3:41) Stax 8531 The Booker T Set.

DANIEL BOONE

1972 #16 *BEAUTIFUL SUNDAY*

    (S) (3:01) Rhino 70929 Super Hits Of The 70's Volume 9.

PAT BOONE

1955 #1 *AIN'T THAT A SHAME*

1955 #8 *AT MY FRONT DOOR (CRAZY LITTLE MAMA)*

1956 #5 *I'LL BE HOME*

    (M) (2:58) Curb 77298 Greatest Hits.

1956 #2 *I ALMOST LOST MY MIND*

    (S) (2:30) Curb 77298 Greatest Hits. *(rerecorded)*

1956 #10 *FRIENDLY PERSUASION (THEE I LOVE)*

    (S) (3:01) Curb 77298 Greatest Hits. *(rerecorded)*

1956 #16 *CHAINS OF LOVE*

1956 #25 *ANASTASIA*

1957 #3 *DON'T FORBID ME*

    (S) (2:12) Curb 77298 Greatest Hits. *(rerecorded)*

1957 #9 *WHY BABY WHY*

1957 #24 *I'M WAITING JUST FOR YOU*

1957 #1 *LOVE LETTERS IN THE SAND*

    (M) (2:22) MCA 31199 Vintage Music Volume 2. *(whistling in the introduction that was not on the original 45)*

    (M) (2:22) MCA 5777 Vintage Music Volumes 1 & 2. *(whistling in the introduction that was not on the original 45)*

    (S) (2:13) Curb 77298 Greatest Hits. *(rerecording)*

    (S) (2:13) Curb 77354 50's Hits Volume 1. *(rerecording)*

    (S) (2:13) Curb 77525 Greatest Hits Of Rock 'N' Roll Volume 2. *(rerecording)*

1957 #20 *BERNADINE*

1957 #10 *REMEMBER YOU'RE MINE*

    (S) (2:15) Curb 77298 Greatest Hits. *(rerecording)*

1957 #15 *THERE'S A GOLDMINE IN THE SKY*

1957 #3 *APRIL LOVE*

    (S) (2:40) Curb 77298 Greatest Hits. *(rerecording)*

1958 #6 *A WONDERFUL TIME UP THERE*

    (S) (2:00) Curb 77298 Greatest Hits. *(rerecording)*

1958 #6 *IT'S TOO SOON TO KNOW*

1958 #9 *SUGAR MOON*

1958 #11 *IF DREAMS CAME TRUE*

1958 #25 *GEE, BUT IT'S LONELY*

1958 #33 *I'LL REMEMBER TONIGHT*

PAT BOONE (Continued)

1959 #17 *WITH THE WIND AND RAIN IN YOUR HAIR*

1959 #21 *FOR A PENNY*

1959 #23 *TWIXT TWELVE AND TWENTY*

1959 #25 *FOOLS HALL OF FAME*

1960 #23 *(WELCOME) NEW LOVERS*

1960 #36 *WALKING THE FLOOR OVER YOU*

1961 #2 *MOODY RIVER*
- (S) (2:35) MCA 31205 Vintage Music Volume 8.
- (S) (2:35) MCA 5805 Vintage Music Volumes 7 & 8.
- (S) (2:35) Curb 77298 Greatest Hits.

1961 #28 *BIG COLD WIND*

1961 #36 *JOHNNY WILL*

1962 #35 *I'LL SEE YOU IN MY DREAMS*

1962 #6 *SPEEDY GONZALES*
- (S) (2:32) MCA 5937 Vintage Music Volumes 13 & 14.
- (S) (2:32) MCA 31211 Vintage Music Volume 14.
- (S) (2:30) Curb 77298 Greatest Hits. *(rerecorded)*

PAT BOONE & FONTANE SISTERS

1956 #39 *VOICES*

JIMMY BOWEN

1957 #12 *I'M STICKIN' WITH YOU*
- (M) (2:06) Collectables 5416 Murray The K - Sing Along With The Golden Gassers. *(truncated fade)*
- (M) (2:06) Collectables 5406 Best Of.

1957 #33 *WARM UP TO ME BABY*
- (M) (2:17) Collectables 5406 Best Of.

DAVID BOWIE

1973 #17 *SPACE ODDITY*
- (S) (5:15) RCA 1732 Changesonebowie.
- (S) (5:13) Rykodisc 20171 Changesbowie.
- (S) (5:13) Rykodisc 10131 Space Oddity.
- (M) (5:07) Rykodisc 90120 Sound + Vision. *(demo version with :14 studio talk)*
- (S) (5:13) RCA 4813 Space Oddity.
- (S) (5:13) RCA 4919 Fame And Fashion.

BOX TOPS

1967 #1 *THE LETTER*
- (S) (1:50) K-Tel 686 Battle Of The Bands Volume 4.
- (S) (1:52) Rhino 70628 Billboard's Top Rock & Roll Hits of 1967.
- (S) (1:50) Warner Special Products 27611 Ultimate.

1967 #24 *NEON RAINBOW*
- (S) (2:58) Warner Special Products 27611 Ultimate.

1968 #2 *CRY LIKE A BABY*
- (S) (2:31) Rhino 70629 Billboard's Top Rock & Roll Hits of 1968.
- (S) (2:31) Rhino 72005 Billboard's Top Rock & Roll Hits 1968-1972 Box Set.
- (S) (2:31) Warner Special Products 27610 More Party Classics.
- (S) (2:31) Warner Special Products 27611 Ultimate.

1968 #17 *CHOO CHOO TRAIN*
- (S) (2:50) Warner Special Products 27611 Ultimate.

1969 #29 *SWEET CREAM LADIES, FORWARD MARCH*
- (S) (2:12) Warner Special Products 27611 Ultimate.

BOX TOPS (Continued)
1969 #13 *SOUL DEEP*
        (S) (2:26) Warner Special Products 27609 Memphis Soul Classics.
        (S) (2:26) Warner Special Products 27611 Ultimate.
1969 #35 *TURN ON A DREAM*
        (S) (2:47) Warner Special Products 27611 Ultimate.

TOMMY BOYCE & BOBBY HART
1967 #34 *OUT & ABOUT*
1968 #7 *I WONDER WHAT SHE'S DOING TONIGHT*
        (S) (2:42) Rhino 75777 More Nuggets.
1968 #16 *ALICE LONG (YOU'RE STILL MY FAVORITE GIRLFRIEND)*

JAN BRADLEY
1963 #14 *MAMA DIDN'T LIE*
        (M) (2:01) MCA 5937 Vintage Music Volumes 13 & 14.
        (M) (2:01) MCA 31210 Vintage Music Volume 13.
        (M) (2:00) MCA 6228 O.S.T. Hairspray.
        (M) (2:00) Chess 31317 Best Of Chess Rhythm & Blues Volume 1.

OWEN BRADLEY QUINTET
1958 #32 *BIG GUITAR*

BRASS RING
1966 #39 *PHOENIX LOVE THEME*

BOB BRAUN
1962 #26 *TILL DEATH DO US PART*

BREAD
1970 #1 *MAKE IT WITH YOU*
        (S) (3:09) Elektra 60414 Anthology.
1970 #7 *IT DON'T MATTER TO ME*
        (S) (2:46) Elektra 60414 Anthology.
1971 #20 *LET YOUR LOVE GO*
        (S) (2:18) Elektra 60414 Anthology.
1971 #6 *IF*
        (S) (2:31) Elektra 60414 Anthology.
1971 #3 *BABY I'M A WANT YOU*
        (S) (2:23) Elektra 60414 Anthology.
        (S) (2:29) Elektra 75015 Baby I'm A Want You.
1972 #6 *EVERYTHING I OWN*
        (S) (3:04) Elektra 60414 Anthology.
        (S) (3:05) Elektra 75015 Baby I'm A Want You.
1972 #15 *DIARY*
        (S) (3:04) Elektra 60414 Anthology.
        (S) (3:05) Elektra 75015 Baby I'm A Want You.
1972 #10 *THE GUITAR MAN*
        (S) (3:41) Elektra 60414 Anthology.
        (S) (3:45) Elektra 60918 Guitar Man.
1972 #11 *SWEET SURRENDER*
        (S) (2:33) Elektra 60414 Anthology.
        (S) (2:35) Elektra 60918 Guitar Man.
1973 #11 *AUBREY*
        (S) (3:34) Elektra 60414 Anthology.
        (S) (3:38) Elektra 60918 Guitar Man.

BEVERLY BREMERS
1972 #16 *DON'T SAY YOU DON'T REMEMBER*
  (S) (3:23) Rhino 70927 Super Hits Of The 70's Volume 7.

BRENDA & THE TABULATIONS
1967 #22 *DRY YOUR EYES*
1971 #14 *RIGHT ON THE TIP OF MY TONGUE*
  (M) (3:15) Rhino 70784 Soul Hits Of The 70's Volume 4. *(mastered from vinyl)*

WALTER BRENNAN
1960 #36 *DUTCHMAN'S GOLD*
1962 #8 *OLD RIVERS*
  (S) (2:44) Rhino 70683 Billboard's Top Country Hits Of 1962.
1962 #31 *MAMA SANG A SONG*

TERESA BREWER
1955 #7 *PLEDGING MY LOVE*
  (M) (2:41) MCA 1545 Best Of.
1956 #6 *A TEAR FELL*
  (M) (2:33) MCA 1545 Best Of.
1956 #10 *A SWEET OLD FASHIONED GIRL*
1956 #24 *MUTUAL ADMIRATION SOCIETY*
1957 #40 *I'M DROWNING MY SORROWS*
1957 #17 *EMPTY ARMS*
  (M) (2:47) MCA 1545 Best Of.
1957 #40 *TEARDROPS IN MY HEART*
1957 #1 *YOU SEND ME*
1958 #37 *THE HULA HOOP SONG*
1960 #24 *ANYMORE*

BREWER & SHIPLEY
1971 #8 *ONE TOKE OVER THE LINE*
  (S) (3:18) Rhino 70924 Super Hits Of The 70's Volume 4.
  (S) (3:18) Rhino 72009 Super Hits Of The 70's Volumes 1-4 Box Set.
  (S) (3:19) Pair 1202 Best Of Buddah.
  (S) (3:18) Priority 8670 Hitchin A Ride/70's Greatest Rock Hits Volume 10.
  (S) (3:20) Pair 1231 Greatest Hits.
  (S) (4:31) Special Music 4920 Best Of. *(LP version)*
1971 #39 *TARKIO ROAD*
  (S) (3:11) Rhino 70926 Super Hits Of The 70's Volume 6.
  (S) (4:31) Pair 1231 Greatest Hits. *(LP version)*
  (S) (4:31) Special Music 4920 Best Of. *(LP version)*

BRIGHTER SIDE OF DARKNESS
1973 #10 *LOVE JONES*
  (S) (3:18) Rhino 70790 Soul Hits Of The 70's Volume 10.

BROOKLYN BRIDGE
1969 #4 *WORST THAT COULD HAPPEN*
  (M) (3:05) Pair 1202 Best Of Buddah.
  (S) (3:07) Collectables 5015 Greatest Hits Of Johnny Maestro & The Brooklyn Bridge.
1969 #40 *BLESSED IS THE RAIN*
  (S) (3:17) Collectables 5015 Greatest Hits Of Johnny Maestro & The Brooklyn Bridge.

BROOKLYN BRIDGE (Continued)
1969 #37 *YOU'LL NEVER WALK ALONE*
  (S) (4:54) Collectables 5015 Greatest Hits Of Johnny Maestro & The Brooklyn Bridge. *(LP length)*

DONNIE BROOKS
1960 #13 *MISSION BELL*
1961 #34 *DOLL HOUSE*

BROTHERHOOD OF MAN
1970 #13 *UNITED WE STAND*
  (S) (2:52) Rhino 70922 Super Hits Of The 70's Volume 2.
  (S) (2:52) Rhino 72009 Super Hits Of The 70's Volumes 1-4 Box Set.

BROTHERS FOUR
1960 #2 *GREENFIELDS*
  (S) (2:54) Columbia 44373 Hollywood Magic The 60's.
  (S) (3:01) Columbia 45017 Radio Classics Of The 50's.
  (S) (3:02) Columbia 8603 Greatest Hits.
  (S) (3:02) Rhino 70264 Troubadours Of The Folk Era Volume 2.

AL BROWN'S TUNETOPPERS
1960 #14 *THE MADISON*

ARTHUR BROWN (see CRAZY WORLD OF ARTHUR BROWN)

BUSTER BROWN
1960 #34 *FANNIE MAE*
  (M) (2:52) Rhino 70646 Billboard's Top R&B Hits Of 1960.
  (S) (2:56) Relic 7009 Raging Harlem Hit Parade.

JAMES BROWN
1961 #40 *LOST SOMEONE*
  (E) (3:26) Polydor 849108 Star Time.
1962 #35 *NIGHT TRAIN*
  (S) (3:31) Rhino 75774 Soul Shots Volume 1.
  (S) (3:31) Polydor 831700 CD Of JB II.
  (M) (3:38) Polydor 849109 Star Time.
  (M) (3:30) Polydor 511326 20 All Time Greatest Hits.
1963 #16 *PRISONER OF LOVE*
  (S) (2:25) Polydor 825714 CD Of JB.
  (S) (2:24) Polydor 849109 Star Time.
  (S) (2:23) Polydor 817304 Roots Of A Revolution.
1964 #26 *OH BABY DON'T YOU WEEP (PART 1)*
  (S) (6:30) Polydor 817304 Roots Of A Revolution. *(Parts 1 & 2; even Part 1 is not the 45 version)*
1964 #21 *OUT OF SIGHT*
  (E) (2:21) Polydor 825714 CD Of JB.
  (M) (2:20) Polydor 849109 Star Time.
1965 #8 *PAPA'S GOT A BRAND NEW BAG (PART 1)*
  (M) (2:05) Polydor 825714 CD Of JB.
  (M) (6:57) Polydor 849109 Star Time. *(much slower than the original version; Parts 1, 2 & 3)*
  (M) (2:07) Polydor 849109 Star Time.
  (M) (2:05) Polydor 511326 20 All Time Greatest Hits.
  (M) (2:05) Special Music 847982 Papa's Got A Brand New Bag.
1965 #2 *I GOT YOU (I FEEL GOOD)*
  (S) (2:44) Rhino 75774 Soul Shots.
  (S) (2:44) Rhino 70651 Billboard's Top R&B Hits Of 1965.
  (S) (2:44) Rhino 72006 Billboard's Top R&B Hits 1965-1969 Box Set.

JAMES BROWN (Continued)

       (S) (2:44) A&M 3913 O.S.T. Good Morning Vietnam.
       (S) (2:25) Polydor 825714 CD Of JB. *(rerecording)*
       (S) (2:27) Polydor 849109 Star Time. *(rerecording)*
       (M) (2:44) Polydor 849109 Star Time.
       (S) (2:42) Priority 7909 Vietnam: Rockin' The Delta.
       (M) (2:45) Polydor 511326 20 All Time Greatest Hits.

1966 #4 *IT'S A MAN'S MAN'S MAN'S WORLD*

       (M) (2:43) Rhino 70652 Billboard's Top R&B Hits Of 1966.
       (M) (2:43) Rhino 72006 Billboard's Top R&B Hits 1965-1969 Box Set.
       (M) (3:13) Polydor 825714 CD Of JB. *(rerecording)*
       (S) (3:17) Polydor 849109 Star Time. *(rerecording)*
       (M) (2:46) Polydor 511326 20 All Time Greatest Hits.

1966 #39 *DON'T BE A DROPOUT*

       (S) (4:31) Polydor 849108 Star Time.

1967 #34 *BRING IT UP*

       (S) (3:48) Polydor 849109 Star Time. *(LP version)*

1967 #10 *COLD SWEAT (PART 1)*

       (S) (3:00) Rhino 70653 Billboard's Top R&B Hits Of 1967.
       (S) (3:00) Rhino 72006 Billboard's Top R&B Hits 1965-1969 Box Set.
       (S) (7:26) Polydor 831700 CD Of JB II. *(Parts 1 & 2)*
       (S) (7:31) Polydor 849109 Star Time. *(Parts 1 & 2; very poor stereo separation)*
       (M) (2:50) Polydor 511326 20 All Time Greatest Hits.
       (M) (2:50) Special Music 847982 Papa's Got A Brand New Bag.

1967 #29 *GET IT TOGETHER (PART 1)*

       (M) (8:57) Polydor 849109 Star Time. *(Parts 1 & 2)*

1968 #32 *I CAN'T STAND MYSELF (WHEN YOU TOUCH ME)*

       (S) (3:25) Polydor 831700 CD Of JB II.
       (S) (3:29) Polydor 849109 Star Time. *(faster than the 45 version)*

1968 #31 *THERE WAS A TIME*

       (S) (4:57) Polydor 849109 Star Time. *(live; tracks into the next selection)*

1968 #9 *I GOT THE FEELIN'*

       (M) (2:39) Polydor 825714 CD Of JB.
       (S) (2:37) Polydor 849109 Star Time.
       (M) (2:37) Polydor 511326 20 All Time Greatest Hits.

1968 #16 *LICKING STICK - LICKING STICK (PART 1)*

       (S) (2:46) Polydor 825714 CD Of JB.
       (S) (4:52) Polydor 849109 Star Time. *(Parts 1 & 2)*

1968 #17 *SAY IT LOUD - I'M BLACK AND I'M PROUD (PART 1)*

       (S) (2:48) Rhino 70654 Billboard's Top R&B Hits Of 1968.
       (S) (2:48) Rhino 72006 Billboard's Top R&B Hits 1965-1969 Box Set.
       (S) (4:46) Polydor 831700 CD Of JB II. *(Parts 1 & 2)*
       (S) (2:59) Polydor 849109 Star Time.
       (S) (2:46) Polydor 511326 20 All Time Greatest Hits.

1968 #36 *GOODBYE MY LOVE*

1969 #24 *GIVE IT UP OR TURN IT A LOOSE*

       (S) (3:16) Polydor 831700 CD Of JB II.
       (S) (3:10) Polydor 849109 Star Time. *(previous selection tracks over introduction)*
       (M) (3:10) Polydor 511326 20 All Time Greatest Hits.
       (S) (6:09) Polydor 829624 In The Jungle Groove. *(remixed)*

JAMES BROWN *(Continued)*

1969 #34 *I DON'T WANT NOBODY TO GIVE ME NOTHING (OPEN UP THE DOOR, I'LL GET IT MYSELF) PART 1*
    (S) (7:01) Polydor 831700 CD Of JB II.
    (S) (5:59) Polydor 849109 Star Time.

1969 #11 *MOTHER POPCORN (YOU GOT TO HAVE A MOTHER FOR ME) (PART 1)*
    (S) (3:10) Polydor 825714 CD Of JB.
    (S) (3:15) Polydor 511326 20 All Time Greatest Hits.
    (S) (6:15) Polydor 849109 Star Time. *(Parts 1 & 2)*

1969 #34 *WORLD (PART 1)*

1969 #31 *LET A MAN COME IN AND DO THE POPCORN (PART 1)*

1970 #40 *AIN'T IT FUNKY NOW (PART 1)*

1970 #26 *IT'S A NEW DAY (PARTS 1 & 2)*
    (S) (3:49) Polydor 849109 Star Time. *(live)*
    (S) (6:18) Polydor 829624 In The Jungle Groove.

1970 #37 *FUNKY DRUMMER (PART 1)*
    (S) (7:01) Polydor 849108 Star Time.
    (S) (9:12) Polydor 829624 In The Jungle Groove.

1970 #30 *BROTHER RAPP (PARTS 1 & 2)*

1970 #17 *GET UP (I FEEL LIKE BEING A) SEX MACHINE (PART 1)*
    (S) (5:03) Polydor 825714 CD Of JB.
    (S) (5:16) Polydor 849109 Star Time.
    (M) (5:15) Polydor 511326 20 All Time Greatest Hits.

1970 #15 *SUPER BAD (PARTS 1 & 2)*
    (M) (4:11) Rhino 70658 Billboard's Top R&B Hits Of 1970.
    (M) (2:57) Polydor 825714 CD Of JB.
    (M) (4:59) Polydor 511326 20 All Time Greatest Hits.

1971 #35 *GET UP, GET INTO IT, GET INVOLVED*
    (S) (7:03) Polydor 849109 Star Time.
    (M) (7:05) Polydor 829624 In The Jungle Groove.

1971 #32 *SOUL POWER (PART 1)*
    (M) (3:00) Polydor 825714 CD Of JB. *(:16 shorter than the 45 version)*
    (S) (4:24) Polydor 849109 Star Time.
    (M) (8:00) Polydor 829624 In The Jungle Groove. *(remixed)*

1971 #40 *ESCAPE-ISM (PART 1)*

1971 #10 *HOT PANTS (SHE GOT TO USE WHAT SHE GOT, TO GET WHAT SHE WANTS)*
    (M) (3:06) Polydor 849109 Star Time.
    (S) (3:06) Polydor 511326 20 All Time Greatest Hits.
    (S) (8:40) Polydor 829624 In The Jungle Groove.

1971 #20 *MAKE IT FUNKY (PART 1)*
    (M) (3:14) Rhino 70659 Billboard's Top R&B Hits Of 1971.
    (S) (7:21) Polydor 831700 CD Of JB II.
    (M) (3:35) Polydor 849109 Star Time.
    (M) (3:15) Polydor 511326 20 All Time Greatest Hits.

1971 #29 *I'M A GREEDY MAN (PART 1)*
    (S) (6:29) Polydor 831700 CD Of JB II.
    (S) (3:35) Polydor 849109 Star Time.

1972 #30 *TALKING LOUD AND SAYING NOTHING (PART 1)*
    (S) (7:42) Polydor 829624 In The Jungle Groove. *(remixed)*
    (S) (9:00) Polydor 849108 Star Time.

1972 #32 *KING HEROIN*
    (S) (3:56) Polydor 849109 Star Time.

1972 #38 *HONKY TONK (PART 1)*

JAMES BROWN (Continued)
1972 #10 *GET ON THE GOOD FOOT (PART 1)*
    (M) (3:32) Rhino 70660 Billboard's Top R&B Hits Of 1972.
    (S) (5:16) Polydor 831700 CD Of JB II.
    (M) (4:08) Polydor 849109 Star Time.
    (M) (3:34) Polydor 511326 20 All Time Greatest Hits.
1972 #32 *I GOT A BAG OF MY OWN*
    (S) (3:47) Polydor 849108 Star Time.
1973 #33 *I GOT ANTS IN MY PANTS (AND I WANT TO DANCE) (PART 1)*
    (S) (3:01) Polydor 849109 Star Time.

MAXINE BROWN
1961 #15 *ALL IN MY MIND*
    (M) (2:32) Capricorn 42003 The Scepter Records Story.
1961 #15 *FUNNY*
    (S) (2:32) Capricorn 42003 The Scepter Records Story.
1964 #22 *OH NO NOT MY BABY*
    (S) (2:35) Capricorn 42003 The Scepter Records Story.

NAPPY BROWN
1955 #9 *DON'T BE ANGRY*
1957 #22 *LITTLE BY LITTLE*

RUTH BROWN
1957 #26 *LUCKY LIPS*
    (M) (2:07) Atlantic 81295 Atlantic Rhythm & Blues Volume 3.
    (M) (2:05) Atlantic 82061 Miss Rhythm.
    (M) (2:07) Atlantic 82305 Atlantic Rhythm And Blues 1947-1974 Box Set.
    (E) (2:05) Rhino 70279 Rare Soul: Beach Music Classics Volume 3.

JACKSON BROWNE
1972 #12 *DOCTOR MY EYES*
    (S) (3:14) Asylum 5051 Saturate Before Using.

BROWNS
1959 #1 *THE THREE BELLS*
    (M) (2:49) RCA 9902 Nipper's #1 Hits 1956-1986.
    (S) (2:49) RCA 8466 Nipper's Greatest Hits Of The 50's Volume 1.
    (S) (2:49) Rhino 70680 Billboard's Top Country Hits Of 1959.
1959 #17 *SCARLET RIBBONS (FOR HER HAIR)*
1960 #8 *THE OLD LAMPLIGHTER*
    (S) (2:20) RCA 8475 Nipper's Greatest Hits Of The 60's Volume 2.

DAVE BRUBECK QUARTET
1961 #23 *TAKE FIVE*
    (S) (5:23) Columbia 40585 Time Out. *(LP version)*

ANITA BRYANT
1959 #14 *TILL THERE WAS YOU*
1960 #7 *PAPER ROSES*
1960 #20 *IN MY LITTLE CORNER OF THE WORLD*
1960 #2 *WONDERLAND BY NIGHT*

RAY BRYANT COMBO
1960 #25 *MADISON TIME (PART 1)*
    (S) (3:05) Rhino 70992 Groove 'n' Grind.
    (M) (3:05) MCA 6228 O.S.T. Hairspray.

BUBBLE PUPPY
1969 #16 *HOT SMOKE & SASAFRASS*
    (S) (2:35) K-Tel 686 Battle Of The Bands Volume 4.

BUCHANAN & GOODMAN
1956 #3 *THE FLYING SAUCER (PARTS 1 & 2)*
     (M) (4:19) Rhino 70599 Billboard's Top Rock & Roll Hits Of 1956.
1957 #37 *FLYING SAUCER THE 2ND*

BUCHANAN BROTHERS
1969 #21 *MEDICINE MAN (PART 1)*

BUCKINGHAMS
1967 #3 *KIND OF A DRAG*
     (S) (2:07) Rhino 70628 Billboard's Top Rock & Roll Hits Of 1967.
          (remixed)
     (S) (2:04) Columbia 45019 Pop Classics Of The 60's. *(remixed)*
     (S) (2:06) Columbia/Legacy 46984 Rock Artifacts Volume 4. *(orignal mix)*
     (S) (2:07) Columbia 9812 Greatest Hits. *(remixed)*
     (S) (2:06) Columbia/Legacy 47718 Mercy, Mercy, Mercy. *(original mix)*

1967 #39 *LAWDY MISS CLAWDY*
     (S) (2:05) Columbia/Legacy 46984 Rock Artifacts Volume 4. *(includes :03 studio talk and :02 guitar intro that was spliced off the 45 version)*
     (S) (1:59) Columbia 9812 Greatest Hits.
     (S) (2:04) Columbia/Legacy 47718 Mercy, Mercy, Mercy. *(includes :03 studio talk and :02 guitar intro that was spliced off the 45 version)*

1967 #6 *DON'T YOU CARE*
     (S) (2:25) Columbia 9812 Greatest Hits.
     (S) (2:27) Columbia/Legacy 47718 Mercy, Mercy, Mercy.

1967 #5 *MERCY, MERCY, MERCY*
     (S) (2:46) Columbia 45018 Rock Classics Of The 60's.
     (S) (2:46) Columbia 9812 Greatest Hits.
     (S) (2:46) Columbia/Legacy 47718 Mercy, Mercy, Mercy.

1967 #5 *HEY BABY (THEY'RE PLAYING OUR SONG)*
     (S) (2:48) Columbia/Legacy 46983 Rock Artifacts Volume 3. *(:04 seconds of studio talk prior to the intro and more talk over the first few seconds of the song; slightly longer fade than the single)*
     (S) (2:37) Columbia 9812 Greatest Hits.
     (S) (2:48) Columbia/Legacy 47718 Mercy, Mercy, Mercy. *(same comments as for Columbia/Legacy 46983)*

1968 #7 *SUSAN*
(dj copies ran (2:17) and (2:48))
     (S) (2:55) Columbia/Legacy 46983 Rock Artifacts Volume 3. *(:07 longer than the 45 or LP)*
     (S) (2:43) Columbia 9812 Greatest Hits. *(:05 shorter than the 45 or LP)*
     (S) (2:55) Columbia/Legacy 47718 Mercy, Mercy, Mercy. *(:07 longer than the 45 or LP)*

BUD & TRAVIS
1960 #35 *BALLAD OF THE ALAMO*

BUFFALO SPRINGFIELD
1967 #7 *FOR WHAT IT'S WORTH (STOP, HEY WHAT'S THAT SOUND)*
     (S) (2:36) Atlantic 81909 Hit Singles 1958-1977.
     (S) (2:33) Atlantic 82032 The Wonder Years.
     (S) (2:34) Atco 33200 Buffalo Springfield.
     (S) (2:37) Atco 38105 Best Of.

BULLET
1972 #25 *WHITE LIES, BLUE EYES*
     (S) (2:51) Rhino 70927 Super Hits Of The 70's Volume 7.

BUOYS
1971 #13 *TIMOTHY*
> (S) (2:45) Rhino 70926 Super Hits Of The 70's Volume 6.
> (S) (2:45) Capricorn 42003 The Scepter Records Story.

ERIC BURDON & THE ANIMALS (*see* ANIMALS)

ERIC BURDON & WAR
1970 #1 *SPILL THE WINE*
> *(dj copies of this 45 ran (4:03) and (4:51); commercial copies ran (4:51))*
> (M) (4:03) Priority 9467 Best Of War.
> (M) (4:03) Rhino 70072 Best Of.
> (S) (4:52) Rhino 71050 Eric Burdon Declares "War".

1971 #37 *THEY CAN'T TAKE AWAY OUR MUSIC*

SOLOMON BURKE
1961 #21 *JUST OUT OF REACH (OF MY TWO EMPTY ARMS)*
> (M) (2:46) Atlantic 81296 Atlantic Rhythm & Blues Volume 4.
> (S) (2:41) Atlantic 8109 Best Of.
> (S) (2:41) Curb 77422 Best Of.
> (S) (2:46) Atlantic 82305 Atlantic Rhythm And Blues 1947-1974 Box Set.
> (S) (2:41) Rhino 70284 Home In Your Heart.

1962 #38 *CRY TO ME*
> (E) (2:31) RCA 6965 More Dirty Dancing.
> (M) (2:31) Atlantic 81296 Atlantic Rhythm & Blues Volume 4.
> (S) (2:31) Curb 77422 Best Of.
> (S) (2:31) Atlantic 8109 Best Of.
> (S) (2:34) Atlantic 82305 Atlantic Rhythm And Blues 1947-1974 Box Set.
> (S) (2:30) Rhino 70284 Home In Your Heart.

1963 #22 *IF YOU NEED ME*
> (M) (2:32) Atlantic 81297 Atlantic Rhythm & Blues Volume 5.
> (S) (2:30) Atlantic 8109 Best Of.
> (S) (2:30) Curb 77422 Best Of.
> (S) (2:30) Atlantic 82305 Atlantic Rhythm And Blues 1947-1974 Box Set.
> (S) (2:30) Rhino 70284 Home In Your Heart.

1963 #37 *YOU'RE GOOD FOR ME*
> (S) (2:48) Rhino 70284 Home In Your Heart.

1964 #32 *GOODBYE BABY (BABY GOODBYE)*
> (S) (3:21) Atlantic 8109 Best Of.
> (S) (3:20) Rhino 70284 Home In Your Heart.

1965 #22 *GOT TO GET YOU OFF MY MIND*
> (S) (1:56) Atlantic 8109 Best Of.
> (S) (1:55) Atlantic 82305 Atlantic Rhythm And Blues 1947-1974 Box Set.
> (S) (1:55) Rhino 70284 Home In Your Heart.

1965 #23 *TONIGHT'S THE NIGHT*
> (S) (2:45) Atlantic 8109 Best Of.
> (S) (2:45) Rhino 70284 Home In Your Heart.

DORSEY BURNETTE
1960 #19 *(THERE WAS A) TALL OAK TREE*
1960 #40 *HEY LITTLE ONE*

JOHNNY BURNETTE
1960 #8 *DREAMIN'*
> (S) (2:18) Enigma 73531 O.S.T. Scandal.

1960 #7 *YOU'RE SIXTEEN*
1961 #19 *LITTLE BOY SAD*
1961 #31 *GOD, COUNTRY AND MY BABY*

BUSTERS
1963 #29 *BUST OUT*

JERRY BUTLER
1958 #22 *FOR YOUR PRECIOUS LOVE*
    (S) (2:43) Rhino 75893 Jukebox Classics Volume 1.
    (S) (2:41) Motown 6215 Hits From The Legendary Vee-Jay Records.
    (S) (2:43) Rhino 75881 Best Of.
    (E) (2:38) Curb 77419 Greatest Hits.

1960 #3 *HE WILL BREAK YOUR HEART*
    (S) (2:46) Rhino 70646 Billboard's Top R&B Hits Of 1960.
    (S) (2:46) Rhino 75894 Jukebox Classics Volume 2.
    (M) (2:41) Motown 6215 Hits From The Legendary Vee-Jay Records.
    (S) (2:46) Rhino 75881 Best Of.
    (E) (2:43) Curb 77419 Greatest Hits.

1961 #21 *FIND ANOTHER GIRL*
    (S) (2:49) Rhino 75881 Best Of.

1961 #35 *I'M A TELLING YOU*
    (S) (2:21) Rhino 75881 Best Of.

1961 #5 *MOON RIVER*
    (M) (2:34) Motown 6215 Hits From The Legendary Vee-Jay Records.
    (S) (2:38) Rhino 75881 Best Of.
    (E) (2:37) Curb 77419 Greatest Hits.

1962 #24 *MAKE IT EASY ON YOURSELF*
    (S) (2:35) Dunhill Compact Classics 028 Sock Hop.
    (S) (2:42) Rhino 75881 Best Of.
    (E) (2:35) Curb 77419 Greatest Hits.

1964 #28 *NEED TO BELONG*
    (S) (2:55) Rhino 75881 Best Of.

1968 #18 *NEVER GIVE YOU UP*
    (S) (3:04) Rhino 75881 Best Of.
    (M) (2:55) Mercury 510967 Very Best Of.
    (M) (2:55) Mercury 510968 Iceman/The Mercury Years.

1968 #24 *HEY, WESTERN UNION MAN*
    (S) (2:42) Rhino 70654 Billboard's Top R&B Hits Of 1968.
    (S) (2:42) Rhino 72006 Billboard's Top R&B Hits 1965-1969 Box Set.
    (S) (2:39) Rhino 75881 Best Of.
    (M) (2:44) Curb 77419 Greatest Hits.
    (S) (2:41) Mercury 510967 Very Best Of.
    (S) (2:41) Mercury 510968 Iceman/The Mercury Years.

1969 #33 *ARE YOU HAPPY*
    (S) (2:36) Mercury 510967 Very Best Of.
    (S) (2:38) Mercury 510968 Iceman/The Mercury Years.

1969 #5 *ONLY THE STRONG SURVIVE*
    (S) (2:35) Rhino 70655 Billboard's Top R&B Hits Of 1969. *(truncated fade)*
    (S) (2:35) Rhino 72006 Billboard's Top R&B Hits 1965-1969 Box Set.
                 (truncated Fade)
    (S) (2:32) Rhino 75881 Best Of.
    (M) (2:35) Curb 77419 Greatest Hits.
    (S) (2:35) Mercury 510967 Very Best Of.
    (S) (2:35) Mercury 510968 Iceman/The Mercury Years.
    (S) (3:12) Mercury 510968 Iceman/The Mercury Years. *(previously*
                 unreleased version)

1969 #22 *MOODY WOMAN*
    (S) (2:20) Mercury 510967 Very Best Of.
    (S) (2:20) Mercury 510968 Iceman/The Mercury Years.

JERRY BUTLER (Continued)
1969 #23 WHAT'S THE USE OF BREAKING UP
>   (S) (2:35) Curb 77419   Greatest Hits.
>   (S) (2:35) Mercury 510967   Very Best Of.
>   (S) (2:35) Mercury 510968   Iceman/The Mercury Years.

JERRY BUTLER & BRENDA LEE EAGER
1972 #24 AIN'T UNDERSTANDING MELLOW
>   (S) (4:18) Rhino 70787   Soul Hits Of The 70's Volume 7.

JERRY BUTLER & BETTY EVERETT
1964 #9 LET IT BE ME
>   (M) (2:48) Dunhill Compact Classics 028   Sock Hop.
>   (M) (2:47) JCI 3102   Love Sixties.
>   (S) (2:42) Motown 6215   Hits From The Legendary Vee-Jay Records.
>   (M) (2:48) Rhino 75881   Best Of Jerry Butler.
>   (M) (2:47) Curb 77419   Jerry Butler's Greatest Hits.

BYRDS
1965 #1 MR. TAMBOURINE MAN
>   (M) (2:17) Rhino 70626   Billboard's Top Rock & Roll Hits Of 1965.
>   (M) (2:17) Rhino 72007   Billboard's Top Rock & Roll Hits 1962-1966 Box Set.
>   (E) (2:17) Columbia 45019   Pop Classics Of The 60's.
>   (E) (2:17) Columbia 9516   Greatest Hits.
>   (M) (2:19) Columbia 9172   Mr. Tambourine Man.
>   (S) (2:16) Columbia/Legacy 46773   The Byrds. *(very poor stereo separation)*
>   (M) (2:17) Columbia 37335   Original Singles 1965-67.
>   (S) (2:16) Murray Hill 21143   Never Before. *(very poor stereo separation)*
>   (S) (2:29) Columbia/Legacy 47884   20 Essential Tracks. *(:10 longer than any previously released version; nice stereo separation)*

1965 #9 ALL I REALLY WANT TO DO
>   (S) (2:00) Columbia 9516   Greatest Hits.
>   (S) (2:01) Columbia 9172   Mr. Tambourine Man.
>   (S) (2:02) Columbia/Legacy 46773   The Byrds.
>   (M) (2:01) Columbia 37335   Original Singles 1965-67.
>   (S) (2:02) Columbia/Legacy 47884   20 Essential Tracks.

1965 #1 TURN! TURN! TURN!
>   (M) (3:34) Rhino 70626   Billboard's Top Rock & Roll Hits Of 1965.
>   (M) (3:34) Rhino 72007   Billboard's Top Rock & Roll Hits 1962-1966 Box Set.
>   (E) (3:33) Columbia 9516   Greatest Hits.
>   (M) (3:41) Columbia 9254   Turn! Turn! Turn! (LP speed)
>   (S) (3:53) Columbia/Legacy 46773   The Byrds. *(:12 longer fade than either the LP or 45; LP speed)*
>   (M) (3:34) Columbia 37335   Original Singles 1965-67.
>   (S) (3:53) Columbia/Legacy 47884   20 Essential Tracks. *(LP speed; :12 longer than either the LP or 45)*

1966 #39 IT WON'T BE WRONG
>   (M) (1:56) Columbia 37335   Original Singles 1965-67.
>   (S) (1:57) Columbia 9254   Turn! Turn! Turn!
>   (S) (1:56) Columbia/Legacy 46773   The Byrds.

1966 #12 EIGHT MILES HIGH
> **(commercial pressings of this 45 had a drum roll at the very end of the song which was missing from the LP and dj 45's)**
>   (S) (3:33) Columbia 9516   Greatest Hits. *(LP version)*
>   (S) (3:33) Columbia/Legacy 46773   The Byrds. *(LP version)*
>   (S) (3:33) Columbia 9349   Fifth Dimension. *(LP version)*

BYRDS (Continued)

    (M) (3:33) Columbia 37335 Original Singles 1965-67. *(Early pressings of this cd had the commercial 45 version but the remastered pressings include the LP version)*

    (S) (3:18) Murray Hill 21143 Never Before. *(alternate take)*

    (S) (3:33) Columbia/Legacy 47884 20 Essential Tracks. *(LP version)*

1966 #39 *5 D (FIFTH DIMENSION)*

    (S) (2:32) Columbia 9349 Fifth Dimension.

    (M) (2:32) Columbia 37335 Original Singles 1965-67.

    (S) (2:32) Columbia 9516 Greatest Hits.

    (S) (2:34) Columbia/Legacy 46773 The Byrds.

    (S) (2:34) Columbia/Legacy 47884 20 Essential Tracks.

1966 #34 *MR. SPACEMAN*

    (S) (2:07) Columbia 9516 Greatest Hits.

    (S) (2:09) Columbia/Legacy 46773 The Byrds.

    (S) (2:07) Columbia 9349 Fifth Dimension.

    (M) (2:07) Columbia 37335 Original Singles 1965-67.

    (S) (2:09) Columbia/Legacy 47884 20 Essential Tracks.

1967 #28 *SO YOU WANT TO BE A ROCK 'N' ROLL STAR*

    (S) (2:02) Columbia 45018 Rock Classics Of The 60's.

    (S) (2:01) Dunhill Compact Classics 045 Golden Age Of Underground Radio.

    (S) (2:03) Columbia 9516 Greatest Hits.

    (S) (2:04) Columbia/Legacy 46773 The Byrds.

    (S) (2:04) Columbia 9442 Younger Than Yesterday.

    (M) (2:03) Columbia 37335 Original Singles 1965-67.

    (S) (2:04) Columbia/Legacy 47884 20 Essential Tracks.

1967 #26 MY BACK PAGES

    (S) (3:06) Columbia 9516 Greatest Hits.

    (S) (3:06) Columbia/Legacy 46773 The Byrds.

    (S) (3:06) Columbia 9442 Younger Than Yesterday.

    (S) (3:06) Sandstone 33001 Reelin' In The Years Volume 2.

    (S) (3:06) Columbia/Legacy 47884 20 Essential Tracks.

EDWARD BYRNES

1959 #3 *KOOKIE, KOOKIE (LEND ME YOUR COMB)*

CADETS
1956 #10 *STRANDED IN THE JUNGLE*

CADILLACS
1959 #33 *PEEK-A-BOO*
    (S) (2:12) Rhino 70955 Best Of.
    (S) (2:09) Collectables 8800 For Collectors Only.

AL CAIOLA
1961 #24 *THE MAGNIFICENT SEVEN*
    (M) (2:02) Curb 77402 All-Time Great Instrumental Hits Volume 2.
1961 #27 *BONANZA*
    (S) (2:16) Curb 77403 All-Time Great Instrumental Hits Volume 1.

J.J. CALE
1972 #35 *CRAZY MAMA*
    (S) (2:21) Mercury 830042 Naturally.

GLEN CAMPBELL
1967 #26 *BY THE TIME I GET TO PHOENIX*
    (S) (2:42) Capitol 46483 Very Best Of. *(this song appears in mono on the original pressings of this cd but stereo on the remastered versions)*
    (S) (2:42) Capitol 94165 Classics Collection.
    (S) (2:42) Capitol 95848 All Time Country Classics.
    (S) (2:41) Pair 1089 All-Time Favorites.
1968 #38 *I WANNA LIVE*
1968 #38 *DREAMS OF THE EVERYDAY HOUSEWIFE*
    (S) (2:33) Capitol 46483 Very Best Of.
    (S) (2:33) Capitol 94165 Classics Collection.
    (S) (2:32) Pair 1089 All-Time Favorites.
1969 #2 *WICHITA LINEMAN*
    (S) (3:04) Capitol 46483 Very Best Of.
    (S) (3:04) Capitol 94165 Classics Collection.
    (S) (3:04) Pair 1089 All-Time Favorites.
1969 #4 *GALVESTON*
    (S) (2:39) Curb 77355 60's Hits Volume 1.
    (S) (2:39) Capitol 46483 Very Best Of.
    (S) (2:39) Capitol 94165 Classics Collection.
    (S) (2:39) Pair 1089 All-Time Favorites.
1969 #13 *WHERE'S THE PLAYGROUND SUSIE*
    (S) (2:54) Capitol 46483 Very Best Of.
    (S) (2:54) Pair 1089 All-Time Favorites.
1969 #34 *TRUE GRIT*
1969 #15 *TRY A LITTLE KINDNESS*
    (S) (2:24) Capitol 46483 Very Best Of.
    (S) (2:23) Pair 1089 All-Time Favorites.
1970 #11 *HONEY COME BACK*
    (S) (2:58) Pair 1089 All-Time Favorites. *(truncated fade)*

GLEN CAMPBELL (Continued)
1970 #34 *OH HAPPY DAY*
1970 #9 *IT'S ONLY MAKE BELIEVE*
     (S) (2:25) Capitol 46483 Very Best Of.
     (S) (2:24) Pair 1089 All-Time Favorites.
1971 #24 *DREAM BABY (HOW LONG MUST I DREAM)*
     (S) (2:30) Capitol 46483 Very Best Of. *(truncated fade)*
     (S) (2:30) Pair 1089 All-Time Favorites. *(truncated fade)*

GLEN CAMPBELL & BOBBIE GENTRY
1970 #31 *ALL I HAVE TO DO IS DREAM*
     (S) (2:33) Capitol 46483 Very Best Of Glen Campbell.

JO ANN CAMPBELL
1962 #37 *(I'M THE GIRL ON) WOLVERTON MOUNTAIN*

CANDY & THE KISSES
1965 #39 *THE 81*

CANNED HEAT
1968 #9 *ON THE ROAD AGAIN*
     (S) (3:21) Dunhill Compact Classics 045 Golden Age Of Underground Radio.
     (S) (3:23) EMI 48377 Best Of.
     (S) (3:20) Priority 8670 Hitchin A Ride/70's Greatest Rock Hits Volume 10.
1969 #9 *GOING UP THE COUNTRY*
     (S) (2:48) JCI 3101 Rockin' 60's.
     (S) (2:49) Polydor 837362 O.S.T. 1969.
     (S) (2:49) EMI 48377 Best Of.
1970 #17 *LET'S WORK TOGETHER*
     (E) (2:46) EMI 48377 Best Of.
     (E) (2:46) Essex 7052 All Time Rock Classics.

CANNIBAL & THE HEADHUNTERS
1965 #30 *LAND OF 1000 DANCES*
     (M) (2:14) Rhino 75772 Son Of Frat Rock.
     (M) (2:14) Rhino 70992 Groove 'n' Grind
     (E) (2:15) JCI 3100 Dance Sixties.
     (M) (2:15) Dunhill Compact Classics 029 Toga Rock.
     (S) (2:30) Original Sound CDGO-5 Golden Oldies Volume 5. *(:16 longer fade than single version and with 1 extra line added to intro, "c'mon everybody just clap with me" that appeared on the LP version but not the 45 version)*

ACE CANNON
1962 #15 *TUFF*
     (S) (3:18) MCA 25226 History Of Hi Records Rhythm & Blues Volume 1. *(LP version)*

FREDDY CANNON
1959 #6 *TALLAHASSEE LASSIE*
     (E) (2:31) JCI 3201 Party Time Fifties.
     (E) (2:32) Critique 5402 His Latest & Greatest.
     (E) (2:30) Essex 7053 A Hot Summer Night In '59.
1960 #3 *WAY DOWN YONDER IN NEW ORLEANS*
     (E) (2:30) Critique 5402 His Latest & Greatest.
1960 #27 *CHATTANOOGA SHOE SHINE BOY*
     (M) (2:18) Critique 5402 His Latest & Greatest.

FREDDY CANNON (Continued)
1960 #24 JUMP OVER
        (E) (2:40) Critique 5402 His Latest & Greatest.
1961 #35 BUZZ BUZZ A-DIDDLE-IT
        (E) (2:25) Critique 5402 His Latest & Greatest.
1961 #31 TRANSISTOR SISTER
        (E) (2:22) Critique 5402 His Latest & Greatest.
1962 #3 PALISADES PARK
        (M) (1:52) Rhino 70623 Billboard Top Rock & Roll Hits Of 1962.
        (M) (1:52) Rhino 72007 Billboard Top Rock & Roll Hits 1962-1966 Box Set.
        (E) (1:53) JCI 3110 Sock Hoppin' Sixties.
        (E) (2:32) Critique 5402 His Latest & Greatest.
1964 #24 ABIGAIL BEECHER
        (S) (2:24) Critique 5402 His Latest & Greatest.
1965 #13 ACTION
        (S) (2:07) Critique 5402 His Latest & Greatest.

CAPITOLS
1966 #5 COOL JERK
        (S) (2:41) Rhino 75757 Soul Shots Volume 3. *(LP length)*
        (S) (2:41) Rhino 75772 Son Of Frat Rock. *(LP length)*
        (S) (2:41) Rhino 70652 Billboard's Top R&B Hits Of 1966. *(LP length)*
        (S) (2:41) Rhino 72006 Billboard's Top R&B Hits 1966-1969 Box Set. *(LP length)*
        (S) (2:41) Rhino 70992 Groove 'n' Grind. *(LP length)*
        (S) (2:25) Garland 011 Footstompin' Oldies. *(edited)*
        (M) (2:33) Atlantic 81297 Atlantic Rhythm & Blues Volume 5. *(45 length)*
        (M) (2:32) Atlantic 82305 Atlantic Rhythm And Blues 1947-1974 Box Set. *(45 length)*

CAPRIS
1961 #7 THERE'S A MOON OUT TONIGHT
        (M) (2:10) Collectables 2507 History Of Rock - The Doo Wop Era Volume 1.
        (M) (2:11) Dunhill Compact Classics 031 Back Seat Jams.

CARAVELLES
1963 #6 YOU DON'T HAVE TO BE A BABY TO CRY
        (M) (1:58) Rhino 70989 Best Of The Girl Groups Volume 2.

CAREFREES
1964 #36 WE LOVE YOU BEATLES

HENSON CARGILL
1968 #22 SKIP A ROPE
        (S) (2:35) Rhino 70689 Billboard's Top Country Hits Of

RUSS CARLYLE
1957 #36 STASHU PANDOWSKI

RENATO CAROSONE
1958 #26 TORERO

CARPENTERS
1970 #1 (THEY LONG TO BE) CLOSE TO YOU
        (S) (4:33) A&M 3184 Close To You. *(LP version)*
        (S) (3:41) A&M 6750 Classics Volume 2. *(45 version)*
        (S) (3:40) A&M 3601 The Singles 1969-1973. *(45 version)*
        (S) (3:41) A&M 6601 Yesterday Once More. *(45 version)*
        (S) (3:41) A&M 6875 From The Top. *(45 version)*

CARPENTERS (Continued)

1970 #1 WE'VE ONLY JUST BEGUN
- (S) (3:05) A&M 3184 Close To You. *(tracks into next selection)*
- (S) (3:03) A&M 6750 Classics Volume 2.
- (S) (3:03) A&M 6601 Yesterday Once More.
- (S) (4:09) A&M 3601 The Singles 1969-1973. *(with 1:05 prelude that tracks over the introduction)*
- (S) (3:03) A&M 6875 From The Top.

1971 #6 FOR ALL WE KNOW
- (S) (2:30) A&M 6750 Classics Volume 2. *(tracks into next selection)*
- (S) (2:30) A&M 6601 Yesterday Once More. *(tracks into next selection)*
- (S) (2:32) A&M 3601 The Singles 1969-1973.
- (S) (2:31) A&M 6875 From The Top. *(remixed; some instrumentation rerecorded)*
- (S) (2:33) A&M 3502 Carpenters.

1971 #2 RAINY DAYS AND MONDAYS
- (S) (3:35) A&M 6750 Classics Volume 2. *(previous selection tracks over introduction)*
- (S) (3:35) A&M 6601 Yesterday Once More. *(previous selection tracks over introduction)*
- (S) (3:19) A&M 3601 The Singles 1969-1973. *(previous selection tracks over introduction; ending is edited and tracks into next selection)*
- (S) (3:35) A&M 6875 From The Top. *(previous song just barely tracks over introduction; some instrumentation rerecorded)*
- (S) (3:35) A&M 3502 Carpenters.

1971 #2 SUPERSTAR
- (S) (3:45) A&M 6750 Classics Volume 2. *(tracks into next selection)*
- (S) (3:40) A&M 3601 The Singles 1969-1973. *(tracks into next selection)*
- (S) (3:45) A&M 6601 Yesterday Once More. *(tracks into next selection)*
- (S) (3:45) A&M 6875 From The Top. *(remixed; tracks into following selection)*
- (S) (3:47) A&M 3502 Carpenters.

1972 #2 HURTING EACH OTHER
- (S) (2:45) A&M 6750 Classics Volume 2.
- (S) (2:45) A&M 6601 Yesterday Once More.
- (S) (2:45) A&M 3601 The Singles 1969-1973.
- (S) (2:46) A&M 3511 A Song For You.
- (S) (2:45) A&M 6875 From The Top. *(remixed; piano track rerecorded)*
- (S) (2:46) MFSL 525 A Song For You.

1972 #17 IT'S GOING TO TAKE SOME TIME
- (S) (2:55) A&M 6750 Classics Volume 2.
- (S) (2:54) A&M 3601 The Singles 1969-1973.
- (S) (2:55) A&M 6601 Yesterday Once More.
- (S) (2:57) A&M 3511 A Song For You.
- (S) (2:57) MFSL 525 A Song For You.

1972 #7 GOODBYE TO LOVE
- (S) (3:55) A&M 6750 Classics Volume 2. *(piano track rerecorded)*
- (S) (3:55) A&M 6601 Yesterday Once More. *(previous selection tracks over introduction; piano track rerecorded)*
- (S) (3:50) A&M 3601 The Singles 1969-1973. *(previous selection tracks over introduction; includes :05 introduction first heard on the vinyl LP "The Singles 1969-1973")*
- (S) (3:54) A&M 3511 A Song For You. *(piano track rerecorded)*
- (S) (3:58) A&M 6875 From The Top. *(remixed; piano track rerecorded; includes countoff)*
- (S) (3:55) MFSL 525 A Song For You. *(piano track rerecorded)*

CARPENTERS (Continued)

1973 #5 SING
- (S) (3:17) A&M 6750 Classics Volume 2.
- (S) (3:16) A&M 3601 The Singles 1969-1973.
- (S) (3:17) A&M 6601 Yesterday Once More.
- (S) (3:17) A&M 3519 Now & Then.

1973 #1 YESTERDAY ONCE MORE
- (S) (3:57) A&M 6750 Classics Volume 2. *(piano track rerecorded)*
- (S) (3:56) A&M 3601 The Singles 1969-1973.
- (S) (3:57) A&M 6601 Yesterday Once More. *(piano track rerecorded)*
- (S) (3:57) A&M 3519 Now & Then. *(tracks into next selection)*
- (S) (3:50) A&M 6875 From The Top. *(piano track rerecorded; tracks into next selection)*

1973 #1 TOP OF THE WORLD
- (S) (2:56) A&M 6750 Classics Volume 2. *(tracks into next selection; 45 version)*
- (S) (2:56) A&M 6601 Yesterday Once More. *(tracks into next selection; 45 version)*
- (S) (2:58) A&M 3601 The Singles 1969-1973. *(tracks into next selection; 45 version)*
- (S) (2:58) A&M 3511 A Song For You. *(45 version)*
- (S) (2:58) A&M 6875 From The Top. *(LP version)*
- (S) (2:58) MFSL 525 A Song For You. *(45 version)*

CATHY CARR

1956 #2 IVORY TOWER
- (M) (2:34) Rhino 75894 Jukebox Classics Volume 2.

1959 #31 FIRST ANNIVERSARY

VALERIE CARR

1958 #36 WHEN THE BOYS TALK ABOUT THE GIRLS

VIKKI CARR

1967 #5 IT MUST BE HIM
- (S) (2:50) EMI 96268 24 Greatest Hits Of All Time.
- (S) (2:51) EMI 92776 Best Of.
- (S) (2:48) Capitol 90231 O.S.T. Moonstruck.
- (S) (2:56) Pair 1082 From The Heart. *(includes :05 silent introduction)*
- (S) (2:50) EMI 93450 Best Of.

1968 #35 THE LESSON
- (S) (2:30) EMI 92776 Best Of.
- (S) (2:29) EMI 93450 Best Of.

DAVID CARROLL

1955 #1 MELODY OF LOVE

MINDY CARSON

1955 #7 WAKE THE TOWN AND TELL THE PEOPLE

CLARENCE CARTER

1968 #11 SLIP AWAY
- (S) (2:29) Atlantic 81911 Golden Age Of Black Music (1960-1970).
- (M) (2:31) Atlantic 81298 Atlantic Rhythm & Blues Volume 6.
- (S) (2:30) Atco 91813 Classic Recordings.
- (S) (2:27) Atlantic 82305 Atlantic Rhythm And Blues 1947-1974 Box Set.
- (S) (2:30) Rhino 70286 Snatching It Back.

CLARENCE CARTER (Continued)
1969 #13 TOO WEAK TO FIGHT
        (S)   (2:15) Atlantic 81911 Golden Age Of Black Music (1960-1970).

        (S)   (2:15) Atlantic 82305 Atlantic Rhythm And Blues 1947-1974 Box Set.

        (S)   (2:15) Rhino 70286 Snatching It Back.

        (S)   (2:15) Rhino 70277 Rare Soul: Beach Music Classics Volume 1.

1969 #17 SNATCHING IT BACK
        (S)   (2:49) Rhino 70286 Snatching It Back.

1969 #39 THE FEELING IS RIGHT
        (S)   (2:52) Rhino 70286 Snatching It Back.

1970 #1 PATCHES
        (S)   (3:09) Atlantic 82305 Atlantic Rhythm And Blues 1947-1974 Box Set.

        (S)   (3:09) Atlantic 81299 Atlantic Rhythm & Blues Volume 7.

        (S)   (3:10) Rhino 70286 Snatching It Back.

1970 #39 IT'S ALL IN YOUR MIND
        (S)   (2:30) Rhino 70286 Snatching It Back.

MEL CARTER
1963 #38 WHEN A BOY FALLS IN LOVE
1965 #12 HOLD ME, THRILL ME, KISS ME
        (S)   (2:29) JCI 3102 Love Sixties.

1965 #35 (ALL OF A SUDDEN) MY HEART SINGS
1966 #37 BAND OF GOLD

CASCADES
1963 #2 RHYTHM OF THE RAIN

AL CASEY
1963 #39 SURFIN' HOOTENANY

ALVIN CASH & THE CRAWLERS
1965 #9 TWINE TIME

JOHNNY CASH
1956 #23 I WALK THE LINE
        (M)   (2:41) Rhino 75884 The Sun Story.

        (M)   (2:43) Rhino 75893 Jukebox Classics Volume 1.

        (M)   (2:41) Rhino 70950 The Sun Years.

        (M)   (2:42) Dunhill Compact Classics 009 Legends.

        (S)   (2:33) Columbia 9478 Greatest Hits Volume 1. *(rerecording)*

        (M)   (2:41) Columbia 47991 Essential.

        (S)   (2:33) Mercury 834526 Classic Cash. *(all selections on this cd are rerecordings)*

        (M)   (2:43) RCA 66059 Sun's Greatest Hits.

1958 #28 BALLAD OF A TEENAGE QUEEN
        (M)   (2:09) Rhino 70950 The Sun Years.

        (M)   (2:10) Dunhill Compact Classics 009 Legends.

        (M)   (2:09) Columbia 47991 Essential.

1958 #24 GUESS THINGS HAPPEN THAT WAY
        (M)   (1:49) Dunhill Compact Classics 009 Legends.

        (M)   (1:47) Rhino 70950 The Sun Years.

        (M)   (1:48) Columbia 47991 Essential.

        (S)   (1:43) Mercury 834526 Classic Cash. *(all selections on this cd are rerecordings)*

1958 #40 WAYS OF A WOMAN IN LOVE
        (M)   (2:22) Rhino 70950 The Sun Years.

        (M)   (2:13) Columbia 47991 Essential.

JOHNNY CASH (Continued)
1959 #19 DON'T TAKE YOUR GUNS TO TOWN
   (S) (3:01) Rhino 70680 Billboard's Top Country Hits Of 1959
   (S) (3:01) Columbia 46031 Columbia Country Classics Volume 3.
   (S) (3:01) Columbia 40637 Columbia Records 1958-1986.
   (S) (3:01) Columbia 9478 Greatest Hits Volume 1.
   (S) (3:00) Columbia 47991 Essential.
   (S) (2:55) Mercury 834526 Classic Cash. (*all selections on this cd are rerecordings*)
   (S) (3:01) CBS Special Products 8122 The Fabulous.

1960 #26 LITTLE DRUMMER BOY
1963 #14 RING OF FIRE
   (S) (2:35) Columbia 46032 Columbia Country Classics Volume 4.
   (S) (2:35) Columbia 40637 Columbia Records 1958-1986.
   (S) (2:36) Columbia 9478 Greatest Hits Volume 1.
   (S) (2:35) Columbia 47991 Essential.
   (S) (2:42) Mercury 834526 Classic Cash. (*all selections on this cd are rerecordings*)

1968 #36 FOLSOM PRISON BLUES
   (M) (2:47) Rhino 75894 Jukebox Classics Volume 2. (*Sun Records studio recording - not the hit single version*)
   (M) (2:47) Rhino 75884 The Sun Records Story. (*Sun Records studio recording - not the hit single version*)
   (M) (2:48) Rhino 70950 The Sun Years. (*Sun Records studio recording - not the hit single version*)
   (M) (2:44) Columbia 40637 Columbia Records 1958-1986.
   (M) (2:47) Dunhill Compact Classics 009 Legends. (*Sun Records studio recording - not the hit single version*)
   (S) (2:39) Columbia 33639 At Folsom Prison And San Quentin.
   (S) (2:41) Columbia 47991 Essential.
   (M) (2:47) Columbia 47991 Essential. (*Sun Records studio recording - not the hit single version*)
   (S) (2:44) Mercury 834526 Classic Cash. (*all selections on this cd are rerecordings*)
   (M) (2:47) RCA 66059 Sun's Greatest Hits. (*Sun Records studio recording - not the hit single version*)

1969 #2 A BOY NAMED SUE
   (S) (3:44) Columbia 46031 Columbia Country Classics Volume 3.
   (S) (3:44) Columbia 40637 Columbia Records 1958-1986.
   (S) (3:42) Columbia 38317 Biggest Hits.
   (S) (3:36) Columbia 33639 At Folsom Prison And San Quentin.
   (S) (3:45) Columbia 47991 Essential.

1969 #40 SEE RUBY FALL
   (S) (2:49) Columbia 47991 Essential.

1970 #11 WHAT IS TRUTH
   (S) (2:36) Columbia 47991 Essential.

JOHNNY CASH & JUNE CARTER
1970 #26 IF I WERE A CARPENTER

CASHMAN & WEST
1972 #28 AMERICAN CITY SUITE
   (S) (7:44) Rhino 70929 Super Hits Of The 70's Volume 9. (*45 version*)

CASINOS
1967 #5 THEN YOU CAN TELL ME GOODBYE
   (M) (3:03) Dunhill Compact Classics 031 Back Seat Jams.
   (S) (3:05) Rhino 70996 One Hit Wonders Of The 60's Volume 2.

DAVID CASSIDY
1972 #3 *CHERISH*
   (S) (3:46) Arista 8604   Partridge Family Greatest Hits.
1972 #15 *COULD IT BE FOREVER*
   (S) (2:18) Arista 8604   Partridge Family Greatest Hits.
1972 #15 *HOW CAN I BE SURE*
1972 #26 *ROCK ME BABY*

CASTAWAYS
1965 #12 *LIAR LIAR*
   (S) (1:50) K-Tel 205   Battle Of The Bands Volume 3.
   (S) (1:50) Rhino 75777   More Nuggets.
   (S) (1:51) A&M 3913   O.S.T. Good Morning Vietnam.
   (S) (1:51) Rhino 70732   Grandson Of Frat Rock.

CASTELLS
1961 #21 *SACRED*
1962 #34 *SO THIS IS LOVE*

JIMMY CASTOR BUNCH
1967 #35 *HEY, LEROY, YOUR MAMA'S CALLIN' YOU*
1972 #2 *TROGLODYTE (CAVE MAN)*
   (S) (3:33) RCA 8476 and 9684   Nipper's Greatest Hits Of The 70's. *(LP length)*
   (S) (3:23) Rhino 70788   Soul Hits Of The 70's Volume 8.
   (S) (3:32) RCA 61144   The RCA Records Label: The First Note In Black Music. *(LP length)*

GEORGE CATES & HIS ORCHESTRA
1956 #1 *MOONGLOW AND THEME FROM "PICNIC"*

CAT MOTHER & THE ALL NIGHT NEWS BOYS
1969 #16 *GOOD OLD ROCK 'N ROLL*
   (S) (3:10) Rhino 70732   Grandson Of Frat Rock.

C COMPANY *featuring* TERRY NELSON
1971 #26 *BATTLE HYMN OF LT. CALLEY*

CHAD & JEREMY
1964 #28 *YESTERDAY'S GONE*
   (M) (2:30) Rhino 70319   History Of British Rock Volume 1.
   (M) (2:30) Rhino 72022   History Of British Rock Box Set.
   (M) (2:30) Rhino 72008   History Of British Rock Volumes 1-4 Box Set.
1964 #8 *A SUMMER SONG*
   (S) (2:36) Rhino 70087   Summer & Sun.
   (S) (2:36) Rhino 70320   History Of British Rock Volume 2.
   (S) (2:36) Rhino 72022   History Of British Rock Box Set.
   (S) (2:36) Rhino 72008   History Of British Rock Volumes 1-4 Box Set.
1965 #22 *WILLOW WEEP FOR ME*
   (S) (2:31) Rhino 70321   History Of British Rock Volume 3.
   (S) (2:31) Rhino 72022   History Of British Rock Box Set.
   (S) (2:31) Rhino 72008   History Of British Rock Volumes 1-4 Box
1965 #20 *IF I LOVED YOU*
1965 #15 *BEFORE AND AFTER*
   (S) (2:41) Rhino 70323   History Of British Rock Volume 5.
   (S) (2:41) Rhino 72022   History Of British Rock Box Set.
   (S) (2:41) Columbia/Legacy 47719   Painted Dayglow Smile.

CHAIRMEN OF THE BOARD
1970 #9 *GIVE ME JUST A LITTLE MORE TIME*
    (S)   (2:37) Dunhill Compact Classics 033 Beachbeat Shaggin'.
    (S)   (2:38) Rhino 70781 Soul Hits Of The 70's Volume 1.
    (S)   (2:39) HDH 3901 Greatest Hits.
1970 #30 *(YOU'VE GOT ME) DANGLING ON A STRING*
    (S)   (2:57) HDH 3901 Greatest Hits. *(LP length)*
    (M)   (2:44) Rhino 70783 Soul Hits Of The 70's Volume 3.
1970 #39 *EVERYTHING'S TUESDAY*
    (M)   (2:46) Rhino 70783 Soul Hits Of The 70's Volume 3.
    (S)   (2:47) HDH 3901 Greatest Hits.
1971 #10 *PAY TO THE PIPER*
    (S)   (3:05) Rhino 70784 Soul Hits Of The 70's Volume 4.
    (S)   (3:03) HDH 3901 Greatest Hits.
1971 #37 *CHAIRMAN OF THE BOARD*
    (S)   (3:07) Rhino 70784 Soul Hits Of The 70's Volume 4. *(neither the LP or 45 version as this is :10 longer than the 45 and :24 shorter than the LP length, yet recorded at the LP speed)*
    (S)   (3:31) HDH 3901 Greatest Hits. *(LP version)*

CHAKACHAS
1972 #6 *JUNGLE FEVER*
    (S)   (4:20) Rhino 70787 Soul Hits Of The 70's Volume 7.

RICHARD CHAMBERLAIN
1962 #13 *THEME FROM DR. KILDARE (THREE STARS WILL SHINE TONIGHT)*
1962 #24 *LOVE ME TENDER*
1963 #20 *ALL I HAVE TO DO IS DREAM*

CHAMBERS BROTHERS
1968 #11 *TIME HAS COME TODAY*
    (dj copies of this song ran (2:37) & (4:45))
    (S)   (4:54) Rhino 75754 Even More Nuggets.
    (S) (11:03) Dunhill Compact Classics 045 Golden Age Of Underground Radio. *(LP version)*
    (S) (11:02) Columbia 30871 Greatest Hits. *(LP version)*
    (S) (11:01) Columbia 9522 The Time Has Come. *(LP version)*
    (M)   (4:47) Columbia 45018 Rock Classics Of The 60's.
    (S)   (3:31) Sandstone 33004 Reelin' In The Years Volume 5. *(neither the LP or 45 version)*
1968 #39 *I CAN'T TURN YOU LOOSE*
    (S)   (4:53) Columbia 30871 Greatest Hits.

CHAMPS
1958 #1 *TEQUILA*
    (M)   (2:10) Rhino 70619 Billboard's Top Rock & Roll Hits Of 1958.
    (M)   (2:10) Rhino 72004 Billboard's Top Rock & Roll Hits 1957-1961 Box Set.
    (E)   (2:10) Dunhill Compact Classics 028 Sock Hop.
    (M)   (2:10) Rhino 70732 Grandson Of Frat Rock.
1958 #21 *EL RANCHO ROCK*
1960 #21 *TOO MUCH TEQUILA*
1962 #33 *LIMBO ROCK*

GENE CHANDLER
1962 #1 *DUKE OF EARL*
    (M)   (2:22) Rhino 70623 Billboard's Top Rock & Roll Hits Of 1962.

GENE CHANDLER (Continued)

      (M) (2:22) Rhino 72007 Billboard's Top Rock & Roll Hits 1962-1966 Box Set.

      (M) (2:21) Motown 6215 Hits From The Legendary Vee-Jay Records.

      (M) (2:22) Dunhill Compact Classics 028 Sock Hop.

1964 #21 *JUST BE TRUE*

1965 #18 *NOTHING CAN STOP ME*

1970 #11 *GROOVY SITUATION*

      (S) (3:12) Rhino 70783 Soul Hits Of The 70's Volume 3.

GENE CHANDLER & BARBARA ACKLIN

1968 #40 *FROM THE TEACHER TO THE PREACHER*

BRUCE CHANNEL

1962 #1 *HEY! BABY*

      (E) (2:22) RCA 6408 O.S.T. Dirty Dancing.

1962 #38 *NUMBER ONE MAN*

CHANTAYS

1963 #5 *PIPELINE*

      (S) (2:16) Rhino 70089 Surfin' Hits.

      (S) (2:17) MCA 31204 Vintage Music Volume 7.

      (S) (2:17) MCA 5805 Vintage Music Volumes 7 & 8.

      (S) (2:18) JCI 3106 Surfin' Sixties.

CHANTELS

1958 #19 *MAYBE*

      (M) (2:51) Rhino 70644 Billboard's Top R&B Hits Of 1958.

      (M) (2:52) Rhino 70954 Best Of.

      (M) (2:48) Collectables 8802 For Collectors Only.

      (M) (2:48) Collectables 5423 The Chantels.

1958 #32 *EVERY NIGHT (I PRAY)*

      (M) (2:03) Rhino 70954 Best Of. *(truncated fade)*

      (M) (2:01) Collectables 8802 For Collectors Only.

      (M) (2:01) Collectables 5423 The Chantels. *(truncated fade)*

1961 #14 *LOOK IN MY EYES*

      (S) (2:16) Rhino 70954 Best Of.

      (M) (2:16) Atlantic 82152 O.S.T. Goodfellas. *(mastered from vinyl)*

      (S) (2:15) Collectables 8802 For Collectors Only.

1961 #28 *WELL, I TOLD YOU*

      (S) (2:24) Rhino 70954 Best Of.

HARRY CHAPIN

1972 #20 *TAXI*

      (S) (6:41) Elektra 75023 Heads & Tales.

      (S) (6:40) Elektra 60773 Gold Medal Collection.

JIMMY CHARLES

1960 #6 *A MILLION TO ONE*

RAY CHARLES

1959 #6 *WHAT'D I SAY (PART 1)*

      (S) (6:25) Warner Special Products 27601 Atlantic Soul Classics. *(LP version of Parts 1 & 2)*

      (S) (6:25) JCI 3202 Rockin' Fifties. *(LP version of Parts 1 & 2)*

      (M) (5:05) Atlantic 81296 Atlantic Rhythm & Blues Volume 4. *(45 edit of Parts 1 & 2)*

      (M) (3:05) Rhino 70732 Grandson Of Frat Rock. *(45 version of just Part 1)*

      (S)   (4:31) Rhino 75759 Anthology. *(rerecording)*
      (M) (5:04) Atlantic 82305 Atlantic Rhythm And Blues 1947-1974 Box Set.
              (45 edit of Parts 1 & 2)
      (S)   (6:25) Atlantic 82310 Birth Of Soul Box Set. *(LP version of Parts 1 & 2)*

1960 #27 STICKS AND STONES
      (S)   (2:11) Rhino 75759 Anthology.

1960 #3 GEORGIA ON MY MIND
      (S)   (3:37) Rhino 75759 Anthology.
      (S)   (3:37) Dunhill Compact Classics 036 His Greatest Volume 1.

1960 #21 RUBY
      (S)   (3:49) Dunhill Compact Classics 037 His Greatest Volume 2. *(LP version)*

1961 #38 THEM THAT GOT
      (S)   (2:46) Dunhill Compact Classics 037 His Greatest Hits Volume 2.

1961 #9 ONE MINT JULEP
      (S)   (3:05) Rhino 75759 Anthology.
      (S)   (3:05) Dunhill Compact Classics 038 Genius + Soul = Jazz.
      (S)   (3:05) Dunhill Compact Classics 036 His Greatest Volume 1.

1961 #1 HIT THE ROAD JACK
      (S)   (1:57) Rhino 75759 Anthology.
      (S)   (1:57) Dunhill Compact Classics 037 His Greatest Volume 2.

1962 #9 UNCHAIN MY HEART
      (S)   (2:49) Rhino 75759 Anthology.
      (S)   (2:49) Dunhill Compact Classics 036 His Greatest Volume 1.

1962 #26 HIDE 'NOR HAIR
      (S)   (3:09) Dunhill Compact Classics 036 His Greatest Volume 1.

1962 #40 AT THE CLUB
      (S)   (2:58) Dunhill Compact Classics 037 His Greatest Hits Volume 2.

1962 #1 I CAN'T STOP LOVING YOU
      (S)   (4:11) Rhino 75759 Anthology. *(LP version)*
      (S)   (4:11) Rhino 70099 Modern Sounds In Country & Western Music. *(LP version)*
      (S)   (4:11) Dunhill Compact Classics 040 Greatest Country & Western Hits. *(LP version)*
      (S)   (4:10) Dunhill Compact Classics 037 His Greatest Volume 2. *(LP version)*

1962 #39 BORN TO LOSE
      (S)   (3:13) Rhino 70099 Modern Sounds In Country & Western Music.
      (S)   (3:14) Dunhill Compact Classics 036 His Greatest Hits Volume 1.
      (S)   (3:13) Rhino 75759 Anthology.

1962 #5 YOU DON'T KNOW ME
      (S)   (3:13) Rhino 70099 Modern Sounds In Country & Western Music.
      (S)   (3:13) Dunhill Compact Classics 040 Greatest Country & Western Hits.
      (S)   (3:14) Dunhill Compact Classics 036 His Greatest Volume 1.

1962 #9 YOU ARE MY SUNSHINE
      (S)   (2:57) Rhino 75759 Anthology.
      (S)   (2:57) Rhino 70099 Modern Sounds In Country & Western Music.
      (S)   (2:57) Dunhill Compact Classics 040 Greatest Country & Western Hits.
      (S)   (2:57) Dunhill Compact Classics 037 His Greatest Volume 2.

1963 #25 DON'T SET ME FREE
      (S)   (2:35) Rhino 75759 Anthology.
      (S)   (2:35) Dunhill Compact Classics 037 His Greatest Volume 2.

RAY CHARLES (Continued)

1963 #11 TAKE THESE CHAINS FROM MY HEART
    (S) (2:54) Dunhill Compact Classics 040 Greatest Country & Western Hits.
    (S) (2:53) Dunhill Compact Classics 037 His Greatest Volume 2.

1963 #22 NO ONE
    (S) (3:07) Dunhill Compact Classics 037 His Greatest Volume 2.

1963 #35 WITHOUT LOVE (THERE IS NOTHING)
    (S) (3:33) Dunhill Compact Classics 037 His Greatest Volume 2.

1963 #2 BUSTED
    (S) (2:05) Rhino 75759 Anthology.
    (S) (2:11) Dunhill Compact Classics 047 Ingredients In A Recipe For Soul. *(with countoff)*
    (S) (2:08) Dunhill Compact Classics 037 His Greatest Volume 2. *(with countoff)*

1964 #20 THAT LUCKY OLD SUN
    (S) (4:20) Rhino 75759 Anthology. *(LP version)*
    (S) (4:20) Rhino 70099 Modern Sounds In Country & Western Music. *(LP version)*
    (S) (4:19) Dunhill Compact Classics 047 Ingredients In A Recipe For Soul. *(LP version)*
    (S) (4:19) Dunhill Compact Classics 036 His Greatest Volume 1. *(LP version)*

1965 #39 MAKIN' WHOOPEE
    (S) (6:16) Dunhill Compact Classics 037 His Greatest Hits Volume 2. *(LP version)*

1966 #6 CRYING TIME
    (S) (2:55) Rhino 75759 Anthology.
    (S) (2:59) Dunhill Compact Classics 040 Greatest Country & Western Hits. *(with countoff)*
    (S) (2:54) Dunhill Compact Classics 036 His Greatest Volume 1.

1966 #22 TOGETHER AGAIN
    (S) (2:36) Dunhill Compact Classics 040 Greatest Country & Western Hits.

1966 #23 LET'S GO GET STONED
    (S) (2:58) Rhino 75759 Anthology. *(truncated fade)*
    (S) (2:58) Dunhill Compact Classics 036 His Greatest Volume 1.

1967 #18 HERE WE GO AGAIN
    (S) (3:14) Rhino 75759 Anthology.
    (S) (3:14) Rhino 70099 Modern Sounds in Country & Western Music.
    (S) (3:14) Dunhill Compact Classics 036 His Greatest Volume 1.

1967 #28 YESTERDAY
    (S) (2:44) Dunhill Compact Classics 036 His Greatest Volume 1.

1968 #39 ELEANOR RIGBY
    (S) (2:56) Rhino 75759 Anthology.
    (S) (2:55) Dunhill Compact Classics 037 His Greatest Volume 2.

1971 #28 DON'T CHANGE ON ME
    (S) (3:02) Dunhill Compact Classics 036 His Greatest Volume 1.

1971 #24 BOOTY BUTT

RAY CHARLES SINGERS
1964 #4 LOVE ME WITH ALL YOUR HEART
1964 #32 AL-DI-LA
1965 #33 ONE MORE TIME

SONNY CHARLES & THE CHECKMATES, LTD.
1969 #16 *BLACK PEARL*
        (S) (3:26) Rhino 75774 Soul Shots.

        (M) (3:17) Abkco 7118 Phil Spector/Back To Mono (1958-1969).

CHARTBUSTERS
1964 #39 *SHE'S THE ONE*

CHASE
1971 #22 *GET IT ON*
        (S) (2:57) Rhino 70925 Super Hits Of The 70's Volume 5.

        (S) (2:57) Columbia/Legacy 46160 Rock Artifacts Volume 1.

CHUBBY CHECKER
1959 #37 *THE CLASS*
1960 #1 *THE TWIST*
        (S) (2:33) Rhino 70621 Billboard's Top Rock & Roll Hits Of 1960. *(rerecording)*

        (S) (2:33) Rhino 72004 Billboard's Top Rock & Roll Hits 1957-1961. *(rerecording)*

        (S) (2:33) Rhino 70992 Groove 'n' Grind. *(rerecording)*

        (S) (2:35) Enigma 73531 O.S.T. Scandal. *(rerecording)*

1960 #13 *THE HUCKLEBUCK*
1961 #1 *PONY TIME*
        (S) (1:30) MCA 6171 Good Time Rock 'N' Roll. *(all selections on this cd are recorded live)*

1961 #16 *DANCE THE MESS AROUND*
1961 #3 *LET'S TWIST AGAIN*
        (S) (3:10) MCA 6171 Good Time Rock 'N' Roll. *(all selections on this cd are recorded live)*

1961 #7 *THE FLY*
1962 #31 *LET'S TWIST AGAIN*
(this song charted in two different years: 1961 & 1962; see 1961 listing)
1962 #1 *THE TWIST*
(yes, this song hit #1 in two different years: 1960 & 1962; see 1960 listing)
1962 #1 *SLOW TWISTIN'*
1962 #14 *DANCIN' PARTY*
1962 #1 *LIMBO ROCK*
        (M) (2:22) MCA 6214 Moonlighting - TV Soundtrack.

1962 #8 *POPEYE THE HITCHHIKER*
1963 #15 *LET'S LIMBO SOME MORE*
1963 #28 *TWENTY MILES*
1963 #14 *BIRDLAND*
1963 #23 *TWIST IT UP*
1963 #15 *LODDY LO*
1964 #16 *HOOKA TOOKA*
1964 #18 *HEY, BOBBA NEEDLE*
1964 #39 *LAZY ELSIE MOLLY*
1965 #40 *LET'S DO THE FREDDIE*

CHUBBY CHECKER & BOBBY RYDELL
1962 #38 *JINGLE BELL ROCK*

CHEECH & CHONG
1973 #13 *BASKETBALL JONES FEATURING TYRONE SHOELACES*
        (S) (4:04) Warner Brothers 3252 Los Cochinos.

        (S) (4:01) Warner Brothers 3614 Greatest Hit.

CHEE-CHEE & PEPPY
1971 #35 *I KNOW I'M IN LOVE*
CHER
1965 #9 **ALL I REALLY WANT TO DO**
    (S) (2:54) EMI 92773 Legendary Masters Series. *(very poor stereo separation)*
    (S) (2:56) EMI 91836 Best Of.
1965 #32 **WHERE DO YOU GO**
    (S) (3:16) EMI 92773 Legendary Masters Series.
    (S) (3:12) EMI 91836 Best Of.
1966 #2 **BANG BANG (MY BABY SHOT ME DOWN)**
    (S) (2:42) EMI 96268 24 Greatest Hits Of All Time.
    (S) (2:46) EMI 92773 Legendary Masters Series. *(with countoff)*
    (S) (2:42) EMI 91836 Best Of.
1966 #32 **ALFIE**
    (S) (2:57) EMI 92773 Legendary Masters Series.
1967 #8 **YOU BETTER SIT DOWN KIDS**
    (S) (4:17) EMI 92773 Legendary Masters Series. *(includes :09 of studio talk; :26 longer fade than either the 45 or LP version)*
    (S) (3:41) EMI 91836 Best Of.
1971 #1 **GYPSIES, TRAMPS & THIEVES**
    (S) (2:36) Rhino 70632 Billboard's Top Rock & Roll Hits Of 1971.
    (S) (2:36) Rhino 72005 Billboard's Top Rock & Roll Hits 1968-1972 Box Set.
    (S) (2:35) MCA 31376 Gypsys, Tramps & Thieves.
    (S) (2:34) MCA 922 Greatest Hits.
1972 #9 **THE WAY OF LOVE**
    (S) (2:29) MCA 31376 Gypsys, Tramps & Thieves.
    (S) (2:29) MCA 922 Greatest Hits.
1972 #21 **LIVING IN A HOUSE DIVIDED**
    (S) (2:54) MCA 922 Greatest Hits.
1973 #1 **HALF BREED**
    (S) (2:42) MCA 922 Greatest Hits.
DON CHERRY
1956 #5 **BAND OF GOLD**
    (M) (2:35) Rhino 70588 Rockin' & Rollin' Wedding songs Volume 1.
1956 #35 **GHOST TOWN**
CHICAGO
1970 #11 **MAKE ME SMILE**
    (S) (2:58) Columbia 33900 Greatest Hits. *(45 version)*
    (S) (3:15) Columbia 24 Chicago II. *(LP version; tracks into next selection)*
    (S) (3:28) Columbia 47416 Group Portrait. *(LP version; tracks into next selection)*
1970 #6 **25 OR 6 TO 4**
    (S) (4:49) Columbia 33900 Greatest Hits. *(LP version)*
    (S) (4:49) Columbia 24 Chicago II. *(LP version)*
    (S) (4:49) Columbia 47416 Group Portrait. *(LP version)*
1971 #5 **DOES ANYBODY REALLY KNOW WHAT TIME IT IS?**
    (S) (3:18) Columbia 33900 Greatest Hits. *(45 version)*
    (S) (4:33) Columbia 00008 Chicago Transit Authority. *(LP version)*
    (S) (4:34) Columbia 47416 Group Portrait. *(LP version)*

CHICAGO (Continued)

1971 #19 *FREE*
- (S) (2:15) Columbia 39579 Take Me Back To Chicago.
- (S) (2:15) Columbia 30110 Chicago III. (*previous selection tracks into introduction; tracks into next selection*)
- (S) (2:15) Columbia 47416 Group Portrait.

1971 #25 *LOWDOWN*
- (S) (3:33) Columbia 39579 Take Me Back To Chicago.
- (S) (3:33) Columbia 30110 Chicago III.
- (S) (3:34) Columbia 47416 Group Portrait.

1971 #11 *BEGINNINGS*
- (S) (7:49) Columbia 33900 Greatest Hits. (*LP version*)
- (S) (7:49) Columbia 00008 Chicago Transit Authority. (*LP version*)
- (S) (7:53) Columbia 47416 Group Portrait. (*LP version*)

1971 #13 *QUESTIONS 67 & 68*
- (S) (3:24) Columbia 37682 Greatest Hits Volume 2. (*45 version*)
- (S) (4:58) Columbia 00008 Chicago Transit Authority. (*LP version*)
- (S) (5:02) Columbia 47416 Group Portrait. (*LP version; tracks into next selection*)

1972 #3 *SATURDAY IN THE PARK*
- (S) (3:52) Columbia 33900 Greatest Hits.
- (S) (3:52) Columbia 31102 Chicago V.
- (S) (3:54) Columbia 47416 Group Portrait.
- (S) (3:52) Epic 48732 O.S.T. My Girl.

1972 #17 *DIALOGUE (PART 1 & 2)*
- (S) (4:07) Columbia 37682 Greatest Hits Volume 2. (*Part II only; not quite the LP version as this ending fades while the LP version ends cold*)
- (S) (2:56) Columbia 31102 Chicago V. (*Part I; tracks into part II just like the vinyl LP version*)
- (S) (4:12) Columbia 31102 Chicago V. (*Part II; Part I tracks right into Part II just like the vinyl LP version*)
- (S) (2:56) Columbia 47416 Group Portrait. (*Part I; tracks into Part II just like the vinyl LP version*)
- (S) (4:12) Columbia 47416 Group Portrait. (*Part II; Part I tracks right into Part II just like the vinyl LP version*)

1973 #8 *FEELIN' STRONGER EVERY DAY*
- (S) (4:12) Columbia 33900 Greatest Hits.
- (S) (4:13) Columbia 32400 Chicago VI.
- (S) (4:13) Columbia 47416 Group Portrait.

1973 #1 *JUST YOU 'N' ME*
- (S) (3:41) Columbia 33900 Greatest Hits.
- (S) (3:41) Columbia 32400 Chicago VI.
- (S) (3:41) Columbia 47416 Group Portrait.

CHIFFONS

1963 #1 *HE'S SO FINE*
- (M) (1:51) Rhino 70624 Billboard's Top Rock & Roll Hits Of 1963.
- (M) (1:51) Rhino 72007 Billboard's Top Rock & Roll Hits 1962-1966 Box Set.
- (M) (1:51) Rhino 70988 Best Of The Girl Groups Volume 1.
- (M) (1:54) JCI 3110 Sock Hoppin' Sixties.
- (M) (1:53) 3C/Laurie 104 Best Of.

1963 #7 *ONE FINE DAY*
- (M) (2:07) Rhino 70988 Best Of The Girl Groups Volume 1.
- (M) (2:08) 3C/Laurie 104 Best Of.

CHIFFONS (Continued)
1963 #38 *A LOVE SO FINE*
> (M) (1:53) 3C/Laurie 104 Best Of.
1964 #37 *I HAVE A BOYFRIEND*
1966 #10 *SWEET TALKIN' GUY*
> (M) (2:26) Warner Special Products 27602 20 Party Classics.
> (S) (2:25) Rhino 70989 Best Of The Girl Groups Volume 2.
> (M) (2:24) 3C/Laurie 104 Best Of.

CHI-LITES
1971 #29 *(FOR GOD'S SAKE) GIVE MORE POWER TO THE PEOPLE*
> (S) (3:05) Rhino 70784 Soul Hits Of The 70's Volume 4. *(an apparant attempt to reproduce the 45 version but several audience noise overdubs are missing)*
> (S) (3:45) Epic 38627 Greatest Hits. *("Greatest Hits" vinyl LP version, which was longer than either the 45 or original LP version)*
> (S) (2:57) Rhino 70532 Greatest Hits.
1971 #5 *HAVE YOU SEEN HER*
> (S) (5:09) Rhino 70659 Billboard's Top R&B Hits Of 1971.
> (S) (5:00) Rhino 70786 Soul Hits Of The 70's Volume 6.
> (S) (5:04) Epic 38627 Greatest Hits.
> (S) (5:08) Rhino 70532 Greatest Hits.
1972 #1 *OH GIRL*
> (S) (3:28) Rhino 70660 Billboard's Top R&B Hits Of 1972. *(:16 longer fade than 45 verion)*
> (S) (3:17) Rhino 70787 Soul Hits Of The 70's Volume 7. *(:05 longer fade than 45 version)*
> (S) (3:40) Epic 38627 Greatest Hits. *(LP version)*
> (S) (3:47) Rhino 70532 Greatest Hits. *(LP version)*

CHIMES
1961 #11 *ONCE IN A WHILE*
> (M) (2:25) Collectables 2507 History Of Rock - The doo Wop Era Volume 1. *(sounds like it was mastered from vinyl)*
1961 #40 *I'M IN THE MOOD FOR LOVE*

CHIPMUNKS
1958 #1 *THE CHIPMUNK SONG*
> (S) (2:20) Rhino 75755 Dr. Demento Presents The Greatest Christmas Novelty CD.
> (S) (2:18) Rhino 70636 Billboard's Greatest Christmas Hits.
> (E) (2:20) EMI 91684 Best Of.
> (E) (2:19) EMI 48378 Christmas With The Chipmunks.
1959 #3 *ALVIN'S HARMONICA*
> (S) (2:41) EMI 91684 Best Of.
1959 #14 *RAGTIME COWBOY JOE*
> (S) (2:06) EMI 91684 Best Of.
1960 #32 *ALVIN'S ORCHESTRA*

CHORDETTES
1956 #8 *BORN TO BE WITH YOU*
> (M) (2:47) Rhino 70849 Best Of.
1956 #18 *LAY DOWN YOUR ARMS*
> (M) (2:27) Rhino 70849 Best Of.
1957 #12 *JUST BETWEEN YOU AND ME*
> (M) (2:07) Rhino 70849 Best Of.

CHORDETTES (Continued)

1958 #2 LOLLIPOP
    (M) (2:09) Atlantic 81677 O.S.T. Stand By Me.
    (M) (2:08) Rhino 75894 Jukebox Classics Volume 2.
    (M) (2:08) Rhino 70849 Best Of.

1958 #21 ZORRO
    (M) (2:01) Rhino 70849 Best Of.

1959 #28 NO OTHER ARMS, NO OTHER LIPS
    (M) (2:32) Rhino 70849 Best Of.

1961 #14 NEVER ON SUNDAY
    (S) (2:40) Rhino 70849 Best Of.

CHRISTIE

1970 #16 YELLOW RIVER
    (S) (2:46) Rhino 70924 Super Hits Of The 70's Volume 4.
    (S) (2:46) Rhino 72009 Super Hits Of The 70's Volumes 1-4 Box Set.
    (S) (2:45) Columbia/Legacy 46160 Rock Artifacts Volume 1.

LOU CHRISTIE

1963 #18 THE GYPSY CRIED
    (M) (2:09) Rhino 70246 Enlightenment: The Best Of. *(truncated fade)*

1963 #3 TWO FACES HAVE I
    (M) (2:43) Rhino 70246 Enlightenment: The Best Of.

1966 #1 LIGHTNIN' STRIKES
    (S) (2:58) Mercury 816555 45's On CD Volume 2.
    (S) (2:58) Rhino 70246 Enlightenment: The Best Of.
    (S) (2:49) MCA 6171 Good Time Rock 'N' Roll. *(all selections on this cd are recorded live)*

1966 #20 RHAPSODY IN THE RAIN
    (M) (2:45) Rhino 70246 Enlightenment: The Best Of. *(uncensored version)*

1969 #7 I'M GONNA MAKE YOU MINE
    (E) (2:39) Pair 1202 Best Of Buddah.
    (E) (2:40) Rhino 70246 Enlightenment: The Best Of.
    (S) (2:23) MCA 6171 Good Time Rock 'N' Roll. *(all selections on this cd are recorded live)*

JIMMY CLANTON

1958 #5 JUST A DREAM
    (M) (2:29) Ace 2039 Very Best Of. *(mastered from vinyl)*

1958 #33 A LETTER TO AN ANGEL

1959 #28 MY OWN TRUE LOVE

1960 #7 GO, JIMMY, GO
    (M) (2:09) Ace 2039 Very Best Of.

1960 #17 ANOTHER SLEEPLESS NIGHT
    (M) (2:07) Ace 2039 Very Best Of.

1962 #10 VENUS IN BLUE JEANS
    (M) (2:21) Ace 2039 Very Best Of.

ERIC CLAPTON

1970 #13 AFTER MIDNIGHT
    (the actual 45 time is (2:51) not (3:15) as stated on the record label)
    (S) (2:50) Polydor 825093 Eric Clapton. *(45 length)*
    (S) (3:08) Polydor 800014 Time Pieces. *(LP length)*
    (S) (3:16) Polydor 835269 Crossroads. *(alternate take)*
    (S) (4:06) Polydor 835269 Crossroads. *(rerecorded in 1987)*

CLAUDINE CLARK

1962 #6 PARTY LIGHTS
    (M) (2:22) Rhino 75891 Wonder Women.
    (M) (2:21) Rhino 70988 Best Of The Girl Groups Volume 1.
    (M) (2:22) Rhino 70648 Billboard's Top R&B Hits Of 1962.
    (M) (2:21) JCI 3110 Sock Hoppin' Sixties.

DAVE CLARK FIVE

1964 #5 GLAD ALL OVER
1964 #4 BITS AND PIECES
1964 #8 DO YOU LOVE ME
1964 #4 CAN'T YOU SEE THAT SHE'S MINE
1964 #7 BECAUSE
1964 #22 EVERYBODY KNOWS (I STILL LOVE YOU)
1964 #9 ANY WAY YOU WANT IT
1965 #13 COME HOME
1965 #15 REELIN' AND ROCKIN'
1965 #6 I LIKE IT LIKE THAT
1965 #6 CATCH US IF YOU CAN
1965 #1 OVER AND OVER
1966 #13 AT THE SCENE
1966 #10 TRY TOO HARD
1966 #18 PLEASE TELL ME WHY
1967 #8 YOU GOT WHAT IT TAKES
1967 #35 YOU MUST HAVE BEEN A BEAUTIFUL BABY

DEE CLARK

1959 #34 NOBODY BUT YOU
1959 #17 JUST KEEP IT UP
1959 #20 HEY LITTLE GIRL
    (S) (2:18) Rhino 75893 Jukebox Classics Volume 1.
    (S) (2:16) Rhino 70645 Billboard's Top R&B Hits Of 1959.
    (S) (2:12) Motown 6215 Hits From The Legendary Vee-Jay Records.
    (S) (2:12) Garland 011 Footstompin' Oldies.
    (M) (2:10) Dunhill Compact Classics 028 Sock Hop.

1960 #31 HOW ABOUT THAT
1960 #40 YOU'RE LOOKING GOOD
1961 #2 RAINDROPS
    (S) (2:52) Rhino 75894 Jukebox Classics Volume 2.
    (S) (2:53) Rhino 70647 Billboard's Top R&B Hits Of 1961.
    (M) (2:49) Motown 6215 Hits From The Legendary Vee-Jay Records.
    (M) (2:52) Dunhill Compact Classics 028 Sock Hop.

PETULA CLARK

1965 #1 DOWNTOWN
    (S) (3:04) Rhino 70323 History Of British Rock Volume 5.
    (S) (3:04) Rhino 72022 History Of British Rock Box Set.
    (S) (3:08) GNP/Crescendo 2170 Greatest Hits Of.

1965 #2 I KNOW A PLACE
    (S) (2:43) Rhino 70324 History Of British Rock Volume 6. *(truncated fade)*
    (S) (2:43) Rhino 72022 History Of British Rock Box Set. *(truncated fade)*
    (S) (2:45) GNP/Crescendo 2170 Greatest Hits Of.
    (S) (2:44) Scotti Brothers 75260 Treasures Volume 1.

1965 #25 YOU'D BETTER COME HOME
    (S) (2:55) GNP/Crescendo 2170 Greatest Hits Of.

PETULA CLARK (Continued)
1965 #23 ROUND EVERY CORNER
> (S) (2:39) GNP/Crescendo 2170 Greatest Hits Of. *(truncated fade)*

1966 #2 MY LOVE
> (S) (2:44) Rhino 70325 History Of British Rock Volume 7.
> (S) (2:44) Rhino 72022 History Of British Rock Box Set.
> (S) (2:45) GNP/Crescendo 2170 Greatest Hits Of.

1966 #15 A SIGN OF THE TIMES
> (S) (2:57) GNP/Crescendo 2170 Greatest Hits Of.

1966 #8 I COULDN'T LIVE WITHOUT YOUR LOVE
> (S) (2:58) GNP/Crescendo 2170 Greatest Hits Of.

1966 #22 WHO AM I
> (S) (2:23) GNP/Crescendo 2170 Greatest Hits Of.

1967 #18 COLOR MY WORLD
> (S) (2:54) GNP/Crescendo 2170 Greatest Hits Of.

1967 #5 THIS IS MY SONG
> (S) (3:18) GNP/Crescendo 2170 Greatest Hits Of. *(LP version)*

1967 #6 DON'T SLEEP IN THE SUBWAY
> (S) (2:58) GNP/Crescendo 2170 Greatest Hits Of.
> (S) (2:57) Scotti Brothers 75260 Treasures Volume 1.

1967 #27 THE CAT IN THE WINDOW (THE BIRD IN THE SKY)
1967 #28 THE OTHER MAN'S GRASS IS ALWAYS GREENER
> (S) (2:56) GNP/Crescendo 2170 Greatest Hits Of.

1968 #12 KISS ME GOODBYE
> (S) (3:56) GNP/Crescendo 2170 Greatest Hits Of. *(slower in pitch than the 45 or LP)*

1968 #27 DON'T GIVE UP

ROY CLARK
1969 #19 YESTERDAY, WHEN I WAS YOUNG

SANFORD CLARK
1956 #8 THE FOOL
> (M) (2:43) Rhino 70599 Billboard's Top Rock & Roll Hits Of 1956.
> (M) (2:43) MCA 5939 Vintage Music Volumes 17 & 18.
> (M) (2:43) MCA 31214 Vintage Music Volume 17.
> (M) (2:43) Rhino 70741 Rock This Town: Rockabilly Hits Volume 1.

TONY CLARKE
1965 #28 THE ENTERTAINER
> (S) (2:32) Rhino 75757 Soul Shots Volume 3.
> (S) (2:33) Chess 31318 Best Of Chess Rhythm & Blues Volume 2.

CLASSICS
1963 #21 TILL THEN
> (M) (2:13) Collectables 2507 History Of Rock - The Doo Wop Era Part 1.

CLASSICS IV
1968 #2 SPOOKY
> (S) (2:52) EMI 91472 Very Best Of.
> (S) (2:51) Capitol 98138 Spring Break Volume 1. *(noisy fade out)*

1968 #2 STORMY
> (S) (2:47) EMI 91472 Very Best Of.
> (S) (2:47) Capitol 98139 Spring Break Volume 2.

1969 #3 TRACES
> (S) (2:45) EMI 90603 Rock Me Gently.
> (S) (2:45) EMI 91472 Very Best Of.

CLASSICS IV (Continued)
1969 #15 EVERYDAY WITH YOU GIRL
> (S) (2:31) EMI 91472 Very Best Of. (*truncated fade*)

1969 #38 MIDNIGHT

1972 #31 WHAT AM I CRYING FOR?

TOM CLAY
1971 #7 WHAT THE WORLD NEEDS NOW IS LOVE/ABRAHAM, MARTIN AND JOHN
> (S) (6:19) Motown 6184 Hard To Find Motown Classics Volume 2.

CLEAN LIVING
1972 #34 IN HEAVEN THERE IS NO BEER

CLEFTONES
1961 #16 HEART AND SOUL
> (S) (1:50) Rhino 70951 Best Of.
> (S) (1:51) Collectables 8806 For Collectors Only.

JIMMY CLIFF
1970 #18 WONDERFUL WORLD, BEAUTIFUL PEOPLE
> (S) (3:12) A&M 6015 Reggae Spectacular.
> (S) (3:14) A&M 3189 Wonderful World, Beautiful People.

BUZZ CLIFFORD
1961 #10 BABY SITTIN' BOOGIE

MIKE CLIFFORD
1962 #13 CLOSE TO CATHY

CLIMAX
1972 #1 PRECIOUS AND FEW
> (S) (2:44) Rhino 70927 Super Hits Of The 70's Volume 7.

PATSY CLINE
1957 #14 WALKIN' AFTER MIDNIGHT
> (M) (1:56) MCA 5939 Vintage Music Volumes 17 & 18. (*rerecording*)
> (M) (1:56) MCA 31214 Vintage Music Volume 17. (*rerecording*)
> (S) (1:57) MCA 4038 Patsy Cline Story. (*rerecording*)
> (M) (2:32) MCA 12 Twelve Greatest Hits.
> (M) (2:33) MCA 4-10421 The Patsy Cline Collection.
> (S) (2:00) MCA 6149 O.S.T. Sweet Dreams. (*rerecording*)
> (S) (1:59) MCA 1467 Remembering. (*rerecording*)
> (M) (2:33) MCA 25200 Patsy Cline.
> (M) (2:33) MCA 8925 Commemorative Collection.
> (E) (2:31) Pair 1236 The Legendary.
> (M) (2:30) Curb 77518 Best Of.

1961 #15 I FALL TO PIECES
> (S) (2:46) MCA 4038 Patsy Cline Story.
> (M) (2:47) MCA 12 Twelve Greatest Hits.
> (S) (2:48) MCA 4-10421 The Patsy Cline Collection.
> (S) (2:47) MCA 6149 O.S.T. Sweet Dreams.
> (M) (2:47) MCA 8925 Commemorative Collection.

1961 #13 CRAZY
> (S) (2:40) MCA 5940 Vintage Music Volumes 19 & 20.
> (S) (2:40) MCA 31216 Vintage Music Volume 19.
> (S) (2:41) MCA 4038 Patsy Cline Story.
> (M) (2:39) MCA 12 Twelve Greatest Hits. (*truncated fade*)
> (S) (2:42) MCA 4-10421 The Patsy Cline Collection.
> (S) (2:41) MCA 6149 O.S.T. Sweet Dreams.
> (M) (2:39) MCA 8925 Commemorative Collection.

PATSY CLINE (Continued)

1962 #11 SHE'S GOT YOU
- (S) (2:57) MCA 4038 Patsy Cline Story.
- (M) (2:57) MCA 12 Twelve Greatest Hits.
- (S) (3:06) MCA 4-10421 The Patsy Cline Collection. *(with countoff)*
- (S) (2:58) MCA 6149 O.S.T. Sweet Dreams.
- (M) (2:57) MCA 8925 Commemorative Collection.

CLIQUE

1969 #20 SUGAR ON SUNDAY

1969 #34 I'LL HOLD OUT MY HAND

ROSEMARY CLOONEY

1957 #23 MANGOS

CLOVERS

1956 #34 LOVE, LOVE, LOVE
- (M) (2:02) Atlantic 81295 Atlantic Rhythm & Blues Volume 3.
- (M) (2:01) Atlantic 82305 Atlantic Rhythm And Blues 1947-1974 Box Set.

1959 #21 LOVE POTION NO. 9
- (S) (1:51) EMI 96268 24 Greatest Hits Of All Time. *(45 version)*
- (M) (1:53) Curb 77323 All Time Greatest Hits Of Rock 'N' Roll. *(45 version)*
- (S) (1:51) EMI 96336 Best Of - Love Potion No. 9. *(45 version)*
- (S) (2:25) EMI 96336 Best Of - Love Potion No. 9. *(LP version; includes :31 of studio talk and a false start)*
- (S) (1:51) Rhino 70593 The Rock 'N' Roll Classics Of Leiber & Stoller. *(45 version)*

COASTERS

1957 #7 SEARCHIN'
- (M) (2:39) Atlantic 81295 Atlantic Rhythm & Blues Volume 3.
- (E) (2:39) Warner Special Products 27604 Ultimate.
- (M) (2:38) Atco 33111 Greatest Hits.
- (M) (2:39) Atlantic 82305 Atlantic Rhythm And Blues 1947-1974 Box Set.

1957 #15 YOUNG BLOOD
- (M) (2:20) Warner Special Products 27602 20 Party Classics.
- (M) (2:19) Atlantic 81295 Atlantic Rhythm & Blues Volume 3. *(first few notes truncated)*
- (M) (2:20) Warner Special Products 27604 Ultimate.
- (M) (2:20) Atco 33111 Greatest Hits.
- (M) (2:19) Atlantic 82305 Atlantic Rhythm And Blues 1947-1974 Box Set. *(first few notes truncated)*

1958 #1 YAKETY YAK
- (S) (1:48) Warner Special Products 27601 Atlantic Soul Classics.
- (S) (1:50) Rhino 70619 Billboard's Top Rock & Roll Hits Of 1958.
- (S) (1:50) Rhino 72004 Billboard's Top Rock & Roll Hits 1957-1961 Box Set.
- (M) (1:48) Atlantic 81295 Atlantic Rhythm & Blues Volume 3. *(45 version)*
- (M) (1:48) Atlantic 81677 O.S.T. Stand By Me. *(45 version)*
- (S) (1:49) Warner Special Products 27604 Ultimate.
- (S) (1:49) Atco 33111 Coasters Greatest Hits.
- (S) (1:49) MCA 6171 Good Time Rock 'N' Roll. *(all selections on this cd are recorded live)*
- (M) (1:48) Atlantic 82305 Atlantic Rhythm And Blues 1947-1974 Box Set. *(45 version)*

1959 #2 *CHARLIE BROWN*

(S) (2:22) Rhino 70620 Billboard's Top Rock & Roll Hits Of 1959. *(LP version)*

(S) (2:22) Rhino 72004 Billboard's Top Rock & Roll Hits 1957-1961 Box Set. *(LP version)*

(M) (2:17) Atlantic 81296 Atlantic Rhythm & Blues Volume 4. *(45 version)*

(M) (2:18) Warner Special Products 27604 Ultimate. *(45 version; truncated fade)*

(M) (2:17) Atco 33111 Greatest Hits. *(LP version; truncated fade)*

(M) (2:15) Rhino 70593 The Rock 'N' Roll Classics Of Leiber & Stoller. *(45 version)*

(S) (2:10) MCA 6171 Good Time Rock 'N' Roll. *(all selections on this cd are recorded live)*

(M) (2:17) Atlantic 82305 Atlantic Rhythm And Blues 1947-1974 Box Set. *(45 version)*

1959 #11 *ALONG CAME JONES*

(M) (2:55) Atlantic 81296 Atlantic Rhythm & Blues Volume 4.

(M) (2:53) Warner Special Products 27604 Ultimate.

(M) (2:55) Atco 33111 Greatest Hits.

(M) (2:55) Atlantic 82305 Atlantic Rhythm And Blues 1947-1974 Box Set.

1959 #9 *POISON IVY*

(S) (2:40) Rhino 70645 Billboard's Top R&B Hits Of 1959. *(alternate take)*

(S) (2:40) Atlantic 81296 Atlantic Rhythm & Blues Volume 4. *(alternate take)*

(M) (2:40) Warner Special Products 27604 Ultimate. *(45 version)*

(S) (2:40) Atco 33111 Greatest Hits. *(alternate take)*

(S) (2:40) Atlantic 82305 Atlantic Rhythm And Blues 1947-1974 Box Set. *(alternate take)*

1960 #33 *WHAT ABOUT US*

1960 #34 *WAKE ME, SHAKE ME*

1961 #30 *LITTLE EGYPT*

(M) (2:50) Atlantic 81296 Atlantic Rhythm & Blues Volume 4. *(45 version)*

(S) (2:50) Warner Special Products 27604 Ultimate. *(alternate take)*

(S) (2:45) Atlantic 82305 Atlantic Rhythm And Blues 1947-1974 Box Set. *(45 version)*

EDDIE COCHRAN

1957 #15 *SITTIN' IN THE BALCONY*

(M) (1:57) EMI 46580 Best Of.

(M) (1:58) EMI 92809 Legendary Masters Series Volume 1.

(M) (1:57) Curb 77371 Greatest Hits.

1958 #11 *SUMMERTIME BLUES*

(M) (1:56) Rhino 70906 American Bandstand Greatest Hits Collection.

(M) (1:56) Rhino 70087 Summer & Fun.

(M) (1:58) EMI 96268 24 Greatest Hits Of All Time. *(with cold ending)*

(E) (1:56) EMI 90614 Non Stop Party Rock.

(M) (1:56) EMI 46580 Best Of.

(M) (1:58) EMI 92809 Legendary Masters Series Volume 1. *(with cold ending)*

(M) (1:55) Curb 77323 All Time Greatest Hits Of Rock 'N' Roll.

(M) (1:56) Curb 77371 Greatest Hits.

(M) (1:55) Capitol 48993 Spuds Mackenzie's Party Faves.

(M) (1:56) Capitol 98138 Spring Break Volume 1.

JOE COCKER

1970 #36 *SHE CAME IN THROUGH THE BATHROOM WINDOW*
   (S) (2:37) A&M 2503 Classics Volume 4.
   (S) (2:36) A&M 3326 Joe Cocker!

1970 #5 *THE LETTER*
   (S) (4:20) A&M 2503 Classics Volume 4. *(from "Mad Dogs & Englishmen" - not the hit single version)*
   (S) (4:16) A&M 3257 Greatest Hits. *(from "Mad Dogs & Englishmen" - not the hit single version)*
   (S) (4:09) A&M 6002 Mad Dogs & Englishmen. *(not the hit single version)*

1970 #16 *CRY ME A RIVER*
   (S) (4:03) Warner Special Products 27616 Classic Rock.
   (S) (4:01) JCI 3401 Live Volume 1.
   (S) (3:53) A&M 2503 Classics Volume 4.
   (S) (3:47) A&M 6002 Mad Dogs & Englishmen.
   (S) (4:03) A&M 3257 Greatest Hits.

1971 #29 *HIGH TIME WE WENT*
   (S) (4:28) A&M 2503 Classics Volume 4.
   (S) (4:26) A&M 3257 Greatest Hits.

1972 #36 *FEELING ALRIGHT*
   (S) (4:01) JCI 3101 Rockin' Sixties.
   (S) (4:11) A&M 2503 Classics Volume 4.
   (S) (4:08) A&M 3106 With A Little Help From My Friends.
   (S) (4:09) A&M 3257 Greatest Hits.
   (S) (3:59) Priority 8662 Hard 'N Heavy/70's Greatest Rock Hits Volume 1.

1972 #31 *MIDNIGHT RIDER*
   (S) (4:00) A&M 2503 Classics Volume 4.

DENNIS COFFEY & THE DETROIT GUITAR BAND

1972 #4 *SCORPIO*
   (S) (4:03) Rhino 70787 Soul Hits Of The 70's Volume 7.

1972 #13 *TAURUS*

COZY COLE

1958 #1 *TOPSY II*
   (M) (3:33) Rhino 70644 Billboard's Top R&B Hits Of 1958.
   (M) (3:34) Curb 77402 All-Time Great Instrumental Hits Volume 2.

1958 #36 *TURVY II*

NAT KING COLE

1955 #7 *DARLING JE VOUS AIME BEAUCOUP*
   (M) (2:48) Capitol 93590 Capitol Collector's Series.
   (S) (2:48) Capitol 95129 Story. *(rerecording)*
   (M) (2:48) Capitol 99230 The Unforgettable.

1955 #3 *A BLOSSOM FELL*
   (M) (2:30) Capitol 93590 Capitol Collector's Series.

1955 #10 *IF I MAY*
   (S) (2:56) Capitol 95129 Story. *(rerecording)*

1956 #17 *THAT'S ALL THERE IS TO THAT*

1956 #17 *NIGHT LIGHTS*
   (S) (2:47) Capitol 95129 Story. *(rerecording)*

1956 #25 *TO THE ENDS OF THE EARTH*
   (S) (2:24) Capitol 95129 Story. *(rerecording)*

1957 #29 *BALLERINA*
   (S) (2:40) Capitol 95129 Story. *(rerecording)*

1957 #34 *YOU ARE MY FIRST LOVE*

NAT KING COLE (Continued)
1957 #7 SEND FOR ME
    (S) (2:29) Capitol 95129   Story. *(rerecording)*
    (M) (2:36) Capitol 93590   Capitol Collector's Series.

1957 #26 MY PERSONAL POSSESSION

1957 #22 WITH YOU ON MY MIND

1958 #28 ANGEL SMILE

1958 #10 LOOKING BACK
    (S) (2:24) Capitol 95129   Story. *(rerecording)*

1958 #25 COME CLOSER TO ME

1958 #22 NON DIMENTICAR (DON'T FORGET)
    (S) (3:06) Capitol 95129   Story. *(rerecording)*
    (S) (3:37) Capitol 93590   Capitol Collector's Series. *(includes :49 of studio talk)*
    (M) (2:47) Capitol 99230   The Unforgettable.

1959 #39 YOU MADE ME LOVE YOU

1959 #32 MIDNIGHT FLYER

1962 #2 RAMBLIN' ROSE
    (S) (2:47) Capitol 93590   Capitol Collector's Series.
    (S) (2:47) Capitol 46651   Ramblin' Rose.
    (S) (2:47) Capitol 98670   Memories Are Made Of This.

1962 #14 DEAR LONELY HEARTS
    (S) (3:07) Capitol 93590   Capitol Collector's Series.
    (S) (3:06) Capitol 46651   Ramblin' Rose.

1963 #7 THOSE LAZY HAZY CRAZY DAYS OF SUMMER
    (S) (2:53) Capitol 93590   Capitol Collector's Series. *(includes :30 of studio talk)*
    (S) (2:23) Enigma 73531   O.S.T. Scandal.

1963 #15 THAT SUNDAY, THAT SUMMER
    (S) (3:09) Capitol 99230   The Unforgettable.

1964 #19 I DON'T WANT TO BE HURT ANYMORE

1964 #34 I DON'T WANT TO SEE TOMORROW

DAVE & ANSIL COLLINS
1971 #27 DOUBLE BARREL
    (M) (2:47) Rhino 70785   Soul Hits Of The 70's Volume 5.

JUDY COLLINS
1968 #8 BOTH SIDES NOW
    (S) (3:13) Elektra 74012   Wildflowers.
    (S) (3:12) Elektra 75030   Colors Of The Day/Best Of.

1969 #40 SOMEDAY SOON
    (S) (3:41) Elektra 74033   Who Knows Where The Time Goes.

1971 #13 AMAZING GRACE
    (S) (4:03) Elektra 75010   Whales & Nightingales.
    (S) (4:06) Elektra 75030   Colors Of The Day/Best Of.

1973 #29 COOK WITH HONEY
    (S) (3:28) Elektra 75053   True Stories And Other Dreams.

CHI COLTRANE
1972 #15 THUNDER AND LIGHTNING
    (S) (3:00) Rhino 70929   Super Hits Of The 70's Volume 9.
    (S) (3:00) Columbia/Legacy 46160   Rock Artifacts Volume 1.

COMMANDER CODY & HIS LOST PLANET AIRMEN
1972 #7 *HOT ROD LINCOLN*
    (S) (2:42) Rhino 70928 Super Hits Of The 70's Volume 8.
    (S) (2:41) MCA 25240 Classic Rock Volume 3.
    (S) (2:41) Rhino 70742 Rock This Town: Rockabilly Hits Volume 2.
    (S) (2:41) MCA 10092 Too Much Fun/Best Of.
    (S) (2:41) MCA 31185 Lost In The Ozone.
    (S) (2:41) Priority 8670 Hitchin A Ride/70's Greatest Rock Hits Volume 10.

NICKY COMO
1960 #13 *LOOK FOR A STAR*

PERRY COMO
1955 #3 *KO KO MO (I LOVE YOU SO)*
1955 #6 *TINA MARIE*
1956 #1 *HOT DIGGITY (DOG ZIGGITY BOOM)*
    (M) (2:21) RCA 8467 Nipper's Greatest Hits Of The 50's Volume 2.
    (E) (2:21) RCA 8323 All Time Greatest Hits.
    (M) (2:21) RCA 0972 Pure Gold.
    (M) (2:21) RCA 53802 Como's Golden Records.
1956 #7 *JUKE BOX BABY*
1956 #9 *MORE*
1956 #18 *GLENDORA*
1956 #29 *SOMEBODY UP THERE LIKES ME*
1956 #33 *MOONLIGHT LOVE*
1957 #2 *ROUND AND ROUND*
    (E) (2:32) RCA 9902 Nipper's #1 Hits 1956-1986.
    (E) (2:33) RCA 8323 All Time Greatest Hits.
    (M) (2:32) RCA 53802 Como's Golden Records.
1957 #22 *THE GIRL WITH THE GOLDEN BRAIDS*
1957 #23 *MY LITTLE BABY*
1957 #14 *JUST BORN (TO BE YOUR BABY)*
1957 #36 *IVY ROSE*
1958 #2 *CATCH A FALLING STAR*
    (S) (2:26) RCA 8466 Nipper's Greatest Hits Of The 50's Volume 1.
    (E) (2:28) RCA 8323 All Time Greatest Hits.
    (M) (2:29) RCA 0972 Pure Gold.
    (M) (2:28) Special Music 2651 It's Impossible.
    (M) (2:28) RCA 53802 Como's Golden Records.
1958 #21 *MAGIC MOMENTS*
    (E) (2:38) RCA 8323 All Time Greatest Hits.
    (M) (2:38) RCA 53802 Como's Golden Records.
1958 #9 *KEWPIE DOLL*
1958 #24 *MOON TALK*
1959 #26 *TOMBOY*
1959 #37 *I KNOW*
1960 #17 *DELEWARE*
1962 #22 *CATERINA*
1965 #29 *DREAM ON LITTLE DREAMER*
    (S) (2:20) RCA 8323 All Time Greatest Hits.
    (S) (2:19) Special Music 2651 It's Impossible. *(truncated fade)*

PERRY COMO (Continued)

1971 #10 IT'S IMPOSSIBLE
     (S) (3:14) RCA 8476 and 9684 Nipper's Greatest Hits Of The 70's.
     (S) (3:13) RCA 8323 All Time Greatest Hits.
     (S) (3:13) RCA 0972 Pure Gold.
     (S) (3:13) Special Music 2651 It's Impossible.

1973 #18 AND I LOVE YOU SO
     (S) (3:17) Special Music 2651 It's Impossible.

ARTHUR CONLEY

1967 #4 SWEET SOUL MUSIC
     (E) (2:19) Warner Special Products 27601 Atlantic Soul Classics.
     (M) (2:20) Atlantic 81911 Golden Age Of Black Music (1960-1970).
     (M) (2:20) Atlantic 81298 Atlantic Rhythm & Blues Volume 6.
     (M) (2:19) Atlantic 82305 Atlantic Rhythm And Blues 1947-1974 Box Set.

1968 #19 FUNKY STREET

RAY CONNIFF & THE SINGERS

1966 #11 SOMEWHERE MY LOVE
     (S) (3:45) Columbia 40214 16 Most Requested Songs. *(rerecording; titled "LARA'S THEME FROM DR. ZHIVAGO" on the cd)*
     (S) (2:28) Columbia 9319 Somewhere My Love.

DICK CONTINO

1957 #15 PLEDGE OF LOVE

CONTOURS

1962 #2 DO YOU LOVE ME
     (M) (2:51) Rhino 75778 Frat Rock.
     (M) (2:53) Rhino 70648 Billboard's Top R&B Hits Of 1962.
     (E) (2:51) RCA 6965 More Dirty Dancing.
     (M) (2:51) Motown 9104 Motown Memories Volume 1.
     (M) (2:51) Motown 6219 Hard To Find Motown Classics Volume 3.
     (M) (2:51) Motown 6160 The Good-Feeling Music Of The Big Chill Generation Volume 2.
     (M) (2:51) Dunhill Compact Classics 043 Toga Rock II.
     (M) (2:52) Rhino 70243 Greatest Movie Rock Hits.
     (M) (2:51) Motown 9017 and 5248 16 #1 Hits From The Early 60's.
     (S) (2:49) Motown 5448 A Collection Of 16 Big Hits Volume 1. *(alternate take)*
     (S) (2:51) Warner Brothers 3359 O.S.T. The Wanderers. *(alternate take)*
     (S) (6:36) Motown 5415 Do You Love Me. *(remixed disco version from the movie "Dirty Dancing")*
     (M) (2:50) Motown 9071 Motown Dance Party Volume 1. *(all selections on this cd are segued together)*

SAM COOKE

1957 #1 YOU SEND ME
     (E) (2:45) RCA 3863 Best Of.
     (E) (2:44) RCA 7127 The Man And His Music.
     (M) (2:42) Pair 1006 You Send Me.

1958 #20 I'LL COME RUNNING BACK TO YOU
     (M) (2:10) RCA 7127 The Man And His Music.

1958 #33 (I LOVE YOU) FOR SENTIMENTAL REASONS
     (M) (2:36) RCA 3863 Best Of.

1958 #39 LONELY ISLAND

1958 #37 LOVE YOU MOST OF ALL

SAM COOKE (Continued)

1959 #29 EVERYBODY LIKES TO CHA CHA CHA
        (M) (2:34) RCA 3863 Best Of.
        (M) (2:36) RCA 7127 The Man And His Music.

1959 #32 ONLY SIXTEEN
        (S) (1:53) RCA 3863 Best Of.
        (S) (1:53) RCA 7127 The Man And His Music.

1960 #40 TEENAGE SONATA

1960 #10 WONDERFUL WORLD
        (M) (2:04) RCA 3863 Best Of.
        (M) (2:04) RCA 7127 The Man And His Music.
        (E) (2:05) MCA 31023 O.S.T. Animal House. *(all selections on this cd are segued together)*
        (E) (2:04) Special Music 2610 The Unforgettable.

1960 #3 CHAIN GANG
        (S) (2:35) RCA 8474 Nipper's Greatest Hits Of The 60's Volume 1.
        (S) (2:33) RCA 3863 Best Of.
        (S) (2:33) RCA 7127 The Man And His Music.
        (S) (2:34) Pair 1186 An Original.

1960 #28 SAD MOOD
        (S) (2:27) RCA 3863 Best Of.
        (S) (2:28) RCA 7127 The Man And His Music.

1961 #28 THAT'S IT-I QUIT-I'M MOVIN' ON

1961 #16 CUPID
        (S) (2:28) RCA 3863 Best Of.
        (S) (2:29) RCA 7127 The Man And His Music.

1962 #6 TWISTIN' THE NIGHT AWAY
        (S) (2:38) RCA 8475 Nipper's Greatest Hits Of The 60's Volume 2.
        (S) (2:39) RCA 3863 Best Of.
        (S) (2:39) RCA 7127 The Man And His Music.
        (E) (2:38) MCA 31023 O.S.T. Animal House. *(all selections on this cd are segued together)*

1962 #16 HAVING A PARTY
        (E) (2:22) RCA 3863 Best Of.
        (E) (2:26) RCA 7127 The Man And His Music.

1962 #9 BRING IT ON HOME TO ME
        (E) (2:39) RCA 3863 Best Of.
        (E) (2:41) RCA 7127 The Man And His Music.

1962 #21 NOTHING CAN CHANGE THIS LOVE
        (S) (2:35) RCA 7127 The Man And His Music.

1963 #20 SEND ME SOME LOVIN'

1963 #14 ANOTHER SATURDAY NIGHT
        (S) (2:25) RCA 7127 The Man And His Music.

1963 #15 FRANKIE AND JOHNNY

1963 #11 LITTLE RED ROOSTER

1964 #9 GOOD NEWS
        (S) (2:29) RCA 7127 The Man And His Music.

1964 #16 GOOD TIMES
        (S) (2:27) RCA 7127 The Man And His Music.

1964 #38 TENNESSEE WALTZ

1964 #24 COUSIN OF MINE

1965 #6 SHAKE
        (S) (2:48) RCA 7127 The Man And His Music.

1965 #36 IT'S GOT THE WHOLE WORLD SHAKIN'

SAM COOKE (Continued)
1965 #30 *SUGAR DUMPLING*
>   (E)   (2:37)   Special Music 2610   The Unforgettable.

COOKIES
1962 #21 *CHAINS*
>   (M)   (2:29)   Rhino 70989   Best Of The Girl Groups Volume 2.
>   (M)   (2:33)   Collectables 5414   Carole King Plus. *(truncated fade)*

1963 #8 *DON'T SAY NOTHIN' BAD (ABOUT MY BABY)*
>   (M)   (2:42)   Rhino 70989   Best Of The Girl Groups Volume 2.
>   (M)   (2:45)   Collectables 5414   Carole King Plus. *(truncated fade)*

EDDIE COOLEY & THE DIMPLES
1956 #25 *PRISCILLA*

ALICE COOPER
1971 #21 *EIGHTEEN*
>   *(LP title was "I'M EIGHTEEN")*
>   (S)   (2:56)   Rhino 70986   Heavy Metal Memories.
>   (S)   (2:53)   JCI 3302   Electric Seventies.
>   (S)   (2:55)   Warner Special Products 27616   Classic Rock.
>   (S)   (2:54)   Warner Brothers 3107   Greatest Hits.
>   (S)   (2:56)   Warner Brothers 1883   Love It To Death.
>   (S)   (2:56)   RCA 8533   O.S.T. Heartbreak Hotel.

1972 #36 *BE MY LOVER*
>   (S)   (3:17)   Warner Brothers 2567   Killer.

1972 #6 *SCHOOL'S OUT*
>   (S)   (3:27)   Warner Brothers 3107   Greatest Hits.
>   (S)   (3:26)   Warner Brothers 2623   School's Out.
>   (S)   (3:25)   Sire 6070   Rock 'N' Roll High School.

1972 #18 *ELECTED*
>   (S)   (4:05)   Warner Brothers 3107   Greatest Hits.
>   (S)   (4:05)   Warner Brothers 2685   Billion Dollar Babies.

1973 #25 *HELLO HURRAY*
>   (S)   (4:15)   Warner Brothers 3107   Greatest Hits.
>   (S)   (4:15)   Warner Brothers 2685   Billion Dollar Babies. *(tracks into the next selection)*

1973 #26 *NO MORE MR. NICE GUY*
>   (S)   (3:06)   Warner Brothers 3107   Greatest Hits.
>   (S)   (3:05)   Warner Brothers 2685   Billion Dollar Babies.

1973 #36 *BILLION DOLLAR BABIES*
>   (S)   (3:38)   Warner Brothers 2685   Billion Dollar Babies.

LES COOPER & THE SOUL ROCKERS
1962 #21 *WIGGLE WOBBLE*
>   (S)   (2:04)   Relic 7009   Raging Harlem Hit Parade.

KEN COPELAND
1957 #14 *PLEDGE OF LOVE*

JILL COREY
1957 #19 *LOVE ME TO PIECES*

CORNELIUS BROTHERS & SISTER ROSE
1971 #2 *TREAT HER LIKE A LADY*
>   (S)   (2:44)   Rhino 70632   Billboard's Top Rock & Roll Hits Of 1971.
>   (S)   (2:44)   Rhino 72005   Billboard's Top Rock & Roll Hits 1968-1972 Box Set.
>   (S)   (2:44)   Rhino 70785   Soul Hits Of The 70's Volume 5.

CORNELIUS BROTHERS & SISTER ROSE (Continued)
>> (S) (2:43) EMI 90603 Rock Me Gently.
>> (S) (2:44) Curb 77356 70's Hits Volume 2.

1972 #1 *TOO LATE TO TURN BACK NOW*
>> (S) (3:20) Rhino 70788 Soul Hits Of The 70's Volume 8.

1972 #23 *DON'T EVER BE LONELY (A POOR LITTLE FOOL LIKE ME)*
>> (S) (2:59) Rhino 70788 Soul Hits Of The 70's Volume 8.

1973 #31 *I'M NEVER GONNA BE ALONE ANYMORE*

DON CORNELL

1955 #10 *THE BIBLE TELLS ME SO*

CORSAIRS

1962 #12 *SMOKY PLACES*
>> (M) (2:58) MCA 5938 Vintage Music Volumes 15 & 16.
>> (M) (2:58) MCA 31213 Vintage Music Volume 16.
>> (M) (2:55) Chess 31317 Best Of Chess Rhythm & Blues Volume 1.

DAVE "BABY" CORTEZ

1959 #1 *THE HAPPY ORGAN*
>> (M) (1:58) Rhino 70620 Billboard's Top Rock & Roll Hits Of 1959.
>> (M) (1:58) Rhino 72004 Billboard's Top Rock & Roll Hits 1957-1961 Box Set.

1962 #11 *RINKY DINK*
>> (M) (2:50) MCA 31205 Vintage Music Volume 8.
>> (M) (2:50) MCA 5805 Vintage Music Volumes 7 & 8.
>> (M) (2:50) Chess 31320 Best Of Chess Rock 'n' Roll Volume 2.

BILL COSBY

1967 #5 *LITTLE OLE MAN (UPTIGHT - EVERYTHING'S ALRIGHT)*

DON COSTA

1960 #18 *THEME FROM "THE UNFORGIVEN" (THE NEED FOR LOVE)*

1960 #12 *NEVER ON SUNDAY*
>> (S) (2:55) Curb 77403 All-Time Great Instrumental Hits Volume 1.

COUNT FIVE

1966 #4 *PSYCHOTIC REACTION*
>> (E) (3:04) K-Tel 713 Battle Of The Bands.
>> (E) (3:05) Warner Special Products 27607 Highs Of The 60's.
>> (M) (3:04) Rhino 75892 Nuggets.
>> (E) (3:05) Novus 3077 O.S.T. Drugstore Cowboy.
>> (E) (3:05) JCI 3103 Electric Sixties.

DON COVAY

1973 #28 *I WAS CHECKIN' OUT, SHE WAS CHECKIN' IN*
>> (S) (4:06) Rhino 70551 Soul Hits Of The 70's Volume 11.
>> (S) (4:20) Mercury 836030 Checkin' In With.

DON COVAY & THE GOODTIMERS

released as by **THE GOODTIMERS:**

1961 #20 *PONY TIME*

released as by **DON COVAY & THE GOODTIMERS:**

1964 #26 *MERCY, MERCY*
>> (M) (2:24) Atlantic 81297 Atlantic Rhythm & Blues Volume 5.
>> (S) (2:24) Atlantic 82305 Atlantic Rhythm And Blues 1947-1974 Box Set.

COVEN

1971 #18 *ONE TIN SOLDIER (THE LEGEND OF BILLY JACK)*
>> (S) (3:20) Rhino 70927 Super Hits Of The 70's Volume 7. (*Warner Brothers hit version which was later released on MGM in a different version*)

COWSILLS
1967 #1 THE RAIN, THE PARK & OTHER THINGS
    (M) (2:56) Mercury 834216 45's On CD Volume 3.
    (S) (3:00) Polydor 833344 Best Of.
1968 #17 WE CAN FLY
    (S) (2:12) Polydor 833344 Best Of.
1968 #6 INDIAN LAKE
    (S) (2:41) Polydor 833344 Best Of.
1968 #33 POOR BABY
    (M) (2:56) Polydor 833344 Best Of.
1969 #1 HAIR
    (S) (3:28) Rhino 70630 Billboard's Top Rock & Roll Hits Of 1969.
    (S) (3:28) Rhino 72005 Billboard's Top Rock & Roll Hits 1968-1972 Box Set.
    (S) (3:28) Polydor 833344 Best Of.

CRABBY APPLETON
1970 #30 GO BACK
    (S) (3:03) Rhino 70926 Super Hits Of The 70's Volume 6.

FLOYD CRAMER
1960 #2 LAST DATE
    (S) (2:27) RCA 8474 Nipper's Greatest Hits Of The 60's Volume 1.
    (S) (2:27) RCA 56322 Best Of.
    (S) (2:27) Pair 1210 Best Of.
1961 #7 ON THE REBOUND
    (S) (2:06) RCA 8475 Nipper's Greatest Hits Of The 60's Volume 2.
    (S) (2:06) RCA 56322 Best Of.
    (S) (2:08) Pair 1210 Best Of.
1961 #15 SAN ANTONIO ROSE
    (S) (2:19) Rhino 70682 Billboard's Top Country Hits Of 1961.
    (S) (2:20) Pair 1210 Best Of.

LES CRANE
1971 #11 DESIDERATA

JOHNNY CRAWFORD
1962 #40 PATTI ANN
1962 #13 CINDY'S BIRTHDAY
1962 #27 YOUR NOSE IS GONNA GROW
1962 #20 RUMORS
1963 #34 PROUD

CRAZY ELEPHANT
1969 #6 GIMME GIMME GOOD LOVIN'
    (S) (2:02) K-Tel 205 Battle Of the Bands Volume 3.
    (S) (2:02) Rhino 70996 One Hit Wonders Of The 60's Volume 2.
    (S) (2:02) Rhino 70732 Grandson Of Frat Rock.

CRAZY WORLD OF ARTHUR BROWN
1968 #2 FIRE
    (S) (2:49) Mercury 834216 45's On CD Volume 3.
    (S) (2:53) Rhino 70327 History Of British Rock Volume 9.
    (S) (2:53) Rhino 72022 History Of British Rock Box Set.
    (M) (3:01) Polydor 833736 The Crazy World of Arthur Brown. *(the cd jacket says this is the mono mix but the U.S. 45 was mono and it wasn't even close to this version; tracks into next selection)*
    (S) (2:53) Polydor 833736 The Crazy World Of Arthur Brown.

CREAM

1968 #6 *SUNSHINE OF YOUR LOVE*
- (S) (4:09) JCI 3103 Electric Sixties. *(LP version)*
- (M) (3:01) Rhino 70326 History of British Rock Volume 8. *(45 version)*
- (M) (3:01) Rhino 72022 History Of British Rock Box Set. *(45 version)*
- (S) (4:09) Polydor 823636 Disraeli Gears. *(LP version)*
- (S) (4:09) Polydor 811639 Strange Brew/Very Best Of. *(LP version)*
- (S) (4:09) Polydor 835268 Crossroads. *(LP version)*
- (S) (4:09) Atlantic 82152 O.S.T. Goodfellas. *(LP version)*

1968 #5 *WHITE ROOM*
- (S) (4:55) Atlantic 81908 Classic Rock 1966-1988. *(LP version)*
- (S) (4:47) Polydor 837362 O.S.T. 1969. *(LP version)*
- (M) (3:02) Rhino 70327 History Of British Rock Volume 9. *(45 version; truncated fade)*
- (M) (3:02) Rhino 72022 History Of British Rock Box Set. *(45 version; truncated fade)*
- (S) (4:57) Polydor 811639 Strange Brew/Very Best Of. *(LP version)*
- (S) (4:57) Polydor 827578 Wheels Of Fire. *(LP version)*
- (S) (4:56) Polydor 835268 Crossroads. *(LP version)*
- (S) (4:55) Atlantic 82306 Atlantic Rock & Roll Box Set. *(LP version)*

1969 #17 *CROSSROADS*
(dj copies of this 45 ran (2:50) and (4:13))
- (S) (4:13) Polydor 811639 Strange Brew/Very Best Of.
- (S) (4:14) Polydor 827578 Wheels Of Fire.
- (S) (4:12) Polydor 835268 Crossroads.

CREEDENCE CLEARWATER REVIVAL

1968 #9 *SUZIE Q (PART 1)*
- (S) (4:34) Fantasy CCR2 Chronicle. *(Part 1)*
- (S) (3:58) Fantasy CCR3 Chronicle Volume 2. *(Part 2)*
- (S) (8:33) Fantasy 9418 Creedence Gold. *(LP version)*
- (S) (8:33) Fantasy 8382 Creedence Clearwater Revival. *(LP version)*

1969 #2 *PROUD MARY*
- (S) (3:06) Fantasy CCR2 Chronicle. *(very poor stereo separation)*
- (S) (3:06) Fantasy 8387 Bayou Country. *(very poor stereo separation)*
- (S) (3:06) Fantasy 9418 Creedence Gold. *(very poor stereo separation)*

1969 #2 *BAD MOON RISING*
- (S) (2:18) Fantasy CCR2 Chronicle. *(very poor stereo separation)*
- (S) (2:19) Fantasy 8393 Green River. *(very poor stereo separation)*
- (S) (2:17) Epic 48732 O.S.T. My Girl. *(very poor stereo separation)*
- (S) (2:18) Motown 6094 More Songs From The Original Soundtrack Of The "Big Chill". *(very poor stereo separation)*
- (S) (2:18) Fantasy 9418 Creedence Gold. *(very poor stereo separation)*

1969 #3 *GREEN RIVER*
- (S) (2:31) Polydor 837362 O.S.T. 1969.
- (S) (2:33) Fantasy CCR2 Chronicle.
- (S) (2:33) Fantasy 8393 Green River.

1969 #40 *COMMOTION*
- (S) (2:41) Fantasy CCR2 Chronicle.
- (S) (2:41) Fantasy 8393 Green River.

1969 #10 *DOWN ON THE CORNER*
- (S) (2:44) Fantasy CCR2 Chronicle.
- (S) (2:44) Fantasy 8397 Willie And The Poor Boys.
- (S) (2:43) Fantasy 9418 Creedence Gold.

CREEDENCE CLEARWATER REVIVAL (Continued)

1969 #6 FORTUNATE SON
- (S) (2:18) Fantasy CCR2 Chronicle.
- (S) (2:19) Fantasy 8397 Willie And The Poor Boys.
- (S) (2:18) Fantasy 9430 More Creedence Gold.

1970 #5 TRAVELIN' BAND
- (S) (2:06) Fantasy CCR2 Chronicle.
- (S) (2:06) Fantasy 8402 Cosmos Factory.

1970 #13 WHO'LL STOP THE RAIN
- (S) (2:27) Fantasy CCR2 Chronicle.
- (S) (2:27) Fantasy 8402 Cosmos Factory.
- (S) (2:26) Fantasy 9430 More Creedence Gold.

1970 #2 UP AROUND THE BEND
- (S) (2:41) Fantasy CCR2 Chronicle.
- (S) (2:41) Fantasy 8402 Cosmos Factory.
- (S) (2:40) Fantasy 9430 More Creedence Gold.

1970 #1 LOOKIN' OUT MY BACK DOOR
- (S) (2:31) Fantasy CCR2 Chronicle.
- (S) (2:31) Fantasy 9430 More Creedence Gold.

1971 #3 HAVE YOU EVER SEEN THE RAIN
- (S) (2:38) Fantasy CCR2 Chronicle.
- (S) (2:38) Fantasy 8410 Pendulum.
- (S) (2:38) Fantasy 9418 Creedence Gold.

1971 #5 SWEET HITCH-HIKER
- (S) (2:55) Fantasy CCR2 Chronicle. *(very poor stereo separation)*
- (S) (2:56) Fantasy 9404 Mardi Gras. *(very poor stereo separation)*
- (S) (2:56) Fantasy 9430 More Creedence Gold. *(very poor stereo separation)*

1972 #25 SOMEDAY NEVER COMES
- (S) (3:59) Fantasy CCR2 Chronicle.
- (S) (3:58) Fantasy 9404 Mardi Gras.

CRESCENDOS

1958 #6 OH JULIE
- (M) (2:41) Rhino 70897 Best Of Excello Records Volume 2.

CRESTS

1959 #3 16 CANDLES
- (M) (2:51) Rhino 70620 Billboard's Top Rock & Roll Hits Of 1959.
- (M) (2:51) Rhino 72004 Billboard's Top Rock & Roll Hits 1957-1961 Box Set.
- (M) (2:49) Rhino 75763 Best Of Doo Wop Ballads.
- (M) (2:51) Garland 012 Remember When.
- (M) (2:52) JCI 3203 Lovin' Fifties.
- (M) (2:48) Rhino 70948 Best Of.
- (M) (2:49) Collectables 5009 Golden Classics.

1959 #29 SIX NIGHTS A WEEK
- (M) (2:45) Rhino 70948 Best Of.
- (M) (2:46) Collectables 5009 Golden Classics.

1959 #15 THE ANGELS LISTENED IN
- (S) (2:00) Rhino 70948 Best Of.
- (S) (2:00) Collectables 5009 Golden Classics.

1960 #13 STEP BY STEP
- (M) (2:27) Rhino 75764 Best Of Doo Wop Uptempo.
- (S) (2:26) Rhino 70948 Best Of.
- (S) (2:26) Collectables 5009 Golden Classics.

CRESTS (Continued)
1960 #20 *TROUBLE IN PARADISE*
> (M) (2:22) Rhino 70948 Best Of.
> (M) (2:23) Collectables 5009 Golden Classics.

CREW-CUTS
1955 #3 *EARTH ANGEL*
1955 #3 *KO KO MO (I LOVE YOU SO)*
1955 #9 *DON'T BE ANGRY*

BOB CREWE GENERATION
1967 #9 *MUSIC TO WATCH GIRLS BY*

CRICKETS (*see* BUDDY HOLLY)

CRITTERS
1966 #21 *YOUNGER GIRL*
> (S) (2:24) MCA 5938 Vintage Music Volumes 15 & 16.
> (S) (2:24) MCA 31213 Vintage Music Volume 16.

1966 #14 *MR. DIEINGLY SAD*
> (S) (2:46) K-Tel 839 Battle Of The Bands Volume 2.
> (S) (2:47) MCA 5939 Vintage Music Volumes 17 & 18.
> (S) (2:47) MCA 31214 Vintage Music Volume 17.

JIM CROCE
1972 #7 *YOU DON'T MESS AROUND WITH JIM*
> (S) (2:59) 21 Records/Atco 90467 Photographs & Memories.

1972 #7 *OPERATOR (THAT'S NOT THE WAY IT FEELS)*
> (S) (3:44) 21 Records/Atco 90467 Photographs & Memories.
> (S) (3:46) 21 Records/Atco 90469 Time In A Bottle/Greatest Love Songs.

1973 #30 *ONE LESS SET OF FOOTSTEPS*
> (S) (2:44) 21 Records/Atco 90467 Photographs & Memories.

1973 #1 *BAD, BAD LEROY BROWN*
> (S) (2:58) Rhino 70634 Billboard's Top Rock & Roll Hits Of 1973.

1973 #3 *I GOT A NAME*
> (S) (3:08) 21 Records/Atco 90467 Photographs & Memories.

BING CROSBY & GRACE KELLY
1956 #4 *TRUE LOVE*
> (M) (3:04) Capitol 98670 Memories Are Made Of This.

DAVID CROSBY & GRAHAM NASH
1972 #31 *IMMIGRATION MAN*
> (S) (2:57) Atlantic 82319 Crosby, Stills & Nash Box Set.

CROSBY, STILLS & NASH
1969 #19 *MARRAKESH EXPRESS*
> (the LP version of this song has :02 studio talk preceeding the music)
> (S) (2:35) Atlantic 19117 Crosby, Stills, Nash. (*LP version*)
> (S) (2:35) Atlantic 82319 Crosby, Stills & Nash Box Set. (*LP version*)

1969 #15 *SUITE:JUDY BLUE EYES*
> (S) (7:23) Atlantic 81908 Classic Rock 1966-1988. (*LP version*)
> (S) (7:23) Atlantic 19117 Crosby, Stills, Nash. (*LP version*)
> (S) (7:22) Atlantic 19119 So Far. (*LP version*)
> (S) (7:23) Atlantic 82306 Atlantic Rock & Roll Box Set. (*LP version*)
> (S) (7:27) Atlantic 82319 Crosby, Stills & Nash Box Set. (*LP version with countoff*)

CROSBY, STILLS, NASH & YOUNG
1970 #13 *WOODSTOCK*
(S) (3:51) Atlantic 19119 So Far.
(S) (3:51) Atlantic 19118 Deja Vu.
(S) (3:50) Atlantic 82319 Crosby, Stills & Nash Box Set.
1970 #16 *TEACH YOUR CHILDREN*
(S) (2:50) Atlantic 82032 The Wonder Years.
(S) (2:51) Atlantic 19119 So Far.
(S) (2:51) Atlantic 19118 Deja Vu.
(S) (2:51) Atlantic 82319 Crosby, Stills & Nash Box Set.
1970 #14 *OHIO*
(S) (2:57) Atlantic 81908 Classic Rock 1966-1988.
(S) (2:57) Atlantic 19119 So Far.
(S) (2:57) Atlantic 82306 Atlantic Rock & Roll Box Set.
(S) (3:01) Atlantic 82319 Crosby, Stills & Nash Box Set.
(S) (2:57) Reprise 2257 Neil Young/Decade.
1970 #20 *OUR HOUSE*
(S) (2:57) Atlantic 19119 So Far.
(S) (2:58) Atlantic 19118 Deja Vu.
(S) (2:58) Atlantic 82319 Crosby, Stills & Nash Box Set.

CROSS COUNTRY
1973 #18 *IN THE MIDNIGHT HOUR*

CROW
1970 #16 *EVIL WOMAN DON'T PLAY YOUR GAMES WITH ME*
1970 #40 *DON'T TRY TO LAY NO BOOGIE WOOGIE ON THE "KING OF ROCK & ROLL"*

CRUSADERS
1972 #40 *PUT IT WHERE YOU WANT IT*

CRYSTALS
1961 #19 *THERE'S NO OTHER LIKE MY BABY*
(M) (2:29) Abkco 7118 Phil Spector/Back To Mono (1958-1969).
1962 #10 *UPTOWN*
(M) (2:19) Abkco 7118 Phil Spector/Back To Mono (1958-1969).
(S) (1:48) MCA 6171 Good Time Rock 'N' Roll. *(all selections on this cd are recorded live)*
1962 #2 *HE'S A REBEL*
(M) (2:25) Abkco 7118 Phil Spector/Back To Mono (1958-1969).
1963 #14 *HE'S SURE THE BOY I LOVE*
(M) (2:43) Abkco 7118 Phil Spector/Back To Mono (1958-1969).
1963 #4 *DA DOO RON RON*
(M) (2:16) Abkco 7118 Phil Spector/Back To Mono (1958-1969).
(S) (1:40) MCA 6171 Good Time Rock 'N' Roll. *(all selections on this cd are recorded live)*
1963 #6 *THEN HE KISSED ME*
(M) (2:34) Abkco 7118 Phil Spector/Back To Mono (1958-1969).

CUFF LINKS
1969 #5 *TRACY*
(the 45 time is (2:05); the LP time (2:14) and is much slower in pitch than the 45 version)
(S) (2:07) K-Tel 205 Battle Of The Bands Volume 3.
(S) (2:14) Rhino 70921 Super Hits Of The 70's Volume 1. *(LP speed)*
(S) (2:14) Rhino 72009 Super Hits Of The 70's Volumes 1-4 Box Set. *(LP speed)*
(S) (2:09) MCA 31207 Vintage Music Volume 10.
(S) (2:09) MCA 5806 Vintage Music Volumes 9 & 10.

CUFF LINKS (Continued)
1970 #31 *WHEN JULIE COMES AROUND*
1970 #40 *RUN SALLY RUN*

MIKE CURB CONGREGATION
1971 #34 *BURNING BRIDGES*
    (S) (2:44) Rhino 70925 Super Hits Of The 70's Volume 5.
    (S) (2:43) Curb 77317 70's Hits Volume 1.
    (S) (2:43) Curb 77443 Greatest Hits.

CYMANDE
1973 #39 *THE MESSAGE*

CYMARRON
1971 #17 *RINGS*
    (S) (2:30) Columbia/Legacy 46763 Rock Artifacts Volume 2.

JOHNNY CYMBAL
1963 #17 *MR. BASS MAN*
    (S) (2:40) MCA 31202 Vintage Music Volume 5.
    (S) (2:40) MCA 5804 Vintage Music Volumes 5 & 6.

CYRKLE
1966 #3 *RED RUBBER BALL*
    (S) (2:17) Rhino 75754 Even More Nuggets.
    (S) (2:18) Columbia 45019 Pop Classics Of The 60's.
    (S) (2:17) Columbia/Legacy 47717 Red Rubber Ball.
1966 #18 *TURN DOWN DAY*
    (S) (2:28) Columbia 45019 Pop Classics Of The 60's.
    (S) (2:32) Columbia/Legacy 47717 Red Rubber Ball.

DADDY DEWDROP
1971 #5 *CHICK-A-BOOM (DON'T YA JES' LOVE IT)*
    (S) (2:50) Rhino 70925 Superhits Of The 70's Volume 5.

DADDY-O'S
1958 #31 *GOT A MATCH*

ALAN DALE
1955 #7 *SWEET AND GENTLE*

DALE AND GRACE
1963 #1 *I'M LEAVING IT UP TO YOU*
1964 #8 *STOP AND THINK IT OVER*

TONY DALLARA
1958 #24 *COME PRIMA*

LIZ DAMON'S ORIENT EXPRESS

1971 #29 *1900 YESTERDAY*

VIC DAMONE

1956 #5 *ON THE STREET WHERE YOU LIVE*
        (S) (2:36) Curb 77476 Best Of. *(rerecording)*

1957 #25 *AN AFFAIR TO REMEMBER*
        (M) (2:45) Columbia 45111 16 Most Requested Songs Of The 50's Volume 2.

1965 #28 *YOU WERE ONLY FOOLING (WHILE I WAS FALLING IN LOVE)*

VIC DANA

1963 #18 *MORE*
        (S) (2:18) EMI 91678 Golden Greats.

1964 #9 *SHANGRI-LA*
        (S) (2:03) EMI 91678 Golden Greats.

1965 #11 *RED ROSES FOR A BLUE LADY*
        (S) (2:47) EMI 91678 Golden Greats.

1970 #39 *IF I NEVER KNEW YOUR NAME*

DANCER, PRANCER & NERVOUS (THE SINGING REINDEER)

1960 #31 *THE HAPPY REINDEER*

CHARLIE DANIELS BAND

1973 #10 *UNEASY RIDER*
        (S) (5:19) Rhino 70758 Super Hits Of The 70's Volume 11.
        (S) (5:18) Epic 38795 Decade Of Hits.

DANLEERS

1958 #9 *ONE SUMMER NIGHT*
        (M) (2:11) Garland 012 Remember When.
        (E) (2:12) Collectables 2508 History Of Rock - The Doo Wop Era Part 2.

DANNY & THE JUNIORS

1958 #1 *AT THE HOP*
        (M) (2:30) Rhino 70619 Billboard's Top Rock & Roll Hits Of 1958.
        (M) (2:30) Rhino 72004 Billboard's Top Rock & Roll Hits 1957-1961 Box Set.
        (M) (2:30) MCA 31198 Vintage Music Volume 1.
        (M) (2:30) MCA 5777 Vintage Music Volumes 1 & 2.
        (M) (2:30) JCI 3201 Party Time Fifties.
        (M) (2:27) MCA 31060 Rockin' With. *(truncated fade)*

1958 #22 *ROCK AND ROLL IS HERE TO STAY*
        (M) (2:28) MCA 31199 Vintage Music Volume 2.
        (M) (2:28) MCA 5777 Vintage Music Volumes 1 & 2.
        (M) (2:27) MCA 31060 Rockin' With.

DANTE & THE EVERGREENS

1960 #1 *ALLEY-OOP*

JOE DARENSBOURG & HIS DIXIE FLYERS

1958 #30 *YELLOW DOG BLUES*

BOBBY DARIN

1958 #2 *SPLISH SPLASH*
      (the stereo mix of this song differs slightly from the mono or 45 mix)
        (M) (2:10) Atlantic 81909 Hit Singles 1958-1977.
        (S) (2:48) Atco 33131 Story. *(includes :43 of talk preceeding and overlapping the song)*
        (M) (2:11) Warner Special Products 27606 Ultimate.

          (S)   (2:05) Curb 77325   Greatest Hits.

          (S)   (2:06) Atco 91794   Splish Splash.

1958 #12 *QUEEN OF THE HOP*

          (S)   (2:10) Atco 33131   Bobby Darin Story.

          (M) (2:05) Warner Special Products 27602   20 Party Classics.

          (S)   (2:10) Warner Special Products 27606   Ultimate.

          (S)   (2:10) Atco 91794   Splish Splash.

1959 #30 *PLAIN JANE*

          (S)   (1:57) Atco 33131   Bobby Darin Story.

          (M) (1:54) Warner Special Products 27606   Ultimate.

1959 #3 *DREAM LOVER*

          (M) (2:30) Elektra 60107   O.S.T. Diner.

          (S)   (2:30) Atco 33131   Bobby Darin Story.

          (M) (2:29) Warner Special Products 27606   Ultimate.

          (M) (2:28) Curb 77325   Greatest Hits.

          (S)   (2:30) Atco 91794   Splish Splash.

1959 #1 *MACK THE KNIFE*

          (the stereo mix of this song differs slightly from the mono or 45 mix)

          (S)   (3:07) Rhino 70620   Billboard's Top Rock & Roll Hits Of 1959.

          (S)   (3:07) Rhino 72004   Billboard's Top Rock & Roll Hits 1957-1961 Box Set.

          (M) (3:03) Atlantic 81909   Hit Singles 1958-1977.

          (S)   (3:05) Atlantic 81769   O.S.T. Big Town.

          (S)   (3:06) JCI 3201   Party Time Fifties.

          (S)   (3:24) Atco 33131   Bobby Darin Story. *(with :22 talk preceeding and running into the music)*

          (S)   (3:05) Warner Special Products 27606   Ultimate. *(bad dropout at (2:53)-(2:54))*

          (S)   (3:31) Curb 77325   Greatest Hits. *(live)*

          (S)   (3:06) Atco 91795   Mack The Knife.

1960 #7 *BEYOND THE SEA*

          (M) (2:49) Elektra 60107   O.S.T. Diner.

          (S)   (2:53) Capitol 91185   O.S.T. Tequila Sunrise.

          (S)   (3:01) Atco 33131   Bobby Darin Story. *(talk over the introduction which is mono and runs longer than either the LP or 45 version; the rest of the song is in stereo!)*

          (S)   (2:52) Atlantic 82152   O.S.T. Goodfellas.

          (S)   (2:53) Warner Special Products 27606   Ultimate.

          (M) (2:48) Atco 91795   Mack The Knife.

1960 #13 *CLEMENTINE*

          (S)   (3:11) Atco 33131   Bobby Darin Story. *(alternate take)*

          (S)   (3:11) Warner Special Products 27606   Ultimate.

          (M) (3:13) Atco 91795   Mack The Knife.

1960 #16 *WON'T YOU COME HOME BILL BAILEY*

          (S)   (2:04) Atco 33131   Bobby Darin Story.

          (M) (2:04) Warner Special Products 27606   Ultimate.

          (S)   (2:03) Atco 91795   Mack The Knife.

1960 #19 *ARTIFICIAL FLOWERS*

          (S)   (3:14) Atco 33131   Bobby Darin Story.

          (M) (3:15) Warner Special Products 27606   Ultimate.

          (M) (3:15) Atco 91795   Mack The Knife.

BOBBY DARIN (Continued)

1961 #18 *LAZY RIVER*
    (S) (2:46) Atco 33131 Bobby Darin Story. *(preceeded by :15 talk but at least the talk does not overlap the music)*
    (M) (2:31) Warner Special Products 27606 Ultimate.
    (M) (2:30) Atco 91795 Mack The Knife.

1961 #31 *NATURE BOY*
    (S) (2:32) Atco 91794 Splish Splash.

1961 #7 *YOU MUST HAVE BEEN A BEAUTIFUL BABY*
    (M) (2:12) Warner Special Products 27606 Ultimate.
    (S) (2:04) Atco 91794 Splish Splash.

1962 #16 *IRRESISTIBLE YOU*
    (S) (2:31) Warner Special Products 27606 Ultimate.
    (S) (2:31) Atco 91794 Splish Splash.

1962 #26 *MULTIPLICATION*
    (S) (2:15) Warner Special Products 27606 Ultimate.
    (S) (2:15) Atco 91794 Splish Splash.

1962 #26 *WHAT'D I SAY (PART 1)*
    (S) (4:04) Atco 91794 Splish Splash. *(Parts 1 & 2)*

1962 #10 *THINGS*
    (S) (2:32) Warner Special Products 27606 Ultimate. *(noise on fade out)*
    (S) (2:33) Atco 91794 Splish Splash. *(noise on fade out)*

1962 #28 *IF A MAN ANSWERS*
    (S) (2:20) Capitol 91625 Capitol Collector's Series.

1962 #38 *BABY FACE*
    (M) (2:05) Atco 91794 Splish Splash.

1963 #5 *YOU'RE THE REASON I'M LIVING*
    (S) (2:26) Capitol 91625 Capitol Collector's Series.
    (S) (2:26) Capitol 98665 When AM Was King.

1963 #12 *18 YELLOW ROSES*
    (S) (2:16) Curb 77355 60's Hits Volume 1.
    (S) (2:16) Capitol 91625 Capitol Collector's Series.
    (S) (2:16) Curb 77325 Greatest Hits.

1963 #38 *TREAT MY BABY GOOD*
    (S) (1:55) Capitol 91625 Capitol Collector's Series.

1964 #39 *MILORD*

1966 #9 *IF I WERE A CARPENTER*
    (S) (3:21) Curb 77325 Greatest Hits. *(live)*
    (S) (2:20) Atco 91794 Splish Splash.

JAMES DARREN

1959 #32 *GIDGET*
1961 #2 *GOODBYE CRUEL WORLD*
1962 #9 *HER ROYAL MAJESTY*
1962 #24 *CONSCIENCE*
1967 #38 *ALL*

DARTELLS

1963 #13 *HOT PASTRAMI*
    (M) (1:44) Rhino 75772 Son Of Frat Rock.
    (S) (1:44) MCA 5936 Vintage Music Volumes 11 & 12.
    (S) (1:44) MCA 31208 Vintage Music Volume 11.

DAVID & JONATHAN

1966 #18 *MICHELLE*

MAC DAVIS
1972 #1 *BABY DON'T GET HOOKED ON ME*
(S) (3:02) Columbia 36317 Greatest Hits.

SAMMY DAVIS JR.
1956 #31 *EARTHBOUND*
1962 #14 *WHAT KIND OF FOOL AM I*
(S) (3:21) Garland 018 Greatest Hits.
(S) (3:38) Curb 77272 Greatest Songs. *(rerecording)*
1964 #19 *THE SHELTER OF YOUR ARMS*
(S) (2:47) Dunhill Compact Classics 048 Greatest Hits Volume 2.
1969 #14 *I'VE GOTTA BE ME*
(S) (2:55) Garland 018 Greatest Hits.
(S) (2:15) Curb 77272 Greatest Songs. *(live)*
1972 #1 *CANDY MAN*
(S) (3:08) Rhino 70928 Super Hits Of The 70's Volume 8.
(S) (3:07) Curb 77317 70's Hits Volume 1.
(S) (3:04) Curb 77443 Mike Curb Congregation Greatest Hits.
(S) (3:09) Garland 018 Greatest Hits.
(S) (3:04) Curb 77444 Best Of Sammy Davis Jr. And The Mike Curb
          Congregation.
(S) (3:06) Curb 77272 Greatest Songs.

SKEETER DAVIS
1960 #35 *(I CAN'T HELP YOU) I'M FALLING TOO*
(S) (2:43) Rhino 70681 Billboard's Top Country Hits Of 1960.
1963 #2 *THE END OF THE WORLD*
(S) (2:36) RCA 8474 Nipper's Greatest Hits Of The 60's Volume 1.
(S) (2:36) Rhino 70684 Billboard's Top Country Hits Of 1963.
(S) (2:36) RCA 5802 Best Of The 60's.
1963 #39 *I'M SAVING MY LOVE*
1963 #6 *I CAN'T STAY MAD AT YOU*
(S) (2:06) Rhino 70988 Best Of The Girl Groups Volume 1.
(S) (2:06) RCA 8475 Nipper's Greatest Hits Of The 60's Volume 2.
1964 #35 *GONNA GET ALONG WITHOUT YOU NOW*

SPENCER DAVIS GROUP
1967 #5 *GIMME SOME LOVIN'*
(M) (2:56) Rhino 70322 History Of British Rock Volume 4.
(M) (2:56) Rhino 72022 History Of British Rock Box Set.
(M) (2:56) Rhino 72008 History Of British Rock Volumes 1-4 Box Set.
(M) (2:56) Rhino 75778 Frat Rock.
(M) (2:56) Rhino 70628 Billboard's Top Rock & Roll Hits Of 1967.
(M) (2:55) Dunhill Compact Classics 043 Toga Rock II.
(M) (2:52) Capitol 48993 Spuds Mackenzie's Party Faves.
(M) (2:53) EMI 46598 Best Of.
(M) (2:51) Motown 6094 More Songs From The Original Soundtrack Of
          The "Big Chill".
(M) (2:52) Capitol 98138 Spring Break Volume 1.
1967 #10 *I'M A MAN*
(M) (2:39) Rhino 70326 History Of British Rock Volume 8.
(M) (2:39) Rhino 72022 History Of British Rock Box Set.
(M) (2:49) EMI 46598 Best Of.

TYRONE DAVIS

1969 #5 *CAN I CHANGE MY MIND*
  (S) (2:47) Rhino 75770 Soul Shots Volume 2.
  (S) (2:46) Rhino 70655 Billboard's Top R&B Hits Of 1969.
  (S) (2:46) Rhino 72006 Billboard's Top R&B Hits 1965-1969 Box Set.
  (S) (2:46) Atlantic 81911 Golden Age Of Black Music (1960-1970).
  (S) (2:52) Epic 38626 Greatest Hits. *(truncated fade)*
  (S) (2:46) Atlantic 82305 Atlantic Rhythm And Blues 1947-1974 Box Set.
  (S) (2:46) Rhino 70533 Greatest Hits.

1969 #22 *IS IT SOMETHING YOU'VE GOT*
  (S) (2:33) Epic 38626 Greatest Hits.
  (S) (2:35) Rhino 70533 Greatest Hits.

1970 #4 *TURN BACK THE HANDS OF TIME*
  (the 45 and LP length was originally (2:39); the extended version running about (2:54) first showed up on a Tyrone Davis "Greatest Hits" vinyl LP in the 80's)
  (S) (2:55) Rhino 70658 Billboard's Top R&B Hits Of 1970.
  (S) (2:53) Dunhill Compact Classics 028 Sock Hop.
  (S) (2:55) Rhino 70782 Soul Hits Of The 70's Volume 2.
  (S) (2:37) Atlantic 81299 Atlantic Rhythm & Blues Volume 7.
  (S) (2:54) Epic 38626 Greatest Hits.
  (S) (2:37) Atlantic 82305 Atlantic Rhythm And Blues 1947-1974 Box Set.
  (S) (2:37) Rhino 70533 Greatest Hits.

1970 #33 *I'LL BE RIGHT HERE*
  (S) (2:36) Epic 38626 Greatest Hits.
  (S) (2:36) Rhino 70533 Greatest Hits.

1973 #39 *THERE IT IS*
  (S) (4:05) Epic 38626 Greatest Hits.
  (S) (4:07) Rhino 70533 Greatest Hits.

DAWN (*also* DAWN *featuring* TONY ORLANDO)

1970 #1 *CANDIDA*
1971 #1 *KNOCK THREE TIMES*
  (S) (2:57) Rhino 70632 Billboard's Top Rock & Roll Hits Of 1971.
  (S) (2:57) Rhino 72005 Billboard's Top Rock & Roll Hits 1968-1972 Box Set.
  (S) (2:56) Priority 8669 #1 Hits/70's Greatest Rock Hits Volume 9.

1971 #22 *I PLAY AND SING*
1971 #19 *SUMMER SAND*

releases from this point on were credited to **DAWN** *featuring* **TONY ORLANDO:**

1971 #26 *WHAT ARE YOU DOING SUNDAY*
1973 #1 *TIE A YELLOW RIBBON ROUND THE OLD OAK TREE*
1973 #4 *SAY, HAS ANYBODY SEEN MY SWEET GYPSY ROSE*
1973 #13 *WHO'S IN THE STRAWBERRY PATCH WITH SALLY*

BOBBY DAY

1957 #9 *LITTLE BITTY PRETTY ONE*
  (M) (2:26) Collectables 5074 Golden Classics.

1958 #4 *ROCK-IN ROBIN*
  (M) (2:33) Rhino 70644 Billboard's Top R&B Hits Of 1958.
  (M) (2:34) Collectables 5074 Golden Classics.

1960 #37 *GEE WHIZ*

DORIS DAY

1956 #3 *WHATEVER WILL BE, WILL BE (QUE SERA, SERA)*
  (M) (2:03) Columbia 45111 16 Most Requested Songs Of The 50's Volume 2.

DORIS DAY *(Continued)*

      (M) (2:03) Columbia 44371 A Day At The Movies.

      (M) (2:03) Columbia 45017 Radio Classics Of The 50's.

      (M) (2:03) Columbia 8635 Greatest Hits.

1956 #40 *JULIE*

1958 #36 *TEACHER'S PET*

      (M) (2:34) Columbia 8635 Greatest Hits.

1958 #6 *EVERYBODY LOVES A LOVER*

      (M) (2:41) Columbia 8635 Greatest Hits.

BILL DEAL & THE RHONDELS

1969 #35 *MAY I*

      (M) (2:29) JCI 3115 Groovin' Sixties

1969 #29 *I'VE BEEN HURT*

      (M) (2:09) Rhino 75770 Soul Shots Volume 2.

      (M) (2:07) JCI 3115 Groovin' Sixties.

1969 #22 *WHAT KIND OF FOOL DO YOU THINK I AM*

      (M) (2:13) Rhino 75772 Son Of Frat Rock.

      (M) (2:11) JCI 3115 Groovin' Sixties.

JIMMY DEAN

1961 #1 *BIG BAD JOHN*

      (the very first pressings of this 45 included the words "hell of a man" which were quickly replaced by "a big big man")

      (M) (2:59) Rhino 70682 Billboard's Top Country Hits Of 1961. *("hell of a man" version)*

      (S) (3:00) Columbia 46031 Columbia Country Classics Volume 3. *("big big man" version)*

      (S) (3:00) Columbia 45077 American Originals. *("big big man" version)*

      (S) (3:00) Columbia 9285 Greatest Hits. *("big big man" version)*

1962 #21 *DEAR IVAN*

      (M) (3:45) Columbia 45077 American Originals.

1962 #23 *THE CAJUN QUEEN*

      (M) (2:35) Columbia 45077 American Originals.

      (S) (2:36) Columbia 9285 Greatest Hits.

1962 #7 *P.T. 109*

      (M) (3:07) Columbia 45077 American Originals.

      (S) (3:10) Rhino 70683 Billboard's Top Country Hits Of 1962.

      (S) (3:10) Columbia 9285 Greatest Hits.

1962 #31 *LITTLE BLACK BOOK*

      (S) (2:23) Columbia 45077 American Originals.

      (S) (2:23) Columbia 9285 Greatest Hits.

DEAN & JEAN

1964 #36 *TRA LA LA LA SUZY*

DE CASTRO SISTERS

1955 #2 *TEACH ME TONIGHT*

JOEY DEE & THE STARLIGHTERS

1962 #2 *PEPPERMINT TWIST (PART 1)*

      (S) (2:00) Rhino 70623 Billboard's Top Rock & Roll Hits Of 1962.

      (S) (2:00) Rhino 72007 Billboard's Top Rock & Roll Hits 1962-1966 Box Set.

      (S) (1:58) Rhino 70992 Groove 'N' Grind.

      (S) (1:58) Rhino 70965 Best Of.

      (S) (1:58) Essex 7052 All Time Rock Classics.

JOEY DEE & THE STARLIGHTERS (Continued)

1962 #37 *HEY LET'S TWIST*
    (M)   (1:58) Rhino 70965 Best Of.

1962 #9 *SHOUT (PART 1)*
    (E)   (2:29) JCI 3110 Sock Hoppin' Sixties.
    (S)   (2:31) Rhino 70965 Best Of.

1962 #17 *WHAT KIND OF LOVE IS THIS*
    (S)   (2:06) Rhino 70965 Best Of.

1963 #40 *HOT PASTRAMI WITH MASHED POTATOES (PART 1)*
    (S)   (4:45) Rhino 70965 Best Of. *(Parts 1 & 2)*

JOHNNY DEE

1957 #15 *SITTIN' IN THE BALCONY*

TOMMY DEE

1959 #16 *THREE STARS*

DEEP PURPLE

1968 #4 *HUSH*
    (the LP version of this song includes 3 wolf calls; the 45 version includes 2)
    (S)   (4:18) Rhino 70327 History Of British Rock Volume 9. *(45 version)*
    (S)   (4:18) Rhino 72022 History Of British Rock Box Set. *(45 version)*
    (S)   (4:22) Warner Brothers 3223 When We Rock, We Rock. *(LP version)*

1968 #28 *KENTUCKY WOMAN*
    (S)   (4:43) Warner Brothers 3223 When We Rock, We Rock. *(LP version)*

1973 #3 *SMOKE ON THE WATER*
    (S)   (6:26) Warner Brothers 3223 When We Rock, We Rock. *(live; an edit from the "Made In Japan" LP)*
    (S)   (5:40) Warner Brothers 3100 Machine Head. *(LP version)*
    (S)   (5:38) Warner Brothers 3486 Deepest Purple/Very Best Of. *(LP version)*
    (S)   (5:39) Capitol 96647 Hearts Of Gold - The Classic Rock Collection. *(LP version)*

DE FRANCO FAMILY

1973 #1 *HEARTBEAT - IT'S A LOVEBEAT*
    (S)   (3:09) Rhino 70930 Super Hits Of The 70's Volume 10.

DE JOHN SISTERS

1955 #6 *(MY BABY DON'T LOVE ME) NO MORE*

DESMOND DEKKER & THE ACES

1969 #8 *ISRAELITES*
    (the original 45 and LP length was (2:35))
    (M)   (2:46) Island 90684 and 842901 The Island Story.
    (E)   (2:46) Novus 3077 O.S.T. Drugstore Cowboy.
    (M)   (2:35) Rhino 70271 Best Of.

DELANEY & BONNIE & FRIENDS

1971 #9 *NEVER ENDING SONG OF LOVE*
    (S)   (3:19) Rhino 70777 Best Of. *(LP version)*

1971 #18 *ONLY YOU KNOW AND I KNOW*
    (S)   (3:24) Rhino 70777 Best Of.
    (S)   (4:42) Atco 33326 On Tour With Eric Clapton. *(live)*

DELEGATES

1972 #9 *CONVENTION '72*

DELFONICS

1968 #4 *LA-LA MEANS I LOVE YOU*
- (S) (3:17) Rhino 75774 Soul Shots.
- (S) (3:18) Rhino 70654 Billboard's Top R&B Hits Of 1968.
- (S) (3:18) Rhino 72006 Billboard's Top R&B Hits 1965-1969 Box Set.
- (S) (3:17) JCI 3102 Love Sixties.
- (S) (3:19) Arista 8333 Best Of.

1969 #31 *READY OR NOT HERE I COME (CAN'T HIDE FROM LOVE)*
(the actual 45 length is (1:59) not (2:55) as stated on the record label)
- (S) (1:59) Arista 8333 Best Of.

1969 #40 *YOU GOT YOURS AND I'LL GET MINE*
- (S) (3:17) Arista 8333 Best Of.

1970 #13 *DIDN'T I (BLOW YOUR MIND THIS TIME)*
- (S) (3:20) Epic 46940 O.S.T. Queenslogic.
- (S) (3:20) Rhino 70781 Soul Hits Of The 70's Volume 1.
- (S) (3:20) Arista 8333 Best Of.

DELLS

1968 #24 *THERE IS*
- (S) (3:30) Chess 9283 Best Of Chess Vocal Groups Volume 2.
- (S) (3:31) Chess 9288 There Is.
- (S) (3:30) JCI/Telstar 3515 Best Of.
- (S) (3:31) Chess 9333 On Their Corner/The Best Of.

1968 #16 *STAY IN MY CORNER*
(dj copies of this 45 ran (3:05) and (6:10); commercial copies ran (6:10))
- (S) (3:05) Rhino 75757 Soul Shots Volume 3.
- (S) (6:09) Rhino 70654 Billboard's Top R&B Hits Of 1968.
- (S) (6:09) Rhino 72006 Billboard's Top R&B Hits 1965-1969 Box Set.
- (S) (6:09) Chess 9288 There Is.
- (S) (6:10) Motown 6215 Hits From The Legendary Vee-Jay Records. (*this is a recording made for Vee-Jay Records and is not the hit version*)
- (S) (6:09) MCA 5936 Vintage Music Volumes 11 & 12.
- (S) (6:09) MCA 31208 Vintage Music Volume 11.
- (S) (6:10) Chess 31318 Best of Chess Rhythm & Blues Volume 2.
- (S) (6:08) JCI/Telstar 3515 Best Of.
- (S) (6:09) MCA 10288 Classic Soul.
- (S) (6:10) Chess 9333 On Their Corner/The Best Of.

1968 #35 *ALWAYS TOGETHER*
- (S) (2:58) JCI/Telstar 3515 Best Of.
- (S) (3:03) Chess 9333 On Their Corner/The Best Of.

1969 #18 *I CAN SING A RAINBOW/LOVE IS BLUE*
- (S) (3:17) JCI/Telstar 3515 Best Of. (*dropouts near the end of the song*)
- (S) (3:23) Chess 9333 On Their Corner/The Best Of. (*noisy fadeout*)

1969 #14 *OH, WHAT A NIGHT*
(this song was originally released in 1956 but never charted; rerecorded and released again in 1969 when it did chart)
- (M) (2:52) Rhino 75763 Best Of Doo Wop Ballads. (*1956 version*)
- (S) (4:03) Rhino 75770 Soul Shots Volume 2. (*1969 version*)
- (S) (4:03) Rhino 70655 Billboard's Top R&B Hits Of 1969. (*1969 version*)
- (S) (4:03) Rhino 72006 Billboard's Top R&B Hits 1965-1969 Box Set. (*1969 version*)
- (S) (4:02) Chess 9283 Best Of Chess Vocal Groups Volume 2. (*1969 version*)
- (S) (4:02) MCA 5937 Vintage Music Volumes 13 & 14. (*1969 version*)
- (S) (4:02) MCA 31211 Vintage Music Volume 14. (*1969 version*)

DELLS *(Continued)*

    (M) (2:51) Dunhill Compact Classics 031 Back Seat Jams. *(1956 version)*
    (M) (2:51) Dunhill Compact Classics 028 Sock Hop. *(1956 version)*
    (M) (2:51) Motown 6215 Hits From The Legendary Vee-Jay Records. *(1956 version)*
    (S) (3:57) JCI/Telstar 3515 Best Of. *(1969 version)*
    (S) (4:03) Chess 9333 On Their Corner/The Best Of. *(1969 version)*

1970 #36 *OH WHAT A DAY*

1971 #33 *THE LOVE WE HAD (STAYS ON MY MIND)*

    (S) (4:47) Rhino 70786 Soul Hits Of The 70's Volume 6.
    (S) (4:14) JCI/Telstar 3515 Best Of. *(edited)*
    (S) (4:48) Chess 9333 On Their Corner/The Best Of.

1973 #20 *GIVE YOUR BABY A STANDING OVATION*

    (the actual commercial 45 time is (4:35) not (3:52) as the record label states)
    (S) (4:02) Rhino 70551 Soul Hits Of The 70's Volume 11.
    (S) (3:57) JCI/Telstar 3515 Best Of.
    (S) (4:35) Chess 9333 On Their Corner/The Best Of.

DELL-VIKINGS

1957 #3 *COME GO WITH ME*

    (M) (2:40) Rhino 75764 Best Of Doo Wop Uptempo.
    (M) (2:40) Rhino 70643 Billboard's Top R&B Hits Of 1957.
    (M) (2:40) MCA 31198 Vintage Music Volume 1.
    (M) (2:40) MCA 5777 Vintage Music Volumes 1 & 2.
    (M) (2:38) Atlantic 81677 O.S.T. Stand By Me.
    (M) (2:39) Elektra 60107 O.S.T. Diner.

1957 #9 *WHISPERING BELLS*

    (M) (2:23) Rhino 75764 Best of Doo Wop Uptempo.
    (M) (2:27) MCA 31199 Vintage Music Volume 2.
    (M) (2:27) MCA 5777 Vintage Music Volumes 1 & 2.
    (M) (2:22) Atlantic 81677 O.S.T. Stand By Me.
    (E) (2:21) Collectables 2508 History Of Rock - The Doo Wop Era Part 2.

DEMENSIONS

1960 #19 *OVER THE RAINBOW*

    (M) (3:14) Collectables 2508 History Of Rock - The Doo Wop Era Part 2.
    (M) (3:14) Relic 7032 Over The Rainbow.

MARTIN DENNY

1959 #3 *QUIET VILLAGE*

    (M) (3:38) Rhino 70774 Best Of. *(this is neither the 45 or LP version)*
    (S) (3:46) Pair 1267 Paradise. *(this is neither the 45 or LP version)*

1959 #39 *THE ENCHANTED SEA*

    (S) (1:57) Rhino 70774 Best Of.
    (S) (1:56) Pair 1267 Paradise.

JOHN DENVER

1971 #1 *TAKE ME HOME, COUNTRY ROADS*

    (S) (3:09) RCA 0374 Greatest Hits.
    (S) (3:07) RCA 5189 Poems, Prayers And Promises.
    (S) (3:07) RCA 52160 Take Me Home, Country Roads & Other Hits.

1972 #27 *FRIENDS WITH YOU*

1973 #7 *ROCKY MOUNTAIN HIGH*

    (S) (4:43) RCA 0374 Greatest Hits.
    (S) (4:40) RCA 5190 Rocky Mountain High.
    (S) (4:42) RCA 52160 Take Me Home, Country Roads & Other Hits.

DEODATO

1973 #4 *ALSO SPRACH ZARATHUSTRA*
      (S) (5:03) Rhino 70758 Super Hits Of The 70's Volume 11.
      (S) (8:57) CBS Associated 40695 Prelude. *(LP version)*

DEREK

1969 #10 *CINNAMON*
      (M) (2:42) Rhino 70996 One Hit Wonders Of The 60's Volume 2.
      (S) (2:43) Columbia/Legacy 46983 Rock Artifacts Volume 3.

DEREK & THE DOMINOS

1972 #14 *LAYLA*
     (dj copies of this 45 ran (2:43) and (7:10))
      (S) (7:05) Atlantic 81908 Classic Rock 1966-1988.
      (S) (7:03) Polydor 823277 Layla And Other Assorted Love Songs.
      (S) (7:06) Polydor 835269 Crossroads.
      (S) (7:03) Sandstone 33004 Reelin' In The Years Volume 5.
      (S) (7:04) Polydor 847083 Layla Sessions. *(remixed)*
      (S) (7:04) Polydor 847090 Layla And Other Assorted Love Songs.
            (remixed)
      (S) (3:52) Atlantic 82152 O.S.T. Goodfellas. *(this is only the piano exit from the LP version)*
      (S) (7:05) Atlantic 82306 Atlantic Rock & Roll Box Set.

JACKIE DESHANNON

1965 #8 *WHAT THE WORLD NEEDS NOW IS LOVE*
      (S) (3:11) Rhino 70738 Best Of.
      (S) (3:04) EMI 91473 Very Best Of.
      (S) (3:11) Pair 1284 Good As Gold.

1968 #35 *THE WEIGHT*
      (S) (2:59) EMI 91473 Very Best Of.
      (S) (2:58) Pair 1284 Good As Gold.

1969 #4 *PUT A LITTLE LOVE IN YOUR HEART*
      (S) (2:31) Rhino 70738 Best Of.
      (S) (2:37) Novus 3077 O.S.T. Drugstore Cowboy.
      (S) (2:34) Curb 77355 60's Hits Volume 1. *(truncated fade)*
      (S) (2:34) EMI 91473 Very Best Of. *(truncated fade)*

1969 #33 *LOVE WILL FIND A WAY*
      (S) (2:33) Rhino 70738 Best Of.
      (S) (2:37) EMI 91473 Very Best Of.
      (S) (2:35) Pair 1284 Good As Gold.

JOHNNY DESMOND

1955 #1 *THE YELLOW ROSE OF TEXAS*

DETERGENTS

1965 #11 *LEADER OF THE LAUNDROMAT*

DETROIT EMERALDS

1972 #35 *YOU WANT IT, YOU GOT IT*
1972 #19 *BABY LET ME TAKE YOU (IN MY ARMS)*

DEVOTIONS

1964 #30 *RIP VAN WINKLE*

TRACEY DEY

1964 #35 *GONNA GET ALONG WITHOUT YOU NOW*

NEIL DIAMOND

1966 #6 CHERRY CHERRY
(studio version)
    (S) (2:41) Columbia 38792 Classics - The Early Years.
    (M) (2:42) Columbia 52703 Greatest Hits 1966-1992.

1966 #23 I GOT THE FEELIN' (OH NO NO)
    (S) (2:09) Columbia 38792 Classics - The Early Years.
    (M) (2:18) Columbia 52703 Greatest Hits 1966-1992.

1967 #22 YOU GOT TO ME
    (S) (2:44) Columbia 38792 Classics - The Early Years.
    (M) (2:48) Columbia 52703 Greatest Hits 1966-1992.

1967 #9 GIRL, YOU'LL BE A WOMAN SOON
    (S) (3:20) Columbia 38792 Classics - The Early Years. *(:24 longer than 45 or LP; this extended version first showed up in 1978 on the "Neil Diamond/ Early Classics" vinyl LP)*
    (M) (2:53) Columbia 52703 Greatest Hits 1966-1992.

1967 #13 THANK THE LORD FOR THE NIGHT TIME
    (S) (3:02) Columbia 38792 Classics - The Early Years.
    (M) (3:01) Columbia 52703 Greatest Hits 1966-1992.
    (S) (3:03) MCA 10502 Glory Road 1968-1972. *(live)*

1967 #12 KENTUCKY WOMAN
    (E) (2:24) Columbia 38792 Classics - The Early Years.
    (M) (2:24) Columbia 52703 Greatest Hits 1966-1992.
    (S) (2:41) MCA 10502 Glory Road 1968-1972. *(live)*

1968 #38 NEW ORLEANS

1969 #13 BROTHER LOVE'S TRAVELLING SALVATION SHOW
    (S) (3:28) MCA 31050 Sweet Caroline.
    (S) (3:25) MCA 37252 His 12 Greatest Hits.
    (S) (5:55) Columbia 52703 Greatest Hits 1966-1992. *(live)*
    (S) (3:28) MCA 10502 Glory Road 1968-1972.

1969 #3 SWEET CAROLINE
(the actual 45 time is (3:23) not (2:50) as stated on the record label)
    (S) (3:22) MCA 31050 Sweet Caroline.
    (S) (3:30) MCA 37252 His 12 Greatest Hits. *(:07 longer fade than 45 or LP)*
    (S) (4:06) Columbia 52703 Greatest Hits 1966-1992. *(live)*
    (S) (3:19) MCA 10502 Glory Road 1968-1972.

1969 #4 HOLLY HOLY
    (S) (4:40) MCA 37252 His 12 Greatest Hits.
    (S) (4:38) MCA 31052 Touching You, Touching Me.
    (S) (5:26) Columbia 52703 Greatest Hits 1966-1992. *(live)*
    (S) (4:40) MCA 10502 Glory Road 1968-1972.

1970 #23 SHILO
    (S) (2:55) MCA 37252 His 12 Greatest Hits. *(rerecording)*
    (S) (3:48) Columbia 38792 Classics - The Early Years. *(hit single version; released earlier as a 45 in a different version which never charted)*
    (M) (3:23) Columbia 52703 Greatest Hits 1966-1992. *(original recording but not the hit single version)*
    (S) (2:58) MCA 10502 Glory Road 1968-1972. *(rerecording)*

1970 #24 SOOLAIMON
    (S) (4:16) MCA 37252 His 12 Greatest Hits.
    (S) (4:25) MCA 31071 Tap Root Manuscript. *(LP version; drum beat tracks into next selection)*
    (S) (4:36) Columbia 52703 Greatest Hits 1966-1992. *(live)*
    (S) (4:12) MCA 10502 Glory Road 1968-1972.

1970 #20 SOLITARY MAN
- (S) (2:33) Columbia 38792 Classics - The Early Years. *(alternate take)*
- (M) (2:32) Columbia 52703 Greatest Hits 1966-1992.
- (S) (3:18) MCA 10502 Glory Road 1968-1972. *(live; includes a :21 spoken introduction)*

1970 #1 CRACKLIN' ROSIE
- (S) (2:56) MCA 37252 His 12 Greatest Hits.
- (S) (3:00) MCA 31071 Tap Root Manuscript.
- (S) (3:06) Columbia 52703 Greatest Hits 1966-1992. *(live)*
- (S) (3:02) MCA 10502 Glory Road 1968-1972. *(includes :04 studio talk)*

1970 #17 HE AIN'T HEAVY, HE'S MY BROTHER
- (S) (4:09) MCA 1606 Rainbow.
- (S) (4:09) MCA 31071 Tap Root Manuscript.
- (S) (4:10) MCA 10502 Glory Road 1968-1972.

1970 #36 DO IT
- (M) (2:21) Columbia 38792 Classics - The Early Years. *(hit 45 version and one of two LP versions)*

1971 #4 I AM I SAID
- (S) (3:31) MCA 37252 His 12 Greatest Hits.
- (S) (5:05) Columbia 52703 Greatest Hits 1966-1992. *(live)*
- (S) (3:32) MCA 10502 Glory Road 1968-1972.

1971 #13 STONES
- (S) (3:03) MCA 37252 His 12 Greatest Hits.
- (S) (3:02) MCA 1607 And The Singer Sings His Song.
- (S) (3:02) MCA 1490 Love Songs.
- (S) (3:03) MCA 10502 Glory Road 1968-1972.

1972 #1 SONG SUNG BLUE
- (S) (3:12) MCA 37252 His 12 Greatest Hits.
- (S) (3:14) MCA 31061 Moods.
- (S) (3:05) Columbia 52703 Greatest Hits 1966-1992. *(live)*
- (S) (3:14) MCA 10502 Glory Road 1968-1972.

1972 #16 PLAY ME
- (S) (3:49) MCA 37252 His 12 Greatest Hits.
- (S) (3:51) MCA 31061 Moods.
- (S) (3:50) MCA 1490 Love Songs.
- (S) (4:01) Columbia 52703 Greatest Hits 1966-1992. *(rerecording)*
- (S) (3:49) MCA 10502 Glory Road 1968-1972.

1972 #16 WALK ON WATER
(the original commercial 45 and LP version both included a (1:37) instrumental ending titled "THEME")
- (S) (3:03) MCA 1607 And The Singer Sings His Song. *(does not include "THEME")*
- (S) (3:05) MCA 31061 Moods. *(tracks into "THEME")*
- (S) (3:05) MCA 10502 Glory Road 1968-1972. *(tracks into "THEME")*

1973 #24 CHERRY CHERRY
(live version)
- (S) (4:43) MCA 6896 Hot August Night. *(LP version)*
- (S) (4:44) MCA 10502 Glory Road 1968-1972. *(LP version)*

1973 #19 BE
- (S) (3:30) Columbia 32550 Jonathan Livingston Seagull.
- (S) (6:29) Columbia 52703 Greatest Hits 1966-1992. *(LP version)*

DIAMONDS
1956 #17 *KA-DING-DONG*
1957 #2 *LITTLE DARLIN'*
      (M) (2:06) Rhino 70618 Billboard's Top Rock & Roll Hits Of 1957.
      (M) (2:06) Rhino 72004 Billboard's Top Rock & Roll Hits 1957-1961 Box Set.
      (M) (2:06) Mercury 832041 45's On CD Volume 1.
      (M) (2:07) Mercury 826448 Oldies Golden Million Sellers.
      (S) (2:01) MCA 6171 Good Time Rock 'N' Roll. *(all selections on this cd are recorded live)*
      (M) (2:06) Atlantic 82155 O.S.T. Book Of Love.
1957 #36 *ZIP ZIP*
1958 #1 *THE STROLL*
      (M) (2:26) Rhino 70992 Groove 'n' Grind.
      (M) (2:28) Mercury 832041 45's On CD Volume 1.
      (M) (2:25) JCI 3201 Party Time Fifties.
1958 #21 *HIGH SIGN*
1958 #37 *KATHY-O*
1958 #19 *WALKING ALONG*
1959 #12 *SHE SAY (OOM DOOBY DOOM)*

MANU DIBANGO
1973 #22 *SOUL MAKOSSA*
      (S) (4:27) Rhino 70552 Soul Hits Of The 70's Volume 12.
      (S) (4:27) Rhino 70274 The Disco Years Volume 3.
      (S) (4:24) Turnstyle/Atlantic 14215 Atlantic Dance Classics.

DICK & DEEDEE
1961 #3 *THE MOUNTAIN'S HIGH*
1962 #23 *TELL ME*
1963 #24 *YOUNG AND IN LOVE*
1964 #22 *TURN AROUND*
1965 #16 *THOU SHALT NOT STEAL*

LITTLE JIMMY DICKENS
1965 #28 *MAY THE BIRD OF PARADISE FLY UP YOUR NOSE*
      (S) (2:26) Columbia 46031 Columbia Country Classics Volume 3.

DICKY DOO & THE DON'TS
1958 #29 *CLICK CLACK*

BO DIDDLEY
1959 #21 *SAY MAN*
      (M) (3:10) Chess 19502 The Chess Box.
      (M) (3:09) Telstar/JCI 3506 Best Of.
      (M) (3:09) Chess 5904 Bo Diddley/Go Bo Diddley.

MARK DINNING
1960 #1 *TEEN ANGEL*
      (M) (2:39) Mercury 832041 45's On CD Volume 1.
      (M) (2:39) JCI 3203 Lovin' Fifties.

DINO, DESI & BILLY
1965 #19 *I'M A FOOL*
      (S) (2:53) Rhino 75754 Even More Nuggets.
1965 #32 *NOT THE LOVIN' KIND*

KENNY DINO
1961 #39 *YOUR MA SAID YOU CRIED IN YOUR SLEEP LAST NIGHT*

DION

1960 #12 *LONELY TEENAGER*
- (S) (2:14) 3C/Laurie 105 The Wanderer.
- (S) (2:17) Arista 8206 24 Original Classics.
- (S) (2:14) 3C/Laurie 103 Classic Old & Gold Volume 4.

1961 #1 *RUNAROUND SUE*
- (S) (2:41) Arista 8206 24 Original Classics.
- (S) (2:41) Rhino 70622 Billboard's Top Rock & Roll Hits Of 1961.
- (S) (2:41) Rhino 72004 Billboard's Top Rock & Roll Hits 1957-1961 Box Set.
- (S) (2:34) Warner Brothers 3359 O.S.T. The Wanderers.
- (S) (2:36) Warner Special Products 27602 20 Party Classics.
- (S) (2:42) 3C/Laurie 105 The Wanderer.
- (S) (2:39) CBS Special Products 46200 Rock Goes To The Movies Volume 3.
- (S) (2:42) 3C/Laurie 103 Classic Old & Gold Volume 4.
- (S) (2:42) Essex 7052 All Time Rock Classics.

1962 #3 *THE WANDERER*
- (S) (2:42) 3C/Laurie 105 The Wanderer.
- (S) (2:46) Arista 8206 24 Original Classics.
- (S) (2:46) Rhino 70623 Billboard's Top Rock & Roll Hits Of 1962.
- (S) (2:46) Rhino 72007 Billboard's Top Rock & Roll Hits 1962-1966 Box Set.
- (S) (2:46) Capitol 48993 Spuds Mackenzie's Party Faves.
- (S) (2:46) JCI 3110 Sock Hoppin' Sixties.
- (S) (2:41) Warner Brothers 3359 O.S.T. The Wanderers.
- (S) (2:42) 3C/Laurie 103 Classic Old & Gold Volume 4.

1962 #5 *LOVERS WHO WANDER*
- (S) (2:22) 3C/Laurie 105 The Wanderer.
- (S) (2:29) Arista 8206 24 Original Classics.
- (S) (2:22) 3C/Laurie 103 Classic Old & Gold Volume 4.

1962 #40 *(I WAS) BORN TO CRY*
- (S) (2:26) 3C/Laurie 105 The Wanderer.
- (S) (2:24) Arista 8206 24 Original Classics.

1962 #14 *LITTLE DIANE*
- (S) (2:40) 3C/Laurie 105 The Wanderer.
- (S) (2:45) Arista 8206 24 Original Classics.
- (S) (2:40) 3C/Laurie 103 Classic Old & Gold Volume 4.

1962 #17 *LOVE CAME TO ME*
- (M) (2:37) 3C/Laurie 105 The Wanderer. *(truncated fade)*
- (S) (2:44) Arista 8206 24 Original Classics.
- (M) (2:37) 3C/Laurie 103 Classic Old & Gold Volume 4. *(truncated fade)*

1963 #3 *RUBY BABY*
- (S) (2:36) Columbia/Legacy 46972 Bronx Blues: The Columbia Recordings (1962-1965).
- (S) (2:36) Arista 8206 24 Original Classics.
- (S) (2:36) Rhino 70593 The Rock 'N' Roll Classics Of Leiber & Stoller.

1963 #23 *SANDY*
- (S) (2:19) Arista 8206 24 Original Classics.
- (S) (2:19) 3C/Laurie 105 The Wanderer. *(truncated fade)*
- (S) (2:19) 3C/Laurie 103 Classic Old & Gold Volume 4. *(truncated fade)*

1963 #19 *THIS LITTLE GIRL*
- (S) (2:35) Columbia/Legacy 46972 Bronx Blues: The Columbia Recordings (1962-1965).
- (S) (2:33) Arista 8206 24 Original Classics.

DION (Continued)
1963 #30 *BE CAREFUL OF STONES THAT YOU THROW*
1963 #6 *DONNA THE PRIMA DONNA*
    (S) (2:52) Columbia/Legacy 46972 Bronx Blues: The Columbia Recordings (1962-1965). *(remixed and in portions does not resemble the previously released 45 or LP version; truncated fade)*
    (S) (2:47) Arista 8206 24 Original Classics.
1963 #5 *DRIP DROP*
    (S) (2:35) Columbia/Legacy 46972 Bronx Blues: The Columbia Recordings (1962-1965).
    (S) (2:34) Arista 8206 24 Original Classics.
    (S) (2:35) Rhino 70593 The Rock 'N' Roll Classics Of Leiber & Stoller.
1968 #2 *ABRAHAM, MARTIN AND JOHN*
    (S) (3:17) Arista 8206 24 Original Classics.
    (S) (3:18) Rhino 70734 Songs Of Protest.

DION & THE BELMONTS
1958 #20 *I WONDER WHY*
    (M) (2:19) 3C/Laurie 105 The Wanderer.
    (M) (2:17) Arista 8206 24 Original Classics.
    (M) (2:17) Rhino 75764 Best Of Doo Wop Uptempo.
    (M) (2:20) Elektra 60107 O.S.T. Diner.
    (M) (2:20) 3C/Laurie 102 Classic Old & Gold Volume 3.
    (M) (2:19) Collectables 2507 History Of Rock - The Doo Wop Era Part 1.
1958 #25 *NO ONE KNOWS*
    (M) (2:34) 3C/Laurie 105 The Wanderer.
    (M) (2:34) 3C/Laurie 102 Classic Old & Gold Volume 3.
1959 #37 *DON'T PITY ME*
    (M) (2:35) 3C/Laurie 105 The Wanderer.
    (M) (2:36) 3C/Laurie 102 Classic Old & Gold Volume 3.
1959 #6 *TEENAGER IN LOVE*
    (S) (2:36) Arista 8206 24 Original Classics.
    (S) (2:36) Rhino 70906 American Bandstand Greatest Hits Collection.
    (S) (2:29) Elektra 60107 O.S.T. Diner.
    (E) (2:36) JCI 3201 Party Time Fifties.
    (S) (2:35) 3C/Laurie 105 The Wanderer.
    (S) (2:36) 3C/Laurie 102 Classic Old & Gold Volume 3.
1960 #4 *WHERE OR WHEN*
    (M) (2:36) 3C/Laurie 105 The Wanderer.
    (M) (2:36) Rhino 75763 Best Of Doo Wop Ballads.
    (M) (2:36) Arista 8206 24 Original Classics.
    (M) (2:36) 3C/Laurie 102 Classic Old & Gold Volume 3.
1960 #25 *WHEN YOU WISH UPON A STAR*
    (S) (2:25) 3C/Laurie 105 The Wanderer.
    (S) (2:26) 3C/Laurie 102 Classic Old & Gold Volume 3.
1960 #35 *IN THE STILL OF THE NIGHT*
    (S) (2:35) 3C/Laurie 105 The Wanderer.
    (S) (2:36) 3C/Laurie 102 Classic Old & Gold Volume 3.

DIXIEBELLES
1963 #13 *(DOWN AT) PAPA JOE'S*
1964 #20 *SOUTHTOWN U.S.A.*

DIXIE CUPS
1964 #1 *CHAPEL OF LOVE*
    (M) (2:46) Warner Brothers 25613 O.S.T. Full Metal Jacket.
    (M) (2:47) Rhino 75891 Wonder Women.

DIXIE CUPS (Continued)
- (M) (2:46) Rhino 70988 Best Of The Girl Groups Volume 1.
- (M) (2:47) Rhino 70650 Billboard's Top R&B Hits Of 1964.
- (M) (2:46) Rhino 70588 Rockin' & Rollin' Wedding Songs Volume 1.
- (E) (2:44) Motown 5322 and 9087 Girl Groups: The Story Of A Sound.

1964 #10 *PEOPLE SAY*
- (M) (2:32) Rhino 75891 Wonder Women. (*:13 longer than the 45 or LP*)
- (M) (2:43) Rhino 70988 Best Of The Girl Groups Volume 1. (*:24 longer than the 45 or LP*)

1965 #19 *IKO IKO*
- (M) (2:02) Rhino 75766 Best Of New Orleans Rhythm & Blues Volume 2.
- (M) (2:04) Rhino 75891 Wonder Women.
- (M) (2:02) Rhino 70243 Greatest Movie Rock Hits.
- (M) (2:00) Mango 539909 O.S.T. The Big Easy.

CARL DOBKINS JR.
1959 #3 *MY HEART IS AN OPEN BOOK*
- (M) (2:07) MCA 5936 Vintage Music Volumes 11 & 12.
- (M) (2:07) MCA 31209 Vintage Music Volume 12.

1960 #32 *LUCKY DEVIL*

DR. HOOK & THE MEDICINE SHOW
1972 #1 *SYLVIA'S MOTHER*
- (S) (3:39) Rhino 70928 Super Hits Of The 70's Volume 8. (*45 version*)
- (S) (3:46) Columbia 45047 Pop Classics Of The 70's. (*LP version*)
- (S) (3:49) Capitol 46620 Greatest Hits. (*LP version*)
- (S) (3:49) Columbia 34147 Revisited. (*LP version*)

1973 #5 *THE COVER OF THE ROLLING STONE*
- (S) (2:53) Rhino 70930 Super Hits Of The 70's Volume 10.
- (S) (2:51) Priority 8665 Southern Comfort/70's Greatest Hits Volume 4.
- (S) (2:51) Capitol 46620 Greatest Hits.
- (S) (2:51) Columbia 34147 Revisited.
- (S) (2:51) Columbia 40695 Sloppy Seconds.

DR. JOHN
1973 #11 *RIGHT PLACE, WRONG TIME*
- (S) (2:50) Warner Special Products 27616 Classic Rock.
- (S) (2:51) Atco 7018 In The Right Place.
- (S) (2:51) Warner Special Products 27612 Ultimate Dr. John.
- (S) (2:51) Sandstone 33001 Reelin' In The Years Volume 2.

BILL DOGGETT
1956 #2 *HONKY TONK (PART 1 & 2)*
1956 #12 *SLOW WALK*

FATS DOMINO
1955 #1 *AIN'T THAT A SHAME*
- (M) (2:31) Rhino 70598 Billboard's Top Rock & Roll Hits Of 1955.
- (M) (2:32) EMI 92808 My Blue Heaven - The Best Of.
- (M) (2:24) JCI 3202 Rockin' Fifties.
- (M) (2:24) EMI 46581 Best Of.
- (S) (2:32) MCA 6170 His Greatest Hits. (*all selections on this cd are recorded live*)
- (M) (2:23) EMI 96785 They Call Me The Fat Man.
- (S) (2:21) Rhino/Tomato 70391 Antoine "Fats" Domino. (*all selections on this cd are live recordings*)
- (M) (2:24) Pair 1123 Whole Lotta Rock 'N' Roll.

FATS DOMINO (Continued)

1956 #4 *I'M IN LOVE AGAIN*
- (M) (1:56) Rhino 70599 Billboard's Top Rock & Roll Hits Of 1956.
- (M) (2:00) Sire 26617 Music From The Film A Rage In Harlem.
- (M) (1:56) EMI 92808 My Blue Heaven - The Best Of.
- (M) (2:00) EMI 46581 Best Of.
- (M) (1:52) EMI 96785 They Call Me The Fat Man.
- (S) (3:12) MCA 6170 His Greatest Hits. (*all selections on this cd are recorded live*)
- (S) (3:31) Rhino/Tomato 70391 Antoine "Fats" Domino. (*all selections on this cd are live recordings*)
- (M) (1:56) Pair 1123 Whole Lotta Rock 'N' Roll.

1956 #21 *WHEN MY DREAMBOAT COMES HOME*
- (M) (2:19) EMI 92808 My Blue Heaven - The Best Of.
- (M) (2:22) EMI 46581 Best Of.
- (M) (2:17) EMI 96785 They Call Me The Fat Man.
- (M) (2:20) Pair 1123 Whole Lotta Rock 'N' Roll.

1956 #4 *BLUEBERRY HILL*
- (M) (2:20) Rhino 70642 Billboard's Top R&B Hits Of 1956.
- (M) (2:18) JCI 3204 Heart & Soul Fifties.
- (M) (2:18) EMI 96268 24 Greatest Hits Of All Time.
- (M) (2:18) Curb 77354 50's Hits Volume 1.
- (M) (2:18) EMI 92808 My Blue Heaven - The Best Of.
- (M) (2:19) EMI 46581 Best Of.
- (M) (2:18) Curb 77378 All Time Greatest Hits.
- (M) (2:20) EMI 96785 They Call Me The Fat Man.
- (M) (2:18) Curb 77525 Greatest Hits Of Rock 'N' Roll Volume 2.
- (S) (2:40) MCA 6170 His Greatest Hits. (*all selections on this cd are recorded live*)
- (S) (2:34) Rhino/Tomato 70391 Antoine "Fats" Domino. (*all selections on this cd are live recordings*)
- (M) (2:19) Pair 1123 Whole Lotta Rock 'N' Roll.

1957 #8 *BLUE MONDAY*
- (M) (2:14) Rhino 70643 Billboard's Top R&B Hits Of 1957.
- (M) (2:15) EMI 92808 My Blue Heaven - The Best Of.
- (M) (2:14) EMI 46581 Best Of.
- (M) (2:14) Curb 77378 All Time Greatest Hits.
- (M) (2:14) EMI 96785 They Call Me The Fat Man.
- (S) (2:33) MCA 6170 His Greatest Hits. (*all selections on this cd are recorded live*)
- (S) (2:40) Rhino/Tomato 70391 Antoine "Fats" Domino. (*all selections on this cd are live recordings*)

1957 #22 *WHAT'S THE REASON I'M NOT PLEASING YOU*
- (M) (2:01) EMI 96785 They Call Me The Fat Man.

1957 #5 *I'M WALKIN'*
- (M) (2:08) Rhino 70643 Billboard's Top R&B Hits Of 1957.
- (M) (2:11) EMI 92808 My Blue Heaven - The Best Of.
- (M) (2:02) EMI 46581 Best Of.
- (M) (2:02) Curb 77378 All Time Greatest Hits.
- (M) (2:11) EMI 96785 They Call Me The Fat Man.
- (S) (2:44) MCA 6170 His Greatest Hits. (*all selections on this cd are recorded live*)
- (M) (2:11) Capitol 98139 Spring Break Volume 2.
- (S) (2:53) Rhino/Tomato 70391 Antoine "Fats" Domino. (*all selections on this cd are live recordings*)

1957 #20 VALLEY OF TEARS

      (M) (2:05) EMI 92808 My Blue Heaven - The Best Of. *(includes :09 of studio talk)*

      (M) (1:51) EMI 46581 Best Of.

      (M) (1:51) EMI 96785 They Call Me The Fat Man.

      (S) (2:42) Rhino/Tomato 70391 Antoine "Fats" Domino. *(all selections on this cd are live recordings)*

1957 #19 IT'S YOU I LOVE

      (M) (2:01) EMI 96785 They Call Me The Fat Man.

1957 #29 WHEN I SEE YOU

      (M) (2:10) EMI 96785 They Call Me The Fat Man.

1957 #34 WAIT AND SEE

      (M) (1:53) EMI 96785 They Call Me The Fat Man.

1957 #37 I WANT YOU TO KNOW

      (M) (1:58) EMI 96785 They Call Me The Fat Man.

1959 #9 WHOLE LOTTA LOVING

      (M) (1:38) Rhino 70644 Billboard's Top R&B Hits Of 1958.

      (M) (1:39) Elektra 60107 O.S.T. Diner.

      (M) (1:38) EMI 92808 My Blue Heaven - The Best Of.

      (M) (1:37) EMI 46581 Best Of.

      (M) (1:37) Curb 77323 All Time Greatest Hits Of Rock 'N' Roll.

      (M) (1:38) Curb 77378 All Time Greatest Hits.

      (M) (1:37) EMI 96785 They Call Me The Fat Man.

      (S) (1:31) MCA 6170 His Greatest Hits. *(all selections on this cd are recorded live)*

      (M) (1:37) Pair 1123 Whole Lotta Rock 'N' Roll.

1959 #40 WHEN THE SAINTS GO MARCHING IN

      (S) (2:25) EMI 96785 They Call Me The Fat Man.

      (S) (3:52) Rhino/Tomato 70391 Antoine "Fats" Domino. *(all selections on this cd are live recordings)*

      (M) (2:22) Pair 1123 Whole Lotta Rock 'N' Roll.

1959 #16 I'M READY

      (M) (2:03) EMI 92808 My Blue Heaven - The Best Of.

      (E) (2:03) EMI 90614 Non Stop Party Rock.

      (M) (2:02) Rhino 70794 KFOG Presents M. Dung's Idiot Show.

      (M) (2:02) Curb 77378 All Time Greatest Hits.

      (M) (2:02) EMI 96785 They Call Me The Fat Man.

      (S) (1:53) MCA 6170 His Greatest Hits. *(all selections on this cd are recorded live)*

      (M) (2:02) Pair 1123 Whole Lotta Rock 'N' Roll.

1959 #32 MARGIE

      (S) (2:14) EMI 96785 They Call Me The Fat Man.

      (S) (2:03) Rhino/Tomato 70391 Antoine "Fats" Domino. *(all selections on this cd are live recordings)*

1959 #9 I WANT TO WALK YOU HOME

      (S) (2:16) Rhino 70645 Billboard's Top R&B Hits Of 1959.

      (S) (2:18) EMI 92808 My Blue Heaven - The Best Of.

      (M) (2:20) EMI 46581 Best Of.

      (M) (2:20) Curb 77378 All Time Greatest Hits.

      (S) (2:17) EMI 96785 They Call Me The Fat Man.

      (S) (2:34) MCA 6170 His Greatest Hits. *(all selections on this cd are recorded live)*

      (S) (2:38) Rhino/Tomato 70391 Antoine "Fats" Domino. *(all selections on this cd are live recordings)*

FATS DOMINO (Continued)

1959 #26 *I'M GONNA BE A WHEEL SOME DAY*
  (M) (2:01) EMI 92808 My Blue Heaven - The Best Of.
  (M) (2:01) EMI 46581 Best Of.
  (M) (2:01) EMI 96785 They Call Me The Fat Man.
  (S) (2:13) MCA 6170 His Greatest Hits. *(all selections on this cd are recorded live)*
  (S) (2:25) Rhino/Tomato 70391 Antoine "Fats" Domino. *(all selections on this cd are live recordings)*

1959 #8 *BE MY GUEST*
  (S) (2:14) EMI 92808 My Blue Heaven - The Best Of.
  (M) (1:59) EMI 46581 Best Of.
  (M) (1:59) Curb 77378 All Time Greatest Hits.
  (S) (2:13) EMI 96785 They Call Me The Fat Man.
  (S) (1:54) Rhino/Tomato 70391 Antoine "Fats" Domino. *(all selections on this cd are live recordings)*

1960 #29 *COUNTRY BOY*
  (S) (2:14) EMI 96785 They Call Me The Fat Man.

1960 #10 *WALKING TO NEW ORLEANS*
  (S) (1:59) Rhino 70646 Billboard's Top R&B Hits Of 1960.
  (S) (1:58) EMI 92808 My Blue Heaven - The Best Of.
  (M) (1:54) EMI 46581 Best Of.
  (M) (1:54) Curb 77378 All Time Greatest Hits.
  (S) (1:58) EMI 96785 They Call Me The Fat Man.
  (S) (2:21) MCA 6170 His Greatest Hits. *(all selections on this cd are recorded live)*
  (S) (3:07) Rhino/Tomato 70391 Antoine "Fats" Domino. *(all selections on this cd are live recordings)*

1960 #30 *DON'T COME KNOCKIN'*
  (S) (1:55) EMI 96785 They Call Me The Fat Man.
  (M) (1:55) Pair 1123 Whole Lotta Rock 'N' Roll.

1960 #18 *THREE NIGHTS A WEEK*
  (S) (1:43) EMI 96785 They Call Me The Fat Man.
  (M) (1:43) Pair 1123 Whole Lotta Rock 'N' Roll.

1960 #16 *MY GIRL JOSEPHINE*
  (M) (2:00) Curb 77378 All Time Greatest Hits.
  (S) (2:03) EMI 96785 They Call Me The Fat Man.
  (S) (1:51) MCA 6170 His Greatest Hits. *(all selections on this cd are recorded live)*
  (M) (2:00) Pair 1123 Whole Lotta Rock 'N' Roll.

1961 #30 *WHAT A PRICE*
  (S) (2:21) EMI 96785 They Call Me The Fat Man.
  (S) (2:12) Rhino/Tomato 70391 Antoine "Fats" Domino. *(all selections on this cd are live recordings)*

1961 #26 *AIN'T THAT JUST LIKE A WOMAN*
  (S) (2:39) EMI 96785 They Call Me The Fat Man.

1961 #34 *SHU RAH*
  (S) (1:41) EMI 96785 They Call Me The Fat Man.

1961 #34 *IT KEEPS RAININ'*
  (S) (2:44) EMI 96785 They Call Me The Fat Man.

1961 #17 *LET THE FOUR WINDS BLOW*
  (S) (2:15) Rhino 70647 Billboard's Top R&B Hits Of 1961.
  (S) (2:15) EMI 92808 My Blue Heaven - The Best Of.
  (M) (2:00) EMI 46581 Best Of.

        (M)   (2:00) Curb 77378   All Time Greatest Hits.

        (S)   (2:15) EMI 96785   They Call Me The Fat Man.

        (S)   (4:23) MCA 6170   His Greatest Hits. *(all selections on this cd are recorded live)*

        (S)   (6:49) Rhino/Tomato 70391   Antoine "Fats" Domino. *(all selections on this cd are live recordings)*

        (M)   (2:01) Pair 1123   Whole Lotta Rock 'N' Roll.

1961 #38 *WHAT A PARTY*

        (S)   (1:57) EMI 92808   My Blue Heaven - The Best Of.

        (S)   (1:57) EMI 96785   They Call Me The Fat Man.

1962 #38 *JAMBALAYA (ON THE BAYOU)*

        (M)   (2:21) Enigma 73531   O.S.T. Scandal.

        (M)   (2:20) EMI 96785   They Call Me The Fat Man.

        (M)   (2:20) Rhino 70587   New Orleans Party Classics.

        (S)   (4:37) MCA 6170   His Greatest Hits. *(all selections on this cd are recorded live)*

        (S)   (8:57) Rhino/Tomato 70391   Antoine "Fats" Domino. *(all selections on this cd are live recordings)*

        (M)   (2:22) Pair 1123   Whole Lotta Rock 'N' Roll.

1962 #30 *YOU WIN AGAIN*

        (S)   (2:12) EMI 96785   They Call Me The Fat Man.

        (E)   (2:12) Pair 1123   Whole Lotta Rock 'N' Roll.

DON AND JUAN

1962 #5 *WHAT'S YOUR NAME*

LONNIE DONEGAN

1956 #9 *ROCK ISLAND LINE*

1961 #6 *DOES YOUR CHEWING GUM LOSE IT'S FLAVOR (ON THE BEDPOST OVERNIGHT)*

        (M)   (2:28) Rhino 75768   Dr. Demento Presents.

        (M)   (2:27) Rhino 70743   Dr. Demento 20th Anniversary Collection.

RAL DONNER

1961 #27 *GIRL OF MY BEST FRIEND*

1961 #10 *YOU DON'T KNOW WHAT YOU'VE GOT (UNTIL YOU LOSE IT)*

1961 #30 *PLEASE DON'T GO*

1962 #10 *SHE'S EVERYTHING (I WANTED YOU TO BE)*

DONOVAN

1965 #28 *CATCH THE WIND*

        (M)   (2:16) Rhino 70320   History Of British Rock Volume 2.

        (M)   (2:16) Rhino 72022   History Of British Rock Box Set.

        (M)   (2:16) Rhino 72008   History Of British Rock Volumes 1-4 Box Set.

        (M)   (2:53) Epic/Legacy 46986   Troubadour. *(LP version)*

        (M)   (2:53) Garland 016   Catch The Wind. *(LP version)*

        (M)   (2:16) Rhino 70262   Troubadours Of The Folk Era Volume 1.

        (S)   (5:01) Epic 26439   Greatest Hits. *(rerecording)*

1965 #40 *COLOURS*

        (S)   (2:43) Rhino 70321   History Of British Rock Volume 3.

        (S)   (2:43) Rhino 72022   History Of British Rock Box Set.

        (S)   (2:43) Rhino 72008   History Of British Rock Volumes 1-4 Box Set.

        (S)   (2:42) Garland 016   Catch The Wind.

        (S)   (2:42) Epic/Legacy 46986   Troubadour.

        (S)   (4:10) Epic 26439   Greatest Hits. *(rerecording)*

1966 #1 SUNSHINE SUPERMAN
    (S) (3:29) Rhino 70323 History Of British Rock Volume 5. *(14 longer than 45 or LP)*
    (S) (3:29) Rhino 72022 History Of British Rock Box Set. *(14 longer than 45 or LP)*
    (M) (3:15) Epic 26217 Sunshine Superman.
    (M) (3:12) Epic/Legacy 46986 Troubadour.
    (S) (4:31) Epic 26439 Greatest Hits. *(this version first appeared on Donovan's "Greatest Hits" vinyl LP)*

1966 #3 MELLOW YELLOW
    (M) (3:41) Rhino 70325 History Of British Rock Volume 7.
    (M) (3:41) Rhino 72022 History Of British Rock Box Set.
    (M) (3:39) Epic/Legacy 46986 Troubadour.
    (E) (3:38) Epic 26439 Greatest Hits.

1967 #10 EPISTLE TO DIPPY
    (S) (3:09) Epic 26439 Greatest Hits.
    (M) (3:07) Epic/Legacy 46986 Troubadour.

1967 #9 THERE IS A MOUNTAIN
    (S) (2:33) Epic 26439 Greatest Hits.
    (M) (2:32) Epic/Legacy 46986 Troubadour.

1967 #26 WEAR YOUR LOVE LIKE HEAVEN
    (S) (2:23) Epic 26439 Greatest Hits.
    (S) (2:23) Epic/Legacy 46986 Troubadour.

1968 #18 JENNIFER JUNIPER
    (S) (2:39) Epic 26439 Greatest Hits.
    (S) (2:39) Epic/Legacy 46986 Troubadour.
    (S) (2:40) Epic 26420 Hurdy Gurdy Man.

1968 #3 HURDY GURDY MAN
    (S) (3:13) Epic/Legacy 46986 Troubadour.
    (S) (3:11) Dunhill Compact Classics 045 Golden Age Of Underground Radio.
    (M) (3:15) Rhino 70326 History Of British Rock Volume 8.
    (M) (3:15) Rhino 72022 History Of British Rock Box Set.
    (S) (3:16) Epic 26439 Greatest Hits.
    (S) (3:13) Epic 26420 Hurdy Gurdy Man.

1968 #31 LALENA
    (M) (2:54) Epic/Legacy 46986 Troubadour.
    (S) (2:54) Rhino 70327 History Of British Rock Volume 9.
    (S) (2:54) Rhino 72022 History Of British Rock Box Set.
    (S) (2:53) Epic 26439 Greatest Hits.

1969 #31 TO SUSAN ON THE WEST COAST WAITING
    (S) (3:10) Epic/Legacy 46986 Troubadour.
    (S) (3:11) Epic 26481 Barabajagal.

1969 #9 ATLANTIS
    (S) (4:56) Dunhill Compact Classics 045 Golden Age Of Underground Radio.
    (S) (4:59) Epic/Legacy 46986 Troubadour.
    (S) (5:02) Rhino 70327 History Of British Rock Volume 9.
    (S) (5:02) Rhino 72022 History Of British Rock Box Set.
    (S) (5:01) Epic 26481 Barabajagal.

1970 #40 RIKI TIKI TAVI
    (S) (2:55) Epic/Legacy 46986 Troubadour.

DONOVAN & THE JEFF BECK GROUP
1969 #28 *GOO GOO BARABAJAGAL*
(the album title was simply "BARABAJAGAL")
    (S) (3:17) Epic/Legacy 46986 Troubadour.
    (S) (3:19) Epic 26481 Barabajagal.

DOOBIE BROTHERS
1972 #9 *LISTEN TO THE MUSIC*
    (S) (3:46) Priority 8667 FM Hits/70's Greatest Rock Hits Volume 6. *(45 version with :20 additional music before fade out)*
    (S) (3:46) Warner Brothers 3112 Best Of. *(45 version with :20 additional music before fade out)*
    (S) (4:32) Warner Brothers 2634 Toulous Street. *(LP version)*
1973 #33 *JESUS IS JUST ALRIGHT*
    (S) (4:33) Warner Brothers 3112 Best Of. *(LP version)*
    (S) (4:32) Warner Brothers 2634 Toulous Street. *(LP version)*
1973 #9 *LONG TRAIN RUNNIN'*
    (S) (3:25) Warner Brothers 3112 Best Of.
    (S) (3:25) Warner Brothers 2694 The Captain And Me.
1973 #8 *CHINA GROVE*
    (S) (3:13) Warner Brothers 3112 Best Of.
    (S) (3:13) Warner Brothers 2694 The Captain And Me.
    (S) (3:14) Sandstone 33001 Reelin' In The Years Volume 2.

DOORS
1967 #1 *LIGHT MY FIRE*
    (S) (7:05) Elektra 60345 Best Of. *(LP version)*
    (S) (7:05) Elektra 74007 The Doors. *(LP version)*
    (S) (7:05) Elektra 61047 O.S.T. The Doors. *(LP version)*
1967 #10 *PEOPLE ARE STRANGE*
    (S) (2:08) Elektra 60345 Best Of.
    (S) (2:08) Elektra 74014 Strange Days.
1968 #25 *LOVE ME TWO TIMES*
    (S) (3:13) Elektra 74014 Strange Days.
    (S) (3:13) Elektra 60345 Best Of.
1968 #22 *THE UNKNOWN SOLDIER*
    (S) (3:21) Elektra 60345 Best Of. *(LP version)*
    (S) (3:19) Elektra 74014 Strange Days. *(LP version)*
1968 #1 *HELLO I LOVE YOU*
    (S) (2:12) Elektra 74014 Strange Days.
    (S) (2:10) Atlantic 81742 O.S.T. Platoon.
    (S) (2:13) Elektra 60345 Best Of.
1969 #1 *TOUCH ME*
    (S) (3:10) Elektra 60345 Best Of. *(LP version)*
    (S) (3:10) Elektra 75005 The Soft Parade. *(LP version)*
1969 #28 *WISHFUL SINFUL*
    (S) (2:54) Elektra 75007 The Soft Parade.
1969 #33 *TELL ALL THE PEOPLE*
    (S) (3:19) Elektra 75007 The Soft Parade.
1969 #40 *RUNNIN' BLUE*
    (S) (2:25) Elektra 75007 The Soft Parade.
1970 #40 *YOU MAKE ME REAL*
    (S) (2:50) Elektra 75007 Morrison Hotel.
1971 #7 *LOVE HER MADLY*
    (S) (3:16) Elektra 60345 Best Of.
    (S) (3:17) Elektra 75011 L.A. Woman.

DOORS (Continued)
1971 #12 *RIDERS ON THE STORM*
- (S) (7:08) Elektra 60345 Best Of. *(LP version)*
- (S) (7:06) Elektra 75011 L.A. Woman. *(LP version)*
- (S) (7:00) Elektra 61047 O.S.T. The Doors. *(LP version)*

HAROLD DORMAN
1960 #17 *MOUNTAIN OF LOVE*

JIMMY DORSEY ORCHESTRA
1957 #2 *SO RARE*

1957 #25 *JUNE NIGHT*

LEE DORSEY
1961 #7 *YA YA*
- (M) (2:25) Rhino 70647 Billboard's Top R&B Hits Of 1961. *(mastered from vinyl)*
- (M) (1:54) Warner Brothers 3359 O.S.T. The Wanderers. *(mastered from a scratchy record; edited)*
- (M) (2:25) Relic 7009 Raging Harlem Hit Parade.
- (M) (2:26) Relic 7013 Ya Ya.

1962 #33 *DO-RE-MI*
- (S) (2:10) Relic 7009 Raging Harlem Hit Parade.
- (S) (2:12) Relic 7013 Ya Ya.

1965 #29 *RIDE YOUR PONY*
- (M) (2:51) Rhino 75766 Best Of New Orleans Rhythm & Blues Volume 2.

1966 #38 *GET OUT OF MY LIFE, WOMAN*

1966 #10 *WORKING IN THE COAL MINE*
- (M) (2:47) Rhino 75766 Best Of New Orleans Rhythm & Blues Volume 2.
- (S) (2:49) Warner Special Projects 27610 More Party Classics.

1966 #29 *HOLY COW*

TOMMY DORSEY ORCHESTRA
1958 #2 *TEA FOR TWO CHA CHA CHA*

1958 #30 *I WANT TO BE HAPPY CHA CHA*

MIKE DOUGLAS
1966 #7 *THE MEN IN MY LITTLE GIRL'S LIFE*

RONNIE DOVE
1964 #31 *SAY YOU*

1964 #21 *RIGHT OR WRONG*

1965 #9 *ONE KISS FOR OLD TIMES SAKE*

1965 #15 *A LITTLE BIT OF HEAVEN*

1965 #25 *I'LL MAKE ALL YOUR DREAMS COME TRUE*

1965 #27 *KISS AWAY*

1966 #17 *WHEN LIKING TURNS TO LOVING*

1966 #25 *LET'S START ALL OVER AGAIN*

1966 #30 *HAPPY SUMMER DAYS*

1966 #29 *I REALLY DON'T WANT TO KNOW*

1966 #17 *CRY*

1967 #40 *MY BABE*

DOVELLS
1961 #3 *BRISTOL STOMP*

1962 #32 *DO THE NEW CONTINENTAL*

1962 #34 *BRISTOL TWISTIN' ANNIE*

1962 #21 *HULLY GULLY BABY*

1963 #3 *YOU CAN'T SIT DOWN*

JOE DOWELL
                (S) (2:01) Mercury 826448 Oldies Golden Million Sellers.
1962 #36 *LITTLE RED RENTED ROWBOAT*

CHARLIE DRAKE
1962 #22 *MY BOOMERANG WON'T COME BACK*

PETE DRAKE
1964 #22 *FOREVER*

DRAMATICS
1971 #14 *WHATCHA SEE IS WHATCHA GET*
                (S) (3:31) Rhino 70786 Soul Hits Of The 70's Volume 6. *(45 version)*
                (S) (3:55) Stax 60-003 Best Of. *(LP version)*
                (S) (3:55) Stax 4111 Whatcha See Is Whatcha Get. *(LP version)*
                (S) (3:32) Stax 88008 Top Of The Stax Volume 2. *(45 version)*
1972 #3 *IN THE RAIN*
                (S) (5:06) Stax 88005 Top Of The Stax.
                (S) (4:30) Rhino 70787 Soul Hits Of The 70's Volume 7. *(neither the LP or 45 version)*
                (S) (5:06) Stax 60-003 Best Of.
                (S) (5:06) Stax 4111 Whatcha See Is Whatcha Get.

RUSTY DRAPER
1955 #5 *THE SHIFTING WHISPERING SANDS*
1956 #22 *IN THE MIDDLE OF THE HOUSE*
1957 #18 *FREIGHT TRAIN*

DREAMLOVERS
1961 #19 *WHEN WE GET MARRIED*
                (M) (2:25) JCI 3115 Groovin' Sixties.
                (M) (2:25) Dunhill Compact Classics 031 Back Seat Jams.
                (M) (2:26) Rhino 70588 Rockin' & Rollin' Wedding Songs Volume 1.
                (E) (2:24) Collectables 2508 History Of Rock - The Doo Wop Era Part 2.
                (M) (2:25) Collectables 5004 Best Of.

DREAM WEAVERS
1956 #4 *IT'S ALMOST TOMORROW*

DRIFTERS
1959 #1 *THERE GOES MY BABY*
                (M) (2:09) Rhino 70906 American Bandstand Greatest Hits Collection.
                (M) (2:09) Atlantic 81296 Atlantic Rhythm & Blues Volume 4.
                (M) (2:09) Atlantic 8153 Golden Hits.
                (M) (2:08) Atlantic 81931 1959-1965 All Time Greatest Hits.
                (M) (2:09) Atlantic 82305 Atlantic Rhythm And Blues 1947-1974 Box Set.
1959 #10 *DANCE WITH ME*
                (M) (2:23) Atlantic 81296 Atlantic Rhythm & Blues Volume 4.
                (M) (2:22) Atlantic 8153 Golden Hits. *(truncated fade)*
                (S) (2:24) Atlantic 81931 1959-1965 All Time Greatest Hits. *(stereo on current pressings, mono on original pressings of this cd; truncated fade)*
                (S) (2:24) Atlantic 82305 Atlantic Rhythm And Blues 1947-1974 Box Set.
1959 #23 *(IF YOU CRY) TRUE LOVE, TRUE LOVE*
                (S) (2:19) Atlantic 8153 Golden Hits.
                (S) (2:19) Atlantic 81931 1959-1965 All Time Greatest Hits.
1960 #9 *THIS MAGIC MOMENT*
                (M) (2:28) Atlantic 81296 Atlantic Rhythm & Blues Volume 4.
                (S) (2:26) Atlantic 8153 Golden Hits.

DRIFTERS (Continued)

        (S)   (2:25) Atlantic 81931 1959-1965 All Time Greatest Hits.
        (S)   (2:25) Atlantic 80213 Ultimate Ben E King Collection.
        (S)   (2:30) Atlantic 82305 Atlantic Rhythm And Blues 1947-1974 Box Set.

1960 #40 *LONELY WINDS*

        (M)   (2:46) Atlantic 81931 1959-1965 All Time Greatest Hits.

1960 #1 *SAVE THE LAST DANCE FOR ME*

        (S)   (2:28) Rhino 70621 Billboard's Top Rock & Roll Hits Of 1960.
        (S)   (2:28) Rhino 72004 Billboard's Top Rock & Roll Hits 1957-1961 Box Set.
        (S)   (2:26) Atlantic 81296 Atlantic Rhythm & Blues Volume 4.
        (S)   (2:25) Atlantic 8153 Golden Hits.
        (S)   (2:26) Atlantic 81931 1959-1965 All Time Greatest Hits.
        (S)   (2:26) Atlantic 80213 Ultimate Ben E King Collection.
        (S)   (2:26) Atlantic 82305 Atlantic Rhythm And Blues 1947-1974 Box Set.

1961 #11 *I COUNT THE TEARS*

        (S)   (2:11) Atlantic 8153 Golden Hits.
        (S)   (2:11) Atlantic 81931 1959-1965 All Time Greatest Hits.
        (S)   (2:11) Atlantic 80213 Ultimate Ben E King Collection.

1961 #11 *SOME KIND OF WONDERFUL*

        (S)   (2:35) RCA 6965 More Dirty Dancing (LP version)
        (S)   (2:35) Atlantic 8153 Golden Hits. *(LP version)*
        (S)   (2:35) Atlantic 81931 1959-1965 All Time Greatest Hits. *(LP version)*

1961 #13 *PLEASE STAY*

        (S)   (2:13) Atlantic 81931 1959-1965 All Time Greatest Hits.

1961 #16 *SWEETS FOR MY SWEET*

        (S)   (2:27) Atlantic 81931 1959-1965 All Time Greatest Hits.

1962 #18 *WHEN MY LITTLE GIRL IS SMILING*

        (S)   (2:29) Atlantic 81931 1959-1965 All Time Greatest Hits.

1963 #6 *UP ON THE ROOF*

        (S)   (2:34) Atlantic 81297 Atlantic Rhythm & Blues Volume 5. *(LP version)*
        (S)   (2:35) Atlantic 8153 Golden Hits. *(LP version)*
        (S)   (2:35) Atlantic 81931 1959-1965 All Time Greatest Hits. *(LP version)*
        (S)   (2:35) Atlantic 82305 Atlantic Rhythm And Blues 1947-1974 Box Set. *(LP version)*

1963 #12 *ON BROADWAY*

        (M)   (2:59) Atlantic 81297 Atlantic Rhythm & Blues Volume 5.
        (S)   (2:59) Warner Special Products 27601 Atlantic Soul Classics.
        (S)   (2:59) Atlantic 8153 Golden Hits.
        (S)   (2:58) Atlantic 81931 1959-1965 All Time Greatest Hits.
        (M)   (2:59) Rhino 70593 The Rock 'N' Roll Classics Of Leiber & Stoller.
        (S)   (2:58) Atlantic 82305 Atlantic Rhythm And Blues 1947-1974 Box Set.

1963 #27 *I'LL TAKE YOU HOME*

        (S)   (2:35) Atlantic 81931 1959-1965 All Time Greatest Hits.

1964 #5 *UNDER THE BOARDWALK*

        (S)   (2:39) Atlantic 81297 Atlantic Rhythm & Blues Volume 5. *(LP version)*
        (S)   (2:39) Atlantic 8153 Golden Hits. *(LP version)*
        (S)   (2:39) Atlantic 81931 1959-1965 All Time Greatest Hits. *(LP version)*
        (S)   (2:39) Atlantic 82305 Atlantic Rhythm And Blues 1947-1974 Box Set. *(LP version)*

1964 #31 *I'VE GOT SAND IN MY SHOES*

        (S)   (2:45) Atlantic 8153 Golden Hits.
        (S)   (2:45) Atlantic 81931 1959-1965 All Time Greatest Hits.
        (S)   (2:45) Rhino 70279 Rare Soul: Beach Music Classics Volume 3.

DRIFTERS (Continued)
1964 #24 *SATURDAY NIGHT AT THE MOVIES*
    (S) (2:29) Atlantic 8153 Golden Hits.
    (S) (2:28) Atlantic 81931 1959-1965 All Time Greatest Hits.

DUALS
1961 #24 *STICK SHIFT*
    (E) (2:28) Capitol 96862 Monster Summer Hits - Drag City.

DUBS
1957 #25 *COULD THIS BE MAGIC*
    (M) (2:15) Collectables 5402 Best Of.

DAVE DUDLEY
1963 #39 *SIX DAYS ON THE ROAD*
    (M) (2:20) Rhino 70723 Legends Of Guitar: Country Volume 2.
    (M) (2:20) Rhino 70684 Billboard's Top Country Hits Of 1963.

PATTY DUKE
1965 #6 *DON'T JUST STAND THERE*
1965 #31 *SAY SOMETHING FUNNY*

DUPREES
1962 #7 *YOU BELONG TO ME*
    (S) (2:42) Rhino 71004 Best Of.
    (S) (2:42) Collectables 5008 Best Of.
1962 #16 *MY OWN TRUE LOVE*
    (S) (2:27) Rhino 71004 Best Of.
    (S) (2:27) Collectables 5008 Best Of.
1963 #28 *WHY DON'T YOU BELIEVE ME*
    (S) (2:36) Rhino 71004 Best Of.
    (S) (2:36) Collectables 5008 Best Of.
1963 #19 *HAVE YOU HEARD*
    (M) (2:28) Rhino 71004 Best Of.
    (M) (2:28) Collectables 5008 Best Of.

BOB DYLAN
1965 #1 *LIKE A ROLLING STONE*
    (dj copies of this 45 were issued in two different configurations; Part 1 (3:02) with Part 2 (3:02) on the flip side and another with the complete version (6:00); commercial copies of the 45 all ran (6:00))
    (S) (6:06) Columbia 9463 Greatest Hits.
    (S) (6:07) Columbia 38830 Biograph.
    (S) (6:08) Columbia 9189 Highway 61 Revisited.
    (S) (5:15) Columbia 30050 Self Portrait. *(Live)*
1965 #9 *POSITIVELY 4TH STREET*
    (S) (3:52) Columbia 9463 Greatest Hits.
    (S) (3:52) Columbia 38830 Biograph.
1966 #2 *RAINY DAY WOMEN #12 & 35*
    (S) (4:32) Columbia 45018 Rock Classics Of The 60's. *(LP version)*
    (S) (4:34) Columbia 9463 Greatest Hits. *(LP version)*
    (S) (4:35) Columbia 0841 Blonde On Blonde. *(LP version)*
1966 #25 *I WANT YOU*
    (S) (3:04) Columbia 9463 Greatest Hits.
    (S) (3:04) Columbia 38830 Biograph.
    (S) (3:05) Columbia 0841 Blonde On Blonde.
1966 #28 *JUST LIKE A WOMAN*
    (S) (4:52) Columbia 9463 Greatest Hits. *(LP version)*
    (S) (4:53) Columbia 38830 Biograph. *(LP version)*
    (S) (4:50) Columbia 0841 Blonde On Blonde. *(LP version)*

BOB DYLAN (Continued)
1969 #8 LAY LADY LAY
      (S) (3:14) Columbia 31120 Greatest Hits Volume 2.
      (S) (3:16) Columbia 38830 Biograph.
      (S) (3:16) Columbia 9825 Nashville Skyline.
1970 #28 WIGWAM
      (S) (3:06) Columbia 30050 Self Portrait.
1971 #31 WATCHING THE RIVER FLOW
      (S) (3:32) Columbia 31120 Greatest Hits Volume 2.
1972 #30 GEORGE JACKSON
1973 #10 KNOCKIN' ON HEAVEN'S DOOR
      (S) (2:28) Columbia 45048 Rock Classics Of The 70's.
      (S) (2:29) Columbia 38830 Biograph.
      (S) (2:29) Columbia 32460 O.S.T. Pat Garrett & Billy The Kid.

DYNAMICS
1963 #40 MISERY

RONNIE DYSON
1970 #10 (IF YOU LET ME MAKE LOVE TO YOU) WHY CAN'T I TOUCH YOU?
      (S) (3:24) Rhino 70783 Soul Hits Of The 70's Volume 3.
1970 #35 I DON'T WANNA CRY
1973 #20 ONE MAN BAND (PLAYS ALL ALONE)

EAGLES
1972 #9 TAKE IT EASY
      (S) (3:31) Asylum 5054 The Eagles. *(LP version)*
      (S) (3:28) Asylum 105 Their Greatest Hits. *(LP version)*
1972 #11 WITCHY WOMAN
      (S) (4:12) Asylum 5054 The Eagles. *(LP version)*
      (S) (4:09) Asylum 105 Their Greatest Hits. *(LP version)*
1973 #20 PEACEFUL EASY FEELING
      (S) (4:19) Asylum 5054 The Eagles.
      (S) (4:14) Asylum 105 Their Greatest Hits.

EARLS
1963 #26 REMEMBER THEN
      (S) (2:06) Collectables 5058 Remember Me Baby.

EASYBEATS
1967 #16 FRIDAY ON MY MIND
   (the 45 time is (2:47); the LP time is (2:45))
      (M) (2:49) K-Tel 839 Battle Of The Bands Volume 2. *(slower than 45 and LP)*
      (S) (2:41) Rhino 75892 Nuggets.

EASYBEATS (Continued)

      (S) (2:41) Rhino 70325   History Of British Rock Volume 7.
      (S) (2:41) Rhino 72022   History Of British Rock Box Set.

ECHOES
1961 #15 BABY BLUE

DUANE EDDY
1958 #7 REBEL-ROUSER

      (M) (1:56) Rhino 70719   Legends Of Guitar - Rock; The 50's. *(missing the first :18 seconds of the song)*
      (M) (2:21) Motown 9068   21 Compact Command Performances.
      (M) (2:21) Motown 5431   Have "Twangy" Guitar Will Travel.

1958 #33 RAMROD

      (M) (1:38) Motown 9068   21 Compact Command Performances.
      (M) (1:39) Motown 5431   Have "Twangy" Guitar Will Travel.

1958 #16 CANNONBALL

      (M) (1:53) Motown 9068   21 Compact Command Performances.
      (M) (1:53) Motown 5431   Have "Twangy" Guitar Will Travel.

1959 #19 THE LONELY ONE

      (M) (1:40) Motown 9068   21 Compact Command Performances.
      (M) (1:40) Motown 5431   Have "Twangy" Guitar Will Travel.

1959 #27 YEP!

      (M) (2:06) Motown 9068   21 Compact Command Performances.

1959 #10 FORTY MILES OF BAD ROAD

      (M) (2:03) Motown 9068   21 Compact Command Performances.
      (M) (2:04) Motown 5424 $1,000,000 Worth Of Twang.

1959 #28 SOME KIND-A-EARTHQUAKE

      (M) (1:17) Motown 9068   21 Compact Command Performances.
      (M) (1:17) Motown 5424 $1,000,000 Worth Of Twang.

1960 #20 BONNIE CAME BACK

      (M) (2:16) Motown 9068   21 Compact Command Performances.
      (M) (2:16) Motown 5424 $1,000,000 Worth Of Twang.

1960 #3 BECAUSE THEY'RE YOUNG

      (M) (1:56) Motown 9068   21 Compact Command Performances.
      (M) (1:56) Motown 5424 $1,000,000 Worth Of Twang.

1960 #39 KOMMOTION

      (M) (2:50) Motown 9068   21 Compact Command Performances.
      (M) (2:50) Motown 5424 $1,000,000 Worth Of Twang.

1960 #26 PETER GUNN

      (M) (2:17) Motown 9068   21 Compact Command Performances.

1961 #19 PEPE

      (M) (2:02) Motown 9068   21 Compact Command Performances.
      (M) (2:03) Motown 5424 $1,000,000 Worth Of Twang.

1961 #37 THEME FROM DIXIE

      (M) (1:54) Motown 9068   21 Compact Command Performances.
      (M) (1:54) Motown 5424 $1,000,000 Worth Of Twang.

1962 #11 (DANCE WITH THE) GUITAR MAN

      (S) (2:36) RCA 8475   Nipper's Greatest Hits Of The 60's Volume 2.

1963 #30 BOSS GUITAR

EDISON LIGHTHOUSE
1970 #4 LOVE GROWS WHERE MY ROSEMARY GOES

      (S) (2:48) Rhino 70922   Super Hits Of The 70's Volume 2.
      (S) (2:48) Rhino 72009   Super Hits Of The 70's Volumes 1-4 Box Set.

DAVE EDMUNDS
1971 #4 *I HEAR YOU KNOCKING*
    (S) (2:47) Rhino 70742 Rock This Town: Rockabilly Hits Volume 2.

EDSELS
1961 #21 *RAMA LAMA DING DONG*
    (M) (2:23) Collectables 2507 History Of Rock - The Doo Wop Era Part 1.

EDWARD BEAR
1973 #3 *LAST SONG*
    (S) (3:11) Rhino 70930 Super Hits Of The 70's Volume 10.
    (S) (3:11) EMI 90603 Rock Me Gently.
    (S) (3:11) Capitol 98665 When AM Was King.
1973 #24 *CLOSE YOUR EYES*

BOBBY EDWARDS
1961 #8 *YOU'RE THE REASON*

JIMMY EDWARDS
1957 #35 *LOVE BUG CRAWL*
    (M) (2:02) Rhino 70741 Rock This Town: Rockabilly Hits Volume 1.

JONATHAN EDWARDS
1972 #5 *SUNSHINE*
    (S) (2:14) Rhino 70927 Super Hits Of The 70's Volume 7.
    (S) (2:15) Atco 862 Jonathan Edwards.

TOMMY EDWARDS
1958 #1 *IT'S ALL IN THE GAME*
    (S) (2:35) Mercury 832041 45's On CD Volume 1.
    (S) (2:35) JCI 3203 Lovin' Fifties.
    (E) (2:37) Elektra 60107 O.S.T. Diner.
1958 #14 *LOVE IS ALL WE NEED*
1959 #18 *PLEASE MR. SUN*
1959 #40 *THE MORNING SIDE OF THE MOUNTAIN*
1959 #21 *MY MELANCHOLY BABY*
1959 #29 *I'VE BEEN THERE*
1960 #21 *I REALLY DON'T WANT TO KNOW*

EIGHTH DAY
1971 #8 *SHE'S NOT JUST ANOTHER WOMAN*
    (M) (3:02) Rhino 70785 Soul Hits Of The 70's Volume 5.
1971 #34 *YOU'VE GOT TO CRAWL (BEFORE YOU WALK)*
    (S) (2:46) Rhino 70786 Soul Hits Of The 70's Volume 6.

DONNIE ELBERT
1971 #30 *WHERE DID OUR LOVE GO*
    (S) (3:20) Rhino 70786 Soul Hits Of The 70's Volume 6.
1972 #19 *I CAN'T HELP MYSELF (SUGAR PIE, HONEY BUNCH)*

EL CHICANO
1970 #27 *VIVA TIRADO (PART 1)*
    (S) (4:40) Rhino 70782 Soul Hits Of The 70's Volume 2.
    (S) (4:40) MCA 25197 Viva El Chicano/Their Very Best.

EL DORADOS
1955 #8 *AT MY FRONT DOOR*
    (M) (2:34) Rhino 75764 Best Of Doo Wop Uptempo.
    (M) (2:34) Rhino 70598 Billboard's Top Rock & Roll Hits Of 1955.
    (M) (2:34) Motown 6215 Hits From The Legendary Vee-Jay Records.
    (M) (2:34) Dunhill Compact Classics 028 Sock Hop. *(song title is incorrectly identified on the cd jacket as "CRAZY LITTLE MAMA")*

ELECTRIC INDIAN
1969 #18 *KEEM-O-SABE*

ELECTRIC PRUNES
1967 #12 *I HAD TOO MUCH TO DREAM (LAST NIGHT)*
   (S) (2:56) Warner Special Products 27607 Highs Of The 60's.
   (S) (2:56) Rhino 75754 Even More Nuggets.
   (S) (2:55) JCI 3103 Electric Sixties.

ELEGANTS
1958 #2 *LITTLE STAR*
   (M) (2:38) Rhino 75764 Best Of Doo Wop Uptempo.
   (M) (2:38) Rhino 70619 Billboard Top Rock & Roll Hits Of 1958.
   (M) (2:38) Rhino 72004 Billboard Top Rock & Roll Hits 1957-1961 Box Set.
   (M) (2:38) MCA 5937 Vintage Music Volumes 13 & 14.
   (M) (2:36) JCI 3203 Lovin' Fifties. *(sounds like it was mastered from vinyl)*
   (M) (2:40) Collectables 5420 Best Of.

JIMMY ELLEDGE
1962 #33 *FUNNY HOW TIME SLIPS AWAY*
   (S) (2:48) RCA 8475 Nipper's Greatest Hits Of The 60's Volume 2.

YVONNE ELLIMAN
1971 #30 *I DON'T KNOW HOW TO LOVE HIM*
   (S) (3:38) MCA 2-10000 Jesus Christ Superstar. *(previous selection tracks over introduction; LP version)*

SHIRLEY ELLIS
1964 #7 *THE NITTY GRITTY*
   (S) (2:15) Rhino 70650 Billboard's Top R&B Hits Of 1964.
   (S) (2:14) MCA 31205 Vintage Music Volume 8. *(missing the fake audience noise overdub that appeared on the original hit version)*
   (S) (2:14) MCA 5805 Vintage Music Volumes 7 & 8. *(missing the fake audience noise overdub that appeared on the original version)*
1965 #3 *THE NAME GAME*
   (S) (3:00) MCA 31204 Vintage Music Volume 7. *(:20 longer than either the 45 or LP)*
   (S) (3:00) MCA 5805 Vintage Music Volumes 7 & 8. *(:20 longer than either the 45 or LP)*
1965 #7 *THE CLAPPING SONG*

EMBERS
1961 #36 *SOLITAIRE*

EMERSON, LAKE & PALMER
1972 #40 *FROM THE BEGINNING*
   (S) (4:12) Atlantic 19123 Trilogy. *(LP version)*

LES EMMERSON
1973 #37 *CONTROL OF ME*

EMOTIONS
1969 #40 *SO I CAN LOVE YOU*
   (S) (2:49) Stax 88005 Top Of The Stax.
   (S) (2:48) Stax 4121 Chronicle: Greatest Hits.
1972 #33 *SHOW ME HOW*
   (S) (3:15) Stax 88008 Top Of The Stax Volume 2.

ENGLISH CONGREGATION
1972 #28 *SOFTLY WHISPERING I LOVE YOU*
   (S) (2:57) Rhino 70927 Super Hits Of The 70's Volume 7.

PRESTON EPPS

1959 #16 *BONGO ROCK*

EQUALS

1968 #26 *BABY COME BACK*

ERNIE

1970 #13 *RUBBER DUCKIE*

ESQUIRES

1967 #20 *GET ON UP*

    (M) (2:21) Rhino 70653 Billboard's Top R&B Hits Of 1967.

    (M) (2:21) Rhino 72006 Billboard's Top R&B Hits 1965-1969 Box Set.

    (S) (2:24) Capricorn 42003 The Scepter Records Story.

1968 #29 *AND GET AWAY*

    (S) (2:40) Capricorn 42003 The Scepter Records Story.

ESSEX

1963 #1 *EASIER SAID THAN DONE*

    (S) (2:07) Rhino 70624 Billboard's Top Rock & Roll Hits Of 1963.

    (S) (2:07) Rhino 72007 Billboard's Top Rock & Roll Hits 1962-1966 Box Set.

    (S) (2:07) Rhino 70989 Best Of The Girl Groups Volume 2.

1963 #10 *A WALKIN' MIRACLE*

ETTA & HARVEY (ETTA JAMES & HARVEY FUQUA)

1960 #32 *IF I CAN'T HAVE YOU*

PAUL EVANS

1959 #5 *SEVEN LITTLE GIRLS SITTING IN THE BACK SEAT*

1960 #16 *MIDNITE SPECIAL*

1960 #11 *HAPPY-GO-LUCKY-ME*

BETTY EVERETT

1964 #40 *YOU'RE NO GOOD*

    (S) (2:18) Motown 6215 Hits From The Legendary Vee-Jay Records.

    (S) (2:21) Rhino 75891 Wonder Women.

1964 #6 *THE SHOOP SHOOP SONG (IT'S IN HIS KISS)*

    (S) (2:15) Rhino 75891 Wonder Women.

    (S) (2:14) Rhino 70988 Best Of The Girl Groups Volume 1.

    (S) (2:14) Rhino 70650 Billboard's Top R&B Hits Of 1964.

    (S) (2:12) Dunhill Compact Classics 028 Sock Hop.

    (S) (2:11) Motown 6215 Hits From The Legendary Vee-Jay Records. *(song incorrectly identified on the cd jacket by its subtitle only, "IT'S IN HIS KISS")*

BETTY EVERETT & JERRY BUTLER

1964 #9 *LET IT BE ME*

    (M) (2:48) Dunhill Compact Classics 028 Sock Hop.

    (M) (2:47) JCI 3102 Love Sixties.

    (S) (2:42) Motown 6215 Hits From The Legendary Vee-Jay Records.

    (M) (2:48) Rhino 75881 Best Of Jerry Butler.

    (M) (2:47) Curb 77419 Jerry Butler's Greatest Hits.

EVERLY BROTHERS

1957 #1 *BYE BYE LOVE*

    (M) (2:25) Rhino 75893 Jukebox Classics Volume 1.

    (M) (2:23) Rhino 5258 Cadence Classics.

    (M) (2:23) Arista 8207 24 Original Classics.

    (S) (2:14) Warner Brothers 1554 Very Best Of. *(rerecorded)*

EVERLY BROTHERS (Continued)

    (M) (2:24) Rhino 70211 The Everly Brothers.
    (M) (2:19) Curb 77311 All Time Greatest Hits.
    (M) (2:21) Essex 7052 All Time Rock Classics. *(some severe dropouts from :53 - :59)*

1957 #1 WAKE UP LITTLE SUSIE

    (M) (2:00) Rhino 70618 Billboard's Top Rock & Roll Hits Of 1957.
    (M) (2:00) Rhino 72004 Billboard's Top Rock & Roll Hits 1957-1961 Box Set.
    (M) (1:59) Rhino 75894 Jukebox Classics Volume 2.
    (M) (1:57) JCI 3201 Party Time Fifties. *(truncated fade)*
    (M) (2:00) Rhino 5258 Cadence Classics.
    (M) (2:01) Arista 8207 24 Original Classics.
    (S) (2:00) Warner Brothers 1554 Very Best Of. *(rerecorded)*
    (M) (2:01) Rhino 70211 The Everly Brothers.
    (M) (1:59) Curb 77311 All Time Greatest Hits.

1958 #34 THIS LITTLE GIRL OF MINE

    (M) (2:15) Rhino 70211 The Everly Brothers.
    (M) (2:15) Rhino 5258 Cadence Classics.

1958 #1 ALL I HAVE TO DO IS DREAM

    (M) (2:18) Rhino 75894 Jukebox Classics Volume 2. *(truncated fade)*
    (M) (2:19) JCI 3203 Lovin' Fifties.
    (M) (2:18) Rhino 5258 Cadence Classics.
    (M) (2:18) Arista 8207 24 Original Classics.
    (S) (2:20) Warner Brothers 1554 Very Best Of. *(rerecorded)*
    (M) (2:18) Rhino 70213 Fabulous Style Of.
    (M) (2:21) Curb 77311 All Time Greatest Hits.
    (S) (2:20) Atlantic 81885 O.S.T. Stealing Home. *(rerecorded)*

1958 #2 BIRD DOG

    (M) (2:14) Rhino 70619 Billboard's Top Rock & Roll Hits Of 1958.
    (M) (2:14) Rhino 72004 Billboard's Top Rock & Roll Hits 1957-1964 Box Set.
    (M) (2:14) Rhino 5258 Cadence Classics.
    (M) (2:13) Arista 8207 24 Original Classics.
    (S) (2:13) Warner Brothers 1554 Very Best Of. *(rerecorded)*
    (M) (2:13) Rhino 70213 Fabulous Style Of.
    (E) (2:14) Curb 77311 All Time Greatest Hits.

1958 #11 DEVOTED TO YOU

    (M) (2:21) Rhino 5258 Cadence Classics.
    (M) (2:21) Arista 8207 24 Original Classics.
    (S) (2:20) Warner Brothers 1554 Very Best Of. *(rerecorded)*
    (M) (2:21) Rhino 70213 Fabulous Style Of.

1958 #7 PROBLEMS

    (M) (1:55) Rhino 5258 Cadence Classics.
    (M) (1:55) Arista 8207 24 Original Classics.
    (M) (1:56) Rhino 70213 Fabulous Style Of.
    (M) (1:55) Curb 77311 All Time Greatest Hits.

1959 #17 TAKE A MESSAGE TO MARY

    (S) (2:23) Rhino 5258 Cadence Classics.
    (S) (2:24) Arista 8207 24 Original Classics.
    (S) (2:24) Rhino 70213 Fabulous Style Of.

1959 #25 POOR JENNY

    (S) (2:07) Rhino 5258 Cadence Classics.
    (S) (2:08) Arista 8207 24 Original Classics.
    (S) (2:08) Rhino 70211 The Everly Brothers.
    (S) (2:16) Rhino 70213 Fabulous Style Of. *(alternate take)*

EVERLY BROTHERS (Continued)

1959 #5 ('TIL) I KISSED YOU
- (S)   (2:23)   Rhino 5258   Cadence Classics.
- (S)   (2:23)   Arista 8207   24 Original Classics.
- (S)   (2:21)   Warner Brothers 1554   Very Best Of. *(rerecorded)*
- (S)   (2:23)   Rhino 70213   Fabulous Style Of.
- (S)   (2:22)   Curb 77311   All Time Greatest Hits.
- (S)   (2:22)   Essex 7053   A Hot Summer Night In '59.

1960 #9 LET IT BE ME
- (S)   (2:35)   Rhino 75893   Jukebox Classics Volume 1.
- (S)   (2:34)   Rhino 5258   Cadence Classics.
- (S)   (2:34)   Arista 8207   24 Original Classics.
- (S)   (2:34)   Rhino 70213   Fabulous Style Of.
- (S)   (2:40)   Curb 77311   All Time Greatest Hits.

1960 #1 CATHY'S CLOWN
- (S)   (2:23)   Rhino 70621   Billboard's Top Rock & Roll Hits Of 1960.
- (S)   (2:23)   Rhino 72004   Billboard's Top Rock & Roll Hits 1957-1961 Box Set.
- (S)   (2:22)   Arista 8207   24 Original Classics.
- (S)   (2:22)   Warner Brothers 1471   Golden Hits Of.
- (S)   (2:22)   Warner Brothers 1554   Very Best Of.
- (S)   (2:23)   Curb 77311   All Time Greatest Hits.

1960 #9 WHEN WILL I BE LOVED
- (M)   (1:57)   JCI 3102   Love Sixties.
- (S)   (2:01)   Rhino 5258   Cadence Classics.
- (S)   (2:01)   Arista 8207   24 Original Classics.
- (S)   (2:01)   Rhino 70213   Fabulous Style Of.
- (M)   (1:57)   Curb 77311   All Time Greatest Hits.

1960 #9 SO SAD (TO WATCH GOOD LOVE GO BAD)
- (S)   (2:32)   Arista 8207   24 Original Classics.
- (S)   (2:32)   Warner Brothers 1471   Golden Hits Of.
- (S)   (2:32)   Warner Brothers 1554   Very Best Of.

1960 #25 LIKE STRANGERS
- (S)   (2:00)   Rhino 5258   Cadence Classics.
- (S)   (1:59)   Rhino 70213   Fabulous Style Of.

1961 #11 WALK RIGHT BACK
- (S)   (2:15)   Arista 8207   24 Original Classics.
- (S)   (2:17)   Warner Brothers 1471   Golden Hits Of.
- (S)   (2:17)   Warner Brothers 1554   Very Best Of.

1961 #8 EBONY EYES
- (E)   (3:03)   Warner Brothers 1471   Golden Hits Of.
- (E)   (3:03)   Warner Brothers 1554   Very Best Of.

1961 #20 TEMPTATION
- (S)   (2:11)   Warner Brothers 1471   Golden Hits Of.

1961 #31 DON'T BLAME ME
- (S)   (3:23)   Warner Brothers 1471   Golden Hits Of. *(lots of tape hiss; "Golden Hits Of" vinyl LP version)*

1962 #7 CRYING IN THE RAIN
- (S)   (1:59)   Arista 8207   24 Original Classics.
- (S)   (1:57)   Warner Brothers 1471   Golden Hits Of.
- (S)   (1:57)   Warner Brothers 1554   Very Best Of.
- (S)   (1:59)   Curb 77311   All Time Greatest Hits.

1962 #15 THAT'S OLD FASHIONED (THAT'S THE WAY LOVE SHOULD BE)
- (S)   (2:20)   Warner Brothers 1471   Golden Hits Of.

EVERLY BROTHERS (Continued)
1964 #33 *GONE, GONE, GONE*
       (S) (2:01) Arista 8207 24 Original Classics.

EVERY MOTHERS SON
1967 #5 *COME ON DOWN TO MY BOAT*
       (S) (2:33) K-Tel 205 Battle Of The Bands Volume 3.
       (S) (2:33) Mercury 834216 45's On CD Volume 3.
1967 #36 *PUT YOUR MIND AT EASE*

EXCITERS
1963 #5 *TELL HIM*
       (S) (2:36) Rhino 70989 Best Of The Girl Groups Volume 2. *(LP version)*
       (S) (2:29) Motown 6120 O.S.T. The Big Chill. *(LP version)*
       (S) (2:33) EMI 96268 24 Greatest Hits Of All Time. *(45 version)*
       (S) (2:33) EMI 95202 Tell Him. *(45 version)*
       (S) (2:48) EMI 95202 Tell HIm. *(LP version; includes :11 of studio talk)*
       (S) (2:33) Capitol 98138 Spring Break Volume 1. *(45 version)*

SHELLEY FABARES
1962 #1 *JOHNNY ANGEL*
       (S) (2:21) Rhino 70623 Billboard's Top Rock & Roll Hits Of 1962.
       (S) (2:21) Rhino 72007 Billboard's Top Rock & Roll Hits 1962-1966 Box Set.
       (S) (2:21) Geffen 24310 O.S.T. Mermaids.
1962 #34 *JOHNNY LOVES ME*

FABIAN
1959 #40 *I'M A MAN*
1959 #8 *TURN ME LOOSE*
       (S) (2:23) Rhino 75893 Jukebox Classics Volume 1.
       (S) (2:21) Garland 012 Remember When.
       (S) (2:19) MCA 6171 Good Time Rock 'N' Roll. *(all selections on this cd are recorded live)*
1959 #6 *TIGER*
       (S) (2:31) Rhino 75894 Jukebox Classics Volume 2.
1959 #34 *COME ON AND GET ME*
1960 #11 *HOUND DOG MAN*
1960 #16 *THIS FRIENDLY WORLD*
1960 #32 *ABOUT THIS THING CALLED LOVE*
1960 #35 *STRING ALONG*

BENT FABRIC
1962 #6 *ALLEY CAT*

TOMMY FACENDA
1959 #30 *HIGH SCHOOL U.S.A.*
(there were 29 different versions of this song each mentioning high schools in different cities)

FACES
1972 #10 *STAY WITH ME*
    (S) (4:36) Warner Brothers 25987 Storyteller.

BARBARA FAIRCHILD
1973 #32 *TEDDY BEAR SONG*

ADAM FAITH
1965 #30 *IT'S ALRIGHT*
    (S) (2:32) Rhino 70319 History Of British Rock Volume 1.
    (S) (2:32) Rhino 72022 History Of British Rock Box Set.
    (S) (2:32) Rhino 72008 History Of British Rock Volumes 1-4 Box Set.

PERCY FAITH & HIS ORCHESTRA
1960 #1 *THEME FROM "A SUMMER PLACE"*
    (M) (2:25) Columbia 44374 Hollywood Magic - The 50's.
    (S) (2:21) Columbia 44398 16 Most Requested Songs.
    (M) (2:25) Columbia 8637 Greatest Hits.

MARIANNE FAITHFULL
1965 #30 *AS TEARS GO BY*
    (M) (2:36) Abkco 7547 Greatest Hits.
1965 #32 *COME AND STAY WITH ME*
    (M) (2:22) Abkco 7547 Greatest Hits.
1965 #34 *THIS LITTLE BIRD*
    (M) (2:00) Abkco 7547 Greatest Hits.
1965 #38 *SUMMER NIGHTS*
    (M) (1:44) Abkco 7547 Greatest Hits.

FAITH, HOPE & CHARITY
1970 #36 *SO MUCH LOVE*

FALCONS
1959 #14 *YOU'RE SO FINE*
    (M) (2:25) Rhino 70645 Billboard's Top R&B Hits Of 1959.
    (M) (2:23) Relic 7003 You're So Fine.
    (M) (2:23) Curb 77323 All Time Greatest Hits Of Rock 'N' Roll.

GEORGIE FAME
1965 #17 *YEH, YEH*
    (M) (2:19) Rhino 70323 History Of British Rock Volume 5.
    (M) (2:19) Rhino 72022 History Of British Rock Box Set.
1968 #6 *THE BALLAD OF BONNIE AND CLYDE*
    (M) (3:08) Columbia/Legacy 46984 Rock Artifacts Volume 4.
    (M) (3:08) Rhino 70326 History Of British Rock Volume 8.
    (M) (3:08) Rhino 72022 History Of British Rock Box Set.

FANNY
1971 #32 *CHARITY BALL*

FANTASTIC JOHNNY C
1967 #9 *BOOGALOO DOWN BROADWAY*
1968 #37 *HITCH IT TO THE HORSE*

DON FARDON
1968 #19 *INDIAN RESERVATION*

DONNA FARGO
1972 #8 *THE HAPPIEST GIRL IN THE WHOLE U.S.A.*
(S) (2:30) MCA 6421 16 Top Country Hits Volume 1.
1973 #9 *FUNNY FACE*
(S) (2:46) Rhino 70758 Super Hits Of The 70's Volume 11.
(S) (2:46) MCA 6421 16 Top Country Hits Volume 1.
1973 #31 *SUPERMAN*

JOSE FELICIANO
1968 #3 *LIGHT MY FIRE*
(S) (3:34) RCA 66024 Light My Fire. *(LP length)*
(S) (3:32) RCA 8474 Nipper's Greatest Hits Of The 60's Volume 1. *(LP length)*
(S) (3:34) RCA 6903 All Time Greatest Hits. *(LP length)*
1968 #13 *HI-HEEL SNEAKERS*
(S) (2:18) RCA 6903 All Time Greatest Hits.
1969 #32 *HEY! BABY*
(S) (2:47) RCA 6903 All Time Greatest Hits.

FENDERMEN
1960 #5 *MULE SKINNER BLUES*

FERRANTE & TEICHER
1960 #9 *THEME FROM THE APARTMENT*
(S) (2:58) Curb 77338 Greatest Hits.
1961 #1 *EXODUS*
(S) (2:53) Curb 77403 All-Time Great Instrumental Hits Volume 1.
(S) (2:53) Curb 77338 Greatest Hits.
1961 #39 *LOVE THEME FROM ONE EYED JACKS*
(S) (3:00) Curb 77338 Greatest Hits.
1961 #6 *TONIGHT*
(S) (3:11) Curb 77338 Greatest Hits.
1970 #10 *MIDNIGHT COWBOY*
(S) (3:14) Curb 77338 Greatest Hits.
(S) (3:17) EMI 91682 Best Of.

ERNIE FIELDS
1959 #7 *IN THE MOOD*
(S) (2:39) Curb 77402 All-Time Great Instrumental Hits Volume 2. *(rerecording)*

FIESTAS
1959 #12 *SO FINE*
(M) (2:20) JCI 3201 Party Time Fifties.

FIFTH DIMENSION
1967 #16 *GO WHERE YOU WANNA GO*
1967 #4 *UP UP AND AWAY*
(S) (2:38) Arista 8335 Greatest Hits On Earth.
1967 #38 *PAPER CUP*
1968 #22 *CARPET MAN*
1968 #6 *STONED SOUL PICNIC*
(S) (3:25) Arista 8335 Greatest Hits On Earth.
1968 #11 *SWEET BLINDNESS*
1969 #23 *CALIFORNIA SOUL*
1969 #1 *AQUARIUS/LET THE SUNSHINE IN*
(dj copies of this 45 ran (3:02) and (4:49))
(S) (4:49) Rhino 70630 Billboard's Top Rock & Roll Hits Of 1969.

117

FIFTH DIMENSION (Continued)

      (S)   (4:49) Rhino 72005 Billboard's Top Rock & Roll Hits 1968-1972 Box Set.
      (S)   (4:46) Arista 8335 Greatest Hits On Earth.
      (S)   (4:49) Polygram 837362 O.S.T. 1969.
      (S)   (4:47) JCI 3104 Mellow Sixties.

1969 #23 WORKIN' ON A GROOVY THING

1969 #1 WEDDING BELL BLUES

      (S)   (2:42) Arista 8335 Greatest Hits On Earth. *(truncated fade)*
      (S)   (2:42) Epic 48732 O.S.T. My Girl.
      (S)   (2:42) Rhino 70588 Rockin' & Rollin' Wedding Songs Volume 1.

1970 #14 BLOWING AWAY

1970 #22 PUPPET MAN

      (S)   (2:55) Arista 8335 Greatest Hits On Earth.

1970 #20 SAVE THE COUNTRY

      (S)   (2:38) Arista 8335 Greatest Hits On Earth.

1970 #2 ONE LESS BELL TO ANSWER

      (S)   (3:29) Arista 8335 Greatest Hits On Earth.

1971 #11 LOVE'S LINES, ANGLES AND RHYMES

      (S)   (4:10) Arista 8335 Greatest Hits On Earth. *(truncated fade; LP version)*

1971 #22 LIGHT SINGS

1971 #14 NEVER MY LOVE

      (dj copies of this 45 ran (3:26) and (3:45))
      (S)   (3:54) Arista 8335 Greatest Hits On Earth. *(tracks into next selection)*

1972 #24 TOGETHER LET'S FIND LOVE

      (S)   (3:35) Arista 8335 Greatest Hits On Earth. *(previous selection tracks over introduction)*

1972 #6 (LAST NIGHT) I DIDN'T GET TO SLEEP AT ALL

      (S)   (3:11) Arista 8335 Greatest Hits On Earth.

1972 #10 IF I COULD REACH YOU

1973 #20 LIVING TOGETHER, GROWING TOGETHER

FIFTH ESTATE

1967 #12 DING DONG THE WITCH IS DEAD

      (S)   (2:04) Rhino 70996 One Hit Wonders Of The 60's Volume 2.

LARRY FINNEGAN

1962 #11 DEAR ONE

FIREBALLS

1959 #35 TORQUAY

1960 #23 BULLDOG

1968 #9 BOTTLE OF WINE

      (M)   (2:08) Rhino 75772 Son Of Frat Rock.

FIREFLIES

1959 #10 YOU WERE MINE

      (M)   (1:54) Dunhill Compact Classics 031 Back Seat Jams.
      (M)   (1:53) Collectables 2508 History Of Rock - The Doo Wop Era Part 2.

FIRST CHOICE

1973 #19 ARMED AND EXTREMELY DANGEROUS

      (S)   (2:47) Rhino 70790 Soul Hits Of The 70's Volume 10.

1973 #38 SMARTY PANTS

FIRST EDITION (see KENNY ROGERS & THE FIRST EDITION)

EDDIE FISHER

1955 #10 *HEART*
> (M) (2:36) RCA 9592   All Time Greatest Hits Volume 1.
> (S) (2:25) MCA 31174   Very Best Of. *(rerecording)*

1956 #9 *DUNGAREE DOLL*
> (M) (2:00) RCA 8466   Nipper's Greatest Hits Of The 50's Volume 1.
> (M) (1:59) RCA 9592   All Time Greatest Hits Volume 1.

1956 #9 *CINDY, OH CINDY*
> (M) (2:58) RCA 9592   All Time Greatest Hits Volume 1.

MISS TONI FISHER

1960 #2 *THE BIG HURT*

1962 #23 *WEST OF THE WALL*

ELLA FITZGERALD

1960 #31 *MACK THE KNIFE*
> (E) (5:12) Verve 825670   Mack The Knife: Ella In Berlin. *(LP length)*
> (E) (5:05) Verve 841765   For The Love Of Ella. *(LP length)*

FIVE AMERICANS

1967 #7 *WESTERN UNION*
> (S) (2:32) K-Tel 205   Battle Of The Bands Volume 3. *(very poor stereo separation; :06 longer than 45 or LP)*
> (M) (2:25) Rhino 75777   More Nuggets. *(truncated fade)*
> (S) (2:34) Sundazed 11004   Western Union. *(:08 longer than 45 or LP)*

1967 #31 *SOUND OF LOVE*
> (S) (2:24) Sundazed 11004   Western Union. *(with countoff)*

FIVE BLOBS

1958 #39 *THE BLOB*
> (M) (2:39) Rhino 71492   Elvira Presents Haunted Hits.
> (M) (2:38) Rhino 70535   Halloween Hits.
> (M) (2:38) CBS Special Products 46200   Rock Goes To The Movies Volume 3.

FIVE BY FIVE

1968 #38 *FIRE*

FIVE FLIGHTS UP

1970 #29 *DO WHAT YOU WANNA DO*

FIVE KEYS

1956 #19 *OUT OF SIGHT, OUT OF MIND*
> (M) (2:15) Capitol 92709   Capitol Collector's Series.

1956 #31 *WISDOM OF A FOOL*
> (M) (2:35) Capitol 92709   Capitol Collector's Series. *(includes :06 of studio talk)*

FIVE MAN ELECTRICAL BAND

1971 #7 *SIGNS*
> (M) (4:01) Rhino 70926   Super Hits Of The 70's Volume 6. *(LP version)*
> (M) (4:01) Rhino 70734   Songs Of Protest. *(LP version)*
> (M) (3:59) Priority 8670   Hitchin A Ride/70's Greatest Rock Hits Volume 10. *(LP version)*

1971 #20 *ABSOLUTELY RIGHT*
> (S) (2:17) Rhino 70926   Super Hits Of The 70's Volume 6.

FIVE SATINS

1956 #32 *IN THE STILL OF THE NIGHT*
> (M) (3:03) Rhino 75763   Best Of Doo Wop Ballads.
> (M) (3:04) Rhino 70642   Billboard's Top R&B Hits Of 1956.

FIVE SATINS (Continued)
      (M)   (3:04) RCA 6408 O.S.T. Dirty Dancing.
      (M)   (3:03) Arista 8605 16 Original Doo-Wop Classics.
      (M)   (3:00) Relic 7001 Greatest Hits.
      (M)   (2:58) Collectables 2508 History Of Rock - The Doo Wop Era Volume 2.
      (M)   (3:00) Collectables 5017 Sing Their Greatest Hits.

1957 #39 *TO THE AISLE*
      (M)   (2:43) Arista 8605 16 Original Doo-Wop Classics.
      (M)   (2:43) Relic 7001 Greatest Hits.
      (M)   (2:42) Rhino 70588 Rockin' & Rollin' Wedding Songs Volume 1.
      (M)   (2:43) Collectables 5017 Sing Their Greatest Hits.

FIVE STAIRSTEPS
1970 #4 *O-o-h CHILD*
      (S)   (2:54) Pair 1202 Best Of Buddah. *(mistakenly identifies the group only as the "Stairsteps"; edit)*
      (S)   (2:54) Pair 1199 Best Of Bubblegum Music. *(mistakenly identifies the group only as the "Stairsteps"; edit)*
      (S)   (3:14) Rhino 70782 Soul Hits Of The 70's Volume 2.
      (S)   (3:16) Collectables 5023 Greatest Hits.

ROBERTA FLACK
1972 #1 *THE FIRST TIME EVER I SAW YOUR FACE*
      (S)   (4:17) Atlantic 81912 Golden Age Of Black Music (1970-1975). *(45 version)*
      (S)   (5:20) Atlantic 8230 First Take. *(LP version)*
      (S)   (4:17) Atlantic 81298 Atlantic Rhythm & Blues Volume 6. *(45 version)*
      (S)   (4:16) Atlantic 19317 Best Of. *(45 version)*
      (S)   (4:17) Atlantic 82305 Atlantic Rhythm And Blues 1947-1974 Box Set. *(45 version)*

1973 #1 *KILLING ME SOFTLY WITH HIS SONG*
      (S)   (4:45) Atlantic 81299 Atlantic Rhythm & Blues Volume 7.
      (S)   (4:45) Atlantic 81912 Golden Age Of Black Music (1970-1975).
      (S)   (4:45) Atlantic 19154 Killing Me Softly.
      (S)   (4:45) Atlantic 19317 Best Of.
      (S)   (4:44) Atlantic 82305 Atlantic Rhythm And Blues 1947-1974 Box Set.

1973 #12 *JESSE*
      (S)   (3:59) Atlantic 19154 Killing Me Softly.
      (S)   (3:59) Atlantic 19317 Best Of.

ROBERTA FLACK & DONNY HATHAWAY
1971 #28 *YOU'VE GOT A FRIEND*
      (S)   (3:23) Atlantic 81299 Atlantic Rhythm & Blues Volume 7.
      (S)   (3:22) Atlantic 19317 Best Of Roberta Flack.
      (S)   (3:23) Atlantic 7216 Roberta Flack & Donny Hathaway.
      (S)   (3:23) Atlantic 82092 Donny Hathaway Collection.
      (S)   (3:23) Atlantic 82305 Atlantic Rhythm And Blues 1947-1974 Box Set.

1972 #7 *WHERE IS THE LOVE*
      (S)   (2:41) Atlantic 81299 Atlantic Rhythm & Blues Volume 7.
      (S)   (2:41) Atlantic 19317 Best Of Roberta Flack.
      (S)   (2:43) Atlantic 7216 Roberta Flack & Donny Hathaway.
      (S)   (2:43) Atlantic 82092 Donny Hathaway Collection.
      (S)   (2:43) Atlantic 82305 Atlantic Rhythm And Blues 1947-1974 Box Set.

FLAMING EMBER
1969 #19 *MIND, BODY AND SOUL*
    (M) (2:58) Rhino 70781   Soul Hits Of The 70's Volume 1.
1970 #23 *WESTBOUND #9*
    (M) (2:48) Rhino 70783   Soul Hits Of The 70's Volume 3. *(this is a highly edited version that bears no resemblence to the original hit version)*
1970 #22 *I'M NOT MY BROTHERS KEEPER*
    (S) (3:01) Rhino 70783   Soul Hits Of The 70's Volume 3.

FLAMINGOS
1959 #10 *I ONLY HAVE EYES FOR YOU*
    (S) (3:19) Rhino 70906   American Bandstand Greatest Hits Collection.
    (S) (3:21) Rhino 75763   Best Of Doo Wop Ballads.
    (S) (3:20) Rhino 70967   Best Of.
    (S) (3:21) Epic 48732   O.S.T. My Girl.
    (S) (3:21) Collectables 5424   Flamingo Serenade.
    (S) (3:20) Collectables 8803   For Collectors Only.
    (S) (3:19) Essex 7053   A Hot Summer Night In '59.
    (S) (3:21) Collectables 5426   The Sound Of. *(truncated fade)*

FLARES
1961 #25 *FOOT STOMPING (PART 1)*
    (E) (2:15) Rhino 75764   Best Of Doo Wop Uptempo.
    (S) (2:15) MCA 6228   O.S.T. Hairspray. *(missing some footstomps and an organ overdub)*

FLASH
1972 #30 *SMALL BEGINNINGS*

FLEETWOODS
1959 #1 *COME SOFTLY TO ME*
    (M) (2:21) Enigma 73531   O.S.T. Scandal.
    (M) (2:24) Rhino 70980   Best Of.
1959 #34 *GRADUATION'S HERE*
    (S) (1:57) Rhino 70980   Best Of.
1959 #1 *MR. BLUE*
    (M) (2:23) Elektra 60107   O.S.T. Diner.
    (E) (2:21) JCI 3203   Lovin' Fifties.
    (M) (2:23) Rhino 70980   Best Of.
1960 #34 *OUTSIDE MY WINDOW*
    (S) (2:05) Rhino 70980   Best Of.
1960 #22 *RUNAROUND*
    (S) (2:32) Rhino 70980   Best Of.
1961 #19 *TRAGEDY*
    (S) (2:43) Rhino 70980   Best Of.
1962 #34 *LOVERS BY NIGHT, STRANGERS BY DAY*
    (S) (2:09) Rhino 70980   Best Of.

SHELBY FLINT
1961 #26 *ANGEL ON MY SHOULDER*

FLIRTATIONS
1969 #31 *NOTHING BUT A HEARTACHE*
    (S) (2:42) Rhino 75770   Soul Shots Volume 2.

EDDIE FLOYD
1966 #31 *KNOCK ON WOOD*
    (M) (3:02) Atlantic Group 88218   Complete Stax/Volt Singles.
    (S) (3:02) Stax 88005   Top Of The Stax.
    (S) (3:02) Warner Special Products 27609   Memphis Soul Classics.

EDDIE FLOYD (Continued)

      (S)   (3:02) JCI 3100 Dance Sixties.

      (S)   (3:02) Atlantic 81298 Atlantic Rhythm & Blues Volume 6.

      (S)   (3:04) Atlantic 80283 Knock On Wood. *(truncated fade)*

      (S)   (3:07) Stax 4122 Chronicle: Greatest Hits.

      (M) (3:02) Atlantic 82305 Atlantic Rhythm And Blues 1947-1974 Box Set.

1968 #20 BRING IT ON HOME TO ME

      (S)   (2:29) Stax 4122 Chronicle: Greatest Hits.

      (S)   (2:29) Stax 8548 Stax Soul Brothers.

FLYING MACHINE

1969 #5 SMILE A LITTLE SMILE FOR ME

      (S)   (2:56) Rhino 70921 Super Hits Of The 70's Volume 1. *(neither the 45 or LP version)*

      (S)   (2:56) Rhino 72009 Super Hits Of The 70's Volumes 1-4 Box Set. *(neither the 45 or LP version)*

      (M) (2:57) Rhino 70327 History Of British Rock Volume 9. *(neither the 45 or LP version)*

      (M) (2:57) Rhino 72022 History Of British Rock Box Set. *(neither the 45 or LP version)*

FOCUS

1973 #4 HOCUS POCUS

      (S)   (3:27) JCI 3302 Electric Seventies.

      (S)   (6:39) IRS 13060 Moving Waves. *(LP version)*

WAYNE FONTANA & THE MINDBENDERS (see MINDBENDERS)

FONTANE SISTERS

1955 #1 HEARTS OF STONE

      (M) (2:03) Rhino 70598 Billboard's Top Rock & Roll Hits Of 1955.

      (M) (2:03) MCA 31201 Vintage Music Volume 4. *(background vocals differ from the hit version)*

      (M) (2:03) MCA 5778 Vintage Music Volumes 3 & 4. *(background vocals differ from the hit version)*

      (M) (2:02) Atlantic 82155 O.S.T. Book Of Love. *(background vocals differ from the hit version)*

1955 #10 ROCK LOVE

1955 #3 SEVENTEEN

1956 #10 DADDY-O

1956 #15 THE BANANA BOAT SONG

FONTANE SISTERS & PAT BOONE

1956 #39 VOICES

FRANKIE FORD

1959 #12 SEA CRUISE

      (M) (2:40) Rhino 75766 Best Of New Orleans Rhythm & Blues Volume 2.

      (M) (2:44) JCI 3202 Rockin' Fifties.

      (M) (2:44) Ace 2036 Let's Take A Sea Cruise. *(mastered from vinyl)*

      (M) (2:30) Rhino 70587 New Orleans Party Classics.

TENNESSEE ERNIE FORD

1955 #1 SIXTEEN TONS

      (E)   (2:33) Capitol 90592 Memories Are Made Of This.

      (M) (2:33) Curb 77330 50's Hits - Country Volume 1.

      (M) (2:34) Rhino 70975 Best Of.

      (M) (2:34) Capitol 95291 Capitol Collector's Series.

      (M) (2:34) Capitol 98665 When AM Was King.

FORTUNES

1965 #7 YOU'VE GOT YOUR TROUBLES
- (S) (3:21) Rhino 70323 History Of British Rock Volume 5. *(LP version)*
- (S) (3:21) Rhino 72022 History Of British Rock Box Set. *(LP version)*

1965 #37 HERE IT COMES AGAIN

1971 #8 HERE COMES THAT RAINY DAY FEELING AGAIN
- (S) (2:48) Rhino 70925 Super Hits Of The 70's Volume 5.
- (S) (2:49) EMI 90603 Rock Me Gently.
- (S) (2:46) Curb 77356 70's Hits Volume 2.
- (S) (2:49) Capitol 98665 When AM Was King.

FOUNDATIONS

1968 #8 BABY, NOW THAT I'VE FOUND YOU
- (M) (2:34) Rhino 70324 History Of British Rock Volume 6.
- (M) (2:34) Rhino 72022 History Of British Rock Box Set.

1969 #1 BUILD ME UP BUTTERCUP
- (M) (2:58) Rhino 70630 Billboard's Top Rock & Roll Hits Of 1969.
- (M) (2:58) Rhino 72005 Billboard's Top Rock & Roll Hits 1968-1972 Box Set.
- (S) (2:57) Rhino 70327 History Of British Rock Volume 9. *(hum noticeable on fade out)*
- (S) (2:57) Rhino 72022 History Of British Rock Box Set. *(hum noticeable on fade out)*

1969 #26 IN THE BAD BAD OLD DAYS

FOUR ACES

1955 #1 MELODY OF LOVE

1955 #10 HEART

1955 #1 LOVE IS A MANY SPLENDORED THING

1956 #38 I ONLY KNOW I LOVE YOU

1956 #10 FRIENDLY PERSUASION (THEE I LOVE)

1957 #39 WRITTEN ON THE WIND

1957 #36 BAHAMA MAMA

1958 #25 THE WORLD OUTSIDE

1959 #28 NO OTHER ARMS, NO OTHER LIPS

FOUR COINS

1957 #15 SHANGRI-LA

1957 #25 MY ONE SIN

1958 #25 THE WORLD OUTSIDE

FOUR ESQUIRES

1957 #29 LOVE ME FOREVER

1958 #19 HIDEAWAY

FOUR FRESHMEN

1956 #6 GRADUATION DAY
- (M) (3:04) Capitol 93197 Capitol Collector's Series. *(includes :02 studio noise preceeding music)*

FOUR JACKS AND A JILL

1968 #10 MASTER JACK

FOUR LADS

1955 #2 MOMENTS TO REMEMBER
- (M) (3:14) Columbia 45110 16 Most Requested Songs Of The 50's Volume 1.
- (M) (3:15) Columbia 45017 Radio Classics Of The 50's.

        (M) (3:14) Columbia/Legacy 46158 16 Most Requested Songs.

        (E) (3:16) Columbia 11369 Moments To Remember.

1956 #1 NO, NOT MUCH!

        (M) (3:16) Columbia/Legacy 46158 16 Most Requested Songs.

        (E) (3:17) Columbia 11369 Moments To Remember.

1956 #3 STANDING ON THE CORNER

        (M) (2:50) Columbia 45111 16 Most Requested Songs Of The 50's Volume 2.

        (M) (2:51) Columbia/Legacy 46158 16 Most Requested Songs.

1956 #18 THE BUS STOP SONG (A PAPER OF PINS)

        (M) (2:10) Columbia 44374 Hollywood Magic - The 1950's.

1956 #20 A HOUSE WITH LOVE IN IT

1957 #9 WHO NEEDS YOU

        (M) (2:57) Columbia/Legacy 46158 16 Most Requested Songs.

        (E) (2:56) Columbia 11369 Moments To Remember.

1957 #28 I JUST DON'T KNOW

1958 #22 PUT A LIGHT IN THE WINDOW

1958 #13 THERE'S ONLY ONE OF YOU

        (S) (2:52) Columbia/Legacy 46158 16 Most Requested Songs.

        (E) (2:54) Columbia 11369 Moments To Remember.

1958 #12 ENCHANTED ISLAND

1959 #31 THE GIRL ON PAGE 44

1959 #34 HAPPY ANNIVERSARY

FOUR PREPS

1958 #4 26 MILES (SANTA CATALINA)

        (E) (2:27) Capitol 90592 Memories Are Made Of This.

        (M) (2:26) Curb 77354 50's Hits Volume 1.

        (M) (2:26) Capitol 91626 Capitol Collector's Series.

        (M) (2:27) Capitol 98665 When AM Was King.

1958 #5 BIG MAN

        (M) (2:21) Capitol 91626 Capitol Collector's Series.

1958 #39 LAZY SUMMER NIGHT

        (M) (2:09) Capitol 91626 Capitol Collector's Series.

1960 #15 DOWN BY THE STATION

        (S) (2:47) Capitol 91626 Capitol Collector's Series. *(with countoff)*

1960 #34 GOT A GIRL

        (S) (2:27) Capitol 91626 Capitol Collector's Series.

1961 #18 MORE MONEY FOR YOU AND ME

        (S) (6:24) Capitol 91626 Capitol Collector's Series. *(LP version)*

FOUR SEASONS

1962 #1 SHERRY

        (S) (2:30) Warner Brothers 3359 O.S.T. The Wanderers. *(very poor stereo separation)*

        (S) (2:31) Rhino 72998 25th Anniversary Collection.

        (S) (2:30) Rhino 71490 Anthology.

        (S) (2:29) Atlantic 81885 O.S.T. Stealing Home. *(truncated fade)*

        (S) (2:30) Rhino 70594 Greatest Hits Volume 1.

        (S) (2:30) Curb 77525 Greatest Hits Of Rock 'N' Roll Volume 2.

        (E) (2:29) Curb 77304 Hits Digitally Enhanced. *(remixed)*

1962 #1 BIG GIRLS DON'T CRY

        (S) (2:24) Rhino 70623 Billboard's Top Rock & Roll Hits Of 1962.

        (S) (2:24) Rhino 72007 Billboard's Top Rock & Roll Hits 1962-1966 Box Set.

FOUR SEASONS (Continued)

 (S) (2:23) RCA 6965 More Dirty Dancing.
 (S) (2:23) Geffen 24310 O.S.T. Mermaids.
 (S) (2:25) Warner Brothers 3359 O.S.T. The Wanderers. *(very poor stereo separation)*
 (S) (2:23) Rhino 72998 25th Anniversary Collection.
 (S) (2:23) Rhino 71490 Anthology.
 (S) (2:23) Rhino 70594 Greatest Hits Volume 1.
 (S) (2:23) Curb 77304 Hits Digitally Enhanced. *(remixed; additional instrumentation added)*
 (E) (5:16) Curb 77304 Hits Digitally Enhanced. *(remixed; additional instrumentation added)*

1963 #28 *SANTA CLAUS IS COMING TO TOWN*

 (S) (1:47) Rhino 70234 The Four Seasons Christmas Album.

1963 #1 *WALK LIKE A MAN*

 (S) (2:15) Rhino 70624 Billboard's Top Rock & Roll Hits Of 1963.
 (S) (2:15) Rhino 72007 Billboard's Top Rock & Roll Hits 1962-1966 Box Set.
 (S) (2:15) Warner Brothers 3359 O.S.T. The Wanderers. *(very poor stereo separation)*
 (S) (2:15) Rhino 72998 25th Anniversary Collection.
 (S) (2:15) Rhino 71490 Anthology.
 (M) (2:15) Rhino 70594 Greatest Hits Volume 1.

1963 #20 *AIN'T THAT A SHAME*

 (S) (2:34) Rhino 72998 25th Anniversary Collection. *(LP version)*
 (M) (2:36) Rhino 70594 Greatest Hits Volume 1. *(45 version)*

1963 #4 *CANDY GIRL*

 (S) (2:37) Rhino 72998 25th Anniversary Collection.
 (S) (2:34) Rhino 71490 Anthology.
 (S) (2:37) Rhino 70594 Greatest Hits Volume 1.

1963 #35 *MARLENA*

 (S) (2:33) Rhino 72998 25th Anniversary Collection.
 (S) (2:33) Rhino 71490 Anthology.
 (S) (2:33) Rhino 70594 Greatest Hits Volume 1.
 (S) (2:31) Curb 77304 Hits Digitally Enhanced. *(remixed)*

1963 #30 *NEW MEXICAN ROSE*

 (M) (2:46) Rhino 72998 25th Anniversary Collection.

1964 #3 *DAWN (GO AWAY)*

 (M) (2:45) Rhino 72998 25th Anniversary Collection. *(45 version)*
 (M) (2:45) Rhino 71490 Anthology. *(45 version)*
 (M) (2:45) Rhino 70594 Greatest Hits Volume 1. *(45 version)*

1964 #15 *STAY*

 (S) (1:55) Rhino 72998 25th Anniversary Collection.
 (S) (1:55) Rhino 71490 Anthology.
 (S) (1:54) Rhino 70594 Greatest Hits Volume 1.
 (E) (1:53) Curb 77304 Hits Digitally Enhanced. *(remixed; extra instrumentation added)*

1964 #6 *RONNIE*

 (M) (2:56) Rhino 72998 25th Anniversary Collection.
 (M) (2:56) Rhino 71490 Anthology.
 (M) (2:56) Rhino 70594 Greatest Hits Volume 1.

1964 #1 *RAG DOLL*

 (M) (2:59) Rhino 70625 Billboard's Top Rock & Roll Hits Of 1964.
 (M) (2:59) Rhino 72007 Billboard's Top Rock & Roll Hits 1962-1966 Box Set.

      (M)   (2:59) Rhino 72998 25th Anniversary Collection.
      (M)   (2:59) Rhino 71490 Anthology.
      (S)   (2:55) Rhino 70595 Greatest Hits Volume 2.

1964 #24 ALONE

      (S)   (2:50) Rhino 72998 25th Anniversary Collection.
      (S)   (2:50) Rhino 70594 Greatest Hits Volume 1.

1964 #9 SAVE IT FOR ME

      (S)   (2:35) Rhino 72998 25th Anniversary Collection.
      (S)   (2:35) Rhino 71490 Anthology.
      (S)   (2:35) Rhino 70594 Greatest Hits Volume 1.

1964 #14 BIG MAN IN TOWN

      (S)   (2:44) Rhino 72998 25th Anniversary Collection.
      (S)   (2:44) Rhino 71490 Anthology.
      (S)   (2:44) Rhino 70594 Greatest Hits Volume 1.

1965 #10 BYE, BYE, BABY (BABY GOODBYE)

      (S)   (2:31) Rhino 72998 25th Anniversary Collection.
      (S)   (2:30) Rhino 71490 Anthology.
      (S)   (2:30) Rhino 70594 Greatest Hits Volume 1.

1965 #27 GIRL COME RUNNING

      (M)   (2:58) Rhino 72998 25th Anniversary Collection.
      (M)   (2:58) Rhino 71490 Anthology.
      (M)   (2:58) Rhino 70594 Greatest Hits Volume 1.

1965 #1 LET'S HANG ON!

      (M)   (3:15) Rhino 72998 25th Anniversary Collection. *(45 version)*
      (M)   (3:15) Rhino 71490 Anthology. *(45 version)*
      (M)   (3:15) Rhino 70595 Greatest Hits Volume 2. *(45 version)*

1966 #10 WORKING MY WAY BACK TO YOU

      (S)   (3:03) Rhino 72998 25th Anniversary Collection.
      (S)   (3:03) Rhino 70247 Working My Way Back To You.
      (S)   (3:03) Rhino 71490 Anthology.
      (S)   (3:02) Rhino 70595 Greatest Hits Volume 2.

1966 #9 OPUS 17 (DON'T YOU WORRY 'BOUT ME)

      (S)   (2:31) Rhino 72998 25th Anniversary Collection.
      (S)   (2:31) Rhino 71490 Anthology.
      (S)   (2:31) Rhino 70595 Greatest Hits Volume 2.

1966 #9 I'VE GOT YOU UNDER MY SKIN

      (S)   (3:37) Rhino 72998 25th Anniversary Collection.
      (S)   (3:37) Rhino 71490 Anthology.
      (S)   (3:37) Rhino 70595 Greatest Hits Volume 2.

1967 #12 TELL IT TO THE RAIN

      (S)   (2:34) Rhino 72998 25th Anniversary Collection.
      (S)   (2:35) Rhino 71490 Anthology.
      (S)   (2:34) Rhino 70595 Greatest Hits Volume 2.

1967 #12 BEGGIN'

      (S)   (2:46) Rhino 72998 25th Anniversary Collection.
      (S)   (2:45) Rhino 71490 Anthology.
      (S)   (2:46) Rhino 70595 Greatest Hits Volume 2.

1967 #9 C'MON MARIANNE

      (S)   (2:33) Rhino 72998 25th Anniversary Collection.
      (S)   (2:33) Rhino 71490 Anthology.
      (S)   (2:33) Rhino 70595 Greatest Hits Volume 2.

1967 #14 WATCH THE FLOWERS GROW

      (S)   (3:17) Rhino 72998 25th Anniversary Collection.

FOUR SEASONS (Continued)
1968 #15 *WILL YOU LOVE ME TOMORROW*
    (S) (3:16) Rhino 72998 25th Anniversary Collection.
    (S) (3:16) Rhino 71490 Anthology.
    (S) (3:16) Rhino 70595 Greatest Hits Volume 2.

1969 #33 *AND THAT REMINDS ME*
    (S) (3:30) Rhino 72998 25th Anniversary Collection.

FOUR TOPS
1964 #15 *BABY I NEED YOUR LOVING*
    (S) (2:43) Rhino 70650 Billboard's Top R&B Hits Of 1964.
    (S) (2:45) Motown 6138 The Composer Series: Holland/Dozier/ Holland.
    (S) (2:46) Motown 5451 A Collection Of 16 Big Hits Volume 4.
    (S) (2:43) Motown 0809 and 6188 Anthology.
    (S) (2:44) Motown 904 and 6106 Compact Command Performances.
            (almost all tracks on this cd have a buzz audible as each song reaches the end of its fade)
    (S) (2:44) MCA 6467 O.S.T. Air America.
    (S) (2:44) Motown 9097 The Most Played Oldies On America's Jukeboxes.
            (buzz noticeable on fadeout)
    (S) (2:46) Motown 5209 Greatest Hits.
    (S) (2:43) Motown 5314 and 9022 Great Songs And Performances That Inspired The Motown 25th Anniversary TV Special.
    (S) (2:44) Motown 5122 Four Tops.
    (S) (2:44) Motown 9098 Radio's #1 Hits. *(buzz noticeable on fade out)*
    (S) (2:44) Motown 8027 and 8127 Four Tops/Four Tops Second Album.
    (S) (2:42) Motown 6192 You Can't Hurry Love: All The Great Love Songs Of The Past 25 Years.
    (S) (2:43) Ripete 392183 Ocean Drive.
    (S) (2:43) Motown 5114 Superstar Series Volume 14.

1965 #26 *ASK THE LONELY*
(the 45 length was (2:55) while the LP length was (2:38))
    (S) (2:36) Motown 0809 and 6188 Anthology. *(LP length)*
    (S) (2:39) Motown 9042 and 6106 Compact Command Performances. *(LP length)*
    (S) (2:57) Motown 5209 Greatest Hits. *(truncated fade; 45 length)*
    (S) (2:38) Motown 5122 Four Tops. *(LP length)*
    (S) (2:37) Motown 8027 and 8127 Four Tops/Four Tops Second Album. *(LP length)*
    (S) (2:39) Motown 5114 Superstar Series Volume 14. *(LP length)*

1965 #1 *I CAN'T HELP MYSELF*
    (S) (2:42) Rhino 70651 Billboard's Top R&B Hits Of 1965.
    (S) (2:42) Rhino 72006 Billboard's Top R&B Hits 1965-1969 Box Set.
    (S) (2:41) Motown 6132 25 #1 Hits From 25 Years.
    (S) (2:40) Motown 6159 The Good-Feeling Music Of The Big Chill Generation Volume 1.
    (S) (2:41) Motown 5452 A Collection Of 16 Big Hits Volume 5.
    (S) (2:41) Motown 6138 The Composer Series: Holland/Dozier/ Holland.
    (S) (2:40) Motown 0809 and 6188 Anthology.
    (S) (2:40) Motown 9042 and 6106 Compact Command Performances.
    (S) (2:40) MCA 10063 Original Television Soundtrack "The Sounds Of Murphy Brown".
    (S) (2:40) Motown 9017 and 5248 16 #1 Hits From The Early 60's. *(buzz noticeable on fade out)*
    (S) (2:40) Motown 9097 The Most Played Oldies On America's Jukeboxes. *(buzz noticeable onfadeout)*

FOUR TOPS (Continued)

    (S) (2:41) Motown 5209 Greatest Hits.

    (S) (2:40) Motown 5314 and 9022 Great Songs And Performances That Inspired The Motown 25th Anniversary TV Special.

    (S) (2:40) Motown 5264 Second Album.

    (S) (2:40) Motown 9098 Radio's #1 Hits. *(buzz noticeable on fade out)*

    (S) (2:39) Motown 8027 and 8127 Four Tops/Four Tops Second Album.

    (S) (2:40) Motown 9060 Motown's Biggest Pop Hits. *(buzz noticeable on fadeout)*

    (S) (2:39) Motown 9071 Motown Dance Party Volume 1. *(all selections on this cd are segued together)*

    (S) (2:40) Ripete 392183 Ocean Drive.

1965 #6 IT'S THE SAME OLD SONG

    (S) (2:46) Rhino 70651 Billboard's Top R&B Hits Of 1965.

    (S) (2:46) Rhino 72006 Billboard's Top R&B Hits 1965-1969 Box Set.

    (S) (2:47) Motown 6138 The Composer Series: Holland/Dozier/ Holland.

    (S) (2:45) Motown 5453 A Collection Of 16 Big Hits Volume 6.

    (S) (2:45) Motown 6120 O.S.T. Big Chill.

    (S) (2:45) Motown 0809 and 6188 Anthology.

    (S) (2:46) Motown 9042 and 6106 Compact Command Performances.

    (S) (2:45) Motown 5209 Greatest Hits.

    (S) (2:46) Motown 5314 and 9022 Great Songs And Performances That Inspired The Motown 25th Anniversary TV Special.

    (S) (2:46) Motown 5264 Second Album.

    (S) (2:45) Motown 6094 More Songs From The Original Soundtrack Of The "Big Chill".

    (S) (2:46) Motown 8027 and 8127 Four Tops/Four Tops Second Album.

    (S) (2:46) Motown 9071 Motown Dance Party Volume 1. *(all selections on this cd are segued together)*

    (S) (2:45) Motown 5114 Superstar Series Volume 14.

1965 #12 SOMETHING ABOUT YOU

(the 45 length was (2:48) while the LP length was (2:40))

    (S) (2:39) Motown 0809 and 6188 Anthology. *(LP length)*

    (S) (2:41) Motown 9042 and 6106 Compact Command Performances. *(LP length)*

    (S) (2:40) Motown 5209 Greatest Hits. *(LP length)*

    (S) (2:48) Motown 5264 Second Album. *(45 length)*

    (S) (2:48) Motown 8027 and 8127 Four Tops/Four Tops Second Album. *(45 length)*

1966 #15 SHAKE ME, WAKE ME (WHEN IT'S OVER)

    (S) (2:37) Motown 5454 A Collection Of 16 Big Hits Volume 7.

    (S) (2:38) Motown 0809 and 6188 Anthology.

    (S) (2:38) Motown 9042 and 6106 Compact Command Performances.

    (S) (2:38) Motown 5209 Greatest Hits.

    (S) (2:38) Motown 5444 On Top. *(truncated fade)*

1966 #1 REACH OUT I'LL BE THERE

    (S) (2:58) Rhino 70627 Billboard's Top Rock & Roll Hits Of 1966.

    (S) (2:58) Rhino 72007 Billboard's Top Rock & Roll Hits 1962-1966 Box Set.

    (S) (2:59) Motown 6132 25 #1 Hits From 25 Years.

    (S) (2:57) Motown 6160 The Good-Feeling Music Of The Big Chill Generation Volume 2.

    (S) (2:58) Motown 6137 20 Greatest Songs In Motown History.

    (S) (2:58) Motown 6138 The Composer Series: Holland/Dozier/ Holland.

    (S) (2:57) Motown 5456 A Collection Of 16 Big Hits Volume 9.

FOUR TOPS (Continued)

(S) (2:57) Priority 7909 Vietnam: Rockin' The Delta.
(S) (2:54) Motown 0809 and 6188 Anthology.
(S) (2:58) Motown 9042 and 6106 Compact Command Performances.
(S) (2:55) Motown 9072 Motown Dance Party Volume 2. *(all selections on this cd are segued together)*
(S) (2:57) Motown 9097 The Most Played Oldies On America's Jukeboxes. *(buzz noticeable on fadeout)*
(S) (2:57) Motown 9018 and 5249 16 #1 Hits From The Late 60's.
(S) (2:59) Motown 5149 Reach Out.
(S) (2:57) Motown 5209 Greatest Hits.
(S) (2:58) Motown 5314 and 9022 Great Songs And Performances That Inspired The Motown 25th Anniversary TV Special.
(S) (2:58) Motown 5343 Every Great Motown Song: The First 25 Years Volume 1. *(most selections on this cd have noise on the fade out)*
(S) (2:58) Motown 8034 and 8134 Every Great Motown Song: The First 25 Years Volumes 1 & 2. *(most selections on this cd have noise on the fade out)*
(S) (2:59) Motown 8007 and 8107 Reach Out/Still Waters Run Deep.

1967 #7 STANDING IN THE SHADOWS OF LOVE

(S) (2:34) Motown 9105 Motown Memories Volume 2.
(S) (2:34) Motown 6137 20 Greatest Songs In Motown History.
(S) (2:35) Motown 6138 The Composer Series: Holland/Dozier/ Holland.
(S) (2:34) Motown 5457 A Collection Of 16 Big Hits Volume 10.
(S) (2:34) Motown 0809 and 6188 Anthology.
(S) (2:34) Motown 9042 and 6106 Compact Command Performances.
(S) (2:33) Motown 9072 Motown Dance Party Volume 2. *(all selections on this cd are segued together)*
(S) (2:35) Motown 5149 Reach Out.
(S) (2:36) Motown 5209 Greatest Hits.
(S) (2:34) Motown 5314 and 9022 Great Songs And Performances That Inspired The Motown 25th Anniversary TV Special.
(S) (2:34) Motown 8034 and 8134 Every Great Motown Song: The First 25 Years Volumes 1 & 2. *(most selections on this cd have noise on the fade out)*
(S) (2:34) Motown 5343 Every Great Motown Song: The First 25 Years Volume 1. *(most selections on this cd have noise on the fade out)*
(S) (2:35) Motown 8007 and 8107 Reach Out/Still Waters Run Deep.

1967 #8 BERNADETTE

(S) (3:01) Motown 6161 The Good-Feeling Music Of The Big Chill Generation Volume 3.
(S) (3:00) Motown 5456 A Collection Of 16 Big Hits Volume 9.
(S) (3:00) Motown 0809 and 6188 Anthology.
(S) (3:01) Motown 9042 and 6106 Compact Command Performances.
(S) (3:00) Motown 5149 Reach Out.
(S) (3:00) Motown 5209 Greatest Hits.
(S) (3:01) Motown 5314 and 9022 Great Songs And Performances That Inspired The Motown 25th Anniversary TV Special.
(S) (3:00) Motown 8007 and 8107 Reach Out/Still Waters Run Deep.

1967 #9 7 ROOMS OF GLOOM

(S) (2:30) Motown 5457 A Collection Of 16 Big Hits Volume 10.
(S) (2:29) Motown 0809 and 6188 Anthology.
(S) (2:33) Motown 5149 Reach Out.
(S) (2:33) Motown 5209 Greatest Hits.
(S) (2:33) Motown 8007 and 8107 Reach Out/Still Waters Run Deep.

FOUR TOPS (Continued)

1967 #18 YOU KEEP RUNNING AWAY
- (S) (2:48) Motown 0809 and 6188 Anthology.
- (M) (2:48) Motown 9042 and 6106 Compact Command Performances.

1968 #8 WALK AWAY RENEE
- (S) (2:42) Motown 0809 and 6188 Anthology.
- (S) (2:43) Motown 9042 and 6106 Compact Command Performances.
- (S) (2:43) Motown 5149 Reach Out.
- (S) (2:42) Motown 5314 and 9022 Great Songs And Performances That Inspired The Motown 25th Anniversary TV Special.
- (S) (2:42) Motown 8007 and 8107 Reach Out/Still Waters Run Deep.

1968 #20 IF I WERE A CARPENTER
- (S) (2:47) Motown 0809 and 6188 Anthology.
- (S) (2:49) Motown 9042 and 6106 Compact Command Performances.
- (S) (2:48) Motown 5149 Reach Out.
- (S) (2:48) Motown 8007 and 8107 Reach Out/Still Waters Run Deep.

1968 #31 YESTERDAY'S DREAMS
- (S) (2:56) Motown 9042 and 6106 Compact Command Performances.
- (S) (2:54) Motown 0809 and 6188 Anthology.

1968 #32 I'M IN A DIFFERENT WORLD
- (S) (2:54) Motown 0809 and 6188 Anthology.

1970 #14 IT'S ALL IN THE GAME
- (S) (2:44) Motown 6110 Motown Grammy R&B Performances Of The 60's & 70's.
- (S) (2:42) Motown 0809 and 6188 Anthology. (truncated fade)
- (S) (2:44) Motown 9042 and 6106 Compact Command Performances.
- (S) (2:44) Motown 5314 and 9022 Great Songs And Performances That Inspired The Motown 25th Anniversary TV Special.
- (S) (2:43) Motown 8007 and 8107 Reach Out/Still Waters Run Deep.
- (S) (2:44) Motown 5224 Still Waters Run Deep.
- (S) (2:42) Motown 5114 Superstar Series Volume 14.

1970 #12 STILL WATER (LOVE)
- (S) (3:05) Motown 0809 and 6188 Anthology.
- (S) (3:08) Motown 9042 and 6106 Compact Command Performances.
- (S) (3:08) Motown 5314 and 9022 Great Songs And Performances That Inspired The Motown 25th Anniversary TV Special.
- (S) (3:08) Motown 8007 and 8107 Reach Out/Still Waters Run Deep.
- (S) (3:08) Motown 5224 Still Waters Run Deep.

1971 #26 JUST SEVEN NUMBERS (CAN STRAIGHTEN OUT MY LIFE)
- (S) (3:03) Motown 0809 and 6188 Anthology.
- (S) (3:05) Motown 9042 and 6106 Compact Command Performances.
- (S) (3:11) Motown 5478 Changing Times. (LP version; tracks into next selection)

1971 #36 MAC ARTHUR PARK (PART 2)
- (S) (6:31) Motown 9042 and 6106 Compact Command Performances. (LP version which is Parts 1 & 2)
- (S) (6:30) Motown 5466 Now! (LP version which is Parts 1 & 2)

1973 #9 KEEPER OF THE CASTLE
- (S) (2:52) Rhino 70789 Soul Hits Of The 70's Volume 9.
- (S) (2:54) MCA 27019 Greatest Hits.
- (S) (2:56) Motown 5428 Keeper Of The Castle.
- (S) (2:55) Motown 8046 and 8146 Keeper Of The Castle/ Nature Planned It.

130

FOUR TOPS (Continued)

1973 #1 AIN'T NO WOMAN (LIKE THE ONE I'VE GOT)
    (S) (3:05) Rhino 70790 Soul Hits Of The 70's Volume 10.
    (S) (3:00) Rhino 70661 Billboard's Top R&B Hits Of 1973.
    (S) (3:05) MCA 27019 Greatest Hits.
    (S) (2:58) Motown 5428 Keeper Of The Castle.
    (S) (2:58) Motown 8046 and 8146 Keeper Of The Castle/ Nature Planned It.
    (S) (3:05) MCA 10288 Classic Soul.

1973 #14 ARE YOU MAN ENOUGH
    (S) (3:23) MCA 27019 Greatest Hits.

1973 #30 SWEET UNDERSTANDING LOVE
    (S) (2:58) MCA 27019 Greatest Hits.

FOUR TOPS & SUPREMES

1971 #15 RIVER DEEP - MOUNTAIN HIGH
(the actual 45 time is (3:13) not (3:05) as stated on the record label)
    (S) (4:47) Motown 6184 20 Hard To Find Motown Classics Volume 2. *(LP version)*
    (M) (3:13) Motown 5491 Best Of The Supremes & Four Tops. *(45 version)*
    (S) (4:50) Motown 5123 Magnificent 7. *(LP version)*
    (E) (4:29) Motown 0809 and 6188 Four Tops Anthology. *(edit of LP version)*

INEZ FOXX

1963 #7 MOCKINGBIRD
    (M) (2:37) Rhino 70649 Billboard's Top R&B Hits Of 1963.
    (E) (2:37) EMI 90614 Non Stop Party Rock.
    (M) (2:35) Curb 77323 All Time Greatest Hits Of Rock 'N' Roll.

CONNIE FRANCIS

1958 #3 WHO'S SORRY NOW
    (M) (2:16) JCI 3203 Lovin' Fifties.
    (M) (2:15) Polydor 827569 Very Best Of.
    (S) (2:11) Malaco 2003 Where The Hits Are. *(all selections on this cd are rerecorded)*

1958 #31 I'M SORRY I MADE YOU CRY
    (M) (2:27) Polydor 827569 Very Best Of.

1958 #16 STUPID CUPID
    (M) (2:12) Mercury 832041 45's On CD Volume 1.
    (M) (2:12) Polydor 827569 Very Best Of.
    (S) (2:10) Malaco 2003 Where The Hits Are. *(all selections on this cd are rerecorded)*

1958 #39 FALLIN'
    (M) (2:12) Polydor 827569 Very Best Of.

1959 #2 MY HAPPINESS
    (S) (2:26) Polydor 827569 Very Best Of.
    (S) (2:18) Malaco 2003 Where The Hits Are. *(all selections on this cd are rerecorded)*

1959 #15 IF I DIDN'T CARE
    (M) (2:36) Polydor 827569 Very Best Of.
    (S) (2:47) Malaco 2003 Where The Hits Are. *(all selections on this cd are rerecorded)*

1959 #3 LIPSTICK ON YOUR COLLAR
    (S) (2:16) Polydor 827569 Very Best Of.
    (S) (2:14) Essex 7053 A Hot Summer Night In '59.
    (S) (2:18) Malaco 2003 Where The Hits Are. *(all selections on this cd are rerecorded)*

CONNIE FRANCIS (Continued)

1959 #9 FRANKIE
        (S)   (2:30) Polydor 827569 Very Best Of.
        (S)   (2:45) Malaco 2003 Where The Hits Are. *(all selections on this cd are rerecorded)*

1959 #32 YOU'RE GONNA MISS ME
        (M)   (2:43) Polydor 827569 Very Best Of.

1959 #5 AMONG MY SOUVENIRS
        (M)   (2:29) Polydor 827569 Very Best Of.
        (S)   (2:18) Malaco 2003 Where The Hits Are. *(all selections on this cd are rerecorded)*

1959 #36 GOD BLESS AMERICA
        (S)   (2:44) Polydor 831699 Very Best Of Volume 2.

1960 #7 MAMA
        (S)   (3:55) Polydor 831699 Very Best Of Volume 2.

1960 #31 TEDDY
        (M)   (2:44) Polydor 827569 Very Best Of.

1960 #1 EVERYBODY'S SOMEBODY'S FOOL
        (S)   (2:37) Polydor 827569 Very Best Of.
        (S)   (2:31) Malaco 2003 Where The Hits Are. *(all selections on this cd are rerecorded)*

1960 #27 JEALOUS OF YOU
        (M)   (2:33) Polydor 831699 Very Best Of Volume 2.

1960 #1 MY HEART HAS A MIND OF ITS OWN
        (S)   (2:30) Polydor 827569 Very Best Of.
        (S)   (2:24) Malaco 2003 Where The Hits Are. *(all selections on this cd are rerecorded)*

1960 #9 MANY TEARS AGO
        (S)   (1:54) Polydor 827569 Very Best Of.
        (S)   (1:56) Malaco 2003 Where The Hits Are. *(all selections on this cd are rerecorded)*

1961 #4 WHERE THE BOYS ARE
        (S)   (2:36) Polydor 827569 Very Best Of.
        (S)   (2:35) Malaco 2003 Where The Hits Are. *(all selections on this cd are rerecorded)*

1961 #5 BREAKIN' IN A BRAND NEW BROKEN HEART
        (S)   (2:36) Polydor 827569 Very Best Of.
        (S)   (2:28) Malaco 2003 Where The Hits Are. *(all selections on this cd are rerecorded)*

1961 #7 TOGETHER
        (S)   (2:53) Polydor 831699 Very Best Of Volume 2.
        (S)   (2:45) Malaco 2003 Where The Hits Are. *(all selections on this cd are rerecorded)*

1961 #22 (HE'S MY) DREAMBOAT
        (S)   (2:41) Polydor 831698 Rocksides.

1961 #26 HOLLYWOOD
        (M)   (2:13) Polydor 831698 Rocksides.

1962 #8 WHEN THE BOY IN YOUR ARMS (IS THE BOY IN YOUR HEART)
        (S)   (2:42) Polydor 831699 Very Best Of Volume 2.

1962 #2 DON'T BREAK THE HEART THAT LOVES YOU
        (S)   (3:01) Polydor 827569 Very Best Of.
        (S)   (2:56) Malaco 2003 Where The Hits Are. *(all selections on this cd are rerecorded)*

CONNIE FRANCIS (Continued)

1962 #7 SECOND HAND LOVE
> (S) (2:49) Polydor 827569 Very Best Of.
> (S) (2:53) Malaco 2003 Where The Hits Are. *(all selections on this cd are rerecorded)*

1962 #10 VACATION
> (S) (2:21) Polydor 827569 Very Best Of.
> (S) (2:39) Malaco 2003 Where The Hits Are. *(all selections on this cd are rerecorded)*

1962 #18 I WAS SUCH A FOOL (TO FALL IN LOVE WITH YOU)
> (M) (2:44) Polydor 831699 Very Best Of Volume 2.

1963 #18 I'M GONNA BE WARM THIS WINTER
> (M) (2:23) Polydor 827569 Very Best Of.
> (S) (2:27) Malaco 2003 Where The Hits Are. *(all selections on this cd are rerecorded)*

1963 #11 FOLLOW THE BOYS
> (E) (2:38) Polydor 827569 Very Best Of.

1963 #16 IF MY PILLOW COULD TALK

1963 #34 DROWNIN' MY SORROWS

1963 #22 YOUR OTHER LOVE

1964 #31 IN THE SUMMER OF HIS YEARS

1964 #16 BLUE WINTER
> (M) (2:24) Polydor 831699 Very Best Of Volume 2.

1964 #23 BE ANYTHING (BUT BE MINE)
> (M) (2:08) Polydor 831699 Very Best Of Volume 2.

1964 #34 LOOKING FOR LOVE
> (M) (2:18) Polydor 831698 Rocksides.
> (S) (2:04) CBS Special Products 46200 Rock Goes To The Movies Volume 3.

1964 #37 DON'T EVER LEAVE ME
> (M) (2:43) Polydor 831698 Rocksides.

1965 #35 FOR MAMA
> (S) (3:25) Polydor 831699 Very Best Of Volume 2.

1965 #29 JEALOUS HEART

ARETHA FRANKLIN

1961 #24 ROCK-A-BYE YOUR BABY WITH A DIXIE MELODY

1967 #10 I NEVER LOVED A MAN (THE WAY I LOVE YOU)
> (M) (2:47) Rhino 70653 Billboard's Top R&B Hits Of 1967. *(45 length)*
> (M) (2:47) Rhino 72006 Billboard's Top R&B Hits 1965-1969 Box Set. *(45 length)*
> (S) (2:40) Atlantic 81911 Golden Age Of Black Music (1960-1970). *(LP length)*
> (M) (2:41) Atlantic 81298 Atlantic Rhythm & Blues Volume 6. *(LP length)*
> (S) (2:41) Atlantic 81668 30 Greatest Hits. *(LP length)*
> (S) (2:41) Atlantic 8139 I Never Loved A Man The Way I Love You. *(LP length)*
> (S) (2:41) Atlantic 81280 Best Of. *(LP length)*
> (S) (2:41) Atlantic 8227 Aretha's Gold. *(LP length)*
> (S) (2:42) Atco 91813 Classic Recordings. *(LP length)*
> (S) (2:40) Atlantic 82305 Atlantic Rhythm And Blues 1947-1974 Box Set. *(LP length)*

1967 #3 RESPECT
> (M) (2:22) Atlantic 81298 Atlantic Rhythm & Blues Volume 6.
> (S) (2:25) Atlantic 81742 O.S.T. Platoon.

ARETHA FRANKLIN (Continued)

      (S) (2:22) Atlantic 81911   Golden Age Of Black Music (1960-1970).
      (S) (2:25) JCI 3105   Soul Sixties.
      (S) (2:25) Warner Special Products 27601   Atlantic Soul Classics.
      (S) (2:25) Atlantic 81668   30 Greatest Hits.
      (S) (2:24) Atlantic 8139   I Never Loved A Man The Way I Love You.
      (S) (2:25) Atlantic 81280   Best Of.
      (S) (2:25) Atlantic 8227   Aretha's Gold.
      (S) (2:23) MCA 10063   Original Television Soundtrack "The Sounds Of
                       Murphy Brown". *(previous selection tracks into introduction)*
      (S) (2:24) Atlantic 82305   Atlantic Rhythm And Blues 1947-1974 Box Set.

1967 #3   BABY I LOVE YOU

      (M) (2:39) Atlantic 81298   Atlantic Rhythm & Blues Volume 6.
      (S) (2:36) Atlantic 81911   Golden Age Of Black Music (1960-1970).
      (S) (2:36) Atlantic 81668   30 Greatest Hits.
      (S) (2:36) Atlantic 8227   Aretha's Gold.
      (S) (2:36) Atlantic 82152   O.S.T. Goodfellas.
      (S) (2:36) Atlantic 82305   Atlantic Rhythm And Blues 1947-1974 Box Set.

1967 #12   A NATURAL WOMAN (YOU MAKE ME FEEL LIKE)

      (S) (2:41) JCI 3102   Love Sixties.
      (S) (2:41) Atlantic 81298   Atlantic Rhythm & Blues Volume 6.
      (S) (2:42) Motown 6120   O.S.T. Big Chill.
      (S) (2:40) Atlantic 81668   30 Greatest Hits.
      (S) (2:41) Atlantic 8176   Lady Soul.
      (S) (2:40) Atlantic 81280   Best Of.
      (S) (2:40) Atlantic 8227   Aretha's Gold.
      (S) (2:40) Atlantic 82305   Atlantic Rhythm And Blues 1947-1974 Box Set.

1968 #1   CHAIN OF FOOLS

      (M) (2:45) Warner Special Products 27602   20 Party Classics.
      (M) (2:44) Atlantic 81298   Atlantic Rhythm & Blues Volume 6.
      (S) (2:44) Atlantic 81911   Golden Age Of Black Music (1960-1970).
      (S) (2:44) Atlantic 81668   30 Greatest Hits.
      (S) (2:44) Atlantic 8176   Lady Soul.
      (S) (2:44) Atlantic 81280   Best Of.
      (S) (2:44) Atlantic 8227   Aretha's Gold.
      (S) (2:45) Atco 91813   Classic Recordings.
      (S) (2:44) Atlantic 82305   Atlantic Rhythm And Blues 1947-1974 Box Set.
                    (truncated fade)

1968 #5   (SWEET SWEET BABY) SINCE YOU'VE BEEN GONE

      (S) (2:22) Atlantic 81911   Golden Age Of Black Music (1960-1970).
      (S) (2:22) Atlantic 81668   30 Greatest Hits.
      (S) (2:21) Atlantic 8176   Lady Soul.
      (S) (2:22) Atlantic 8227   Aretha's Gold.
      (S) (2:22) Atlantic 82305   Atlantic Rhythm And Blues 1947-1974 Box Set.

1968 #7   THINK

      (S) (2:15) Atlantic 81298   Atlantic Rhythm & Blues Volume 6.
      (S) (2:16) Atlantic 81911   Golden Age Of Black Music (1960-1970).
      (S) (2:16) JCI 3100   Dance Sixties.
      (S) (2:15) Atlantic 81668   30 Greatest Hits.
      (S) (2:16) Atlantic 81280   Best Of.
      (S) (2:16) Atlantic 8227   Aretha's Gold.
      (S) (2:16) Atlantic 82305   Atlantic Rhythm And Blues 1947-1974 Box Set.

1968 #9   THE HOUSE THAT JACK BUILT

      (S) (2:17) Atlantic 81668   30 Greatest Hits.
      (S) (2:17) Atlantic 8227   Aretha's Gold.

ARETHA FRANKLIN (Continued)

1968 #18 I SAY A LITTLE PRAYER
- (S) (3:30) Atlantic 81911 Golden Age Of Black Music (1960-1970). (*LP version*)
- (S) (3:30) Atlantic 81668 30 Greatest Hits. (*LP version*)
- (S) (3:30) Atlantic 81280 Best Of. (*LP version*)
- (S) (3:30) Atlantic 8227 Aretha's Gold. (*LP version*)

1968 #12 SEE SAW
- (S) (2:40) Atlantic 81668 30 Greatest Hits.
- (S) (2:40) Atlantic 8227 Aretha's Gold.

1969 #10 THE WEIGHT
- (S) (2:55) Atlantic 81668 30 Greatest Hits.

1969 #21 I CAN'T SEE MYSELF LEAVING YOU

1969 #18 SHARE YOUR LOVE WITH ME
- (S) (3:17) Atlantic 81668 30 Greatest Hits.

1969 #23 ELEANOR RIGBY
- (S) (2:32) Atlantic 81668 30 Greatest Hits.

1970 #13 CALL ME
- (S) (3:52) Atlantic 81668 30 Greatest Hits. (*LP version*)
- (S) (3:51) Atlantic 82305 Atlantic Rhythm And Blues 1947-1974 Box Set. (*LP version*)

1970 #25 SPIRIT IN THE DARK
- (S) (3:59) Atlantic 81668 30 Greatest Hits. (*LP version*)

1970 #10 DON'T PLAY THAT SONG
- (S) (2:57) Atlantic 81299 Atlantic Rhythm & Blues Volume 7.
- (S) (2:57) Atlantic 81912 Golden Age Of Black Music (1970-1975).
- (S) (2:56) Atlantic 81668 30 Greatest Hits.
- (S) (2:56) Atlantic 82305 Atlantic Rhythm And Blues 1947-1974 Box Set.

1970 #23 BORDER SONG (HOLY MOSES)

1971 #15 YOU'RE ALL I NEED TO GET BY
- (S) (3:33) Atlantic 81668 30 Greatest Hits.

1971 #2 BRIDGE OVER TROUBLED WATER
- (S) (5:27) Atlantic 81668 30 Greatest Hits. (*LP version*)

1971 #1 SPANISH HARLEM
- (S) (3:26) Rhino 70659 Billboard's Top R&B Hits Of 1971.
- (S) (3:29) Atlantic 81668 30 Greatest Hits.
- (S) (3:29) Atlantic 81280 Best Of.

1971 #7 ROCK STEADY
- (S) (3:10) Atlantic 81299 Atlantic Rhythm & Blues Volume 7.
- (S) (3:11) Atlantic 81668 30 Greatest Hits.
- (S) (3:11) Atlantic 81280 Best Of.
- (S) (3:10) Atlantic 82305 Atlantic Rhythm And Blues 1947-1974 Box Set.

1972 #5 DAYDREAMING
- (S) (3:57) Atlantic 81912 Golden Age Of Black Music (1970-1975). (*LP version*)
- (S) (3:57) Atlantic 81668 30 Greatest Hits. (*LP version*)
- (S) (3:59) Atlantic 82305 Atlantic Rhythm And Blues 1947-1974 Box Set. (*LP version*)

1972 #20 ALL THE KING'S HORSES

1973 #36 MASTER OF EYES (THE DEEPNESS OF YOUR EYES)

1973 #16 ANGEL
- (S) (4:25) Atlantic 81668 30 Greatest Hits. (*LP version*)

STAN FREBERG
1957 #30 *BANANA BOAT (DAY-O)*
    (M) (3:27) Capitol 91627 Capitol Collector's Series.
1957 #22 *WUN'ERFUL WUN'ERFUL! (PARTS 1 & 2)*
    (M) (3:39) Capitol 91627 Capitol Collector's Series. *(Part 1)*
    (M) (3:25) Capitol 91627 Capitol Collector's Series. *(Part 2)*
1959 #34 *GREEN CHRISTMAS*
    (M) (6:52) Rhino 75755 Dr. Demento Presents The Greatest Christmas Novelty CD.
    (M) (6:50) Capitol 91627 Capitol Collector's Series.

JOHN FRED & HIS PLAYBOY BAND
1968 #1 *JUDY IN DISGUISE (WITH GLASSES)*
    (S) (2:55) Rhino 70629 Billboard's Top Rock & Roll Hits Of 1968. *(mastered from vinyl)*
    (S) (2:55) Rhino 72006 Billboard's Top R&B Hits 1965-1969 Box Set. *(mastered from vinyl)*
    (S) (2:55) Novus 3077 O.S.T. Drugstore Cowboy. *(mastered from vinyl)*
    (S) (2:54) Paula 9000 History Of. *(most of this song has very poor stereo separation but smaller segments have very wide stereo separation)*

FREDDIE & THE DREAMERS
1965 #1 *I'M TELLING YOU NOW*
    (S) (2:06) Rhino 70319 History Of British Rock Volume 1.
    (S) (2:06) Rhino 72022 History Of British Rock Box Set.
    (S) (2:06) Rhino 72008 History Of British Rock Volumes 1-4 Box Set.
    (S) (2:05) EMI 96979 Best Of.
1965 #15 *DO THE FREDDIE*
    (S) (2:03) Rhino 70321 History Of British Rock Volume 3.
    (S) (2:03) Rhino 72022 History Of British Rock Box Set.
    (S) (2:03) Rhino 72008 History Of British Rock Volumes 1-4 Box Set.
    (S) (2:04) EMI 96979 Best Of.
1965 #17 *YOU WERE MADE FOR ME*
    (S) (2:08) Rhino 70320 History Of British Rock Volume 2. *(LP version)*
    (S) (2:08) Rhino 72022 History Of British Rock Box Set. *(LP version)*
    (S) (2:08) Rhino 72008 History Of British Rock Volumes 1-4 Box Set. *(LP version)*
    (S) (2:17) EMI 96979 Best Of. *(45 version)*

FREE
1970 #3 *ALL RIGHT NOW*
(dj copies of this 45 were issued with times of either (4:13), (3:32) or (3:12); commercial copies were all (4:13); reissue copies are (3:45))
    (S) (4:12) Island 90684 and 842901 The Island Story. *(original commercial 45 version)*
    (S) (5:30) Priority 8668 Rough And Ready/70's Greatest Rock Hits Volume 7. *(LP version)*
    (S) (5:30) A&M 3663 Best Of. *(LP version)*
    (S) (5:29) A&M 3126 Fire And Water. *(LP version)*

BOBBY FREEMAN
1958 #5 *DO YOU WANT TO DANCE*
    (M) (2:32) Rhino 70644 Billboard's Top R&B Hits Of 1958.
    (M) (2:32) Collectables 5417 Do You Wanna Dance.
1958 #31 *BETTY LOU GOT A NEW PAIR OF SHOES*
    (S) (2:26) Collectables 5417 Do You Wanna Dance.

BOBBY FREEMAN (Continued)
1964 #6 C'MON AND SWIM
(M) (2:44) Rhino 70992 Groove 'n' Grind.
(S) (3:04) Collectables 5417 Do You Wanna Dance. *(Part 1 and Part 2)*

ERNIE FREEMAN
1957 #1 RAUNCHY
(M) (2:14) Rhino 70644 Billboard's Top R&B Hits Of 1958.
(M) (2:15) Curb 77402 All-Time Great Instrumental Hits Volume 2.

FREE MOVEMENT
1971 #6 I'VE FOUND SOMEONE OF MY OWN
(S) (3:38) Rhino 70786 Soul Hits Of The 70's Volume 6.

FRIEND AND LOVER
1968 #7 REACH OUT OF THE DARKNESS
(S) (3:05) Mercury 834216 45's On CD Volume 3.

FRIENDS OF DISTINCTION
1969 #6 GRAZING IN THE GRASS
(S) (2:52) RCA 8474 Nipper's Greatest Hits Of The 60's Volume 1.
(S) (2:55) Rhino 70781 Soul Hits Of The 70's Volume 1.
(S) (2:56) Collectables 5102 Golden Classics.
1969 #23 GOING IN CIRCLES
(S) (4:13) Rhino 70781 Soul Hits Of The 70's Volume 1.
(S) (4:13) Collectables 5102 Golden Classics.
1970 #8 LOVE OR LET ME BE LONELY
(the actual 45 time is (3:11) not (3:15) as stated on the record label)
(S) (3:21) RCA 8476 and 9684 Nipper's Greatest Hits Of The 70's. *(LP length)*
(S) (3:11) Rhino 70782 Soul Hits Of The 70's Volume 2. *(45 length)*
(S) (3:19) Collectables 5102 Golden Classics. *(LP length)*

FRIJID PINK
1970 #6 HOUSE OF THE RISING SUN
1970 #39 SING A SONG FOR FREEDOM

FROGMEN
1961 #34 UNDERWATER
(M) (2:24) Dunhill Compact Classics 030 Beach Classics. *(alternate take)*

MAX FROST & THE TROOPERS
1968 #17 SHAPE OF THINGS TO COME
(S) (1:54) K-Tel 686 Battle Of The Bands Volume 4.
(S) (1:54) Rhino 75754 Even More Nuggets.

BOBBY FULLER FOUR
1966 #9 I FOUGHT THE LAW
(the actual 45 time is (2:17) not (2:07) as the record label states)
(S) (2:19) K-Tel 713 Battle Of The Bands.
(S) (2:16) Dunhill Compact Classics 029 Toga Rock.
(M) (2:16) Rhino 75772 Son Of Frat Rock.
(E) (2:12) Warner Special Products 27607 Highs Of The 60's. *(faster than 45 or LP)*
(S) (2:16) Rhino 70174 Best Of.

FUZZ
1971 #20 I LOVE YOU FOR ALL SEASONS
(S) (3:06) Rhino 70784 Soul Hits Of The 70's Volume 4.

G

GAINORS
1958 #39 *THE SECRET*

GALLAHADS
1956 #8 *THE FOOL*

GALLERY
1972 #1 *NICE TO BE WITH YOU*
  (S) (2:36) Rhino 70928 Super Hits Of The 70's Volume 8.
1972 #13 *I BELIEVE IN MUSIC*
  (S) (2:35) Rhino 70929 Super Hits Of The 70's Volume 9.
1973 #12 *BIG CITY MISS RUTH ANN*
  (S) (2:23) Rhino 70758 Super Hits Of The 70's Volume 11.

FRANK GALLOP
1958 #31 *GOT A MATCH?*

DAVE GARDNER
1957 #36 *WHITE SILVER SANDS*

DON GARDNER & DEE DEE FORD
1962 #16 *I NEED YOUR LOVING*
  (S) (2:53) Relic 7009 Raging Harlem Hit Parade.

ART GARFUNKEL
1973 #6 *ALL I KNOW*
  (S) (3:47) Columbia 45008 Garfunkel.
  (S) (3:43) Columbia 31474 Angel Clare.

FRANK GARI
1961 #36 *UTOPIA*
1961 #40 *LULLABY OF LOVE*

GALE GARNETT
1964 #1 *WE'LL SING IN THE SUNSHINE*
  (S) (2:56) RCA 8475 Nipper's Greatest Hits Of The 60's Volume 2.
1965 #36 *LOVIN' PLACE*

DAVID GATES
1973 #36 *CLOUDS*

MARVIN GAYE
1962 #36 *STUBBORN KIND OF FELLOW*
  (E) (2:47) Motown 5448 A Package Of 16 Big Hits.
  (S) (2:45) Motown 0791 and 6199 Anthology.
  (S) (2:43) Motown 6201 Compact Command Performances Volume 2.
  (M) (2:49) Motown 6311 The Marvin Gaye Collection.
  (S) (2:43) Motown 5218 That Stubborn Kind Of Fellow.
  (S) (2:46) Motown 5301 Super Hits.
  (E) (2:42) Motown 8057 and 8157 How Sweet It Is To Be Loved By
       You/That Stubborn Kind Of Fellow. (*truncated fade*)
  (S) (2:42) Ripete 392183 Ocean Drive.

MARVIN GAYE (Continued)
1963 #10 PRIDE AND JOY
    (S) (2:06) Rhino 70649 Billboard's Top R&B Hits Of 1963. *(45 version)*
    (S) (2:04) Motown 5448 A Package Of 16 Original Big Hits. *(45 version)*
    (S) (2:05) Motown 0791 and 6199 Anthology. *(45 version with first note truncated)*
    (M) (2:26) Motown 6201 Compact Command Performances Volume 2. *(LP version)*
    (M) (2:28) Motown 6311 The Marvin Gaye Collection. *(alternate take)*
    (S) (2:05) Motown 5218 That Stubborn Kind Of Fellow. *(45 version with first note truncated)*
    (S) (2:06) Motown 5301 Super Hits. *(45 version)*
    (E) (2:35) Motown 8057 and 8157 How Sweet It Is To Be Loved By You/That Stubborn Kind Of Fellow. *(LP version)*

1963 #18 CAN I GET A WITNESS
    (S) (2:48) Motown 6138 The Composer Series: Holland/Dozier/ Holland.
    (S) (2:46) Motown 5450 A Collection Of 16 Big Hits Volume 3.
    (S) (2:46) Motown 0791 and 6199 Anthology.
    (S) (2:47) Motown 6201 Compact Command Performances Volume 2.
    (M) (2:46) Motown 6311 The Marvin Gaye Collection.
    (S) (2:47) Motown 5191 Greatest Hits.
    (S) (2:49) Motown 5301 Super Hits.

1964 #18 YOU'RE A WONDERFUL ONE
    (S) (2:45) Motown 5450 A Collection Of 16 Big Hits Volume 3.
    (S) (2:46) Motown 0791 and 6199 Anthology.
    (S) (2:43) Motown 6201 Compact Command Performances Volume 2.
    (M) (2:45) Motown 6311 The Marvin Gaye Collection.
    (S) (2:44) Motown 5419 How Sweet It Is To Be Loved By You.
    (S) (2:43) Motown 5301 Super Hits.
    (S) (2:41) Motown 8057 and 8157 How Sweet It Is To Be Loved By You/That Stubborn Kind Of Fellow. *(badly distorted)*

1964 #19 TRY IT BABY
    (S) (2:57) Motown 5451 A Collection Of 16 Big Hits Volume 4. *(45 length)*
    (S) (2:45) Motown 0791 and 6199 Anthology. *(LP length)*
    (S) (2:46) Motown 6201 Compact Command Performances Volume 2. *(LP length)*
    (M) (2:58) Motown 6311 The Marvin Gaye Collection. *(45 length)*
    (S) (2:46) Motown 6255 A Musical Testament 1964 - 1984. *(LP length)*
    (S) (2:49) Motown 5419 How Sweet It Is To Be Loved By You. *(LP length)*
    (S) (2:57) Motown 5301 Super Hits. *(45 length)*
    (S) (2:50) Motown 8057 and 8157 How Sweet It Is To Be Loved By You/That Stubborn Kind Of Fellow. *(LP length)*

1964 #27 BABY DON'T YOU DO IT
    (S) (2:37) Motown 0791 and 6199 Anthology.
    (S) (2:37) Motown 6201 Compact Command Performances Volume 2.
    (S) (2:37) Motown 6255 A Musical Testament 1964 - 1984.
    (S) (2:37) Motown 5419 How Sweet It Is To Be Loved By You.
    (S) (2:33) Motown 5301 Super Hits.
    (S) (2:38) Motown 8057 and 8157 How Sweet It Is To Be Loved By You/That Stubborn Kind Of Fellow.

1965 #9 HOW SWEET IT IS TO BE LOVED BY YOU
    (S) (2:58) Motown 6138 The Composer Series: Holland/Dozier/ Holland.
    (S) (2:57) Motown 6137 20 Greatest Songs In Motown History.
    (S) (2:50) Motown 5452 A Collection Of 16 Big Hits Volume 5.
    (S) (2:57) Motown 6069 Compact Command Performances.
    (S) (2:54) Motown 0791 and 6199 Anthology.

MARVIN GAYE (Continued)

  (M) (2:55) Motown 6311 The Marvin Gaye Collection.
  (S) (2:57) Motown 5324 and 9035 Top Ten With A Bullet: Motown Love
       Songs.
  (S) (2:58) Motown 5359 and 9084 Motown Legends.
  (S) (2:57) Motown 5191 Greatest Hits.
  (S) (2:56) Motown 5419 How Sweet It Is To Be Loved By You.
  (S) (2:57) Motown 5343 Every Great Motown Song: The First 25 Years
       Volume 1. (*most selections on this cd have noise on the fade out*)
  (S) (2:57) Motown 8034 and 8134 Every Great Motown Song: The First 25
       Years Volumes 1 & 2. (*most selections on this cd have noise on the
       fade out*)
  (S) (2:50) Motown 5301 Super Hits. (*buzz noticeable on fadeout*)
  (S) (2:58) Motown 6058 Every Great Motown Hit.
  (S) (2:57) Motown 8057 and 8157 How Sweet It Is To Be Loved By
       You/That Stubborn Kind Of Fellow.
  (S) (2:56) Motown 6192 You Can't Hurry Love: All The Great Love Songs
       Of The Past 25 Years.

1965 #10 *I'LL BE DOGGONE*

  (S) (2:46) Rhino 70651 Billboard's Top R&B Hits Of 1965.
  (S) (2:46) Rhino 72006 Billboard's Top R&B Hits 1965-1969 Box Set.
  (S) (2:45) Motown 6159 The Good-Feeling Music Of The Big Chill
       Generation Volume 1.
  (S) (2:47) Motown 5452 A Collection Of 16 Big Hits Volume 5.
  (S) (2:43) Motown 5454 A Collection Of 16 Big Hits Volume 7.
  (S) (2:44) Motown 0791 and 6199 Anthology.
  (S) (2:44) Motown 6201 Compact Command Performances Volume 2.
  (M) (2:47) Motown 6311 The Marvin Gaye Collection.
  (S) (2:46) Motown 5296 Moods Of.
  (S) (2:45) Motown 5359 and 9084 Motown Legends.
  (S) (2:48) Motown 5301 Super Hits. (*buzz noticeable on fadeout*)
  (S) (2:44) Motown 8161 and 8061 Moods Of/That's The Way Love Is.

1965 #20 *PRETTY LITTLE BABY*

  (S) (2:35) Motown 0791 and 6199 Anthology.
  (S) (2:35) Motown 6201 Compact Command Performances Volume 2.

1965 #10 *AIN'T THAT PECULIAR*

  (S) (2:59) Rhino 70651 Billboard's Top R&B Hits Of 1965.
  (S) (2:59) Rhino 72006 Billboard's Top R&B Hits 1965-1969 Box Set.
  (S) (2:59) Motown 6159 The Good-Feeling Music Of The Big Chill
       Generation Volume 1.
  (S) (3:00) Motown 6139 The Composer Series: Smokey Robinson.
  (S) (2:57) Motown 5453 A Collection Of 16 Big Hits Volume 6.
  (S) (2:59) Motown 6069 Compact Command Performances.
  (S) (2:57) Motown 0791 and 6199 Anthology.
  (M) (2:56) Motown 6311 The Marvin Gaye Collection.
  (S) (2:59) Motown 5296 Moods Of.
  (S) (2:59) Motown 5359 and 9084 Motown Legends.
  (S) (2:58) Motown 5301 Super Hits.
  (S) (2:58) Motown 8161 and 8061 Moods Of/That's The Way Love Is.
  (S) (2:59) Motown 5311 Great Songs And Performances That Inspired The
       Motown 25th Anniversary TV Special.
  (S) (2:58) Motown 9071 Motown Dance Party Volume 1. (*all selections on
       this cd are segued together*)

MARVIN GAYE (Continued)

1966 #23 ONE MORE HEARTACHE
- (S) (2:39) Motown 0791 and 6199 Anthology.
- (S) (2:39) Motown 6201 Compact Command Performances Volume 2.
- (S) (2:39) Motown 5296 Moods Of.
- (S) (2:39) Motown 5359 and 9084 Motown Legends.
- (S) (2:39) Motown 8161 and 8061 Moods Of/That's The Way Love Is.

1966 #32 TAKE THIS HEART OF MINE
- (S) (2:45) Motown 0791 and 6199 Anthology.
- (S) (2:45) Motown 6201 Compact Command Performances Volume 2.
- (S) (2:46) Motown 5296 Moods Of.
- (S) (2:46) Motown 5359 and 9084 Motown Legends.
- (S) (2:45) Motown 8161 and 8061 Moods Of/That's The Way Love Is.

1967 #34 YOUR UNCHANGING LOVE
- (S) (3:17) Motown 5455 A Collection Of 16 Big Hits Volume 8. *(45 length)*
- (S) (3:09) Motown 0791 and 6199 Anthology. *(LP length)*
- (S) (3:09) Motown 6201 Compact Command Performances Volume 2. *(LP length)*
- (S) (3:10) Motown 5296 Moods Of. *(LP length)*
- (S) (3:11) Motown 5359 and 9084 Motown Legends. *(LP length)*
- (S) (3:10) Motown 8161 and 8061 Moods Of/That's The Way Love Is. *(LP length)*

1968 #30 YOU
- (S) (2:23) Motown 5457 A Collection Of 16 Big Hits Volume 10.
- (S) (2:24) Motown 0791 and 6199 Anthology.
- (S) (2:24) Motown 6201 Compact Command Performances Volume 2.
- (S) (2:24) Motown 5395 I Heard It Through The Grapevine.
- (S) (2:25) Motown 5301 Super Hits. *(truncated fade)*
- (S) (2:25) Motown 8010 and 8110 I Heard It Through The Grapevine/I Want You.

1968 #34 CHAINED
- (S) (2:37) Motown 0791 and 6199 Anthology.
- (S) (2:37) Motown 6201 Compact Command Performances Volume 2.
- (S) (2:37) Motown 5395 I Heard It Through The Grapevine.
- (S) (2:37) Motown 5301 Super Hits.
- (S) (2:37) Motown 8010 and 8110 I Heard It Through The Grapevine/I Want You.

1968 #1 I HEARD IT THROUGH THE GRAPEVINE
- (S) (3:14) Rhino 70629 Billboard's Top Rock & Roll Hits Of 1968.
- (S) (3:14) Rhino 72005 Billboard's Top Rock & Roll Hits 1968-1972 Box Set.
- (S) (3:15) Motown 6132 25 #1 Hits From 25 Years.
- (S) (3:15) Motown 6161 The Good-Feeling Music Of The Big Chill Generation Volume 3.
- (S) (3:14) Motown 6137 20 Greatest Songs In Motown History.
- (S) (5:01) Motown 6120 Music from O.S.T. Big Chill. *(this extended version made its debut on this cd)*
- (S) (3:14) Motown 6069 Compact Command Performances.
- (S) (3:14) Motown 0791 and 6199 Anthology.
- (M) (3:12) Motown 6311 The Marvin Gaye Collection.
- (S) (3:14) Motown 9097 The Most Played Oldies On America's Jukeboxes.
- (S) (3:14) Motown 5395 I Heard It Through The Grapevine.
- (S) (3:14) Motown 6255 A Musical Testament 1964 - 1984.
- (S) (3:14) Motown 5191 Greatest Hits.
- (S) (3:14) Motown 9098 Radio's #1 Hits.

MARVIN GAYE (Continued)

(S) (3:14) Motown 5301 Super Hits.
(S) (3:14) Motown 6058 Every Great Motown Hit.
(S) (3:13) Motown 8010 and 8110 I Heard It Through The Grapevine/I Want You.
(S) (3:15) Motown 9060 Motown's Biggest Pop Hits.
(S) (3:14) Motown 5311 Great Songs And Performances That Inspired The Motown 25th Anniversary TV Special.
(S) (3:13) Motown 9071 Motown Dance Party Volume 1. *(all selections on this cd are segued together)*
(S) (3:13) Ripete 392183 Ocean Drive.

1969 #5 *TOO BUSY THINKING ABOUT MY BABY*

(S) (2:56) Motown 6161 The Good-Feeling Music Of The Big Chill Generation Volume 3.
(S) (2:56) Rhino 70655 Billboard's Top R&B Hits Of 1969.
(S) (2:56) Rhino 72006 Billboard's Top R&B Hits 1965-1969 Box Set.
(S) (2:56) Motown 6069 Compact Command Performances.
(S) (2:55) Motown 0791 and 6199 Anthology.
(M) (2:53) Motown 6311 The Marvin Gaye Collection.
(S) (2:56) Motown 5359 and 9084 Motown Legends.
(S) (2:55) Motown 5125 M.P.G.
(S) (2:54) Motown 5301 Super Hits.
(S) (2:55) Motown 6058 Every Great Motown Hit.
(S) (2:55) Motown 5311 Great Songs And Performances That Inspired The Motown 25th Anniversary TV Special.

1969 #10 *THAT'S THE WAY LOVE IS*

(E) (3:35) Motown 6069 Compact Command Performances.
(E) (3:41) Motown 0791 and 6199 Anthology.
(M) (3:38) Motown 6311 The Marvin Gaye Collection.
(E) (3:41) Motown 6255 A Musical Testament 1964 - 1984.
(E) (3:41) Motown 5125 M.P.G.
(E) (3:32) Motown 5422 That's The Way Love Is.
(E) (3:36) Motown 5301 Super Hits.
(E) (3:35) Motown 6058 Every Great Motown Hit.
(E) (3:32) Motown 8161 and 8061 Moods Of/That's The Way Love Is.

1970 #27 *HOW CAN I FORGET*

(S) (1:55) Motown 0791 and 6199 Anthology.
(S) (1:55) Motown 6201 Compact Command Performances Volume 2.
(S) (1:57) Motown 5422 That's The Way Love Is.
(S) (1:57) Motown 8161 and 8061 Moods Of/That's The Way Love Is.

1970 #28 *THE END OF OUR ROAD*

(S) (2:48) Motown 0791 and 6199 Anthology.
(S) (2:48) Motown 6201 Compact Command Performances Volume 2.
(S) (2:44) Motown 6255 A Musical Testament 1964 - 1984.
(S) (2:44) Motown 5125 M.P.G.
(S) (2:50) Motown 5301 Super Hits.

1971 #1 *WHAT'S GOING ON*

(S) (3:52) Motown 6132 25 #1 Hits From 25 Years. *(LP version)*
(S) (3:51) Motown 6120 O.S.T. Big Chill. *(LP version)*
(S) (3:52) Rhino 70659 Billboard's Top R&B Hits Of 1971. *(LP version)*
(S) (3:51) Motown 6069 Compact Command Performances. *(LP version)*
(S) (3:48) Motown 0791 and 6199 Anthology. *(LP version)*
(S) (3:50) Motown 6311 The Marvin Gaye Collection. *(LP version)*
(S) (3:52) Motown 5339 What's Going On. *(all selections on this cd are segued together; LP version)*

MARVIN GAYE (Continued)

    (S) (3:51) Motown 5191 Greatest Hits. *(LP version)*
    (S) (3:49) Motown 6094 More Songs From The Original Soundtrack Of The "Big Chill". *(LP version)*
    (S) (3:51) Motown 6058 Every Great Motown Hit. *(LP version)*
    (S) (3:50) Motown 0937 20/20 Twenty No. 1 Hits From Twenty Years At Motown. *(LP version)*
    (S) (3:49) Motown 5311 Great Songs And Performances That Inspired The Motown 25th Anniversary TV Special. *(LP version)*

1971 #4 MERCY MERCY ME (THE ECOLOGY)

    (S) (3:12) Motown 6069 Compact Command Performances.
    (S) (3:11) Motown 0791 and 6199 Anthology.
    (S) (3:12) Motown 6311 The Marvin Gaye Collection.
    (S) (3:12) MCA 10063 Original Television Soundtrack "The Sounds Of Murphy Brown".
    (S) (3:12) Motown 5339 What's Going On. *(all selections on this cd are segued together)*
    (S) (3:12) Motown 5191 Greatest Hits.
    (S) (3:12) Motown 6058 Every Great Motown Hit.
    (S) (3:12) Motown 5311 Great Songs And Performances That Inspired The Motown 25th Anniversary TV Special.

1971 #6 INNER CITY BLUES (MAKE ME WANNA HOLLER)

    (S) (3:05) Motown 6069 Compact Command Performances.
    (S) (3:01) Motown 0791 and 6199 Anthology.
    (S) (3:04) Motown 6311 The Marvin Gaye Collection.
    (S) (5:25) Motown 5339 What's Going On. *(all selections on this cd are segued together; LP version)*
    (S) (3:05) Motown 6058 Every Great Motown Hit.
    (S) (3:04) Motown 5311 Great Songs And Performances That Inspired The Motown 25th Anniversary TV Special.

1973 #8 TROUBLE MAN

    (S) (3:49) Motown 9104 Motown Memories Volume 1.
    (S) (3:48) Motown 6069 Compact Command Performances.
    (S) (3:45) Motown 0791 and 6199 Anthology.
    (S) (3:48) Motown 6311 The Marvin Gaye Collection.
    (S) (3:48) Motown 5191 Greatest Hits.
    (S) (3:48) Motown 6058 Every Great Motown Hit.
    (S) (3:49) Motown 5241 O.S.T. Trouble Man. *(previous and following tracks are segued together)*

1973 #1 LET'S GET IT ON

    (S) (4:00) Rhino 70634 Billboard's Top Rock & Roll Hits Of 1973.
    (S) (4:01) Motown 6132 25 #1 Hits From 25 Years.
    (S) (3:59) Epic 46940 O.S.T. Queenslogic
    (S) (3:59) Priority 7909 Vietnam: Rockin' The Delta.
    (S) (4:01) Motown 6069 Compact Command Performances.
    (S) (3:56) Motown 0791 and 6199 Anthology.
    (S) (4:00) Motown 6311 The Marvin Gaye Collection.
    (S) (3:59) Motown 5191 Greatest Hits.
    (S) (4:00) Motown 6058 Every Great Motown Hit.
    (S) (4:51) Motown 5192 Let's Get It On. *(LP version)*
    (S) (4:00) Motown 9060 Motown's Biggest Pop Hits.
    (S) (4:00) Motown 0937 20/20 Twenty No. 1 Hits From Twenty Years At Motown.
    (S) (3:59) Motown 5311 Great Songs And Performances That Inspired The Motown 25th Anniversary TV Special.

MARVIN GAYE (Continued)

1973 #18 *COME GET TO THIS*
 (S) (2:39) Motown 0791 and 6199 Anthology.
 (S) (2:39) Motown 6201 Compact Command Performances Volume 2.
 (S) (2:40) Motown 5192 Let's Get It On.
 (S) (2:39) Ripete 392183 Ocean Drive.

MARVIN GAYE & DIANA ROSS

1973 #14 *YOU'RE A SPECIAL PART OF ME*
 (S) (3:36) Motown 9109 Motown Memories Volume 3.
 (S) (3:37) Motown 6153 and 9053 Marvin Gaye & His Women.
 (S) (4:36) Motown 6311 The Marvin Gaye Collection. *(previously unreleased extended version)*
 (S) (3:36) Motown 6197 and 6049 Diana Ross Anthology.
 (S) (3:36) Motown 9090 and 5124 Diana & Marvin.

MARVIN GAYE & TAMMI TERRELL

1967 #22 *AIN'T NO MOUNTAIN HIGH ENOUGH*
 (S) (2:26) Motown 6137 20 Greatest Songs In Motown History.
 (S) (2:25) Motown 5456 A Collection Of 16 Big Hits Volume 9.
 (S) (2:27) Motown 6110 Motown Grammy R&B Performances Of The 60's & 70's.
 (S) (2:24) Motown 0791 and 6199 Marvin Gaye Anthology.
 (S) (2:26) Motown 6153 and 9053 Marvin Gaye & His Women.
 (M) (2:25) Motown 6311 The Marvin Gaye Collection.
 (S) (2:27) Motown 9009 and 5200 United.
 (S) (2:27) Motown 8047 and 8147 You're All I Need/United.
 (S) (2:27) Motown 5225 Greatest Hits.

1967 #6 *YOUR PRECIOUS LOVE*
 (S) (3:01) Rhino 70653 Billboard's Top R&B Hits Of 1967.
 (S) (3:01) Rhino 72006 Billboard's Top R&B Hits 1965-1969 Box Set.
 (S) (3:00) Motown 5456 A Collection Of 16 Big Hits Volume 9.
 (S) (3:02) Motown 6140 The Composer Series: Ashford & Simpson.
 (S) (3:01) Motown 6160 The Good-Feeling Music Of The Big Chill Generation Volume 2.
 (S) (3:01) Motown 6069 Compact Command Performances.
 (S) (2:59) Motown 0791 and 6199 Marvin Gaye Anthology.
 (S) (3:01) Motown 6153 and 9053 Marvin Gaye & His Women.
 (M) (2:58) Motown 6311 The Marvin Gaye Collection.
 (S) (3:01) Motown 5324 and 9035 Top Ten With A Bullet: Motown Love Songs.
 (S) (3:02) Motown 9009 and 5200 United.
 (S) (2:58) Motown 6058 Every Great Motown Hit.
 (S) (2:58) Motown 5246 Marvin Gaye And His Girls.
 (S) (3:02) Motown 8047 and 8147 You're All I Need/United.
 (S) (3:02) Motown 5225 Greatest Hits.

1968 #18 *IF I COULD BUILD MY WHOLE WORLD AROUND YOU*
 (S) (2:17) Motown 5457 A Collection Of 16 Big Hits Volume 10.
 (S) (2:18) Motown 0791 and 6199 Marvin Gaye Anthology.
 (S) (2:19) Motown 6153 and 9053 Marvin Gaye & His Women.
 (M) (2:20) Motown 6311 The Marvin Gaye Collection.
 (S) (2:20) Motown 9009 and 5200 United.
 (S) (2:19) Motown 6058 Every Great Motown Hit.
 (S) (2:20) Motown 8047 and 8147 You're All I Need/United.
 (S) (2:20) Motown 5225 Greatest Hits.

MARVIN GAYE & TAMMI TERRELL (Continued)
1968 #9 AIN'T NOTHING LIKE THE REAL THING
- (S) (2:13) Motown 6160 The Good-Time Feeling Of The Big Chill Generation Volume 2.
- (S) (2:13) Motown 6140 The Composer Series: Ashford & Simpson.
- (S) (2:12) Motown 0791 and 6199 Marvin Gaye Anthology.
- (S) (2:13) Motown 6153 and 9053 Marvin Gaye & His Women.
- (M) (2:15) Motown 6311 The Marvin Gaye Collection.
- (S) (2:13) Motown 5142 You're All I Need.
- (S) (2:13) Motown 6058 Every Great Motown Hit.
- (S) (2:13) Motown 8047 and 8147 You're All I Need/United.
- (S) (2:13) Motown 5225 Greatest Hits.

1968 #7 YOU'RE ALL I NEED TO GET BY
- (S) (2:47) Motown 6161 The Good-Time Feeling Of The Big Chill Generation Volume 3. *(LP length)*
- (S) (2:47) Motown 6177 Endless Love. *(LP length)*
- (S) (2:48) Motown 6140 The Composer Series: Ashford & Simpson. *(LP length)*
- (S) (2:46) SBK 93744 China Beach - Music & Memories. *(LP length)*
- (S) (2:48) Rhino 70654 Billboard's Top R&B Hits Of 1968. *(LP length)*
- (S) (2:48) Rhino 72006 Billboard's Top R&B Hits 1965-1969 Box Set. *(LP length)*
- (S) (2:47) Motown 6069 Compact Command Performances. *(LP length)*
- (S) (2:48) Motown 0791 and 6199 Marvin Gaye Anthology. *(LP length)*
- (S) (2:47) Motown 6153 and 9053 Marvin Gaye & His Women. *(LP length)*
- (M) (2:39) Motown 6311 The Marvin Gaye Collection. *(45 length)*
- (S) (2:48) Motown 5142 You're All I Need. *(LP length)*
- (S) (2:47) Motown 6058 Every Great Motown Hit. *(LP length)*
- (S) (2:48) Motown 8047 and 8147 You're All I Need/United. *(LP length)*
- (S) (2:47) Motown 5225 Greatest Hits. *(LP length)*

1968 #25 KEEP ON LOVIN' ME HONEY
- (S) (2:29) Motown 6153 and 9053 Marvin Gaye & His Women.
- (S) (2:29) Motown 5142 You're All I Need.
- (S) (2:29) Motown 8047 and 8147 You're All I Need/United.
- (S) (2:29) Motown 5225 Greatest Hits.

MARVIN GAYE & MARY WELLS
1964 #27 ONCE UPON A TIME
- (S) (2:29) Motown 0791 and 6199 Marvin Gaye Anthology.
- (S) (2:29) Motown 6153 and 9053 Marvin Gaye & His Women.
- (M) (2:29) Motown 6311 The Marvin Gaye Collection.
- (S) (2:27) Motown 5451 A Collection Of 16 Big Hits Volume 4.
- (S) (2:30) Motown 5246 Marvin Gaye And His Girls.
- (S) (2:28) Motown 5260 Marvin Gaye & Mary Wells Together.

1964 #25 WHAT'S THE MATTER WITH YOU BABY
- (S) (2:21) Motown 5451 A Collection Of 16 Big Hits Volume 4.
- (S) (2:25) Motown 0791 and 6199 Marvin Gaye Anthology.
- (S) (2:26) Motown 6153 and 9053 Marvin Gaye & His Women.
- (M) (2:21) Motown 6311 The Marvin Gaye Collection.
- (S) (2:24) Motown 5246 Marvin Gaye And His Girls.
- (S) (2:21) Motown 5260 Marvin Gaye & Mary Wells Together.

G-CLEFS
1956 #17 KA-DING DONG
1961 #16 I UNDERSTAND (JUST HOW YOU FEEL)

J. GEILS BAND
1972 #37 *LOOKING FOR A LOVE*
    (S) (3:45) Warner Special Products 27614 Highs Of The Seventies. (*LP version*)
    (S) (3:42) JCI 3301 Rockin' 70's. (*LP version*)
    (S) (3:45) Atlantic 8297 The Morning After. (*LP version*)
    (S) (5:01) Atlantic 19234 Best Of. (*live*)
1973 #15 *GIVE IT TO ME*
(45's were pressed in lengths of (3:07) and (6:28) even though the labels always stated (3:07))
    (S) (6:28) Atlantic 81908 Classic Rock 1966-1988.
    (S) (6:28) Atlantic 7260 Bloodshot.
    (S) (6:26) Atlantic 19234 Best Of.
    (S) (6:27) Atlantic 82306 Atlantic Rock & Roll Box Set.

GENE & DEBBE
1968 #14 *PLAYBOY*

GENIES
1959 #33 *WHO'S THAT KNOCKING*

BOBBIE GENTRY
1967 #1 *ODE TO BILLY JOE*
    (S) (4:13) Curb 77355 60's Hits Volume 1.
    (S) (4:13) Curb 77343 60's Hits - Country Volume 1.
    (S) (4:12) Curb 77387 Greatest Hits.
    (S) (4:12) Capitol 95848 All Time Country Classics.
    (S) (4:13) Capitol 91628 Greatest.
    (S) (4:12) Capitol 98665 When AM Was King.
1970 #31 *FANCY*
    (S) (4:14) Capitol 95848 All Time Country Classics. (*LP version*)
    (E) (4:03) Curb 77387 Greatest Hits. (*45 version*)

BOBBIE GENTRY & GLEN CAMPBELL
1970 #13 *ALL I HAVE TO DO IS DREAM*
    (S) (2:33) Capitol 46483 Very Best Of Glen Campbell.

GENTRYS
1965 #5 *KEEP ON DANCING*
    (M) (2:08) K-Tel 713 Battle Of The Bands.
    (M) (2:09) Warner Special Projects 27610 More Party Classics.
    (M) (2:09) Rhino 75778 Frat Rock.
    (M) (2:09) Mercury 816555 45's On CD Volume 2.
1966 #37 *SPREAD IT ON THICK*
    (M) (2:23) K-Tel 839 Battle Of The Bands Volume 2.

BARBARA GEORGE
1962 #3 *I KNOW (YOU DON'T LOVE ME NO MORE)*
    (M) (2:22) Rhino 75766 Best Of New Orleans Rhythm & Blues Volume 2.
    (M) (2:22) Rhino 70648 Billboard's Top R&B Hits Of 1962.

GERRY & THE PACEMAKERS
1964 #6 *DON'T LET THE SUN CATCH YOU CRYING*
    (S) (2:34) Rhino 70319 History Of British Rock Volume 1.
    (S) (2:34) Rhino 72022 History Of British Rock Box Set.
    (S) (2:34) Rhino 72008 History Of British Rock Volumes 1-4 Box Set.
    (S) (2:34) EMI 46583 Great Hits.
    (S) (2:34) EMI 96093 Best Of.

1964 #10 *HOW DO YOU DO IT?*
    (S) (1:53) Rhino 70319 History Of British Rock Volume 1.
    (S) (1:53) Rhino 72022 History Of British Rock Box Set.
    (S) (1:53) Rhino 72008 History Of British Rock Volumes 1-4 Box Set.
    (M) (1:52) Atlantic 81905 O.S.T. Buster.
    (S) (1:53) EMI 46583 Great Hits.
    (S) (1:53) EMI 96093 Best Of.

1964 #23 *I LIKE IT*
    (M) (2:13) Rhino 70320 History Of British Rock Volume 2.
    (M) (2:13) Rhino 72022 History Of British Rock Box Set.
    (M) (2:13) Rhino 72008 History Of British Rock Volumes 1-4 Box.
    (M) (2:12) EMI 46583 Great Hits.
    (S) (2:44) EMI 96093 Best Of. *(includes :31 false start)*

1965 #19 *I'LL BE THERE*
    (S) (3:12) Rhino 70320 History Of British Rock Volume 2. *(alternate take)*
    (S) (3:12) Rhino 72022 History Of British Rock Box Set. *(alternate take)*
    (S) (3:12) Rhino 72008 History Of British Rock Volumes 1-4 Box Set.
          (alternate take)
    (S) (3:09) EMI 46583 Great Hits. *(alternate take)*
    (S) (3:12) EMI 96093 Best Of. *(alternate take)*

1965 #4 *FERRY ACROSS THE MERSEY*
    (S) (2:22) Rhino 70322 History Of British Rock Volume 4.
    (S) (2:22) Rhino 72022 History Of British Rock Box Set.
    (S) (2:22) Rhino 72008 History Of British Rock Volumes 1-4 Set.
    (S) (2:22) EMI 46583 Great Hits.
    (S) (2:22) EMI 96093 Best Of.

1965 #20 *IT'S GONNA BE ALRIGHT*
    (S) (2:09) Rhino 70321 History Of British Rock Volume 3.
    (S) (2:09) Rhino 72022 History Of British Rock Box Set.
    (S) (2:09) Rhino 72008 History Of British Rock Volumes 1-4 Box Set.
    (S) (2:08) EMI 46583 Great Hits.
    (S) (2:23) EMI 96093 Best Of. *(neither the 45 or LP version)*

STAN GETZ & CHARLIE BYRD
1962 #11 *DESAFINADO*
    (S) (5:48) Verve 810061 Jazz Samba. *(LP version)*
    (S) (5:49) Verve 823611 The Girl From Ipanema/The Bossa Nova Years.
          (LP version)
    (S) (4:00) Verve 833289 Best Of Bossa Nova. *(rerecording)*
    (S) (5:48) Verve 831368 Stan Getz: Compact Jazz. *(LP version)*

STAN GETZ & ASTRUD GILBERTO
1964 #5 *THE GIRL FROM IPANEMA*
    (S) (2:45) Rhino 70995 One Hit Wonders Of The 60's Volume 1. *(45 version)*
    (S) (5:12) Verve 810048 Stan Getz/Joao Gilberto. *(LP version)*
    (S) (5:21) Verve 823611 The Girl From Ipanema/The Bossa Nova Years. *(LP version)*
    (S) (2:52) Sony Music Special Products 52420 Get Yourself A College Girl. *(rerecording)*
    (S) (6:35) Verve 831368 Stan Getz: Compact Jazz. *(live)*
    (S) (5:12) Verve 831369 Astrud Gilberto: Compact Jazz. *(LP version)*

GEORGIA GIBBS
1955 #2 *TWEEDLE DEE*
1955 #3 *DANCE WITH ME HENRY (WALLFLOWER)*
1956 #30 *HAPPINESS STREET*
1956 #36 *TRA LA LA*
1958 #37 *THE HOOLA HOOP SONG*

DON GIBSON
1958 #10 *OH LONESOME ME*
    (M) (2:28) RCA 8466 Nipper's Greatest Hits Of The 50's Volume 1.
    (E) (2:29) RCA 2295 All Time Greatest Hits.
    (S) (2:34) Curb 77440 Best Of Volume 1. *(rerecording)*
    (S) (2:34) Curb 77474 18 Greatest Hits. *(rerecording)*
1958 #38 *BLUE BLUE DAY*
    (E) (1:52) RCA 2295 All Time Greatest Hits.
    (S) (1:56) Curb 77440 Best Of Volume 1. *(rerecording)*
    (S) (1:56) Curb 77474 18 Greatest Hits. *(rerecording)*
1960 #33 *JUST ONE TIME*
    (S) (2:42) RCA 2295 All Time Greatest Hits.
    (S) (2:18) Curb 77474 18 Greatest Hits. *(rerecording)*
1961 #20 *SEA OF HEARTBREAK*
    (S) (2:31) RCA 2295 All Time Greatest Hits.
    (S) (2:15) Curb 77474 18 Greatest Hits. *(rerecording)*

GINNY GIBSON
1956 #37 *MIRACLE OF LOVE*

TERRY GILKYSON & THE EASY RIDERS
1957 #2 *MARIANNE*
    (M) (2:22) Columbia 45111 16 Most Requested Songs Of The 50's
        Volume 2.
    (M) (2:22) Columbia 45017 Radio Classics Of The 50's.

JIMMY GILMER & THE FIREBALLS
1963 #1 *SUGAR SHACK*
    (S) (1:59) Rhino 70624 Billboard's Top Rock & Roll Hits Of 1963.
    (S) (1:59) Rhino 72007 Billboard's Top Rock & Roll Hits 1962-1966 Box
        Set.
1964 #15 *DAISY PETAL PICKIN'*

JAMES GILREATH
1963 #28 *LITTLE BAND OF GOLD*

GINO & GINA
1958 #28 *(IT'S BEEN A LONG TIME) PRETTY BABY*

GIORGIO
1972 #34 *SON OF MY FATHER*
    (S) (3:42) Rhino 70927 Super Hits Of The 70's Volume 7.

CAESAR GIOVANNINI
1956 #29 *PETTICOATS OF PORTUGAL*

GLADSTONE
1972 #38 *A PIECE OF PAPER*

WILL GLAHE
1958 #11 *LIECHTENSTEINER POLKA*

GLASS BOTTLE
1971 #26 *I AIN'T GOT TIME ANYMORE*
>   (S)   (2:25) Rhino 70924   Super Hits Of The 70's Volume 4.
>   (S)   (2:25) Rhino 72009   Super Hits Of The 70's Volumes 1-4 Box Set.

TOM GLAZER & THE DO-RE-MI CHILDREN'S CHORUS
1963 #16 *ON TOP OF SPAGHETTI*

GLENCOVES
1963 #39 *HOOTENANNY*

GARY GLITTER
1972 #3 *ROCK AND ROLL (PART 2)*
>   (S)   (2:55) Rhino 70929   Super Hits Of The 70's Volume 9. *(LP length)*
>   (S)   (2:59) Dunhill Compact Classics 043   Toga Rock II. *(LP length)*
>   (S)   (3:01) Rhino 70729   Greatest Hits. *(LP length)*

1972 #30 *I DIDN'T KNOW I LOVED YOU (TILL I SAW YOU ROCK AND ROLL)*
>   (S)   (3:23) Rhino 70729   Greatest Hits.

GODSPELL
1972 #9 *DAY BY DAY*
>   (S)   (3:14) Rhino 70928   Super Hits Of The 70's Volume 8.
>   (S)   (3:13) Arista 8304   A Musical Based On The Gospel According To St. Matthew.

BOBBY GOLDSBORO
1964 #10 *SEE THE FUNNY LITTLE CLOWN*
>   (S)   (2:34) Curb 77327   All Time Greatest Hits.
>   (S)   (2:35) EMI 48055   Greatest Hits.
>   (S)   (2:35) EMI 96094   Best Of Bobby Goldsboro/Honey.

1965 #12 *LITTLE THINGS*
>   (S)   (2:24) Novus 3077   O.S.T. Drugstore Cowboy.
>   (S)   (2:24) Curb 77327   All Time Greatest Hits.
>   (S)   (2:24) EMI 96094   Best Of Bobby Goldsboro/Honey.

1965 #27 *VOODOO WOMAN*
>   (S)   (2:19) EMI 96094   Best Of Bobby Goldsboro/Honey.

1966 #28 *IT'S TOO LATE*
>   (S)   (2:27) Curb 77327   All Time Greatest Hits.
>   (S)   (2:28) EMI 48055   Greatest Hits.
>   (S)   (2:32) EMI 96094   Best Of Bobby Goldsboro/Honey.

1967 #37 *BLUE AUTUMN*
>   (S)   (3:05) EMI 48055   Greatest Hits. *(rerecording)*
>   (S)   (2:27) EMI 96094   Best Of Bobby Goldsboro/Honey.

1968 #1 *HONEY*
>   (S)   (3:58) EMI 96268   24 Greatest Hits Of All Time.
>   (S)   (3:58) Curb 77343   60's Hits - Country Volume 1.
>   (S)   (3:57) Curb 77327   All Time Greatest Hits.
>   (S)   (3:58) EMI 48055   Greatest Hits.
>   (S)   (3:56) EMI 96094   Best Of Bobby Goldsboro/Honey.

1968 #14 *AUTUMN OF MY LIFE*
>   (S)   (3:26) Curb 77327   All Time Greatest Hits.
>   (S)   (3:25) EMI 48055   Greatest Hits.
>   (S)   (3:24) EMI 96094   Best Of Bobby Goldsboro/Honey.

1968 #29 *THE STRAIGHT LIFE*
>   (S)   (2:38) Curb 77327   All Time Greatest Hits.
>   (S)   (2:37) EMI 96094   Best Of Bobby Goldsboro/Honey.

1971 #8 *WATCHING SCOTTY GROW*
>   (S)   (2:33) Curb 77327   All Time Greatest Hits.
>   (S)   (2:33) EMI 96094   Best Of Bobby Goldsboro/Honey.

BOBBY GOLDSBORO (Continued)

1973 #17 *SUMMER (THE FIRST TIME)*
       (S) (4:36) Curb 77327 All Time Greatest Hits.
       (S) (4:38) EMI 96094 Best Of Bobby Goldsboro/Honey.

DICKIE GOODMAN

1961 #32 *THE TOUCHABLES*

GOODTIMERS (see DON COVAY & THE GOODTIMERS)

RON GOODWIN ORCHESTRA

1957 #30 *SWINGING SWEETHEARTS*

LESLEY GORE

1963 #1 *IT'S MY PARTY*
       (S) (2:19) Rhino 70624 Billboard's Top Rock & Roll Hits Of 1963.
       (S) (2:19) Rhino 72007 Billboard's Top Rock & Roll Hits 1962-1966 Box Set.
       (S) (2:19) Geffen 24310 O.S.T. Mermaids.
       (S) (2:19) Mercury 826448 Oldies Golden Million Sellers.
       (S) (2:14) Mercury 810370 Golden Hits Of. *(:05 shorter than 45 and LP)*
       (S) (2:09) MCA 6171 Good Time Rock 'N' Roll. *(all selections on this cd are recorded live)*
       (S) (2:14) Special Music 836688 It's My Party. *(:05 shorter than 45 and LP)*

1963 #4 *JUDY'S TURN TO CRY*
       (S) (2:10) Mercury 810370 Golden Hits Of.

1963 #6 *SHE'S A FOOL*
       (S) (2:10) Mercury 810370 Golden Hits Of.

1964 #2 *YOU DON'T OWN ME*
       (S) (2:30) Mercury 826448 Oldies Golden Million Sellers.
       (S) (2:28) Mercury 810370 Golden Hits Of.
       (S) (2:08) MCA 6171 Good Time Rock 'N' Roll. *(all selections on this cd are recorded live)*
       (S) (2:28) Special Music 836688 It's My Party.

1964 #14 *THAT'S THE WAY BOYS ARE*
       (S) (2:13) Mercury 810370 Golden Hits Of.
       (S) (2:13) Special Music 836688 It's My Party.

1964 #10 *MAYBE I KNOW*
       (S) (2:35) Mercury 810370 Golden Hits Of.
       (S) (2:35) Special Music 836688 It's My Party.

1965 #20 *LOOK OF LOVE*
       (S) (2:07) Mercury 810370 Golden Hits Of. *(LP version)*
       (S) (2:07) Special Music 836688 It's My Party. *(LP version)*

1965 #19 *SUNSHINE, LOLLIPOPS AND RAINBOWS*
       (S) (1:36) Mercury 810370 Golden Hits Of.

1965 #39 *MY TOWN, MY GUY AND ME*
       (S) (2:25) Mercury 810370 Golden Hits Of.

1967 #11 *CALIFORNIA NIGHTS*
       (S) (2:45) Rhino 70087 Summer & Sun.
       (S) (2:45) Mercury 810370 Golden Hits Of.
       (S) (2:46) Special Music 836688 It's My Party.

EYDIE GORME

1956 #31 *MAMA, TEACH ME TO DANCE*

1957 #29 *LOVE ME FOREVER*

1958 #21 *YOU NEED HANDS*
       (E) (2:26) Curb 77413 Best Of. *(faster than original recording)*

1963 #6 *BLAME IT ON THE BOSSA NOVA*

EYDIE GORME & STEVE LAWRENCE
released as by **STEVE & EYDIE:**
1963 #28 *I WANT TO STAY HERE*
ROBERT GOULET
1965 #15 *MY LOVE, FORGIVE ME (AMORE, SCUSAMI)*
        (S) (2:45) Columbia 9815 Greatest Hits.
        (S) (2:46) Columbia 44402 16 Most Requested Songs.
CHARLIE GRACIE
1957 #3 *BUTTERFLY*
1957 #14 *FABULOUS*
BILLY GRAMMER
1959 #6 *GOTTA TRAVEL ON*
GERRY GRANAHAN
1958 #14 *NO CHEMISE, PLEASE*
ROCCO GRANATA & THE INTERNATIONAL QUINTET
1959 #12 *MARINA*
GRAND FUNK RAILROAD
1970 #27 *CLOSER TO HOME*
      (the LP title of this song was "I'M YOUR CAPTAIN")
        (S) (10:08) Capitol 90608 Capitol Collector's Series. *(includes :16 studio talk; LP version)*
        (S) (9:54) Capitol 48429 Closer To Home. *(LP version)*
1972 #40 *FOOTSTOMPIN' MUSIC*
        (S) (3:45) Sandstone 33004 Reelin' In The Years Volume 5.
        (S) (3:44) Capitol 90608 Capitol Collector's Series.
        (S) (3:44) Capitol 98138 Spring Break Volume 1.
        (S) (3:46) Pair 1178 Great!
1972 #24 *ROCK 'N ROLL SOUL*
        (S) (3:24) Capitol 90608 Capitol Collector's Series.
        (S) (3:28) Capitol 46623 Grand Funk Hits.
released as by **GRAND FUNK:**
1973 #1 *WE'RE AN AMERICAN BAND*
        (S) (3:24) Rhino 70799 O.S.T. Spirit Of '76.
        (S) (3:24) JCI 3302 Electric Seventies.
        (S) (3:24) Sandstone 33001 Reelin' In The Years Volume 2.
        (S) (3:24) Capitol 90608 Capitol Collector's Series.
        (S) (3:24) Capitol 46623 Grand Funk Hits.
        (S) (3:23) Rhino 70519 Todd Rundgren: An Elpees Worth Of Productions.
        (S) (3:25) Capitol 98665 When AM Was King.
EARL GRANT
1958 #10 *THE END*
GOGI GRANT
1955 #8 *SUDDENLY THERE'S A VALLEY*
1956 #1 *THE WAYWARD WIND*
JANIE GRANT
1961 #23 *TRIANGLE*
GRASS ROOTS
1966 #33 *WHERE WERE YOU WHEN I NEEDED YOU*
        (S) (2:57) MCA 5938 Vintage Music Volumes 15 & 16. *(alternate take from the "Let's Live For Today" vinyl LP)*

GRASS ROOTS (Continued)

    (S) (2:57) MCA 31212 Vintage Music Volume 15. (*alternate take from the* "*Let's Live For Today*" *vinyl LP*)

    (S) (2:58) MCA 31132 Greatest Hits Volume 1. (*alternate take from the* "*Let's Live For Today*" *vinyl LP*)

    (S) (2:59) Rhino 70746 Anthology.

    (S) (2:58) MCA 31132 Greatest Hits Volume 1. (*alternate take from the* "*Let's Live For Today*" *vinyl LP*)

    (S) (2:59) Rhino 70746 Anthology (1965-1975).

    (S) (2:58) MCA 31325 Let's Live For Today. (*alternate take*)

1967 #5 *LET'S LIVE FOR TODAY*

    (S) (2:45) K-Tel 839 Battle Of The Bands Volume 2.

    (S) (2:46) Rhino 75754 Even More Nuggets.

    (S) (3:04) MCA 31207 Vintage Music Volume 10. (*:19 longer ending than either 45 or LP*)

    (S) (3:04) MCA 5806 Vintage Music Volumes 9 & 10. (*:19 longer ending than either 45 or LP*)

    (S) (2:46) MCA 31132 Greatest Hits Volume 1.

    (S) (2:46) Rhino 70746 Anthology (1965-1975).

    (S) (2:46) MCA 31325 Let's Live For Today.

1967 #36 *THINGS I SHOULD HAVE SAID*

    (S) (2:30) MCA 5936 Vintage Music Volumes 11 & 12.

    (S) (2:30) MCA 31208 Vintage Music Volume 11.

    (S) (2:27) MCA 31133 Greatest Hits Volume 2.

    (S) (2:29) Rhino 70746 Anthology (1965-1975).

    (S) (2:29) MCA 31325 Let's Live For Today.

1968 #5 *MIDNIGHT CONFESSIONS*

    (S) (2:49) MCA 31206 Vintage Music Volume 9.

    (S) (2:49) MCA 5806 Vintage Music Volumes 9 & 10.

    (S) (2:44) MCA 31133 Greatest Hits Volume 2.

    (S) (2:43) Rhino 70746 Anthology (1965-1975).

1969 #20 *BELLA LINDA*
(the actual 45 time is (2:53) not (2:47) as stated on the record label)

    (S) (2:56) MCA 5940 Vintage Music Volumes 19 & 20.

    (S) (2:56) MCA 31217 Vintage Music Volume 20.

    (S) (2:51) MCA 31132 Greatest Hits Volume 1.

    (S) (3:03) Rhino 70746 Anthology (1965-1975). (*LP length*)

1969 #35 *LOVIN' THINGS*

    (S) (2:48) Rhino 70746 Anthology (1965-1975).

    (S) (2:42) MCA 31133 Greatest Hits Volume 2.

1969 #16 *THE RIVER IS WIDE*

    (S) (2:44) MCA 31132 Greatest Hits Volume 1.

    (S) (2:50) Rhino 70746 Anthology (1965-1975).

1969 #12 *I'D WAIT A MILLION YEARS*
(the LP title of this song was "WAIT A MILLION YEARS")

    (S) (2:41) MCA 31133 Greatest Hits Volume 2. (*45 version*)

    (S) (2:44) Rhino 70746 Anthology (1965-1975). (*45 version*)

1969 #13 *HEAVEN KNOWS*

    (S) (2:21) MCA 31133 Greatest Hits Volume 2.

    (S) (2:25) Rhino 70746 Anthology (1965-1975).

1970 #30 *WALKING THROUGH THE COUNTRY*

    (S) (2:58) Rhino 70746 Anthology (1965-1975).

    (S) (2:58) MCA 31132 Greatest Hits Volume 1.

GRASS ROOTS (Continued)

1970 #25 BABY HOLD ON
    (S) (2:32) MCA 31133 Greatest Hits Volume 2.
    (S) (2:37) Rhino 70746 Anthology (1965-1975).

1970 #39 COME ON AND SAY IT
    (S) (2:26) MCA 31133 Greatest Hits Volume 2.
    (S) (2:28) Rhino 70746 Anthology (1965-1975).

1971 #16 TEMPTATION EYES
    (S) (2:31) MCA 31132 Greatest Hits Volume 1.
    (S) (2:37) Rhino 70746 Anthology (1965-1975).

1971 #12 SOONER OR LATER
    (S) (2:39) MCA 31132 Greatest Hits Volume 1.
    (S) (2:38) Rhino 70746 Anthology (1965-1975).
    (S) (2:39) Priority 7066 #1 Groups/70's Greatest Rock Hits Volume 12.

1971 #8 TWO DIVIDED BY LOVE
    (S) (2:34) MCA 31132 Greatest Hits Volume 1.
    (S) (2:34) Rhino 70746 Anthology (1965-1975).

1972 #22 GLORY BOUND
    (S) (2:33) Rhino 70746 Anthology (1965-1975).

1972 #29 THE RUNAWAY
    (S) (2:51) Rhino 70746 Anthology (1965-1975).

1973 #32 LOVE IS WHAT YOU MAKE IT
    (S) (2:51) Rhino 70746 Anthology (1965-1975).

DOBIE GRAY

1965 #17 THE "IN" CROWD

1973 #8 DRIFT AWAY
    (S) (3:54) Rhino 70930 Super Hits Of The 70's Volume 10.
    (S) (3:55) MCA 31273 Classic Rock Volume 1.
    (S) (3:49) RCA 8533 O.S.T. Heartbreak Hotel.

1973 #36 LOVING ARMS

CHARLES RANDOLPH GREAN SOUNDE

1969 #8 QUENTIN'S THEME

R.B. GREAVES

1969 #3 TAKE A LETTER MARIA
    (S) (2:40) Atlantic 81298 Atlantic Rhythm & Blues Volume 6.
    (S) (2:42) Rhino 70781 Soul Hits Of The 70's Volume 1.
    (S) (2:40) Atlantic 82305 Atlantic Rhythm And Blues 1947-1974 Box Set.

1970 #22 ALWAYS SOMETHING THERE TO REMIND ME

AL GREEN

1971 #6 TIRED OF BEING ALONE
    (S) (2:51) Motown 6111 Compact Command Performances.
    (S) (2:50) Motown 5283 and 9019 Greatest Hits Volume 1.

1972 #1 LET'S STAY TOGETHER
    (both the LP and 45 originally ran (3:16); the (4:46) version first appeared on Al Green's "Greatest Hits" vinyl LP)
    (S) (3:16) MCA 25226 History Of Hi Records Rhythm & Blues Volume 1.
    (S) (3:38) Rhino 70660 Billboard's Top R&B Hits Of 1972. *(:22 longer than either the 45 or LP)*
    (S) (3:16) Motown 6111 Compact Command Performances.
    (S) (4:46) Motown 5283 and 9019 Greatest Hits Volume 1.
    (S) (3:13) JCI 3303 Love Seventies.
    (S) (3:16) Motown 5290 Let's Stay Together.
    (S) (3:16) Motown 8018 and 8118 Let's Stay Together/I'm Still In Love With You.

AL GREEN (Continued)

1972 #3 LOOK WHAT YOU'VE DONE FOR ME
- (S) (3:04) Motown 6111   Compact Command Performances.
- (S) (3:03) Motown 5283 and 9019   Greatest Hits Volume 1.
- (S) (3:03) Motown 5284   I'm Still In Love With You.
- (S) (3:03) Motown 8018 and 8118   Let's Stay Together/I'm Still In Love With You.

1972 #1 I'M STILL IN LOVE WITH YOU
- (S) (3:10) MCA 25227   History Of Hi Records Rhythm & Blues Volume 2.
- (S) (3:12) Motown 6111   Compact Command Performances.
- (S) (3:12) Motown 5283 and 9019   Greatest Hits Volume 1.
- (S) (3:11) Motown 5284   I'm Still In Love With You.
- (S) (3:09) Motown 6192   You Can't Hurry Love: All The Great Love Songs Of The Past 25 Years.
- (S) (3:11) Motown 8018 and 8118   Let's Stay Together/I'm Still In Love With You.

1972 #2 YOU OUGHT TO BE WITH ME
- (S) (3:14) Motown 6111   Compact Command Performances.
- (S) (3:16) Motown 5283 and 9019   Greatest Hits Volume 1.
- (S) (3:14) Motown 5286   Call Me.
- (S) (3:13) Motown 8040 and 8140   Call Me/Livin' For You.

1973 #9 CALL ME (COME BACK HOME)
- (S) (3:01) MCA 25227   History Of Hi Records Rhythm & Blues Volume 2.
- (S) (3:04) Motown 6111   Compact Command Performances.
- (S) (3:03) Motown 5283 and 9019   Greatest Hits Volume 1.
- (S) (3:00) Motown 5286   Call Me.
- (S) (3:01) Motown 8040 and 8140   Call Me/Livin' For You.

1973 #10 HERE I AM (COME AND TAKE ME)
- (S) (4:14) Rhino 70661   Billboard's Top R&B Hits Of 1973.
- (S) (3:11) Motown 6111   Compact Command Performances. *(neither the commercial 45 or LP version)*
- (S) (3:10) Motown 5283 and 9019   Greatest Hits Volume 1. *(neither the commercial 45 or LP version)*
- (S) (4:13) Motown 5286   Call Me.
- (S) (4:14) Motown 8040 and 8140   Call Me/Livin' For You.

GARLAND GREEN

1969 #29 JEALOUS KIND OF FELLA

NORMAN GREENBAUM

1970 #1 SPIRIT IN THE SKY
- (S) (4:00) Rhino 70922   Super Hits Of The 70's Volume 2.
- (S) (4:00) Rhino 72009   Super Hits Of The 70's Volumes 1-4 Box Set.
- (S) (4:00) Rhino 70631   Billboard's Top Rock & Roll Hits Of 1970.
- (S) (4:00) Rhino 72005   Billboard's Top Rock & Roll Hits 1968-1972 Box Set.
- (S) (3:59) Warner Special Projects 27610   More Party Classics.
- (S) (3:57) JCI 3304   Mellow Seventies.

1970 #32 CANNED HAM

LORNE GREENE

1964 #1 RINGO
- (S) (3:13) RCA 8475   Nipper's Greatest Hits Of The 60's Volume 2.
- (S) (3:13) RCA 9902   Nipper's #1 Hits (1956-1986).

BOBBY GREGG & HIS FRIENDS

1962 #34 THE JAM (PART 1)

VINCE GUARALDI TRIO
1963 #31 *CAST YOUR FATE TO THE WIND*
    (S) (3:04) Fantasy 7706   Greatest Hits.
    (S) (3:04) Fantasy 437   Jazz Impressions Of Black Orpheus.

GUESS WHO
1965 #19 *SHAKIN' ALL OVER*
    (M) (2:41) Rhino 70732   Grandson Of Frat Rock.

1969 #4 *THESE EYES*
    (S) (3:41) RCA 8474   Nipper's Greatest Hits Of The 60's Volume 1.
    (S) (3:43) RCA 4141   Wheatfield Soul.
    (S) (3:43) RCA 2076   American Woman, These Eyes & Other Hits.
    (S) (3:44) RCA 3746   Greatest Of.
    (S) (3:44) RCA 3662   Best Of.
    (S) (3:36) RCA 61077   Track Record.
    (S) (3:44) RCA 61133 and 61152   These Eyes.

1969 #8 *LAUGHING*
    (S) (2:34) RCA 4157   Canned Wheat.
    (S) (2:38) RCA 2076   American Woman, These Eyes & Other Hits.
    (S) (2:38) RCA 3746   Greatest Of.
    (S) (2:37) RCA 3662   Best Of.
    (S) (2:42) RCA 61077   Track Record.

1969 #26 *UNDUN*
    (S) (3:41) Sandstone 33001   Reelin' In The Years Volume 2. *(LP version)*
    (S) (3:41) RCA 4157   Canned Wheat. *(LP version)*
    (S) (3:26) RCA 2076   American Woman, These Eyes & Other Hits. *(45 version)*
    (S) (3:26) RCA 3746   Greatest Of. *(45 version)*
    (S) (3:26) RCA 3662   Best Of. *(45 version)*
    (S) (3:28) RCA 61077   Track Record. *(45 version)*
    (S) (3:25) RCA 61133 and 61152   These Eyes. *(45 version)*

1970 #4 *NO TIME*
    (S) (3:37) Priority 8668   Rough And Ready/70's Greatest Rock Hits Volume 7.
    (S) (5:30) RCA 4157   Canned Wheat. *("Canned Wheat" vinyl LP version)*
    (S) (3:28) RCA 2076   American Woman, These Eyes & Other Hits. *(edited)*
    (S) (3:40) RCA 3746   Greatest Of.
    (S) (3:39) RCA 3662   Best Of.
    (S) (3:46) RCA 4266   American Woman.
    (S) (3:43) RCA 61077   Track Record.

1970 #1 *AMERICAN WOMAN*
    (S) (3:51) Rhino 70906   American Bandstand Greatest Hits Collection. *(45 version)*
    (S) (3:48) RCA 9902   Nipper's Greatest Hits 1956-1986. *(45 version)*
    (S) (3:49) RCA 8476   and 9684 Nipper's Greatest Hits Of The 70's. *(45 version)*
    (S) (5:05) RCA 2076   American Woman, These Eyes & Other Hits. *(LP version)*
    (S) (5:05) RCA 3746   Greatest Of. *(LP version)*
    (S) (5:05) RCA 3662   Best Of. *(LP version)*
    (S) (5:06) RCA 4266   American Woman. *(LP version)*
    (S) (5:05) RCA 61077   Track Record. *(LP version)*
    (S) (5:05) RCA 61133 and 61152   These Eyes. *(LP version)*
    (S) (5:05) Priority 7066   #1 Groups/70's Greatest Rock Hits Volume 12.

GUESS WHO (Continued)

1970 #39 NO SUGAR TONIGHT

(the LP version of this song is actually a medley of "NO SUGAR TONIGHT" and "NEW MOTHER NATURE")

(S) (4:49) RCA 3662 Best Of. (LP version)
(S) (4:51) RCA 4266 American Woman. (LP version)
(S) (4:51) RCA 61077 Track Record. (LP version)
(S) (4:49) RCA 61133 and 61152 These Eyes. (LP version)

1970 #13 HAND ME DOWN WORLD

(S) (3:21) RCA 2076 American Woman, These Eyes & Other Hits.
(S) (3:21) RCA 3746 Greatest Of.
(S) (3:21) RCA 3662 Best Of.
(S) (3:25) RCA 61077 Track Record.

1970 #5 SHARE THE LAND

(S) (3:52) RCA 2076 American Woman, These Eyes & Other Hits.
(S) (3:52) RCA 3662 Best Of.
(S) (3:30) RCA 61077 Track Record. (fades :22 earlier than LP and 45)
(S) (3:52) RCA 61133 and 61152 These Eyes.

1971 #35 HANG ON TO YOUR LIFE

(S) (4:09) RCA 3662 Best Of. (LP version)
(S) (4:07) RCA 61077 Track Record. (LP version)

1971 #35 ALBERT FLASHER

(S) (2:25) RCA 3746 Greatest Of.
(S) (2:23) RCA 61077 Track Record.

1971 #15 RAIN DANCE

(S) (2:40) RCA 61077 Track Record.

1972 #26 HEARTBROKEN BOPPER

(S) (4:54) RCA 61077 Track Record. (LP version)

BONNIE GUITAR

1957 #5 DARK MOON

GUNHILL ROAD

1973 #25 BACK WHEN MY HAIR WAS SHORT

ARLO GUTHRIE

1972 #21 THE CITY OF NEW ORLEANS

(S) (4:28) Warner Special Products 27615 Storytellers: Singers & Songwriters.
(S) (4:28) Priority 8670 Hitchin A Ride/70's Greatest Rock Hits Volume 10.
(S) (4:29) Warner Brothers 3117 Best Of.
(S) (4:27) JCI 3304 Mellow Seventies.
(S) (4:30) Rising Son 2060 Hobo's Lullaby.

BILL HALEY & HIS COMETS
1955 #1 *(WE'RE GONNA) ROCK AROUND THE CLOCK*
    (M) (2:10) Rhino 70598 Billboard's Top Rock & Roll Hits Of 1955. *(with countoff)*
    (M) (2:10) RCA 5463 Rock & Roll - The Early Days.
    (M) (2:10) MCA 31200 Vintage Music Volume 3. *(with countoff)*
    (M) (2:10) MCA 5778 Vintage Music Volumes 3 & 4. *(with countoff)*
    (M) (2:10) JCI 3201 Partytime 50's.
    (M) (2:11) Curb 77323 All Time Greatest Hits Of Rock 'N' Roll. *(with countoff)*
    (M) (2:11) MCA 5539 From The Original Master Tapes. *(with countoff)*
    (M) (2:10) MCA 0161 Greatest Hits. *(with countoff)*
1956 #5 *SEE YOU LATER, ALLIGATOR*
    (M) (2:44) Rhino 70599 Billboard's Top Rock & Roll Hits Of 1956. *(noise at very end of song)*
    (M) (2:45) MCA 5936 Vintage Music Volumes 11 & 12.
    (M) (2:45) MCA 31208 Vintage Music Volume 11.
    (M) (2:44) MCA 5539 From The Original Master Tapes.
    (M) (2:44) MCA 0161 Greatest Hits.
1956 #24 *RIP IT UP*
    (M) (2:23) MCA 5539 From The Original Master Tapes.
1956 #38 *RUDY'S ROCK*
    (M) (2:40) MCA 5939 Vintage Music Volumes 17 & 18.
    (M) (2:40) MCA 31214 Vintage Music Volume 17.
    (M) (2:47) MCA 5539 From The Original Master Tapes.
1958 #25 *SKINNY MINNIE*
    (M) (2:56) MCA 0161 Greatest Hits.
1959 #35 *JOEY'S SONG*
    (M) (2:54) MCA 0161 Greatest Hits.

LARRY HALL
1960 #19 *SANDY*

HALOS
1961 #34 *NAG*

GEORGE HAMILTON IV
1956 #6 *A ROSE AND A BABY RUTH*
    (E) (1:58) MCA 5936 Vintage Music Volumes 11 & 12.
    (E) (1:58) MCA 31209 Vintage Music Volume 12.
1957 #23 *ONLY ONE LOVE*
1958 #9 *WHY DON'T THEY UNDERSTAND*
1958 #35 *NOW AND FOR ALWAYS*
1963 #21 *ABILENE*
    (S) (2:11) RCA 8475 Nipper's Greatest Hits Of The 60's Volume 2.
    (S) (2:11) Rhino 70684 Billboard's Top Country Hits Of 1963.
    (S) (2:11) RCA 5802 Best Of The 60's.

ROY HAMILTON
1955 #1 *UNCHAINED MELODY*
    (E) (2:57) Collectables 5150 Golden Classics.
1958 #13 *DON'T LET GO*
    (S) (2:30) Collectables 5150 Golden Classics.
1961 #12 *YOU CAN HAVE HER*
    (S) (2:44) Collectables 5150 Golden Classics.

RUSS HAMILTON
1957 #6 *RAINBOW*

HAMILTON, JOE FRANK & REYNOLDS
1971 #1 *DON'T PULL YOUR LOVE*
    (S) (2:40) Rhino 70925 Super Hits Of The 70's Volume 5.
    (S) (2:41) Priority 8666 Kickin' Back/70's Greatest Rock Hits Volume 5.
1972 #39 *DAISY MAE*

ALBERT HAMMOND
1972 #2 *IT NEVER RAINS IN SOUTHERN CALIFORNIA*
    (S) (3:36) Rhino 70930 Super Hits Of The 70's Volume 10. *(neither the LP or 45 version)*
    (S) (3:49) Columbia/Legacy 46763 Rock Artifacts Volume 2. *(LP version)*

KEITH HAMPSHIRE
1973 #40 *THE FIRST CUT IS THE DEEPEST*

HAPPENINGS
1966 #4 *SEE YOU IN SEPTEMBER*
1966 #13 *GO AWAY LITTLE GIRL*
1967 #1 *I GOT RHYTHM*
1967 #16 *MY MAMMY*
1969 #38 *WHERE DO I GO/BE-IN/HARE KRISHNA*

JOE HARNELL
1963 #17 *FLY ME TO THE MOON BOSSA NOVA*

JANICE HARPER
1957 #28 *BON VOYAGE*

HARPERS BIZARRE
1967 #14 *THE 59TH STREET BRIDGE SONG (FEELIN' GROOVY)*

SLIM HARPO
1961 #24 *RAININ' IN MY HEART*
    (M) (2:31) Rhino 70896 Best Of Excello Records Volume 1.
    (M) (2:31) Rhino 70169 Best Of.
1966 #13 *BABY SCRATCH MY BACK*
    (M) (2:51) Rhino 70896 Best Of Excello Records Volume 1.
    (M) (2:52) Rhino 70169 Best Of.

BETTY HARRIS
1963 #27 *CRY TO ME*

RICHARD HARRIS
1968 #2 *MAC ARTHUR PARK*

ROLF HARRIS
1963 #4 *TIE ME KANGAROO DOWN, SPORT*

THURSTON HARRIS
1957 #9 *LITTLE BITTY PRETTY ONE*
    (M) (2:21) Rhino 70643 Billboard's Top R&B Hits Of 1957.
    (M) (2:21) JCI 3204 Heart & Soul Fifties.

GEORGE HARRISON

1970 #1 *MY SWEET LORD*
- (S) (4:36) Capitol 46682 Best Of.
- (S) (4:36) Capitol 46688 All Things Must Pass.

1971 #7 *WHAT IS LIFE*
- (S) (4:14) Capitol 46682 Best Of.
- (S) (4:15) Capitol 46688 All Things Must Pass.

1971 #20 *BANGLA-DESH*
- (S) (3:55) Capitol 46682 Best Of.

1973 #1 *GIVE ME LOVE (GIVE ME PEACE ON EARTH)*
- (S) (3:33) Capitol 46682 Best Of.
- (S) (3:34) Capitol 94110 Living In The Material World.

NOEL HARRISON

1966 #38 *A YOUNG GIRL*

WILBERT HARRISON

1959 #1 *KANSAS CITY*
- (M) (2:24) Rhino 70620 Billboard's Top Rock & Roll Hits Of 1959.
- (M) (2:24) Rhino 72004 Billboard's Top Rock & Roll Hits 1957-1961 Box Set.
- (M) (2:22) Rhino 70719 Legends Of Guitar - Rock; The 50's. *(first note chopped off)*
- (M) (2:26) Relic 7009 Raging Harlem Hit Parade.
- (M) (2:26) Relic 7035 Kansas City.
- (S) (2:42) Grudge 4510 Greatest Classic R&B Hits. *(rerecording)*
- (M) (2:25) Rhino 70593 The Rock 'N' Roll Classics Of Leiber & Stoller.

1970 #30 *LET'S WORK TOGETHER (PART 1)*
- (M) (5:24) Grudge 4510 Greatest Classic R&B Hits. *(LP version which is Parts 1 & 2)*

FREDDIE HART

1971 #12 *EASY LOVING*

HARVEY & THE MOONGLOWS (see THE MOONGLOWS)

RICHIE HAVENS

1971 #15 *HERE COMES THE SUN*
(some dj copies of this 45 ran (2:36) and others (3:43))
- (M) (2:30) Rhino 70925 Super Hits Of The 70's Volume 5.
- (S) (2:42) Rykodisc 20035 Sings Beatles And Dylan. *(rerecording)*
- (E) (3:47) Rykodisc 20036 Collection. *(with audience applause in stereo on introduction but there was no audience applause on the introduction of the 45 or LP version; stereo audience applause on the ending but not the same applause as found on the 45 and LP)*

DALE HAWKINS

1958 #35 *LA-DO-DADA*

EDWIN HAWKINS SINGERS

1969 #3 *OH HAPPY DAY*
(both the LP and commercial 45 version ran (5:06))
- (S) (3:06) Pair 1202 Best Of Buddah.
- (S) (5:08) Rhino 70781 Soul Hits Of The 70's Volume 1.
- (S) (5:07) Pair 3301 Oh Happy Day.

RONNIE HAWKINS & THE HAWKS

1959 #24 *MARY LOU*
- (S) (2:08) Rhino 70742 Rock This Town: Rockabilly Hits Volume 2.
- (S) (2:08) Rhino 70966 Best Of.

DEANE HAWLEY
1960 #13 *LOOK FOR A STAR*

BILL HAYES
1955 #1 *THE BALLAD OF DAVY CROCKETT*
1957 #12 *WRINGLE, WRANGLE*

ISAAC HAYES
1970 #38 *I STAND ACCUSED*
    (S) (11:34) Stax 60001 Best Of Volume 1. *(LP version)*
    (S) (4:02) Stax 8515 Greatest Hit Singles.
    (S) (11:36) Stax 4129 Isaac Hayes Movement. *(LP version)*

1971 #33 *NEVER CAN SAY GOODBYE*
    (S) (3:35) Stax 8515 Greatest Hit Singles.
    (S) (5:06) Stax 88006 Black Moses. *(LP version)*
    (S) (3:36) Stax 60-002 Best Of Volume 2.
    (S) (3:35) Stax 88008 Top Of The Stax Volume 2.

1971 #1 *THEME FROM SHAFT*
    (S) (3:15) Rhino 70786 Soul Hits Of The 70's Volume 6.
    (S) (4:35) Stax 88005 Top Of The Stax. *(LP version)*
    (S) (3:15) Stax 8515 Greatest Hit Singles.
    (S) (4:35) Stax 60-001 Best Of Volume 1. *(LP version)*
    (S) (4:35) Stax 88002 Shaft. *(LP version)*
    (S) (3:15) Atco 91813 Classic Recordings.

1972 #23 *DO YOUR THING*
    (S) (3:17) Rhino 70788 Soul Hits Of The 70's Volume 8.
    (S) (3:16) Stax 8515 Greatest Hit Singles.
    (S) (19:30) Stax 60-001 Best Of Volume 1. *(LP version)*
    (S) (19:30) Stax 88002 Shaft. *(LP version)*

1972 #36 *THEME FROM THE MEN*
    (S) (3:58) Stax 8515 Greatest Hit Singles.
    (S) (4:02) Stax 60-002 Best Of Volume 2.

RICHARD HAYMAN
1957 #10 *TAMMY*

MURRAY HEAD
1971 #8 *SUPERSTAR*
    (S) (4:15) Rhino 70925 Super Hits Of The 70's Volume 5.
    (S) (4:15) MCA 2-10000 Jesus Christ Superstar. *(previous selection barely tracks over introduction)*

ROY HEAD
1965 #3 *TREAT HER RIGHT*
    (M) (2:03) Rhino 70626 Billboard's Top Rock & Roll Hits Of 1965.
    (M) (2:03) Rhino 72007 Billboard's Top Rock & Roll Hits 1962-1966 Box Set.
    (S) (2:03) MCA 31204 Vintage Music Volume 7. *(missing some overdubs)*
    (S) (2:03) MCA 5805 Vintage Music Volumes 7 & 8. *(missing some overdubs)*

1965 #38 *JUST A LITTLE BIT*
    (S) (1:42) Capricorn 42003 The Scepter Records Story.

HEARTBEATS
1956 #36 *A THOUSAND MILES AWAY*
    (M) (2:24) Rhino 75763 Best Of The Doo Wop Ballads.
    (M) (2:26) Elektra 60107 O.S.T. Diner.
    (M) (2:24) Rhino 70952 Best Of.

HEARTBEATS (Continued)

(M) (2:25) Collectables 5416 Murray The K - Sing Along With The Golden Greats. *(truncated fade)*
(M) (2:24) Collectables 8805 Heartbeats/Shep & The Limelights For Collectors Only.

JOEY HEATHERTON
1972 #26 *GONE*

BOBBY HEBB
1966 #1 *SUNNY*

(S) (2:45) Rhino 70652 Billboard's Top R&B Hits Of 1966.
(S) (2:45) Rhino 72006 Billboard's Top R&B Hits 1965-1969 Box Set.
(S) (2:43) Mercury 826448 Oldies Golden Million Sellers.
(S) (2:44) Mercury 816555 45's On CD Volume 2.

1966 #40 *A SATISFIED MIND*

NEAL HEFTI
1966 #32 *BATMAN THEME*

(S) (2:17) RCA 3573 Neal Hefti.

BOBBY HELMS
1957 #8 *MY SPECIAL ANGEL*

(M) (2:57) MCA 31199 Vintage Music Volume 2.
(M) (2:57) MCA 5777 Vintage Music Volumes 1 & 2.

1958 #11 *JINGLE BELL ROCK*

(M) (2:09) Rhino 70192 Christmas Classics.
(M) (2:09) Rhino 70636 Billboard's Greatest Christmas Hits.
(M) (2:09) Rhino 70639 Billboard's Greatest Country Christmas Hits.
(M) (2:09) MCA 25991 Christmas Hits.
(M) (2:09) Curb 77515 Christmas All-Time Greatest Records Volume 2.

JOE HENDERSON
1962 #7 *SNAP YOUR FINGERS*

JIMI HENDRIX EXPERIENCE
1968 #18 *ALL ALONG THE WATCHTOWER*

(S) (3:59) Polydor 837362 O.S.T. 1969.
(S) (3:57) Reprise 6307 Electric Ladyland.
(S) (3:57) Reprise 2276 Smash Hits.
(S) (3:57) Reprise 26035 Essential Volumes One & Two.
(S) (3:57) Reprise 25119 Kiss The Sky.

1968 #36 *CROSSTOWN TRAFFIC*

(S) (2:16) Reprise 2276 Smash Hits.
(S) (2:24) Reprise 6307 Electric Ladyland. *(LP length with ending audience applause)*
(S) (2:16) Reprise 26035 Essential Volumes One & Two.
(S) (2:16) Reprise 25119 Kiss The Sky.

CLARENCE HENRY
1957 #30 *AIN'T GOT NO HOME*

(M) (2:19) Rhino 75766 Best Of New Orleans Rhythm & Blues Volume 2.
(M) (2:18) MCA 31199 Vintage Music Volume 2.
(M) (2:18) MCA 5777 Vintage Music Volumes 1 & 2.
(M) (2:18) Garland 011 Footstompin' Oldies.
(M) (2:18) Chess 31319 Best Of Chess Rock 'n' Roll Volume 1.
(M) (2:20) Elektra 60107 O.S.T. Diner.
(M) (2:18) Sire 26617 Music From The Film A Rage In Harlem.

CLARENCE HENRY *(Continued)*
1961 #4 *(I DON'T KNOW WHY) BUT I DO*
    (M) (2:17) Rhino 75766 Best Of New Orleans Rhythm & Blues Volume 2.
    (S) (2:17) MCA 31203 Vintage Music Volume 6.
    (S) (2:17) MCA 5804 Vintage Music Volumes 5 & 6.
    (S) (2:17) Garland 012 Remember When.
    (S) (2:17) Chess 31317 Best Of Chess Rhythm & Blues Volume 1.
1961 #12 *YOU ALWAYS HURT THE ONE YOU LOVE*

HERMAN'S HERMITS
1964 #7 *I'M INTO SOMETHING GOOD*
    (M) (2:31) Abkco 4227 Their Greatest Hits.
1965 #1 *CAN'T YOU HEAR MY HEARTBEAT*
    (M) (2:13) Abkco 4227 Their Greatest Hits.
1965 #1 *MRS. BROWN YOU'VE GOT A LOVELY DAUGHTER*
    (M) (2:44) Abkco 4227 Their Greatest Hits.
1965 #5 *SILHOUETTES*
    (M) (1:57) Abkco 4227 Their Greatest Hits.
1965 #5 *WONDERFUL WORLD*
    (M) (1:58) Abkco 4227 Their Greatest Hits.
1965 #1 *I'M HENRY VIII I AM*
    (M) (1:48) Abkco 4227 Their Greatest Hits.
1965 #8 *JUST A LITTLE BIT BETTER*
    (M) (2:51) Abkco 4227 Their Greatest Hits.
1966 #6 *A MUST TO AVOID*
    (M) (1:54) Abkco 4227 Their Greatest Hits.
1966 #3 *LISTEN PEOPLE*
    (M) (2:29) Abkco 4227 Their Greatest Hits.
1966 #8 *LEANING ON THE LAMP POST*
    (M) (2:32) Abkco 4227 Their Greatest Hits. *(LP version)*
1966 #10 *THIS DOOR SWINGS BOTH WAYS*
    (M) (2:05) Abkco 4227 Their Greatest Hits.
1966 #8 *DANDY*
    (M) (1:57) Abkco 4227 Their Greatest Hits.
1967 #15 *EAST WEST*
1967 #3 *THERE'S A KIND OF HUSH*
    (M) (2:33) Abkco 4227 Their Greatest Hits.
1967 #33 *NO MILK TODAY*
    (M) (2:52) Abkco 4227 Their Greatest Hits.
1967 #13 *DON'T GO OUT INTO THE RAIN (YOU'RE GOING TO MELT)*
1967 #21 *MUSEUM*
1968 #21 *I CAN TAKE OR LEAVE YOUR LOVING*

HESITATIONS
1968 #36 *BORN FREE*

EDDIE HEYWOOD
1956 #11 *SOFT SUMMER BREEZE*

AL HIBBLER
1955 #1 *UNCHAINED MELODY*
    (M) (2:53) MCA 5937 Vintage Music Volumes 13 & 14.
    (M) (2:53) MCA 31211 Vintage Music Volume 14.

AL HIBBLER (Continued)
1955 #4 HE
1956 #15 *AFTER THE LIGHTS GO DOWN LOW*
> (M) (2:38) Atlantic 82305 Atlantic Rhythm And Blues 1947-1974 Box Set.
> *(earlier recording than the hit version; sounds muddy)*
> (M) (2:38) Atlantic 1251 After The Lights Go Down Low. *(earlier recording than the hit version)*

ERSEL HICKEY
1958 #39 *BLUEBIRDS OVER THE MOUNTAIN*
> (M) (1:26) CBS Special Products 37618 Rockabilly Stars Volume 1.

HIGHLIGHTS (*featuring* FRANK PISANI)
1956 #24 *CITY OF ANGELS*

HIGHWAYMEN
1961 #1 *MICHAEL*
> (S) (2:45) EMI 96268 24 Greatest Hits Of All Time.
> (S) (2:43) Rhino 70264 Troubadours Of The Folk Era Volume 2.
> (S) (2:44) EMI 96334 Michael Row The Boat Ashore: Best Of.
1962 #13 *COTTON FIELDS*
> (S) (2:30) EMI 96334 Michael Row The Boat Ashore: Best Of. *(includes :18 of studio talk)*

BUNKER HILL
1962 #39 *HIDE & GO SEEK (PART 1)*

JESSE HILL
1960 #32 *OOH POO PAH DOO (PART 2)*
> (M) (2:19) Rhino 75765 Best Of New Orleans Rhythm & Blues Volume 1.
> *(this is Part 1 but Part 2 was the hit side)*

HILLSIDE SINGERS
1972 #16 *I'D LIKE TO TEACH THE WORLD TO SING (IN PERFECT HARMONY)*

HILLTOPPERS
1956 #17 *KA-DING-DONG*
1957 #2 *MARIANNE*
1957 #24 *A FALLEN STAR*
1957 #20 *THE JOKER (THAT'S WHAT THEY CALL ME)*

JOE HINTON
1964 #12 *FUNNY*
> (M) (3:02) MCA 5938 Vintage Music Volumes 15 & 16.
> (M) (3:02) MCA 31212 Vintage Music Volume 15.
> (M) (3:02) Stax 8559 Superblues Volume 2.
> (S) (3:02) MCA 10288 Classic Soul.

AL HIRT
1964 #4 *JAVA*
> (S) (1:56) RCA 8474 Nipper's Greatest Hits Of The 60's Volume 1.
> (S) (1:55) RCA 9593 All Time Greatest Hits.
1964 #15 *COTTON CANDY*
> (S) (2:13) RCA 9593 All Time Greatest Hits.
1964 #20 *SUGAR LIPS*
> (S) (2:00) RCA 9593 All Time Greatest Hits.
1965 #37 *FANCY PANTS*
> (S) (1:53) RCA 9593 All Time Greatest Hits.

CHRIS HODGE

1972 #36 *WE'RE ON OUR WAY*

EDDIE HODGES

1961 #13 *I'M GONNA KNOCK ON YOUR DOOR*
1962 #20 *(GIRLS, GIRLS, GIRLS) MADE TO LOVE*
1965 #36 *NEW ORLEANS*

RON HOLDEN

1960 #5 *LOVE YOU SO*
    (M) (3:06) Original Sound 1960 Memories Of El Monte.

EDDIE HOLLAND

1962 #40 *JAMIE*
    (E) (2:25) Motown 6184 Hard To Find Motown Classics Volume 2.
    (E) (2:25) Motown 5448 A Collection Of 16 Big Hits Volume 1.

HOLLIES

1966 #34 *LOOK THROUGH ANY WINDOW*
    (M) (2:15) Rhino 70324 History Of British Rock Volume 6. *(45 version)*
    (M) (2:15) Rhino 72022 History Of British Rock Box Set. *(45 version)*
    (S) (2:16) Curb 77377 All Time Greatest Hits. *(LP version)*
    (S) (2:16) Epic 32061 Greatest Hits. *(LP version)*
    (S) (2:16) EMI 46584 Best Of Volume 1. *(LP version)*

1966 #5 *BUS STOP*
    (E) (2:52) JCI 3101 Rockin' Sixties.
    (S) (2:52) Rhino 70321 History Of British Rock Volume 3.
    (S) (2:52) Rhino 72022 History Of British Rock Box Set.
    (S) (2:52) Rhino 72008 History Of British Rock Volumes 1-4 Box Set.
    (S) (2:53) Curb 77377 All Time Greatest Hits.
    (S) (2:54) Epic 32061 Greatest Hits.
    (S) (2:53) EMI 46584 Best Of Volume 1.

1966 #8 *STOP STOP STOP*
    (S) (2:48) Rhino 70322 History Of British Rock Volume 4.
    (S) (2:48) Rhino 72022 History Of British Rock Box Set.
    (S) (2:48) Rhino 72008 History Of British Rock Volumes 1-4 Box Set.
    (S) (2:48) Curb 77377 All Time Greatest Hits.
    (S) (2:49) Epic 32061 Greatest Hits.
    (S) (2:48) EMI 46584 Best Of Volume 1.

1967 #7 *ON A CAROUSEL*
    (S) (3:12) Rhino 70324 History Of British Rock Volume 6.
    (S) (3:12) Rhino 72022 History Of British Rock Box Set.
    (S) (3:12) Curb 77377 All Time Greatest Hits.
    (S) (3:10) Epic 32061 Greatest Hits.
    (S) (3:12) EMI 46584 Best Of Volume 1.

1967 #29 *PAY YOU BACK WITH INTEREST*
    (S) (2:39) Rhino 70322 History Of British Rock Volume 4.
    (S) (2:39) Rhino 72022 History Of British Rock Box Set.
    (S) (2:39) Rhino 72008 History Of British Rock Volumes 1-4 Box Set.
    (S) (2:40) Epic 32061 Greatest Hits.
    (S) (2:40) EMI 46584 Best Of Volume 1.

1967 #10 *CARRIE-ANNE*
    (S) (2:54) JCI 3104 Mellow Sixties.
    (M) (2:54) Rhino 70325 History Of British Rock Volume 7.
    (M) (2:54) Rhino 72022 History Of British Rock Box Set.
    (S) (2:53) Curb 77377 All Time Greatest Hits.

        (S) (3:03) Epic 46161   Epic Anthology. *(with :09 studio talk and countoff)*
        (S) (2:55) Epic 32061   Greatest Hits.
        (S) (2:54) EMI 46584   Best Of Volume 1.

1970 #8 *HE AIN'T HEAVY, HE'S MY BROTHER*
        (S) (4:19) Rhino 70327   History Of British Rock Volume 9.
        (S) (4:19) Rhino 72022   History Of British Rock Box Set.
        (S) (4:18) Curb 77377   All Time Greatest Hits.
        (S) (4:17) Epic 46161   Epic Anthology.
        (S) (4:18) Epic 32061   Greatest Hits.
        (S) (4:18) EMI 48831   Best Of Volume 2.

1972 #1 *LONG COOL WOMAN (IN A BLACK DRESS)*
        (S) (3:16) Rhino 70633   Billboard's Top Rock & Roll Hits Of 1972.
        (S) (3:16) Rhino 72005   Billboard's Top Rock & Roll Hits 1968-1972 Box Set.
        (S) (3:15) Rhino 70327   History Of British Rock Volume 9.
        (S) (3:15) Rhino 72022   History Of British Rock Box Set.
        (S) (3:16) JCI 3301   Rockin' Seventies.
        (S) (3:15) Sandstone 33004   Reelin' In The Years Volume 5.
        (S) (3:16) Curb 77377   All Time Greatest Hits.
        (S) (3:15) Epic 30958   Distant Light.
        (S) (3:15) Epic 46161   Epic Anthology.
        (S) (3:16) Epic 32061   Greatest Hits.
        (S) (3:15) EMI 48831   Best Of Volume 2.

1972 #24 *LONG DARK ROAD*
        (S) (4:15) Curb 77377   All Time Greatest Hits. *(LP version)*
        (S) (4:14) Epic 30958   Distant Light. *(LP version)*
        (S) (4:15) Epic 46161   Epic Anthology. *(LP version)*
        (S) (3:24) Epic 32061   Greatest Hits. *(45 version)*
        (S) (4:16) EMI 48831   Best Of Volume 2. *(LP version)*

BRENDA HOLLOWAY

1964 #18 *EVERY LITTLE BIT HURTS*
        (S) (2:51) Motown 9105   Motown Memories Volume 2.
        (E) (2:53) Motown 6184   Hard To Find Motown Classics Volume 2.
        (S) (2:48) Motown 5450   A Collection Of 16 Big Hits Volume 3.
        (M) (2:54) Motown 5485   Greatest Hits And Rare Classics.

1965 #26 *WHEN I'M GONE*
        (S) (2:06) Rhino 75757   Soul Shots Volume 3.
        (E) (2:10) Motown 6184   Hard To Find Motown Classics Volume 2.
        (E) (2:09) Motown 5452   A Collection Of 16 Big Hits Volume 5.
        (S) (2:04) Motown 5485   Greatest Hits And Rare Classics.

BUDDY HOLLY (*also* CRICKETS)

released as by THE CRICKETS:

1957 #3 *THAT'LL BE THE DAY*
        (M) (2:14) Rhino 70618   Billboard's Top Rock & Roll Hits Of 1957.
        (M) (2:14) Rhino 72004   Billboard's Top Rock & Roll Hits 1957-1961 Box Set.
        (M) (2:14) MCA 31198   Vintage Music Volume 1.
        (M) (2:14) MCA 5777   Vintage Music Volumes 1 & 2.
        (M) (2:14) JCI 3201   Party Time Favorites.
        (M) (2:15) MCA 5540   Buddy Holly From The Original Master Tapes.
        (E) (2:27) MCA 31037   The Great Buddy Holly. *(rerecording)*
        (M) (2:14) MCA 31182   The "Chirping" Crickets.

released as by BUDDY HOLLY:
1958 #2 *PEGGY SUE*
- (M) (2:28) Rhino 70618 Billboard's Top Rock & Roll Hits Of 1957.
- (M) (2:28) Rhino 72004 Billboard's Top Rock & Roll Hits 1957-1961 Box Set.
- (M) (2:28) MCA 31199 Vintage Music Volume 2.
- (M) (2:28) MCA 5777 Vintage Music Volumes 1 & 2.
- (M) (2:28) JCI 3202 Rockin' Fifties. *(sounds muddy)*
- (M) (2:28) Curb 77323 All Time Greatest Hits Of Rock 'N' Roll.
- (M) (2:29) MCA 5540 From The Original Master Tapes.
- (M) (2:28) MCA 25239 Buddy Holly.

released as by THE CRICKETS:
1958 #13 *OH BOY!*
- (M) (2:06) MCA 31200 Vintage Music Volume 3.
- (M) (2:06) MCA 5778 Vintage Music Volumes 3 & 4.
- (M) (2:06) Rhino 70741 Rock This Town: Rockabilly Hits Volume 1.
- (M) (2:07) MCA 5540 Buddy Holly From The Original Master Tapes.
- (M) (2:06) MCA 31182 The "Chirping" Crickets.

released as by THE CRICKETS:
1958 #11 *MAYBE BABY*
- (M) (2:00) MCA 31201 Vintage Music Volume 4.
- (M) (2:00) MCA 5778 Vintage Music Volumes 3 & 4.
- (M) (2:01) MCA 5540 Buddy Holly From The Original Master Tapes.
- (M) (2:01) MCA 31182 The "Chirping" Crickets.

released as by BUDDY HOLLY:
1958 #25 *EARLY IN THE MORNING*
1959 #30 *IT DOESN'T MATTER ANYMORE*
- (S) (2:05) MCA 5540 From The Original Master Tapes. *(with countoff)*

HOLLYWOOD ARGYLES
1960 #1 *ALLEY-OOP*
- (M) (2:42) Rhino 70621 Billboard's Top Rock & Roll Hits Of 1960.
- (M) (2:42) Rhino 72004 Billboard's Top Rock & Roll Hits 1957-1961 Box Set.
- (M) (2:42) Rhino 70794 KFOG Presents M. Dung's Idiot Show.

HOLLYWOOD FLAMES
1958 #18 *BUZZ BUZZ BUZZ*
- (M) (2:13) Rhino 75764 Best Of Doo Wop Uptempo.
- (M) (2:15) Specialty 7021 The Hollywood Flames.

1960 #18 *DEVIL OR ANGEL*

EDDIE HOLMAN
1970 #2 *HEY THERE LONELY GIRL*
- (S) (3:33) Rhino 75770 Soul Shots Volume 2.
- (S) (3:33) Rhino 70781 Soul Hits Of The 70's Volume 1.
- (S) (3:33) MCA 5938 Vintage Music Volumes 15 & 16.
- (S) (3:33) MCA 31213 Vintage Music Volume 16.
- (S) (3:32) MCA 10288 Classic Soul.

CLINT HOLMES
1973 #2 *PLAYGROUND IN MY MIND*
- (S) (2:55) Rhino 70758 Super Hits Of The 70's Volume 11.
- (S) (2:53) Columbia/Legacy 46763 Rock Artifacts Volume 2.

JAKE HOLMES
1970 #29 *SO CLOSE*

LEROY HOLMES
1956 #16 *WHEN THE LILACS BLOOM AGAIN*

RICHARD "GROOVE" HOLMES
1966 #32 *MISTY*

HOMBRES
1967 #7 *LET IT OUT (LET IT ALL HANG OUT)*
    (S) (2:06) K-Tel 205 Battle Of The Bands Volume 3.
    (M) (2:02) Mercury 834216 45's On CD Volume 3.
    (S) (2:06) Rhino 70996 One Hit Wonders Of The 60's Volume 2.

HOMER & JETHRO
1959 #16 *THE BATTLE OF KOOKAMONGA*
    (S) (2:36) RCA 8467 Nipper's Greatest Hits Of The 50's Volume 2.
    (S) (2:36) Rhino 70743 Dr. Demento 20th Anniversary Collection.

HONDELLS
1964 #10 *LITTLE HONDA*
    (S) (2:03) Mercury 826448 Oldies Golden Million Sellers.
    (S) (2:03) Mercury 816555 45's On CD Volume 2.
    (S) (2:03) Dunhill Compact Classics 030 Beach Classics.
1966 #38 *YOUNGER GIRL*

HONEYCOMBS
1964 #4 *HAVE I THE RIGHT*
    (M) (2:55) Rhino 70906 American Bandstand Greatest Hits Collection.
    (M) (2:56) Rhino 70319 History Of British Rock Volume 1.
    (M) (2:56) Rhino 72022 History Of British Rock Box Set.
    (M) (2:56) Rhino 72008 History Of British Rock Volumes 1-4 Box Set.

HONEYCONE
1971 #1 *WANT ADS*
    (M) (2:33) Pair 1202 Best Of Buddah. (*cd jacket mistakenly identifies the group as "Honeycomb"; 45 length*)
    (S) (2:45) Rhino 70785 Soul Hits Of The 70's Volume 5. (*"Sweet Replies" LP length; :09 longer fade than the single*)
    (S) (3:46) H-D-H 3902 Greatest Hits. (*"Soulful Tapestry" LP version*)
1971 #7 *STICK UP*
    (S) (2:49) Rhino 70785 Soul Hits Of The 70's Volume 5.
    (S) (3:00) H-D-H 3902 Greatest Hits. (*LP version*)
1972 #14 *ONE MONKEY DON'T STOP NO SHOW (PART 1)*
    (S) (3:42) Rhino 70787 Soul Hits Of The 70's Volume 7. (*45 version but :11 longer than the 45*)
    (S) (3:27) H-D-H 3902 Greatest Hits. (*LP version*)
1972 #15 *THE DAY I FOUND MYSELF*
    (S) (3:06) Rhino 70788 Soul Hits Of The 70's Volume 8.
    (S) (4:14) H-D-H 3902 Greatest Hits. (*LP version*)

MARY HOPKIN
1968 #1 *THOSE WERE THE DAYS*
    (S) (5:07) Capitol 97578 Post Card.
1969 #17 *GOODBYE*

JOHNNY HORTON
1959 #1 *THE BATTLE OF NEW ORLEANS*
    (S) (2:30) Rhino 70680 Billboard's Top Country Hits Of 1959.
    (S) (2:29) Columbia 45017 Radio Classics Of The 50's.

JOHNNY HORTON (Continued)

      (S) (2:29) Columbia 46031   Columbia Country Classics Volume 3.

      (S) (2:31) Columbia 45071   American Originals.

      (S) (2:31) Columbia 40665   Greatest Hits.

1960 #5 *SINK THE BISMARK*

      (S) (3:12) Rhino 70681   Billboard's Top Country Hits Of 1960.

      (S) (3:14) Columbia 45071   American Originals.

      (S) (3:14) Columbia 40665   Greatest Hits.

      (S) (3:14) CBS Special Products 46200   Rock Goes To The Movies Volume 3.

1960 #6 *NORTH TO ALASKA*

      (S) (2:48) Rhino 70682   Billboard's Top Country Hits Of 1961.

      (M) (2:48) Columbia 44373   Hollywood Magic - The 1960's.

      (M) (2:46) Columbia 46031   Columbia Country Classics Volume 3.

      (S) (2:49) Columbia 45071   American Originals.

      (S) (2:49) Columbia 40665   Greatest Hits.

      (S) (2:49) CBS Special Products 46200   Rock Goes To The Movies Volume 3.

HOT BUTTER

1972 #11 *POPCORN*

      (S) (2:30) Rhino 70929   Super Hits Of The 70's Volume 9.

HOTLEGS

1970 #20 *NEANDERTHAL MAN*

      (the actual 45 time is (4:18) not (4:29) as stated on the record label; the LP version is the same as the 45 version except that it fades out instead of ending cold)

      (S) (4:18) Rhino 70923   Super Hits Of The 70's Volume 3. *(LP version)*

      (S) (4:18) Rhino 72009   Super Hits Of The 70's Volumes 1-4 Box Set. *(LP version)*

DAVID HOUSTON

1966 #27 *ALMOST PERSUADED*

      (S) (2:54) Rhino 70687   Billboard's Top Country Hits Of 1966.

      (S) (2:53) Columbia 46032   Columbia Country Classics Volume 4.

      (S) (2:56) Columbia 45074   American Originals.

DON HOWARD

1958 #4 *OH HAPPY DAY*

HUES CORPORATION

1973 #38 *FREEDOM FOR THE STALLION*

      (S) (3:54) Collectables 5215   Rock The Boat/Golden Classics.

FRED HUGHES

1965 #25 *OO WEE BABY, I LOVE YOU*

      (E) (2:17) Motown 6215   Hits From The Legendary Vee-Jay Records.

JIMMY HUGHES

1964 #12 *STEAL AWAY*

      (M) (2:24) Stax 8559   Superblues Volume 2.

HUGO & LUIGI

1957 #40 *SHENANDOAH ROSE*

1958 #18 *CHA-HUA-HUA*

1959 #33 *LA PLUME DE MA TANTE*

HUMAN BEINZ
1968 #5 *NOBODY BUT ME*
(E) (2:18) K-Tel 839 Battle Of The Bands Volume 2. *(slightly longer intro than the LP or 45)*
(M) (2:15) Rhino 75772 Frat Rock.
(E) (2:16) EMI 90614 Non-Stop Party Rock.
(S) (2:16) Dunhill Compact Classics 029 Toga Rock.
(M) (2:15) Capitol 48993 Spuds Mackenzie's Party Faves.
(M) (2:15) Capitol 98138 Spring Break Volume 1.

ENGELBERT HUMPERDINCK
1967 #3 *RELEASE ME (AND LET ME LOVE AGAIN)*
(S) (3:20) London 820367 Greatest Hits.
(S) (3:20) London 820459 Release Me.
1967 #24 *THERE GOES MY EVERYTHING*
(S) (2:53) London 820367 Greatest Hits.
1967 #21 *THE LAST WALTZ*
(S) (2:58) London 820367 Greatest Hits.
1968 #24 *AM I THAT EASY TO FORGET*
(S) (3:07) London 820367 Greatest Hits.
1968 #18 *A MAN WITHOUT LOVE*
(S) (3:19) London 820367 Greatest Hits.
1968 #22 *LES BICYCLETTES DE BELSIZE*
(S) (3:11) London 820367 Greatest Hits.
1969 #26 *THE WAY IT USED TO BE*
(S) (3:09) London 820367 Greatest Hits.
1969 #39 *I'M A BETTER MAN*
(S) (2:48) London 820367 Greatest Hits.
1970 #13 *WINTER WORLD OF LOVE*
(S) (3:20) London 820367 Greatest Hits.
1970 #27 *MY MARIE*
1970 #38 *SWEETHEART*
1971 #37 *WHEN THERE'S NO YOU*
1971 #40 *ANOTHER TIME, ANOTHER PLACE*

PAUL HUMPHREY & HIS COOL AID CHEMISTS
1971 #22 *COOL AID*
(S) (2:41) Rhino 70785 Soul Hits Of The 70's Volume 5.

IVORY JOE HUNTER
1956 #12 *SINCE I MET YOU BABY*
(M) (2:42) JCI 3204 Heart & Soul Fifties. *(sounds muddy)*
(M) (2:42) Atlantic 81295 Atlantic Rhythm & Blues Volume 3.
(M) (2:41) Atlantic 81769 O.S.T. Big Town.
(M) (2:41) Atlantic 82305 Atlantic Rhythm And Blues 1947-1974 Box Set.
1957 #17 *EMPTY ARMS*
(M) (2:40) Atlantic 81295 Atlantic Rhythm & Blues Volume 3.
(M) (2:40) Atlantic 82305 Atlantic Rhythm And Blues 1947-1974 Box Set.
(S) (1:57) Collectables 5226 I'm Coming Down With The Blues.
(rerecorded)

TAB HUNTER
1957 #1 *YOUNG LOVE*
1957 #16 *NINETY-NINE WAYS*
1959 #22 *(I'LL BE WITH YOU) IN APPLE BLOSSOM TIME*

FERLIN HUSKY

1957 #6 GONE
    (M) (2:22) Curb 77330 50's Hits - Country Volume 1.
    (M) (2:22) Curb 77341 Greatest Hits.
    (M) (2:22) Capitol 91629 Capitol Collector's Series.

1957 #24 A FALLEN STAR
    (M) (2:22) Capitol 91629 Capitol Collector's Series.

1961 #11 WINGS OF A DOVE
    (S) (2:17) Curb 77343 60's Hits - Country Volume 1.
    (S) (2:17) Curb 77341 Greatest Hits.
    (S) (2:16) Capitol 91629 Capitol Collector's Series.

BRIAN HYLAND

1960 #1 ITSY BITSY TEENIE WEENIE YELLOW POLKA DOT BIKINI
    (S) (2:20) MCA 31202 Vintage Music Volume 5.
    (S) (2:20) MCA 5804 Vintage Music Volumes 5 & 6.

1961 #23 LET ME BELONG TO YOU

1962 #28 GINNY COME LATELY

1962 #3 SEALED WITH A KISS
    (M) (2:40) MCA 31207 Vintage Music Volume 10. *(noisy intro)*
    (M) (2:40) MCA 5806 Vintage Music Volumes 9 & 10. *(noisy intro)*

1962 #24 WARMED OVER KISSES (LEFT OVER LOVE)

1966 #29 THE JOKER WENT WILD

1970 #3 GYPSY WOMAN
    (M) (2:33) Rhino 70923 Super Hits Of The 70's Volume 3.
    (M) (2:33) Rhino 72009 Super Hits Of The 70's Volumes 1-4 Box Set.

DICK HYMAN & HIS ELECTRIC ECLECTICS

1969 #34 THE MINOTAUR

DICK HYMAN TRIO

1956 #7 MORITAT - A THEME FROM THE "THREE PENNY OPERA"

I

JANIS IAN
1967 #13 *SOCIETY'S CHILD*
    (M) (3:10) Rhino 70734 Songs Of Protest.
    (M) (3:11) Warner Special Products 27615 Storytellers: Singers &
                  Songwriters.
    (M) (3:11) Mercury 834216 45's On CD Volume 3.

IDES OF MARCH
1970 #6 *VEHICLE*
    (S) (2:53) Rhino 70631 Billboard's Top Rock & Roll Hits Of 1970.
    (S) (2:53) Rhino 72005 Billboard's Top Rock & Roll Hits 1968-1972 Box
                  Set.
    (S) (2:53) JCI 3101 Rockin' Sixties.

FRANK IFIELD
1962 #9 *I REMEMBER YOU*
    (M) (2:02) Enigma 73531 O.S.T. Scandal.
    (E) (2:02) Curb 77453 Best Of.

IKETTES
1962 #16 *I'M BLUE (THE GONG GONG SONG)*
    (M) (2:28) MCA 6228 O.S.T. Hairspray.
    (M) (2:29) Atlantic 82305 Atlantic Rhythm And Blues 1947-1974 Box Set.
    (M) (2:31) Curb 77332 Ike & Tina Turner's Greatest Hits. *(sounds like it was mastered from vinyl)*

ILLUSION
1969 #30 *DID YOU SEE HER EYES*

IMPALAS
1959 #2 *SORRY (I RAN ALL THE WAY HOME)*

IMPRESSIONS
1961 #17 *GYPSY WOMAN*
    (S) (2:18) Rhino 70647 Billboard's Top R&B Hits Of 1961.
    (S) (2:18) MCA 31203 Vintage Music Volume 6.
    (S) (2:18) MCA 5804 Vintage Music Volumes 5 & 6.
    (S) (2:19) MCA 31338 Greatest Hits.
1963 #4 *IT'S ALL RIGHT*
    (S) (2:46) Rhino 70649 Billboard's Top R&B Hits Of 1963.
    (S) (2:46) Rhino 75757 Soul Shots Volume 3.
    (S) (2:48) MCA 31202 Vintage Music Volume 5.
    (S) (2:48) MCA 5804 Vintage Music Volumes 5 & 6.
    (S) (2:48) MCA 31338 Greatest Hits.
    (S) (2:48) Ripete 392183 Ocean Drive.
1964 #13 *TALKING ABOUT MY BABY*
    (S) (2:29) MCA 5940 Vintage Music Volumes 19 & 20.
    (S) (2:29) MCA 31217 Vintage Music Volume 20.
    (S) (2:29) MCA 31338 Greatest Hits.

IMPRESSIONS (Continued)
1964 #16 *I'M SO PROUD*
    (S) (2:47) Rhino 75757 Soul Shots Volume 3.
    (S) (2:47) MCA 5939 Vintage Music Volumes 17 & 18.
    (S) (2:47) MCA 31214 Vintage Music Volume 17.
    (S) (2:47) MCA 31338 Greatest Hits.

1964 #10 *KEEP ON PUSHING*
    (S) (2:32) Rhino 70650 Billboard's Top R&B Hits Of 1964.
    (S) (2:30) MCA 5936 Vintage Music Volumes 11 & 12.
    (S) (2:30) MCA 31208 Vintage Music Volume 11.
    (S) (2:31) MCA 31338 Greatest Hits.

1964 #14 *YOU MUST BELIEVE ME*
    (S) (2:31) MCA 31338 Greatest Hits.

1964 #8 *AMEN*
    (S) (3:27) MCA 31204 Vintage Music Volume 7.
    (S) (3:27) MCA 5805 Vintage Music Volumes 7 & 8.
    (S) (3:26) MCA 31338 Greatest Hits.
    (S) (3:25) MCA 25991 Christmas Hits.

1965 #15 *PEOPLE GET READY*
    (S) (2:36) MCA 31338 Greatest Hits.

1965 #29 *WOMAN'S GOT SOUL*
    (S) (2:21) MCA 31207 Vintage Music Volume 10.
    (S) (2:21) MCA 5806 Vintage Music Volumes 9 & 10.
    (S) (2:21) MCA 31338 Greatest Hits.

1966 #36 *YOU'VE BEEN CHEATIN'*
    (E) (2:33) MCA 31338 Greatest Hits.

1968 #11 *WE'RE A WINNER*
    (S) (2:22) Rhino 70654 Billboard's Top R&B Hits Of 1968.
    (S) (2:22) Rhino 72006 Billboard's Top R&B Hits 1965-1969 Box Set.
    (S) (2:21) MCA 31338 Greatest Hits.
    (S) (2:21) MCA 10288 Classic Soul.

1968 #18 *FOOL FOR YOU*
1969 #27 *THIS IS MY COUNTRY*
1969 #21 *CHOICE OF COLORS*
1970 #21 *CHECK OUT YOUR MIND*

INDEPENDENTS
1973 #18 *LEAVING ME*
    (S) (3:07) Rhino 70790 Soul Hits Of The 70's Volume 10.

1973 #36 *BABY I'VE BEEN MISSING YOU*

JORGEN INGMANN
1961 #4 *APACHE*

LUTHER INGRAM
1972 #3 *(IF LOVING YOU IS WRONG) I DON'T WANT TO BE RIGHT*
    (M) (3:25) Rhino 70788 Soul Hits Of The 70's Volume 8.

1973 #32 *I'LL BE YOUR SHELTER (IN TIME OF STORM)*

INNOCENTS
1960 #37 *HONEST I DO*
1961 #33 *GEE WHIZ*

INTRIGUES
1969 #37 *IN A MOMENT*
    (S) (2:47) Collectables 5180 In A Moment/Golden Classics.

INTRUDERS
1968 #5 *COWBOYS TO GIRLS*
     (S) (2:36) Rhino 75774 Soul Shots.

     (S) (2:36) Philadelphia International 32131 Super Hits.
1973 #25 *I'LL ALWAYS LOVE MY MAMA (PART 1)*
     (S) (9:46) Philadelphia International 34940 Philadelphia Classics. *(this version first appeared on the vinyl album "Philadelphia Classics" in 1977)*

IRISH ROVERS
1968 #6 *THE UNICORN*
     (S) (3:18) MCA 5940 Vintage Music Volumes 19 & 20.

     (S) (3:18) MCA 31216 Vintage Music Volume 19.

     (S) (3:18) MCA 15 The Unicorn.

BIG DEE IRWIN
1963 #21 *SWINGING ON A STAR*
     (M) (2:36) Collectables 5407 Best Of Little Eva.

ISLANDERS
1959 #16 *THE ENCHANTED SEA*

ISLEY BROTHERS
1959 #28 *SHOUT (PART 1)*
     (S) (4:24) RCA 8467 Nipper's Greatest Hits Of The 50's Volume 2. *(Parts 1 & 2)*

     (S) (4:38) Rhino 70732 Grandson Of Frat Rock. *(Parts 1 & 2; Part 2 is :13 longer than the LP length and :08 longer than the 45 length)*

     (S) (2:14) Warner Brothers 3359 O.S.T. The Wanderers.

     (S) (2:14) Dunhill Compact Classics 043 Toga Rock II.

     (S) (4:38) Rhino 70908 Isley Brothers Story Volume 1. *(Parts 1 & 2; Part 2 is :13 longer than the LP length and :08 longer than the 45 length)*

     (S) (4:40) RCA 9901 Shout! The Complete Victor Sessions. *(Parts 1 & 2; Part 2 is :15 longer than the LP length and :10 longer than the 45 length)*

     (E) (4:39) RCA 61144 The RCA Records Label: The First Note In Black Music. *(Parts 1 & 2; Part 2 is :14 longer than the LP length and :09 longer than the 45 length)*

     (S) (2:16) Essex 7052 All Time Rock Classics.

     (S) (4:25) Collectables 5103 Shout. *(Parts 1 & 2)*
1962 #7 *TWIST AND SHOUT*
     (S) (2:28) Dunhill Compact Classics 029 Toga Rock.

     (M) (2:29) Dunhill Compact Classics 028 Sock Hop.

     (S) (2:28) Rhino 70732 Grandson Of Frat Rock.

     (M) (2:28) Curb 77333 Best Of.

     (S) (2:28) Rhino 70908 Isley Brothers Story Volume 1.

     (M) (2:27) Motown 5483 Greatest Hits And Rare Classics.

     (S) (2:31) Capricorn 42003 The Scepter Records Story.

1966 #15 *THIS OLD HEART OF MINE (IS WEAK FOR YOU)*
     (S) (2:51) Motown 6219 Hard To Find Motown Classics Volume 3. *(LP length)*

     (S) (2:51) Motown 6159 The Good Feeling Music Of The Big Chill Generation Volume 1. *(LP length)*

     (S) (2:52) Motown 6138 The Composer Series: Holland/Dozier/Holland. *(LP length)*

     (S) (2:36) Motown 5453 A Collection Of 16 Big Hits Volume 6. *(45 length)*

     (S) (2:51) MCA 6214 Moonlighting - TV Soundtrack. *(LP length)*

     (S) (2:51) Curb 77333 Best Of. *(LP length)*

ISLEY BROTHERS (Continued)

        (S) (2:53) Rhino 70908 Isley Brothers Story Volume 1. *(LP length)*
        (M) (2:42) Motown 5483 Greatest Hits And Rare Classics. *(45 length)*
        (S) (2:51) MCA 10063 Original Television Soundtrack "The Sounds Of Murphy Brown". *(LP length)*
        (S) (2:51) Motown 5128 This Old Heart Of Mine. *(LP length)*
        (S) (2:49) Motown 9071 Motown Dance Party Volume 1. *(all selections on this cd are segued together; LP length)*
        (S) (2:51) Ripete 392183 Ocean Drive.

1969 #2 *IT'S YOUR THING*

        (S) (2:49) Rhino 70655 Billboard's Top R&B Hits Of 1969.
        (S) (2:49) Rhino 72006 Billboard's Top R&B Hits 1965-1969 Box Set.
        (S) (2:46) Rhino 70909 Isley Brothers Story Volume 2.
        (S) (2:44) Motown 5483 Greatest Hits And Rare Classics.

1969 #17 *I TURNED YOU ON*

        (S) (2:36) Rhino 70909 Isley Brothers Story Volume 2.

1971 #10 *LOVE THE ONE YOU'RE WITH*

        (S) (3:38) Rhino 70909 Isley Brothers Story Volume 2.

1971 #39 *SPILL THE WINE*

        (S) (6:35) Rhino 70909 Isley Brothers Story Volume 2. *(LP version; truncated fade)*

1972 #36 *LAY AWAY*

        (S) (3:23) Rhino 70909 Isley Brothers Story Volume 2.

1972 #23 *POP THAT THANG*

        (S) (2:55) Rhino 70909 Isley Brothers Story Volume 2.

1973 #6 *THAT LADY (PART 1)*

        (S) (3:18) Rhino 70661 Billboard's Top R&B Hits Of 1973.
        (S) (5:35) Columbia/Legacy 46160 Rock Artifacts Volume 1. *(Parts 1 & 2)*
        (S) (5:34) T-Neck 39240 Greatest Hits Volume 1. *(Parts 1 & 2)*
        (M) (2:47) Curb 77333 Best Of. *(1964 noncharting version)*
        (S) (2:47) Rhino 70908 Isley Brothers Story Volume 1. *(1964 noncharting version)*
        (S) (2:47) EMI 95203 The Complete UA Sessions. *(1964 noncharting version)*
        (S) (2:47) EMI 96286 24 Greatest Hits Of All Time. *(1964 noncharting version)*
        (S) (5:34) Rhino 70909 Isley Brothers Story Volume 2. *(Parts 1 & 2)*

BURL IVES

1962 #7 *A LITTLE BITTY TEAR*

        (M) (2:03) MCA 2-8025 30 Years Of Hits 1958-1974.

1962 #11 *FUNNY WAY OF LAUGHIN'*
1962 #22 *CALL ME MR. IN-BETWEEN*
1962 #39 *MARY ANN REGRETS*

IVY THREE

1960 #10 *YOGI*

J

CHUCK JACKSON
1961 #24 I DON'T WANT TO CRY
- (M) (2:14) Collectables 5115 Golden Classics.
- (S) (2:18) Capricorn 42003 The Scepter Records Story.
1962 #12 ANY DAY NOW (MY WILD BEAUTIFUL BIRD)
- (S) (3:18) Collectables 5115 Golden Classics.
- (S) (3:24) Capricorn 42003 The Scepter Records Story.

DEON JACKSON
1966 #12 LOVE MAKES THE WORLD GO ROUND
- (S) (2:28) Rhino 75770 Soul Shots Volume 2.

JERMAINE JACKSON
1973 #7 DADDY'S HOME
- (S) (2:57) Motown 0868 and 6194 Jackson Five Anthology.
- (S) (3:03) Motown 5484 Greatest Hits And Rare Classics.

J J JACKSON
1966 #26 BUT IT'S ALRIGHT
- (E) (2:47) Rhino 75774 Soul Shots.
- (E) (2:47) JCI 3105 Soul Sixties.

MICHAEL JACKSON
1972 #1 GOT TO BE THERE
- (S) (3:22) Motown 0868 and 6194 Jackson Five Anthology.
- (S) (3:22) Motown 9040 Compact Command Performances.
- (S) (3:22) Motown 5402 and 6195 Anthology.
- (S) (3:22) Motown 5416 Got To Be There.
- (S) (3:21) Motown 5312 Great Songs And Performances That Inspired The Motown 25th Anniversary TV Special.
- (S) (3:21) Motown 8000 and 8100 Got To Be There/Ben.
- (S) (3:22) Motown 5194 and 9079 Best Of.
- (S) (3:21) Motown 6250 Original Soul Of.
1972 #1 ROCKIN' ROBIN
- (S) (2:30) Motown 0868 and 6194 Jackson Five Anthology.
- (S) (2:31) Motown 9040 Compact Command Performances.
- (S) (2:30) Motown 5402 and 6195 Anthology.
- (S) (2:31) Motown 5416 Got To Be There.
- (S) (2:30) Motown 5312 Great Songs And Performances That Inspired The Motown 25th Anniversary TV Special.
- (S) (2:30) Motown 8000 and 8100 Got To Be There/Ben.
- (S) (2:31) Motown 5194 and 9079 Best Of.
- (S) (2:30) Motown 6250 Original Soul Of.
1972 #7 I WANNA BE WHERE YOU ARE
- (S) (2:52) Motown 9105 Motown Memories Volume 2.
- (S) (2:58) Motown 0868 and 6194 Jackson Five Anthology.

MICHAEL JACKSON (Continued)

(S) (2:58) Motown 9040 Compact Command Performances.
(S) (2:54) Motown 5402 and 6195 Anthology.
(S) (2:59) Motown 5416 Got To Be There.
(S) (2:55) Motown 5312 Great Songs And Performances That Inspired The Motown 25th Anniversary TV Special.
(S) (2:59) Motown 8000 and 8100 Got To Be There/Ben.
(S) (2:55) Motown 5194 and 9079 Best Of.

1972 #2 BEN

(S) (2:43) Motown 0868 and 6194 Jackson Five Anthology.
(S) (2:44) Motown 9040 Compact Command Performances.
(S) (2:43) Motown 5344 Every Great Motown Song: The First 25 Years Volume 2.
(S) (2:43) Motown 5402 and 6195 Anthology.
(S) (2:43) Motown 5153 Ben.
(S) (2:43) Motown 5275 12 #1 Hits From The 70's.
(S) (2:43) Motown 5312 Great Songs And Performances That Inspired The Motown 25th Anniversary TV Special.
(S) (2:43) Motown 8000 and 8100 Got To Be There/Ben.
(S) (2:43) Motown 5194 and 9079 Best Of.
(S) (2:43) Motown 0937 20/20 Twenty No. 1 Hits From Twenty Years At Motown.

1973 #37 WITH A CHILD'S HEART

(S) (3:31) Motown 9040 Compact Command Performances.
(S) (3:30) Motown 5402 and 6195 Anthology.
(S) (3:30) Motown 5194 and 9079 Best Of.

MILLIE JACKSON

1972 #19 ASK ME WHAT YOU WANT
1972 #34 MY MAN, A SWEET MAN
1973 #18 HURTS SO GOOD

(S) (3:45) Rhino 70553 Soul Hits Of The 70's Volume 13.

STONEWALL JACKSON

1959 #3 WATERLOO

(S) (2:27) Rhino 70680 Billboard's Top Country Hits Of 1959.
(M) (2:27) Columbia 46031 Columbia Country Classics Volume 3.
(S) (2:26) Columbia 45070 American Originals.
(S) (2:27) CBS Special Products 8186 The Dynamic.

WANDA JACKSON

1960 #37 LET'S HAVE A PARTY

(E) (2:08) EMI 90614 Non Stop Party Rock.
(M) (2:08) Rhino 70742 Rock This Town: Rockabilly Hits Volume 2.
(M) (2:07) JCI 3201 Partytime Fifties.
(E) (2:07) Curb 77398 Greatest Hits.
(M) (2:08) Rhino 70990 Rockin' In The Country: Best Of.

1961 #29 IN THE MIDDLE OF A HEARTACHE

(S) (2:32) Curb 77398 Greatest Hits.
(S) (2:32) Rhino 70990 Rockin' In The Country: Best Of.

JACKSON FIVE

1970 #1 I WANT YOU BACK

(S) (2:58) Rhino 70631 Billboard's Top Rock & Roll Hits Of 1970.
(S) (2:58) Rhino 72005 Billboard's Top Rock & Roll Hits 1968-1972 Box Set.
(S) (2:57) Motown 6132 25 #1 Hits From 25 Years.

JACKSON FIVE (Continued)

(S) (2:58) Motown 0868 and 6194 Anthology.
(S) (2:58) Motown 9040 Compact Command Performances.
(S) (2:55) Motown 5129 Diana Ross Presents.
(S) (2:56) Motown 5275 12 #1 Hits From The 70's.
(S) (2:56) Motown 5312 Great Songs And Performances That Inspired The Motown 25th Anniversary TV Special.
(S) (2:57) Motown 8019 and 8119 Diana Ross Presents/ABC.
(S) (2:57) Motown 5201 Greatest Hits.
(S) (2:56) Motown 0937 20/20 Twenty No. 1 Hits From Twenty Years At Motown.
(S) (2:50) Motown 9071 Motown Dance Party Volume 1. *(all selections on this cd are segued together)*
(S) (2:54) Pair 1272 Original Motown Classics.

1970 #1 ABC

(S) (2:57) Motown 6132 25 #1 Hits From 25 Years.
(S) (2:57) Motown 0868 and 6194 Anthology.
(S) (2:57) Motown 9040 Compact Command Performances.
(S) (2:56) Motown 5275 12 #1 Hits From The 70's.
(S) (2:56) Motown 5312 Great Songs And Performances That Inspired The Motown 25th Anniversary TV Special.
(S) (2:56) Motown 8019 and 8119 Diana Ross Presents/ABC.
(S) (2:54) Motown 5152 ABC. *(truncated fade)*
(S) (2:57) Motown 5201 Greatest Hits.
(S) (2:57) Motown 9060 Motown's Biggest Pop Hits.
(S) (2:53) Motown 9071 Motown Dance Party Volume 1. *(all selections on this cd are segued together)*
(S) (2:56) Pair 1272 Original Motown Classics.

1970 #1 THE LOVE YOU SAVE

(S) (3:03) Rhino 70658 Billboard's Top R&B Hits Of 1970.
(S) (3:03) Motown 0868 and 6194 Anthology.
(S) (3:02) Motown 9040 Compact Command Performances.
(S) (3:00) Motown 9072 Motown Dance Party Volume 2. *(all selections on this cd are segued together)*
(S) (3:01) Motown 5312 Great Songs And Performances That Inspired The Motown 25th Anniversary TV Special.
(S) (3:02) Motown 8019 and 8119 Diana Ross Presents/ABC.
(S) (2:58) Motown 5152 ABC.
(S) (3:02) Motown 5201 Greatest Hits.
(S) (2:58) Pair 1272 Original Motown Classics.

1970 #1 I'LL BE THERE

(S) (3:54) Motown 9110 Motown Memories Volume 4.
(S) (3:56) Motown 6132 25 #1 Hits From 25 Years.
(S) (3:56) Rhino 70658 Billboard's Top R&B Hits Of 1970.
(S) (3:56) Motown 0868 and 6194 Anthology.
(S) (3:56) Motown 9040 Compact Command Performances.
(S) (3:57) Motown 5157 Third Album.
(S) (3:55) Motown 5402 and 6195 Michael Jackson Anthology.
(S) (3:54) Motown 5275 12 #1 Hits From The 70's.
(S) (3:54) Motown 5312 Great Songs And Performances That Inspired The Motown 25th Anniversary TV Special.
(S) (3:56) Motown 8011 and 8111 Third Album/Maybe Tomorrow.
(S) (3:56) Motown 5201 Greatest Hits.
(S) (3:55) Motown 9060 Motown's Biggest Pop Hits.
(S) (3:55) Motown 0937 20/20 Twenty No. 1 Hits From Twenty Years At Motown.

JACKSON FIVE (Continued)

1971 #1 MAMA'S PEARL
- (S) (3:02) Motown 0868 and 6194 Anthology. (*:09 shorter than 45 or LP*)
- (S) (3:12) Motown 9040 Compact Command Performances.
- (S) (3:07) Motown 5157 Third Album.
- (S) (3:07) Motown 8011 and 8111 Third Album/Maybe Tomorrow.
- (S) (3:11) Motown 5201 Greatest Hits.

1971 #1 NEVER CAN SAY GOODBYE
- (S) (2:57) Motown 6137 20 Greatest Songs In Motown History.
- (S) (2:58) Rhino 70659 Billboard's Top R&B Hits Of 1971.
- (S) (2:57) Motown 0868 and 6194 Anthology.
- (S) (2:59) Motown 9040 Compact Command Performances.
- (S) (2:59) Motown 5324 and 9035 Top Ten With A Bullet: Motown Love Songs.
- (S) (2:57) Motown 5344 Every Great Motown Song: The First 25 Years Volume 2. (*most selections on this cd have noise on the fade out*)
- (S) (2:57) Motown 5228 Maybe Tomorrow.
- (S) (2:56) Motown 5402 and 6195 Michael Jackson Anthology.
- (S) (2:57) Motown 8034 Every Great Motown Song: The First 25 Years Volumes 1 & 2. (*most selections on this cd have noise on the fade out*)
- (S) (2:57) Motown 8011 and 8111 Third Album/Maybe Tomorrow.
- (S) (2:59) Motown 5201 Greatest Hits.
- (S) (2:57) Motown 0937 20/20 Twenty No. 1 Hits From Twenty Years At Motown.
- (S) (2:57) Pair 1272 Original Motown Classics.

1971 #16 MAYBE TOMORROW
- (S) (4:39) Motown 0868 and 6194 Anthology.
- (S) (4:38) Motown 9040 Compact Command Performances.
- (S) (4:40) Motown 5228 Maybe Tomorrow.
- (S) (4:37) Motown 5402 and 6195 Michael Jackson Anthology.
- (S) (4:37) Motown 5312 Great Songs And Performances That Inspired The Motown 25th Anniversary TV Special.
- (S) (4:39) Motown 8011 and 8111 Third Album/Maybe Tomorrow.
- (S) (4:38) Motown 5201 Greatest Hits.

1972 #6 SUGAR DADDY
- (S) (2:30) Motown 0868 and 6194 Anthology.
- (S) (2:29) Motown 9040 Compact Command Performances.
- (S) (2:29) Motown 5201 Greatest Hits.

1972 #5 LITTLE BITTY PRETTY ONE
- (S) (2:44) Motown 0868 and 6194 Anthology.

1972 #15 LOOKIN' THROUGH THE WINDOWS
- (S) (3:35) Motown 0868 and 6194 Anthology.
- (S) (3:31) Motown 9040 Compact Command Performances.

1972 #12 CORNER OF THE SKY
- (S) (3:29) Motown 0868 and 6194 Anthology.
- (S) (3:33) Motown 5469 Skywriter.

1973 #21 HALLELUJAH DAY
- (S) (2:45) Motown 0868 and 6194 Anthology.
- (S) (2:46) Motown 5469 Skywriter.

1973 #24 GET IT TOGETHER
- (S) (2:46) Motown 0868 and 6194 Anthology.
- (S) (2:48) Motown 9040 Compact Command Performances.

DICK JACOBS & HIS ORCHESTRA
1956 #21 *PETTICOATS OF PORTUGAL*
1957 #12 *FASCINATION*
JAGGERZ
1970 #2 *THE RAPPER*
      (S) (2:42) Rhino 70921   Super Hits Of The 70's Volume 1. *(LP version)*
      (S) (2:42) Rhino 72009   Super Hits Of The 70's Volumes 1-4 Box Set. *(LP version)*
      (S) (2:42) Rhino 70631   Billboard's Top Rock & Roll Hits Of 1970. *(LP version)*
      (S) (2:42) Rhino 72005   Billboard's Top Rock & Roll Hits 1968 - 1972 Box Set. *(LP version)*
      (M) (2:40) Pair 1202   Best Of Buddah. *(45 version)*
      (M) (2:40) Pair 1199   Best Of Bubblegum Music. *(45 version)*
      (M) (2:41) K-Tel 839   Battle Of The Bands Volume 2. *(45 version)*
      (M) (2:40) Priority 7997   Super Songs/70's Greatest Rock Hits Volume 8. *(45 version)*
      (M) (2:40) Special Music 4914   Best Of The Bubblegum Years. *(45 version)*
ETTA JAMES
1960 #23 *ALL I COULD DO WAS CRY*
      (M) (2:56) Chess 9280   The Sweetest Peaches/Chess Years Volume 1.
      (E) (2:53) Chess 9266   At Last!
      (E) (2:51) Telstar/JCI 3505   Best Of.
1960 #25 *MY DEAREST DARLING*
      (S) (3:00) Chess 9266   At Last!
      (S) (2:57) Telstar/JCI 3505   Best Of.
1961 #30 *AT LAST*
      (S) (2:57) Chess 9266   At Last!
      (S) (2:56) Telstar/JCI 3505   Best Of.
1961 #25 *TRUST IN ME*
      (S) (2:57) Chess 9266   At Last!
      (S) (2:56) Telstar/JCI 3505   Best Of.
1962 #20 *SOMETHING'S GOT A HOLD ON ME*
      (M) (2:46) Chess 31317   Best Of Chess Rhythm & Blues Volume 1.
      (M) (2:46) Chess 9280   The Sweetest Peaches/Chess Years Volume 1.
      (M) (2:45) Telstar/JCI 3505   Best Of.
1962 #22 *STOP THE WEDDING*
      (M) (2:40) Chess 9280   The Sweetest Peaches/Chess Years Volume 1.
      (M) (2:30) Telstar/JCI 3505   Best Of.
1963 #24 *PUSHOVER*
      (M) (2:54) Chess 9280   The Sweetest Peaches/Chess Years Volume 1.
      (E) (2:54) Telstar/JCI 3505   Best Of.
1968 #27 *TELL MAMA*
      (S) (2:20) MCA 31205   Vintage Music Volume 8.
      (S) (2:20) MCA 5805   Vintage Music Volumes 7 & 8.
      (S) (2:20) Garland 011   Footstompin' Oldies.
      (S) (2:20) Chess 31318   Best Of Chess Rhythm & Blues Volume 2.
      (M) (2:19) Chess 9269   Tell Mama.
      (S) (2:20) Chess 9281   The Sweetest Peaches/Chess Years Volume 2.
      (M) (2:19) Telstar/JCI 3505   Best Of.
1968 #37 *SECURITY*
      (M) (2:44) Chess 9269   Tell Mama. *(LP version)*
      (S) (2:27) Chess 9281   The Sweetest Peaches/Chess Years Volume 2. *(edit of LP version in an unsuccessful attempt to recreate the 45 version)*
      (M) (2:44) Telstar/JCI 3505   Best Of. *(LP version)*

ETTA JAMES & HARVEY FUQUA (ETTA & HARVEY)
1960 #32 *IF I CAN'T HAVE YOU*
        (M) (2:50) Chess 9280 The Sweetest Peaches/Chess Years Volume 1.

JONI JAMES
1955 #5   *HOW IMPORTANT CAN IT BE?*
1955 #9   *YOU ARE MY LOVE*
1956 #30 *GIVE US THIS DAY*
1958 #21 *THERE GOES MY HEART*
1959 #28 *THERE MUST BE A WAY*

SONNY JAMES
1957 #1 *YOUNG LOVE*
        (M) (2:29) Curb 77354 50's Hits Volume 1.
        (M) (2:29) Curb 77330 50's Hits - Country Volume 1.
        (M) (2:30) JCI 3203 Lovin' Fifties.
        (M) (2:29) Curb 77359 Greatest Hits.
        (M) (2:28) Capitol 91630 Capitol Collector's Series.
        (M) (2:29) Curb 77525 Greatest Hits Of Rock 'N' Roll Volume 2.
1957 #31 *FIRST DATE, FIRST KISS, FIRST LOVE*
        (M) (2:26) Capitol 91630 Capitol Collector's Series.

TOMMY JAMES
1971 #2 *DRAGGIN' THE LINE*
        (S) (2:47) Rhino 70632 Billboard's Top Rock & Roll Hits Of 1971.
        (S) (2:47) Rhino 72005 Billboard's Top Rock & Roll Hits 1968-1972 Box Set.
        (S) (2:43) Rhino 70925 Super Hits Of The 70's Volume 5.
        (S) (2:44) Rhino 70735 The Solo Years (1970 - 1981).
        (S) (2:43) Rhino 70920 Tommy James & The Shondells Anthology.
        (S) (2:44) Pair 1278 Very Best Of.
1971 #23 *I'M COMIN' HOME*
        (S) (2:02) Rhino 70735 The Solo Years (1970 - 1981).
        (S) (2:03) Pair 1278 Very Best Of.
1972 #25 *NOTHING TO HIDE*
        (S) (2:39) Rhino 70735 The Solo Years (1970 - 1981).
1973 #40 *BOO, BOO, DON'T 'CHA BE BLUE*
        (S) (3:28) Rhino 70735 The Solo Years (1970 - 1981).

TOMMY JAMES & THE SHONDELLS
1966 #1 *HANKY PANKY*
        (M) (2:52) Rhino 70627 Billboard's Top Rock & Roll Hits Of 1966. *(mastered from vinyl)*
        (M) (2:52) Rhino 72007 Billboard's Top Rock & Roll Hits 1962-1966 Box Set. *(mastered from vinyl)*
        (M) (2:51) Priority 7909 Vietnam: Rockin' the Delta. *(mastered from vinyl)*
        (M) (2:51) Rhino 70920 Anthology. *(mastered from vinyl)*
1966 #15 *SAY I AM (WHAT I AM)*
        (S) (2:29) Rhino 70920 Anthology.
        (S) (2:29) Pair 1278 Very Best Of.
1966 #27 *IT'S ONLY LOVE*
        (the actual 45 time is (2:07); the actual LP time is (2:13) not (2:07) as stated on the LP label)
        (S) (2:15) Rhino 70920 Anthology.
        (S) (2:15) Pair 1278 Very Best Of.

TOMMY JAMES & THE SHONDELLS (Continued)

1967 #3 I THINK WE'RE ALONE NOW
- (M) (2:07) Rhino 70628 Billboard's Top Rock & Roll Hits Of 1967.
- (M) (2:07) Rhino 72007 Billboard's Top Rock & Roll Hits 1962-1966 Box Set.
- (M) (2:07) Rhino 70920 Anthology.

1967 #10 MIRAGE
- (S) (2:36) Rhino 70920 Anthology.
- (S) (2:36) Pair 1278 Very Best Of.

1967 #30 I LIKE THE WAY
- (S) (2:40) Rhino 70920 Anthology.
- (S) (2:40) Pair 1278 Very Best Of.

1967 #14 GETTIN' TOGETHER
- (S) (2:13) Rhino 70920 Anthology.
- (S) (2:13) Pair 1278 Very Best Of.

1967 #37 OUT OF THE BLUE
- (S) (2:23) Rhino 70920 Anthology.
- (S) (2:23) Pair 1278 Very Best Of.

1968 #38 GET OUT NOW
- (S) (2:10) Rhino 70920 Anthology.
- (S) (2:10) Pair 1278 Very Best Of.

1968 #3 MONY MONY
(the actual 45 time is (2:55) not (2:45) as stated on the record label)
- (S) (2:51) Rhino 70629 Billboard's Top Rock & Roll Hits Of 1968.
- (S) (2:51) Rhino 72005 Billboard's Top Rock & Roll Hits 1968-1972 Box Set.
- (S) (2:51) Rhino 70906 American Bandstand Greatest Hits Collection.
- (S) (2:49) Dunhill Compact Classics 029 Toga Rock. (*remixed*)
- (S) (3:17) Rhino 75772 Son Of Frat Rock. (*:26 longer than either the LP or 45 version; remixed*)
- (S) (2:50) Warner Special Products 27610 More Party Classics. (*LP mix*)
- (S) (2:52) Rhino 70920 Anthology.
- (S) (2:51) Essex 7052 All Time Rock Classics. (*LP mix*)

1968 #38 SOMEBODY CARES
- (S) (2:39) Rhino 70920 Anthology.
- (S) (2:39) Pair 1278 Very Best Of.

1968 #24 DO SOMETHING TO ME
- (S) (2:28) Rhino 70920 Anthology.
- (S) (3:17) Rhino 70534 Crimson & Clover/Cellophane Symphony. (*LP version running (2:27) + :50 LP reprise*)
- (S) (2:28) Pair 1278 Very Best Of.

1969 #1 CRIMSON AND CLOVER
- (S) (3:23) Rhino 70630 Billboard's Top Rock & Roll Hits Of 1969. (*45 version*)
- (S) (3:23) Rhino 72005 Billboard's Top Rock & Roll Hits 1968-1972 Box Set. (*45 version*)
- (S) (3:26) K-Tel 686 Battle Of The Bands Volume 4. (*45 version*)
- (S) (3:26) Rhino 70920 Anthology. (*45 version*)
- (S) (5:30) Rhino 70534 Crimson & Clover/Cellophane Symphony. (*LP version with :07 studio talk*)
- (S) (3:27) Pair 1278 Very Best Of. (*45 version*)

TOMMY JAMES & THE SHONDELLS (Continued)

1969 #10 SWEET CHERRY WINE
(dj copies of this 45 ran (4:22) not (3:59) as stated on the record label; commercial copies ran (4:14) not (4:25) as stated on the record label; the difference in time between the dj and commercial 45's is due to the fact that the dj copies were :08 slower in pitch)
- (S) (4:28) Rhino 70920 Anthology. *(neither the LP or 45 version)*
- (S) (4:19) Rhino 70534 Crimson & Clover/Cellophane Symphony.
- (S) (4:28) Pair 1278 Very Best Of. *(neither the 45 or LP version)*

1969 #2 CRYSTAL BLUE PERSUASION
(the actual 45 time is (3:52) not (3:45) as stated on the record label)
- (S) (4:01) Rhino 70920 Anthology. *(remixed 45 version but LP length)*
- (S) (4:01) Rhino 70534 Crimson & Clover/Cellophane Symphony. *(LP version)*
- (S) (4:01) Pair 1278 Very Best Of. *(remixed 45 version but LP length)*

1969 #11 BALL OF FIRE
(the actual 45 time is (2:55); the actual LP time is (2:47))
- (S) (3:04) Rhino 70920 Anthology.
- (S) (3:04) Pair 1278 Very Best Of.

1970 #19 SHE
- (S) (2:01) Rhino 70920 Anthology.
- (S) (2:01) Pair 1278 Very Best Of.

1970 #28 GOTTA GET BACK TO YOU
- (S) (3:02) Rhino 70920 Anthology.
- (S) (3:02) Pair 1278 Very Best Of.

1970 #36 COME TO ME
(the actual 45 and LP time is (2:35) not (2:56) as the LP label states)
- (S) (3:11) Rhino 70735 The Solo Years (1970 - 1981). *(rerecording)*
- (S) (2:35) Pair 1278 Very Best Of.

JAMES GANG

1971 #29 WALK AWAY
- (S) (2:50) Rhino 70986 Heavy Metal Memories. *(45 version)*
- (S) (3:33) MCA 31274 Classic Rock Volume 2. *(LP version)*
- (S) (3:31) MCA 6012 15 Greatest Hits. *(LP version)*

JAMIES

1958 #26 SUMMERTIME SUMMERTIME
- (S) (1:59) Rhino 70087 Summer & Sun.

JAN & ARNIE

1958 #3 JENNIE LEE
- (S) (1:57) EMI 46885 Best Of Jan & Dean. *(rerecording)*

JAN & DEAN

1959 #7 BABY TALK
- (E) (2:22) Curb 77374 All Time Greatest Hits.
- (E) (2:23) EMI 46885 Best Of Jan & Dean.
- (M) (2:25) Essex 7053 A Hot Summer Night In '59.

1960 #39 WE GO TOGETHER
- (E) (2:43) EMI 46885 Best Of.

1961 #16 HEART AND SOUL
- (E) (2:06) Curb 77374 All Time Greatest Hits.
- (E) (2:06) EMI 46885 Best Of Jan & Dean.

1963 #26 LINDA
- (S) (2:33) Curb 77374 All Time Greatest Hits.
- (S) (2:46) EMI 92772 Legendary Masters Series. *(with :11 studio talk)*

JAN & DEAN (Continued)
1963 #1 SURF CITY
- (S) (2:26) Rhino 70624 Billboard's Top Rock & Roll Hits Of 1963.
- (S) (2:26) Rhino 72007 Billboard's Top Rock & Roll Hits 1962-1966 Box Set.
- (S) (2:26) JCI 3106 Surfin' Sixties.
- (S) (2:40) EMI 92772 Legendary Masters Series. *(:14 longer than either the 45 or LP)*
- (S) (2:40) EMI 96268 24 Greatest Hits Of All Time. *(:14 longer than either the 45 or LP)*
- (S) (2:26) EMI 90604 Beach Party Blasts.
- (S) (2:26) Curb 77355 60's Hits Volume 1.
- (S) (2:26) Rhino 70089 Surfin' Hits.
- (S) (2:26) Capitol 96861 Monster Summer Hits - Wild Surf.
- (M) (2:28) Curb 77374 All Time Greatest Hits. *(rerecording)*
- (S) (2:40) Capitol 98139 Spring Break Volume 2. *(:14 longer than either the 45 or LP)*

1963 #10 HONOLULU LULU
- (S) (2:12) Curb 77374 All Time Greatest Hits.
- (S) (2:16) EMI 92772 Legendary Masters Series.

1963 #10 DRAG CITY
- (S) (2:17) EMI 90604 Beach Party Blasts.
- (S) (2:15) Capitol 96862 Monster Summer Hits - Drag City.
- (S) (2:18) Curb 77374 All Time Greatest Hits.
- (S) (2:15) EMI 92772 Legendary Masters Series. *(with stereo LP version sound effects)*

1964 #9 DEAD MAN'S CURVE
(the actual 45 time is (2:33) not (2:21) as stated on the record label)
- (S) (2:27) Capitol 96862 Monster Summer Hits - Drag City.
- (S) (2:44) Curb 77374 All Time Greatest Hits. *(noncharting version from the "Drag City" vinyl LP)*
- (S) (2:27) EMI 92772 Legendary Masters Series.

1964 #26 THE NEW GIRL IN SCHOOL
- (S) (3:03) EMI 92772 Legendary Masters Series. *(with :08 studio talk and :27 longer ending than either the 45 or LP)*

1964 #5 THE LITTLE OLD LADY FROM PASADENA
- (S) (2:22) Rhino 70625 Billboard's Top Rock & Roll Hits Of 1964.
- (S) (2:22) Rhino 72007 Billboard's Top Rock & Roll Hits 1962-1966 Box Set.
- (S) (2:42) Capitol 96862 Monster Summer Hits - Drag City. *(:17 longer than either the LP or 45)*
- (S) (2:22) Curb 77374 All Time Greatest Hits.
- (S) (2:42) EMI 92772 Legendary Masters Series. *(:17 longer ending than either the LP or 45)*

1964 #23 RIDE THE WILD SURF
- (S) (2:17) Rhino 70089 Surfin' Hits.
- (M) (2:15) JCI 3106 Surfin' Sixties.
- (S) (2:16) Capitol 96861 Monster Summer Hits - Wild Surf.
- (S) (2:18) Curb 77374 All Time Greatest Hits.
- (S) (2:21) EMI 92772 Legendary Masters Series. *(with :05 countoff)*

1964 #28 SIDEWALK SURFIN'
- (S) (2:15) Capitol 96861 Monster Summer Hits - Wild Surf. *(LP version)*
- (S) (2:34) EMI 92772 Legendary Masters Series. *(45 version but :14 longer than 45 version and :19 longer than LP version)*

JAN & DEAN (Continued)
1965 #39 *I FOUND A GIRL*
      (S) (2:31) EMI 92772 Legendary Masters Series.
1966 #24 *POPSICLE*
      (S) (2:33) EMI 92772 Legendary Masters Series. *(LP length)*

HORST JANKOWSKI
1965 #9 *A WALK IN THE BLACK FOREST*

JARMELS
1961 #13 *A LITTLE BIT OF SOAP*
      (E) (2:11) Collectables 5044 14 Golden Classics.

JAY & THE AMERICANS
1962 #4 *SHE CRIED*
      (S) (2:53) EMI 93448 Come A Little Bit Closer/Best Of.
1963 #28 *ONLY IN AMERICA*
      (S) (1:58) EMI 48384 Greatest Hits.
      (S) (2:01) EMI 93448 Come A Little Bit Closer/Best Of.
      (M) (2:07) Rhino 70593 The Rock 'N' Roll Classics Of Leiber & Stoller.
              (slightly slower in pitch than the 45; much slower in pitch than the LP)
1964 #4 *COME A LITTLE BIT CLOSER*
      (E) (2:44) EMI 48384 Greatest Hits.
      (M) (2:45) EMI 93448 Come A Little Bit Closer/Best Of.
1965 #10 *LET'S LOCK THE DOOR (AND THROW AWAY THE KEY)*
      (E) (2:29) EMI 93448 Come A Little Bit Closer/Best Of.
1965 #4 *CARA MIA*
      (S) (2:30) EMI 48384 Greatest Hits.
      (S) (2:32) EMI 93448 Come A Little Bit Closer/Best Of.
1965 #15 *SOME ENCHANTED EVENING*
      (E) (2:12) EMI 48384 Greatest Hits.
      (S) (2:16) EMI 93448 Come A Little Bit Closer/Best Of.
1965 #20 *SUNDAY AND ME*
      (S) (2:55) EMI 93448 Come A Little Bit Closer/Best Of. *(includes :32 of studio talk)*
1966 #32 *CRYING*
      (S) (3:08) EMI 93448 Come A Little Bit Closer/Best Of. *(includes :31 of studio talk and a false start)*
1969 #5 *THIS MAGIC MOMENT*
      (S) (3:02) EMI 96268 24 Greatest Hits Of All Time.
      (S) (3:02) EMI 93448 Come A Little Bit Closer/Best Of.
      (S) (3:02) Capitol 98139 Spring Break Volume 2. *(truncated fade)*
1970 #14 *WALKIN' IN THE RAIN*
      (S) (2:46) EMI 93448 Come A Little Bit Closer/Best Of.

JAY & THE TECHNIQUES
1967 #4 *APPLES, PEACHES, PUMPKIN PIE*
      (S) (2:24) Mercury 834216 45's On CD Volume 3.
1967 #10 *KEEP THE BALL ROLLIN'*
1968 #29 *STRAWBERRY SHORTCAKE*

JERRY JAYE
1967 #27 *MY GIRL JOSEPHINE*

JAYHAWKS
1956 #10 *STRANDED IN THE JUNGLE*

JAYNETTES
1963 #3 *SALLY GO 'ROUND THE ROSES*
    (M) (3:14) Rhino 70988 Best Of The Girl Groups Volume 1. *(neither the LP or 45 version)*
    (S) (3:12) Chess 31320 Best Of Chess Rock 'n' Roll Volume 2. *(missing an organ overdub; :09 longer fade than the 45 or LP)*
    (S) (3:12) MCA 31203 Vintage Music Volume 6. *(missing an organ overdub; :09 longer fade than the 45 or LP)*
    (S) (3:12) MCA 5804 Vintage Music Volumes 5 & 6. *(missing an organ overdub; :09 longer fade than the 45 or LP)*

CATHY JEAN & THE ROOMMATES
1961 #12 *PLEASE LOVE ME FOREVER*

JEFFERSON
1970 #19 *BABY TAKE ME IN YOUR ARMS*

JEFFERSON AIRPLANE
1967 #5 *SOMEBODY TO LOVE*
    (S) (2:57) RCA 8474 Nipper's Greatest Hits Of The 60's Volume 1.
    (S) (2:59) RCA 3766 Surrealistic Pillow.
    (S) (2:58) RCA 5724 2400 Fulton Street.
    (S) (2:55) RCA 4459 Worst Of.
    (S) (2:55) RCA 2078 White Rabbit & Other Hits.
1967 #6 *WHITE RABBIT*
    (S) (2:30) Atlantic 81742 O.S.T. Platoon.
    (S) (2:32) RCA 3766 Surrealistic Pillow.
    (S) (2:32) RCA 5724 2400 Fulton Street.
    (S) (2:31) RCA 4459 Worst Of.
    (S) (2:31) RCA 2078 White Rabbit & Other Hits.
    (S) (2:31) Pair 1090 Time Machine.
1967 #24 *BALLAD OF YOU & ME & POONEIL*
    (S) (4:35) RCA 5724 2400 Fulton Street. *(tracks into next selection)*
    (S) (4:38) RCA 4459 Worst Of.
    (S) (4:37) RCA 4545 After Bathing At Baxter's. *(LP version which tracks into "A SMALL PACKAGE OF VALUE WILL COME TO YOU SHORTLY" and "YOUNG GIRL SUNDAY BLUES" for a total time of (9:42))*
1967 #37 *WATCH HER RIDE*
    (S) (3:12) RCA 4545 After Bathing At Baxter's. *(LP version which tracks into "SPARE CHAYNGE" for a total time of (12:22))*
1971 #35 *PRETTY AS YOU FEEL*
    (S) (4:28) RCA 5724 2400 Fulton Street. *(LP version)*

JOE JEFFREY GROUP
1969 #13 *MY PLEDGE OF LOVE*
    (S) (2:44) Rhino 75774 Soul Shots. *(this song begins in mono but ends in true stereo!)*
    (S) (2:40) Capricorn 42003 The Scepter Records Story. *(this song begins in electronic stereo but ends in true stereo!)*

JELLY BEANS
1964 #10 *I WANNA LOVE HIM SO BAD*
    (M) (2:43) Rhino 75891 Wonder Women.
    (M) (2:42) Rhino 70988 Best Of The Girl Groups Volume 1.

KRIS JENSEN
1962 #20 *TORTURE*

JETHRO TULL
1973 #15 *LIVING IN THE PAST*
    (S) (3:19) Warner Special Products 27614 Highs Of The Seventies.
    (S) (4:05) Chrysalis 21655 and 41655 20 Years Of Jethro Tull. *(Live)*
    (S) (3:19) Chrysalis 21078 and 41078 M.U. The Best Of.
    (S) (3:18) Chrysalis 21035 and 41035 Living In The Past.
    (S) (3:16) Chrysalis 21515 and 41515 Original Masters.
    (S) (4:05) Chrysalis 21653 and 41653 20 Years Of Tull Box Set. *(live)*

JOSE JIMENEZ
1961 #19 *THE ASTRONAUT (PARTS 1 & 2)*
    (S) (5:52) Rhino 70749 Best Of.

JIVE BOMBERS
1957 #24 *BAD BOY*

JIVE FIVE
1961 #6 *MY TRUE STORY*
    (M) (2:31) Relic 7007 My True Story.
    (M) (2:33) Rhino 75763 Best Of Doo Wop Ballads.
    (M) (2:33) Rhino 70647 Billboard's Top R&B Hits Of 1961.
    (M) (2:33) Dunhill Compact Classics 031 Back Seat Jams.
    (S) (2:23) Collectables 5022 Their Greatest Hits. *(missing some overdubs)*
    (S) (2:47) Relic 7007 My True Story. *(includes :17 false start; missing some overdubs)*

1965 #35 *I'M A HAPPY MAN*

DAMITA JO
1960 #17 *I'LL SAVE THE LAST DANCE FOR YOU*
1961 #30 *I'LL BE THERE*

ELTON JOHN
1971 #8 *YOUR SONG*
    (S) (4:00) MCA 31105 Elton John.
    (S) (3:59) MCA 37215 Greatest Hits.
    (S) (3:59) MCA 10110 To Be Continued.
    (S) (3:58) MCA 31016 Your Songs.
    (S) (3:59) JCI 3303 Love Seventies.

1971 #17 *FRIENDS*
    (S) (2:22) MCA 10110 To Be Continued.
    (S) (2:21) MCA 31016 Your Songs.

1972 #17 *LEVON*
· *the actual 45 time is (5:08) not (4:59) as stated on the record label)*
    (S) (5:21) MCA 31190 Madman Across The Water. *(LP length)*
    (S) (5:20) MCA 37216 Greatest Hits Volume 2. *(LP length)*
    (S) (5:21) MCA 10110 To Be Continued. *(LP length)*
    (S) (5:20) MFSL 516 Madman Across The Water. *(LP length)*

1972 #29 *TINY DANCER*
    (S) (6:14) MCA 31190 Madman Across The Water.
    (S) (6:13) MCA 10110 To Be Continued.
    (S) (6:12) MCA 31016 Your Songs.
    (S) (6:16) MFSL 516 Madman Across The Water.

1972 #11 *ROCKET MAN*
    (S) (4:40) MCA 25240 Classic Rock Volume 3.
    (S) (4:38) MCA 31104 Honky Chateau.

ELTON JOHN (Continued)

      (S) (4:40) MCA 37215 Greatest Hits.
      (S) (4:40) MCA 10110 To Be Continued.
      (S) (4:41) MFSL 536 Honky Chateau. *(truncated fade)*

1972 #18 *HONKY CAT*

      (S) (5:11) MCA 31104 Honky Chateau. *(tracks into next selection)*
      (S) (5:11) MCA 37215 Greatest Hits. *(glitch at end of fade)*
      (S) (5:11) MCA 10110 To Be Continued.
      (S) (5:15) MFSL 536 Honky Chateau. *(tracks into next selection)*

1973 #1 *CROCODILE ROCK*

      (S) (3:54) Rhino 70634 Billboard's Top Rock & Roll Hits Of 1973.
      (S) (3:53) JCI 3301 Rockin' Seventies.
      (S) (3:55) MCA 31077 Don't Shoot Me I'm Only The Piano Player.
      (S) (3:54) MCA 37215 Greatest Hits.
      (S) (3:54) MCA 10110 To Be Continued.

1973 #2 *DANIEL*

      (S) (3:50) Sandstone 33003 Reelin' In The Years Volume 4.
      (S) (3:53) MCA 31077 Don't Shoot Me I'm Only The Piano Player.
      (S) (3:52) MCA 37215 Greatest Hits.
      (S) (3:52) MCA 10110 To Be Continued.

1973 #9 *SATURDAY NIGHT'S ALRIGHT FOR FIGHTING*

      (S) (4:52) MCA 31274 Classic Rock Volume 2.
      (S) (4:46) MCA 2-6894 Goodbye Yellow Brick Road.
      (S) (4:52) MCA 37215 Greatest Hits.
      (S) (4:53) MCA 10110 To Be Continued.
      (S) (4:53) MFSL 526 Goodbye Yellow Brick Road.

1973 #1 *GOODBYE YELLOW BRICK ROAD*

      (S) (3:13) Rhino 70634 Billboard's Top Rock & Roll Hits Of 1973. *(glitch at 3:13)*
      (S) (3:12) MCA 2-6894 Goodbye Yellow Brick Road.
      (S) (3:13) MCA 37215 Greatest Hits.
      (S) (3:13) MCA 10110 To Be Continued.
      (S) (3:12) MFSL 526 Goodbye Yellow Brick Road.

LITTLE WILLIE JOHN

1956 #24 *FEVER*

      (M) (2:39) Atlantic 81769 O.S.T. Big Town.

1960 #27 *HEARTBREAK (IT'S HURTIN' ME)*

1960 #18 *SLEEP*

ROBERT JOHN

1968 #34 *IF YOU DON'T WANT MY LOVE*

      (S) (2:18) CBS Special Products 37915 Endless Beach.

1972 #2 *THE LION SLEEPS TONIGHT*

      (S) (2:32) Atlantic 81909 Hit Singles 1958 - 1977.
      (S) (3:38) Curb 77532 Your Favorite Songs. *(rerecording)*
      (S) (2:33) Curb 77543 Greatest Hits.

JOHNNIE & JOE

1957 #22 *OVER THE MOUNTAIN; ACROSS THE SEA*

      (M) (2:16) Rhino 70643 Billboard's Top R&B Hits Of 1957.
      (M) (2:15) Chess 31320 Best Of Chess Rock 'n' Roll Volume 2.

JOHNNY & THE HURRICANES

1959 #26 *CROSSFIRE*

1959 #5 *RED RIVER ROCK*

      (M) (2:10) Curb 77402 All-Time Great Instrumental Hits Volume 2.

JOHNNY & THE HURRICANES (Continued)
1959 #22 *REVEILLE ROCK*
1960 #10 *BEATNIK FLY*
1960 #31 *DOWN YONDER*

BETTY JOHNSON
1957 #20 *I DREAMED*
1958 #25 *THE LITTLE BLUE MAN*

MARV JOHNSON
1959 #30 *COME TO ME*
       (M) (2:17) Collectables 5236 Marvelous Marv/Golden Classics.
       (M) (2:17) EMI 98895 Best Of.

1960 #5 *YOU GOT WHAT IT TAKES*
       (M) (2:40) EMI 98895 Best Of.
       (M) (2:41) EMI 96268 24 Greatest Hits Of All Time.
       (M) (2:39) Rhino 70646 Billboard's Top R&B Hits Of 1960.
       (M) (2:39) JCI 3204 Heart & Soul Fifties.
       (M) (2:39) Curb 77323 All Time Greatest Hits Of Rock 'N' Roll.
       (M) (2:40) Collectables 5236 Marvelous Marv/Golden Classics.

1960 #8 *I LOVE THE WAY YOU LOVE*
       (M) (2:37) EMI 98895 Best Of.
       (M) (2:36) Collectables 5236 Marvelous Marv/Golden Classics.

1960 #22 *(YOU'VE GOT TO) MOVE TWO MOUNTAINS*
       (S) (2:43) EMI 98895 Best Of.
       (S) (2:43) Collectables 5236 Marvelous Marv/Golden Classics.

1961 #39 *HAPPY DAYS*
       (M) (2:17) EMI 98895 Best Of.
       (S) (2:38) Collectables 5236 Marvelous Marv/Golden Classics.

JO JO GUNNE
1972 #31 *RUN RUN RUN*
       (S) (2:32) Rhino 70928 Super Hits Of The 70's Volume 8.

JON & ROBIN & THE IN CROWD
1967 #21 *DO IT AGAIN A LITTLE BIT SLOWER*
       (S) (2:30) Rhino 70995 One Hit Wonders Of The 60's Volume 1.

DAVY JONES
1971 #32 *RAINY JANE*

ETTA JONES
1960 #36 *DON'T GO TO STRANGERS*

JACK JONES
1963 #12 *WIVES AND LOVERS*
       (S) (2:28) Curb 77324 Greatest Hits.

1965 #15 *DEAR HEART*
1965 #12 *THE RACE IS ON*
       (S) (1:46) Curb 77324 Greatest Hits.

1966 #32 *THE IMPOSSIBLE DREAM*
       (S) (2:16) Curb 77324 Greatest Hits.

1967 #34 *LADY*

JIMMY JONES
1960 #2 *HANDY MAN*
(M)(1:59) Rhino 70621 Billboard's Top Rock & Roll Hits Of 1960.
(M)(1:59) Rhino 72004 Billboard's Top Rock & Roll Hits 1957-1961 Box Set.
(M)(1:59) Mercury 832041 45's On CD Volume 1.
1960 #3 *GOOD TIMIN'*
(S)(2:07) Mercury 816555 45's On CD Volume 2.

JOE JONES
1960 #2 *YOU TALK TOO MUCH*
(M) (2:35) Collectables 5416 Murray The K - Sing Along With The Golden Greats.

LINDA JONES
1967 #29 *HYPNOTIZED*
(S) (2:39) Rhino 75770 Soul Shots Volume 2.

TOM JONES
1965 #10 *IT'S NOT UNUSUAL*
(M) (2:00) Rhino 70323 History Of British Rock Volume 5.
(M) (2:00) Rhino 72022 History Of British Rock Box Set.
(S) (2:00) London 810192 Golden Hits.
1965 #2 *WHAT'S NEW PUSSYCAT*
(S) (2:04) London 810192 Golden Hits. *(LP version)*
1965 #25 *WITH THESE HANDS*
(S) (2:42) London 810192 Golden Hits.
1966 #22 *THUNDERBALL*
(S) (3:00) EMI 46079 James Bond 13 Original Themes.
(S) (3:00) EMI 90628 O.S.T. Thunderball.
1967 #10 *GREEN, GREEN GRASS OF HOME*
(S) (3:10) London 810192 Golden Hits. *(first :06 of song are silent)*
(S) (3:03) London 820182 Green, Green Grass Of Home.
1967 #22 *DETROIT CITY*
(S) (3:33) London 810192 Golden Hits.
(S) (3:29) London 820182 Green, Green Grass Of Home.
1968 #20 *DELILAH*
(S) (3:22) London 810192 Golden Hits.
(S) (3:23) London 820486 Delilah.
1968 #31 *HELP YOURSELF*
(S) (2:53) London 810192 Golden Hits.
1969 #38 *A MINUTE OF YOUR TIME*
(S) (2:57) London 810192 Golden Hits.
1969 #7 *LOVE ME TONIGHT*
(S) (3:11) London 810192 Golden Hits.
1969 #6 *I'LL NEVER FALL IN LOVE AGAIN*
(this 45 was issued in two lengths, (4:18) and (2:55))
(S) (4:12) London 810192 Golden Hits.
1970 #5 *WITHOUT LOVE (THERE IS NOTHING)*
(S) (3:44) London 810192 Golden Hits.
1970 #10 *DAUGHTER OF DARKNESS*
1970 #11 *I (WHO HAVE NOTHING)*
(S) (2:56) Rhino 70593 The Rock 'N' Roll Classics Of Leiber & Stoller.
1970 #23 *CAN'T STOP LOVING YOU*
1971 #1 *SHE'S A LADY*

TOM JONES *(Continued)*
 1971 #14 *PUPPET MAN*
 1971 #40 *RESURRECTION SHUFFLE*
 1971 #40 *TILL*
 1973 #34 *LETTER TO LUCILLE*

JANIS JOPLIN
 1969 #39 *KOZMIC BLUES*
      (S) (4:21) Columbia 9913 I Got Dem Ol' Kozmic Blues Again Mama!
 1971 #1 *ME AND BOBBY MC GEE*
      (S) (4:29) Columbia 45048 Rock Classics Of The 70's.
      (S) (4:30) Columbia 32168 Greatest Hits.
      (S) (4:29) Columbia 30322 Pearl.
      (S) (4:28) Sony Music Special Products 48621 Kris Kristofferson: Singer/Songwriter.
 1971 #20 *CRY BABY*
      (S) (3:56) Columbia 32168 Greatest Hits.
      (S) (3:57) Columbia 30322 Pearl.

BILL JUSTIS
 1957 #1 *RAUNCHY*
      (M) (2:21) Rhino 75884 The Sun Story.
      (S) (2:24) Mercury 832041 45's On CD Volume 1. *(rerecording)*
      (M) (2:20) RCA 66059 Sun's Greatest Hits.
 1958 #37 *COLLEGE MAN*

BERT KAEMPFERT
 1961 #1 *WONDERLAND BY NIGHT*
 1962 #37 *AFRIKAAN BEAT*
 1965 #9 *RED ROSES FOR A BLUE LADY*
      (S) (2:19) MFSL 795 Best Of.
 1965 #29 *THREE O'CLOCK IN THE MORNING*

KALIN TWINS
 1958 #5 *WHEN*
      (M) (2:25) MCA 31198 Vintage Music Volume 1.
      (M) (2:25) MCA 5777 Vintage Music Volumes 1 & 2.
      (M) (2:25) Curb 77354 50's Hits Volume 1.
      (M) (2:25) Curb 77525 Greatest Hits Of Rock 'N' Roll Volume 2.
 1958 #29 *FORGET ME NOT*

KITTY KALLEN
1959 #25 *IF I GIVE MY HEART TO YOU*
1963 #13 *MY COLORING BOOK*

KASENETZ KATZ SINGING ORCHESTRAL CIRCUS
1968 #18 *QUICK JOEY SMALL*
    (E) (2:21) Pair 1199 Best Of Bubblegum Music. *(group incorrectly identified on the cd as the "KASENETZ KATZ SUPER CIRCUS")*
    (E) (2:21) Special Music 4914 Best Of The Bubblegum Years.

SAMMY KAYE & HIS ORCHESTRA
1964 #31 *CHARADE*

ERNIE K-DOE
1961 #1 *MOTHER-IN-LAW*
    (M) (2:34) Rhino 75765 Best Of New Orleans Rhythm & Blues Volume 1.
    (M) (2:35) Rhino 70622 Billboard's Top Rock & Roll Hits Of 1961.
    (M) (2:35) Rhino 72004 Billboard's Top Rock & Roll Hits 1957-1961 Box Set.
    (E) (2:33) EMI 90614 Non-Stop Party Rock.
    (M) (2:32) Curb 77323 All Time Greatest Hits Of Rock 'N' Roll.

KEITH
1966 #31 *AIN'T GONNA LIE*
1967 #7 *98.6*
    (S) (3:02) Mercury 834216 45's On CD Volume 3.
1967 #31 *TELL ME TO MY FACE*

JERRY KELLER
1959 #24 *HERE COMES SUMMER*
    (S) (2:07) MCA 5937 Vintage Music Volumes 13 & 14.
    (S) (2:07) MCA 31211 Vintage Music Volume 14.

MONTY KELLY & HIS ORCHESTRA
1960 #27 *SUMMER SET*

EDDIE KENDRICKS
1973 #1 *KEEP ON TRUCKIN' (PART 1)*
    (the actual 45 time is (3:33) not (3:21) as stated on the record label)
    (S) (3:33) Rhino 70661 Billboard's Top R&B Hits Of 1973.
    (S) (3:33) Rhino 70551 Soul Hits Of The 70's Volume 11.
    (S) (3:34) Motown 6132 25 #1 Hits From 25 Years.
    (S) (3:32) Priority 7909 Vietnam: Rockin' The Delta.
    (S) (7:58) Motown 5481 At His Best. *(LP version)*
    (S) (3:30) Motown 9072 Motown Dance Party Volume 2. *(all selections on this cd are segued together)*
    (S) (3:33) Motown 9021 and 5309 25 Years Of Grammy Greats.
    (S) (3:28) Motown 5275 12 #1 Hits From The 70's.
    (S) (3:33) Motown 9060 Motown's Biggest Pop Hits.
    (S) (3:28) Motown 0937 20/20 Twenty No. 1 Hits From Twenty Years At Motown.

CHRIS KENNER
1961 #2 *I LIKE IT LIKE THAT (PART 1)*
    (M) (1:55) Warner Brothers 25613 O.S.T. Full Metal Jacket.
    (M) (1:55) Rhino 75766 Best Of New Orleans Rhythm & Blues Volume 2.
    (M) (1:55) Rhino 70647 Billboard's Top R&B Hits Of 1961.
    (E) (2:11) Collectables 5166 I Like It Like That/Golden Classics. *(mastered from vinyl; includes :12 studio talk)*

STAN KENTON
1962 #31 *MAMA SANG A SONG*

THEOLA KILGORE
1963 #21 *THE LOVE OF MY MAN*

ANDY KIM
1968 #16 *HOW'D WE EVER GET THIS WAY*
1968 #35 *SHOOT 'EM UP BABY*
1969 #6 *BABY, I LOVE YOU*
1969 #20 *SO GOOD TOGETHER*
1970 #12 *BE MY BABY*

B.B. KING
1964 #28 *ROCK ME BABY*
1970 #15 *THE THRILL IS GONE*
    (S) (5:24) Stax 8551 Superblues Volume 1. *(LP length)*
    (S) (5:25) MCA 31040 Best Of. *(LP length)*
    (S) (5:24) MCA 31039 Completely Well. *(LP length)*
    (S) (5:24) MCA 10288 Classic Soul. *(LP length)*
1973 #38 *TO KNOW YOU IS TO LOVE YOU*

BEN E. KING
1961 #9 *SPANISH HARLEM*
    (M) (2:53) Atlantic 81296 Atlantic Rhythm & Blues Volume 4.
    (M) (2:50) Abkco 7118 Phil Spector/Back To Mono (1958-1969).
    (S) (2:57) Atlantic 80213 Ultimate Collection.
    (S) (2:56) Atlantic 82305 Atlantic Rhythm And Blues 1947-1974 Box Set.
1961 #3 *STAND BY ME*
    (S) (2:58) Rhino 70647 Billboard's Top R&B Hits Of 1961.
    (M) (2:54) Atlantic 81296 Atlantic Rhythm & Blues Volume 4.
    (M) (2:53) Atlantic 81677 O.S.T. Stand By Me.
    (S) (2:58) Atlantic 81911 Golden Age Of Black Music (1960-1970).
    (S) (2:58) Warner Brothers 3359 O.S.T. The Wanderers.
    (S) (2:58) Warner Special Products 27601 Atlantic Soul Classics.
    (M) (2:51) Rhino 70593 The Rock 'N' Roll Classics Of Leiber & Stoller.
    (S) (2:58) Atlantic 80213 Ultimate Collection.
    (S) (2:58) Atlantic 82305 Atlantic Rhythm And Blues 1947-1974 Box Set.
1961 #19 *AMOR*
    (S) (3:04) Atlantic 81296 Atlantic Rhythm & Blues Volume 4.
    (S) (3:04) Atlantic 80213 Ultimate Collection.
    (S) (3:04) Atlantic 82305 Atlantic Rhythm And Blues 1947-1974 Box Set.
1962 #11 *DON'T PLAY THAT SONG (YOU LIED)*
    (M) (2:50) Atlantic 81296 Atlantic Rhythm & Blues Volume 4.
    (S) (2:47) Atlantic 80213 Ultimate Collection.
    (S) (2:47) Atlantic 82305 Atlantic Rhythm And Blues 1947-1974 Box Set.
1963 #25 *I (WHO HAVE NOTHING)*
    (M) (2:27) Atlantic 81297 Atlantic Rhythm & Blues Volume 5.
    (M) (2:26) Atlantic 80213 Ultimate Collection.
    (M) (2:26) Atlantic 82305 Atlantic Rhythm And Blues 1947-1974 Box Set.

CAROLE KING
1962 #29 *IT MIGHT AS WELL RAIN UNTIL SEPTEMBER*
    (M) (2:21) Rhino 70989 Best Of The Girl Groups Volume 2.
    (M) (2:24) Collectables 5414 Carole King Plus.
1971 #1 *IT'S TOO LATE*
    (S) (3:52) Epic/Ode 34946 Tapestry.
    (S) (3:53) Epic/Ode 34967 Her Greatest Hits.

CAROLE KING (Continued)
1971 #10 SO FAR AWAY
      (S) (3:55) Epic/Ode 34946 Tapestry.
      (S) (3:57) Epic/Ode 34967 Her Greatest Hits.
1972 #8 SWEET SEASONS
      (S) (3:13) Epic/Ode 34949 Music.
      (S) (3:15) Epic/Ode 34967 Her Greatest Hits.
1973 #20 BEEN TO CANAAN
      (S) (3:37) Epic/Ode 34950 Rhymes & Reasons.
      (S) (3:39) Epic/Ode 34967 Her Greatest Hits.
1973 #24 BELIEVE IN HUMANITY
      (S) (3:19) Epic/Ode 34962 Fantasy. *(all selections on this cd are segued together)*
      (S) (3:19) Epic/Ode 34967 Her Greatest Hits.
1973 #27 CORAZON
      (S) (4:05) Epic/Ode 34962 Fantasy. *(LP version where previous selection overlaps introduction; tracks into next selection)*
      (S) (3:57) Epic/Ode 34967 Her Greatest Hits. *(45 version)*

CLAUDE KING
1962 #5 WOLVERTON MOUNTAIN
      (S) (2:55) Rhino 70683 Billboard's Top Country Hits Of 1962.
      (S) (2:58) Columbia 46031 Columbia Country Classics Volume 3.
      (S) (2:57) Columbia 45075 American Originals.

JONATHAN KING
1965 #12 EVERYONE'S GONE TO THE MOON
      (S) (2:27) Rhino 70325 History Of British Rock Volume 7.
      (S) (2:27) Rhino 72022 History Of British Rock Box Set.

KING CURTIS
1962 #14 SOUL TWIST
      (M) (2:45) Rhino 70648 Billboard's Top R&B Hits Of 1962.
      (S) (2:47) Relic 7009 Raging Harlem Hit Parade.
      (S) (2:35) Capitol 91631 Best Of. *(rerecording)*
      (S) (2:45) Collectables 5119 Soul Twist And Other Golden Classics.
1967 #39 MEMPHIS SOUL STEW
      (S) (2:57) Warner Special Products 27609 Memphis Soul Classics.
      (S) (2:56) Atlantic 81298 Atlantic Rhythm & Blues Volume 6.
      (S) (2:54) JCI 3553 Soul Serenade.
      (S) (2:56) Atlantic 82305 Atlantic Rhythm And Blues 1947-1974 Box Set.
1967 #34 ODE TO BILLY JOE
      (S) (2:47) JCI 3553 Soul Serenade.

KING FLOYD
1971 #4 GROOVE ME
      (S) (2:59) Rhino 70659 Billboard's Top R&B Hits Of 1971.
      (S) (2:58) Rhino 70784 Soul Hits Of The 70's Volume 4.
      (S) (3:00) Atlantic 81299 Atlantic Rhythm & Blues Volume 7.
      (S) (3:00) Atlantic 81912 Golden Age Of Black Music (1970-1975).
      (S) (2:59) Atlantic 82305 Atlantic Rhythm And Blues 1947-1974 Box Set.
1971 #19 BABY LET ME KISS YOU
      (S) (2:49) Rhino 70785 Soul Hits Of The 70's Volume 5.

KING HARVEST
1973 #10 DANCING IN THE MOONLIGHT

KINGSMEN

1964 #1 *LOUIE LOUIE*
- (E) (2:42) Warner Special Products 27607 Highs Of The 60's.
- (M) (2:43) Rhino 75778 Frat Rock.
- (M) (2:43) Rhino 70624 Billboard's Top Rock & Roll Hits Of 1963.
- (M) (2:43) Rhino 72007 Billboard's Top Rock & Roll Hits 1962-1966 Box Set.
- (M) (2:43) Dunhill Compact Classics 029 Toga Rock.
- (M) (2:42) Capitol 48993 Spuds Mackenzie's Party Faves.
- (M) (2:42) Rhino 70605 Best Of Louie Louie.
- (M) (2:43) Rhino 70794 KFOG Presents M. Dung's Idiot Show.
- (M) (2:43) Rhino 70745 Greatest Hits.
- (M) (2:43) Collectables 5073 Louie Louie And Other Golden Classics.
- (M) (2:42) Essex 7052 All Time Rock Classics.
- (M) (2:43) Capricorn 42003 The Scepter Records Story.

1964 #17 *MONEY*
- (M) (2:29) Rhino 70745 Greatest Hits.
- (M) (2:29) Collectables 5073 Louie Louie And Other Golden Classics.

1964 #33 *DEATH OF AN ANGEL*
- (M) (2:31) Rhino 70745 Greatest Hits.
- (M) (2:33) Collectables 5073 Louie Louie And Other Golden Classics. *(live; mastered from vinyl)*

1965 #8 *JOLLY GREEN GIANT*
- (M) (1:57) Rhino 70745 Greatest Hits.
- (M) (1:57) Collectables 5073 Louie Louie And Other Golden Classics.
- (M) (1:57) Capricorn 42003 The Scepter Records Story.

KINGSTON TRIO

1958 #1 *TOM DOOLEY*
- (E) (3:01) Capitol 90592 Memories Are Made Of This.
- (M) (3:01) Curb 77354 50's Hits Volume 1.
- (M) (3:01) Curb 77385 Greatest Hits.
- (M) (3:01) Capitol 46624 Very Best Of.
- (M) (3:02) Capitol 92710 Capitol Collector's Series.
- (M) (3:01) Capitol 96748 The Kingston Trio/From the Hungry "i".
- (M) (3:02) Rhino 70264 Troubadours Of The Folk Era Volume 2.
- (M) (3:00) Pair 1067 Early American Heroes.
- (M) (3:02) Capitol 98665 When AM Was King.

1959 #18 *THE TIJUANA JAIL*
- (S) (2:48) Curb 77385 Greatest Hits.
- (S) (2:46) Capitol 46624 Very Best Of. *(this song appears in mono on cd's that were pressed in Japan)*
- (S) (2:48) Capitol 92710 Capitol Collector's Series.
- (E) (2:48) Pair 1067 Early American Heroes.

1959 #17 *M.T.A.*
- (S) (3:12) Curb 77385 Greatest Hits.
- (S) (3:11) Capitol 46624 Very Best Of. *(this song appears in mono on cd's that were pressed in Japan)*
- (S) (3:14) Capitol 92710 Capitol Collector's Series.
- (S) (3:13) Capitol 96749 At Large/Here We Go Again.
- (S) (3:13) Pair 1067 Early American Heroes.

1959 #20 *A WORRIED MAN*
- (S) (2:50) Curb 77385 Greatest Hits.
- (S) (2:47) Capitol 46624 Very Best Of. *(this song appears in mono on cd's that were pressed in Japan)*

    (S) (3:25) Capitol 92710 Capitol Collector's Series. *(with :33 false start and studio talk)*

    (S) (2:51) Capitol 96749 At Large/Here We Go Again.

    (E) (2:50) Pair 1067 Early American Heroes.

1962 #22 *WHERE HAVE ALL THE FLOWERS GONE*

    (S) (3:00) Rhino 70734 Songs Of Protest.

    (S) (3:01) Curb 77385 Greatest Hits.

    (S) (2:58) Capitol 46624 Very Best Of. *(this song appears in mono on cd's that were pressed in Japan)*

    (S) (3:01) Capitol 92710 Capitol Collector's Series.

    (S) (3:01) Pair 1067 Early American Heroes.

1963 #17 *GREENBACK DOLLAR*

    (S) (2:49) Curb 77385 Greatest Hits. *(uncensored LP version)*

    (S) (2:48) Capitol 46624 Very Best Of. *(this song appears in mono on cd's that were pressed in Japan; uncensored LP version)*

    (S) (2:49) Capitol 92710 Capitol Collector's Series. *(uncensored LP version)*

    (S) (2:49) Pair 1067 Early American Heroes. *(uncensored LP version)*

1963 #7 *REVEREND MR. BLACK*

    (S) (3:01) Curb 77385 Greatest Hits.

    (S) (2:58) Capitol 46624 Very Best Of. *(this song appears in mono on cd's that were pressed in Japan)*

    (S) (3:12) Capitol 92710 Collector's Series. *(with countoff and :13 longer fade than either the 45 or LP)*

    (S) (3:01) Pair 1221 Made In The USA.

1963 #36 *DESERT PETE*

    (S) (2:42) Capitol 46624 Very Best Of. *(this song appears in mono on cd's that were pressed in Japan)*

    (S) (2:47) Capitol 92710 Capitol Collector's Series.

    (S) (2:43) Pair 1221 Made In The USA.

KINKS

1964 #5 *YOU REALLY GOT ME*

    (M) (2:12) Rhino 70906 American Bandstand Greatest Hits Collection.

    (M) (2:13) Rhino 70086 Greatest Hits.

    (M) (2:12) Rhino 70319 History Of British Rock Volume 1.

    (M) (2:12) Rhino 72022 History Of British Rock Box Set.

    (M) (2:12) Rhino 72008 History Of British Rock Volumes 1-4 Box Set.

    (M) (2:12) Rhino 75772 Son Of Frat Rock.

    (M) (2:12) Rhino 70720 Legends Of Guitar - Rock; The 60's.

    (M) (2:12) Rhino 70315 You Really Got Me.

1965 #6 *ALL DAY AND ALL OF THE NIGHT*

    (M) (2:22) Rhino 70320 History Of British Rock Volume 2.

    (M) (2:22) Rhino 72022 History Of British Rock Box Set.

    (M) (2:22) Rhino 72008 History Of British Rock Volumes 1-4 Box Set.

    (M) (2:21) Rhino 70086 Greatest Hits.

    (M) (2:21) Rhino 70316 Kinda Kinks.

1965 #5 *TIRED OF WAITING FOR YOU*

    (M) (2:30) Rhino 70321 History Of British Rock Volume 3.

    (M) (2:30) Rhino 72022 History Of British Rock Box Set.

    (M) (2:30) Rhino 72008 History Of British Rock Volumes 1-4 Box Set.

    (M) (2:30) Rhino 70086 Greatest Hits.

    (M) (2:29) Rhino 70316 Kinda Kinks.

KINKS (Continued)
1965 #24 *SET ME FREE*
    (M) (2:10) Rhino 70086 Greatest Hits.
    (M) (2:10) Rhino 75769 Kinkdom.
1965 #40 *WHO'LL BE THE NEXT IN LINE*
    (M) (2:00) Rhino 70086 Greatest Hits.
    (M) (2:00) Rhino 75769 Kinkdom.
1966 #9 *A WELL RESPECTED MAN*
    (M) (2:40) Rhino 70322 Hitory Of British Rock Volume 4.
    (M) (2:40) Rhino 72022 History Of British Rock Box Set.
    (M) (2:40) Rhino 72008 History Of British Rock Volumes 1-4 Box Set.
    (M) (2:41) Rhino 70086 Greatest Hits.
    (M) (2:41) Rhino 75769 Kinkdom.
1966 #11 *SUNNY AFTERNOON*
    (M) (3:32) Rhino 70086 Greatest Hits.
    (E) (3:33) Reprise 6454 Kink Kronikles.
1970 #8 *LOLA*
    (S) (4:02) Reprise 6423 Lola Versus Powerman And The Moneygoround.
        (Coca Cola version)
    (S) (4:01) Reprise 6454 Kink Kronikles. *(Coca Cola version)*
1971 #39 *APEMAN*
    (S) (3:52) Reprise 6423 Lola Versus Powerman And The Moneygoround.
    (S) (3:52) Reprise 6454 Kink Kronikles.

MAC & KATIE KISSOON
1971 #18 *CHIRPY CHIRPY CHEEP CHEEP*

KNICKERBOCKERS
1966 #24 *LIES*
    (S) (2:40) K-Tel 713 Battle Of The Bands.
    (S) (2:42) Rhino 75892 Nuggets.
    (S) (2:42) JCI 3100 Dance Sixties.
    (S) (2:41) Warner Special Products 27607 Highs Of The 60's.
    (S) (2:40) Sundazed 11002 The Fabulous Knickerbockers.

FREDERICK KNIGHT
1972 #20 *I'VE BEEN LONELY FOR SO LONG*
    (S) (3:19) Stax 88005 Top Of The Stax.
    (S) (3:18) Stax 8548 Stax Soul Brothers.
    (S) (3:18) Rhino 70788 Soul Hits Of The 70's Volume 8.

GLADYS KNIGHT & THE PIPS (*also* THE PIPS)
released as by THE PIPS:
1961 #13 *EVERY BEAT OF MY HEART*
    (M) (2:00) Rhino 70647 Billboard's Top R&B Hits Of 1961. *(Vee Jay label hit version)*
    (M) (2:00) Motown 6215 Hits From the Legendary Vee-Jay Records. *(Vee Jay label hit version)*
    (E) (1:59) JCI 3102 Love Sixties. *(Fury label noncharting version)*
    (M) (2:04) Arista 8605 16 Original Doo Wop Classics. *(Fury label noncharting version)*
    (S) (2:03) Relic 7009 Raging Harlem Hit Parade. *(Fury label noncharting version)*
    (E) (2:00) Curb 77321 Greatest Hits. *(Vee Jay label hit version)*
    (S) (1:52) Motown 6200 and 0792 Gladys Knight & The Pips Anthology. *(rerecording)*

***released as by* GLADYS KNIGHT & THE PIPS:**

1962 #17 *LETTER FULL OF TEARS*
    (M) (2:48) Arista 8605 16 Original Doo-Wop Classics.
    (M) (2:48) Relic 7009 Raging Harlem Hit Parade.
    (E) (2:42) Curb 77321 Greatest Hits.
    (S) (3:48) Motown 6200 and 0792 Anthology. *(rerecording)*

1968 #1 *I HEARD IT THROUGH THE GRAPEVINE*
    (S) (2:46) Rhino 70653 Billboard's Top R&B Hits Of 1967.
    (S) (2:46) Rhino 72006 Billboard's Top R&B Hits 1965-1969 Box Set.
    (S) (2:44) Motown 6160 The Good-Feeling Music Of The Big Chill Generation Volume 2.
    (S) (2:43) Motown 5457 A Collection Of 16 Big Hits Volume 10.
    (S) (2:46) Curb 77321 Greatest Hits.
    (S) (2:47) Motown 6109 Compact Command Performances.
    (S) (2:43) Motown 6200 and 0792 Anthology.
    (S) (2:44) MCA 10063 Original Television Soundtrack "The Sounds Of Murphy Brown".
    (S) (2:44) Motown 9097 The Most Played Oldies On America's Jukeboxes.
    (S) (2:44) Motown 9018 and 5249 16 #1 Hits From the Late 60's.
    (S) (2:45) Motown 5126 Everybody Needs Love.
    (S) (2:47) Motown 9086 and 5303 All The Greatest Hits.
    (S) (2:44) Motown 5343 Every Great Motown Song: The First 25 Years Volume 1. *(most selections on this cd have noise on the fade out)*
    (S) (2:44) Motown 8034 and 8134 Every Great Motown Song: The First 25 Years Volumes 1 & 2. *(most selections on this cd have noise on the fade out)*
    (S) (2:44) Motown 9095 and 5325 Motown Girl Groups: Top 10 With A Bullet!
    (S) (2:44) Motown 8031 and 8131 Everybody Needs Love/If I Were Your Woman.
    (S) (2:43) Motown 9071 Motown Dance Party Volume 1. *(all selections on this cd are segued together)*

1968 #11 *THE END OF OUR ROAD*
    (S) (2:18) Motown 6109 Compact Command Performances.
    (S) (2:15) Motown 6200 and 0792 Anthology.
    (S) (2:17) Motown 9086 and 5303 All The Greatest Hits.
    (S) (2:16) Motown 5467 Feelin' Bluesy.

1968 #38 *IT SHOULD HAVE BEEN ME*
    (S) (2:47) Motown 6109 Compact Command Performances.
    (S) (2:58) Motown 6200 and 0792 Anthology.
    (S) (2:46) Motown 9000 and 5113 Motown Superstar Series.
    (S) (2:46) Motown 5467 Feelin' Bluesy.

1969 #27 *THE NITTY GRITTY*
    (S) (2:59) Motown 9109 Motown Memories Volume 3.
    (S) (3:00) Motown 6109 Compact Command Performances.
    (S) (2:53) Motown 6200 and 0792 Anthology.
    (S) (2:59) Motown 5148 Nitty Gritty.
    (S) (2:59) Motown 9086 and 5303 All The Greatest Hits.

1969 #25 *FRIENDSHIP TRAIN*
    (the actual 45 time is (3:45) not (3:30) as stated on the record label)
    (S) (3:46) Curb 77321 Greatest Hits.
    (S) (3:47) Motown 6109 Compact Command Performances.
    (S) (3:45) Motown 6200 and 0792 Anthology.
    (S) (3:47) Motown 9086 and 5303 All The Greatest Hits.

released as by GLADYS KNIGHT & THE PIPS (Continued)

1970 #28 *YOU NEED LOVE LIKE I DO (DON'T YOU)*
- (S) (3:39) Motown 6109 Compact Command Performances.
- (S) (3:38) Motown 6200 and 0792 Anthology.
- (S) (3:35) Motown 9072 Motown Dance Party Volume 2. *(all selections on this cd are segued together)*
- (S) (3:38) Motown 9086 and 5303 All The Greatest Hits.

1971 #5 *IF I WERE YOUR WOMAN*
- (S) (3:14) Motown 9104 Motown Memories Volume 1.
- (S) (3:14) Curb 77321 Greatest Hits.
- (S) (3:15) Motown 6109 Compact Command Performances.
- (S) (3:12) Motown 6200 and 0792 Anthology.
- (S) (3:14) MCA 10063 Original Television Soundtrack "The Sounds Of Murphy Brown".
- (M) (3:11) Motown 5344 Every Great Motown Song: The First 25 Years Volume 2. *(most selections on this cd have noise on the fade out)*
- (S) (3:14) Motown 9086 and 5303 All The Greatest Hits.
- (S) (3:13) Motown 5388 If I Were Your Woman.
- (M) (3:11) Motown 8034 and 8134 Every Great Motown Song: The First 25 Years Volumes 1 & 2. *(most selections on this cd have noise on the fade out)*
- (S) (3:14) Motown 8031 and 8131 Everybody Needs Love/If I Were Your Woman.

1971 #9 *I DON'T WANT TO DO WRONG*
- (S) (3:19) Motown 6109 Compact Command Performances.
- (S) (3:17) Motown 6200 and 0792 Anthology.
- (S) (3:19) Motown 9086 and 5303 All The Greatest Hits.
- (S) (3:19) Motown 9000 and 5113 Motown Superstar Series.
- (S) (3:18) Motown 5388 If I Were Your Woman.
- (S) (3:19) Motown 8031 and 8131 Everybody Needs Love/If I Were Your Woman.

1972 #22 *MAKE ME THE WOMAN THAT YOU GO HOME TO*
- (S) (3:47) Motown 6109 Compact Command Performances. *(hum noticeable on the fade out)*
- (S) (3:44) Motown 6200 and 0792 Anthology.
- (S) (3:46) Motown 9086 and 5303 All The Greatest Hits. *(hum noticeable on the fadeout)*

1972 #37 *HELP ME MAKE IT THROUGH THE NIGHT*
- (S) (4:19) Motown 6109 Compact Command Performances. *(hum noticeable on the fade out)*
- (S) (4:17) Motown 6200 and 0792 Anthology.

1973 #1 *NEITHER ONE OF US (WANTS TO BE THE FIRST TO SAY GOODBYE)*
- (S) (4:21) Rhino 70661 Billboard's Top R&B Hits Of 1973.
- (S) (4:21) Motown 6110 Motown Grammy R&B Performances Of The 60's & 70's.
- (S) (4:21) Curb 77321 Greatest Hits.
- (S) (4:21) Motown 6109 Compact Command Performances.
- (S) (4:20) Motown 6200 and 0792 Anthology.
- (S) (4:21) Motown 8008 and 8108 Neither One Of Us/All I Need Is Time.
- (S) (4:21) Motown 9086 and 5303 All The Greatest Hits.
- (S) (4:21) Motown 5193 Neither One Of Us.

1973 #15 *DADDY COULD SWEAR, I DECLARE*
- (S) (3:42) Motown 9109 Motown Memories Volume 3.
- (S) (3:43) Motown 6109 Compact Command Performances.

released as by GLADYS KNIGHT & THE PIPS (Continued)

       (S) (3:39) Motown 6200 and 0792 Anthology.
       (S) (3:42) Motown 8008 and 8108 Neither One Of Us/All I Need Is Time.
       (S) (3:42) Motown 9086 and 5303 All The Greatest Hits.
       (S) (3:42) Motown 5193 Neither One Of Us.

1973 #23 *WHERE PEACEFUL WATERS FLOW*

       (S) (4:24) Rhino 70756 Soul Survivors: The Best Of.
       (S) (4:25) Pair 1198 Best Of.
       (S) (4:23) Pair 3304 Imagination.

1973 #1 *MIDNIGHT TRAIN TO GEORGIA*

       (S) (4:38) Rhino 70634 Billboard's Top Rock & Roll Hits Of 1973. *(LP version)*
       (S) (4:37) Rhino 70551 Soul Hits Of The 70's Volume 11. *(LP version)*
       (S) (4:37) Pair 1202 Best Of Buddah. *(LP version)*
       (S) (4:38) Curb 77321 Greatest Hits. *(LP version)*
       (S) (4:37) Rhino 70756 Soul Survivors: The Best Of. *(LP version)*
       (S) (4:37) Pair 1198 Best Of. *(LP version)*
       (S) (4:37) Pair 3304 Imagination. *(LP version)*

JEAN KNIGHT

1971 #2 *MR. BIG STUFF*

       (S) (2:44) Stax 88005 Top Of The Stax. *(LP length)*
       (S) (2:43) Stax 8543 Stax Soul Sisters. *(LP length)*
       (S) (2:27) Rhino 70659 Billboard's Top R&B Hits Of 1971. *(45 length)*
       (S) (2:28) Rhino 70785 Soul Hits Of The 70's Volume 5. *(45 length)*
       (S) (2:44) Stax 8554 Mr. Big Stuff. *(LP length)*

ROBERT KNIGHT

1967 #11 *EVERLASTING LOVE*

       (S) (2:57) Rhino 70996 One Hit Wonders Of The 60's Volume 2.

SONNY KNIGHT

1956 #20 *CONFIDENTIAL*

KNOCKOUTS

1960 #35 *DARLING LORRAINE*

BUDDY KNOX

1957 #1 *PARTY DOLL*

       (M) (2:11) Rhino 70741 Rock This Town: Rockabilly Hits Volume 1.
       (M) (2:12) Rhino 70618 Billboard's Top Rock & Roll Hits Of 1957.
       (M) (2:12) Rhino 72004 Billboard's Top Rock & Roll Hits 1957-1961 Box Set.
       (M) (2:11) Rhino 70964 Best Of.
       (M) (2:12) Collectables 5416 Murray The K - Sing Along With The Golden Greats.

1957 #25 *ROCK YOUR LITTLE BABY TO SLEEP*

       (M) (2:21) Rhino 70964 Best Of.

1957 #16 *HULA LOVE*

       (M) (2:19) Rhino 70964 Best Of.

1958 #30 *SOMEBODY TOUCHED ME*

       (M) (2:15) Rhino 70964 Best Of.

MOE KOFFMAN QUARTET

1958 #18 *THE SWINGIN' SHEPHERD BLUES*

KOKOMO

1961 #14 *ASIA MINOR*

BILLY J KRAMER WITH THE DAKOTAS

1964 #7 *LITTLE CHILDREN*
    (M) (2:46) Rhino 70319 History Of British Rock Volume 1.
    (M) (2:46) Rhino 72022 History Of British Rock Box Set.
    (M) (2:46) Rhino 72008 History Of British Rock Volumes 1-4 Box Set.
    (M) (2:45) EMI 96055 Best Of.

1964 #10 *BAD TO ME*
    (M) (2:19) Rhino 70319 History Of British Rock Volume 1.
    (M) (2:19) Rhino 72022 History Of British Rock Box Set.
    (M) (2:19) Rhino 72008 History Of British Rock Volumes 1-4 Box Set.
    (S) (2:17) EMI 96055 Best Of.

1964 #39 *I'LL KEEP YOU SATISFIED*
    (M) (2:04) Rhino 70320 History Of British Rock Volume 2.
    (M) (2:04) Rhino 72022 History Of British Rock Box Set.
    (M) (2:04) Rhino 72008 History Of British Rock Volumes 1-4 Box Set.
    (S) (2:05) EMI 96055 Best Of.

1964 #29 *FROM A WINDOW*
    (S) (1:55) Rhino 70321 History Of British Rock Volume 3.
    (S) (1:55) Rhino 72022 History Of British Rock Box Set.
    (S) (1:55) Rhino 72008 History Of British Rock Volumes 1-4 Box Set.
    (S) (1:53) EMI 96055 Best Of.

KRIS KRISTOFFERSON

1971 #33 *LOVING HER WAS EASIER (THAN ANYTHING I'LL EVER DO AGAIN)*
    (S) (3:46) CBS Special Products 44352 The Silver Tongued Devil And I.
    (S) (3:46) CBS Special Products 44350 Songs Of Kristofferson.
    (S) (3:45) CBS Special Products 46807 Rock Goes To The Movies
                Volume 4.
    (S) (3:44) Sony Music Special Products 48621 Singer/ Songwriter.

1973 #32 *WHY ME*
    (S) (3:25) Sony Music Special Products 47064 Jesus Was A Capricorn.
    (S) (3:27) CBS Special Products 44350 Songs Of Kristofferson.
    (S) (3:26) Sony Music Special Products 48621 Singer/ Songwriter.
    (S) (3:26) Pair 1078 My Songs.

BOB KUBAN & THE IN MEN

1966 #15 *THE CHEATER*
    (S) (2:38) Rhino 70995 One Hit Wonders Of The 60's Volume 1.

L

PATTI LA BELLE & THE BLUE BELLES
1963 #39 *DOWN THE AISLE (WEDDING SONG)*

FRANCIS LAI & HIS ORCHESTRA
1971 #36 *THEME FROM LOVE STORY*

FRANKIE LAINE
1955 #6 *HUMMING BIRD*
1957 #6 *MOONLIGHT GAMBLER*
        (M) (2:53) Columbia 45029 16 Most Requested Songs.
        (E) (2:54) Columbia 8636 Greatest Hits.
1957 #19 *LOVE IS A GOLDEN RING*
        (M) (2:29) Columbia 45029 16 Most Requested Songs.
1969 #19 *YOU GAVE ME A MOUNTAIN*

MAJOR LANCE
1963 #7 *MONKEY TIME*
        (M) (2:46) Rhino 75770 Soul Shots Volume 2.
        (M) (2:45) Rhino 70992 Groove 'n' Grind.
        (M) (2:45) CBS Special Products 37321 Okeh Soul.
1963 #17 *HEY LITTLE GIRL*
        (M) (2:27) CBS Special Products 37321 Okeh Soul.
1964 #4 *UM, UM, UM, UM, UM, UM*
        (M) (2:19) CBS Special Products 37321 Okeh Soul.
1964 #21 *THE MATADOR*
        (M) (2:23) CBS Special Products 37321 Okeh Soul.
1964 #23 *RYHTHM*
        (M) (2:15) CBS Special Products 37321 Okeh Soul.

MICKEY LEE LANE
   1964 #38 *SHAGGY DOG*
MARIO LANZA
   1958 #32 *ARRIVEDERCI ROMA*
            (M)   (3:15)   RCA 60889   Collection.
LARKS
   1965 #6   *THE JERK*
            (S)   (2:32)   Rhino 70992   Groove 'n' Grind. *(alternate vocal take)*
JULIUS LA ROSA
   1955 #10 *DOMANI (TOMORROW)*
   1955 #8   *SUDDENLY THERE'S A VALLEY*
   1956 #31 *PRISCILLA*
   1957 #36 *STASHU PANDOWSKI*
DENISE LA SALLE
   1971 #13 *TRAPPED BY A THING CALLED LOVE*
   1972 #33 *NOW RUN AND TELL THAT*
   1972 #40 *MAN SIZED JOB*
ROD LAUREN
   1960 #24 *IF I HAD A GIRL*
EDDIE LAWRENCE
   1956 #33 *THE OLD PHILOSOPHER*
STEVE LAWRENCE
   1957 #5   *THE BANANA BOAT SONG*
   1957 #1   *PARTY DOLL*
   1957 #38 *CAN'T WAIT FOR SUMMER*
   1960 #7   *PRETTY BLUE EYES*
   1960 #9   *FOOTSTEPS*
   1961 #11 *PORTRAIT OF MY LOVE*
   1963 #1   *GO AWAY LITTLE GIRL*
   1963 #19 *DON'T BE AFRAID LITTLE DARLIN'*
   1963 #36 *POOR LITTLE RICH GIRL*
   1963 #27 *WALKING PROUD*

STEVE LAWRENCE & EYDIE GORME
released as by **STEVE & EYDIE:**
   1963 #28 *I WANT TO STAY HERE*
VICKI LAWRENCE
   1973 #1   *THE NIGHT THE LIGHTS WENT OUT IN GEORGIA*
            (S)   (3:33)   Rhino 70930   Super Hits Of The 70's Volume 10.
JOY LAYNE
   1957 #29 *YOUR WILD HEART*
   1957 #35 *AFTER SCHOOL*
LED ZEPPELIN
   1970 #2   *WHOLE LOTTA LOVE*
            (both commercial and dj 45's were pressed with times of either (3:10) or (5:33))
            (S)   (5:33)   Atlantic 81908   Classic Rock 1966 - 1988.
            (S)   (5:34)   Atlantic 19127   Led Zeppelin II.
            (S)   (5:33)   Atlantic 82144   Led Zeppelin Box.
            (S) (14:23)   Swan Song 201   O.S.T. The Song Remains The Same. *(live version)*

202

LED ZEPPELIN (Continued)

        (S) (5:33) Atlantic 82306   Atlantic Rock & Roll Box Set.
        (S) (5:32) Atlantic 82371   Remasters.

1971 #8 IMMIGRANT SONG

        (S) (2:24) Atlantic 19128   Led Zeppelin III.
        (S) (2:23) Atlantic 82144   Led Zeppelin Box. *(tracks into next selection)*
        (S) (2:23) Atlantic 82371   Remasters. *(tracks into next selection)*

1972 #9 BLACK DOG

        (S) (4:54) Atlantic 19129   Led Zeppelin.
        (S) (4:53) Atlantic 82144   Led Zeppelin Box.
        (S) (4:53) Atlantic 82371   Remasters.

1973 #28 OVER THE HILLS AND FAR AWAY

        (S) (4:49) Atlantic 19130   Houses Of The Holy.
        (S) (4:46) Atlantic 82144   Led Zeppelin Box.

1973 #16 D'YER MAK'ER

        (S) (4:23) Atlantic 19130   Houses Of The Holy.
        (S) (4:21) Atlantic 82144   Led Zeppelin Box.
        (S) (4:21) Atlantic 82371   Remasters.

BRENDA LEE

1960 #3 SWEET NOTHIN'S

        (S) (2:21) MCA 31203   Vintage Music Volume 6.
        (S) (2:21) MCA 5804   Vintage Music Volumes 5 & 6.
        (S) (2:22) MCA 10384   Anthology.
        (S) (2:21) MCA 4012   Brenda Lee Story. *(buzz can be heard throughout the song)*

1960 #1 I'M SORRY

        (S) (2:38) MCA 31202   Vintage Music Volume 5.
        (S) (2:38) MCA 5804   Vintage Music Volumes 5 & 6.
        (S) (2:37) MCA 2-8025   30 Years Of Hits 1958 - 1974.
        (S) (2:39) MCA 10384   Anthology.
        (S) (2:36) MCA 4012   Brenda Lee Story.

1960 #11 THAT'S ALL YOU GOTTA DO

        (S) (2:27) MCA 10384   Anthology.
        (S) (2:26) MCA 4012   Brenda Lee Story. *(truncated fade)*

1960 #2 I WANT TO BE WANTED

        (M) (3:02) MCA 5939   Vintage Music Volumes 17 & 18.
        (M) (3:02) MCA 31215   Vintage Music Volume 18.
        (S) (3:03) MCA 10384   Anthology.
        (S) (3:02) MCA 4012   Brenda Lee Story.

1961 #22 ROCKIN' AROUND THE CHRISTMAS TREE

        (S) (2:03) Rhino 70192   Christmas Classics
        (S) (2:03) Rhino 70636   Billboard's Greatest Christmas Hits.
        (S) (2:02) MCA 25991   Christmas Hits.
        (S) (2:05) MCA 10384   Anthology.
        (S) (2:07) Warner Brothers 26660   A Brenda Lee Christmas. *(rerecording; tracks into next selection)*
        (M) (2:04) Curb 77515   Christmas All-Time Greatest Records Volume 2.

1961 #6 EMOTIONS

        (M) (2:49) MCA 5937   Vintage Music Volumes 13 & 14.
        (M) (2:49) MCA 31210   Vintage Music Volume 13.
        (S) (2:48) MCA 10384   Anthology.
        (S) (2:47) MCA 4012   Brenda Lee Story.

1961 #7 YOU CAN DEPEND ON ME

        (S) (3:31) MCA 10384   Anthology.
        (S) (3:29) MCA 4012   Brenda Lee Story.

BRENDA LEE (Continued)

1961 #4 _DUM DUM_
    (S) (2:24) MCA 10384 Anthology.
    (S) (2:23) MCA 4012 Brenda Lee Story.

1961 #6 _FOOL #1_
    (S) (2:26) MCA 10384 Anthology.
    (S) (2:24) MCA 4012 Brenda Lee Story.

1961 #23 _ANYBODY BUT ME_
    (S) (2:23) MCA 4012 Brenda Lee Story.

1962 #6 _BREAK IT TO ME GENTLY_
    (S) (2:36) MCA 10384 Anthology.
    (S) (2:35) MCA 4012 Brenda Lee Story.

1962 #6 _EVERYBODY LOVES ME BUT YOU_
    (S) (2:29) MCA 10384 Anthology.

1962 #21 _HEART IN HAND_
    (S) (2:27) MCA 5939 Vintage Music Volumes 17 & 18.
    (S) (2:27) MCA 31214 Vintage Music Volume 17.
    (S) (2:26) MCA 10384 Anthology.

1962 #26 _IT STARTED ALL OVER AGAIN_

1962 #3 _ALL ALONE AM I_
    (M) (2:42) MCA 5936 Vintage Music Volumes 11 & 12.
    (M) (2:42) MCA 31708 Vintage Music Volume 11.
    (S) (2:42) MCA 10384 Anthology.
    (S) (2:41) MCA 4012 Brenda Lee Story.

1962 #38 _SAVE ALL YOUR LOVIN' FOR ME_

1963 #23 _YOUR USED TO BE_

1963 #10 _LOSING YOU_
    (S) (2:31) MCA 10384 Anthology.
    (S) (2:29) MCA 4012 Brenda Lee Story.

1963 #22 _MY WHOLE WORLD IS FALLING DOWN_
    (S) (1:54) MCA 10384 Anthology.
    (S) (1:52) MCA 4012 Brenda Lee Story.

1963 #23 _I WONDER_
    (S) (2:57) MCA 10384 Anthology.

1963 #21 _THE GRASS IS GREENER_
    (S) (2:43) MCA 10384 Anthology.

1964 #11 _AS USUAL_
    (S) (2:33) MCA 10384 Anthology.
    (S) (2:32) MCA 4012 Brenda Lee Story.

1964 #18 _THINK_

1964 #27 _ALONE WITH YOU_

1964 #36 _WHEN YOU LOVED ME_

1964 #14 _IS IT TRUE_
    (S) (2:29) MCA 10384 Anthology.

1965 #34 _THANKS A LOT_
    (S) (2:40) MCA 4012 Brenda Lee Story.

1965 #15 _TOO MANY RIVERS_
    (S) (2:48) MCA 10384 Anthology.
    (S) (2:47) MCA 4012 Brenda Lee Story.

1965 #30 _RUSTY BELLS_

1966 #18 _COMING ON STRONG_
    (S) (2:01) MCA 10384 Anthology.
    (S) (1:59) MCA 4012 Brenda Lee Story.

BRENDA LEE (Continued)
1969 #34 *JOHNNY ONE TIME*
>> (S) (3:36) MCA 10384 Anthology.
>> (S) (3:15) MCA 4012 Brenda Lee Story.

CURTIS LEE
1961 #6 *PRETTY LITTLE ANGEL EYES*
>> (M) (2:44) Abkco 7118 Phil Spector/Back To Mono (1958-1969).

DICKEY LEE
1962 #4 *PATCHES*
1963 #8 *I SAW LINDA YESTERDAY*
>> (M) (2:02) Mercury 816555 45's On CD Volume 2.
1965 #11 *LAURIE (STRANGE THINGS HAPPEN)*

JACKIE LEE
1966 #13 *THE DUCK*
>> (M) (2:22) Dunhill Compact Classics 028 Sock Hop.

LAURA LEE
1971 #20 *WOMEN'S LOVE RIGHTS*
>> (S) (3:11) Rhino 70786 Soul Hits Of The 70's Volume 6.
>> (S) (3:11) HDH 3903 Greatest Hits.

LEAPY LEE
1968 #16 *LITTLE ARROWS*

PEGGY LEE
1958 #6 *FEVER*
>> (S) (3:19) Capitol 90592 Memories Are Made Of This.
>> (M) (3:18) Curb 77379 All-Time Greatest Hits.
>> (S) (2:59) Capitol 98670 Memories Are Made Of This. *(live)*
1969 #10 *IS THAT ALL THERE IS*
>> (S) (4:19) Curb 77379 All-Time Greatest Hits.

RAYMOND LEFEVRE & HIS ORCHESTRA
1958 #17 *THE DAY THE RAINS CAME*
1968 #36 *AME CALINE (SOUL COAXING)*

LEFT BANKE
1966 #2 *WALK AWAY RENEE*
>> (S) (2:40) Warner Special Products 27607 Highs Of The 60's.
>> (S) (2:41) Mercury 848095 There's Gonna Be A Storm.
1967 #12 *PRETTY BALLERINA*
>> (S) (2:34) Mercury 848095 There's Gonna Be A Storm.

LEMON PIPERS
1968 #1 *GREEN TAMBOURINE*
>> (S) (2:24) Rhino 70629 Billboard's Top Rock & Roll Hits Of 1968.
>> (S) (2:24) Rhino 72005 Billboard's Top Rock & Roll Hits 1968-1972 Box Set.
>> (S) (2:24) Pair 1202 Best Of Buddah.
>> (S) (2:24) Pair 1199 Best Of Bubblegum Music.
>> (S) (2:24) K-Tel 205 Battle Of The Bands Volume 3.
>> (S) (2:24) Special Music 4914 Best Of The Bubblegum Years.
1968 #30 *JELLY JUNGLE (OF ORANGE MARMALADE)*

LENNON SISTERS
1956 #3 *TONIGHT YOU BELONG TO ME*

JOHN LENNON (and PLASTIC ONO BAND)
released as by THE PLASTIC ONO BAND:
1969 #11 *GIVE PEACE A CHANCE*
    (S) (:58) Capitol 46642 Shaved Fish. *(introduction only)*
    (S) (4:51) Capitol 90803 Music From The Original Motion Picture "Imagine". *(with countoff)*
    (S) (4:50) Capitol 91516 Collection. *(with countoff)*
    (S) (4:50) Capitol 95220 Lennon. *(with countoff)*
1970 #32 *COLD TURKEY*
    (S) (5:00) Capitol 46642 Shaved Fish.
    (S) (5:01) Capitol 91516 Collection.
    (S) (5:00) Capitol 95220 Lennon.

released as by JOHN ONO LENNON:
1970 #3 *INSTANT KARMA (WE ALL SHINE ON)*
    (S) (3:19) Capitol 46642 Shaved Fish.
    (S) (3:19) Capitol 91516 Collection.
    (S) (3:19) Capitol 95220 Lennon.

released as by JOHN LENNON/PLASTIC ONO BAND:
1971 #19 *MOTHER*
    (S) (5:33) Parlophone 46770 Plastic Ono Band. *(LP version)*
    (S) (5:01) Capitol 46642 Shaved Fish. *(edit of LP version)*
    (S) (4:44) Capitol 90803 Music From The Original Motion Picture "Imagine". *(live version)*
    (S) (5:33) Capitol 95220 Lennon. *(LP version)*
1971 #10 *POWER TO THE PEOPLE*
    (S) (3:19) Capitol 46642 Shaved Fish.
    (S) (3:15) Capitol 91516 Collection.
    (S) (3:15) Capitol 95220 Lennon.
1971 #2 *IMAGINE*
    (S) (3:01) Capitol 46642 Shaved Fish.
    (S) (3:01) Capitol 90803 Music From The Original Motion Picture "Imagine".
    (S) (3:01) Capitol 91516 Collection.
    (S) (3:01) Capitol 95220 Lennon.
    (S) (3:01) Capitol 46641 Imagine.

released as by JOHN & YOKO WITH THE HARLEM COMMUNITY CHOIR:
1972 #36 *HAPPY XMAS (WAR IS OVER)*
    (S) (4:11) Capitol 46642 Shaved Fish. *(with "GIVE PEACE A CHANCE" reprise found on the "Shaved Fish" vinyl LP)*
    (S) (3:31) Capitol 91516 Collection. *(45 version)*
    (S) (3:31) Capitol 95220 Lennon. *(45 version)*

released as by JOHN LENNON:
1973 #10 *MIND GAMES*
    (S) (4:11) Parlophone 46769 Mind Games.
    (S) (4:11) Capitol 46642 Shaved Fish.
    (S) (4:11) Capitol 91516 Collection.
    (S) (4:10) Capitol 95220 Lennon.

KETTY LESTER
1962 #7 *LOVE LETTERS*

LETTERMEN
1961 #8 *THE WAY YOU LOOK TONIGHT*
    (S) (2:19) Capitol 46626 All-Time Greatest Hits.
    (S) (2:19) Capitol 48438 Best Of.

LETTERMEN (Continued)
1961 #13 WHEN I FALL IN LOVE
  (S) (2:26) Capitol 46626   All-Time Greatest Hits.
  (S) (2:26) Capitol 48438   Best Of.
  (S) (2:21) Capitol 98670   Memories Are Made Of This. *(live)*
1962 #19 COME BACK SILLY GIRL
1965 #17 THEME FROM "A SUMMER PLACE"
  (M) (2:02) Capitol 46626   All-Time Greatest Hits.
  (S) (2:04) Capitol 48438   Best Of.
1968 #7 GOIN' OUT OF MY HEAD/CAN'T TAKE MY EYES OFF YOU
  (S) (3:10) Capitol 46626   All-Time Greatest Hits.
1968 #35 SHERRY DON'T GO
1969 #14 HURT SO BAD
  (S) (2:17) Capitol 46626   All-Time Greatest Hits.

BARBARA LEWIS
1963 #4 HELLO STRANGER
  (S) (2:40) Rhino 70649   Billboard's Top R&B Hits Of 1963.
  (S) (2:40) Atlantic 81297   Atlantic Rhythm & Blues Volume 5.
  (M) (2:40) Rhino 75891   Wonder Women.
  (S) (2:40) Atlantic 82305   Atlantic Rhythm And Blues 1947-1974 Box Set.
  (S) (2:38) Collectables 5104   Golden Classics.
1965 #10 BABY, I'M YOURS
  (S) (2:29) Atlantic 81297   Atlantic Rhythm & Blues Volume 5.
  (S) (2:29) Atlantic 82305   Atlantic Rhythm And Blues 1947-1974 Box Set.
  (S) (2:27) Collectables 5104   Golden Classics. *(truncated fade)*
1965 #19 MAKE ME YOUR BABY
  (S) (2:29) Warner Special Products 27601   Atlantic Soul Classics.
  (S) (2:30) Rhino 75891   Wonder Women.
  (E) (2:28) Collectables 5104   Golden Classics.

BOBBY LEWIS
1961 #1 TOSSIN' AND TURNIN'
  (S) (2:33) Rhino 75893   Jukebox Classics Volume 1. *(with spoken intro)*
  (S) (2:33) Rhino 70622   Billboard's Top Rock & Roll Hits Of 1961. *(with spoken intro)*
  (S) (2:33) Rhino 72004   Billboard's Top Rock & Roll Hits 1957-1961 Box Set. *(with spoken intro)*
  (S) (2:33) JCI 3110   Sock Hoppin' Sixties. *(sounds muddy)*
  (M) (2:14) MCA 31023   O.S.T. Animal House. *(edited; all tracks on this cd are segued together)*
1961 #24 ONE TRACK MIND
  (S) (2:06) Rhino 75894   Jukebox Classics Volume 2.

GARY LEWIS & THE PLAYBOYS
1965 #1 THIS DIAMOND RING
  (S) (2:07) Rhino 70626   Billboard's Top Rock & Roll Hits Of 1965.
  (S) (2:07) Rhino 72007   Billboard's Top Rock & Roll Hits 1962-1966 Box Set.
  (S) (2:13) EMI 96268   24 Greatest Hits Of All Time. *(:12 longer than either the 45 or LP; truncated fade)*
  (S) (2:01) EMI 91474   Golden Greats. *(noise on fade out)*
  (S) (2:13) EMI 93449   Legendary Masters Series. *(:12 longer than either the 45 or LP; truncated fade)*
  (S) (2:13) Capitol 98139   Spring Break Volume 2. *(:12 longer than either the 45 or LP; truncated fade)*

GARY LEWIS & THE PLAYBOYS (Continued)

1965 #3 COUNT ME IN
    (S) (2:31) EMI 93449 Legendary Masters Series. *(with countoff)*

1965 #4 SAVE YOUR HEART FOR ME
    (S) (1:54) EMI 91474 Golden Greats.
    (S) (2:01) EMI 93449 Legendary Masters Series. *(with countoff)*

1965 #6 EVERYBODY LOVES A CLOWN
    (S) (2:17) EMI 91474 Golden Greats.
    (S) (2:23) EMI 93449 Legendary Masters Series. *(:05 longer than either the 45 or LP)*

1966 #4 SHE'S JUST MY STYLE
    (S) (2:51) EMI 91474 Golden Greats.
    (S) (3:10) EMI 93449 Legendary Masters Series. *(with countoff; :15 longer than either the 45 or LP)*

1966 #10 SURE GONNA MISS HER
    (S) (2:12) EMI 91474 Golden Greats. *(stereo LP version)*
    (S) (2:30) EMI 93449 Legendary Masters Series. *(45 and mono LP version)*

1966 #9 GREEN GRASS
    (S) (2:13) EMI 93449 Legendary Masters Series.

1966 #15 MY HEART'S SYMPHONY
    (S) (3:01) EMI 93449 Legendary Masters Series. *(with countoff; :20 longer than either the 45 or LP)*

1966 #16 (YOU DON'T HAVE TO) PAINT ME A PICTURE
    (S) (2:32) EMI 93449 Legendary Masters Series. *(includes :10 of studio talk)*

1967 #20 WHERE WILL THE WORDS COME FROM
    (S) (1:59) EMI 93449 Legendary Masters Series.

1967 #31 THE LOSER
    (S) (2:17) EMI 93449 Legendary Masters Series.

1967 #35 GIRLS IN LOVE
    (S) (2:24) EMI 93449 Legendary Masters Series.

1967 #31 JILL
    (S) (2:18) EMI 93449 Legendary Masters Series.

1968 #8 SEALED WITH A KISS
    (S) (2:25) EMI 93449 Legendary Masters Series.

JERRY LEWIS

1956 #9 ROCK-A-BYE YOUR BABY WITH A DIXIE MELODY
    (M) (5:26) Capitol 93196 Capitol Collector's Series. *(includes 2 false starts ((2:53) so the actual song length is (2:33))*

JERRY LEE LEWIS

1957 #5 WHOLE LOTTA SHAKIN' GOING ON
    (M) (2:51) Rhino 70618 Billboard's Top Rock & Roll Hits Of 1957.
    (M) (2:51) Rhino 72004 Billboard's Top Rock & Roll Hits 1957-1961 Box Set.
    (M) (2:51) Rhino 75893 Jukebox Classics Volume 1.
    (M) (2:50) Rhino 75884 The Sun Story.
    (M) (2:52) Elektra 60107 O.S.T. Diner.
    (M) (2:50) Dunhill Compact Classics 009 Legends.
    (M) (2:51) Rhino 70255 and 5255 18 Original Sun Greatest Hits.
    (M) (2:50) Rhino 70656 Jerry Lee Lewis.
    (S) (2:38) Mercury 826251 Golden Rock Hits. *(all selections on this cd are rerecordings)*
    (S) (3:57) Polydor 839516 O.S.T. Great Balls Of Fire. *(rerecording)*
    (M) (2:51) RCA 66059 Sun's Greatest Hits.

JERRY LEE LEWIS (Continued)
1958 #2 GREAT BALLS OF FIRE
- (M) (1:49) Rhino 70243 Greatest Movie Rock Hits.
- (M) (1:49) Rhino 70619 Billboard's Top Rock & Roll Hits Of 1958.
- (M) (1:49) Rhino 72004 Billboard's Top Rock & Roll Hits 1957-1961 Box Set.
- (M) (1:49) Rhino 70906 American Bandstand Greatest Hits Collection.
- (M) (1:49) Rhino 75884 The Sun Story.
- (M) (1:50) Rhino 75894 Jukebox Classics Volume 2.
- (M) (1:50) RCA 5463 Rock & Roll - The Early Days.
- (M) (1:52) Capitol 48993 Spuds Mackenzie's Party Faves.
- (S) (1:47) Mercury 826448 Oldies Golden Million Sellers (rerecording)
- (M) (1:48) Atlantic 81677 O.S.T. Stand By Me.
- (M) (1:49) JCI 3202 Rockin' Fifties.
- (M) (1:50) Dunhill Compact Classics 009 Legends.
- (M) (1:50) Warner Special Products 27602 20 Party Classics.
- (M) (1:49) Atlantic 81885 O.S.T. Stealing Home.
- (M) (1:49) Rhino 70657 Jerry Lee's Greatest.
- (M) (1:50) Rhino 70255 and 5255 18 Original Sun Greatest Hits.
- (S) (1:46) Mercury 826251 Golden Rock Hits. *(all selections on this cd are rerecordings)*
- (S) (2:31) Polydor 839516 O.S.T. Great Balls Of Fire. *(rerecording)*
- (M) (1:50) RCA 66059 Sun's Greatest Hits.

1958 #10 BREATHLESS
- (M) (2:40) Rhino 75884 The Sun Story.
- (M) (2:41) Dunhill Compact Classics 009 Legends.
- (M) (2:41) Rhino 70255 and 5255 18 Original Sun Greatest Hits.
- (S) (2:39) Mercury 826251 Golden Rock Hits. *(all selections on this cd are rerecordings)*
- (S) (2:49) Polydor 839516 O.S.T. Great Balls Of Fire. *(rerecording)*
- (M) (2:41) RCA 66059 Sun's Greatest Hits.

1958 #20 HIGH SCHOOL CONFIDENTIAL
- (M) (2:27) Rhino 70741 Rock This Town: Rockabilly Hits Volume 1.
- (M) (2:28) Rhino 70255 and 5255 18 Original Sun Greatest Hits.
- (M) (2:26) Rhino 70656 Jerry Lee Lewis.
- (S) (2:20) Mercury 826251 Golden Rock Hits. *(all selections on this cd are rerecordings)*
- (S) (2:17) Polydor 839516 O.S.T. Great Balls Of Fire. *(rerecording)*

1961 #33 WHAT'D I SAY
- (M) (2:23) Rhino 70657 Jerry Lee's Greatest.
- (M) (2:24) Rhino 70255 and 5255 18 Original Sun Greatest Hits.

1973 #25 DRINKING WINE SPO-DEE-O'DEE

RAMSEY LEWIS TRIO
1965 #4 THE "IN" CROWD
- (S) (3:18) Rhino 75774 Soul Shots. *(edit of the album version made to resemble the single version)*
- (S) (3:16) Chess 31318 Best Of Chess Rhythm & Blues Volume 2. *(:10 longer than the 45 version)*
- (S) (5:50) Chess 6021 Greatest Hits Of. *(LP version)*
- (S) (5:51) Chess 9185 The "In" Crowd. *(LP version)*

1965 #12 HANG ON SLOOPY
(the actual 45 time is (2:57) not (2:50) as stated on the record label)
- (S) (3:16) MCA 5940 Vintage Music Volumes 19 & 20. *(LP length)*
- (S) (3:16) MCA 31217 Vintage Music Volume 20. *(LP length)*
- (S) (3:07) Chess 6021 Greatest Hits Of. *(edit of LP length)*

RAMSEY LEWIS TRIO (Continued)
1966 #29 *A HARD DAY'S NIGHT*
    (S) (4:57) Chess 6021 Greatest Hits Of. (*LP version*)

1966 #18 *WADE IN THE WATER*
    (S) (3:46) MCA 5938 Vintage Music Volumes 15 & 16. (*LP version*)
    (S) (3:46) MCA 31213 Vintage Music Volume 16. (*LP version*)
    (S) (3:48) Chess 6021 Greatest Hits Of. (*LP version*)
    (S) (3:49) Chess 6025 Best Of Chess Jazz. (*LP version*)

ENOCH LIGHT & THE LIGHT BRIGADE
1958 #30 *I WANT TO BE HAPPY CHA CHA*

GORDON LIGHTFOOT
1971 #5 *IF YOU COULD READ MY MIND*
    (S) (3:47) Warner Special Products 27615 Storytellers: Singers & Songwriters.
    (S) (3:47) Reprise 2237 Gord's Gold.
    (S) (3:47) Reprise 6392 If You Could Read My Mind.

LIGHTHOUSE
1971 #16 *ONE FINE MORNING*
    (S) (5:15) Rhino 70926 Super Hits Of The 70's Volume 6. (*alternate bass line; LP version*)

1972 #37 *SUNNY DAYS*

1973 #31 *PRETTY LADY*

BOB LIND
1966 #7 *ELUSIVE BUTTERFLY*

KATHY LINDEN
1958 #14 *BILLY*

1959 #14 *GOODBYE JIMMY, GOODBYE*

MARK LINDSAY
1970 #9 *ARIZONA*
    (S) (3:05) Rhino 70921 Super Hits Of The 70's Volume 1.
    (S) (3:05) Rhino 72009 Super Hits Of The 70's Volumes 1-4 Box Set.

1970 #31 *MISS AMERICA*

1970 #20 *SILVER BIRD*
    (S) (3:00) Rhino 70924 Super Hits Of The 70's Volume 4.
    (S) (3:00) Rhino 72009 Super Hits Of The 70's Volumes 1-4 Box Set.

1970 #37 *AND THE GRASS WON'T PAY NO MIND*

LITTLE ANTHONY & THE IMPERIALS
1958 #7 *TEARS ON MY PILLOW*
    (M) (2:16) Rhino 70644 Billboard's Top R&B Hits Of 1958.
    (M) (2:15) Rhino 70919 Best Of.
    (S) (2:12) EMI 91475 Best Of. (*rerecording*)
    (S) (2:03) MCA 6171 Good Time Rock 'N' Roll. (*all selections on this cd are recorded live*)
    (M) (2:15) Collectables 5422 Imperials Featuring Little Anthony.
    (M) (2:15) Collectables 8804 For Collectors Only.

1960 #21 *SHIMMY, SHIMMY, KO-KO-BOP*
    (S) (2:07) Rhino 70919 Best Of. (*alternate take*)
    (S) (2:08) EMI 91475 Best Of. (*alternate take*)
    (S) (2:06) Collectables 8804 For Collectors Only. (*alternate take*)

1964 #20 *I'M ON THE OUTSIDE (LOOKING IN)*
    (M) (3:00) Rhino 70919 Best Of.
    (S) (3:10) EMI 91475 Best Of.

LITTLE ANTHONY & THE IMPERIALS (Continued)
1964 #5 *GOIN' OUT OF MY HEAD*
(S) (2:28) EMI 96268 24 Greatest Hits Of All Time.
(S) (2:28) Curb 77355 60's Hits Volume 1.
(S) (2:27) Rhino 70919 Best Of.
(S) (2:29) EMI 91475 Best Of.
(S) (2:18) MCA 6171 Good Time Rock 'N' Roll. *(all selections on this cd are recorded live)*

1965 #14 *HURT SO BAD*
(S) (2:16) Rhino 70919 Best Of.
(S) (2:19) EMI 91475 Best Of.
(S) (1:48) MCA 6171 Good Time Rock 'N' Roll. *(all selections on this cd are recorded live)*

1965 #22 *TAKE ME BACK*
(M) (2:37) Rhino 70919 Best Of.
(S) (2:36) EMI 91475 Best Of.

1965 #40 *I MISS YOU SO*
(S) (2:33) Rhino 70919 Best Of.
(S) (2:36) EMI 91475 Best Of.

LITTLE CAESAR & THE ROMANS
1961 #9 *THOSE OLDIES BUT GOODIES (REMIND ME OF YOU)*
(M) (3:24) Dunhill Compact Classics 031 Back Seat Jams.

LITTLE DIPPERS
1960 #11 *FOREVER*

LITTLE EVA
1962 #1 *THE LOCO-MOTION*
(M) (2:27) Rhino 70623 Billboard's Top Rock & Roll Hits Of 1962. *(significant dropout at :15)*
(M) (2:27) Rhino 72007 Billboard's Top Rock & Roll Hits 1962-1966 Box Set. *(significant dropout at :15)*
(M) (2:24) Rhino 70989 Best Of The Girl Groups Volume 2. *(missing a handclapping overdub)*
(M) (2:27) Rhino 70992 Groove 'n' Grind. *(significant dropout at :15)*
(M) (2:26) Rhino 70906 American Bandstand Greatest Hits Collection. *(significant dropout at :15)*
(M) (2:26) Collectables 5414 Carole King Plus. *(truncated fade)*
(M) (2:24) Collectables 5407 Best Of.

1962 #15 *KEEP YOUR HANDS OFF MY BABY*
(M) (2:34) Collectables 5414 Carole King Plus.
(M) (2:32) Collectables 5407 Best Of.

1963 #21 *LET'S TURKEY TROT*
(M) (2:29) Collectables 5407 Best Of.

LITTLE JOE & THE THRILLERS
1957 #32 *PEANUTS*
(M) (2:27) Collectables 5076 Little Joe & The Thrillers Meet The Schoolboys.
(M) (2:25) CBS Special Products 37649 Okeh Rhythm & Blues.

LITTLE JOEY & THE FLIPS
1962 #30 *BONGO STOMP*

LITTLE MILTON
1965 #18 *WE'RE GONNA MAKE IT*
(S) (2:39) Chess 31317 Best Of Chess Rhythm & Blues Volume 1.
(S) (2:39) Chess 5906 We're Gonna Make It/Little Milton Sings the Blues.

LITTLE RICHARD

1956 #7 *LONG TALL SALLY*
- (M) (2:07) Rhino 70642 Billboard's Top R&B Hits Of 1956.
- (M) (2:07) Rhino 75893 Jukebox Classics Volume 1.
- (M) (2:07) Rhino 75899 18 Greatest Hits.
- (M) (2:07) Specialty 8508 The Specialty Sessions.
- (M) (2:07) Specialty 2154 Essential.
- (E) (2:01) Motown 9066 Compact Command Performances. *(rerecorded)*
- (M) (2:07) Specialty 7012 The Georgia Peach.
- (M) (2:19) Epic 40389 Greatest Hits. *(all selections on this cd are live with a lot of dialog preceeding each song)*

1956 #21 *RIP IT UP*
- (M) (2:21) Warner Special Products 27602 20 Party Classics.
- (M) (2:21) Rhino 75899 18 Greatest Hits.
- (M) (2:20) Specialty 8508 The Specialty Sessions.
- (M) (2:21) Specialty 2154 Essential.
- (E) (1:58) Motown 9066 Compact Command Performances. *(rerecorded)*
- (M) (2:21) Specialty 7012 The Georgia Peach.
- (M) (2:20) Atlantic 82155 O.S.T. Book Of Love.

1956 #32 *READY TEDDY*
- (M) (2:06) Rhino 75899 18 Greatest Hits.
- (M) (2:06) Specialty 8508 The Specialty Sessions.
- (M) (2:06) Specialty 2154 Essential.
- (M) (2:07) Specialty 7012 The Georgia Peach.

1957 #22 *LUCILLE*
- (M) (2:25) JCI 3204 Heart & Soul Fifties. *(sounds muddy)*
- (M) (2:27) Rhino 70643 Billboard's Top R&B Hits Of 1957.
- (M) (2:27) Rhino 75899 18 Greatest Hits.
- (M) (2:23) Specialty 8508 The Specialty Sessions.
- (M) (2:21) Specialty 2154 Essential.
- (E) (2:14) Motown 9066 Compact Command Performances. *(rerecorded)*
- (M) (2:23) Specialty 7012 The Georgia Peach.
- (M) (2:02) Epic 40389 Greatest Hits. *(all selections on this cd are live with a lot of dialog preceeding each song)*

1957 #27 *JENNY, JENNY*
- (M) (2:01) Rhino 75899 18 Greatest Hits.
- (M) (2:02) Specialty 8508 The Specialty Sessions.
- (M) (2:00) Specialty 2154 Essential.
- (E) (1:57) Motown 9066 Compact Command Performances. *(rerecorded)*
- (M) (2:01) Specialty 7012 The Georgia Peach.
- (M) (2:44) Epic 40389 Greatest Hits. *(all selections on this cd are live with a lot of dialog preceeding each song)*

1957 #12 *KEEP A KNOCKIN'*
- (M) (2:19) JCI 3202 Rockin' Fifties.
- (M) (2:22) Rhino 70643 Billboard's Top R&B Hits Of 1957.
- (M) (2:21) Rhino 75899 18 Greatest Hits.
- (M) (2:17) Specialty 8508 The Specialty Sessions.
- (M) (2:16) Specialty 2154 Essential.
- (E) (2:10) Motown 9066 Compact Command Performances. *(rerecorded)*
- (M) (2:15) Specialty 7012 The Georgia Peach.

1958 #18 *GOOD GOLLY MISS MOLLY*
- (E) (2:08) JCI 3201 Partytime Fifties.
- (M) (2:08) Rhino 75899 18 Greatest Hits.
- (M) (2:48) Specialty 8508 The Specialty Sessions. *(includes :39 false start and studio talk)*

LITTLE RICHARD (Continued)
        (M) (2:06) Specialty 2154 Essential.
        (E) (2:04) Motown 9066 Compact Command Performances. *(rerecorded)*
        (M) (2:08) Specialty 7012 The Georgia Peach.
        (M) (1:43) Epic 40389 Greatest Hits. *(all selections on this cd are live with a lot of dialog preceeding each song)*

LITTLE SISTER
1970 #20 *YOU'RE THE ONE (PART 2)*
1971 #22 *SOMEBODY'S WATCHING YOU*
        (S) (2:49) Rhino 70784 Soul Hits Of The 70's Volume 4.

LOBO
1971 #8 *ME AND YOU AND A DOG NAMED BOO*
        (S) (2:50) Rhino 70925 Super Hits Of The 70's Volume 5.
        (S) (2:49) Priority 8670 Hitchin A Ride/70's Greatest Rock Hits Volume 10.
        (S) (2:53) Curb 77302 Greatest Hits.
1972 #1 *I'D LOVE YOU TO WANT ME*
        (S) (4:01) Rhino 70929 Super Hits Of The 70's Volume 9.
        (S) (4:03) Curb 77302 Greatest Hits.
1973 #4 *DON'T EXPECT ME TO BE YOUR FRIEND*
        (S) (3:34) Curb 77302 Greatest Hits.
1973 #27 *IT SURE TOOK A LONG, LONG TIME*
1973 #20 *HOW CAN I TELL HER*
        (S) (4:14) Curb 77302 Greatest Hits.

HANK LOCKLIN
1960 #6 *PLEASE HELP ME I'M FALLING*
        (S) (2:21) RCA 8475 Nipper's Greatest Hits Of The 60's Volume 2.
        (S) (2:21) Rhino 70681 Billboard's Top Country Hits Of 1960.
        (S) (2:21) RCA 5802 Best Of The 60's.

LOGGINS & MESSINA
1973 #5 *YOUR MAMA DON'T DANCE*
        (S) (2:47) Columbia 45047 Pop Classics Of The 70's.
        (S) (2:46) JCI 3301 Rockin' Seventies.
        (S) (2:47) Columbia 34388 Best Of Friends.
        (S) (2:47) Columbia 31748 Loggins & Messina.
1973 #11 *THINKING OF YOU*
        (S) (2:18) Columbia 34388 Best Of Friends.
        (S) (2:18) Columbia 31748 Loggins & Messina.
1973 #13 *MY MUSIC*
        (S) (3:02) Columbia 32540 Full Sail.
        (S) (3:03) Columbia 34388 Best Of Friends.

LOLITA
1960 #7 *SAILOR (YOUR HOME IS THE SEA)*

LAURIE LONDON
1958 #1 *HE'S GOT THE WHOLE WORLD (IN HIS HANDS)*
        (M) (2:19) Capitol 98665 When AM Was King.

SHORTY LONG
1968 #10 *HERE COMES THE JUDGE*
        (S) (2:37) Motown 6184 Hard To Find Motown Classics Volume 2.

LOOKING GLASS
1972 #1 BRANDY (YOU'RE A FINE GIRL)
    (S) (3:03) Rhino 70929 Super Hits Of The 70's Volume 9. *(LP version)*
    (S) (3:06) Rhino 70633 Billboard's Top Rock & Roll Hits Of 1972. *(LP version)*
    (S) (3:06) Rhino 72005 Billboard's Top Rock & Roll Hits Of 1968-1972 Box Set. *(LP version)*
    (S) (2:55) Columbia/Legacy 46763 Rock Artifacts Volume 2. *(45 version)*
1973 #31 JIMMY LOVES MARY-ANNE
    (S) (3:23) Rhino 70930 Super Hits Of The 70's Volume 10.
    (S) (3:24) Columbia/Legacy 46160 Rock Artifacts Volume 1.

TRINI LOPEZ
1963 #3 IF I HAD A HAMMER
    (S) (3:22) WEA Latina 72868 25th Anniversary Album. *(Live)*
1964 #26 KANSAS CITY
    (S) (3:54) WEA Latina 72868 25th Anniversary Album. *(Live)*
1965 #22 LEMON TREE
    (S) (2:44) WEA Latina 72868 25th Anniversary Album. *(Live)*

LOS BRAVOS
1966 #3 BLACK IS BLACK
    (S) (2:56) Rhino 70325 History Of British Rock Volume 7.
    (S) (2:56) Rhino 72022 History Of British Rock Box Set.
1968 #34 BRING A LITTLE LOVIN'

LOS INDIOS TABAJARAS
1963 #7 MARIA ELENA
    (S) (3:09) RCA 8474 Nipper's Greatest Hits Of The 60's Volume 1.

LOST GENERATION
1970 #39 THE SLY, SLICK, AND THE WICKED
    (S) (2:56) Rhino 70784 Soul Hits Of The 70's Volume 4.

JOHN D. LOUDERMILK
1961 #28 LANGUAGE OF LOVE

LOVE
1966 #35 MY LITTLE RED BOOK
    (S) (2:28) JCI 3101 Rockin' Sixties.
    (S) (2:28) Warner Special Products 27610 More Party Classics.
    (S) (2:29) Elektra 74001 Love.
1966 #33 7 AND 7 IS
    (S) (2:13) Warner Special Products 27607 Highs Of The 60's.
    (S) (2:13) Elektra 74005 Da Capo.

DARLENE LOVE
1963 #38 (TODAY I MET) THE BOY I'M GONNA MARRY
    (M) (2:46) Abkco 7118 Phil Spector/Back To Mono (1958-1969).
1963 #27 WAIT TIL MY BOBBY GETS HOME
    (M) (2:21) Abkco 7118 Phil Spector/Back To Mono (1958-1969).

LOVE UNLIMITED
1972 #7 WALKIN' IN THE RAIN WITH THE ONE I LOVE
    (S) (4:47) Rhino 70551 Soul Hits Of The 70's Volume 11.

LOVIN' SPOONFUL
1965 #8 DO YOU BELIEVE IN MAGIC
    (S) (2:04) K-Tel 839 Battle Of The Bands Volume 2.
    (S) (2:02) Pair 1202 Best Of Buddah.

LOVIN' SPOONFUL (Continued)

    (S) (2:04) Rhino 70944 Anthology.
    (S) (2:03) Special Music 4916 All The Best.
    (S) (2:04) Pair 1200 Best Of.
    (S) (2:03) Buddah 68002 Very Best Of.

1966 #11 YOU DIDN'T HAVE TO BE SO NICE

    (S) (2:26) Rhino 70944 Anthology.
    (S) (2:26) Special Music 4916 All The Best.
    (S) (2:26) Pair 1200 Best Of.
    (S) (2:25) Buddah 68002 Very Best Of.

1966 #1 DAYDREAM

    (S) (2:19) Rhino 70944 Anthology.
    (S) (2:18) Special Music 4916 All The Best.
    (S) (2:18) Pair 1200 Best Of.
    (S) (2:18) Buddah 68002 Very Best Of.

1966 #4 DID YOU EVER HAVE TO MAKE UP YOUR MIND?

    (S) (1:57) Rhino 70944 Anthology.
    (S) (1:57) JCI 3104 Mellow Sixties.
    (S) (1:57) Special Music 4916 All The Best.
    (S) (1:57) Pair 1200 Best Of.
    (S) (1:57) Buddah 68002 Very Best Of.

1966 #1 SUMMER IN THE CITY

    (S) (2:38) Rhino 70087 Summer & Sun.
    (S) (2:39) Rhino 70944 Anthology.
    (S) (2:38) Rhino 70627 Billboard's Top Rock & Roll Hits Of 1966.
    (S) (2:38) Rhino 72007 Billboard's Top Rock & Roll Hits 1962-1966 Box Set.
    (S) (2:35) Pair 1202 Best Of Buddah.
    (S) (2:39) K-Tel 686 Battle Of The Bands Volume 4.
    (S) (2:37) Warner Special Products 27610 More Party Classics.
    (S) (2:39) Special Music 4916 All The Best.
    (S) (2:39) Pair 1200 Best Of.
    (S) (2:38) Pair 3305 Hums Of.
    (S) (2:38) Buddah 68002 Very Best Of.

1966 #9 RAIN ON THE ROOF
(the LP title was "YOU AND ME AND RAIN ON THE ROOF")

    (S) (2:12) Rhino 70944 Anthology.
    (S) (2:11) Special Music 4916 All The Best.
    (S) (2:11) Pair 1200 Best Of.
    (S) (2:11) Pair 3305 Hums Of.
    (S) (2:11) Buddah 68002 Very Best Of.

1967 #10 NASHVILLE CATS

    (S) (2:35) Rhino 70944 Anthology.
    (S) (2:35) Special Music 4916 All The Best.
    (S) (2:34) Pair 1200 Best Of.
    (S) (2:34) Pair 3305 Hums Of.
    (S) (2:33) Buddah 68002 Very Best Of.

1967 #15 DARLING BE HOME SOON

    (S) (3:32) Rhino 70944 Anthology.
    (S) (3:29) Special Music 4916 All The Best.
    (S) (3:32) Pair 1200 Best Of.
    (S) (3:30) Buddah 68002 Very Best Of. (*sounds like it was mastered from vinyl*)

1967 #17 SIX O'CLOCK

    (S) (2:41) Rhino 70944 Anthology.
    (S) (2:40) Special Music 4916 All The Best.

LOVIN' SPOONFUL (Continued)
>   (S)   (2:41)   Pair 1200   Best Of.
>   (S)   (2:41)   Buddah 68002   Very Best Of.

1967 #16 SHE IS STILL A MYSTERY
>   (S)   (3:00)   Rhino 70944   Anthology.
>   (S)   (2:57)   Special Music 4916   All The Best.
>   (S)   (2:58)   Pair 1200   Best Of.
>   (S)   (2:58)   Buddah 68002   Very Best Of. *(poor sound quality; sounds like it was mastered from vinyl)*

1968 #40 MONEY
>   (S)   (1:54)   Rhino 70944   Anthology.
>   (S)   (1:52)   Pair 1200   Best Of.

JIM LOWE
1956 #2 GREEN DOOR
>   (M)   (2:11)   Rhino 70599   Billboard's Top Rock & Roll Hits Of 1956.

1957 #11 FOUR WALLS
1957 #33 TALKIN' TO THE BLUES

ROBIN LUKE
1958 #6 SUSIE DARLIN'
>   (M)   (2:36)   MCA 31202   Vintage Music Volume 5.
>   (M)   (2:36)   MCA 5804   Vintage Music Volumes 5 & 6.
>   (M)   (2:36)   Curb 77354   50's Hits Volume 1.
>   (M)   (2:36)   Curb 77525   Greatest Hits Of Rock 'N' Roll Volume 2.

LULU
1967 #1 TO SIR WITH LOVE
>   (S)   (2:44)   Columbia 44373   Hollywood Magic - The 1960's.
>   (S)   (2:44)   Columbia/Legacy 46983   Rock Artifacts Volume 3.
>   (S)   (2:41)   Rhino 70324   History Of British Rock Volume 6. *(noise on fadeout)*
>   (S)   (2:41)   Rhino 72022   History Of British Rock Box Set. *(noise on fadeout)*

1968 #37 BEST OF BOTH WORLDS
>   (S)   (3:00)   Columbia/Legacy 46984   Rock Artifacts Volume 4.

1970 #18 OH ME OH MY (I'M A FOOL FOR YOU BABY)
>   (S)   (2:41)   Rhino 70926   Super Hits Of The 70's Volume 6.

BOB LUMAN
1960 #5 LET'S THINK ABOUT LIVIN'

VICTOR LUNDBERG
1967 #6 AN OPEN LETTER TO MY TEENAGE SON

ARTHUR LYMAN
1959 #36 TABOO
>   (S)   (4:53)   Dunhill Compact Classics 613   Exotic Sound Of. *(LP version)*

released as by THE ARTHUR LYMAN GROUP:
1961 #6 YELLOW BIRD
>   (S)   (2:43)   Dunhill Compact Classics 613   Exotic Sound Of.

FRANKIE LYMON & THE TEENAGERS
released as by THE TEENAGERS featuring FRANKIE LYMON:
1956 #6 WHY DO FOOLS FALL IN LOVE
>   (M)   (2:17)   Rhino 70642   Billboard's Top R&B Hits Of 1956.
>   (M)   (2:16)   Rhino 70599   Billboard's Top Rock & Roll Hits Of 1956.
>   (M)   (2:15)   Rhino 70906   American Bandstand Greatest Hits Collection.
>   (M)   (2:16)   Rhino 75764   Best Of Doo Wop Uptempo.

THE TEENAGERS featuring FRANKIE LYMON (Continued)
>>(M) (2:16) Rhino 70918 Best Of.
>>(M) (2:17) MCA 10063 Original Television Soundtrack "The Sounds Of Murphy Brown".
>>(M) (2:16) Atlantic 82155 O.S.T. Book Of Love.
>>(M) (2:16) Collectables 5416 Murray The K - Sing Along With The Golden Greats.
>>(M) (2:17) Pair 1279 Goody Goody.

released as by **FRANKIE LYMON & THE TEENAGERS:**
1957 #20 *GOODY GOODY*
>>(M) (2:09) Rhino 70918 Best Of.
>>(M) (2:09) Pair 1279 Goody Goody.

BARBARA LYNN
1962 #4 *YOU'LL LOSE A GOOD THING*
>>(M) (2:20) Rhino 70648 Billboard's Top R&B Hits Of 1962. (*sounds like it was mastered from vinyl*)
>>(M) (2:17) MCA 6228 O.S.T. Hairspray. (*sounds like it was mastered from vinyl*).

VERA LYNN
1957 #40 *DON'T CRY MY LOVE (THE FAITHFUL HUSSAR)*

GLORIA LYNNE
1964 #22 *I WISH YOU LOVE*
>>(S) (3:39) Collectables 5138 Golden Classics. (*truncated fade*)

LONNIE MACK
1963 #5 *MEMPHIS*
>>(M) (2:30) Warner Special Projects 27610 More Party Classics.
>>(M) (2:29) Curb 77402 All-Time Great Instrumental Hits Volume 2.
1963 #28 *WHAM!*

GISELE MacKENZIE
1955 #3 *HARD TO GET*

GORDON MacRAE
1958 #31 *THE SECRET*

JOHNNY MADDOX
1955 #1 *THE CRAZY OTTO MEDLEY*

BETTY MADIGAN
1958 #27 *DANCE EVERYONE DANCE*

JOHNNY MAESTRO
1961 #36 *MODEL GIRL*
>>(S) (2:16) Rhino 70948 Best Of The Crests.

MAGIC LANTERNS
1968 #17 *SHAME, SHAME*
        (S)   (3:01) Rhino 70277 Rare Soul: Beach Music Classics Volume 1.

GEORGE MAHARIS
1962 #31 *TEACH ME TONIGHT*

MAIN INGREDIENT
1972 #1 *EVERYBODY PLAYS THE FOOL*
        (S)   (3:18) RCA 8476 and 9684 Nipper's Greatest Hits Of The 70's.
        (S)   (3:19) Rhino 70789 Soul Hits Of The 70's Volume 9.
        (S)   (3:22) RCA 9591 All Time Greatest Hits.
        (S)   (3:22) RCA 61144 The RCA Records Label: The First Note In Black Music.
        (S)   (3:21) Collectables 5101 Golden Classics.

MAJORS
1962 #20 *A WONDERFUL DREAM*
        (M)   (2:00) Collectables 5249 A Golden Classics Edition.

MIRIAM MAKEBA
1967 #13 *PATA PATA*

MALO
1972 #12 *SUAVECITO*
        (S)   (3:23) Rhino 70787 Soul Hits Of The 70's Volume 7. *(45 version)*
        (S)   (6:32) GNP Crescendo 2205 Best Of. *(LP version)*
        (S)   (3:24) GNP Crescendo 2205 Best Of. *(45 version)*

MAMA CASS
1968 #10 *DREAM A LITTLE DREAM OF ME*
        (S)   (3:12) MCA 31147 Mama's Big Ones.
        (S)   (3:12) MCA 10195 Creeque Alley/History Of The Mama's & Papa's.
        (S)   (3:13) MCA 31335 The Papa's & The Mama's.
        (S)   (3:12) MCA 5701 16 Of Their Greatest Hits. *(missing the MC introduction)*
1969 #35 *IT'S GETTING BETTER*
        (S)   (2:57) MCA 31147 Mama's Big Ones.
        (S)   (3:00) MCA 10195 Creeque Alley/History Of The Mama's & Papa's.
1969 #25 *MAKE YOUR OWN KIND OF MUSIC*
        (S)   (2:18) MCA 31147 Mama's Big Ones.
        (S)   (2:23) MCA 10195 Creeque Alley/History Of The Mama's & Papa's.
1970 #30 *NEW WORLD COMING*
        (S)   (2:09) MCA 31147 Mama's Big Ones.

MAMA'S & PAPA'S
1966 #4 *CALIFORNIA DREAMIN'*
        (S)   (2:37) MCA 31207 Vintage Music Volume 10.
        (S)   (2:37) MCA 5806 Vintage Music Volumes 9 & 10.
        (S)   (2:37) MCA 25240 Classic Rock Volume 3.
        (S)   (2:37) JCI 3104 Mellow Sixties.
        (S)   (2:39) Motown 6159 The Good-Feeling Music Of The Big Chill Generation Volume 1.
        (S)   (2:38) MCA 10195 Creeque Alley/History Of.
        (S)   (2:37) MCA 31042 If You Can Believe Your Eyes And Ears.
        (S)   (2:39) MCA 5701 16 Of Their Greatest Hits.
        (S)   (2:37) MCA 6467 O.S.T. Air America.

MAMA'S & PAPA'S (Continued)
1966 #1 MONDAY MONDAY
    (S) (3:22) Rhino 70627 Billboard's Top Rock & Roll Hits Of 1966.
    (S) (3:22) Rhino 72007 Billboard's Top Rock & Roll Hits 1962-1966 Box Set.
    (S) (3:25) Motown 6159 The Good-Feeling Music Of The Big Chill Generation Volume 1.
    (S) (3:23) MCA 31206 Vintage Music Volume 9.
    (S) (3:23) MCA 5806 Vintage Music Volumes 9 & 10.
    (S) (3:25) MCA 10195 Creeque Alley/History Of.
    (S) (3:24) MCA 31042 If You Can Believe Your Eyes And Ears.
    (S) (3:24) MCA 5701 16 Of Their Greatest Hits.

1966 #6 I SAW HER AGAIN
    (S) (3:11) MCA 10195 Creeque Alley/History Of. (LP version)
    (S) (3:12) MCA 5701 16 Of Their Greatest Hits. (LP version)
    (S) (3:11) MCA 31043 The Mama's & Papa's. (LP version)

1966 #14 LOOK THROUGH MY WINDOW
    (S) (3:05) MCA 5938 Vintage Music Volumes 15 & 16.
    (S) (3:05) MCA 31212 Vintage Music Volume 15.
    (S) (3:03) MCA 10195 Creeque Alley/History Of.
    (S) (3:06) MCA 31044 Deliver.
    (S) (3:20) MCA 5701 16 Of Their Greatest Hits. (:15 longer than any previously issued version of this song)

1967 #6 WORDS OF LOVE
    (S) (2:12) MCA 5939 Vintage Music Volumes 17 & 18. (LP version)
    (S) (2:12) MCA 31215 Vintage Music Volume 18. (LP version)
    (S) (2:12) MCA 10195 Creeque Alley/History Of. (LP version)
    (S) (2:12) MCA 31147 Mama's Big Ones. (LP version)
    (S) (2:15) MCA 5701 16 Of Their Greatest Hits. (LP version)
    (S) (2:13) MCA 31043 The Mama's & Papa's. (LP version)

1967 #2 DEDICATED TO THE ONE I LOVE
    (S) (2:56) MCA 5937 Vintage Music Volumes 13 & 14.
    (S) (2:56) MCA 31210 Vintage Music Volume 13.
    (S) (2:56) MCA 10195 Creeque Alley/History Of.
    (S) (2:58) MCA 31044 Deliver.
    (S) (2:59) MCA 5701 16 Of Their Greatest Hits.

1967 #5 CREEQUE ALLEY
    (S) (3:46) MCA 10195 Creeque Alley/History Of.
    (S) (3:47) MCA 31044 Deliver.
    (S) (3:48) MCA 5701 16 Of Their Greatest Hits.

1967 #15 TWELVE THIRTY (YOUNG GIRLS ARE COMING TO THE CANYON)
    (S) (3:23) MCA 10195 Creeque Alley/History Of.
    (S) (3:23) MCA 31335 The Papa's & The Mama's.
    (S) (3:23) MCA 5701 16 Of Their Greatest Hits.

1967 #23 GLAD TO BE UNHAPPY
    (S) (1:41) MCA 5940 Vintage Music Volumes 19 & 20.
    (S) (1:41) MCA 31216 Vintage Music Volume 19.
    (S) (1:41) MCA 10195 Creeque Alley/History Of.
    (S) (1:42) MCA 5701 16 Of Their Greatest Hits.

1968 #36 DANCING BEAR
    (S) (4:08) MCA 10195 Creeque Alley/History Of. (LP version)
    (S) (4:08) MCA 31043 The Mama's & Papa's. (LP version)

HENRY MANCINI

1960 #20 *MR. LUCKY*
    (S) (2:12) RCA 8321 All Time Greatest Hits Volume 1.
    (S) (2:12) RCA 3667 Pure Gold.
    (S) (2:13) RCA 2198 Music From "Mr. Lucky".

1961 #5 *MOON RIVER*
    (S) (2:39) RCA 8321 All Time Greatest Hits Volume 1.
    (S) (2:43) RCA 5938 Mancini's Classic Movie Scores.
    (S) (2:40) RCA 3667 Pure Gold.
    (S) (2:39) RCA 2077 Moon River, The Pink Panther & Other Hits.
    (S) (2:40) RCA 2362 Breakfast At Tiffany's.
    (S) (2:39) MCA 6340 O.S.T. Born On The Fourth Of July.
    (S) (2:41) RCA 55938 Pink Panther And Other Hits.
    (S) (2:40) Pair 1092 Collection.
    (S) (2:41) Pair 1213 Academy Award Collection.

1963 #29 *DAYS OF WINE AND ROSES*
    (S) (2:05) RCA 8321 All Time Greatest Hits Volume 1.
    (S) (2:06) RCA 3667 Pure Gold.
    (S) (2:06) Pair 1092 Collection.
    (S) (2:08) Pair 1213 Academy Award Collection.

1969 #1 *LOVE THEME FROM ROMEO & JULIET*
    (S) (2:31) RCA 8474 Nipper's Greatest Hits Of The 60's Volume 1.
    (S) (2:31) RCA 8321 All Time Greatest Hits Volume 1.
    (S) (2:31) RCA 3667 Pure Gold.
    (S) (2:31) Pair 1187 Mancini Magic.
    (S) (2:32) Pair 1092 Collection.

1971 #11 *THEME FROM LOVE STORY*
    (S) (2:49) RCA 8321 All Time Greatest Hits Volume 1.

MANFRED MANN

1964 #1 *DO WAH DIDDY DIDDY*
    (S) (2:21) Rhino 70320 History Of British Rock Volume 2.
    (S) (2:21) Rhino 72022 History Of British Rock Box Set.
    (S) (2:21) Rhino 72008 History Of British Rock Volumes 1-4 Box Set.
    (S) (2:21) Rhino 70625 Billboard's Top Rock & Roll Hits Of 1964.
    (S) (2:21) Rhino 72007 Billboard's Top Rock & Roll Hits 1962-1966 Box Set.
    (M) (2:21) Curb 77355 60's Hits Volume 1.
    (M) (2:21) Epic 48732 O.S.T. My Girl.
    (M) (2:21) EMI 48397 Best Of.
    (M) (2:21) Capitol 98138 Spring Break Volume 1.
    (M) (2:31) EMI 96096 Best Of. *(includes :09 studio talk; original unedited version which was not the hit version)*
    (S) (2:21) EMI 96096 Best Of.

1965 #15 *SHA LA LA*
    (M) (2:29) Rhino 70321 History Of British Rock Volume 3.
    (M) (2:29) Rhino 72022 History Of British Rock Box Set.
    (M) (2:29) Rhino 72008 History Of British Rock Volumes 1-4 Box Set.
    (M) (2:30) EMI 48397 Best Of.
    (M) (2:29) EMI 96096 Best Of.

1966 #27 *PRETTY FLAMINGO*
    (S) (2:32) Rhino 70322 History Of British Rock Volume 4.
    (S) (2:32) Rhino 72022 History Of British Rock Box Set.

MANFRED MANN (Continued)
>> (S) (2:32) Rhino 72008 History Of British Rock Volumes 1-4 Box Set.
>> (M) (2:33) EMI 48397 Best Of.
>> (S) (2:29) EMI 96096 Best Of.

1968 #4 *MIGHTY QUINN (QUINN THE ESKIMO)*

MANHATTANS

1973 #29 *THERE'S NO ME WITHOUT YOU*
>> (S) (3:37) Columbia 36861 Greatest Hits. *(truncated fade)*

BARRY MANN

1961 #7 *WHO PUT THE BOMP (IN THE BOMP, BOMP, BOMP)*
>> (S) (2:43) MCA 31202 Vintage Music Volume 5.
>> (S) (2:43) MCA 5804 Vintage Music Volumes 5 & 6.

CARL MANN

1959 #30 *MONA LISA*
>> (M) (2:26) Rhino 75884 The Sun Story.
>> (M) (2:26) RCA 66059 Sun's Greatest Hits.

GLORIA MANN

1956 #6 *TEEN AGE PRAYER*

MANTOVANI & HIS ORCHESTRA

1957 #6 *AROUND THE WORLD*
>> (S) (2:03) London 800085 Golden Hits.

1960 #3 *MAIN THEME FROM EXODUS*

MARATHONS

1961 #21 *PEANUT BUTTER*
>> (M) (2:00) Rhino 75772 Son Of Frat Rock.
>> (M) (1:57) Chess 9283 Best Of Chess Vocal Groups Volume 2.
>> (M) (2:01) Dunhill Compact Classics 057 Olympics All-Time Greatest Hits.
>> (E) (2:01) Collectables 5081 The Olympics Meet The Marathons.

MARCELS

1961 #1 *BLUE MOON*
>> (S) (2:13) Rhino 75764 Best Of Doo Wop Uptempo.
>> (S) (2:13) Rhino 70622 Billboard's Top Rock & Roll Hits Of 1961.
>> (S) (2:13) Rhino 72004 Billboard's Top Rock & Roll Hits 1957-1961 Box Set.
>> (S) (2:14) Rhino 70953 Best Of.

1961 #16 *HEARTACHES*
>> (S) (2:31) Rhino 70953 Best Of.

LITTLE PEGGY MARCH

1963 #1 *I WILL FOLLOW HIM*
>> (S) (2:27) RCA 8474 Nipper's Greatest Hits Of The 60's Volume 1.
>> (S) (2:25) RCA 9902 Nipper's #1 Hits 1956 - 1986.

1963 #33 *HELLO HEARTACHE, GOODBYE LOVE*
>> (S) (2:26) RCA 8475 Nipper's Greatest Hits Of The 60's Volume 2.

BOBBY MARCHAN

1960 #19 *THERE'S SOMETHING ON YOUR MIND (PART 2)*
>> (M) (2:45) Rhino 70646 Billboard's Top R&B Hits Of 1960.
>> (M) (4:50) Relic 7009 Raging Harlem Hit Parade. *(Parts 1 & 2)*

ERNIE MARESCA

1962 #11 *SHOUT! SHOUT! (KNOCK YOURSELF OUT)*
>> (S) (2:09) Rhino 75772 Son Of Frat Rock.
>> (M) (2:10) JCI 3110 Sock Hoppin' Sixties.

MARK IV
1959 #9 *I GOT A WIFE*

MARKETTS
1962 #31 *SURFER'S STOMP*
    (S) (1:56) Rhino 70089   Surfin' Hits.
    (S) (1:56) EMI 90604   Beach Party Blasts.
    (S) (1:56) Curb 77402   All-Time Great Instrumental Hits Volume 2.
    (S) (1:56) Capitol 96861   Monster Summer Hits - Wild Surf.

1964 #3 *OUT OF LIMITS*
    (S) (2:04) Rhino 70089   Surfin' Hits.
    (S) (2:05) Rhino 71492   Elvira Presents Haunted Hits.
    (S) (2:04) Rhino 70625   Billboard's Top Rock & Roll Hits Of 1964.
    (S) (2:04) Rhino 72007   Billboard's Top Rock & Roll Hits 1962-1966 Box Set.
    (S) (2:04) Warner Special Products 27607   Highs Of The 60's.
    (S) (2:04) JCI 3106   Surfin' Sixties.

1966 #14 *BATMAN THEME*
    (S) (2:39) Warner Special Projects 27610   More Party Classics.

MAR-KEYS
1961 #3 *LAST NIGHT*
    (M) (2:36) Atlantic Group 88218   Complete Stax/Volt Singles.
    (M) (2:34) Warner Special Products 27609   Memphis Soul Classics.
    (M) (2:34) Atlantic 81296   Atlantic Rhythm & Blues Volume 4.
    (M) (2:36) Stax 88008   Top Of The Stax Volume 2.
    (M) (2:36) Atlantic 82305   Atlantic Rhythm And Blues 1947-1974 Box Set.

PIGMEAT MARKHAM
1968 #23 *HERE COMES THE JUDGE*

MARMALADE
1970 #7 *REFLECTIONS OF MY LIFE*
    (dj copies of this 45 ran (3:12) while commercial copies were (4:18))
    (S) (4:14) Rhino 70922   Super Hits Of The 70's Volume 2.
    (S) (4:14) Rhino 72009   Super Hits Of The 70's Volumes 1-4 Box Set.
    (S) (4:14) Rhino 70327   History Of British Rock Volume 9.
    (S) (4:14) Rhino 72022   History Of British Rock Box Set.

RALPH MARTERIE & HIS ORCHESTRA
1957 #31 *SHISH-KEBAB*

MARTHA & THE VANDELLAS
1963 #20 *COME AND GET THESE MEMORIES*
    (S) (2:26) Motown 9105   Motown Memories Volume 2.
    (S) (2:26) Motown 5448   A Package Of 16 Original Big Hits.
    (S) (2:27) Motown 9057 and 6170   Compact Command Performances.
    (S) (2:27) Motown 9011 and 5204   Greatest Hits.
    (S) (2:26) Pair 1275   Original Motown Classics.

1963 #4 *HEAT WAVE*
    (E) (2:43) Motown 6159   The Good-Feeling Music Of The Big Chill Generation Volume 1.
    (E) (2:44) Motown 6138   The Composer Series: Holland/Dozier/ Holland.
    (S) (2:41) Motown 5449   A Collection Of 16 Big Hits Volume 2. *(neither the 45 or LP version!)*
    (E) (2:43) Motown 6110   Motown Grammy R&B Performances Of The 60's & 70's.
    (E) (2:44) Rhino 70649   Billboard's Top R&B Hits Of 1963.
    (E) (2:43) Motown 9057 and 6170   Compact Command Performances.

    (E) (2:45) Motown 8049 and 8149 Heat Wave/Dance Party.

    (E) (2:43) Motown 9017 and 5248 16 #1 Hits From The Early 60's.

    (E) (2:43) Motown 9021 and 5309 25 Years Of Grammy Greats.

    (E) (2:43) Motown 9011 and 5204 Greatest Hits.

    (E) (2:43) Motown 5343 Every Great Motown Song: The First 25 Years Volume 1. *(most selections on this cd have noise on the fade out)*

    (E) (2:43) Motown 8034 and 8134 Every Great Motown Song: The First 25 Years Volumes 1 & 2. *(most selections on this cd have noise on the fade out)*

    (E) (2:43) Motown 9098 Radio's #1 Hits.

    (E) (2:43) Motown 9095 and 5325 Motown Girl Groups: Top 10 With A Bullet!

    (E) (2:44) Motown 5145 Heat Wave.

    (E) (2:41) Motown 9071 Motown Dance Party Volume 1. *(all selections on this cd are segued together)*

    (E) (2:43) Pair 1275 Original Motown Classics.

1964 #14 *QUICKSAND*

    (S) (2:42) Motown 5450 A Collection Of 16 Big Hits Volume 3. *(LP version)*

    (S) (2:33) Motown 9057 and 6170 Compact Command Performances. *(45 version)*

    (S) (2:33) Motown 9011 and 5204 Greatest Hits. *(45 version)*

1964 #34 *LIVE WIRE*

    (S) (2:35) Motown 9057 and 6170 Compact Command Performances.

    (S) (2:34) Motown 9011 and 5204 Greatest Hits.

1964 #4 *DANCING IN THE STREET*

    (S) (2:37) Motown 6137 20 Greatest Songs In Motown History.

    (S) (2:39) Motown 5450 A Collection Of 16 Big Hits Volume 3.

    (S) (2:37) Motown 6120 O.S.T. The Big Chill.

    (S) (2:39) Rhino 70650 Billboard's Top R&B Hits Of 1964.

    (S) (2:37) Motown 9057 and 6170 Compact Command Performances.

    (S) (2:37) Motown 8049 and 8149 Heat Wave/Dance Party.

    (S) (2:36) Motown 9072 Motown Dance Party Volume 2. *(all selections on this cd are segued together)*

    (S) (2:37) Motown 9011 and 5204 Greatest Hits.

    (S) (2:37) Motown 5433 Dance Party.

    (S) (2:37) Motown 5343 Every Great Motown Song: The First 25 Years Volume 1. *(most selections on this cd have noise on the fade out)*

    (S) (2:37) Motown 8034 and 8134 Every Great Motown Song: The First 25 Years Volumes 1 & 2. *(most selections on this cd have noise on the fade out)*

    (S) (2:37) Motown 9098 Radio's #1 Hits.

    (S) (2:36) Motown 6094 More Songs From The Original Soundtrack Of The "Big Chill".

    (S) (2:38) Motown 9095 and 5325 Motown Girl Groups: Top 10 With A Bullet!

    (S) (2:39) Motown 5322 and 9087 Girl Groups: The Story Of A Sound. *(highly distorted)*

    (S) (2:37) Pair 1275 Original Motown Classics.

1965 #31 *WILD ONE*

    (S) (2:42) Motown 9057 and 6170 Compact Command Performances.

    (S) (2:43) Motown 8049 and 8149 Heat Wave/Dance Party.

    (S) (2:42) Motown 9011 and 5204 Greatest Hits.

    (S) (2:43) Motown 5433 Dance Party.

1965 #9 NOWHERE TO RUN
    (S) (2:54) A&M 3913 O.S.T. Good Morning Vietnam.
    (S) (2:55) Motown 5452 A Collection Of 16 Big Hits Volume 5.
    (S) (2:53) Priority 7909 Vietnam: Rockin' The Delta. *(truncated fade)*
    (S) (2:55) Motown 9057 and 6170 Compact Command Performances.
    (S) (2:55) MCA 10063 Original Television Soundtrack "The Sounds Of Murphy Brown".
    (S) (2:56) Motown 8049 and 8149 Heat Wave/Dance Party.
    (S) (2:53) Motown 9072 Motown Dance Party Volume 2. *(all selections on this cd are segued together)*
    (S) (2:55) Motown 9011 and 5204 Greatest Hits.
    (S) (2:55) Motown 5433 Dance Party.

1966 #23 MY BABY LOVES ME
    (S) (3:01) Motown 9109 Motown Memories Volume 3.
    (S) (3:01) Motown 5453 A Collection Of 16 Big Hits Volume 6.
    (S) (3:01) Motown 9057 and 6170 Compact Command Performances.
    (S) (3:02) Motown 9011 and 5204 Greatest Hits. *(noise on fadeout)*
    (S) (3:01) Motown 5111 Superstar Series Volume 11.

1966 #11 I'M READY FOR LOVE
    (S) (2:49) Motown 5454 A Collection Of 16 Big Hits Volume 7.
    (S) (2:54) Motown 9057 and 6170 Compact Command Performances.
    (S) (2:51) Motown 6767 Watchout.

1967 #6 JIMMY MACK
    (S) (2:41) Motown 9104 Motown Memories Volume 1. *(alternate take)*
    (S) (2:48) Motown 5455 A Collection Of 16 Big Hits Volume 8. *(alternate take)*
    (S) (2:41) Motown 6161 The Good-Feeling Music Of The Big Chill Generation Volume 3. *(alternate take)*
    (M) (2:48) Rhino 70653 Billboard's Top R&B Hits Of 1967. *(45 version)*
    (M) (2:48) Rhino 72006 Billboard's Top R&B Hits 1965-1969 Box Set. *(45 version)*
    (S) (2:41) Motown 9057 and 6170 Compact Command Performances. *(alternate take)*
    (S) (2:42) Motown 6767 Watchout. *(LP version)*
    (S) (2:41) Motown 9095 and 5325 Motown Girl Groups: Top 10 With A Bullet! (LP version)
    (M) (2:50) Motown 9071 Motown Dance Party Volume 1. *(45 version; all selections on this cd are segued together)*
    (M) (2:48) Ripete 392183 Ocean Drive. *(45 version)*

1967 #27 LOVE BUG LEAVE MY HEART ALONE
    (S) (2:03) Motown 5457 A Collection Of 16 Big Hits Volume 10.
    (S) (2:07) Motown 9057 and 6170 Compact Command Performances.

1967 #12 HONEY CHILE
    (S) (2:56) Motown 5456 A Collection Of 16 Big Hits Volume 9.
    (S) (2:57) Motown 9057 and 6170 Compact Command Performances.
    (S) (2:54) Motown 5111 Superstar Series Volume 11.

1968 #37 I PROMISE TO WAIT MY LOVE
    (S) (2:05) Motown 9057 and 6170 Compact Command Performances.
    (S) (2:04) Motown 5111 Superstar Series Volume 11.

1968 #40 I CAN'T DANCE TO THAT MUSIC YOU'RE PLAYIN'
    (E) (2:36) Motown 9057 and 6170 Compact Command Performances.

BOBBI MARTIN
1965 #18 *DON'T FORGET I STILL LOVE YOU*
1970 #9 *FOR THE LOVE OF HIM*
        (S)   (2:35) Rhino 70922 Super Hits Of The 70's Volume 2.
        (S)   (2:35) Rhino 72009 Super Hits Of The 70's Volumes 1-4 Box Set.

DEAN MARTIN
1956 #1 *MEMORIES ARE MADE OF THIS*
        (E)   (2:17) Capitol 90592 Memories Are Made Of This.
        (M)   (2:16) Curb 77354 50's Hits Volume 1.
        (M)   (2:14) Capitol 46627 Best Of.
        (M)   (2:15) Capitol 91633 Capitol Collector's Series.
        (E)   (2:15) Pair 1029 Dreams And Memories.
        (M)   (2:14) Capitol 98670 Memories Are Made Of This.
1958 #3 *RETURN TO ME*
        (S)   (2:41) Capitol 46627 Best Of. *(rerecording)*
        (M)   (2:23) Capitol 91633 Capitol Collector's Series.
        (E)   (2:22) Pair 1029 Dreams And Memories.
1958 #38 *ANGEL BABY*
        (M)   (2:44) Capitol 91633 Capitol Collector's Series.
1958 #1 *VOLARE (NEL BLU DIPINTO DI BLU)*
        (M)   (2:57) Capitol 46627 Best Of.
        (M)   (2:58) Capitol 91633 Capitol Collector's Series.
        (E)   (2:58) Pair 1029 Dreams And Memories.
1959 #36 *ON AN EVENING IN ROMA*
        (M)   (2:42) Capitol 91633 Capitol Collector's Series. *(includes :19 of studio talk)*
1964 #1 *EVERYBODY LOVES SOMEBODY*
1964 #8 *THE DOOR IS STILL OPEN TO MY HEART*
1965 #26 *YOU'RE NOBODY TILL SOMEBODY LOVES YOU*
        (S)   (2:11) Capitol 46627 Best Of. *(Capitol recording - not the hit Reprise version)*
        (S)   (2:11) Pair 1029 Dreams And Memories. *(Capitol recording - not the hit Reprise version)*
1965 #20 *SEND ME THE PILLOW YOU DREAM ON*
1965 #35 *(REMEMBER ME) I'M THE ONE WHO LOVES YOU*
1965 #24 *HOUSTON*
1965 #11 *I WILL*
1966 #34 *SOMEWHERE THERE'S A SOMEONE*
1966 #40 *COME RUNNING BACK*
1967 #30 *IN THE CHAPEL IN THE MOONLIGHT*

TRADE MARTIN
1962 #39 *THAT STRANGER USED TO BE MY GIRL*

VINCE MARTIN (WITH THE TARRIERS)
1956 #9 *CINDY, OH CINDY*

WINK MARTINDALE
1959 #4 *DECK OF CARDS*

AL MARTINO
1963 #3 *I LOVE YOU BECAUSE*
        (S)   (2:41) Capitol 91145 Best Of.
        (S)   (2:40) Curb 77401 Greatest Hits.
        (S)   (2:41) Capitol 96430 Capitol Collector's Series.
        (S)   (2:40) Capitol 98670 Memories Are Made Of This.

AL MARTINO (Continued)
1963 #19 *PAINTED, TAINTED ROSE*
       (M) (2:46) Capitol 91145 Best Of.
       (M) (2:46) Capitol 96430 Capitol Collector's Series.
1963 #23 *LIVING A LIE*
       (S) (2:29) Capitol 91145 Best Of.
       (S) (2:28) Capitol 96430 Capitol Collector's Series.
1964 #11 *I LOVE YOU MORE AND MORE EVERY DAY*
       (S) (2:13) Capitol 91145 Best Of.
       (S) (2:13) Curb 77401 Greatest Hits.
       (S) (2:13) Capitol 96430 Capitol Collector's Series.
1964 #18 *TEARS AND ROSES*
       (S) (2:17) Capitol 96430 Capitol Collector's Series.
1966 #16 *SPANISH EYES*
       (S) (2:44) Curb 77355 60's Hits Volume 1.
       (S) (2:45) Capitol 91145 Best Of.
       (S) (2:44) Curb 77401 Greatest Hits.
       (S) (3:52) Capitol 96430 Capitol Collector's Series. *(includes 2 false starts of (1:06) total time)*
1966 #33 *THINK I'LL GO SOMEWHERE AND CRY MYSELF TO SLEEP*
       (S) (2:45) Capitol 96430 Capitol Collector's Series.
1967 #27 *MARY IN THE MORNING*
       (S) (2:49) Capitol 91145 Best Of.
       (S) (2:49) Curb 77401 Greatest Hits.
       (S) (2:54) Capitol 96430 Capitol Collector's Series.

MARVELETTES
1961 #2 *PLEASE MR. POSTMAN*
       (M) (2:26) Rhino 70622 Billboard's Top Rock & Roll Hits Of 1961.
       (M) (2:26) Rhino 72004 Billboard's Top Rock & Roll Hits 1957-1961 Box Set.
       (M) (2:27) Motown 6132 25 #1 Hits From 25 Years.
       (M) (2:26) Motown 6159 The Good-Feeling Music Of The Big Chill Generation Volume 1.
       (S) (2:20) Motown 5448 A Package Of 16 Big Hits. *(missing the overdub near the end of the song that went "deliver de letter")*
       (M) (2:26) Motown 9056 and 6169 Compact Command Performances.
       (M) (2:26) Motown 9017 and 5248 16 #1 Hits From The Early 60's.
       (M) (2:26) Motown 9097 Most Played Oldies On America's Jukeboxes.
       (M) (2:26) Motown 5180 Greatest Hits. *(noise on fadeout)*
       (M) (2:26) Motown 5343 Every Great Motown Song: The First 25 Years Volume 1. *(most selections on this cd have noise on the fade out)*
       (M) (2:26) Motown 8034 and 8134 Every Great Motown Song: The First 25 Years Volumes 1 & 2. *(most selections on this cd have noise on the fade out)*
       (M) (2:25) Motown 9098 Radio's #1 Hits.
       (M) (2:27) Motown 5266 Please Mr. Postman.
       (M) (2:26) Motown 5322 and 9087 Girl Groups: The Story Of A Sound.
1962 #32 *TWISTIN' POSTMAN*
       (S) (2:29) Motown 9056 and 6169 Compact Command Performances.
       (S) (2:29) Motown 5180 Greatest Hits.
1962 #8 *PLAYBOY*
       (S) (2:46) Motown 5449 A Collection Of 16 Big Hits Volume 2.
       (E) (2:45) Motown 9056 and 6169 Compact Command Performances.
       (S) (2:43) Motown 5473 Playboy.
       (E) (2:45) Motown 5180 Greatest Hits.

MARVELETTES (Continued)
1962 #18 *BEECHWOOD 4-5789*
    (S) (2:08) Motown 5448 A Package Of 16 Big Hits.
    (E) (2:10) Motown 9056 and 6169 Compact Command Performances.
    (S) (2:09) Motown 5473 Playboy.
    (E) (2:10) Motown 5180 Greatest Hits.

1965 #21 *TOO MANY FISH IN THE SEA*
    (S) (2:19) Motown 5451 A Collection Of 16 Big Hits Volume 4.
    (S) (2:27) Motown 6120 O.S.T. Big Chill.
    (S) (2:27) Motown 9056 and 6169 Compact Command Performances.
    (S) (2:28) Motown 5180 Greatest Hits.
    (S) (2:26) Motown 6094 More Songs From The Original Soundtrack Of The "Big Chill".
    (S) (2:26) Motown 9071 Motown Dance Party Volume 1. (*all selections on this cd are segued together*)

1965 #36 *I'LL KEEP HOLDING ON*
    (E) (2:25) Motown 5452 A Collection Of 16 Big Hits Volume 5.
    (E) (2:25) Motown 9056 and 6169 Compact Command Performances.

1966 #9 *DON'T MESS WITH BILL*
    (S) (2:48) Motown 9104 Motown Memories Volume 1.
    (S) (2:49) Motown 5453 A Collection Of 16 Big Hits Volume 6.
    (S) (2:48) Motown 9056 and 6169 Compact Command Performances.
    (S) (2:49) Motown 5180 Greatest Hits.
    (S) (2:48) Motown 9095 and 5325 Motown Girl Groups: Top 10 With A Bullet!

1967 #16 *THE HUNTER GETS CAPTURED BY THE GAME*
    (S) (2:46) Motown 5454 A Collection Of 16 Big Hits Volume 7.
    (S) (2:47) Motown 9056 and 6169 Compact Command Performances.
    (S) (2:47) Motown 5421 The Marvelettes.
    (S) (2:47) Motown 8055 and 8155 Sophisticated Soul/ Marvelettes.

1967 #30 *WHEN YOU'RE YOUNG AND IN LOVE*
    (S) (2:35) Motown 9056 and 6169 Compact Command Performances.
    (S) (2:34) Motown 5421 The Marvelettes.
    (S) (2:34) Motown 8055 and 8155 Sophisticated Soul/ Marvelettes.

1968 #10 *MY BABY MUST BE A MAGICIAN*
    (S) (2:32) Motown 5456 A Collection Of 16 Big Hits Volume 9.
    (S) (2:33) Motown 9056 and 6169 Compact Command Performances.
    (S) (2:34) Motown 5430 Sophisticated Soul.
    (S) (2:33) Motown 8055 and 8155 Sophisticated Soul/ Marvelettes.

MARVELOWS
1965 #32 *I DO*
    (M) (2:25) Rhino 75757 Soul Shots Volume 3.
    (E) (2:25) MCA 5937 Vintage Music Volumes 13 & 14.
    (E) (2:25) MCA 31210 Vintage Music Volume 13.

HUGH MASEKELA
1968 #1 *GRAZING IN THE GRASS*
    (S) (2:37) Rhino 70629 Billboard's Top Rock & Roll Hits Of 1968.
    (S) (2:37) Rhino 72005 Billboard's Top Rock & Roll Hits 1968-1972 Box Set.
    (S) (2:35) MCA 5940 Vintage Music Volumes 19 & 20.
    (S) (2:35) MCA 31216 Vintage Music Volume 19.
    (S) (2:36) MCA 10288 Classic Soul.

MASHMAKHAN

1970 #30 *AS THE YEARS GO BY*
> (S) (3:44) Columbia/Legacy 46160 Rock Artifacts Volume 1. (*neither the LP or 45 version*)

BARBARA MASON

1965 #3 *YES, I'M READY*
1965 #33 *SAD, SAD GIRL*
1973 #18 *GIVE ME YOUR LOVE*

DAVE MASON

1970 #37 *ONLY YOU KNOW AND I KNOW*
> (S) (4:05) MCA 31273 Classic Rock Volume 1.
> (S) (4:06) MCA 31170 Alone Together.
> (S) (4:02) MCA 31169 Very Best Of.

TOBIN MATHEWS & CO.

1960 #27 *RUBY DUBY DU*

JOHNNY MATHIS

1957 #12 *WONDERFUL! WONDERFUL!*
> (M) (2:45) Columbia 34667 Johnny's Greatest Hits.
> (M) (2:46) Columbia 40217 16 Most Requested Songs.

1957 #2 *IT'S NOT FOR ME TO SAY*
> (M) (3:03) Columbia 45111 16 Most Requested Songs Of The 50's Volume 2.
> (M) (3:02) Columbia 34667 Johnny's Greatest Hits.
> (M) (3:02) Columbia 40217 16 Most Requested Songs.

1957 #1 *CHANCES ARE*
> (S) (3:00) Columbia 45110 16 Most Requested Songs Of The 50's Volume 1.
> (S) (3:00) Columbia 45017 Radio Classics Of The 50's.
> (M) (3:00) Columbia 34667 Johnny's Greatest Hits.
> (M) (3:01) Columbia 40217 16 Most Requested Songs.

1957 #38 *THE TWELFTH OF NEVER*
> (M) (2:27) Columbia 34667 Johnny's Greatest Hits.
> (M) (2:27) Columbia 40217 16 Most Requested Songs.

1957 #20 *WILD IS THE WIND*
> (M) (2:25) Columbia 44374 Hollywood Magic - The 50's.
> (M) (2:25) Columbia 34667 Johnny's Greatest Hits.
> (M) (2:25) Columbia 40217 16 Most Requested Songs.

1957 #26 *NO LOVE (BUT YOUR LOVE)*
> (M) (2:17) Columbia 34667 Johnny's Greatest Hits.

1958 #23 *COME TO ME*
> (M) (3:02) Columbia 34667 Johnny's Greatest Hits.

1958 #35 *ALL THE TIME*
> (M) (2:42) Columbia 34667 Johnny's Greatest Hits.

1958 #20 *TEACHER, TEACHER*
> (S) (2:38) Columbia 8150 More Johnny's Greatest Hits.

1958 #15 *A CERTAIN SMILE*
> (M) (2:48) Columbia 44374 Hollywood Magic - The 50's.
> (S) (2:46) Columbia 8150 More Johnny's Greatest Hits.
> (S) (2:45) Columbia 40217 16 Most Requested Songs.

1958 #14 *CALL ME*
> (S) (2:45) Columbia 8150 More Johnny's Greatest Hits.

228

JOHNNY MATHIS (Continued)
1959 #40 LET'S LOVE
    (S) (2:43) Columbia 8150 More Johnny's Greatest Hits.
1959 #33 SOMEONE
    (S) (2:55) Columbia 8150 More Johnny's Greatest Hits.
1959 #19 SMALL WORLD
    (S) (3:18) Columbia 8150 More Johnny's Greatest Hits.
    (S) (3:16) Columbia 40217 16 Most Requested Songs.
1959 #14 MISTY
    (S) (3:32) Columbia 40217 16 Most Requested Songs.
1960 #24 STARBRIGHT
1960 #35 MY LOVE FOR YOU
1962 #8 GINA
    (S) (2:45) Columbia 40217 16 Most Requested Songs.
1963 #9 WHAT WILL MY MARY SAY
    (S) (3:08) Columbia 40217 16 Most Requested Songs.
1963 #40 EVERY STEP OF THE WAY

MATTHEWS SOUTHERN COMFORT
1971 #17 WOODSTOCK
    (S) (4:27) Rhino 70924 Super Hits Of The 70's Volume 4.
    (S) (4:27) Rhino 72009 Super Hits Of The 70's Volumes 1-4 Box Set.
    (S) (4:27) MCA 10519 Best Of.

PAUL MAURIAT
1968 #1 LOVE IS BLUE
    (S) (2:36) Philips 830769 Love Is Blue. *(rerecording)*
    (S) (2:35) Philips 834259 Love Is Blue/20th Anniversary Collection.
          (rerecording)

ROBERT MAXWELL
1964 #9 SHANGRI-LA

NATHANIEL MAYER & THE FABULOUS TWILIGHTS
1962 #26 VILLAGE OF LOVE

CURTIS MAYFIELD
1971 #24 (DON'T WORRY) IF THERE'S A HELL BELOW WE'RE ALL GOING TO GO
    (S) (7:03) Curtom 2902 Of All Time/Classic Collection. *(LP version)*
1972 #6 FREDDIE'S DEAD
    (S) (3:46) Rhino 70660 Billboard's Top R&B Hits Of 1972.
    (S) (3:46) Rhino 70789 Soul Hits Of The 70's Volume 9.
    (S) (5:26) Curtom 2002 Superfly. *(LP version)*
1973 #6 SUPERFLY
    (S) (3:12) Rhino 70790 Soul Hits Of The 70's Volume 10.
    (S) (3:53) Curtom 2002 Superfly. *(LP length)*
1973 #39 FUTURE SHOCK

PAUL McCARTNEY (and WINGS)
1971 #6 ANOTHER DAY
    (S) (3:40) Capitol 48287 All The Best.
    (S) (3:41) Capitol 46056 Wings Greatest.

released as by WINGS:
1972 #38 GIVE IRELAND BACK TO THE IRISH
1973 #6 HI HI HI
    (S) (3:07) Capitol 46056 Wings Greatest.

WINGS (Continued)
1973 #1 LIVE AND LET DIE
      (S) (3:10) EMI 46079 James Bond 13 Original Themes.
      (S) (3:11) EMI 90629 O.S.T. Live And Let Die.
      (S) (3:10) Capitol 48287 All The Best.
      (S) (3:10) Capitol 46056 Wings Greatest.

released as by PAUL McCARTNEY & WINGS:
1973 #1 MY LOVE
      (S) (4:07) Capitol 52026 Red Rose Speedway.
      (S) (4:07) Capitol 48287 All The Best.
      (S) (4:07) Capitol 46056 Wings Greatest.

PAUL & LINDA McCARTNEY
1971 #1 UNCLE ALBERT/ADMIRAL HALSEY
      (S) (4:54) Capitol 46612 Ram. (*LP length; tracks into next selection just like the "Ram" vinyl LP*)
      (S) (4:39) Capitol 48287 All The Best. (*:08 shorter than 45 length*)
      (S) (4:40) Capitol 46056 Wings Greatest. (*:07 shorter than 45 length*)

McCOYS
1965 #1 HANG ON SLOOPY

(the original 45 and LP time was (3:02) even though the record label stated (2:57); the (3:52) version first appeared on the "Bang And Shout" Superhits" various artist compilation LP in 1970)
      (M) (3:02) Rhino 70626 Billboard's Top Rock & Roll Hits Of 1965.
      (M) (3:02) Rhino 72007 Billboard's Top Rock & Roll Hits 1962-1966 Box Set.
      (M) (3:52) Rhino 70996 One Hit Wonders Of The 60's Volume 2.
      (M) (3:52) Rhino 70732 Grandson Of Frat Rock.
      (E) (2:59) SBK 93744 China Beach - Music & Memories.
      (M) (3:02) K-Tel 713 Battle Of The Bands.
      (E) (3:01) Sony Music Special Products 46994 The Immediate Singles Collection Volume 2. (*numerous droupouts*)

1965 #9 FEVER
      (E) (2:50) Sony Music Special Products 46994 The Immediate Singles Collection Volume 2.

1966 #17 COME ON LET'S GO
      (M) (2:37) Sony Music Special Products 47351 The Immediate Singles Collection Volume 1.

JIMMY McCRACKLIN
1958 #26 THE WALK
      (M) (2:44) Rhino 70992 Groove 'n' Grind. (*some vocal distortion*)
      (M) (2:44) Chess 31317 Best Of Chess Rhythm & Blues Volume 1.

GENE McDANIELS
1961 #3 A HUNDRED POUNDS OF CLAY
      (S) (2:18) EMI 91681 Golden Greats.
1961 #24 A TEAR
      (S) (2:07) EMI 91681 Golden Greats.
1961 #9 TOWER OF STRENGTH
      (S) (2:15) EMI 91681 Golden Greats.
1962 #16 CHIP CHIP
      (S) (2:17) EMI 91681 Golden Greats.
1962 #32 POINT OF NO RETURN
      (S) (2:13) EMI 91681 Golden Greats.
1962 #38 SPANISH LACE
      (S) (2:21) EMI 91681 Golden Greats.

MAUREEN McGOVERN
1973 #3 *THE MORNING AFTER*
    (S) (2:20) Rhino 70758 Super Hits Of The 70's Volume 11.
    (S) (2:19) Curb 77337 Greatest Hits.

JIMMY McGRIFF
1962 #34 *I'VE GOT A WOMAN (PART 1)*

McGUINNESS FLINT
1971 #35 *WHEN I'M DEAD AND GONE*

BARRY McGUIRE
1965 #1 *EVE OF DESTRUCTION*
    (S) (3:35) Rhino 70734 Songs Of Protest. *(lots of tape hiss)*
    (S) (3:35) Rhino 70626 Billboard's Top Rock & Roll Hits Of 1965. *(noisy intro)*
    (S) (3:35) Rhino 72007 Billboard's Top Rock & Roll Hits 1962-1966 Box Set. *(noisy intro)*
    (S) (3:35) Motown 6161 The Good-Feeling Music Of The Big Chill Generation Volume 3. *(noisy intro)*
    (S) (3:32) MCA 31206 Vintage Music Volume 9. *(noisy intro)*
    (S) (3:32) MCA 5806 Vintage Music Volumes 9 & 10. *(noisy intro)*

McGUIRE SISTERS
1955 #1 *SINCERELY*
    (M) (2:58) MCA 31341 Greatest Hits.
1955 #3 *SOMETHING'S GOTTA GIVE*
    (M) (2:51) MCA 31341 Greatest Hits.
1955 #4 *HE*
    (M) (2:34) MCA 31341 Greatest Hits.
1956 #33 *EV'RY DAY OF MY LIFE*
    (M) (2:37) MCA 31341 Greatest Hits.
1956 #36 *ENDLESS*
1957 #23 *GOODNIGHT MY LOVE, PLESANT DREAMS*
1957 #36 *KID STUFF*
1958 #7 *SUGARTIME*
    (M) (2:31) MCA 31200 Vintage Music Volume 3. *(numerous dropouts)*
    (M) (2:31) MCA 5778 Vintage Music Volumes 3 & 4. *(numerous dropouts)*
    (M) (2:31) MCA 31341 Greatest Hits.
1959 #21 *MAY YOU ALWAYS*
    (S) (2:56) MCA 31341 Greatest Hits.
1961 #17 *JUST FOR OLD TIME'S SAKE*
    (S) (2:48) MCA 31341 Greatest Hits. *(hum noticeable on fadeout)*

SCOTT McKENZIE
1967 #4 *SAN FRANCISCO (BE SURE TO WEAR FLOWERS IN YOUR HAIR)*
    (S) (2:57) Columbia/Legacy 46983 Rock Artifacts Volume 3.
1967 #18 *LIKE AN OLD TIME MOVIE*
    (S) (3:14) Columbia/Legacy 46983 Rock Artifacts Volume 3.

TOMMY McLAIN
1966 #17 *SWEET DREAMS*

DON McLEAN
1972 #1 *AMERICAN PIE (PARTS 1 & 2)*
    (S) (8:23) MCA 6340 O.S.T. Born On The Fourth Of July.
    (S) (8:33) EMI 46555 American Pie.
    (S) (8:33) EMI 91476 Best Of.

DON McLEAN (Continued)
      (S) (8:31) EMI 46586 Then & Now.
      (S) (8:33) Curb 77547 Classics.
      (S) (8:56) Curb 77547 Classics. *(rerecording)*
1972 #11 *VINCENT*
      (S) (3:58) EMI 46555 American Pie.
      (S) (3:58) EMI 91476 Best Of.
      (S) (3:58) EMI 46586 Then & Now.
      (S) (5:16) Curb 77547 Classics. *(rerecording)*
1973 #19 *DREIDEL*
      (S) (3:44) EMI 91476 Best Of.

PHIL McLEAN
1962 #20 *SMALL SAD SAM*

ROBIN McNAMARA
1970 #7 *LAY A LITTLE LOVIN' ON ME*
      (S) (3:00) Rhino 70922 Super Hits Of The 70's Volume 2.
      (S) (3:00) Rhino 72009 Super Hits Of The 70's Volumes 1-4 Box Set.

CLYDE McPHATTER
1956 #29 *TREASURE OF LOVE*
      (M) (2:07) Rhino 70642 Billboard's Top R&B Hits Of 1956.
      (M) (2:07) Atlantic 81295 Atlantic Rhythm & Blues Volume 3.
      (M) (2:08) Curb 77417 Greatest Hits.
      (M) (2:08) Atlantic 82314 Deep Sea Ball.
      (M) (2:08) Atlantic 82305 Atlantic Rhythm And Blues 1947-1974 Box Set.
1957 #33 *LONG LONELY NIGHTS*
      (M) (2:22) Atlantic 82314 Deep Sea Ball.
      (M) (2:22) Atlantic 82305 Atlantic Rhythm And Blues 1947-1974 Box Set.
1959 #10 *A LOVER'S QUESTION*
      (M) (2:32) Atlantic 81295 Atlantic Rhythm & Blues Volume 3.
      (M) (2:32) Curb 77417 Greatest Hits.
      (M) (2:33) Atlantic 82314 Deep Sea Ball.
      (M) (2:33) Atlantic 82305 Atlantic Rhythm And Blues 1947-1974 Box Set.
1959 #31 *SINCE YOU'VE BEEN GONE*
      (M) (2:25) Atlantic 82314 Deep Sea Ball.
1960 #23 *TA TA*
      (S) (2:13) Mercury 838243 Mercury R&B '46 - '62.
      (M) (2:12) Curb 77417 Greatest Hits.
1962 #7 *LOVER PLEASE*
      (S) (1:54) Mercury 838243 Mercury R&B '46 - '62.
      (S) (1:54) JCI 3204 Heart & Soul Fifties.
      (M) (1:45) Curb 77417 Greatest Hits. *(noise on fadeout)*
1962 #26 *LITTLE BITTY PRETTY ONE*
      (S) (2:14) Mercury 838243 Mercury R&B '46 - '62.
      (M) (2:10) Curb 77417 Greatest Hits.

MEL & TIM
1969 #12 *BACKFIELD IN MOTION*
1972 #18 *STARTING ALL OVER AGAIN*
      (S) (3:29) Stax 88005 Top Of The Stax.
      (S) (3:32) Rhino 70789 Soul Hits Of The 70's Volume 9.

MELANIE

1970 #3 LAY DOWN (CANDLES IN THE RAIN)
- (S) (3:59) Rhino 70923 Super Hits Of The 70's Volume 3. (:13 *longer than 45 and "Candles In The Rain" LP*)
- (S) (3:59) Rhino 72009 Super Hits Of The 70's Volumes 1-4 Box Set. (:13 *longer than 45 and "Candles In The Rain" LP*)
- (S) (3:47) Pair 1202 Best Of Buddah.
- (S) (3:45) Rhino 70991 Best Of.
- (S) (3:47) Pair 1203 Best Of.
- (S) (3:46) Pair 3302 Candles In The Rain. (*truncated fade*)

1970 #20 PEACE WILL COME (ACCORDING TO PLAN)
- (M) (3:18) Rhino 70991 Best Of.
- (E) (3:20) Pair 1203 Best Of.

1971 #34 RUBY TUESDAY
- (S) (4:34) Rhino 70991 Best Of.
- (S) (4:35) Pair 1203 Best Of.

1971 #1 BRAND NEW KEY
- (S) (2:23) Rhino 70991 Best Of.
- (S) (2:22) Rhino 70927 Super Hits Of The 70's Volume 7.

1972 #21 RING THE LIVING BELL
- (S) (5:01) Rhino 70991 Best Of. (*LP version*)

1972 #25 THE NICKEL SONG
- (S) (3:43) Rhino 70991 Best Of.
- (S) (3:48) Pair 1203 Best Of.

1973 #30 BITTER BAD
- (S) (2:29) Rhino 70991 Best Of.

MELLO-TONES

1957 #27 ROSIE LEE

HAROLD MELVIN & THE BLUE NOTES

1972 #40 I MISS YOU (PART 1)
- (S) (8:27) Philadelphia International 34232 Collector's Item. (*Parts 1 & 2*)

1972 #2 IF YOU DON'T KNOW ME BY NOW
- (S) (3:25) Rhino 70789 Soul Hits Of The 70's Volume 9.
- (S) (3:25) Rhino 70660 Billboard's Top R&B Hits Of 1972.
- (S) (3:25) Philadelphia International 39255 Philly Ballads Volume 1.
- (S) (3:25) Epic 48732 O.S.T. My Girl.
- (S) (3:25) Philadelphia International 34232 Collector's Item.

1973 #9 THE LOVE I LOST (PART 1)
- (S) (3:41) Rhino 70661 Billboard's Top R&B Hits Of 1973.
- (S) (3:37) Rhino 70552 Soul Hits Of The 70's Volume 12.
- (S) (6:22) Philadelphia International 34232 Collector's Item. (*LP version; Parts 1 & 2*)

SERGIO MENDES & BRASIL '66

1968 #5 THE LOOK OF LOVE
- (S) (2:41) A&M 6012 Four Sider.
- (S) (2:39) A&M 2516 Classics Volume 18.
- (S) (2:41) A&M 3258 Greatest Hits.

1968 #7 THE FOOL ON THE HILL
- (S) (3:09) A&M 6012 Four Sider.
- (S) (3:10) A&M 2516 Classics Volume 18.
- (S) (3:13) A&M 3258 Greatest Hits.
- (S) (3:13) A&M 3108 Fool On The Hill.

SERGIO MENDES & BRASIL '66 (Continued)
1968 #19 SCARBOROUGH FAIR
    (S) (3:17) A&M 2516 Classics Volume 18.
    (S) (3:18) A&M 3258 Greatest Hits.
    (S) (3:17) A&M 3108 Fool On The Hill.

MERCY
1969 #2 LOVE (CAN MAKE YOU HAPPY)
    (S) (3:12) Rhino 70996 One Hit Wonders Of The 60's Volume 2. *(this is the original "Sundi" label recording)*

METERS
1969 #33 CISSY STRUT
    (S) (2:59) Rhino 75766 Best Of New Orleans Rhythm & Blues Volume 2.

LEE MICHAELS
1971 #4 DO YOU KNOW WHAT I MEAN
    (S) (3:12) Rhino 70927 Super Hits Of The 70's Volume 7.
    (S) (3:12) Dunhill Compact Classics 045 Golden Age Of Underground Radio.
    (S) (3:12) Warner Special Products 27616 Classic Rock.
1971 #39 CAN I GET A WITNESS

MICKEY & SYLVIA
1957 #7 LOVE IS STRANGE
    (M) (2:54) Rhino 70643 Billboard's Top R&B Hits Of 1957.
    (M) (2:53) RCA 6408 O.S.T. Dirty Dancing.
    (M) (2:55) RCA 8467 Nipper's Greatest Hits Of The 50's Volume 2. *(contains some female background overdubs that were not on the original hit)*
    (M) (2:55) Geffen 24310 O.S.T. Mermaids.
    (M) (2:54) Rhino 70561 Legends Of Guitar - Rock: The 50's Volume 2.
    (M) (2:55) RCA 9900 Love Is Strange & Other Hits.
    (M) (2:54) RCA 61144 The RCA Records Label: The First Note In Black Music.
1957 #39 DEAREST
    (M) (2:56) RCA 9900 Love Is Strange & Other Hits.

BETTE MIDLER
1973 #13 DO YOU WANT TO DANCE?
    (S) (2:42) Atlantic 7238 The Divine Miss M.
1973 #6 BOOGIE WOOGIE BUGLE BOY
    (M) (2:22) Atlantic 7238 The Divine Miss M.
1973 #40 FRIENDS
    (S) (2:53) Atlantic 7238 The Divine Miss M.

GARRY MILES
1960 #13 LOOK FOR A STAR

JODY MILLER
1965 #22 QUEEN OF THE HOUSE
1965 #31 HOME OF THE BRAVE

MITCH MILLER
1955 #1 YELLOW ROSE OF TEXAS
    (M) (3:00) Columbia 45110 16 Most Requested Songs Of The 50's Volume 1.
    (M) (3:01) Columbia 44374 Hollywood Magic - The 1950's.
    (M) (3:00) Columbia 1544 Mitch's Greatest Hits.
    (M) (3:00) Columbia 44406 16 Most Requested Songs.

MITCH MILLER (Continued)

1956 #9 *THEME SONG FROM "SONG FOR A SUMMER NIGHT"*
    (M) (3:09) Columbia 1544 Mitch's Greatest Hits.

1958 #15 *MARCH FROM THE RIVER KWAI AND COLONEL BOGEY*
    (M) (2:24) Columbia 44374 Hollywood Magic - The 1950's.
    (M) (2:25) Columbia 1544 Mitch's Greatest Hits.
    (M) (2:24) Columbia 44406 16 Most Requested Songs.

1959 #5 *THE CHILDREN'S MARCHING SONG*
    (M) (2:48) Columbia 1544 Mitch's Greatest Hits.
    (M) (2:46) Columbia 44406 16 Most Requested Songs.

NED MILLER

1963 #6 *FROM A JACK TO A KING*
    (M) (2:09) Rhino 70684 Billboard's Top Country Hits Of 1963. *(alternate take)*

ROGER MILLER

1964 #7 *DANG ME*
    (S) (1:48) Mercury 826261 Golden Hits.
    (S) (1:48) Mercury 314512646 Best Of Volume Two.
    (S) (1:41) Curb 77511 Best Of. *(all selections on this cd are rerecordings)*

1964 #6 *CHUG-A-LUG*
    (S) (2:02) Rhino 70732 Grandson Of Frat Rock.
    (S) (2:02) Mercury 826261 Golden Hits.
    (S) (2:02) Mercury 314512646 Best Of Volume Two.
    (S) (1:58) Curb 77511 Best Of. *(all selections on this cd are rerecordings)*

1965 #34 *DO-WACKA-DO*
    (S) (1:44) Mercury 826261 Golden Hits.
    (S) (1:44) Mercury 314512646 Best Of Volume Two.
    (S) (1:44) Curb 77511 Best Of. *(all selections on this cd are rerecordings)*

1965 #3 *KING OF THE ROAD*
    (S) (2:25) Mercury 314512646 Best Of Volume Two.
    (S) (2:26) Mercury 826261 Golden Hits.
    (S) (2:21) Curb 77511 Best Of. *(all selections on this cd are rerecordings)*

1965 #9 *ENGINE ENGINE #9*
    (S) (2:16) Mercury 314512646 Best Of Volume Two.
    (S) (2:16) Mercury 826261 Golden Hits.
    (S) (1:58) Curb 77511 Best Of. *(all selections on this cd are rerecordings)*

1965 #30 *ONE DYIN' AND A BURYIN'*
    (S) (2:00) Mercury 826261 Golden Hits.

1965 #38 *KANSAS CITY STAR*
    (S) (2:15) Mercury 314512646 Best Of Volume Two.
    (S) (2:15) Mercury 826261 Golden Hits.
    (S) (2:17) Curb 77511 Best Of. *(all selections on this cd are rerecordings)*

1966 #8 *ENGLAND SWINGS*
    (S) (1:52) Mercury 826261 Golden Hits.
    (S) (1:51) Mercury 314512646 Best Of Volume Two.
    (S) (1:50) Curb 77511 Best Of. *(all selections on this cd are rerecordings)*

1966 #20 *HUSBANDS AND WIVES*
    (S) (2:21) Mercury 848977 Best Of.
    (S) (2:22) Curb 77511 Best Of. *(all selections on this cd are rerecordings)*

1967 #39 *WALKIN' IN THE SUNSHINE*

MILLS BROTHERS
1968 #21 *CAB DRIVER*
    (M) (2:55) Ranwood 7035 22 Great Hits. *(rerecorded)*

GARRY MILLS
1960 #13 *LOOK FOR A STAR*

HAYLEY MILLS
1961 #5 *LET'S GET TOGETHER*
1962 #31 *JOHNNY JINGO*

GARNET MIMMS & THE ENCHANTERS
1963 #4 *CRY BABY*
    (S) (3:25) Rhino 70649 Billboard's Top R&B Hits Of 1963.
    (S) (3:24) Collectables 5248 Garnett Mimms & The Enchanters.
1963 #40 *BABY DON'T YOU WEEP*
    (S) (3:27) Collectables 5248 Garnett Mimms & The Enchanters.
1964 #34 *FOR YOUR PRECIOUS LOVE*
    (S) (3:02) Collectables 5248 Garnett Mimms & The Enchanters.

released as by GARNET MIMMS:
1966 #34 *I'LL TAKE GOOD CARE OF YOU*
    (S) (3:17) Collectables 5248 Garnett Mimms & The Enchanters.

MINDBENDERS (*also* WAYNE FONTANA & THE MINDBENDERS)
released as by WAYNE FONTANA & THE MINDBDENDERS:
1965 #1 *GAME OF LOVE*
    (M) (2:06) Mercury 816555 45's On CD Volume 2.
    (M) (2:04) A&M 3913 O.S.T. Good Morning Vietnam. *(the preceeding dialog overlaps the first music note)*
    (M) (2:06) Rhino 70323 History Of British Rock Volume 5.
    (M) (2:06) Rhino 72022 History Of British Rock Box Set.

released as by THE MINDBENDERS:
1966 #1 *A GROOVY KIND OF LOVE*
    (M) (1:57) Mercury 816555 45's On CD Volume 2.
    (M) (1:59) Rhino 70324 History Of British Rock Volume 6.
    (M) (1:59) Rhino 72022 History Of British Rock Box Set.

SAL MINEO
1957 #6 *START MOVIN' (IN MY DIRECTION)*
1957 #38 *LASTING LOVE*

MIRACLES (*also* SMOKEY ROBINSON & THE MIRACLES)
released as by THE MIRACLES:
1961 #2 *SHOP AROUND*
    (M) (2:44) Motown 9041 and 6071 Compact Command Performances.
    (M) (2:47) Rhino 70647 Billboard's Top R&B Hits Of 1961.
    (M) (2:43) Motown 6159 The Good-Feeling Music Of The Big Chill Generation Volume 1.
    (M) (2:44) Motown 6139 The Composer Series: Smokey Robinson.
    (M) (2:44) Motown 5448 A Package Of 16 Big Hits. *(cd jacket mistakenly credits this song to the Contours)*
    (M) (2:44) Motown 6196 and 0793 Anthology.
    (M) (2:43) Motown 9017 and 5248 16 #1 Hits From The Early 60's.
    (M) (2:44) Motown 5316 Great Songs And Performances That Inspired The Motown 25th Anniversary TV Special.

THE MIRACLES (Continued)

    (M) (2:43) Motown 5343 Every Great Motown Song: The First 25 Years Volume 1. *(most selections on this cd have noise on the fade out)*

    (M) (2:43) Motown 8034 and 8134 Every Great Motown Song: The First 25 Years Volumes 1 & 2. *(most selections on this cd have noise on the fade out)*

    (M) (2:47) Motown 5160 Hi We're The Miracles.

1962 #22 *WHAT'S SO GOOD ABOUT GOOD-BY*

    (S) (2:59) Motown 9105 Motown Memories Volume 2.

    (S) (3:04) Motown 5450 A Collection Of 16 Big Hits Volume 3.

    (S) (2:59) Motown 6202 Compact Command Performances Volume 2.

    (S) (3:00) Motown 6196 and 0793 Anthology.

1962 #33 *I'LL TRY SOMETHING NEW*

    (E) (2:35) Motown 9041 and 6071 Compact Command Performances.

    (E) (2:38) Motown 6196 and 0793 Anthology.

1963 #6 *YOU'VE REALLY GOT A HOLD ON ME*

    (E) (2:56) Motown 6160 The Good-Feeling Music Of The Big Chill Generation Volume 2.

    (E) (2:57) Motown 6139 The Composer Series: Smokey Robinson.

    (M) (2:57) Geffen 24310 O.S.T. Mermaids.

    (S) (2:50) Motown 5448 A Package Of 16 Big Hits.

    (M) (2:56) Rhino 70649 Billboard's Top R&B Hits Of 1963.

    (E) (2:56) Motown 9041 and 6071 Compact Command Performances.

    (S) (2:49) Motown 6196 and 0793 Anthology.

    (E) (2:56) Motown 9017 and 5248 16 #1 Hits From The Early 60's.

    (S) (2:56) Motown 5316 Great Songs And Performances That Inspired The Motown 25th Anniversary TV Special.

1963 #9 *MICKEY'S MONKEY*

    (S) (2:47) Rhino 70992 Groove 'N' Grind.

    (S) (2:45) Motown 5450 A Collection Of 16 Big Hits Volume 3.

    (S) (2:45) Motown 9041 and 6071 Compact Command Performances.

    (S) (2:47) Motown 6196 and 0793 Anthology.

    (S) (2:45) Motown 5316 Great Songs And Performances That Inspired The Motown 25th Anniversary TV Special.

    (S) (2:44) Motown 5439 Doin' Mickey's Monkey.

    (S) (2:45) Motown 8050 and 8150 Doin' Mickey's Monkey / Away We A Go-Go.

    (S) (2:42) Motown 9071 Motown Dance Party Volume 1. *(all selections on this cd are segued together)*

    (S) (2:47) Rhino 70291 Bo Diddley Beats.

1964 #25 *I LIKE IT LIKE THAT*

    (S) (2:41) Motown 6202 Compact Command Performances Volume 2.

    (S) (2:42) Motown 6196 and 0793 Anthology.

1964 #37 *THAT'S WHAT LOVE IS MADE OF*

    (S) (2:53) Motown 5451 A Collection Of 16 Big Hits Volume 4.

    (S) (2:47) Motown 6202 Compact Command Performances Volume 2.

    (S) (2:49) Motown 6196 and 0793 Anthology.

1965 #16 *OOO BABY BABY*

    (S) (2:44) Motown 6161 The Good-Feeling Music Of The Big Chill Generation Volume 3.

    (S) (2:45) Motown 6139 The Composer Series: Smokey Robinson.

    (S) (2:44) Motown 6202 Compact Command Performances Volume 2.

    (S) (2:44) Motown 6196 and 0793 Anthology.

    (S) (2:44) Motown 9097 The Most Played Oldies On America's Jukeboxes.

THE MIRACLES (Continued)

        (S)   (2:44) Motown 5316 Great Songs And Performances That Inspired The Motown 25th Anniversary TV Special.

        (S)   (2:45) Motown 5210 Greatest Hits Volume 2.

        (S)   (2:44) Motown 5269 Going To A Go-Go.

        (S)   (2:44) Motown 5343 Every Great Motown Song: The First 25 Years Volume 1. *(most selections on this cd have noise on the fade out)*

        (S)   (2:44) Motown 8034 and 8134 Every Great Motown Song: The First 25 Years Volumes 1 & 2. *(most selections on this cd have noise on the fade out)*

        (S)   (2:43) Motown 8004 and 8104 Going To A Go-Go/ Tears Of A Clown.

1965 #16 *THE TRACKS OF MY TEARS*

        (S)   (2:53) Motown 6137 20 Greatest Songs In Motown History.

        (S)   (2:53) Atlantic 81742 O.S.T. Platoon.

        (S)   (2:54) Motown 6120 O.S.T. The Big Chill.

        (S)   (2:52) Motown 5452 A Collection Of 16 Big Hits Volume 5.

        (S)   (2:53) Motown 6139 The Composer Series: Smokey Robinson.

        (S)   (2:53) Rhino 70651 Billboard's Top R&B Hits Of 1965.

        (S)   (2:53) Rhino 72006 Billboard's Top R&B Hits 1965-1969 Box Set.

        (S)   (2:53) MCA 10063 Original Television Soundtrack "The Sounds Of Murphy Brown".

        (S)   (2:53) Motown 9041 and 6071 Compact Command Performances.

        (S)   (2:53) Motown 6196 and 0793 Anthology.

        (S)   (2:53) Motown 9097 The Most Played Oldies On America's Jukeboxes.

        (S)   (2:53) Motown 5316 Great Songs And Performances That Inspired The Motown 25th Anniversary TV Special.

        (S)   (2:54) Motown 5210 Greatest Hits Volume 2.

        (S)   (2:53) Motown 5269 Going To A Go-Go.

        (S)   (2:56) Motown 5275 12 #1 Hits From The 70's.

        (S)   (2:53) Motown 8004 and 8104 Going To A Go-Go/ Tears Of A Clown.

1965 #21 *MY GIRL HAS GONE*

        (S)   (2:52) Motown 5454 A Collection Of 16 Big Hits Volume 7.

        (S)   (2:49) Motown 6202 Compact Command Performances Volume 2.

        (S)   (2:49) Motown 6196 and 0793 Anthology.

        (S)   (2:50) Motown 5210 Greatest Hits Volume 2.

        (S)   (2:49) Motown 5269 Going To A Go-Go.

        (S)   (2:49) Motown 8004 and 8104 Going To A Go-Go/ Tears Of A Clown.

1966 #10 *GOING TO A GO-GO*

        (S)   (2:45) Rhino 70652 Billboard's Top R&B Hits Of 1966.

        (S)   (2:45) Rhino 72006 Billboard's Top R&B Hits 1965-1969 Box Set.

        (S)   (2:46) Motown 6139 The Composer Series: Smokey Robinson.

        (S)   (2:44) Motown 5453 A Collection Of 16 Big Hits Volume 6.

        (S)   (2:45) Motown 9041 and 6071 Compact Command Performances.

        (S)   (2:44) Motown 6196 and 0793 Anthology.

        (S)   (2:43) Motown 9072 Motown Dance Party Volume 2. *(all selections on this cd are segued together)*

        (S)   (2:45) Motown 5316 Great Songs And Performances That Inspired The Motown 25th Anniversary TV Special.

        (S)   (2:46) Motown 5210 Greatest Hits Volume 2.

        (S)   (2:45) Motown 5269 Going To A Go-Go.

        (S)   (2:45) Motown 8004 and 8104 Going To A Go-Go/ Tears Of A Clown.

1966 #25 *(COME 'ROUND HERE) I'M THE ONE YOU NEED*

        (S)   (2:29) Motown 5455 A Collection Of 16 Big Hits Volume 8.

        (S)   (2:28) Motown 6202 Compact Command Performances Volume 2.

        (S)   (2:30) Motown 6196 and 0793 Anthology.

THE MIRACLES (Continued)

      (S)   (2:30) Motown 5210   Greatest Hits Volume 2.
      (S)   (2:28) Motown 5136   Away We A Go Go.
      (S)   (2:30) Motown 8050 and 8150   Doin' Mickey's Monkey/ Away We A Go-Go.

releases from this point on were credited to **SMOKEY ROBINSON & THE MIRACLES:**

1967 #19 *MORE LOVE*

      (S)   (2:45) Motown 5456   A Collection Of 16 Big Hits Volume 9.
      (S)   (2:46) Motown 6139   The Composer Series: Smokey Robinson.
      (S)   (2:43) Motown 6202   Compact Command Performances Volume 2.
      (S)   (2:44) Motown 6196 and 0793   Anthology.
      (S)   (2:44) Motown 5210   Greatest Hits Volume 2.
      (S)   (2:46) Motown 9092 and 5156   Tears Of A Clown.
      (S)   (2:46) Motown 8004 and 8104   Going To A Go-Go/ Tears Of A Clown.

1967 #3 *I SECOND THAT EMOTION*

      (S)   (2:45) Motown 6160   The Good-Feeling Music Of The Big Chill Generation Volume 2.
      (S)   (2:46) Motown 6139   The Composer Series: Smokey Robinson.
      (S)   (2:46) Motown 6110   Motown Grammy R&B Performances Of The 60's & 70's.
      (S)   (2:43) Motown 5456   A Collection Of 16 Big Hits Volume 9.
      (S)   (2:46) Motown 6120   O.S.T. The Big Chill.
      (S)   (2:44) Rhino 70654   Billboard's Top R&B Hits Of 1968.
      (S)   (2:44) Rhino 72006   Billboard's Top R&B Hits 1965-1969 Box Set.
      (S)   (2:46) Motown 9041 and 6071   Compact Command Performances.
      (S)   (2:43) Motown 6196 and 0793   Anthology.
      (S)   (2:45) Motown 9018 and 5249   16 #1 Hits From The Late 60's.
      (S)   (2:45) Motown 9021 and 5309   25 Years Of Grammy Greats.
      (S)   (2:45) Motown 5316   Great Songs And Performances That Inspired The Motown 25th Anniversary TV Special.
      (S)   (2:45) Motown 5210   Greatest Hits Volume 2.

1968 #17 *IF YOU CAN WANT*

      (S)   (2:42) Motown 9041 and 6071   Compact Command Performances.
      (S)   (2:41) Motown 6196 and 0793   Anthology.
      (S)   (2:42) Motown 8043 and 8143   Time Out For/ Special Occasion.
      (S)   (2:42) Motown 5418   Special Occasion.

1968 #24 *YESTER LOVE*

      (S)   (2:17) Motown 6202   Compact Command Performances Volume 2.
      (S)   (2:13) Motown 6196 and 0793   Anthology.
      (S)   (2:17) Motown 8043 and 8143   Time Out For/ Special Occasion.
      (S)   (2:17) Motown 5418   Special Occasion.

1968 #24 *SPECIAL OCCASION*

      (S)   (2:19) Motown 6202   Compact Command Performances Volume 2.
      (S)   (2:19) Motown 6196 and 0793   Anthology.
      (S)   (2:20) Motown 8043 and 8143   Time Out For/ Special Occasion.
      (S)   (2:20) Motown 5418   Special Occasion.

1969 #9 *BABY, BABY DON'T CRY*

      (the actual 45 time is (3:54) not (3:29) as stated on the record label; the actual LP time is (3:58) not (3:29) as stated on the record label)
      (S)   (4:01) Motown 9041 and 6071   Compact Command Performances.
      (S)   (4:01) Motown 6196 and 0793   Anthology.
      (S)   (3:55) Motown 8043 and 8143   Time Out For/ Special Occasion.
      (S)   (4:01) Motown 5437   Time Out For.

SMOKEY ROBINSON & THE MIRACLES (Continued)
1969 #36 DOGGONE RIGHT
    (S) (2:56) Motown 9041 and 6071 Compact Command Performances.
    (S) (2:56) Motown 6196 and 0793 Anthology.
    (S) (2:56) Motown 8043 and 8143 Time Out For/Special Occasion.
    (S) (2:56) Motown 5437 Time Out For.

1970 #1 *TEARS OF A CLOWN*
    (S) (2:58) Rhino 70631 Billboard's Top Rock & Roll Hits Of 1970.
    (S) (2:58) Rhino 72005 Billboard's Top Rock & Roll Hits 1968-1972 Box Set.
    (S) (2:59) Motown 6132 25 #1 Hits From 25 Years.
    (S) (2:58) Motown 6177 Endless Love.
    (S) (2:59) Motown 6139 The Composer Series: Smokey Robinson.
    (S) (2:59) Motown 9041 and 6071 Compact Command Performances.
    (S) (2:58) Motown 6196 and 0793 Anthology.
    (S) (2:58) Motown 9097 The Most Played Oldies On America's Jukeboxes.
    (S) (2:58) Motown 5316 Great Songs And Performances That Inspired The Motown 25th Anniversary TV Special.
    (S) (3:00) Motown 9092 and 5156 Tears Of A Clown.
    (S) (3:01) Motown 8004 and 8104 Going To A Go-Go/ Tears Of A Clown.
    (S) (2:58) Motown 9060 Motown's Biggest Pop Hits.
    (S) (2:58) Motown 0937 20/20 Twenty No. 1 Hits From Twenty Years At Motown.
    (S) (2:54) Motown 9071 Motown Dance Party Volume 1. *(all selections on this cd are segued together)*

1971 #18 *I DON'T BLAME YOU AT ALL*
    (S) (3:09) Motown 9041 and 6071 Compact Command Performances.
    (S) (3:08) Motown 6196 and 0793 Anthology.

CHAD MITCHELL TRIO
1962 #35 *LIZZIE BORDEN*

GUY MITCHELL
1956 #1 *SINGING THE BLUES*
    (M) (2:24) Columbia 45110 16 Most Requested Songs Of The 50's Volume 1.
    (M) (2:24) Columbia 45017 Radio Classics Of The 50's.
    (M) (2:24) Columbia 46096 16 Most Requested Songs.

1957 #15 *KNEE DEEP IN THE BLUES*
    (M) (2:10) Columbia 46096 16 Most Requested Songs.

1957 #13 *ROCK-A-BILLY*

1959 #1 *HEARTACHES BY THE NUMBER*

JONI MITCHELL
1973 #20 *YOU TURN ME ON, I'M A RADIO*
    (S) (2:38) Asylum 5057 For The Roses.

WILLIE MITCHELL
1964 #33 *20-75*
    (S) (2:12) MCA 25226 History Of Hi Records Rhythm & Blues Volume 1.

1968 #27 *SOUL SERENADE*
    (S) (2:17) MCA 25226 History Of Hi Records Rhythm & Blues Volume 1.
    (S) (2:17) Rhino 70562 Legends Of Guitar - Rock: The 60's Volume 2.

DOMENICO MODUGNO
1958 #1 *NEL BLU DIPINTO DI BLUE*

1958 #24 *COME PRIMA*

MOJO MEN
1967 #39 *SIT DOWN, I THINK I LOVE YOU*
      (M) (2:20) Warner Special Projects 27610 More Party Classics.
      (M) (2:19) Rhino 70536 San Francisco Nights.

MOMENTS
1970 #8 *LOVE ON A TWO WAY STREET*
      (S) (3:26) Rhino 70658 Billboard's Top R&B Hits Of 1970. *(some distortion on the lead vocals)*
      (S) (3:26) Rhino 70782 Soul Hits Of The 70's Volume 2. *(some distortion on the lead vocals)*

1970 #37 *IF I DIDN'T CARE*

MONKEES
1966 #1 *LAST TRAIN TO CLARKSVILLE*
      (S) (2:44) Arista 8313 Greatest Hits. *(truncated fade)*
      (S) (2:44) Arista 8524 The Monkees. *(truncated fade)*
      (M) (2:41) Arista 8432 Then & Now...The Best Of.
      (S) (2:43) Rhino 70566 Listen To The Band.

1966 #1 *I'M A BELIEVER*
      (S) (2:45) Rhino 70627 Billboard's Top Rock & Roll Hits Of 1966.
      (S) (2:45) Rhino 72007 Billboard's Top Rock & Roll Hits 1962-1966 Box Set.
      (S) (2:44) Arista 8313 Greatest Hits.
      (S) (2:44) Arista 8525 More Of The Monkees.
      (S) (2:44) Arista 8432 Then & Now...The Best Of.
      (S) (2:43) Rhino 70566 Listen To The Band.

1966 #25 *(I'M NOT YOUR) STEPPIN' STONE*
      (S) (2:21) Arista 8313 Greatest Hits. *(LP version)*
      (S) (2:21) Arista 8525 More Of The Monkees. *(LP version)*
      (S) (2:22) Arista 8432 Then & Now...The Best Of. *(LP version)*
      (S) (2:20) Rhino 70566 Listen To The Band. *(45 version)*

1967 #1 *A LITTLE BIT ME, A LITTLE BIT YOU*
      (S) (2:48) K-Tel 839 Battle Of The Bands Volume 2. *(LP version)*
      (S) (2:49) Arista 8313 Greatest Hits. *(LP version)*
      (S) (2:49) Arista 8432 Then & Now...The Best Of. *(LP Version)*
      (M) (2:47) Rhino 70566 Listen To The Band. *(45 version)*

1967 #3 *PLEASANT VALLEY SUNDAY*
      (S) (3:13) Rhino 75892 Nuggets. *(LP version without "PET PIG PORKY" introduction)*
      (S) (3:13) Arista 8313 Greatest Hits. *(LP version without "PET PIG PORKY" introduction)*
      (S) (3:13) Arista 8432 Then & Now...The Best Of. *(LP version without "PET PIG PORKY" introduction)*
      (S) (3:40) Arista 8603 Pices, Aquarius, Capricorn & Jones Ltd. *(LP version with :27 "PET PIG PORKY" introduction)*
      (S) (3:16) Rhino 70566 Listen To The Band. *(neither the LP or 45 version; remixed; slightly longer fade than 45 or LP version)*

1967 #5 *WORDS*
      (S) (2:52) Arista 8432 Then & Now...The Best Of.
      (S) (2:50) Arista 8334 More Greatest Hits.
      (S) (2:51) Arista 8603 Pices, Aquarius, Capricorn & Jones Ltd. *(previous selection tracks over introduction)*
      (S) (2:53) Rhino 70566 Listen To The Band.

MONKEES (Continued)

1967 #1 DAYDREAM BELIEVER
        (S) (3:05) Rhino 70628 Billboard's Top Rock & Roll Hits Of 1967.
        (S) (3:04) Arista 8313 Greatest Hits.
        (S) (3:05) Arista 8432 Then & Now...The Best Of.
        (S) (3:08) Rhino 70566 Listen To The Band.

1968 #1 VALLERI
        (S) (2:12) Warner Special Products 27602 20 Party Classics.
        (S) (2:18) Arista 8432 Then & Now...The Best Of. *(cold ending unlike the 45 & LP and slightly longer because of the different ending)*
        (S) (2:18) Rhino 75892 Nuggets. *(same comments as for Arista 8432)*
        (S) (2:16) Arista 8334 More Greatest Hits. *(same comments as for Arista 8432)*
        (S) (2:19) Rhino 70566 Listen To The Band. *(same comments as for Arista 8432)*

1968 #10 D.W. WASHBURN
        (S) (2:47) Arista 8432 Then & Now...The Best Of.
        (S) (2:47) Rhino 70566 Listen To The Band. *(truncated fade)*

1968 #26 IT'S NICE TO BE WITH YOU
        (S) (2:50) Rhino 70566 Listen To The Band.

1969 #37 TEAR DROP CITY
        (S) (2:04) Rhino 70566 Listen To The Band.

MONOTONES

1958 #7 BOOK OF LOVE
        (M) (2:18) Rhino 75764 Best Of Doo Wop Uptempo.
        (M) (2:18) Rhino 70644 Billboard's Top R&B Hits Of 1958.
        (M) (2:19) MCA 31198 Vintage Music Volume 1.
        (M) (2:19) MCA 5777 Vintage Music Volumes 1 & 2.
        (M) (2:17) Chess 31320 Best Of Chess Rock 'n' Roll Volume 2.
        (E) (2:16) Collectables 2508 History Of Rock - The Doo Wop Era Part 2.
        (M) (2:18) Collectables 5427 Who Wrote The Book Of Love.
        (M) (2:23) Collectables 5427 Who Wrote The Book Of Love. *(alternate take)*

MATT MONROE

1961 #38 MY KIND OF GIRL
        (S) (2:54) Enigma 73531 O.S.T. Scandal. *(rerecording)*

1965 #24 WALK AWAY

VAUGHN MONROE

1956 #22 IN THE MIDDLE OF THE HOUSE

LOU MONTE

1958 #12 LAZY MARY (LUNA MEZZO MARE)
        (S) (2:38) RCA 8466 Nipper's Greatest Hits Of The 50's Volume 1.

1963 #7 PEPINO THE ITALIAN MOUSE

HUGO MONTENEGRO

1968 #4 THE GOOD, THE BAD AND THE UGLY
        (S) (2:43) RCA 8475 Nipper's Greatest Hits Of The 60's Volume 2.
        (S) (2:44) RCA 66019 Light My Fire. *(LP length)*

CHRIS MONTEZ

1962 #6 LET'S DANCE
        (M) (2:15) MCA 31023 O.S.T. Animal House. *(no countoff; all selections on this cd are segued together)*
        (S) (2:27) Dunhill Compact Classics 056 All-Time Greatest Hits.

CHRIS MONTEZ (Continued)
1966 #22 CALL ME
    (S) (2:46) Dunhill Compact Classics 056 All-Time Greatest Hits.
1966 #19 THE MORE I SEE YOU
    (S) (2:54) Dunhill Compact Classics 056 All-Time Greatest Hits.
1966 #37 THERE WILL NEVER BE ANOTHER YOU
    (S) (2:52) Dunhill Compact Classics 056 All-Time Greatest Hits.
1966 #34 TIME AFTER TIME
    (S) (2:29) Dunhill Compact Classics 056 All-Time Greatest Hits.

MOODY BLUES
1965 #6 GO NOW!
    (M) (3:10) Rhino 70323 History Of British Rock Volume 5.
    (M) (3:10) Rhino 72022 History Of British Rock Box Set.
    (M) (3:10) London 820758 Magnificent Moodies.
1968 #26 TUESDAY AFTERNOON (FOREVER AFTERNOON)
    (S) (5:05) Polygram 837362 O.S.T. 1969. *(edit of LP version)*
    (S) (8:23) Deram 820006 Days Of Future Passed. *(complete LP version which according to the cd jacket is a medley of "FOREVER AFTERNOON (TUESDAY)" and "(EVENING) TIME TO GET AWAY"; the vinyl LP jacket simply called the track "FOREVER AFTERNOON (TUESDAY)")*
    (S) (4:50) Threshold/Polydor 840659 Greatest Hits. *(edit of LP version)*
    (S) (4:01) Threshold 820007 This Is The Moody Blues. *(edit of LP version; all selections on this cd are segued together)*
    (S) (8:22) MFSL 512 Days Of Future Passed. *(LP version)*
1970 #19 QUESTION
    (S) (5:42) Warner Special Products 27614 Highs Of The 70's. *(LP version)*
    (S) (5:43) Threshold/Polydor 840659 Greatest Hits. *(LP version)*
    (S) (5:39) Threshold 820007 This Is The Moody Blues. *(LP version; all selections on this cd are segued together)*
    (S) (5:48) Threshold 820211 Question Of Balance. *(LP version; all selections on this cd are segued together)*
1971 #14 THE STORY IN YOUR EYES
    (S) (3:03) Threshold/Polydor 840659 Greatest Hits.
    (S) (2:44) Threshold 820007 This Is The Moody Blues. *(edit)*
    (S) (2:56) Threshold 820160 Every Good Boy Deserves Favour. *(all selections on this cd are segued together)*
1972 #20 ISN'T LIFE STRANGE
    (S) (6:37) Threshold/Polydor 840659 Greatest Hits. *(:37 longer than either the 45 or LP)*
    (S) (5:59) Threshold 820155 Voices In The Sky/Best Of.
    (S) (5:32) Threshold 820007 This Is The Moody Blues. *(:28 shorter than either the 45 or LP; all selections on this cd are segued together)*
    (S) (6:00) Threshold 820159 Seventh Sojourn. *(all selections on this cd are segued together)*
1972 #1 NIGHTS IN WHITE SATIN
    (at least some of the 45 dj copies had a printed label time of (4:20) when the real time was (3:13); commercial copies were (4:26))
    (S) (5:50) Rhino 70633 Billboard's Top Rock & Roll Hits Of 1972. *(neither the 45 or LP version)*
    (S) (5:50) Rhino 72005 Billboard's Top Rock & Roll Hits 1968-1972 Box Set. *(neither the 45 or LP version)*
    (M) (4:26) Rhino 70326 History Of British Rock Volume 8.
    (M) (4:26) Rhino 72022 History Of British Rock Box Set.

MOODY BLUES (Continued)

      (S) (4:25) Threshold 820155 Voices In The Sky/Best Of.
      (S) (7:24) Deram 820006 Days Of Future Passed. *(LP version)*
      (S) (7:23) Sandstone 33003 Reelin' In The Years Volume 4. *(LP version)*
      (S) (7:22) Milan 35609 O.S.T. Shattered. *(LP version)*
      (S) (7:38) Threshold/Polydor 840659 Greatest Hits. *(slightly longer than the LP version)*
      (S) (4:32) Threshold 820007 This Is The Moody Blues. *(this song segues into the next track which is given the title "LATE LAMENT" but in reality this is a portion of the full album length version of "NIGHTS IN WHITE SATIN")*
      (S) (7:23) MFSL 512 Days Of Future Passed. *(LP version)*

1973 #8 I'M JUST A SINGER (IN A ROCK AND ROLL BAND)

      (S) (4:16) Threshold/Polydor 840659 Greatest Hits.
      (S) (4:14) Threshold 820155 Voices In The Sky/Best Of.
      (S) (4:10) Threshold 820007 This Is The Moody Blues. *(all selections on this cd are segued together)*
      (S) (4:16) Threshold 820159 Seventh Sojourn. *(all selections on this cd are segued together)*

ART MOONEY

1955 #5 HONEY-BABE

1958 #22 THE RIVER KWAI MARCH AND COLONEL BOGEY

MOONGLOWS (also HARVEY & THE MOONGLOWS)

1956 #25 SEE SAW

      (M) (2:24) MCA 5937 Vintage Music Volumes 13 & 14.
      (M) (2:24) MCA 31210 Vintage Music Volume 13.
      (M) (2:24) Chess 9283 Best Of Chess Vocal Groups Volume 2.
      (M) (2:23) Chess 31270 From The Motion Picture "Rock, Rock, Rock".

released as by HARVEY & THE MOONGLOWS:

1958 #39 TEN COMMANDMENTS OF LOVE

      (M) (3:40) Rhino 75763 Best Of Doo Wop Ballads.
      (M) (4:02) MCA 31198 Vintage Music Volume 1
      (M) (4:02) MCA 5777 Vintage Music Volumes 1 & 2.
      (M) (4:01) Chess 31320 Best Of Chess Rock 'n' Roll Volume 2.
      (M) (3:38) Chess 31267 Look, It's The Moonglows.

BOB MOORE

1961 #6 MEXICO

BOBBY MOORE & THE RHYTHM ACES

1966 #25 SEARCHING FOR MY BABY

      (M) (2:30) Rhino 75770 Soul Shots Volume 2.
      (M) (2:29) MCA 31204 Vintage Music Volume 7.
      (M) (2:29) MCA 5805 Vintage Music Volumes 7 & 8.
      (M) (2:29) Chess 31317 Best Of Chess Rhythm & Blues Volume 1.

JACKIE MOORE

1971 #11 PRECIOUS PRECIOUS

      (S) (3:26) Atlantic 81912 Golden Age Of Black Music (1970-1975).
      (S) (3:23) Rhino 70784 Soul Hits Of The 70's Volume 4.
      (S) (3:25) Atlantic 82305 Atlantic Rhythm And Blues 1947-1974 Box Set.

1973 #32 SWEET CHARLIE BABE

JANE MORGAN
1957 #5 *FASCINATION*
    (S) (2:20) Elektra 60107 O.S.T. Diner. *(rerecording)*
    (E) (2:21) Curb 77405 Greatest Hits.
1958 #17 *THE DAY THE RAINS CAME*
    (S) (2:57) Curb 77405 Greatest Hits.
1959 #34 *HAPPY ANNIVERSARY*

JANE MORGAN & ROGER WILLIAMS
1956 #22 *TWO DIFFERENT WORLDS*

JAYE P. MORGAN
1955 #3 *THAT'S ALL I WANT FROM YOU*
1955 #8 *THE LONGEST WALK*

JAYE P. MORGAN & EDDY ARNOLD
1956 #24 *MUTUAL ADMIRATION SOCIETY*

MORMON TABERNACLE CHOIR
1959 #11 *BATTLE HYMN OF THE REPUBLIC*

VAN MORRISON
1967 #8 *BROWN EYED GIRL*
    (S) (3:06) JCI 3104 Mellow Sixties. *(with "making love" lyric)*
    (S) (3:06) Atlantic 82032 The Wonder Years. *(with "making love" lyric)*
    (S) (3:05) MCA 6340 O.S.T. Born On The Fourth Of July. *(with "making love" lyric)*
    (M) (3:02) Mercury 841970 Best Of. *(with "laughin' and runnin'" lyric)*
    (S) (3:03) Epic/Legacy 47041 Bang Masters. *(with "making love" lyric)*
    (M) (3:00) Columbia 46093 T.B. Sheets. *(with "laughin' and runnin'" lyric)*
    (S) (3:02) Columbia 47380 O.S.T. Sleeping With The Enemy. *(with "making love" lyric)*
1970 #30 *COME RUNNING*
    (S) (2:30) Warner Brothers 3103 Moondance.
1971 #9 *DOMINO*
    (S) (3:06) Warner Brothers 1884 His Band And The Street Choir.
    (S) (3:03) Mercury 841970 Best Of.
1971 #23 *BLUE MONEY*
    (S) (3:43) Warner Brothers 1884 His Band And The Street Choir.
1971 #25 *WILD NIGHT*
    (S) (3:31) Warner Brothers 1950 Tupelo Honey.
    (S) (3:31) Mercury 841970 Best Of.

MOTHERLODE
1969 #12 *WHEN I DIE*
    (S) (3:20) Pair 1202 Best Of Buddah.

MOTT THE HOOPLE
1972 #34 *ALL THE YOUNG DUDES*
    (S) (3:29) JCI 3302 Electric Seventies. *("Marks & Sparks" version)*
    (S) (3:29) Columbia 45048 Rock Classics Of The 70's. *("Marks & Sparks" version)*
    (S) (3:28) Epic 46490 O.S.T. Queens Logic. *("Marks & Sparks" version)*
    (S) (3:30) Columbia 34368 Greatest Hits. *("Marks & Sparks" version)*
    (S) (3:29) Columbia 31750 All The Young Dudes. *("Marks & Sparks" version; previous song tracks into introduction)*
    (S) (3:29) Priority 7055 Heavy Hitters/70's Greatest Rock Hits Volume 11. *("Marks & Sparks" version)*

MOUNTAIN
1970 #24 *MISSISSIPPI QUEEN*
        (S)   (2:28) Columbia 45048   Rock Classics Of The 70's.
        (S)   (2:29) Priority 7942 Hard Rockin' 70's.
        (S)   (2:29) Priority 8662 Hard 'N Heavy/70's Greatest Rock Hits Volume 1.
        (S)   (2:30) Rhino 70921 Super Hits Of The 70's Volume 1. *(hum noticeable on the introduction)*
        (S)   (2:30) Rhino 72009 Super Hits Of The 70's Volumes 1-4 Box Set. *(hum noticeable on the introduction)*
        (S)   (2:29) Rhino 70986 Heavy Metal Memories. *(hum noticeable on the introduction)*
        (S)   (2:29) JCI 3302 Electric Seventies. *(hum noticeable on the introduction)*
        (S)   (2:29) CBS Special Products 46806 Rock Goes To The Movies Volume 1.
        (S)   (2:29) Columbia 32079 Best Of.

MOUTH & MACNEAL
1972 #5 *HOW DO YOU DO*
        (S)   (3:13) Rhino 70928 Super Hits Of The 70's Volume 8.

MICKEY MOZART QUINTET
1959 #25 *LITTLE DIPPER*

MUNGO JERRY
1970 #2 *IN THE SUMMERTIME*
        (S)   (3:30) Rhino 70923 Super Hits Of The 70's Volume 3.
        (S)   (3:30) Rhino 72009 Super Hits Of The 70's Volumes 1-4 Box Set.
        (S)   (3:30) Rhino 70087 Summer & Sun.

JERRY MURAD'S HARMONICATS
1961 #30 *CHERRY PINK AND APPLE BLOSSOM WHITE*
        (S)   (1:45) Columbia 9511 Greatest Hits.

MURMAIDS
1964 #3 *POPSICLES AND ICICLES*
        (M)   (2:31) Rhino 70989 Best Of The Girl Groups Volume 2.

ANNE MURRAY
1970 #6 *SNOWBIRD*
        (S)   (2:09) Capitol 46058 Greatest Hits.
        (S)   (2:08) Capitol 95954 Fifteen Of The Best.
1973 #6 *DANNY'S SONG*
        (S)   (3:04) Capitol 48446 Danny's Song.
        (S)   (3:03) Capitol 46058 Greatest Hits.
        (S)   (3:04) Capitol 95954 Fifteen Of The Best.
1973 #37 *WHAT ABOUT ME*
        (S)   (3:13) Capitol 48446 Danny's Song. *(LP length)*

MUSIC EXPLOSION
1967 #2 *LITTLE BIT O' SOUL*
        (M)   (2:20) Warner Special Products 27602 20 Party Classics.
        (S)   (2:19) Rhino 75772 Son Of Frat Rock.
        (S)   (2:19) Rhino 70628 Billboard Top Rock & Roll Hits Of 1967.
        (E)   (2:18) Pair 1199 Best Of Bubblegum Music.
        (S)   (2:19) Dunhill Compact Classics 029 Toga Rock.
        (S)   (2:19) K-Tel 713 Battle Of The Bands.
        (E)   (2:18) Special Music 4914 Best Of The Bubblegum Years.

MUSIC MACHINE
1966 #21 *TALK TALK*
> (S) (1:55) Rhino 75777 More Nuggets.
> (M) (1:55) K-Tel 713 Battle Of The Bands.

BILLY MYLES
1957 #20 *THE JOKER (THAT'S WHAT THEY CALL ME)*

MYSTICS
1959 #22 *HUSHABYE*
> (S) (2:30) Rhino 75764 Best Of Doo Wop Uptempo.
> (S) (2:32) Collectables 2507 History Of Rock - The Doo Wop Era Part 1.
> (S) (2:31) Essex 7053 A Hot Summer Night In '59.
> (S) (2:31) Collectables 5043 16 Golden Classics. *(sounds like it was mastered from vinyl)*

NAPOLEON XIV
1966 #1 *THEY'RE COMING TO TAKE ME AWAY, HA HAAA!*
> (S) (2:10) Rhino 75768 Dr. Demento Presents.
> (S) (2:09) Rhino 70743 Dr. Demento 20th Anniversary Collection.

GRAHAM NASH
1971 #29 *CHICAGO*
> (S) (2:51) Atlantic 7204 Songs For Beginners.
> (S) (3:57) Atlantic 82319 Crosby, Stills & Nash Box Set. *(LP version which is a medley with "WE CAN CHANGE THE WORLD")*

GRAHAM NASH & DAVID CROSBY
1972 #31 *IMMIGRATION MAN*
> (S) (2:57) Atlantic 82319 Crosby, Stills & Nash Box Set.

JOHNNY NASH
1958 #30 *A VERY SPECIAL LOVE*
1968 #7 *HOLD ME TIGHT*
1970 #36 *CUPID*
1972 #1 *I CAN SEE CLEARLY NOW*
> (S) (2:46) Rhino 70633 Billboard's Top Rock & Roll Hits Of 1972.
> (S) (2:46) Rhino 72005 Billboard's Top Rock & Roll Hits 1969-1972 Box Set.
> (S) (2:42) Columbia/Legacy 46763 Rock Artifacts Volume 2.
> (S) (2:45) Rhino 70789 Soul Hits Of The 70's Volume 9.
> (S) (2:38) Columbia/Legacy 47966 Rhythm Come Forward Volume 2. *(tracks into next selection)*
> (S) (2:44) JCI 3304 Mellow Seventies.
> (S) (2:44) Epic 31067 I Can See Clearly Now.

JOHNNY NASH (Continued)
1973 #11 *STIR IT UP*
      (S) (3:02) Epic 46490 O.S.T. Queens Logic.
      (S) (3:01) Columbia/Legacy 46763 Rock Artifacts Volume 2.
      (S) (2:58) Rhino 70790 Soul Hits Of The 70's Volume 10.
      (S) (3:02) Epic 31067 I Can See Clearly Now.

NASHVILLE TEENS
1964 #14 *TOBACCO ROAD*

SAM NEELY
1972 #31 *LOVING YOU JUST CROSSED MY MIND*
      (S) (3:16) EMI 90603 Rock Me Gently.

NEIGHBORHOOD
1970 #24 *BIG YELLOW TAXI*

RICK NELSON
released as by **RICKY NELSON:**
1957 #12 *I'M WALKING*
      (M) (1:56) Mercury 832041 45's On CD Volume 1.
      (M) (1:56) Curb 77372 All-Time Greatest Hits.
      (S) (1:40) MCA 6163 All My Best. *(all tracks on this cd are rerecordings)*
1957 #8 *A TEENAGER'S ROMANCE*
      (M) (2:16) Curb 77372 All-Time Greatest Hits.
1957 #23 *YOU'RE MY ONE AND ONLY LOVE*
      (M) (2:04) Curb 77372 All-Time Greatest Hits.
1957 #6 *BE-BOP BABY*
      (M) (2:02) EMI 46588 Best Of.
      (M) (2:22) EMI 92771 Legendary Masters Volume 1. *(includes :21 studio talk
            and false start)*
1957 #21 *HAVE I TOLD YOU THAT I LOVE YOU*
      (M) (1:56) EMI 92771 Legendary Masters Volume 1.
1958 #3 *STOOD UP*
      (M) (1:51) EMI 46588 Best Of.
      (M) (1:50) EMI 92771 Legendary Masters Volume 1.
      (M) (1:50) Curb 77372 All-Time Greatest Hits.
      (S) (1:40) MCA 6163 All My Best. *(all tracks on this cd are rerecordings)*
1958 #6 *WAITIN' IN SCHOOL*
      (M) (2:00) Rhino 70561 Legends Of Guitar - Rock: The 50's Volume 2.
      (M) (2:01) EMI 46588 Best Of.
      (M) (2:01) EMI 92771 Legendary Masters Volume 1.
1958 #12 *BELIEVE WHAT YOU SAY*
      (M) (2:03) Rhino 70741 Rock This Town: Rockabilly Hits Volume 1. *(45
            version)*
      (M) (2:02) Rhino 70561 Legends Of Guitar - Rock: The 50's Volume 2. *(45
            version)*
      (M) (2:02) EMI 46588 Best Of. *(LP version)*
      (M) (2:03) EMI 92771 Legendary Masters Volume 1. *(45 version)*
      (M) (2:02) Curb 77372 All-Time Greatest Hits. *(LP version)*
      (S) (2:09) MCA 6163 All My Best. *(all tracks on this cd are rerecordings)*
1958 #20 *MY BUCKET'S GOT A HOLE IN IT*
      (M) (2:01) EMI 92771 Legendary Masters Volume 1.
1958 #2 *POOR LITTLE FOOL*
      (E) (2:30) EMI 96268 24 Greatest Hits Of All Time.
      (M) (2:30) Curb 77354 50's Hits Volume 1.

RICKY NELSON (Continued)

       (M) (2:30) EMI 46588 Best Of.
       (M) (2:30) EMI 92771 Legendary Masters Volume 1.
       (S) (2:32) MCA 6163 All My Best. *(all tracks on this cd are rerecordings)*
       (M) (2:30) Curb 77525 Greatest Hits Of Rock 'N' Roll Volume 2.

1958 #7 LONESOME TOWN
       (M) (2:13) EMI 46588 Best Of.
       (M) (2:12) EMI 92771 Legendary Masters Volume 1.
       (M) (2:13) Curb 77372 All-Time Greatest Hits.
       (S) (2:14) MCA 6163 All My Best. *(all tracks on this cd are rerecordings)*

1958 #15 I GOT A FEELING
       (M) (2:03) EMI 92771 Legendary Masters Volume 1.
       (S) (1:57) MCA 6163 All My Best. *(all tracks on this cd are rerecordings)*

1959 #5 NEVER BE ANYONE ELSE BUT YOU
       (M) (2:13) EMI 46588 Best Of.
       (S) (2:16) EMI 92771 Legendary Masters Volume 1. *(alternate take)*
       (M) (2:13) Curb 77372 All-Time Greatest Hits.
       (S) (2:15) MCA 6163 All My Best. *(all tracks on this cd are rerecordings)*

1959 #6 IT'S LATE
       (M) (1:56) EMI 46588 Best Of.
       (M) (2:27) EMI 92771 Legendary Masters Volume 1. *(includes :31 false start and countoff)*
       (S) (2:00) MCA 6163 All My Best. *(all tracks on this cd are rerecordings)*

1959 #18 JUST A LITTLE TOO MUCH
       (M) (2:10) EMI 46588 Best Of.
       (S) (2:09) EMI 92771 Legendary Masters Volume 1.
       (S) (2:03) MCA 6163 All My Best. *(all tracks on this cd are rerecordings)*

1959 #11 SWEETER THAN YOU
       (S) (2:09) EMI 92771 Legendary Masters Volume 1. *(alternate take)*

1960 #21 I WANNA BE LOVED
       (M) (2:43) EMI 92771 Legendary Masters Volume 1. *(background hum noticeable)*

1960 #11 YOUNG EMOTIONS
       (M) (2:32) EMI 46588 Best Of.
       (M) (2:32) EMI 92771 Legendary Masters Volume 1.

1960 #40 I'M NOT AFRAID
       (M) (2:36) EMI 92771 Legendary Masters Volume 1.

1961 #29 YOU ARE THE ONLY ONE
       (S) (2:39) EMI 95219 Best Of Volume 2.

1961 #1 TRAVELIN' MAN
       (S) (2:20) EMI 46588 Best Of. *(ends cold)*
       (S) (2:20) EMI 95219 Best Of Volume 2. *(ends cold)*
       (S) (2:23) MCA 6163 All My Best. *(all tracks on this cd are rerecordings)*

1961 #9 HELLO MARY LOU
       (S) (2:17) Curb 77532 Your Favorite Songs.
       (S) (2:17) EMI 46588 Best Of.
       (S) (2:41) EMI 95219 Best Of Volume 2. *(includes :24 false start and countoff)*
       (S) (2:18) MCA 6163 All My Best. *(all tracks on this cd are rerecordings)*

singles from this point on were released as by RICK NELSON:

1961 #11 A WONDER LIKE YOU
       (M) (2:34) EMI 95219 Best Of Volume 2.

1961 #20 EVERLOVIN'
       (M) (2:06) EMI 95219 Best Of Volume 2.

RICK NELSON (Continued)
1962 #9 YOUNG WORLD
　　　　　(M)　(2:23)　EMI　46588　Best Of.
　　　　　(M)　(2:24)　EMI　95219　Best Of Volume 2.
　　　　　(S)　(2:20)　MCA　6163　All My Best. *(all tracks on this cd are rerecordings)*

1962 #9 TEEN AGE IDOL
　　　　　(M)　(2:26)　EMI　46588　Best Of.
　　　　　(M)　(2:26)　EMI　95219　Best Of Volume 2.
　　　　　(S)　(2:30)　MCA　6163　All My Best. *(all tracks on this cd are rerecordings)*

1963 #7 IT'S UP TO YOU
　　　　　(S)　(2:44)　EMI　46588　Best Of.
　　　　　(S)　(2:56)　EMI　95219　Best Of Volume 2. *(:13 longer than 45)*
　　　　　(S)　(2:49)　MCA　6163　All My Best. *(all tracks on this cd are rerecordings)*

1963 #17 STRING ALONG
　　　　　(S)　(2:18)　MCA　10098　Best Of (1963-1975).

1963 #12 FOOLS RUSH IN
　　　　　(S)　(2:30)　MCA　10098　Best Of (1963-1975).
　　　　　(S)　(2:30)　MCA　31363　Sings "For You".
　　　　　(S)　(2:31)　Curb　77372　All-Time Greatest Hits.
　　　　　(S)　(2:39)　MCA　6163　All My Best. *(all tracks on this cd are rerecordings)*

1964 #8 FOR YOU
　　　　　(S)　(2:14)　MCA　10098　Best Of (1963-1975).
　　　　　(S)　(2:15)　MCA　31363　Sings "For You".
　　　　　(S)　(2:15)　Curb　77372　All-Time Greatest Hits.

1964 #19 THE VERY THOUGHT OF YOU
　　　　　(S)　(1:54)　MCA　10098　Best Of (1963-1975).

1970 #30 SHE BELONGS TO ME
　　　　　(S)　(3:01)　MCA　10098　Best Of (1963-1975).

released as by RICK NELSON & THE STONE CANYON BAND:
1972 #3 GARDEN PARTY
　　　　　(S)　(3:45)　MCA　10098　Best Of (1963-1975).
　　　　　(S)　(3:45)　MCA　31364　Garden Party.
　　　　　(S)　(3:45)　Curb　77372　All-Time Greatest Hits.
　　　　　(S)　(4:02)　MCA　6163　All My Best. *(all tracks on this cd are rerecordings)*

SANDY NELSON
1959 #4 TEEN BEAT
1961 #9 LET THERE BE DRUMS
　　　　　(M)　(2:18)　Curb　77402　All-Time Great Instrumental Hits Volume 2.
1964 #37 TEEN BEAT '65

NEON PHILHARMONIC
1969 #15 MORNING GIRL
　　　　　(S)　(2:11)　Rhino　70996　One Hit Wonders Of The 60's Volume 2.

PETER NERO
1972 #21 THEME FROM "SUMMER OF '42"
　　　　　(S)　(2:51)　Columbia　31105　Summer Of '42.
　　　　　(S)　(2:50)　Columbia　33136　Greatest Hits.

NERVOUS NORVUS
1956 #35 TRANSFUSION
　　　　　(M)　(2:23)　Rhino　75768　Dr. Demento Presents.
　　　　　(M)　(2:24)　Rhino　70743　Dr. Demento 20th Anniversary Collection.
　　　　　(M)　(2:24)　MCA　31200　Vintage Music Volume 3.
　　　　　(M)　(2:24)　MCA　5778　Vintage Music Volumes 3 & 4.
1956 #37 APE CALL

MICHAEL NESMITH & THE FIRST NATIONAL BAND
1970 #17 *JOANNE*
    (S) (3:10) Rhino 70763 The Older Stuff/Best Of The Early Years.
1971 #28 *SILVER MOON*
    (S) (3:10) Rhino 70763 The Older Stuff/Best Of The Early Years.

AARON NEVILLE
1967 #3 *TELL IT LIKE IT IS*
    (M) (2:40) Rhino 70653 Billboard's Top R&B Hits Of 1967.
    (M) (2:40) Rhino 72006 Billboard's Top R&B Hits 1965-1969 Box Set.
    (S) (4:15) Mango 539909 O.S.T. The Big Easy. *(live)*
    (M) (2:38) Curb 77303 Greatest Hits.
    (S) (2:38) Ripete 2392163 Ebb Tide. *(mastered from vinyl)*
    (E) (2:40) Curb 77491 Tell It Like It Is.

NEWBEATS
1964 #2 *BREAD AND BUTTER*
    (S) (1:57) Rhino 70625 Billboard's Top Rock & Roll Hits Of 1964.
    (S) (1:57) Rhino 72007 Billboard's Top Rock & Roll Hits 1962-1966 Box Set.
    (S) (1:56) Rhino 70732 Grandson Of Frat Rock.
1964 #16 *EVERYTHING'S ALRIGHT*
1965 #34 *BREAK AWAY (FROM THAT BOY)*
1965 #14 *RUN, BABY RUN (BACK INTO MY ARMS)*

NEW BIRTH
1973 #28 *I CAN UNDERSTAND IT*
    (S) (6:20) Collectables 5100 Golden Classics.

NEW CHRISTY MINSTRELS
1963 #14 *GREEN GREEN*
    (S) (2:07) Columbia 9279 Greatest Hits.
    (S) (2:07) Rhino 70264 Troubadours Of The Folk Era Volume 2. *(truncated fade)*
    (S) (2:07) Columbia 8855 Ramblin'.
1963 #38 *SATURDAY NIGHT*
1964 #20 *TODAY*
    (S) (2:43) Columbia 9279 Greatest Hits.

NEW COLONY SIX
1968 #22 *I WILL ALWAYS THINK ABOUT YOU*
    (S) (2:22) Mercury 834216 45's On CD Volume 3.
1969 #13 *THINGS I'D LIKE TO SAY*
1969 #40 *I COULD NEVER LIE TO YOU*

JIMMY NEWMAN
1957 #24 *A FALLEN STAR*

TED NEWMAN
1957 #28 *PLAYTHING*

NEW SEEKERS
1970 #10 *LOOK WHAT THEY'VE DONE TO MY SONG MA*
1972 #11 *I'D LIKE TO TEACH THE WORLD TO SING (IN PERFECT HARMONY)*
1973 #21 *PINBALL WIZARD/SEE ME, FEEL ME*

WAYNE NEWTON
1963 #12 *DANKE SHOEN*
    (S) (2:34) Curb 77355 60's Hits Volume 1.
    (S) (2:34) Curb 77270 Best Of Now. *(rerecording)*

WAYNE NEWTON (Continued)

(S) (2:34) Capitol 91634 Capitol Collector's Series.
(S) (2:34) Capitol 98670 Memories Are Made Of This.

1965 #11 *RED ROSES FOR A BLUE LADY*

(S) (2:50) Curb 77270 Best Of Now. *(rerecording)*
(S) (2:21) Capitol 91634 Capitol Collector's Series.

1972 #1 *DADDY DON'T YOU WALK SO FAST*

(S) (3:24) Curb 77317 70's Hits Volume 1.
(S) (3:17) Curb 77270 Best Of Now. *(rerecording)*

1972 #38 *CAN'T YOU HEAR THE SONG?*

OLIVIA NEWTON-JOHN

1971 #23 *IF NOT FOR YOU*

(S) (2:51) MCA 5226 Greatest Hits.

NEW VAUDEVILLE BAND

1966 #1 *WINCHESTER CATHEDRAL*

(M) (2:23) Rhino 70325 History Of British Rock Volume 7.
(M) (2:23) Rhino 72022 History Of British Rock Box Set.

NEW YORK CITY

1973 #12 *I'M DOIN' FINE NOW*

(S) (2:51) Rhino 70790 Soul Hits Of The 70's Volume 10.

NILSSON

1969 #7 *EVERYBODY'S TALKIN'*

(S) (2:30) EMI 48409 O.S.T. Midnight Cowboy. *(alternate take)*
(S) (2:43) RCA 8475 Nipper's Greatest Hits Of The 60's Volume 2.
(S) (2:43) RCA 9670 All Time Greatest Hits.
(S) (2:43) Pair 1214 Best Of. *(truncated fade)*

1969 #35 *I GUESS THE LORD MUST BE IN NEW YORK CITY*

(S) (2:42) RCA 9670 All Time Greatest Hits.
(S) (2:42) Pair 1214 Best Of. *(truncated fade)*
(S) (2:42) RCA 61138 and 61155 Songwriter.

1971 #27 *ME AND MY ARROW*

(S) (2:10) RCA 9670 All Time Greatest Hits. *(includes :05 introductory narration)*
(S) (2:04) RCA 2593 The Point.
(S) (2:10) RCA 61138 and 61155 Songwriter. *(includes :05 introductory narration)*

1972 #1 *WITHOUT YOU*

(S) (3:13) RCA 9902 Nipper's #1 Hits 1956-1986.
(S) (3:16) RCA 8476 and 9684 Nipper's Greatest Hits Of The 70's.
(S) (3:17) RCA 9670 All Time Greatest Hits.
(S) (3:20) RCA 4515 Nilsson Schmilsson.
(S) (3:20) MFSL 541 Nilsson Schmilsson.
(S) (3:18) Pair 1214 Best Of.

1972 #22 *JUMP INTO THE FIRE*

(S) (2:54) RCA 9670 All Time Greatest Hits.
(S) (7:01) RCA 4515 Nilsson Schmilsson. *(LP version)*
(S) (7:05) MFSL 541 Nilsson Schmilsson. *(LP version)*
(M) (3:32) Pair 1214 Best Of. *(commercial 45 version)*
(S) (2:54) RCA 61138 and 61155 Songwriter.

1972 #12 *COCONUT*

(S) (3:49) RCA 9670 All Time Greatest Hits.
(S) (3:51) RCA 4515 Nilsson Schmilsson.
(S) (3:50) MFSL 541 Nilsson Schmilsson.
(S) (3:50) RCA 61138 and 61155 Songwriter.

NILSSON (Continued)
1972 #23 SPACEMAN
    (S) (3:30) RCA 9670 All Time Greatest Hits.
    (S) (3:34) RCA 3812 Son Of Schmilsson.
    (S) (3:30) RCA 61138 and 61155 Songwriter.
1973 #40 REMEMBER (CHRISTMAS)
    (S) (4:05) RCA 9670 All Time Greatest Hits.
    (S) (4:07) RCA 3812 Son Of Schmilsson.

1910 FRUITGUM COMPANY
1968 #2 SIMON SAYS
    (S) (2:14) Pair 1202 Best Of Buddah.
    (S) (2:14) Pair 1199 Best Of Bubblegum Music.
    (S) (2:14) Special Music 4914 Best Of The Bubblegum Years.
1968 #3 1,2,3 RED LIGHT
    (S) (2:06) Pair 1199 Best Of Bubblegum Music. (the group is incorrectly identified as the "OHIO EXPRESS" on the cd jacket)
    (S) (2:06) Special Music 4914 Best Of The Bubblegum Years.
1968 #31 GOODY GOODY GUMDROPS
    (S) (2:15) Pair 1199 Best Of Bubblegum Music.
    (S) (2:15) Special Music 4914 Best Of The Bubblegum Years.
1969 #4 INDIAN GIVER
    (S) (2:40) Pair 1199 Best Of Bubblegum Music.
    (S) (2:40) K-Tel 205 Battle Of The Bands Volume 3.
    (S) (2:40) Special Music 4914 Best Of The Bubblegum Years.
1969 #31 SPECIAL DELIVERY
    (S) (2:36) Pair 1199 Best Of Bubblegum Music.
    (S) (2:36) Special Music 4914 Best Of The Bubblegum Years.

NITE-LITERS
1971 #39 K-JEE
    (S) (3:59) Collectables 5214 K-Jee/Golden Classics.
1972 #39 AFRO STRUT
    (S) (2:50) Collectables 5214 K-Jee/Golden Classics.

NITTY GRITTY DIRT BAND
1971 #9 MR. BOJANGLES
    (S) (3:34) Rhino 70924 Super Hits Of The 70's Volume 4.
    (S) (3:34) Rhino 72009 Super Hits Of The 70's Volumes 1-4 Box Set.
    (S) (3:33) Priority 8665 High Times/70's Greatest Rock Hits Volume 4.
    (S) (3:24) EMI 90603 Rock Me Gently. (alternate take)
    (S) (3:34) Curb 77356 70's Hits Volume 2.
    (S) (5:13) EMI 46591 Best Of. (LP version with prologue)
    (S) (3:33) Curb 77357 Greatest Hits.
    (S) (5:02) Warner Brothers 25382 Twenty Years Of Dirt. (LP version with prologue)
1971 #38 HOUSE AT POOH CORNER
    (S) (2:37) EMI 46591 Best Of.
    (S) (2:37) Curb 77357 Greatest Hits.

JACK NITZSCHE
1963 #37 THE LONELY SURFER
    (S) (2:33) Rhino 70089 Surfin' Hits.
    (S) (2:33) JCI 3106 Surfin' Sixties.

NICK NOBLE
1955 #10 THE BIBLE TELLS ME SO
1957 #35 A FALLEN STAR

CLIFF NOBLES & COMPANY
1968 #4 *THE HORSE*
(S) (2:39) Rhino 70629   Billboard's Top Rock & Roll Hits Of 1968.
(S) (2:39) Rhino 72005   Billboard's Top Rock & Roll Hits 1966-1972 Box
Set.

JACKY NOGUEZ & HIS ORCHESTRA
1959 #18 *CIAO, CIAO BAMBINA*

FREDDIE NORTH
1971 #30 *SHE'S ALL I GOT*

NU TORNADOS
1958 #22 *PHILADELPHIA, U.S.A.*

NUTTY SQUIRRELS
1959 #3 *UH! OH! (PART 2)*

OCEAN
1971 #2 *PUT YOUR HAND IN THE HAND*
(S) (2:55) Rhino 70924   Super Hits Of The 70's Volume 4.
(S) (2:55) Rhino 72009   Super Hits Of The 70's Volumes 1-4 Box Set.
(S) (2:20) Pair 1202   Best Of Buddah. *(edited)*

KENNY O'DELL
1967 #35 *BEAUTIFUL PEOPLE*

OHIO EXPRESS
1967 #23 *BEG, BORROW AND STEAL*
1968 #4 *YUMMY YUMMY YUMMY*
(S) (2:20) Rhino 70629   Billboard's Top Rock & Roll Hits Of 1968.
(S) (2:20) Rhino 72005   Billboard's Top Rock & Roll Hits 1968-1972 Box
Set.
(S) (2:18) Pair 1202   Best Of Buddah.
(S) (2:18) Pair 1199   Best Of Bubblegum Music.
(S) (2:18) Special Music 4914   Best Of The Bubblegum Years.
1968 #25 *DOWN AT LULU'S*
(S) (1:53) Pair 1199   Best Of Bubblegum Music.
(S) (1:53) Special Music 4914   Best Of The Bubblegum Years.
1968 #8 *CHEWY CHEWY*
(S) (2:36) Pair 1199   Best Of Bubblegum Music.
(S) (2:36) Special Music 4914   Best Of The Bubblegum Years.
1969 #26 *MERCY*
(S) (2:21) Pair 1199   Best Of Bubblegum Music.
(S) (2:21) Special Music 4914   Best Of The Bubblegum Years.

OHIO PLAYERS
1973 #13 *FUNKY WORM*
1973 #31 *ECSTASY*

O'JAYS
1972 #1 *BACK STABBERS*
    (S) (3:06) Rhino 70633 Billboard's Top Rock & Roll Hits Of 1972.
    (S) (3:06) Rhino 72005 Billboard's Top Rock & Roll Hits 1968-1972 Box Set.
    (S) (3:05) Rhino 70788 Soul Hits Of The 70's Volume 8.
    (S) (3:06) Philadelphia International 35024 Collector's Items.
    (S) (3:06) Philadelphia International 39251 Greatest Hits.

1973 #1 *LOVE TRAIN*
    (the original 45 and LP length was (2:58); a (6:15) version first surfaced on the "Philadelphia Classics" vinyl LP in 1977)
    (S) (2:58) Rhino 70634 Billboard's Top Rock & Roll Hits Of 1973.
    (S) (2:58) Rhino 70552 Soul Hits Of The 70's Volume 12.
    (S) (6:15) Philadelphia International 34940 Philadelphia Classics.
    (S) (2:57) Philadelphia International 35024 Collector's Items.
    (S) (2:57) Philadelphia International 39251 Greatest Hits.

1973 #30 *TIME TO GET DOWN*

O'KAYSIONS
1968 #5 *GIRL WATCHER*

DANNY O'KEEFE
1972 #10 *GOOD TIME CHARLIE'S GOT THE BLUES*
    (S) (2:38) JCI 3304 Mellow Seventies. *(rerecording)*

OLIVER
1969 #4 *GOOD MORNING STARSHINE*
    (S) (2:35) JCI 3104 Mellow Sixties.

1969 #2 *JEAN*
1969 #23 *SUNDAY MORNIN'*

OLYMPICS
1958 #11 *WESTERN MOVIES*
    (M) (2:19) Curb 77323 All Time Greatest Hits Of Rock 'N' Roll.
    (M) (2:19) Dunhill Compact Classics 057 All-Time Greatest Hits.

1960 #20 *BIG BOY PETE*
    (M) (2:26) Dunhill Compact Classics 057 All-Time Greatest Hits.
    (M) (2:08) Collectables 5081 The Olympics Meet The Marathons.

1960 #33 *SHIMMY LIKE KATE*
    (M) (2:20) Dunhill Compact Classics 057 All-Time Greatest Hits.
    (M) (2:21) Collectables 5081 The Olympics Meet The Marathons.

1961 #25 *DANCE BY THE LIGHT OF THE MOON*
    (M) (2:12) Dunhill Compact Classics 057 All-Time Greatest Hits.
    (M) (2:12) Collectables 5081 The Olympics Meet The Marathons.

100 PROOF AGED IN SOUL
1970 #6 *SOMEBODY'S BEEN SLEEPING IN MY BED*
    (S) (2:45) Rhino 70783 Soul Hits Of The 70's Volume 3. *(45 version)*
    (S) (4:09) HDH 3904 Greatest Hits. *(LP version)*

ROY ORBISON
1960 #2 *ONLY THE LONELY (KNOW HOW I FEEL)*
    (S) (2:25) Rhino 71493 For The Lonely: 18 Greatest Hits.
    (S) (2:26) CBS Special Products 44348 All-Time Greatest Hits Volume 1.
    (S) (2:25) CBS Special Products 45116 All-Time Greatest Hits.

      (S)   (2:25) CBS Special Products 46809 Legendary.
      (S)   (2:26) Virgin 90604 In Dreams: The Greatest Hits. *(all selections on this cd are rerecorded)*
      (S)   (2:23) CBS Special Products 21427 Sings Lonely And Blue.

1960 #13 *BLUE ANGEL*

      (S)   (2:49) Rhino 71493 For The Lonely: 18 Greatest Hits.
      (S)   (2:49) CBS Special Products 44348 All-Time Greatest Hits Volume 1.
      (S)   (2:49) CBS Special Products 45116 All-Time Greatest Hits.
      (S)   (2:49) CBS Special Products 46809 Legendary.
      (S)   (2:46) Virgin 90604 In Dreams: The Greatest Hits. *(all selections on this cd are rerecorded)*
      (S)   (2:50) CBS Special Products 21427 Sings Lonely And Blue.

1961 #28 *I'M HURTIN'*

      (S)   (2:42) CBS Special Products 44349 All-Time Greatest Hits Volume 2.
      (S)   (2:42) Rhino 71493 For The Lonely: 18 Greatest Hits.
      (S)   (2:42) CBS Special Products 45116 All-Time Greatest Hits.
      (S)   (2:41) CBS Special Products 46809 Legendary.
      (S)   (2:46) Virgin 90604 In Dreams: The Greatest Hits. *(all selections on this cd are rerecorded)*
      (S)   (2:41) CBS Special Products 21427 Sings Lonely And Blue.

1961 #1 *RUNNING SCARED*

      (S)   (2:11) CBS Special Products 44349 All-Time Greatest Hits Volume 2.
      (S)   (2:10) Rhino 71493 For The Lonely: 18 Greatest Hits.
      (S)   (2:10) CBS Special Products 45116 All-Time Greatest Hits.
      (S)   (2:10) CBS Special Products 46809 Legendary.
      (S)   (2:12) Virgin 90604 In Dreams: The Greatest Hits. *(all selections on this cd are rerecorded)*
      (S)   (2:10) CBS Special Products 21428 Crying.

1961 #1 *CRYING*

      (S)   (2:44) Rhino 71493 For The Lonely: 18 Greatest Hits.
      (S)   (2:44) CBS Special Products 44348 All-Time Greatest Hits Volume 1.
      (S)   (2:44) CBS Special Products 45116 All-Time Greatest Hits.
      (S)   (2:44) CBS Special Products 46809 Legendary.
      (S)   (2:45) Virgin 90604 In Dreams: The Greatest Hits. *(all selections on this cd are rerecorded)*
      (S)   (2:44) CBS Special Products 21428 Crying.

1961 #34 *CANDY MAN*

      (S)   (2:43) Rhino 71493 For The Lonely: 18 Greatest Hits.
      (S)   (2:43) CBS Special Products 44348 All-Time Greatest Hits Volume 1.
      (S)   (2:43) CBS Special Products 45116 All-Time Greatest Hits.
      (S)   (2:43) CBS Special Products 46809 Legendary.
      (S)   (2:57) Virgin 90604 In Dreams: The Greatest Hits. *(all selections on this cd are rerecorded)*

1962 #9 *DREAM BABY (HOW LONG MUST I DREAM)*

      (S)   (2:30) Rhino 71493 For The Lonely: 18 Greatest Hits.
      (S)   (2:31) CBS Special Products 44348 All-Time Greatest Hits Volume 1.
      (S)   (2:31) CBS Special Products 45116 All-Time Greatest Hits.
      (S)   (2:31) CBS Special Products 46809 Legendary.
      (S)   (2:48) Virgin 90604 In Dreams: The Greatest Hits. *(all selections on this cd are rerecorded)*

1962 #21 *THE CROWD*

      (S)   (2:21) CBS Special Products 44349 All-Time Greatest Hits Volume 2.
      (S)   (2:21) CBS Special Products 45116 All-Time Greatest Hits.
      (S)   (2:21) CBS Special Products 46809 Legendary.

ROY ORBISON (Continued)

1962 #27 LEAH
- (S) (2:38) Rhino 71493 For The Lonely: 18 Greatest Hits.
- (S) (2:38) CBS Special Products 44348 All-Time Greatest Hits Volume 1.
- (S) (2:38) CBS Special Products 45116 All-Time Greatest Hits.
- (S) (2:38) CBS Special Products 46809 Legendary.
- (S) (2:42) Virgin 90604 In Dreams: The Greatest Hits. *(all selections on this cd are rerecorded)*

1962 #32 WORKIN' FOR THE MAN
- (S) (2:25) Rhino 71493 For The Lonely: 18 Greatest Hits.
- (S) (2:25) CBS Special Products 44348 All-Time Greatest Hits Volume 1.
- (S) (2:24) CBS Special Products 45116 All-Time Greatest Hits.
- (S) (2:24) CBS Special Products 46809 Legendary.
- (S) (2:43) Virgin 90604 In Dreams: The Greatest Hits. *(all selections on this cd are rerecorded)*

1963 #10 IN DREAMS
- (S) (2:47) Rhino 71493 For The Lonely: 18 Greatest Hits.
- (S) (2:47) CBS Special Products 44348 All-Time Greatest Hits Volume 1.
- (S) (2:47) CBS Special Products 45116 All-Time Greatest Hits.
- (S) (2:47) CBS Special Products 46809 Legendary.
- (S) (2:48) Virgin 90604 In Dreams: The Greatest Hits. *(all selections on this cd are rerecorded)*
- (S) (2:47) CBS Special Products 21429 In Dreams.

1963 #23 FALLING
- (S) (2:21) CBS Special Products 44349 All-Time Greatest Hits Volume 2.
- (S) (2:20) CBS Special Products 45116 All-Time Greatest Hits.
- (S) (2:21) CBS Special Products 46809 Legendary.
- (S) (2:24) Virgin 90604 In Dreams: The Greatest Hits. *(all selections on this cd are rerecorded)*

1963 #7 MEAN WOMAN BLUES
- (S) (2:24) CBS Special Products 44349 All-Time Greatest Hits Volume 2.
- (S) (2:23) Rhino 71493 For The Lonely: 18 Greatest Hits.
- (S) (2:23) CBS Special Products 45116 All-Time Greatest Hits.
- (S) (2:23) CBS Special Products 46809 Legendary.
- (S) (2:24) Virgin 90604 In Dreams: The Greatest Hits. *(all selections on this cd are rerecorded)*

1963 #21 BLUE BAYOU
- (S) (2:27) CBS Special Products 44349 All-Time Greatest Hits Volume 2.
- (S) (2:28) Rhino 71493 For The Lonely: 18 Greatest Hits.
- (S) (2:27) CBS Special Products 45116 All-Time Greatest Hits.
- (S) (2:25) CBS Special Products 46809 Legendary.
- (S) (2:48) Virgin 90604 In Dreams: The Greatest Hits. *(all selections on this cd are rerecorded)*
- (S) (2:25) CBS Special Products 21429 In Dreams.

1964 #16 PRETTY PAPER
- (S) (2:45) Rhino 70192 Christmas Classics.
- (S) (2:44) CBS Special Products 44349 All-Time Greatest Hits Volume 2.
- (S) (2:45) Rhino 71493 For The Lonely: 18 Greatest Hits.
- (S) (2:44) CBS Special Products 45116 All-Time Greatest Hits.
- (S) (2:45) CBS Special Products 46809 Legendary.

1964 #10 IT'S OVER
- (S) (2:46) Rhino 71493 For The Lonely: 18 Greatest Hits.
- (S) (2:46) CBS Special Products 44348 All-Time Greatest Hits Volume 1.
- (S) (2:46) CBS Special Products 45116 All-Time Greatest Hits.

ROY ORBISON (Continued)

        (S) (2:46) CBS Special Products 46809 Legendary.
        (S) (2:50) Virgin 90604 In Dreams: The Greatest Hits. *(all selections on this cd are rerecorded)*

1964 #1 OH, PRETTY WOMAN

        (S) (2:56) EMI 93492 O.S.T. Pretty Woman. *(LP version)*
        (S) (2:56) CBS Special Products 46808 Rock Goes To The Movies Volume 5. *(LP version)*
        (S) (2:56) CBS Special Products 44349 All-Time Greatest Hits Volume 2. *(LP version)*
        (S) (2:55) Rhino 71493 For The Lonely: 18 Greatest Hits. *(LP version)*
        (S) (2:55) CBS Special Products 45116 All-Time Greatest Hits. *(LP version)*
        (M) (2:55) CBS Special Products 46809 Legendary. *(45 version)*
        (S) (3:01) Virgin 90604 In Dreams: The Greatest Hits. *(all selections on this cd are rerecorded)*

1965 #20 GOODNIGHT

        (S) (2:27) CBS Special Products 45113 Our Love Song.
        (S) (2:27) CBS Special Products 46809 Legendary.

1965 #18 RIDE AWAY

        (S) (3:27) Mercury 816555 45's On CD Volume 2.
        (S) (3:27) Polydor 839234 Singles Collection (1965-1973).
        (S) (3:27) Rhino 70711 Classic Roy Orbison (1965-1968).
        (S) (3:27) CBS Special Products 46809 Legendary.

1965 #36 CRAWLING BACK

        (S) (3:10) Polydor 839234 Singles Collection (1965-1973).
        (S) (3:14) Rhino 70711 Classic Roy Orbison (1965-1968).
        (S) (3:14) CBS Special Products 46809 Legendary.

1966 #31 BREAKIN' UP IS BREAKIN' MY HEART

        (S) (2:06) Polydor 839234 Singles Collection (1965-1973).
        (S) (2:06) Rhino 70711 Classic Roy Orbison (1965-1968).
        (S) (2:06) CBS Special Products 46809 Legendary.

1966 #40 TWINKLE TOES

        (S) (2:34) Polydor 839234 Singles Collection (1965-1973).
        (S) (2:34) Rhino 70711 Classic Roy Orbison (1965-1968).

ORIGINAL CASUALS

1958 #28 SO TOUGH

        (M) (2:14) MCA 31202 Vintage Music Volume 5.
        (M) (2:14) MCA 5804 Vintage Music Volumes 5 & 6.

ORIGINALS

1969 #16 BABY I'M FOR REAL

        (S) (3:16) Motown 6183 Hard To Find Motown Classics Volume 1.
        (S) (3:17) Rhino 70655 Billboard's Top R&B Hits Of 1969.
        (S) (3:17) Rhino 72006 Billboard's Top R&B Hits 1965-1969 Box Set.
        (S) (3:17) Motown 5462 Baby I'm For Real.
        (S) (3:18) Motown 5110 Motown Superstar Series Volume 10.

1970 #18 THE BELLS

        (S) (3:00) Motown 9105 Motown Memories Volume 2.
        (S) (3:02) Motown 6183 Hard To Find Motown Classics Volume 1.
        (S) (3:04) Rhino 70782 Soul Hits Of The 70's Volume 2.
        (S) (2:58) Motown 5461 Portrait Of.
        (S) (3:03) Motown 5110 Motown Superstar Series Volume 10.

TONY ORLANDO
1961 #17 *HALFWAY TO PARADISE*
1961 #17 *BLESS YOU*

ORLONS
1962 #2 *THE WAH WATUSI*
1962 #6 *DON'T HANG UP*
1963 #3 *SOUTH STREET*
1963 #12 *NOT ME*
1963 #20 *CROSS FIRE!*

FRANK ORTEGA TRIO
1959 #38 *77 SUNSET STRIP*

DONNY OSMOND
1971 #7 *SWEET AND INNOCENT*
    (E) (2:52) Curb 77510 Greatest Hits.
1971 #1 *GO AWAY LITTLE GIRL*
    (S) (2:30) Curb 77510 Greatest Hits.
1972 #9 *HEY GIRL*
    (S) (3:10) Curb 77510 Greatest Hits. *(truncated fade)*
1972 #3 *PUPPY LOVE*
    (S) (3:03) Curb 77510 Greatest Hits.
1972 #8 *TOO YOUNG*
    (E) (3:05) Curb 77510 Greatest Hits.
1972 #16 *WHY*
    (S) (2:42) Curb 77510 Greatest Hits.
1973 #5 *THE TWELFTH OF NEVER*
    (S) (2:40) Curb 77510 Greatest Hits.
1973 #28 *A MILLION TO ONE*
    (E) (2:58) Curb 77510 Greatest Hits.

MARIE OSMOND
1973 #6 *PAPER ROSES*
    (S) (2:36) Curb 77263 Best Of. *(rerecording)*

OSMONDS
1971 #1 *ONE BAD APPLE*
    (S) (2:43) Rhino 70632 Billboard's Top Rock & Roll Hits Of 1971.
    (S) (2:43) Rhino 72005 Billboard's Top Rock & Roll Hits 1968-1972 Box Set.
    (S) (2:43) Curb 77529 Osmond Brothers Greatest Hits.
1971 #9 *DOUBLE LOVIN'*
    (S) (2:32) Curb 77529 Osmond Brothers Greatest Hits.
1971 #2 *YO-YO*
    (S) (3:12) Curb 77529 Osmond Brothers Greatest Hits.
1972 #3 *DOWN BY THE LAZY RIVER*
    (S) (2:41) Curb 77529 Osmond Brothers Greatest Hits.
1972 #15 *HOLD HER TIGHT*
    (S) (3:13) Curb 77529 Osmond Brothers Greatest Hits.
1972 #19 *CRAZY HORSES*
    (S) (2:28) Curb 77529 Osmond Brothers Greatest Hits.
1973 #21 *GOIN' HOME*
    (S) (2:27) Curb 77529 Osmond Brothers Greatest Hits.
1973 #19 *LET ME IN*
    (S) (3:38) Curb 77529 Osmond Brothers Greatest Hits.

GILBERT O'SULLIVAN
1972 #1 *ALONE AGAIN (NATURALLY)*
    (S) (3:37) Rhino 70928 Super Hits Of The 70's Volume 8.
    (S) (3:38) Rhino 70633 Billboard's Top Rock & Roll Hits Of 1972.
    (S) (3:38) Rhino 72005 Billboard's Top Rock & Roll Hits 1968-1972 Box Set.
    (S) (3:36) Priority 8669 #1 Hits/70's Greatest Rock Hits Volume 9.
    (S) (3:36) Rhino 70560 Best Of.
1972 #3 *CLAIR*
    (S) (2:59) Rhino 70929 Super Hits Of The 70's Volume 9.
    (S) (3:00) Rhino 70560 Best Of.
1973 #22 *OUT OF THE QUESTION*
    (S) (2:56) Rhino 70560 Best Of.
1973 #4 *GET DOWN*
    (S) (2:39) Rhino 70758 Super Hits Of The 70's Volume 11.
    (S) (2:39) Rhino 70560 Best Of.
1973 #11 *OOH BABY*
    (S) (3:13) Rhino 70560 Best Of.

JOHNNY OTIS SHOW
1958 #16 *WILLIE AND THE HAND JIVE*
    (M) (2:34) Rhino 70644 Billboard's Top R&B Hits Of 1958.
    (M) (2:35) Rhino 70719 Legends Of Guitar - Rock; The 50's.
    (E) (2:34) EMI 90614 Non Stop Party Rock.
    (M) (2:34) Capitol 48993 Spuds Mackenzie's Party Faves.
    (E) (2:32) Curb 77323 All Time Greatest Hits Of Rock 'N' Roll.
    (M) (2:34) Capitol 92858 The Capitol Years.
    (M) (2:33) Capitol 98138 Spring Break Volume 1.
    (M) (2:34) Rhino 70291 Bo Diddley Beats.

OTIS & CARLA (OTIS REDDING & CARLA THOMAS)
1967 #19 *TRAMP*
    (M) (2:59) Atlantic Group 88218 Complete Stax/Volt Singles.
    (S) (2:59) Atlantic 81762 The Otis Redding Story.
    (S) (2:57) Warner Special Products 27608 Ultimate Otis Redding.
    (S) (2:59) Atco 80254 The Dock Of The Bay.
    (S) (2:59) Atlantic 82256 Otis Redding & Carla Thomas: King & Queen.
    (S) (2:59) Atlantic 82305 Atlantic Rhythm And Blues 1947-1974 Box Set.

OUTSIDERS
1966 #6 *TIME WON'T LET ME*
    (S) (2:48) EMI 90614 Non-Stop Party Rock.
    (S) (2:48) Capitol 48993 Spuds Mackenzie's Party Faves.
    (M) (2:48) K-Tel 839 Battle Of The Bands Volume 2. *(truncated fade)*
    (S) (3:01) Capitol 94076 Capitol Collector's Series. *(includes :02 countoff; :10 longer than 45 or LP)*
    (S) (3:01) Capitol 98138 Spring Break Volume 1. *(includes :02 countoff; :10 longer than 45 or LP)*
    (S) (2:59) Capitol 98665 When AM Was King. *(:10 longer than 45 or LP)*
1966 #24 *GIRL IN LOVE*
    (S) (3:18) Capitol 94076 Capitol Collector's Series.
1966 #13 *RESPECTABLE*
    (S) (2:00) Capitol 94076 Capitol Collector's Series.
    (S) (2:00) Capitol 98139 Spring Break Volume 2.
1966 #40 *HELP ME GIRL*
    (S) (2:45) Capitol 94076 Capitol Collector's Series.

REG OWEN & HIS ORCHESTRA
1959 #14 *MANHATTAN SPIRITUAL*
BUCK OWENS
1965 #31 *I'VE GOT A TIGER BY THE TAIL*
        (S) (2:09) Rhino 70686 Billboard's Top Country Hits Of 1965.
        (S) (2:09) Curb 77342 All-Time Greatest Hits.
DONNIE OWENS
1958 #20 *NEED YOU*

P

PACIFIC GAS & ELECTRIC
1970 #12 *ARE YOU READY?*
        (dj copies of this 45 ran (2:40) while the commercial copies ran (5:47))
        (S) (5:47) Rhino 70782 Soul Hits Of The 70's Volume 2.
        (S) (5:46) Columbia/Legacy 46160 Rock Artifacts Volume 1.
        (S) (5:45) Sandstone 33002 Reelin' In The Years Volume 3.
PACKERS
1965 #29 *HOLE IN THE WALL*
PATTI PAGE
1956 #6 *ALLEGHENY MOON*
        (M) (2:50) Mercury 510434 The Mercury Years Volume 2.
        (S) (2:56) Columbia 9326 Greatest Hits. *(rerecording)*
1956 #14 *MAMA FROM THE TRAIN*
        (M) (2:50) Mercury 510434 The Mercury Years Volume 2.
1957 #25 *A POOR MAN'S ROSES (OR A RICH MAN'S GOLD)*
        (M) (2:28) Mercury 510434 The Mercury Years Volume 2.
1957 #8 *OLD CAPE COD*
        (M) (2:34) Mercury 510434 The Mercury Years Volume 2.
        (S) (3:08) Columbia 9326 Greatest Hits. *(rerecording)*
        (S) (3:06) Columbia 44401 16 Most Requested Songs. *(rerecording)*
1957 #18 *I'LL REMEMBER TODAY*
        (M) (2:39) Mercury 510434 The Mercury Years Volume 2.
1958 #28 *BELONGING TO SOMEONE*
1958 #38 *ANOTHER TIME, ANOTHER PLACE*
1958 #9 *LEFT RIGHT OUT OF YOUR HEART*
        (S) (2:39) Mercury 510434 The Mercury Years Volume 2.
1958 #28 *FIBBIN'*
1959 #36 *TRUST IN ME*

1960 #32 *ONE OF US (WILL WEEP TONIGHT)*
> (S) (2:31) Mercury 510434 The Mercury Years Volume 2.

1962 #35 *GO ON HOME*

1962 #26 *MOST PEOPLE GET MARRIED*
> (S) (2:03) Mercury 510434 The Mercury Years Volume 2.

1965 #10 *HUSH, HUSH, SWEET CHARLOTTE*
> (S) (2:31) Columbia 44401 16 Most Requested Songs. *(rerecording)*

NICK PAONE
1959 #36 *BLAH, BLAH, BLAH*

PARADE
1967 #26 *SUNSHINE GIRL*
> (S) (2:43) Rhino 75777 More Nuggets.

PARADONS
1960 #17 *DIAMONDS AND PEARLS*
> (M) (2:14) Dunhill Compact Classics 031 Back Seat Jams.

PARIS SISTERS
1961 #7 *I LOVE HOW YOU LOVE ME*
> (M) (2:05) Rhino 70989 Best Of The Girl Groups Volume 2.
> (M) (2:04) Abkco 7118 Phil Spector/Back To Mono (1958-1969).

FESS PARKER
1957 #12 *WRINGLE WRANGLE*

ROBERT PARKER
1966 #11 *BAREFOOTIN'*
> (M) (2:33) Rhino 70652 Billboard's Top R&B Hits Of 1966.
> (M) (2:33) Rhino 72006 Billboard's Top R&B Hits 1965-1969 Box Set.
> (M) (2:29) Garland 011 Footstompin' Oldies.

MICHAEL PARKS
1970 #13 *LONG LONESOME HIGHWAY*

PARLIAMENTS
1967 #18 *(I WANNA) TESTIFY*

BILL PARSONS
1959 #10 *THE ALL AMERICAN BOY*

PARTRIDGE FAMILY
1970 #1 *I THINK I LOVE YOU*
> *(the actual 45 time is (2:50) not (2:28) as stated on the record label)*
> (S) (2:50) Rhino 70923 Super Hits Of The 70's Volume 3.
> (S) (2:50) Rhino 72009 Super Hits Of The 70's Volumes 1-4 Box Set.
> (S) (2:50) Rhino 70631 Billboard's Top Rock & Roll Hits Of 1970.
> (S) (2:50) Rhino 72005 Billboard's Top Rock & Roll Hits 1968-1972 Box
> Set.
> (S) (2:51) Priority 8669 #1 Hits/70's Greatest Rock Hits Volume 9.
> (S) (2:51) Arista 8604 Greatest Hits.

1971 #1 *DOESN'T SOMEBODY WANT TO BE WANTED*
> (S) (2:45) Arista 8604 Greatest Hits.

1971 #2 *I'LL MEET YOU HALFWAY*
> (S) (3:47) Arista 8604 Greatest Hits. *(LP length)*

1971 #9 *I WOKE UP IN LOVE THIS MORNING*
> (S) (2:37) Arista 8604 Greatest Hits.

1972 #13 *IT'S ONE OF THOSE NIGHTS (YES LOVE)*
> (S) (3:33) Arista 8604 Greatest Hits.

PARTRIDGE FAMILY (Continued)
1972 #31 *AM I LOSING YOU*
          (S) (2:21) Arista 8604 Greatest Hits.
1972 #25 *BREAKING UP IS HARD TO DO*
1973 #25 *LOOKING THROUGH THE EYES OF LOVE*
          (S) (3:04) Arista 8604 Greatest Hits.

PASTEL SIX
1963 #22 *THE CINNAMON CINDER (IT'S A VERY NICE DANCE)*

JOHNNY PATE
1958 #18 *SWINGING SHEPHERD BLUES*

PATIENCE & PRUDENCE
1956 #3 *TONIGHT YOU BELONG TO ME*
1956 #13 *GONNA GET ALONG WITHOUT YOU NOW*

PATTY & THE EMBLEMS
1964 #28 *MIXED-UP, SHOOK-UP, GIRL*

BILLY PAUL
1972 #1 *ME AND MRS. JONES*
          (S) (4:46) Rhino 70660 Billboard's Top R&B Hits Of 1972.
          (S) (4:45) Rhino 70789 Soul Hits Of The 70's Volume 9.
          (S) (4:46) Philadelphia International 39307 Ten Years Of #1 Hits.

LES PAUL & MARY FORD
1955 #6 *HUMMINGBIRD*
          (M) (2:37) Capitol 97654 The Legend And The Legacy.
          (M) (2:37) Capitol 99617 Best Of The Capitol Masters.
1957 #24 *CINCO ROBLES*
          (M) (3:04) Capitol 97654 The Legend And The Legacy.

PAUL & PAULA
1963 #1 *HEY PAULA*
          (M) (2:29) Mercury 826448 Oldies Golden Million Sellers.
          (E) (2:36) MCA 31023 O.S.T. Animal House. (*sound effects added to the introduction; all tracks on this cd are segued together*)
          (M) (2:28) Rhino 70588 Rockin' & Rollin' Wedding Songs Volume 1.
1963 #7 *YOUNG LOVERS*
1963 #21 *FIRST QUARREL*

RITA PAVONE
1964 #35 *REMEMBER ME*

FREDA PAYNE
1970 #2 *BAND OF GOLD*
          (S) (2:51) Dunhill Compact Classics 033 Beachbeat Shaggin'.
          (S) (2:53) Rhino 70782 Soul Hits Of The 70's Volume 2.
          (S) (2:53) HDH 3905 Greatest Hits.
1970 #21 *DEEPER & DEEPER*
          (S) (3:01) Rhino 70784 Soul Hits Of The 70's Volume 4. (*LP version*)
          (S) (3:00) HDH 3905 Greatest Hits. (*LP version*)
1971 #36 *CHERISH WHAT IS DEAR TO YOU*
          (S) (3:55) HDH 3905 Greatest Hits. (*LP version*)
1971 #7 *BRING THE BOYS HOME*
          (S) (3:28) Rhino 70785 Soul Hits Of The 70's Volume 5. (*LP version*)
          (S) (3:28) HDH 3905 Greatest Hits. (*LP version*)

PEACHES & HERB

1967 #39 *LET'S FALL IN LOVE*
1967 #12 *CLOSE YOUR EYES*
1967 #22 *FOR YOUR LOVE*
1967 #13 *LOVE IS STRANGE*
1968 #37 *TWO LITTLE KIDS*

ANN PEEBLES

1970 #27 *PART TIME LOVE*
        (S) (2:50) Hi 25226 History Of Hi R&B Volume 1.
        (S) (2:50) MCA 25225 Greatest Hits.

PENGUINS

1955 #3 *EARTH ANGEL (WILL YOU BE MINE)*
        (M) (2:55) Rhino 75763 Best Of Doo Wop Ballads.
        (M) (2:55) Rhino 70598 Billboard's Top Rock & Roll Hits Of 1955.
        (M) (2:48) Original Sound 1960 Memories Of El Monte. *(first note overlaps previous song)*
        (M) (2:54) Collectables 5045 Golden Classics. *(truncated fade)*
        (M) (2:54) Collectables 5048 Dootone Rhythm And Blues. *(truncated fade)*

PEOPLE

1968 #13 *I LOVE YOU*
(radio station copies of the 45 ran (2:43) and (4:37); commercial copies were all (4:37))
        (E) (4:29) K-Tel 686 Battle Of The Bands Volume 4.

PEPPERMINT RAINBOW

1969 #21 *WILL YOU BE STAYING AFTER SUNDAY*

EMILIO PERICOLI

1962 #6 *AL DI LA*

CARL PERKINS

1956 #2 *BLUE SUEDE SHOES*
        (M) (2:13) Rhino 70599 Billboard's Top Rock & Roll Hits Of 1956.
        (M) (2:13) RCA 5463 Rock & Roll - The Early Days. *(echo added)*
        (M) (2:13) Rhino 75884 The Sun Story.
        (M) (2:13) Dunhill Compact Classics 009 Legends.
        (M) (2:13) Rhino 75893 Jukebox Classics Volume 1. *(echo added)*
        (M) (2:13) Rhino 70741 Rock This Town: Rockabilly Hits Volume 1.
        (M) (2:12) JCI 3202 Rockin' Fifties.
        (M) (2:13) Rhino 75890 Original Sun Greatest Hits.
        (M) (2:14) RCA 66059 Sun's Greatest Hits.

PERSUADERS

1971 #10 *THIN LINE BETWEEN LOVE AND HATE*
        (S) (3:21) Rhino 70786 Soul Hits Of The 70's Volume 6.
        (S) (3:21) Rhino 70659 Billboard's Top R&B Hits Of 1971.
        (S) (3:23) Atlantic 81299 Atlantic Rhythm & Blues Volume 7.
        (S) (3:22) Atlantic 82305 Atlantic Rhythm And Blues 1947-1974 Box Set.
1973 #39 *SOME GUYS HAVE ALL THE LUCK*

PETER & GORDON

1964 #1 *A WORLD WITHOUT LOVE*
        (S) (2:39) Rhino 70319 History Of British Rock Volume 1.
        (S) (2:39) Rhino 72022 History Of British Rock Box Set.
        (S) (2:39) Rhino 72008 History Of British Rock Volumes 1-4 Box Set.
        (S) (2:38) Rhino 70748 Best Of.
        (S) (2:37) Capitol 98665 When AM Was King.

PETER & GORDON (Continued)
1964 #12 *NOBODY I KNOW*
    (S) (2:28) Rhino 70319 History Of British Rock Volume 1.
    (S) (2:28) Rhino 72022 History Of British Rock Box Set.
    (S) (2:28) Rhino 72008 History Of British Rock Volumes 1-4 Box Set.
    (S) (2:27) Rhino 70748 Best Of.

1964 #18 *I DON'T WANT TO SEE YOU AGAIN*
    (S) (1:59) Rhino 70320 History Of British Rock Volume 2.
    (S) (1:59) Rhino 72022 History Of British Rock Box Set.
    (S) (1:59) Rhino 72008 History Of British Rock Volumes 1-4 Box Set.
    (S) (1:59) Rhino 70748 Best Of.

1965 #6 *I GO TO PIECES*
    (S) (2:21) Rhino 70321 History Of British Rock Volume 3.
    (S) (2:21) Rhino 72022 History Of British Rock Box Set.
    (S) (2:21) Rhino 72008 History Of British Rock Volumes 1-4 Box Set.
    (S) (2:20) Rhino 70748 Best Of.

1965 #13 *TRUE LOVE WAYS*
    (S) (2:37) Rhino 70321 History Of British Rock Volume 3.
    (S) (2:37) Rhino 72022 History Of British Rock Box Set.
    (S) (2:37) Rhino 72008 History Of British Rock Volumes 1-4 Box Set.
    (S) (2:37) Rhino 70748 Best Of.

1965 #25 *TO KNOW YOU IS TO LOVE YOU*
    (S) (2:35) Rhino 70320 History Of British Rock Volume 2.
    (S) (2:35) Rhino 72022 History Of British Rock Box Set.
    (S) (2:35) Rhino 72008 History Of British Rock Volumes 1-4 Box Set.
    (S) (2:34) Rhino 70748 Best Of.

1966 #17 *WOMAN*
    (M) (2:27) Rhino 70322 History Of British Rock Volume 4.
    (M) (2:27) Rhino 72022 History Of British Rock Box Set.
    (M) (2:27) Rhino 72008 History Of British Rock Volumes 1-4 Box Set.
    (M) (2:25) Rhino 70748 Best Of.

1966 #5 *LADY GODIVA*
    (S) (2:24) Rhino 70322 History Of British Rock Volume 4.
    (S) (2:24) Rhino 72022 History Of British Rock Box Set.
    (S) (2:24) Rhino 72008 History Of British Rock Volumes 1-4 Box Set.
    (S) (2:24) Rhino 70748 Best Of.

1967 #13 *KNIGHT IN RUSTY ARMOUR*
    (M) (2:36) Rhino 70326 History Of British Rock Volume 8. *(45 version)*
    (M) (2:36) Rhino 72022 History Of British Rock Box Set. *(45 version)*
    (S) (2:36) Rhino 70748 Best Of. *(LP version)*

1967 #22 *SUNDAY FOR TEA*
    (S) (2:19) Rhino 70748 Best Of.

PETER, PAUL & MARY
1962 #13 *IF I HAD A HAMMER*
    (S) (2:09) Warner Brothers 1449 Peter, Paul & Mary. *(LP version)*
    (S) (2:09) Warner Brothers 3105 Best Of/Ten Years Together. *(LP version)*

1963 #2 *PUFF THE MAGIC DRAGON*
    (S) (3:36) Warner Brothers 1785 Peter, Paul And Mommy. *(rerecording)*
    (S) (3:26) Warner Brothers 1473 Moving.
    (S) (3:26) Warner Brothers 3105 Best Of/Ten Years Together.

1963 #2 *BLOWIN' IN THE WIND*
    (S) (2:55) Warner Brothers 26224 In The Wind.
    (S) (2:55) Warner Brothers 3105 Best Of/Ten Years Together.

PETER, PAUL & MARY (Continued)
1963 #15 DON'T THINK TWICE, IT'S ALL RIGHT
    (S) (3:12) Warner Brothers 26224 In The Wind.
    (S) (3:12) Warner Brothers 3105 Best Of/Ten Years Together.
1964 #38 STEWBALL
    (S) (3:08) Warner Brothers 26224 In The Wind.
    (S) (3:08) Warner Brothers 3105 Best Of/Ten Years Together.
1964 #31 TELL IT ON THE MOUNTAIN
    (S) (2:54) Warner Brothers 26224 In The Wind.
1965 #25 FOR LOVIN' ME
    (S) (2:07) Warner Brothers 26225 A Song Will Rise.
    (S) (2:07) Warner Brothers 3105 Best Of/Ten Years Together.
1967 #11 I DIG ROCK AND ROLL MUSIC
    (S) (2:29) Warner Brothers 1700 Album 1700.
    (S) (2:30) Warner Brothers 3105 Best Of/Ten Years Together.
1969 #20 DAY IS DONE
    (S) (3:12) Warner Brothers 1785 Peter, Paul And Mommy. *(LP version)*
    (S) (3:20) Warner Brothers 3105 Best Of/Ten Years Together. *(45 version)*
1969 #1 LEAVING ON A JET PLANE
    (S) (3:26) Warner Brothers 1700 Album 1700.
    (S) (3:26) Warner Brothers 3105 Best Of/Ten Years Together.

PAUL PETERSON
1962 #32 SHE CAN'T FIND HER KEYS
1963 #6 MY DAD

RAY PETERSON
1959 #19 THE WONDER OF YOU
    (M) (2:34) RCA 8467 Nipper's Greatest Hits Of The 50's Volume 2.
1960 #5 TELL LAURA I LOVE HER
    (S) (2:54) RCA 8474 Nipper's Greatest Hits Of The 60's Volume 1.
1961 #7 CORINNA, CORINNA
    (M) (2:39) Abkco 7118 Phil Spector/Back To Mono (1958-1969).
1961 #27 MISSING YOU

NORMAN PETTY TRIO
1957 #18 ALMOST PARADISE

PETS
1958 #18 CHA-HUA-HUA

JOHN PHILLIPS
1970 #37 MISSISSIPPI
    (S) (3:33) MCA 10195 Creeque Alley/History Of The Mama's & Papa's.

LITTLE ESTHER PHILLIPS
1962 #8 RELEASE ME
    (S) (3:16) Rhino 70648 Billboard's Top R&B Hits Of 1962.
    (M) (3:16) Atlantic 81297 Atlantic Rhythm & Blues Volume 5.
    (S) (3:16) Atlantic 82305 Atlantic Rhythm And Blues 1947-1974 Box Set.

PHIL PHILLIPS WITH THE TWILIGHTS
1959 #2 SEA OF LOVE
    (M) (2:20) Mercury 842170 O.S.T. Sea Of Love.
    (M) (2:20) Rhino 70645 Billboard's Top R&B Hits Of 1959.
    (M) (2:20) Mercury 832041 45's On CD Volume 1.
    (M) (2:20) Garland 012 Remember When.
    (M) (2:19) Essex 7053 A Hot Summer Night In '59.

BOBBY "BORIS" PICKETT

1962 #1 *MONSTER MASH*

 (S) (3:10) Rhino 71492 Elvira Presents Haunted Hits.
 (S) (3:10) Rhino 75768 Dr. Demento Presents.
 (S) (3:10) Dunhill Compact Classics 050 Monster Rock 'N Roll Show.
 (S) (3:10) Rhino 70743 Dr. Demento 20th Anniversary Collection.
 (S) (3:09) Rhino 70535 Halloween Hits.
 (S) (3:11) Deram 844147 The Original Monster Mash.

1962 #29 *MONSTER'S HOLIDAY*

 (M) (3:07) Rhino 70192 Christmas Classics.
 (M) (3:08) Deram 844147 The Original Monster Mash.

1973 #10 *MONSTER MASH*

 (this song was a hit in 1962 and 1973; see 1962 listings)

WILSON PICKETT

1963 #31 *IT'S TOO LATE*

 (M) (3:05) Atlantic 81737 Greatest Hits.
 (M) (3:07) Rhino 70287 A Man And A Half.

1965 #22 *IN THE MIDNIGHT HOUR*

 (E) (2:29) JCI 3100 Dance Sixties.
 (E) (2:26) Atlantic 81297 Atlantic Rhythm & Blues Volume 5.
 (E) (2:29) Warner Special Products 27601 Atlantic Soul Classics.
 (M) (2:32) Atco 91813 Classic Recordings.
 (M) (2:35) Atlantic 81737 Greatest Hits. *(missing the opening drum roll; :06 longer than 45 or LP)*
 (E) (2:26) Atlantic 81283 Best Of.
 (M) (2:36) Atlantic 82305 Atlantic Rhythm And Blues 1947-1974 Box Set. *(:07 longer than 45 or LP)*
 (M) (2:31) Rhino 70287 A Man And A Half.
 (S) (8:09) Rhino 70287 A Man And A Half. *(live)*

1966 #9 *634-5789 (SOULSVILLE U.S.A.)*

 (M) (2:54) Rhino 70652 Billboard's Top R&B Hits Of 1966.
 (M) (2:54) Rhino 72006 Billboard's Top R&B Hits 1965-1969 Box Set.
 (M) (2:55) Warner Special Products 27609 Memphis Soul Classics.
 (M) (2:55) Atlantic 81737 Greatest Hits.
 (M) (2:55) Atlantic 81283 Best Of.
 (M) (2:55) Atlantic 82305 Atlantic Rhythm And Blues 1947-1974 Box Set.
 (M) (2:56) Rhino 70287 A Man And A Half.

1966 #9 *LAND OF 1000 DANCES*

 (M) (2:25) Atlantic 81298 Atlantic Rhythm & Blues Volume 6.
 (M) (2:25) Warner Special Products 27602 20 Party Classics.
 (M) (2:23) Atlantic 81737 Greatest Hits.
 (M) (2:23) Atlantic 81283 Best Of.
 (M) (2:23) Atlantic 82305 Atlantic Rhythm And Blues 1947-1974 Box Set.
 (M) (2:24) Rhino 70287 A Man And A Half.

1966 #16 *MUSTANG SALLY*

 (M) (3:04) Atlantic 81298 Atlantic Rhythm & Blues Volume 6.
 (E) (3:04) JCI 3105 Soul Sixties. *(sounds awful)*
 (M) (3:05) Atco 91813 Classic Recordings.
 (M) (3:04) Atlantic 81737 Greatest Hits.
 (M) (3:04) Atlantic 81283 Best Of.
 (M) (3:04) Atlantic 82305 Atlantic Rhythm And Blues 1947-1974 Box Set.
 (M) (3:05) Rhino 70287 A Man And A Half.

WILSON PICKETT (Continued)

1967 #40 EVERYBODY NEEDS SOMEBODY TO LOVE
- (M) (2:16) Atlantic 81737 Greatest Hits.
- (M) (2:16) Atlantic 81283 Best Of.
- (M) (2:17) Rhino 70287 A Man And A Half.

1967 #38 I FOUND A LOVE (PART 1)
- (M) (2:54) Atlantic 81283 Best Of. *(mastered from vinyl; not the hit recording but a different song released in 1963 when Wilson Pickett sang with the Falcons)*
- (M) (2:54) Atlantic 81737 Greatest Hits. *(same comments as for Atlantic 81283)*

1967 #10 FUNKY BROADWAY
- (M) (2:31) Atlantic 81298 Atlantic Rhythm & Blues Volume 6.
- (S) (2:33) Atlantic 81737 Greatest Hits.
- (S) (2:33) Atlantic 81283 Best Of.
- (S) (2:33) Atlantic 82305 Atlantic Rhythm And Blues 1947-1974 Box Set.
- (M) (2:35) Rhino 70287 A Man And A Half.

1967 #17 STAG-O-LEE
- (S) (2:20) Rhino 70287 A Man And A Half.

1968 #40 I'M IN LOVE
- (S) (2:27) Atlantic 81298 Atlantic Rhythm & Blues Volume 6.
- (S) (2:27) Atlantic 81737 Greatest Hits.
- (S) (2:27) Atlantic 81283 Best Of.
- (S) (2:27) Atlantic 82305 Atlantic Rhythm And Blues 1947-1974 Box Set.
- (S) (2:29) Rhino 70287 A Man And A Half.

1968 #23 SHE'S LOOKIN' GOOD
- (M) (2:19) Atlantic 81737 Greatest Hits.
- (S) (2:26) Rhino 70287 A Man And A Half.

1968 #23 I'M A MIDNIGHT MOVER
- (S) (2:23) Atlantic 81737 Greatest Hits.
- (S) (2:23) Atlantic 81283 Best Of.
- (S) (2:23) Rhino 70287 A Man And A Half.

1969 #20 HEY JUDE
- (S) (4:03) Atlantic 81737 Greatest Hits.
- (S) (4:05) Rhino 70287 A Man And A Half.

1969 #40 HEY JOE
- (S) (3:02) Rhino 70287 A Man And A Half. *(truncated fade)*

1970 #16 SUGAR SUGAR
- (S) (2:55) Atlantic 81737 Greatest Hits.
- (S) (2:55) Rhino 70287 A Man And A Half.

1970 #14 ENGINE NUMBER 9
(LP title is "GET ME BACK ON TIME, ENGINE NUMBER 9")
- (S) (6:24) Rhino 70287 A Man And A Half. *(LP version)*

1971 #40 DON'T LET THE GREEN GRASS FOOL YOU
- (S) (2:45) Atlantic 81912 Golden Age Of Black Music (1970-1975).
- (S) (2:45) Atlantic 81737 Greatest Hits.
- (S) (3:03) Rhino 70287 A Man And A Half. *(includes :16 studio talk)*

1971 #7 DON'T KNOCK MY LOVE (PART 1)
- (S) (2:21) Atlantic 81912 Golden Age Of Black Music (1970-1975).
- (S) (2:20) Atlantic 81737 Greatest Hits.
- (S) (2:20) Atlantic 82305 Atlantic Rhythm And Blues 1947-1974 Box Set.
- (S) (2:15) Rhino 70287 A Man And A Half.

WILSON PICKETT (Continued)
1972 #17 FIRE AND WATER
>> (S) (3:29) Rhino 70287 A Man And A Half. (*tracks into the next selection which is "(YOUR LOVE HAS BROUGHT ME) A MIGHTY LONG WAY," just like the vinyl LP did*)

PICKETTYWITCH
1970 #40 THAT SAME OLD FEELING

WEBB PIERCE
1959 #25 I AIN'T NEVER
>> (S) (1:52) MCA 5939 Vintage Music Volumes 17 & 18.
>> (S) (1:52) MCA 31215 Vintage Music Volume 18.
>> (S) (1:53) Rhino 70680 Billboard Top Country Hits Of 1959.
>> (S) (1:53) MCA 2-8025 30 Years Of Hits 1958 - 1974.

PINK FLOYD
1973 #10 MONEY
>> (S) (6:24) Capitol 46001 Dark Side Of The Moon. (*LP version; tracks into next selection*)
>> (S) (6:22) Capitol 96647 Hearts Of Gold - The Classic Rock Collection. (*LP version*)
>> (S) (6:22) MFSL 517 Dark Side Of The Moon. (*LP version; tracks into next selection*)

PIPKINS
1970 #7 GIMME DAT DING
>> (S) (2:10) Rhino 70926 Super Hits Of The 70's Volume 6.

PIPS (see GLADYS KNIGHT & THE PIPS)

GENE PITNEY
1961 #31 (I WANNA) LOVE MY LIFE AWAY
>> (M) (1:52) Rhino 75896 Anthology.
>> (M) (1:52) Collectables 5084 His Golden Classics.
1961 #34 EVERY BREATH I TAKE
>> (M) (2:39) Garland 012 Remember When.
>> (M) (2:44) Rhino 75896 Anthology.
>> (M) (2:42) Abkco 7118 Phil Spector/Back To Mono (1958-1969).
>> (M) (2:44) Collectables 5084 His Golden Classics.
1962 #11 TOWN WITHOUT PITY
>> (M) (2:51) MCA 6228 O.S.T. Hairspray.
>> (M) (2:53) Rhino 75896 Anthology.
>> (M) (2:52) Collectables 5084 His Golden Classics.
1962 #8 (THE MAN WHO SHOT) LIBERTY VALANCE
>> (S) (2:55) Rhino 75896 Anthology.
>> (S) (2:55) Collectables 5084 His Golden Classics.
1962 #5 ONLY LOVE CAN BREAK A HEART
>> (S) (2:48) JCI 3102 Love Sixties.
>> (S) (2:49) Rhino 75896 Anthology.
>> (S) (2:49) Collectables 5084 His Golden Classics.
1963 #14 HALF HEAVEN — HALF HEARTACHE
>> (S) (2:42) Rhino 75896 Anthology.
>> (S) (2:42) Collectables 5084 His Golden Classics.
1963 #13 MECCA
>> (S) (2:19) Rhino 75896 Anthology.
>> (S) (2:19) Collectables 5084 His Golden Classics.

GENE PITNEY (Continued)

1963 #30 TRUE LOVE NEVER RUNS SMOOTH
    (S) (2:24) Rhino 75896 Anthology.
    (S) (2:24) Collectables 5084 His Golden Classics.

1963 #18 TWENTY FOUR HOURS FROM TULSA
    (S) (2:57) Rhino 75896 Anthology.
    (S) (2:57) Collectables 5084 His Golden Classics.

1964 #7 IT HURTS TO BE IN LOVE
    (M) (2:31) Garland 012 Remember When.
    (M) (2:31) Rhino 75896 Anthology. *(truncated fade)*
    (M) (2:31) Collectables 5084 His Golden Classics.

1964 #11 I'M GONNA BE STRONG
    (S) (2:12) Rhino 75896 Anthology.
    (S) (2:12) Collectables 5084 His Golden Classics.

1965 #26 I MUST BE SEEING THINGS

1965 #16 LAST CHANCE TO TURN AROUND
    (S) (3:04) Rhino 75896 Anthology.

1965 #23 LOOKING THROUGH THE EYES OF LOVE
    (S) (3:14) Rhino 75896 Anthology. *(truncated fade)*

1965 #34 PRINCESS IN RAGS

1966 #24 BACKSTAGE

1968 #16 SHE'S A HEARTBREAKER
    (S) (3:15) Rhino 75896 Anthology.
    (S) (3:15) Collectables 5084 His Golden Classics.

PLASTIC ONO BAND (see JOHN LENNON)

EDDIE PLATT & HIS ORCHESTRA

1958 #18 CHA-HUA-HUA

PLATTERS

1955 #3 ONLY YOU (AND YOU ALONE)
    (M) (2:36) Rhino 70598 Billboard's Top Rock & Roll Hits Of 1955.
    (M) (2:36) Mercury 826448 Oldies Golden Million Sellers.
    (M) (2:34) JCI 3203 Lovin' Fifties.
    (M) (2:36) Mercury 826447 Golden Hits.
    (M) (2:36) Mercury 510317 Very Best Of.
    (M) (2:36) Mercury 510314 The Magic Touch: An Anthology.

1956 #1 THE GREAT PRETENDER
    (M) (2:37) Rhino 70642 Billboard's Top R&B Hits Of 1956.
    (M) (2:36) Mercury 826447 Golden Hits.
    (M) (2:37) Mercury 510317 Very Best Of.
    (M) (2:37) Mercury 510314 The Magic Touch: An Anthology.
    (M) (2:37) Atlantic 82155 O.S.T. Book Of Love.

1956 #3 (YOU'VE GOT) THE MAGIC TOUCH
    (M) (2:25) Mercury 826447 Golden Hits.
    (M) (2:27) Mercury 510317 Very Best Of.
    (M) (2:27) Mercury 510314 The Magic Touch: An Anthology.

1956 #1 MY PRAYER
    (M) (2:44) Mercury 832041 45's On CD Volume 1.
    (M) (2:42) Mercury 826447 Golden Hits.
    (M) (2:44) Mercury 510317 Very Best Of.
    (M) (2:44) Mercury 510314 The Magic Touch: An Anthology.

1956 #14 YOU'LL NEVER NEVER KNOW
    (S) (1:54) Mercury 830773 More Golden Hits. *(this is not the song "YOU'LL NEVER NEVER KNOW" as the cd jacket states but a similarly titled song, "YOU'LL NEVER KNOW")*

PLATTERS (Continued)

(M) (2:37) Mercury 826447 Golden Hits.
(M) (2:37) Mercury 510317 Very Best Of.
(M) (2:37) Mercury 510314 The Magic Touch: An Anthology.

1956 #14 IT ISN'T RIGHT
(M) (2:24) Mercury 830773 More Golden Hits.
(M) (2:24) Mercury 510314 The Magic Touch: An Anthology.

1957 #24 ON MY WORD OF HONOR
(M) (2:41) Mercury 510317 Very Best Of.
(M) (2:41) Mercury 510314 The Magic Touch: An Anthology.

1957 #36 ONE IN A MILLION
(M) (2:52) Mercury 830773 More Golden Hits.
(M) (2:52) Mercury 510314 The Magic Touch: An Anthology.

1957 #15 I'M SORRY
(E) (2:52) Mercury 830773 More Golden Hits.
(M) (2:51) Mercury 510317 Very Best Of.
(M) (2:51) Mercury 510314 The Magic Touch: An Anthology.

1957 #31 HE'S MINE
(M) (2:21) Mercury 510314 The Magic Touch: An Anthology.

1957 #22 MY DREAM
(E) (2:37) Mercury 830773 More Golden Hits.
(M) (2:36) Mercury 510314 The Magic Touch: An Anthology.

1958 #38 HELPLESS
(S) (2:40) Mercury 830773 More Golden Hits.
(S) (2:39) Mercury 510314 The Magic Touch: An Anthology.

1958 #1 TWILIGHT TIME
(M) (2:43) Mercury 826447 Golden Hits. *(45 lyrics)*
(S) (2:44) Mercury 510317 Very Best Of. *(LP lyrics)*
(S) (2:44) Mercury 510314 The Magic Touch: An Anthology. *(LP lyrics)*

1958 #32 YOU'RE MAKING A MISTAKE
(M) (2:44) Mercury 510314 The Magic Touch: An Anthology.

1958 #34 I WISH
(S) (2:44) Mercury 830773 More Golden Hits.
(S) (2:41) Mercury 510314 The Magic Touch: An Anthology.

1959 #1 SMOKE GETS IN YOUR EYES
(M) (2:38) Mercury 826448 Oldies Golden Million Sellers.
(M) (2:38) Mercury 826447 Golden Hits.
(S) (2:37) Mercury 510317 Very Best Of. *(very poor stereo separation)*
(S) (2:36) Mercury 510314 The Magic Touch: An Anthology. *(very poor stereo separation)*

1959 #12 ENCHANTED
(E) (2:52) Mercury 830773 More Golden Hits.
(S) (2:51) Mercury 510317 Very Best Of. *(very poor stereo separation)*
(S) (2:51) Mercury 510314 The Magic Touch: An Anthology. *(very poor stereo separation)*

1959 #26 REMEMBER WHEN
(S) (2:47) Mercury 830773 More Golden Hits.
(M) (2:47) Mercury 510314 The Magic Touch: An Anthology.

1959 #38 WHERE
(M) (2:40) Mercury 510314 The Magic Touch: An Anthology.

1960 #7 HARBOR LIGHTS
(E) (3:06) Mercury 826447 Golden Hits. *(LP version)*
(S) (3:09) Mercury 510317 Very Best Of. *(LP version)*
(S) (3:09) Mercury 510314 The Magic Touch: An Anthology. *(LP version)*

271

PLATTERS (Continued)

1960 #38 EBB TIDE
- (M) (2:22) Mercury 826447 Golden Hits.
- (S) (2:24) Mercury 510314 The Magic Touch: An Anthology. *(very poor stereo separation)*

1960 #27 RED SAILS IN THE SUNSET
- (E) (2:23) Mercury 826447 Golden Hits.
- (S) (2:20) Mercury 510314 The Magic Touch: An Anthology. *(very poor stereo separation)*

1960 #14 TO EACH HIS OWN
- (S) (2:48) Mercury 830773 More Golden Hits.
- (S) (2:47) Mercury 510314 The Magic Touch: An Anthology. *(very poor stereo separation)*

1961 #35 IF I DIDN'T CARE
- (S) (3:06) Mercury 830773 More Golden Hits.
- (S) (3:07) Mercury 510317 Very Best Of.
- (S) (3:06) Mercury 510314 The Magic Touch: An Anthology.

1961 #32 I'LL NEVER SMILE AGAIN
- (S) (2:51) Mercury 830773 More Golden Hits.
- (S) (2:51) Mercury 510314 The Magic Touch: An Anthology. *(very poor stereo separation)*

1966 #35 I LOVE YOU 1000 TIMES
1967 #19 WITH THIS RING
- (S) (2:41) Rhino 70589 Rockin' & Rollin' Wedding Songs Volume 2.

PLAYBOYS

1958 #29 OVER THE WEEKEND

PLAYMATES

1958 #19 JO-ANN
- (M) (2:34) Collectables 5418 Golden Classics.

1958 #23 DON'T GO HOME
- (M) (2:33) Collectables 5418 Golden Classics.

1958 #4 BEEP BEEP
- (S) (2:42) Rhino 70743 Dr. Demento 20th Anniversary Collection. *(45 version)*
- (S) (3:04) Collectables 5416 Murray The K - Sing Along With The Golden Gassers. *(LP version)*
- (S) (3:04) Collectables 5418 Golden Classics. *(LP version)*

1959 #15 WHAT IS LOVE?
- (S) (2:16) Collectables 5418 Golden Classics.
- (M) (2:11) Essex 7053 A Hot Summer Night In '59.

1960 #28 WAIT FOR ME
- (S) (2:49) Collectables 5418 Golden Classics.

POETS

1966 #38 SHE BLEW A GOOD THING

POINTER SISTERS

1973 #10 YES WE CAN CAN
- (S) (3:05) Rhino 70551 Soul Hits Of The 70's Volume 11.
- (S) (5:59) MCA 31377 The Pointer Sisters. *(LP version)*

PONI TAILS

1957 #35 YOUR WILD HEART
1958 #10 BORN TOO LATE
- (S) (2:17) MCA 31201 Vintage Music Volume 4.
- (S) (2:17) MCA 5778 Vintage Music Volumes 3 & 4.

PONI TAILS (Continued)
>   (S)   (2:17)   Curb 77354   50's Hits Volume 1.
>   (S)   (2:16)   Curb 77525   Greatest Hits Of Rock 'N' Roll Volume 2.

POPPY FAMILY
1970 #2 *WHICH WAY YOU GOIN' BILLY?*
>   *(the actual 45 time is (3:25) not (3:10) as stated on the record label)*
>   (S)   (3:20)   Rhino 70922   Super Hits Of The 70's Volume 2. *(LP length)*
>   (S)   (3:20)   Rhino 72009   Super Hits Of The 70's Volumes 1-4 Box Set. *(LP length)*

1970 #20 *THAT'S WHERE I WENT WRONG*

SANDY POSEY
1966 #12 *BORN A WOMAN*
1967 #13 *SINGLE GIRL*
1967 #39 *WHAT A WOMAN IN LOVE WON'T DO*
1967 #17 *I TAKE IT BACK*

FRANK POURCEL
1959 #8 *ONLY YOU*
>   (M)   (2:29)   Capitol 98670   Memories Are Made Of This.

JANE POWELL
1956 #4 *TRUE LOVE*

JOEY POWERS
1964 #10 *MIDNIGHT MARY*
>   (M)   (2:24)   Rhino 70995   One Hit Wonders Of The 60's Volume 1. *(alternate take)*

PEREZ PRADO
1955 #1 *CHERRY PINK AND APPLE BLOSSOM WHITE*
>   (M)   (3:01)   RCA 8466   Nipper's Greatest Hits Of The 50's Volume 1.
1958 #1 *PATRICIA*
>   (S)   (2:19)   RCA 8467   Nipper's Greatest Hits Of The 50's Volume 2.
1958 #18 *GUAGLIONE*

PREMIERS
1964 #19 *FARMER JOHN*
>   (S)   (2:32)   Warner Special Projects 27610   More Party Classics. *(includes :20 LP introduction)*
>   (M)   (2:12)   Rhino 75772   Son Of Frat Rock.

PRESIDENTS
1970 #7 *5-10-15-20 (25-30 YEARS OF LOVE)*
>   (S)   (3:07)   Rhino 70783   Soul Hits Of The 70's Volume 3. *(sounds like it is mastered from vinyl)*

ELVIS PRESLEY
1956 #1 *HEARTBREAK HOTEL*
>   (M)   (2:06)   RCA 8466   Nipper's Greatest Hits Of The 50's Volume 1.
>   (M)   (2:06)   RCA 8533   O.S.T. Heartbreak Hotel.
>   (M)   (2:06)   RCA 6383   The Top Ten Hits.
>   (M)   (2:05)   RCA 6382   The Number One Hits.
>   (M)   (2:06)   RCA 6401   50 Worldwide Gold Award Hits.
>   (E)   (2:08)   RCA 2227   The Great Performances.
>   (S)   (1:57)   RCA 3114   Collectors Gold. *(live)*
>   (M)   (2:06)   RCA 5196   Elvis' Golden Records.
>   (M)   (2:05)   RCA 2079   Heartbreak Hotel, Hound Dog & Other Top Ten Hits.
>   (M)   (2:05)   Pair 1251   Great Performances.
>   (M)   (2:05)   Special Music 2705   A Legendary Performer Volume 1.

ELVIS PRESLEY (Continued)

    (M) (2:07) RCA 66050 The Complete 50's Masters.
    (M) (2:33) RCA 66050 The Complete 50's Masters. *(live; includes :35 introduction)*

1956 #4 *I WANT YOU, I NEED YOU, I LOVE YOU*

    (M) (2:36) RCA 6383 The Top Ten Hits.
    (M) (2:36) RCA 6382 The Number One Hits.
    (M) (2:36) RCA 6401 50 Worldwide Gold Award Hits.
    (M) (2:38) RCA 5196 Elvis' Golden Records.
    (M) (2:40) Pair 1251 Great Performances. *(alternate take)*
    (M) (2:40) Special Music 2706 A Legendary Performer Volume 2. *(alternate take)*
    (M) (2:39) RCA 66050 The Complete 50's Masters.
    (M) (2:39) RCA 66050 The Complete 50's Masters. *(alternate take)*

1956 #1 *DON'T BE CRUEL*

    (M) (2:02) RCA 53732 Pure Gold.
    (M) (2:01) Rhino 70599 Billboard's Top Rock & Roll Hits Of 1956.
    (E) (2:03) Elektra 60107 O.S.T. Diner.
    (M) (2:01) RCA 8467 Nipper's Greatest Hits Of The 50's Volume 2.
    (M) (2:01) RCA 6383 The Top Ten Hits.
    (M) (2:00) RCA 6382 The Number One Hits.
    (M) (2:01) RCA 6401 50 Worldwide Gold Award Hits.
    (M) (2:02) RCA 2227 The Great Performances.
    (M) (2:02) RCA 5196 Elvis' Golden Records.
    (M) (2:00) RCA 2079 Heartbreak Hotel, Hound Dog & Other Top Ten Hits.
    (M) (2:00) Pair 1251 Great Performances.
    (M) (2:00) Special Music 2705 A Legendary Performer Volume 1.
    (M) (2:00) RCA 66050 The Complete 50's Masters.

1956 #1 *HOUND DOG*

    (M) (2:16) Rhino 70599 Billboard's Top Rock & Roll Hits Of 1956.
    (M) (2:14) RCA 6383 The Top Ten Hits.
    (M) (2:14) RCA 6382 The Number One Hits.
    (M) (2:14) RCA 6401 50 Worldwide Gold Award Hits.
    (M) (2:14) RCA 5182 Rocker.
    (S) (0:58) RCA 6985 The Alternate Aloha. *(all selections on this cd are live)*
    (M) (2:14) RCA 5196 Elvis' Golden Records.
    (M) (2:13) RCA 3026 Sings Leiber & Stoller.
    (M) (2:14) RCA 2079 Heartbreak Hotel, Hound Dog & Other Top Ten Hits.
    (M) (2:14) RCA 66050 The Complete 50's Masters.

1956 #1 *LOVE ME TENDER*

    (M) (2:40) RCA 53732 Pure Gold.
    (M) (2:44) RCA 6383 The Top Ten Hits.
    (M) (2:43) RCA 6382 The Number One Hits.
    (M) (2:43) RCA 6401 50 Worldwide Gold Award Hits.
    (M) (2:40) RCA 6738 Essential Elvis.
    (M) (1:11) RCA 6738 Essential Elvis. *(alternate take)*
    (S) (3:14) RCA 3114 Collectors Gold. *(live)*
    (M) (2:44) RCA 5196 Elvis' Golden Records.
    (M) (2:43) RCA 2079 Heartbreak Hotel, Hound Dog & Other Top Ten Hits.
    (M) (2:43) Pair 1251 Great Performances.
    (M) (2:43) Special Music 2705 A Legendary Performer Volume 1.
    (M) (2:40) RCA 66050 The Complete 50's Masters.

1956 #10 *LOVE ME*

    (M) (2:41) Rhino 70593 The Rock 'N' Roll Classics Of Leiber & Stoller.
    (M) (2:41) RCA 6383 The Top Ten Hits.
    (M) (2:42) RCA 5199 Elvis.

ELVIS PRESLEY (Continued)

    (S) (1:42) RCA 6985 The Alternate Aloha. *(all selections on this cd are live)*
    (M) (2:42) RCA 5196 Elvis' Golden Records.
    (M) (2:41) RCA 3026 Sings Leiber & Stoller.
    (M) (2:42) RCA 66050 The Complete 50's Masters.

1957 #1 TOO MUCH

    (M) (2:30) RCA 6383 The Top Ten Hits.
    (M) (2:30) RCA 6382 The Number One Hits.
    (M) (2:30) RCA 6401 50 Worldwide Gold Award Hits.
    (M) (2:31) RCA 5196 Elvis' Golden Records.
    (M) (2:30) RCA 66050 The Complete 50's Masters.

1957 #33 PLAYING FOR KEEPS

    (M) (2:48) RCA 6401 50 Worldwide Gold Award Hits.
    (M) (2:51) RCA 1990 For LP Fans Only.
    (M) (2:49) RCA 5353 A Valentine Gift For You.
    (M) (2:49) RCA 66050 The Complete 50's Masters.

1957 #1 ALL SHOOK UP

    (M) (1:56) RCA 53732 Pure Gold.
    (M) (1:56) Rhino 70618 Billboard's Top Rock & Roll Hits Of 1957.
    (M) (1:56) Rhino 72004 Billboard's Top Rock & Roll Hits 1957-1961 Box Set.
    (M) (1:56) RCA 6383 The Top Ten Hits.
    (M) (1:56) RCA 6382 The Number One Hits.
    (M) (1:56) RCA 6401 50 Worldwide Gold Award Hits.
    (M) (1:57) RCA 5196 Elvis' Golden Records.
    (M) (1:56) RCA 9589 Stereo '57/Essential Elvis Volume 2.
    (M) (1:57) RCA 61144 The RCA Records Label: The First Note In Black Music.
    (M) (1:56) RCA 66050 The Complete 50's Masters.

1957 #32 (THERE'LL BE) PEACE IN THE VALLEY (FOR ME)

    (M) (1:40) RCA 9586 Elvis Gospel 1957-1971. *(mastered from vinyl; live)*
    (M) (3:20) RCA 3758 How Great Thou Art.
    (M) (3:20) Pair 1251 Great Performances.
    (M) (3:19) Special Music 2472 You'll Never Walk Alone.
    (M) (3:20) Special Music 2705 A Legendary Performer Volume 1.
    (M) (3:22) Pair 1010 Double Dynamite.
    (M) (3:19) RCA 66050 The Complete 50's Masters.

1957 #1 (LET ME BE YOUR) TEDDY BEAR

    (M) (1:47) RCA 6383 The Top Ten Hits.
    (M) (1:46) RCA 6382 The Number One Hits.
    (M) (1:47) RCA 6401 50 Worldwide Gold Award Hits.
    (M) (1:46) RCA 2227 The Great Performances.
    (M) (1:46) RCA 6738 Essential Elvis.
    (M) (1:46) RCA 1515 Loving You.
    (M) (1:47) RCA 5196 Elvis' Golden Records.
    (M) (1:46) RCA 2079 Heartbreak Hotel, Hound Dog & Other Top Ten Hits.
    (M) (1:45) Special Music 2704 Sings For Children.
    (M) (1:45) RCA 66050 The Complete 50's Masters.

1957 #21 LOVING YOU

    (M) (2:11) RCA 53732 Pure Gold.
    (M) (2:14) RCA 6401 50 Worldwide Gold Award Hits.
    (M) (2:12) RCA 6738 Essential Elvis. *(with :22 studio talk; alternate take)*
    (M) (2:07) RCA 6738 Essential Elvis. *(with :42 studio talk; alternate take)*
    (M) (1:45) RCA 6738 Essential Elvis. *(with :06 studio talk; alternate take)*
    (M) (1:51) RCA 6738 Essential Elvis. *(alternate take)*
    (M) (1:26) RCA 6738 Essential Elvis. *(alternate take)*

(M) (2:14) RCA 1515 Loving You.
(M) (2:15) RCA 5196 Elvis' Golden Records.
(M) (2:13) RCA 3026 Sings Leiber & Stoller.
(M) (2:15) Pair 1185 Forever.
(M) (2:11) RCA 66050 The Complete 50's Masters.
(M) (1:47) RCA 66050 The Complete 50's Masters. *(alternate take)*
(M) (1:24) RCA 66050 The Complete 50's Masters. *(alternate take)*

1957 #1 JAILHOUSE ROCK

(M) (2:26) RCA 53732 Pure Gold.
(M) (2:25) Rhino 70618 Billboard's Top Rock & Roll Hits Of 1957.
(M) (2:25) Rhino 72004 Billboard's Top Rock & Roll Hits 1957-1961 Box Set.
(M) (2:26) Rhino 70593 The Rock 'N' Roll Classics Of Leiber & Stoller.
(M) (2:27) RCA 6383 The Top Ten Hits.
(M) (2:25) RCA 6382 The Number One Hits.
(M) (2:26) RCA 6401 50 Worldwide Gold Award Hits.
(M) (2:25) RCA 5182 Rocker.
(M) (2:25) RCA 2227 The Great Performances.
(M) (2:35) RCA 6738 Essential Elvis. *(alternate take)*
(M) (1:56) RCA 6738 Essential Elvis. *(alternate take)*
(M) (2:25) RCA 5196 Elvis' Golden Records.
(M) (2:29) RCA 3026 Sings Leiber & Stoller.
(M) (2:23) RCA 2079 Heartbreak Hotel, Hound Dog & Other Top Ten Hits.
(M) (2:22) Pair 1251 Great Performances.
(M) (2:22) Special Music 2706 A Legendary Performer Volume 2.
(M) (2:26) RCA 66050 The Complete 50's Masters.

1958 #1 DON'T

(M) (2:47) RCA 6383 The Top Ten Hits.
(M) (2:47) RCA 6382 The Number One Hits.
(M) (2:48) RCA 6401 50 Worldwide Gold Award Hits.
(M) (2:49) RCA 5197 50,000,000 Elvis Fans Can't Be Wrong.
(M) (2:52) RCA 3026 Sings Leiber & Stoller. *(includes :05 of studio talk)*
(M) (2:47) RCA 66050 The Complete 50's Masters.

1958 #9 I BEG OF YOU

(M) (1:52) RCA 6383 The Top Ten Hits.
(M) (1:52) RCA 6401 50 Worldwide Gold Award Hits.
(M) (1:53) RCA 5197 50,000,000 Elvis Fans Can't Be Wrong.
(S) (2:08) RCA 9589 Stereo '57/Essential Elvis Volume 2. *(alternate take)*
(S) (2:46) RCA 9589 Stereo '57/Essential Elvis Volume 2. *(alternate take)*
(S) (1:59) RCA 9589 Stereo '57/Essential Elvis Volume 2. *(alternate take)*
(M) (1:50) RCA 66050 The Complete 50's Masters.
(M) (1:51) RCA 66050 The Complete 50's Masters. *(alternate take)*

1958 #4 WEAR MY RING AROUND YOUR NECK

(M) (2:13) RCA 6383 The Top Ten Hits. *(LP version)*
(M) (2:13) RCA 6401 50 Worldwide Gold Award Hits. *(LP version)*
(M) (2:14) RCA 5197 50,000,000 Elvis Fans Can't Be Wrong. *(LP version)*
(M) (2:13) RCA 2229 Hits Like Never Before/Essential Elvis Volume 3. *(LP version)*
(M) (2:13) RCA 2229 Hits Like Never Before/Essential Elvis Volume 3. *(45 version)*
(M) (2:13) RCA 66050 The Complete 50's Masters. *(45 version)*

1958 #3 HARD HEADED WOMAN

(M) (1:52) Rhino 70619 Billboard's Top Rock & Roll Hits Of 1958.
(M) (1:52) Rhino 72004 Billboard's Top Rock & Roll Hits 1957-1961 Box Set.

ELVIS PRESLEY (Continued)

    (M) (1:52) RCA 9902 Nipper's #1 Hits 1956-1986.
    (M) (1:52) RCA 6383 The Top Ten Hits.
    (M) (1:52) RCA 6382 The Number One Hits.
    (M) (1:52) RCA 6401 50 Worldwide Gold Award Hits.
    (M) (1:52) RCA 3733 King Creole.
    (M) (1:52) RCA 66050 The Complete 50's Masters.

1958 #20 KING CREOLE

    (M) (2:07) RCA 2227 The Great Performances.
    (M) (2:06) RCA 3733 King Creole.
    (M) (2:15) RCA 2229 Hits Like Never Before/Essential Elvis Volume 3.
              (alternate take)
    (M) (2:04) RCA 2229 Hits Like Never Before/Essential Elvis Volume 3.
              (alternate take; mastered from vinyl)
    (M) (1:39) RCA 2229 Hits Like Never Before/Essential Elvis Volume 3.
              (instrumental; mastered from vinyl)
    (M) (2:07) RCA 3026 Sings Leiber & Stoller.
    (M) (2:07) RCA 66050 The Complete 50's Masters.
    (M) (2:04) RCA 66050 The Complete 50's Masters. *(alternate take)*

1958 #3 ONE NIGHT

    (M) (2:30) RCA 8533 O.S.T. Heartbreak Hotel.
    (M) (2:30) RCA 6383 The Top Ten Hits.
    (M) (2:31) RCA 5197 50,000,000 Elvis Fans Can't Be Wrong.
    (M) (2:42) RCA 5418 Reconsider Baby. *(alternate take; :07 studio talk)*
    (M) (2:32) RCA 9965 Great American Vocalists.
    (M) (2:29) RCA 66050 The Complete 50's Masters.

1958 #5 I GOT STUNG

    (M) (1:48) RCA 6383 The Top Ten Hits.
    (M) (1:49) RCA 6401 50 Worldwide Gold Award Hits.
    (M) (1:50) RCA 5197 50,000,000 Elvis Fans Can't Be Wrong.
    (M) (1:30) RCA 2229 Hits Like Never Before/Essential Elvis Volume 3.
              (:06 studio talk; alternate take)
    (M) (2:00) RCA 2229 Hits Like Never Before/Essential Elvis Volume 3.
              (:09 false start; alternate take)
    (M) (1:49) RCA 2229 Hits Like Never Before/Essential Elvis Volume 3.
              (alternate take)
    (M) (1:49) RCA 66050 The Complete 50's Masters.

1959 #2 (NOW AND THEN THERE'S) A FOOL SUCH AS I

    (M) (2:28) RCA 6383 The Top Ten Hits.
    (M) (2:29) RCA 6401 50 Worldwide Gold Award Hits.
    (M) (2:30) RCA 5197 50,000,000 Elvis Fans Can't Be Wrong.
    (M) (2:38) RCA 2229 Hits Like Never Before/Essential Elvis Volume 3.
              (alternate take)
    (M) (2:36) RCA 66050 The Complete 50's Masters.

1959 #6 I NEED YOUR LOVE TONIGHT

    (M) (2:02) RCA 6383 The Top Ten Hits.
    (M) (2:03) RCA 5197 50,000,000 Elvis Fans Can't Be Wrong.
    (M) (2:07) RCA 2229 Hits Like Never Before/Essential Elvis Volume 3.
              (:08 false start; alternate take)
    (M) (1:57) RCA 2229 Hits Like Never Before/Essential Elvis Volume 3.
              (alternate take)
    (M) (2:03) RCA 66050 The Complete 50's Masters.

1959 #2 A BIG HUNK O' LOVE

    (M) (2:13) Rhino 70620 Billboard's Top Rock & Roll Hits Of 1959.
    (M) (2:13) Rhino 72004 Billboard's Top Rock & Roll Hits 1957-1961 Box
              Set.

ELVIS PRESLEY (Continued)

        (M) (2:10) RCA 6382   The Number One Hits.
        (M) (2:07) RCA 6401   50 Worldwide Gold Award Hits.
        (S) (2:34) RCA 6985   The Alternate Aloha. *(all selections on this cd are live)*
        (M) (2:05) RCA 5197   50,000,000 Elvis Fans Can't Be Wrong.
        (M) (2:16) RCA 2229   Hits Like Never Before/Essential Elvis Volume 3.
                                  (alternate take)
        (M) (2:11) RCA 8468   Elvis In Nashvillle.
        (M) (2:12) RCA 66050   The Complete 50's Masters.

1959 #23 MY WISH CAME TRUE

        (M) (2:35) RCA 5197   50,000,000 Elvis Fans Can't Be Wrong.
        (M) (2:33) RCA 66050   The Complete 50's Masters.

1960 #1 STUCK ON YOU

        (S) (2:14) Rhino 70621   Billboard's Top Rock & Roll Hits Of 1960.
        (S) (2:14) Rhino 72004   Billboard's Top Rock & Roll Hits 1957-1961 Box
                                  Set.
        (S) (2:15) RCA 6383   The Top Ten Hits.
        (S) (2:14) RCA 6382   The Number One Hits.
        (S) (2:18) RCA 6401   50 Worldwide Gold Award Hits.
        (S) (2:17) RCA 5600   Return Of The Rocker.
        (S) (2:17) RCA 2765   Elvis' Golden Records Volume 3.

1960 #40 FAME AND FORTUNE

        (S) (2:30) RCA 2227   The Great Performances.
        (S) (2:32) RCA 5353   A Valentine Gift For You.
        (S) (2:31) RCA 2765   Elvis' Golden Records Volume 3.

1960 #1 IT'S NOW OR NEVER

        (S) (3:13) Rhino 70621   Billboard's Top Rock & Roll Hits Of 1960.
        (S) (3:13) Rhino 72004   Billboard's Top Rock & Roll Hits 1957-1961 Box
                                  Set.
        (S) (3:15) RCA 8474   Nipper's Greatest Hits Of The 60's Volume 1.
        (S) (3:13) RCA 6383   The Top Ten Hits.
        (S) (3:13) RCA 6382   The Number One Hits.
        (S) (3:13) RCA 6401   50 Worldwide Gold Award Hits.
        (S) (3:16) RCA 2765   Elvis' Golden Records Volume 3.
        (M) (3:12) Pair 1251   Great Performances.
        (M) (3:12) Special Music 2706   A Legendary Performer Volume 2.

1960 #1 ARE YOU LONESOME TONIGHT?

        (S) (3:05) RCA 6383   The Top Ten Hits.
        (S) (3:05) RCA 6382   The Number One Hits.
        (S) (3:06) RCA 6401   50 Worldwide Gold Award Hits.
        (S) (3:07) RCA 5353   A Valentine Gift For You.
        (S) (3:03) RCA 2765   Elvis' Golden Records Volume 3.

1961 #1 SURRENDER

        (S) (1:50) RCA 6383   The Top Ten Hits.
        (S) (1:51) RCA 6382   The Number One Hits.
        (S) (1:50) RCA 6401   50 Worldwide Gold Award Hits.
        (S) (1:53) RCA 2765   Elvis' Golden Records Volume 3.

1961 #30 FLAMING STAR

1961 #5 I FEEL SO BAD

        (S) (2:50) RCA 6383   The Top Ten Hits.
        (S) (2:50) RCA 6401   50 Worldwide Gold Award Hits.
        (S) (2:51) RCA 5418   Reconsider Baby.
        (S) (2:51) RCA 2765   Elvis' Golden Records Volume 3.

ELVIS PRESLEY (Continued)

1961 #5 LITTLE SISTER
    (S) (2:28) RCA 6383 The Top Ten Hits.
    (S) (2:29) RCA 6401 50 Worldwide Gold Award Hits.
    (S) (2:29) RCA 5600 Return Of The Rocker.
    (S) (2:28) RCA 2765 Elvis' Golden Records Volume 3.

1961 #21 (MARIE'S THE NAME) HIS LATEST FLAME
    (S) (2:03) RCA 6383 The Top Ten Hits.
    (S) (2:04) RCA 5600 Return Of The Rocker.
    (S) (2:04) RCA 2765 Elvis' Golden Records Volume 3.

1962 #4 CAN'T HELP FALLING IN LOVE
    (S) (3:00) RCA 6383 The Top Ten Hits.
    (S) (3:00) RCA 6401 50 Worldwide Gold Award Hits.
    (S) (3:04) RCA 6985 The Alternate Aloha. *(all selections on this cd are live)*
    (S) (3:00) RCA 5353 A Valentine Gift For You.
    (S) (2:59) RCA 3683 O.S.T. Blue Hawaii.
    (S) (2:59) Pair 1251 Great Performances.
    (S) (2:58) Special Music 2705 A Legendary Performer Volume 1.

1962 #28 ROCK-A-HULA-BABY
    (S) (1:58) RCA 6401 50 Worldwide Gold Award Hits.
    (S) (1:58) RCA 3683 O.S.T. Blue Hawaii.

1962 #1 GOOD LUCK CHARM
    (S) (2:23) RCA 6383 The Top Ten Hits.
    (S) (2:23) RCA 6382 The Number One Hits.
    (S) (2:21) RCA 6401 50 Worldwide Gold Award Hits.
    (S) (2:20) RCA 2765 Elvis' Golden Records Volume 3.

1962 #18 FOLLOW THAT DREAM
    (E) (1:35) RCA 5600 Return Of The Rocker.
    (M) (1:37) Pair 1010 Double Dynamite.

1962 #4 SHE'S NOT YOU
    (S) (2:07) RCA 6383 The Top Ten Hits.
    (S) (2:07) RCA 6401 50 Worldwide Gold Award Hits.
    (S) (2:06) RCA 2765 Elvis' Golden Records Volume 3.

1962 #31 KID GALAHAD

1962 #1 RETURN TO SENDER
    (E) (2:06) RCA 6383 The Top Ten Hits.
    (E) (2:04) RCA 6401 50 Worldwide Gold Award Hits.
    (S) (2:06) RCA 2227 The Great Performances.
    (E) (2:08) RCA 5600 Return Of The Rocker.

1963 #10 ONE BROKEN HEART FOR SALE
    (E) (1:34) RCA 6401 50 Worldwide Gold Award Hits.
    (S) (2:20) RCA 3114 Collectors Gold. *(alternate take)*

1963 #3 (YOU'RE THE) DEVIL IN DISGUISE
    (E) (2:16) RCA 6383 The Top Ten Hits.
    (S) (2:19) RCA 1297 Elvis' Gold Records Volume 4.
    (E) (2:16) RCA 6401 50 Worldwide Gold Award Hits.
    (S) (2:19) RCA 61024 The Lost Album.

1963 #8 BOSSA NOVA BABY
    (S) (1:59) RCA 6383 The Top Ten Hits.
    (S) (1:59) RCA 6401 50 Worldwide Gold Award Hits.
    (S) (2:01) RCA 3026 Sings Leiber & Stoller.

ELVIS PRESLEY (Continued)

1963 #33 WITCHCRAFT
        (S)   (2:21)   RCA 1297   Elvis' Gold Records Volume 4.
        (S)   (2:18)   RCA 61024   The Lost Album.
        (S)   (2:30)   RCA 3114   Collectors Gold. *(alternate take)*
        (S)   (2:27)   RCA 5600   Return Of The Rocker.

1964 #10 KISSIN' COUSINS
        (S)   (2:11)   RCA 6401   50 Worldwide Gold Award Hits.

1964 #38 KISS ME QUICK
        (S)   (2:44)   RCA 2523   Pot Luck With Elvis.
        (S)   (2:46)   Pair 1037   Remembering.

1964 #13 WHAT'D I SAY
        (S)   (3:03)   RCA 1297   Elvis' Gold Records Volume 4.
        (S)   (5:43)   RCA 3114   Collectors Gold. *(live)*

1964 #16 VIVA LAS VEGAS
        (M)   (2:10)   RCA 6401   50 Worldwide Gold Award Hits.

1964 #16 SUCH A NIGHT
        (S)   (2:59)   RCA 2231   Elvis Is Back.
        (S)   (3:47)   Pair 1251   Great Performances. *(includes 2 false starts of :50)*
        (S)   (3:48)   Special Music 2706   A Legendary Performer Volume 2. *(includes 2 false starts of :50)*

1964 #10 ASK ME
        (S)   (2:05)   RCA 1297   Elvis' Gold Records Volume 4.
        (S)   (2:05)   RCA 61024   The Lost Album.
        (S)   (2:06)   RCA 3114   Collectors Gold. *(alternate take)*

1964 #13 AIN'T THAT LOVING YOU BABY
        (M)   (2:22)   RCA 1297   Elvis' Gold Records Volume 4.
        (M)   (2:21)   RCA 6401   50 Worldwide Gold Award Hits.
        (M)   (2:33)   RCA 5418   Reconsider Baby. *(alternate take)*
        (M)   (2:23)   RCA 2229   Hits Like Never Before / Essential Elvis Volume 3. *(alternate take)*
        (M)   (2:06)   RCA 2229   Hits Like Never Before / Essential Elvis Volume 3. *(:18 studio talk and false start; alternate take)*

1965 #16 DO THE CLAM

1965 #4 CRYING IN THE CHAPEL
        (M)   (2:22)   RCA 6383   The Top Ten Hits.
        (M)   (2:22)   RCA 6401   50 Worldwide Gold Award Hits.
        (M)   (2:22)   RCA 3758   How Great Thou Art.

1965 #14 (SUCH AN) EASY QUESTION
        (S)   (2:16)   RCA 2523   Pot Luck With Elvis.
        (S)   (2:19)   Pair 1037   Remembering.

1965 #9 I'M YOURS
        (S)   (2:20)   RCA 2523   Pot Luck With Elvis. *(LP version)*

1965 #15 PUPPET ON A STRING
        (S)   (2:38)   Special Music 2704   Sings For Children.

1966 #20 TELL ME WHY
        (M)   (2:08)   RCA 5353   A Valentine Gift For You.
        (M)   (2:08)   RCA 9589   Stereo '57 / Essential Elvis Volume 2.

1966 #19 FRANKIE AND JOHNNY
        (S)   (2:32)   Pair 1010   Double Dynamite.

1966 #19 LOVE LETTERS
        (S)   (2:49)   RCA 1297   Elvis' Gold Records Volume 4.
        (S)   (3:38)   RCA 3114   Collectors Gold. *(alternate take; includes :46 of false starts)*
        (S)   (2:51)   RCA 5353   A Valentine Gift For You.

ELVIS PRESLEY (Continued)

1966 #32 *SPINOUT*

1966 #39 *ALL THAT I AM*

1967 #26 *INDESCRIBABLY BLUE*
     (S) (2:47) RCA 1297 Elvis' Gold Records Volume 4.

1967 #35 *LONG LEGGED GIRL (WITH THE SHORT DRESS ON)*

1967 #35 *YOU DON'T KNOW ME*

1968 #39 *GUITAR MAN*
     (M) (2:14) RCA 8468 Elvis In Nashville.
     (S) (2:17) Pair 1250 Double Feature: Speedway/Clambake.

1968 #26 *U.S. MALE*
     (S) (2:41) Pair 1010 Double Dynamite.

1969 #9 *IF I CAN DREAM*
     (E) (3:07) RCA 8533 O.S.T. Heartbreak Hotel.
     (E) (3:07) RCA 6401 50 Worldwide Gold Award Hits.
     (S) (3:09) RCA 2227 The Great Performances.
     (E) (3:19) RCA 61021 NBC-TV Special. (*LP version which features ending audience applause*)
     (S) (3:10) RCA 4941 Gold Records Volume 5.
     (E) (3:15) Pair 1251 Great Performances. (*LP version which features ending audience applause*)
     (E) (3:15) Special Music 2706 A Legendary Performer Volume 2. (*LP version which features ending audience applause*)

1969 #24 *MEMORIES*
     (E) (2:19) RCA 2227 The Great Performances. (*highly edited*)
     (S) (2:43) RCA 3114 Collectors Gold. (*live; rerecording*)
     (E) (3:16) RCA 61021 NBC-TV Special. (*LP version which features audience applause on intro and ending*)

1969 #1 *IN THE GHETTO*
     (S) (2:46) RCA 53732 Pure Gold.
     (S) (2:43) RCA 6383 The Top Ten Hits.
     (E) (2:45) RCA 6401 50 Worldwide Gold Award Hits.
     (S) (2:45) RCA 6221 The Memphis Record.
     (S) (2:46) RCA 51456 From Elvis In Memphis.
     (S) (2:46) RCA 4941 Gold Records Volume 5.

1969 #25 *CLEAN UP YOUR OWN BACK YARD*
     (S) (3:09) RCA 4941 Gold Records Volume 5.

1969 #1 *SUSPICIOUS MINDS*
     (S) (4:16) RCA 9902 Nipper's #1 Hits 1956-1986.
     (S) (4:18) RCA 8475 Nipper's Greatest Hits Of The 60's Volume 2.
     (S) (3:21) RCA 6383 The Top Ten Hits. (*edited*)
     (S) (3:38) RCA 6382 The Number One Hits. (*edited*)
     (S) (4:26) RCA 6401 50 Worldwide Gold Award Hits.
     (S) (3:24) RCA 6221 The Memphis Record. (*edited*)
     (S) (3:59) RCA 6985 The Alternate Aloha. (*all selections on this cd are live*)
     (S) (4:20) RCA 4941 Gold Records Volume 5.

1970 #6 *DON'T CRY DADDY*
     (E) (2:48) RCA 6383 The Top Ten Hits.
     (E) (2:45) RCA 6401 50 Worldwide Gold Award Hits.
     (E) (2:48) RCA 6221 The Memphis Record.
     (E) (2:46) RCA 5430 Always On My Mind.

ELVIS PRESLEY (Continued)

1970 #10 *KENTUCKY RAIN*
    (E) (3:22) RCA 53732 Pure Gold.
    (S) (3:12) RCA 6401 50 Worldwide Gold Award Hits.
    (S) (3:15) RCA 6221 The Memphis Record.
    (S) (3:23) RCA 4941 Gold Records Volume 5.

1970 #10 *THE WONDER OF YOU*
    (S) (2:36) RCA 6383 The Top Ten Hits. *(audience applause tracks into next selection)*
    (S) (2:38) RCA 54362 Elvis On Stage.

1970 #18 *I'VE LOST YOU*
    (S) (3:39) RCA 5430 Always On My Mind. *(live)*
    (S) (3:40) MFSL 560 That's The Way It Is. *(live)*

1970 #30 *THE NEXT STEP IS LOVE*
    (S) (3:31) MFSL 560 That's The Way It Is.

1970 #10 *YOU DON'T HAVE TO SAY YOU LOVE ME*
    (S) (2:29) MFSL 560 That's The Way It Is.

1971 #13 *I REALLY DON'T WANT TO KNOW*
    (S) (2:44) RCA 52274 Welcome To My World.

1971 #34 *WHERE DID THEY GO, LORD*

1971 #40 *LIFE*

1971 #36 *I'M LEAVIN'*

1972 #31 *UNTIL IT'S TIME FOR YOU TO GO*

1972 #1 *BURNING LOVE*
    (S) (2:53) RCA 8476 and 9684 Nipper's Greatest Hits Of The 70's.
    (S) (2:51) RCA 8533 O.S.T. Heartbreak Hotel.
    (S) (2:52) RCA 6383 The Top Ten Hits.
    (S) (2:55) RCA 6985 The Alternate Aloha. *(all selections on this cd are live)*
    (S) (2:53) RCA 4941 Gold Records Volume 5.
    (S) (2:50) Pair 1010 Double Dynamite.

1973 #15 *SEPARATE WAYS*
    (E) (2:33) RCA 5430 Always On My Mind.
    (S) (2:35) Pair 1010 Double Dynamite.

1973 #10 *STEAMROLLER BLUES*
    (S) (3:15) RCA 6985 The Alternate Aloha. *(all selections on this cd are live; alternate take)*

1973 #27 *RAISED ON ROCK*

BILLY PRESTON

1972 #1 *OUT A-SPACE*
    (S) (4:08) A&M 3205 Best Of.

1973 #1 *WILL IT GO ROUND IN CIRCLES*
    (S) (3:43) Rhino 70634 Billboard's Top Rock & Roll Hits Of 1973.
    (S) (3:47) Rhino 70551 Soul Hits Of The 70's Volume 11.
    (S) (3:43) A&M 3205 Best Of.

1973 #6 *SPACE RACE*
    (S) (3:26) A&M 3205 Best Of.

JOHNNY PRESTON

1960 #1 *RUNNING BEAR*
    (M) (2:36) Rhino 70621 Billboard's Top Rock & Roll Hits Of 1960.
    (M) (2:36) Rhino 72004 Billboard's Top Rock & Roll Hits 1957-1961 Box Set.
    (M) (2:35) Mercury 832041 45's On CD Volume 1.
    (M) (2:36) Mercury 826448 Oldies Golden Million Sellers.

JOHNNY PRESTON (Continued)
1960 #6 *CRADLE OF LOVE*
1960 #9 *FEEL SO FINE*

ANDRE PREVIN
1959 #31 *LIKE YOUNG*

LLOYD PRICE
1957 #22 *JUST BECAUSE*
   (M) (2:45) Rhino 75766 Best Of New Orleans Rhythm & Blues Volume 2.
   (M) (2:44) Sire 26617 Music From The Film A Rage In Harlem.
1959 #1 *STAGGER LEE*
   (S) (2:20) Rhino 70620 Billboard's Top Rock & Roll Hits Of 1959.
   (S) (2:20) Rhino 72004 Billboard's Top Rock & Roll Hits 1957-1961 Box
         Set.
   (S) (2:20) MCA 31199 Vintage Music Volume 2.
   (S) (2:20) MCA 5777 Vintage Music Volumes 1 & 2.
   (S) (2:20) Garland 011 Footstompin' Oldies
   (S) (2:17) JCI 3204 Heart & Soul Fifties.
   (S) (2:20) Curb 77525 Greatest Hits Of Rock 'N' Roll Volume 2.
   (S) (2:20) Curb 77305 Greatest Hits.
   (S) (2:20) Pair 1257 Greatest Hits.
1959 #19 *WHERE WERE YOU (ON OUR WEDDING DAY)?*
1959 #2 *PERSONALITY*
   (S) (2:33) Rhino 70645 Billboard's Top R&B Hits Of 1959.
   (S) (2:33) Garland 012 Remember When.
   (S) (2:33) MCA 31201 Vintage Music Volume 4.
   (S) (2:33) MCA 5778 Vintage Music Volumes 3 & 4.
   (S) (2:33) Curb 77305 Greatest Hits.
   (S) (2:33) Pair 1257 Greatest Hits.
1959 #2 *I'M GONNA GET MARRIED*
   (E) (2:18) MCA 5938 Vintage Music Volumes 15 & 16.
   (E) (2:18) MCA 31212 Vintage Music Volume 15.
   (S) (2:18) Rhino 70589 Rockin' & Rollin' Wedding Songs Volume 2.
   (E) (2:18) Curb 77305 Greatest Hits.
1959 #16 *COME INTO MY HEART*
1960 #11 *LADY LUCK*
1960 #38 *NO IF'S - NO AND'S*
1960 #21 *QUESTION*
1963 #21 *MISTY*

RAY PRICE
1971 #13 *FOR THE GOOD TIMES*
   (S) (3:47) Rhino 70924 Super Hits Of The 70's Volume 4.
   (S) (3:47) Rhino 72009 Super Hits Of The 70's Volumes 1-4 Box Set.
   (M) (3:46) Columbia 46032 Columbia Country Classics Volume 4.
   (S) (3:47) Columbia 45068 American Originals.
   (S) (3:47) Sony Music Special Products 48621 Kris Kristofferson:
         Singer/Songwriter.

CHARLEY PRIDE
1972 #19 *KISS AN ANGEL GOOD MORNIN'*

LOUIS PRIMA
1960 #2 *WONDERLAND BY NIGHT*

LOUIS PRIMA & KEELY SMITH

1958 #13 *THAT OLD BLACK MAGIC*

    (M) (2:55) Rhino 70225 Best Of.

    (M) (2:55) Capitol 94072 Capitol Collectors Series.

    (M) (2:54) Capitol 98670 Memories Are Made Of This.

P.J. PROBY

1967 #33 *NIKI HOEKY*

PROCOL HARUM

1967 #5 *A WHITER SHADE OF PALE*

    (E) (4:03) Motown 6120 O.S.T. The Big Chill.

    (M) (3:57) Rhino 70326 History Of British Rock Volume 8.

    (M) (3:57) Rhino 72022 History Of British Rock Box Set.

    (E) (4:03) A&M 2515 Classics Volume 17.

1967 #35 *HOMBURG*

    (M) (3:55) A&M 2515 Classics Volume 17.

1972 #18 *CONQUISTADOR*

    (the actual LP time is (5:06) not (4:16) as stated on the record label)

    (S) (4:11) JCI 3402 Live Volume 2.

    (S) (4:09) Rhino 70326 History Of British Rock Volume 8.

    (S) (4:09) Rhino 72022 History Of British Rock Box Set.

    (S) (4:13) A&M 2515 Classics Volume 17.

    (S) (5:07) MFSL 788 Live. *(includes :03 silent lead into selection; LP length)*

JEANNE PRUETT

1973 #24 *SATIN SHEETS*

    (S) (3:20) MCA 2-8025 30 Years Of Hits 1958-1974.

    (S) (3:20) MCA 6421 16 Top Country Hits Volume 1.

GARY PUCKETT & THE UNION GAP (*also* UNION GAP)

released as by THE UNION GAP *featuring* GARY PUCKETT:

1968 #3 *WOMAN WOMAN*

    (S) (3:33) Columbia/Legacy 46984 Rock Artifacts Volume 4. *(:20 longer than either the LP or 45)*

    (S) (3:14) Columbia 1042 Greatest Hits.

    (S) (3:33) Columbia/Legacy 48959 Looking Glass. *(:20 longer than either the 45 or LP)*

1968 #1 *YOUNG GIRL*

    (the actual 45 time is (3:07) not (3:12) as the record label states)

    (S) (3:03) Columbia 45019 Pop Classics Of The 60's. *(LP speed but :09 shorter than LP length)*

    (S) (3:11) Columbia 1042 Greatest Hits. *(LP speed; LP length)*

    (S) (3:11) Columbia/Legacy 48959 Looking Glass. *(LP speed; LP length)*

released as by GARY PUCKETT & THE UNION GAP:

1968 #1 *LADY WILLPOWER*

    (S) (2:36) Columbia 1042 Greatest Hits.

    (S) (2:45) Columbia/Legacy 48959 Looking Glass.

1968 #5 *OVER YOU*

    (S) (2:21) Columbia 1042 Greatest Hits.

    (S) (2:23) Columbia/Legacy 48959 Looking Glass.

1969 #12 *DON'T GIVE IN TO HIM*

    (the actual 45 time is (2:21) not (2:25) as stated on the record label; LP length is (2:18))

    (S) (2:11) Columbia 1042 Greatest Hits.

    (S) (2:29) Columbia/Legacy 48959 Looking Glass.

GARY PUCKETT & THE UNION GAP (Continued)
1969 #5 *THIS GIRL IS A WOMAN NOW*
        (S) (3:06) Columbia 1042 Greatest Hits.
        (S) (3:07) Columbia/Legacy 48959 Looking Glass.
1970 #38 *LET'S GIVE ADAM AND EVE ANOTHER CHANCE*
        (S) (2:46) Columbia 1042 Greatest Hits.
        (S) (2:44) Columbia/Legacy 48959 Looking Glass.

JAMES & BOBBY PURIFY
1966 #6 *I'M YOUR PUPPET*
        (M) (2:59) Rhino 75774 Soul Shots.
        (M) (2:59) JCI 3102 Love Sixties.
1967 #35 *WISH YOU DIDN'T HAVE TO GO*
1967 #27 *SHAKE A TAIL FEATHER*
        (M) (2:08) JCI 3105 Soul Sixties.
        (S) (2:07) Rhino 70732 Grandson Of Frat Rock
1967 #30 *LET LOVE COME BETWEEN US*
        (S) (2:24) Rhino 75757 Soul Shots Volume 3.

BILL PURSELL
1963 #7 *OUR WINTER LOVE*

PYRAMIDS
1964 #17 *PENETRATION*
        (M) (2:00) Rhino 70089 Surfin' Hits.
        (M) (1:57) Dunhill Compact Classics 030 Beach Classics.

QUAKER CITY BOYS
1959 #33 *TEASIN'*

? & THE MYSTERIANS
1966 #1 *96 TEARS*
1966 #22 *I NEED SOMEBODY*

QUIN-TONES
1958 #24 *DOWN THE AISLE OF LOVE*
        (M) (2:48) Rhino 70589 Rockin' & Rollin' Wedding Songs Volume 2.

R

RADIANTS
1965 #38 *VOICE YOUR CHOICE*
    (S) (2:32) Rhino 75757 Soul Shots Volume 3.
    (S) (2:32) Chess 31318 Best Of Chess R&B Volume 2.

RAIDERS (see PAUL REVERE & THE RAIDERS)

RAINDROPS
1963 #34 *WHAT A GUY*
1963 #15 *THE KIND OF BOY YOU CAN'T FORGET*
    (S) (2:08) Rhino 70989 Best Of The Girl Groups Volume 2.

MARVIN RAINWATER
1957 #24 *GONNA FIND ME A BLUEBIRD*

DON RALKE
1959 #38 *77 SUNSET STRIP*

EDDIE RAMBEAU
1965 #12 *CONCRETE AND CLAY*

RAMRODS
1961 #25 *(GHOST) RIDERS IN THE SKY*

TEDDY RANDAZZO
1960 #30 *THE WAY OF A CLOWN*

RAN-DELLS
1963 #13 *MARTIAN HOP*
    (M) (2:10) Rhino 70535 Halloween Hits.

BOOTS RANDOLPH
1963 #33 *YAKETY SAX*
    (S) (2:01) CBS Special Products 44356 Yakety Sax.
    (S) (2:01) CBS Special Products 44355 Greatest Hits.

RANDY & THE RAINBOWS
1963 #13 *DENISE*
    (M) (1:59) Rhino 75764 Best Of Doo Wop Uptempo.
    (M) (1:55) Collectables 2508 History Of Rock - The Doo Wop Era Part 2.

RARE EARTH
1970 #2 *GET READY*
    (E) (2:46) Motown 6183 Hard To Find Motown Classics Volume 1.
    (E) (2:47) JCI 3100 Dance Sixties.
    (E) (2:45) Priority 8662 Hard 'N Heavy/70's Greatest Rock Hits Volume 1.
    (S) (2:57) Dunhill Compact Classics 043 Toga Rock II. *(:11 longer fade than the 45; missing the fake crowd noise overdub at the introduction)*
    (S) (20:04) Motown 8033 and 8133 Get Ready/Ecology. *(edit of LP version)*
    (S) (21:27) Motown 5229 Get Ready. *(LP version)*
    (E) (2:46) Motown 5482 Greatest Hits And Rare Classics.
    (E) (2:45) Motown 9071 Motown Dance Party Volume 1. *(all selections on this cd are segued together)*

RARE EARTH (Continued)

1970 #5 (I KNOW) I'M LOSING YOU
- (M) (3:35) Motown 6183 Hard To Find Motown Classics Volume 1.
- (E) (3:35) Motown 8033 and 8133 Get Ready/Ecology.
- (S) (10:54) Motown 5202 Ecology. *(LP version)*
- (E) (3:35) Motown 5482 Greatest Hits And Rare Classics.

1971 #18 BORN TO WANDER
- (S) (2:56) Motown 6184 Hard To Find Motown Classics Volume 2.
- (S) (3:09) Motown 8033 and 8133 Get Ready/Ecology. *(edit of LP length)*
- (S) (3:20) Motown 5202 Ecology. *(LP length; truncated fade)*
- (S) (3:18) Motown 5482 Greatest Hits And Rare Classics. *(LP length)*

1971 #7 I JUST WANT TO CELEBRATE
- (S) (3:33) Motown 6184 Hard To Find Motown Classics Volume 2.
- (S) (3:33) MCA 25240 Classic Rock Volume 3.
- (S) (3:35) Motown 5482 Greatest Hits And Rare Classics.
- (S) (3:35) Priority 7055 Heavy Hitters/70's Greatest Rock Hits Volume 11.

1972 #24 HEY BIG BROTHER
(dj copies of this 45 ran (2:48) and (4:45); commercial copies were all (2:59))
- (S) (4:43) Motown 5482 Greatest Hits And Rare Classics.

RASCALS (*also* YOUNG RASCALS)

released as by THE YOUNG RASCALS:

1966 #1 GOOD LOVIN'
- (S) (2:28) JCI 3101 Rockin' Sixties.
- (S) (2:28) Atlantic 81909 Hit Singles 1958-1977.
- (S) (2:28) Motown 6120 O.S.T. Big Chill.
- (S) (2:28) Warner Special Products 27602 20 Party Classics.
- (S) (2:28) Epic 48732 O.S.T. My Girl.
- (S) (2:27) Warner Special Products 27605 Ultimate.
- (S) (2:27) Atlantic 8190 Greatest Hits/Time Peace.
- (S) (2:27) Warner Special Products 27617 The Young Rascals.
- (M) (2:30) Rhino 71031 Anthology (1965-1972).

1966 #23 YOU BETTER RUN
- (S) (2:25) Warner Special Products 27605 Ultimate.
- (S) (2:25) Atlantic 8190 Greatest Hits/Time Peace.
- (S) (2:24) Warner Special Products 27619 Groovin'.
- (M) (2:26) Rhino 71031 Anthology (1965-1972).

1967 #17 I'VE BEEN LONELY TOO LONG
(LP title was simply "LONELY TOO LONG")
- (S) (2:58) SBK 93744 China Beach - Music & Memories. *(LP version)*
- (S) (2:59) Warner Special Products 27605 Ultimate. *(LP version)*
- (S) (2:58) Atlantic 8190 Greatest Hits/Time Peace. *(LP version)*
- (S) (2:59) Warner Special Products 27618 Collections. *(LP version)*
- (M) (2:04) Rhino 71031 Anthology (1965-1972). *(45 version)*

1967 #1 GROOVIN'
- (E) (2:27) Atlantic 81742 O.S.T. Platoon.
- (S) (2:29) Atlantic 81909 Hit Singles 1958-1977.
- (S) (2:29) Warner Special Products 27605 Ultimate.
- (S) (2:28) Atlantic 8190 Greatest Hits/Time Peace.
- (S) (2:29) Warner Special Products 27619 Groovin'.
- (M) (2:28) Rhino 71031 Anthology (1965-1972).

1967 #8 A GIRL LIKE YOU
- (S) (2:47) Warner Special Products 27605 Ultimate.
- (S) (2:46) Atlantic 8190 Greatest Hits/Time Peace.
- (S) (2:48) Warner Special Products 27619 Groovin'.
- (M) (2:46) Rhino 71031 Anthology (1965-1972).

THE YOUNG RASCALS (Continued)
1967 #2 *HOW CAN I BE SURE*
- (S) (2:50) Warner Special Products 27605 Ultimate.
- (S) (2:50) Atlantic 8190 Greatest Hits/Time Peace.
- (S) (2:51) Warner Special Products 27619 Groovin'.
- (M) (2:52) Rhino 71031 Anthology (1965-1972).

1968 #15 *IT'S WONDERFUL*
- (S) (2:16) Warner Special Products 27605 Ultimate. *(neither the LP or 45 version; LP speed but missing the intro and outro sound effects)*
- (S) (2:14) Atlantic 8190 Greatest Hits/Time Peace. *(neither the LP or 45 version; LP speed but missing the intro and outro sound effects)*
- (M) (3:21) Rhino 71031 Anthology (1965-1972). *(commercial 45 version)*

releases from this point on were released as by **THE RASCALS:**
1968 #3 *A BEAUTIFUL MORNING*
- (S) (2:32) JCI 3104 Mellow Sixties.
- (S) (2:32) Warner Special Products 27605 Ultimate.
- (S) (2:31) Atlantic 8190 Greatest Hits/Time Peace.
- (S) (2:33) Rhino 71031 Anthology (1965-1972).

1968 #1 *PEOPLE GOT TO BE FREE*
- (S) (2:58) Atlantic 81909 Hit Singles 1958-1977.
- (M) (2:59) Rhino 70734 Songs Of Protest.
- (S) (2:57) Warner Special Products 27610 More Party Classics.
- (S) (2:57) Priority 7909 Vietnam: Rockin' The Delta.
- (S) (2:57) Warner Special Products 27605 Ultimate.
- (S) (2:58) Rhino 71031 Anthology (1965-1972).

1968 #12 *A RAY OF HOPE*
- (S) (3:39) Warner Special Products 27605 Ultimate.
- (S) (3:41) Rhino 71031 Anthology (1965-1972).

1969 #17 *HEAVEN*
- (S) (3:21) Warner Special Products 27605 Ultimate.
- (S) (3:21) Rhino 71031 Anthology (1965-1972).

1969 #13 *SEE*
- (S) (5:01) Warner Special Products 27605 Ultimate. *(LP version)*
- (S) (4:44) Rhino 71031 Anthology (1965-1972). *(:06 longer than the 45 version)*

1969 #12 *CARRY ME BACK*
- (S) (2:49) Warner Special Products 27605 Ultimate.
- (S) (2:49) Rhino 71031 Anthology (1965-1972).

1970 #29 *HOLD ON*

RASPBERRIES
1972 #4 *GO ALL THE WAY*
- (S) (3:17) JCI 3301 Rockin' Seventies.
- (S) (3:19) Capitol 92126 Capitol Collectors Series.
- (S) (3:19) Capitol 98139 Spring Break Volume 2.
- (S) (3:19) Capitol 98665 When AM Was King.

1973 #10 *I WANNA BE WITH YOU*
- (S) (3:04) Capitol 92126 Capitol Collectors Series.

1973 #18 *LET'S PRETEND*
- (S) (3:39) Capitol 92126 Capitol Collectors Series.

1973 #37 *TONIGHT*
- (S) (3:39) Capitol 92126 Capitol Collectors Series.

LOU RAWLS
1966 #16 *LOVE IS A HURTIN' THING*
    (S) (2:11) Rhino 75774   Soul Shots.
    (S) (2:16) Curb 77355   60's Hits Volume 1.
    (S) (2:15) Capitol 91147   Best Of.
    (S) (2:16) Curb 77380   Greatest Hits.
    (S) (2:12) Capitol 98306   The Legendary Lou Rawls. *(truncated fade)*

1967 #31 *DEAD END STREET*
    (S) (3:57) Capitol 91147   Best Of. *(this cd splits this song into two separate tracks: track 5 is the "DEAD END STREET MONOLOGUE" (1:37) and track 6 which is "DEAD END STREET" (2:20); LP version)*
    (*) (****) Curb 77380   Greatest Hits. *(cd jacket claims this song is included on the cd but it is not)*
    (S) (3:57) Capitol 98306   The Legendary Lou Rawls. *(LP version)*

1969 #23 *YOUR GOOD THING (IS ABOUT TO END)*
    (S) (4:24) Curb 77380   Greatest Hits. *(LP version)*
    (S) (2:51) Capitol 98306   The Legendary Lou Rawls. *(45 version)*

1971 #27 *A NATURAL MAN*
    (S) (3:34) Rhino 70786   Soul Hits Of The 70's Volume 6.
    (S) (3:38) Curb 77443   Mike Curb Congregation Greatest Hits.
    (S) (3:39) Curb 77380   Greatest Hits.

DIANE RAY
1963 #33 *PLEASE DON'T TALK TO THE LIFEGUARD*

JAMES RAY
1962 #18 *IF YOU GOTTA MAKE A FOOL OF SOMEBODY*

JOHNNIE RAY
1956 #3 *JUST WALKING IN THE RAIN*
    (M) (2:36) Columbia 45110   16 Most Requested Songs Of The 50's Volume 1.
    (M) (2:37) Columbia 30609   Best Of.
    (M) (2:37) Columbia/Legacy 46095   16 Most Requested Songs.

1957 #10 *YOU DON'T OWE ME A THING*
1957 #24 *YES TONIGHT, JOSEPHINE*
1957 #31 *BUILD YOUR LOVE (ON A STRONG FOUNDATION)*

MARGIE RAYBURN
1957 #16 *I'M AVAILABLE*

RAYS
1957 #3 *SILHOUETTES*

REBELS
1963 #8 *WILD WEEKEND*

REDBONE
1972 #19 *THE WITCH QUEEN OF NEW ORLEANS*
    (S) (2:45) Rhino 70927   Super Hits Of The 70's Volume 7.
    (S) (2:55) Columbia/Legacy 46160   Rock Artifacts Volume 1. *(neither the LP or 45 version.)*
    (S) (2:42) Dunhill Compact Classics 050   Monster Rock 'n' Roll Show. *(tracks into next selection)*

OTIS REDDING
1965 #15 *I'VE BEEN LOVING YOU TOO LONG (TO STOP NOW)*
    (M) (2:52) Atlantic Group 88218   Complete Stax/Volt Singles. *(45 version)*
    (M) (3:11) Atlantic 81297   Atlantic Rhythm & Blues Volume 5. *(LP version)*

    (S) (3:11) Warner Special Products 27615 Atlantic Soul Classics. (*LP version*)

    (M) (2:53) Atco 80318 Otis Blue. (*45 version*)

    (S) (3:11) Atlantic 81762 Otis Redding Story. (*LP version*)

    (S) (3:12) Warner Special Products 27608 Ultimate. (*LP version*)

    (S) (3:11) Atlantic 82305 Atlantic Rhythm And Blues 1947-1974 Box Set. (*LP version*)

1965 #38 *RESPECT*

    (M) (2:06) Atlantic Group 88218 Complete Stax/Volt Singles. (*45 version*)

    (S) (2:05) JCI 3100 Dance Sixties. (*some dropouts on introduction; LP version*)

    (M) (2:04) Atlantic 81297 Atlantic Rhythm & Blues Volume 5. (*45 version*)

    (M) (2:04) Stax 88008 Top Of The Stax Volume 2. (*45 version*)

    (M) (2:04) Atco 80318 Otis Blue. (*45 version*)

    (S) (2:05) Atlantic 81762 Otis Redding Story. (*LP version*)

    (S) (2:06) Warner Special Products 27608 Ultimate. (*LP version*)

    (M) (2:04) Atlantic 82305 Atlantic Rhythm And Blues 1947-1974 Box Set. (*45 version*)

    (M) (1:53) Stax 8572 Remember Me. (*alternate take*)

1966 #30 *SATISFACTION*

    (M) (2:43) Atlantic Group 88218 Complete Stax/Volt Singles.

    (M) (2:43) Atco 80318 Otis Blue.

    (S) (2:43) Atlantic 81762 Otis Redding Story.

    (S) (2:45) Warner Special Products 27608 Ultimate.

1966 #38 *FA-FA-FA-FA-FA (SAD SONG)*

    (M) (2:40) Atlantic Group 88218 Complete Stax/Volt Singles. (*truncated fade*)

    (S) (2:38) Atlantic 81762 Otis Redding Story.

    (M) (2:39) Atco 91707 Dictionary Of Soul.

    (M) (2:39) Warner Special Products 27608 Ultimate.

1967 #20 *TRY A LITTLE TENDERNESS*

    (M) (3:17) Atlantic Group 88218 Complete Stax/Volt Singles. (*45 length*)

    (S) (3:46) JCI 3105 Soul Sixties. (*LP length*)

    (S) (3:47) Atlantic 81298 Atlantic Rhythm & Blues Volume 6. (*LP length*)

    (S) (3:46) Warner Special Products 27609 Memphis Soul Classics. (*LP length*)

    (M) (3:46) Atco 91813 Classic Recordings. (*LP length*)

    (S) (3:46) Atlantic 81762 Otis Redding Story. (*LP length*)

    (M) (3:46) Atco 91707 Dictionary Of Soul. (*LP length*)

    (S) (3:48) Warner Special Products 27608 Ultimate. (*LP length*)

    (S) (3:47) Atlantic 82305 Atlantic Rhythm And Blues 1947-1974 Box Set. (*LP length*)

    (S) (3:59) Stax 8572 Remember Me. (*alternate take; 2 severe dropouts on the introduction*)

1968 #3 *(SITTIN' ON) THE DOCK OF THE BAY*

    (M) (2:38) Atlantic Group 88218 Complete Stax/Volt Singles.

    (M) (2:41) Atlantic 81298 Atlantic Rhyhtm & Blues Volume 6.

    (E) (2:41) Atlantic 81742 O.S.T. Platoon.

    (S) (2:41) Atlantic 81911 Golden Age Of Black Music (1960-1970).

    (S) (2:39) Stax 88005 Top Of The Stax.

    (S) (2:40) Atlantic 81762 Otis Redding Story.

    (S) (2:41) Atco 80254 The Dock Of The Bay.

    (S) (2:40) Warner Special Products 27608 Ultimate.

OTIS REDDING (Continued)

  (S) (2:40) Atlantic 82305 Atlantic Rhythm And Blues 1947-1974 Box Set.
 - (S) (2:58) Stax 8572 Remember Me. *(includes :07 studio talk; alternate take)*
  (S) (2:42) Stax 8572 Remember Me. *(includes :02 countoff; alternate take)*

1968 #24 THE HAPPY SONG (DUM-DUM)
  (M) (2:41) Atlantic Group 88218 Complete Stax/Volt Singles.
  (S) (2:37) Atlantic 81762 Otis Redding Story.
  (S) (2:40) Atco 80270 The Immortal Otis Redding.

1968 #37 AMEN
  (S) (3:01) Atlantic 81762 Otis Redding Story.
  (S) (3:02) Atco 80270 The Immortal Otis Redding.

1968 #37 I'VE GOT DREAMS TO REMEMBER
  (S) (3:13) Atco 91813 Classic Recordings.
  (S) (3:11) Atlantic 81762 Otis Redding Story.
  (S) (3:14) Atco 80270 The Immortal Otis Redding.

1968 #22 PAPA'S GOT A BRAND NEW BAG
  (M) (2:29) Atlantic 81762 Otis Redding Story.

1969 #38 A LOVER'S QUESTION
  (S) (2:52) Rhino 70294 Love Man.

OTIS REDDING & CARLA THOMAS
released as by OTIS & CARLA:

1967 #19 TRAMP
  (M) (2:59) Atlantic Group 88218 Complete Stax/Volt Singles.
  (S) (2:59) Atlantic 82256 King & Queen.
  (S) (2:59) Atlantic 81762 Otis Redding Story.
  (S) (2:59) Atco 80254 The Dock Of The Bay.
  (S) (2:57) Warner Special Products 27608 Ultimate Otis Redding.
  (S) (2:59) Atlantic 82305 Atlantic Rhythm And Blues 1947-1974 Box Set.

HELEN REDDY

1971 #19 I DON'T KNOW HOW TO LOVE HIM
  (S) (3:15) Capitol 46490 Greatest Hits (And More).
  (S) (3:15) Pair 1066 Lust For Life.

1971 #38 CRAZY LOVE
1972 #1 I AM WOMAN
  (S) (3:22) Capitol 46490 Greatest Hits (And More).
  (S) (3:19) Pair 1066 Lust For Life.

1973 #14 PEACEFUL
  (S) (2:49) Capitol 46490 Greatest Hits (And More).

1973 #1 DELTA DAWN
  (S) (3:06) Capitol 46490 Greatest Hits (And More).
  (S) (3:06) Pair 1066 Lust For Life.
  (S) (3:06) Capitol 98665 When AM Was King.

REDEYE

1971 #22 GAMES
  (S) (3:00) Rhino 70925 Super Hits Of The 70's Volume 5. *(LP version)*

JERRY REED

1971 #8 AMOS MOSES
  (S) (2:19) Rhino 70923 Super Hits Of The 70's Volume 3.
  (S) (2:19) Rhino 72009 Super Hits Of The 70's Volumes 1-4 Box Set.
  (S) (2:17) RCA 8476 and 9684 Nipper's Greatest Hits Of The 70's.
  (S) (2:15) RCA 54109 Best Of.

1971 #9 WHEN YOU'RE HOT, YOU'RE HOT
  (S) (2:18) Rhino 70925 Super Hits Of The 70's Volume 5.
  (S) (2:16) RCA 54109 Best Of.

LOU REED

1973 #17 *WALK ON THE WILD SIDE*
    (S)   (4:09)   Priority 7997   Super Songs/70's Greatest Rock Hits Volume 8. *(LP version)*
    (S)   (4:11)   RCA 3753   Walk On The Wild Side: The Best Of. *(LP version)*
    (S)   (4:09)   RCA 52162   Walk On The Wild Side & Other Hits. *(LP version)*
    (S)   (4:12)   RCA 2356   Between Thought And Expression. *(LP version)*

DELLA REESE

1957 #15 *AND THAT REMINDS ME*
1959 #1 *DON'T YOU KNOW*
    (S)   (2:31)   RCA 8467   Nipper's Greatest Hits Of The 50's Volume 2.
1960 #15 *NOT ONE MINUTE MORE*
1960 #31 *SOMEDAY (YOU'LL WANT ME TO WANT YOU)*

JIM REEVES

1957 #11 *FOUR WALLS*
    (M)   (2:49)   RCA 8467   Nipper's Greatest Hits Of The 50's Volume 2.
    (M)   (2:49)   RCA 2493   Four Walls - The Legend Begins.
    (M)   (2:49)   RCA 3936   Pure Gold Volume 1.
    (M)   (2:49)   RCA 58451   Best Of.
    (M)   (2:49)   RCA 52301   He'll Have To Go And Other Favorites.

1960 #2 *HE'LL HAVE TO GO*
    (S)   (2:19)   RCA 8466   Nipper's Greatest Hits Of The 50's Volume 1.
    (S)   (2:19)   RCA 58451   Best Of.
    (S)   (2:19)   RCA 52301   He'll Have To Go And Other Favorites.

1960 #29 *AM I LOSING YOU*
    (M)   (2:43)   RCA 2493   Four Walls - The Legend Begins.
    (S)   (2:15)   RCA 58451   Best Of. *(rerecording)*
    (S)   (2:15)   RCA 52301   He'll Have To Go And Other Favorites. *(rerecording)*

REFLECTIONS

1964 #9 *(JUST LIKE) ROMEO AND JULIET*

REGENTS

1961 #13 *BARBARA ANN*
    (M)   (2:13)   Rhino 70906   American Bandstand Greatest Hits Collection.
    (M)   (2:13)   Collectables 5403   Barbara-Ann.
    (M)   (2:13)   Essex 7052   All Time Rock Classics.

1961 #32 *RUNAROUND*
    (S)   (2:19)   Collectables 5403   Barbara-Ann. *(truncated fade)*

CLARENCE REID

1969 #36 *NOBODY BUT YOU BABE*

DIANE RENAY

1964 #6 *NAVY BLUE*
1964 #28 *KISS ME SAILOR*

RENE & RENE

1964 #38 *ANGELITO*
1969 #15 *LO MUCHO QUE TE QUIERO (THE MORE I LOVE YOU)*
    (M)   (2:58)   Original Sound 1960   Memories Of El Monte.

REVELS

1959 #35 *MIDNIGHT STROLL*
    (M)   (2:33)   Dunhill Compact Classics 050   Monster Rock 'n Roll Show.

PAUL REVERE & THE RAIDERS (*also* RAIDERS)

1961 #38 *LIKE, LONG HAIR*
- (M) (1:55) Columbia 45311 The Legend Of Paul Revere. (*mastered from vinyl*)

1966 #11 *JUST LIKE ME*
- (M) (2:21) Columbia 45019 Pop Classics Of The 60's.
- (M) (2:21) Rhino 75778 Frat Rock.
- (E) (2:21) Columbia 35593 Greatest Hits.
- (S) (2:23) Columbia 45311 The Legend Of Paul Revere. (*remixed*)

1966 #4 *KICKS*
- (E) (2:21) Columbia 45018 Rock Classics Of The 60's.
- (E) (2:21) Columbia 35593 Greatest Hits.
- (S) (2:26) Columbia 45311 The Legend Of Paul Revere. (*remixed*)
- (S) (2:25) Columbia 9308 Midnight Ride. (*remixed*)

1966 #6 *HUNGRY*
- (M) (2:58) Rhino 75778 Frat Rock.
- (S) (2:54) Columbia 35593 Greatest Hits.
- (S) (2:54) Columbia 45311 The Legend Of Paul Revere. (*remixed*)

1966 #20 *THE GREAT AIRPLANE STRIKE*
- (S) (3:06) Columbia 35593 Greatest Hits. (*LP version*)
- (S) (2:54) Columbia 45311 The Legend Of Paul Revere. (*remixed 45 version*)

1967 #4 *GOOD THING*
- (M) (3:02) Rhino 70628 Billboard's Top Rock & Roll Hits Of 1967.
- (E) (3:00) Columbia 35593 Greatest Hits.
- (S) (3:01) Columbia 45311 The Legend Of Paul Revere. (*remixed*)

1967 #22 *UPS AND DOWNS*
- (E) (2:44) Columbia 35593 Greatest Hits.
- (M) (2:48) Columbia 45311 The Legend Of Paul Revere.

1967 #5 *HIM OR ME - WHAT'S IT GONNA BE?*
- (M) (2:38) Columbia 45311 The Legend Of Paul Revere.

1967 #17 *I HAD A DREAM*
- (S) (2:17) Columbia 45311 The Legend Of Paul Revere.

1967 #35 *PEACE OF MIND*
- (M) (2:25) Columbia 45311 The Legend Of Paul Revere.

1968 #19 *TOO MUCH TALK*
- (M) (2:13) Columbia 45311 The Legend Of Paul Revere. (*with :15 intro*)

1968 #27 *DON'T TAKE IT SO HARD*
- (S) (2:23) Columbia 45311 The Legend Of Paul Revere.

1969 #18 *MR. SUN, MR. MOON*
- (S) (2:43) Columbia 45311 The Legend Of Paul Revere.

1969 #20 *LET ME*
- (S) (2:39) Columbia 45311 The Legend Of Paul Revere.

1969 #25 *WE GOTTA ALL GET TOGETHER*
- (S) (2:58) Columbia 45311 The Legend Of Paul Revere.

releases from this point on were credited simply to THE RAIDERS:

1971 #1 *INDIAN RESERVATION*
- (S) (2:52) Rhino 70632 Billboard's Top Rock & Roll Hits Of 1971.
- (S) (2:52) Rhino 72005 Billboard's Top Rock & Roll Hits 1968-1972 Box Set.
- (S) (2:53) Rhino 70925 Super Hits Of The 70's Volume 5.
- (S) (2:51) Columbia 45047 Pop Classics Of The 70's.
- (S) (2:51) Columbia 45311 The Legend Of Paul Revere.

THE RAIDERS (Continued)
1971 #23 *BIRDS OF A FEATHER*
    (S) (2:36) Columbia 45311 The Legend Of Paul Revere.

1972 #28 *COUNTRY WINE*
    (S) (2:29) Columbia 45311 The Legend Of Paul Revere.

ANN REYNOLDS
1957 #38 *WIND IN THE WILLOW*

DEBBIE REYNOLDS
1957 #1 *TAMMY*
    (M) (3:04) Curb 77435 Best Of.

1958 #30 *A VERY SPECIAL LOVE*
    (M) (2:36) Curb 77435 Best Of.

1960 #19 *AM I THAT EASY TO FORGET*
    (S) (2:18) Curb 77435 Best Of.

JODY REYNOLDS
1958 #10 *ENDLESS SLEEP*

LAWRENCE REYNOLDS
1969 #31 *JESUS IS A SOUL MAN*

EMITT RHODES
1971 #38 *FRESH AS A DAISY*

CHARLIE RICH
1960 #27 *LONELY WEEKENDS*
    (M) (2:07) Rhino 75884 The Sun Story.
    (M) (2:07) Dunhill Compact Classics 009 Legends.
    (M) (2:07) RCA 66059 Sun's Greatest Hits.

1965 #18 *MOHAIR SAM*
    (S) (2:07) Mercury 314512643 The Complete "Smash" Sessions.

1973 #17 *BEHIND CLOSED DOORS*
    (S) (2:55) Columbia 46032 Columbia Country Classics Volume 4.
    (S) (2:52) JCI 3304 Mellow Seventies.
    (S) (2:54) Epic 34240 Greatest Hits.
    (S) (2:54) Epic 32247 Behind Closed Doors.
    (S) (2:53) Columbia 45073 American Originals.

1973 #1 *THE MOST BEAUTIFUL GIRL*
    (S) (2:41) Columbia 46032 Columbia Country Classics Volume 4.
    (S) (2:43) Epic 34240 Greatest Hits.
    (S) (2:42) Epic 32247 Behind Closed Doors.
    (S) (2:41) Columbia 45073 American Originals.

CLIFF RICHARD
1959 #38 *LIVING DOLL*

1964 #24 *IT'S ALL IN THE GAME*

NELSON RIDDLE & HIS ORCHESTRA
1956 #1 *LISBON ANTIGUA*
    (M) (2:33) Capitol 90592 Memories Are Made Of This.
    (M) (2:34) Curb 77403 All-Time Great Instrumental Hits Volume 1.
    (M) (2:34) Capitol 91228 Best Of.
    (M) (2:33) Capitol 98670 Memories Are Made Of This.

1956 #27 *THEME FROM "THE PROUD ONES"*

1962 #40 *ROUTE 66 THEME*
    (S) (2:08) Capitol 91228 Best Of.
    (S) (2:07) Pair 1173 The Riddle Touch.

RIGHTEOUS BROTHERS
1965 #1 *YOU'VE LOST THAT LOVIN' FEELIN'*
- (S) (3:43) Rhino 70626 Billboard's Top Rock & Roll Hits Of 1965.
- (S) (3:43) Rhino 72007 Billboard's Top Rock & Roll Hits 1962-1966 Box Set.
- (M) (3:45) Abkco 7118 Phil Spector/Back To Mono (1958-1969).
- (S) (4:27) Curb 42257 Best Of Bill Medley. *(rerecorded)*
- (S) (3:43) Verve 847248 Very Best Of.
- (S) (3:43) Rhino 71488 Anthology.
- (S) (3:49) Curb 77423 Reunion. *(rerecorded)*
- (S) (3:40) Curb 77381 Best Of.
- (S) (3:43) Special Music 511078 You've Lost That Lovin' Feelin'.

1965 #10 *JUST ONCE IN MY LIFE*
- (M) (3:52) Abkco 7118 Phil Spector/Back To Mono (1958-1969).
- (S) (3:47) Verve 847248 Very Best Of.
- (S) (3:47) Rhino 71488 Anthology.
- (S) (4:02) Curb 77423 Reunion. *(rerecorded)*
- (S) (4:04) Curb 77381 Best Of. *(rerecorded)*
- (S) (3:47) Special Music 511078 You've Lost That Lovin' Feelin'.

1965 #5 *UNCHAINED MELODY*
- (M) (3:35) Abkco 7118 Phil Spector/Back To Mono (1958-1969).
- (S) (3:36) Curb 77532 Your Favorite Songs. *(rerecorded)*
- (S) (3:35) Verve 847248 Very Best Of.
- (S) (3:35) Rhino 71488 Anthology.
- (S) (3:35) Curb 77423 Reunion. *(rerecorded)*
- (S) (6:33) Curb 77423 Reunion. *(rerecorded)*
- (S) (3:37) Curb 77381 Best Of. *(rerecorded)*
- (S) (3:35) Special Music 511078 You've Lost That Lovin' Feelin'.

1966 #4 *EBB TIDE*
- (M) (2:48) Abkco 7118 Phil Spector/Back To Mono (1958-1969).
- (S) (2:47) Verve 847248 Very Best Of.
- (S) (2:47) Rhino 71488 Anthology.
- (S) (2:49) Curb 77423 Reunion. *(rerecorded)*
- (S) (2:50) Curb 77381 Best Of. *(rerecorded)*
- (S) (2:47) Special Music 511078 You've Lost That Lovin' Feelin'.

1966 #1 *(YOU'RE MY) SOUL AND INSPIRATION*
- (S) (3:04) Rhino 70627 Billboard's Top Rock & Roll Hits Of 1966.
- (S) (3:04) Rhino 72007 Billboard's Top Rock & Roll Hits 1962-1966 Box Set.
- (S) (3:19) Verve 847248 Very Best Of. *(:15 longer than either the 45 or LP version)*
- (S) (3:19) Rhino 71488 Anthology. *(:15 longer than either the 45 or LP version)*
- (S) (3:22) Curb 77423 Reunion. *(rerecorded)*
- (S) (3:19) Curb 77381 Best Of. *(:15 longer than either the 45 or LP version)*
- (S) (3:19) Special Music 511078 You've Lost That Lovin' Feelin'.

1966 #15 *HE*
- (S) (3:00) Verve 847248 Very Best Of.
- (S) (2:59) Rhino 71488 Anthology.

1966 #30 *GO AHEAD AND CRY*
- (S) (2:35) Verve 847248 Very Best Of.
- (S) (2:34) Rhino 71488 Anthology. *(truncated fade)*

JEANNIE C. RILEY
1968 #1 *HARPER VALLEY P.T.A.*
(S) (3:09) Rhino 70689 Billboard's Top Country Hits Of 1968.

RINKY DINKS
1958 #25 *EARLY IN THE MORNING*
(M) (2:14) Warner Special Products 27606 Ultimate Bobby Darin.

MIGUEL RIOS
1970 #9 *A SONG OF JOY*

RIP CHORDS
1964 #4 *HEY LITTLE COBRA*
(M) (2:00) Dunhill Compact Classics 030 Beach Classics.
(S) (1:57) Columbia 45018 Rock Classics Of The 60's.
1964 #29 *THREE WINDOW COUPE*
(S) (1:57) Columbia/Legacy 46984 Rock Artifacts Volume 4.

TEX RITTER
1961 #28 *I DREAMED OF A HILL-BILLY HEAVEN*
(S) (3:07) Curb 77397 Greatest Hits.
(S) (3:08) Capitol 95036 Capitol Collector's Series.

JOHNNY RIVERS
1964 #2 *MEMPHIS*
(S) (2:30) Rhino 70793 Anthology 1964-1977. *(no audience applause at the end; 45 version)*
(S) (2:31) EMI 90727 Very Best Of. *(audience applause at the end; LP version)*
(S) (2:33) EMI 46594 Best Of. *(audience applause at the end; LP version)*
1964 #11 *MAYBELLINE*
(S) (2:13) Rhino 70793 Anthology 1964-1977. *(ends with :03 of different audience applause than found on the LP version)*
(S) (2:14) EMI 90727 Very Best Of. *(LP version which has ending audience applause)*
(S) (2:16) EMI 46594 Best Of. *(LP version which has ending audience applause)*
(S) (2:17) Pair 1195 Good Rockin'. *(LP version which has ending audience applause)*
1964 #10 *MOUNTAIN OF LOVE*
(S) (2:39) Rhino 70793 Anthology 1964-1977.
(S) (2:38) EMI 46594 Best Of.
1965 #37 *MIDNIGHT SPECIAL*
(S) (2:29) Rhino 70793 Anthology 1964-1977. *(LP version with audience applause at the end)*
(S) (2:29) EMI 90727 Very Best Of. *(LP version which has audience applause at the end)*
(S) (2:29) EMI 46594 Best Of. *(LP version which has audience applause at the end)*
(S) (2:34) Pair 1195 Good Rockin'. *(LP version which has audience applause at the end)*
1965 #7 *SEVENTH SON*
(S) (2:47) Rhino 70793 Anthology 1964-1977.
(S) (2:49) EMI 90727 Very Best Of.
(S) (2:47) EMI 46594 Best Of.
1965 #34 *WHERE HAVE ALL THE FLOWERS GONE*
(S) (3:16) Rhino 70793 Anthology 1964-1977. *(45 version but :14 longer fade)*
(S) (3:45) EMI 46594 Best Of. *(LP version)*

JOHNNY RIVERS (Continued)

1966 #4 SECRET AGENT MAN
- (S) (3:04) Rhino 70793 Anthology 1964-1977.
- (S) (3:04) EMI 90727 Very Best Of.
- (S) (3:04) EMI 46594 Best Of.

1966 #18 (I WASHED MY HANDS IN) MUDDY WATER
- (S) (3:00) Rhino 70793 Anthology 1964-1977.
- (S) (3:04) EMI 46594 Best Of.

1966 #1 POOR SIDE OF TOWN
- (S) (3:45) Rhino 70793 Anthology 1964-1977. *(:10 longer than LP length)*
- (S) (3:44) EMI 99900 Changes/Rewind. *(:09 longer than LP length)*
- (S) (3:05) EMI 90727 Very Best Of.
- (S) (3:35) EMI 46594 Best Of. *(LP length)*

1967 #6 BABY I NEED YOUR LOVIN'
- (S) (3:17) Rhino 70793 Anthology 1964-1977. *(45 version but :10 longer)*
- (S) (3:24) EMI 99900 Changes/Rewind. *(:18 longer than 45 or LP)*
- (S) (3:05) EMI 90727 Very Best Of. *(LP version)*
- (S) (3:07) EMI 46594 Best Of. *(LP version)*

1967 #10 THE TRACKS OF MY TEARS
- (S) (2:56) Rhino 70793 Anthology 1964-1977.
- (S) (2:59) EMI 99900 Changes/Rewind.
- (S) (2:54) EMI 90727 Very Best Of.
- (S) (2:54) EMI 46594 Best Of.
- (S) (2:52) Pair 1195 Good Rockin'.

1968 #10 SUMMER RAIN
- (S) (3:49) Rhino 70793 Anthology 1964-1977. *(:12 longer than either the 45 or LP)*
- (S) (3:37) EMI 46594 Best Of.
- (S) (3:52) Pair 1195 Good Rockin'. *(:15 longer than either the 45 or LP)*

1968 #25 LOOK TO YOUR SOUL
- (S) (3:30) Rhino 70793 Anthology 1964-1977. *(:30 longer than 45 version)*
- (S) (3:12) EMI 46594 Best Of. *(sound effects on intro and ending; LP version)*

1969 #30 MUDDY RIVER
- (S) (3:14) Rhino 70793 Anthology 1964-1977.

1970 #38 INTO THE MYSTIC
- (S) (4:40) Rhino 70793 Anthology 1964-1977.

1973 #5 ROCKIN' PNEUMONIA - BOOGIE WOOGIE FLU
- (S) (3:11) Rhino 70793 Anthology 1964-1977. *(edited; :15 shorter than either the LP or 45)*
- (S) (3:25) EMI 90727 Very Best Of.
- (S) (3:26) EMI 46594 Best Of.

1973 #27 BLUE SUEDE SHOES
- (S) (2:46) Rhino 70793 Anthology 1964-1977.
- (S) (2:49) EMI 90727 Very Best Of.
- (S) (2:45) EMI 46594 Best Of.
- (S) (2:48) Capitol 98139 Spring Break Volume 2.

RIVIERAS

1964 #6 CALIFORNIA SUN
- (M) (2:22) Rhino 70087 Summer & Sun.
- (M) (2:22) Rhino 75772 Son Of Frat Rock.
- (M) (2:21) JCI 3106 Surfin' Sixties.
- (M) (2:22) Dunhill Compact Classics 030 Beach Classics.
- (M) (2:22) A&M 3913 O.S.T. Good Morning Vietnam.

RIVINGTONS
1962 #35 *PAPA-OOM-MOW-MOW*
    (S) (2:21) EMI 90614 Non-Stop Party Rock.
    (S) (2:21) EMI 96268 24 Greatest Hits Of All Time.
    (S) (2:22) Capitol 48993 Spuds Mackenzie's Party Faves.
    (S) (2:22) Capitol 96861 Monster Summer Hits - Wild Surf.
    (S) (2:23) Dunhill Compact Classics 043 Toga Rock II.
    (S) (2:20) EMI 95204 The Liberty Years.
    (S) (2:22) Capitol 98138 Spring Break Volume 1.

MARTY ROBBINS
1956 #36 *SINGING THE BLUES*
    (M) (2:24) Columbia 46032 Columbia Country Classics Volume 4.
    (M) (2:25) Columbia 38870 A Lifetime Of Song.
    (M) (2:25) Columbia 45069 American Originals.
    (M) (2:25) Columbia 48537 Essential Marty Robbins.
1957 #3 *A WHITE SPORT COAT (AND A PINK CARNATION)*
    (M) (2:27) Columbia 45111 16 Most Requested Songs Of The 50's Volume
            2.
    (M) (2:28) Columbia 38870 A Lifetime Of Song.
    (M) (2:28) Columbia 48537 Essential Marty Robbins.
1958 #32 *THE STORY OF MY LIFE*
    (M) (2:30) Columbia 38870 A Lifetime Of Song.
    (M) (2:31) Columbia 48537 Essential Marty Robbins.
1960 #2 *EL PASO*
(stereo versions of El Paso omit several lines that are found on the mono or 45 version of this song; those lines start 1:28 into the mono version with "just for a moment..." and go to 1:43 "...and that was to run")
    (S) (4:19) Columbia 45017 Radio Classics Of The 50's.
    (M) (4:39) Rhino 70681 Billboard's Top Country Hits Of 1960.
    (M) (4:39) Rhino 70718 Legends Of Guitar - Country Volume 1.
    (S) (4:19) Columbia 46031 Columbia Country Classics Volume 3.
    (S) (4:22) Columbia 08435 More Greatest Hits.
    (S) (4:20) Columbia 38309 Biggest Hits.
    (S) (4:20) Columbia 00116 Gunfighter Ballads.
    (M) (4:39) Columbia 38870 A Lifetime Of Song.
    (S) (4:20) Columbia 31361 All Time Greatest.
    (M) (4:38) Columbia 48537 Essential Marty Robbins.
1960 #26 *BIG IRON*
    (S) (3:57) Columbia 46031 Columbia Country Classics Volume 3.
    (S) (3:57) Columbia 08435 More Greatest Hits.
    (S) (3:57) Columbia 00116 Gunfighter Ballads.
    (M) (3:54) Columbia 38870 A Lifetime Of Song.
    (S) (3:56) Columbia 31361 All Time Greatest.
    (M) (3:52) Columbia 48537 Essential Marty Robbins.
1960 #35 *BALLAD OF THE ALAMO*
    (S) (3:39) Columbia 08435 More Greatest Hits.
1961 #3 *DON'T WORRY*
    (S) (3:13) Columbia 08435 More Greatest Hits.
    (M) (3:09) Columbia 38870 A Lifetime Of Song.
    (S) (3:12) Columbia 31361 All Time Greatest.
    (M) (3:08) Columbia 48537 Essential Marty Robbins.
1962 #16 *DEVIL WOMAN*
    (S) (2:50) Columbia 46032 Columbia Country Classics Volume 4.
    (M) (2:51) Columbia 38870 A Lifetime Of Song.
    (S) (2:51) Columbia 31361 All Time Greatest.
    (S) (2:50) Columbia 48537 Essential Marty Robbins.

MARTY ROBBINS (Continued)
1962 #26 RUBY ANN
>   (M)   (1:58)   Columbia 38870   A Lifetime Of Song.
>   (M)   (1:58)   Columbia 45069   American Originals.
>   (M)   (1:59)   Columbia 48537   Essential Marty Robbins.

1970 #38 MY WOMAN MY WOMAN, MY WIFE
>   (S)   (3:31)   Columbia 38870   A Lifetime Of Song.
>   (S)   (3:30)   Columbia 31361   All Time Greatest.
>   (S)   (3:31)   Columbia 48537   Essential Marty Robbins.

AUSTIN ROBERTS
1972 #10 SOMETHING'S WRONG WITH ME
>   (S)   (3:07)   Rhino 70929   Super Hits Of The 70's Volume 9.

1973 #39 KEEP ON SINGING

DON ROBERTSON
1956 #8 THE HAPPY WHISTLER

IVO ROBIC
1959 #12 MORGEN

FLOYD ROBINSON
1959 #17 MAKIN' LOVE
>   (S)   (1:54)   RCA 8466   Nipper's Greatest Hits Of The 50's Volume 1.

SMOKEY ROBINSON & THE MIRACLES (see MIRACLES)

ROCHELL & THE CANDLES
1961 #27 ONCE UPON A TIME

ROCK-A-TEENS
1959 #18 WOO-HOO
>   (M)   (2:05)   Rhino 70742   Rock This Town: Rockabilly Hits Volume 2.

ROCKY FELLERS
1963 #16 KILLER JOE
>   (M)   (2:18)   Garland 011   Footstompin' Oldies.
>   (M)   (2:19)   Capricorn 42003   The Scepter Records Story.

EILEEN RODGERS
1956 #24 MIRACLE OF LOVE

JIMMIE RODGERS
1957 #1 HONEYCOMB
>   (M)   (2:14)   Rhino 70942   Best Of.
>   (M)   (2:14)   Collectables 5416   Murray The K - Sing Along With The Golden
>   Gassers. (*truncated fade*)
>   (S)   (2:11)   MCA 31086   Best Of. (*rerecording*)
>   (S)   (2:11)   Curb 77442   Best Of. (*rerecording*)

1957 #5 KISSES SWEETER THAN WINE
>   (M)   (2:19)   Rhino 70942   Best Of.
>   (S)   (2:16)   MCA 31086   Best Of. (*rerecording*)
>   (S)   (2:16)   Curb 77442   Best Of. (*rerecording*)

1958 #15 OH-OH, I'M FALLING IN LOVE AGAIN
>   (M)   (2:12)   Rhino 70942   Best Of.
>   (S)   (2:15)   MCA 31086   Best Of. (*rerecording*)
>   (S)   (2:15)   Curb 77442   Best Of. (*rerecording*)

1958 #4 SECRETLY
>   (M)   (2:34)   Rhino 70942   Best Of.
>   (M)   (2:34)   Curb 77442   Best Of.

JIMMIE RODGERS (Continued)
    1958 #31 *MAKE ME A MIRACLE*
              (M) (2:00) Rhino 70942 Best Of.
              (M) (2:00) Curb 77442 Best Of.
    1958 #14 *ARE YOU REALLY MINE*
              (S) (2:25) Rhino 70942 Best Of.
              (S) (2:15) MCA 31086 Best Of. *(rerecording)*
              (S) (2:15) Curb 77442 Best Of. *(rerecording)*
    1958 #11 *BIMBOMBEY*
              (M) (2:14) Rhino 70942 Best Of.
              (S) (2:10) MCA 31086 Best Of. *(rerecording)*
              (S) (2:10) Curb 77442 Best Of. *(rerecording)*
    1959 #39 *I'M NEVER GONNA TELL*
              (M) (1:50) Rhino 70942 Best Of.
    1959 #30 *BECAUSE YOU'RE YOUNG*
    1959 #38 *RING-A-LING-A-LARIO*
              (S) (2:20) Rhino 70942 Best Of.
    1959 #34 *TUCUMCARI*
               (S) (2:12) Rhino 70942 Best Of.
              (S) (2:12) Curb 77442 Best Of.
    1960 #27 *TENDER LOVE AND CARE (T.L.C.)*
              (S) (2:14) Rhino 70942 Best Of.
    1967 #30 *CHILD OF CLAY*
              (S) (4:07) Rhino 70942 Best Of.

TOMMY ROE
    1962 #2 *SHIELA*
              (S) (1:59) Rhino 70623 Billboard's Top Rock & Roll Hits Of 1962.
              (S) (1:59) Rhino 72007 Billboard's Top Rock & Roll Hits 1962-1966 Box
                         Set.
              (S) (2:02) MCA 31203 Vintage Music Volume 6.
              (S) (2:02) MCA 5804 Vintage Music Volumes 5 & 6.
              (S) (2:02) Curb 77525 Greatest Hits Of Rock 'N' Roll Volume 2.
              (S) (2:03) Curb 77299 Best Of.
    1962 #34 *SUSIE DARLIN'*
    1963 #5 *EVERYBODY*
              (E) (1:49) MCA 5938 Vintage Music Volumes 15 & 16.
              (E) (1:49) MCA 31212 Vintage Music Volume 15.
              (S) (3:11) Curb 77299 Best Of. *(rerecording)*
    1964 #27 *COME ON*
    1966 #8 *SWEET PEA*
              (S) (2:08) MCA 5939 Vintage Music Volumes 17 & 18.
              (S) (2:08) MCA 31215 Vintage Music Volume 18.
              (S) (2:08) Curb 77299 Best Of.
    1966 #6 *HOORAY FOR HAZEL*
    1967 #22 *IT'S NOW WINTERS DAY*
    1969 #1 *DIZZY*
              (S) (2:57) Rhino 70630 Billboard's Top Rock & Roll Hits Of 1969.
              (S) (2:57) Rhino 72005 Billboard's Top Rock & Roll Hits 1968-1972 Box
                         Set.
              (S) (2:57) MCA 31207 Vintage Music Volume 10.
              (S) (2:57) MCA 5806 Vintage Music Volumes 9 & 10.
              (S) (2:56) Curb 77299 Best Of.

TOMMY ROE (Continued)

1969 #14 *HEATHER HONEY*
1969 #40 *JACK AND JILL*
1970 #5 *JAM UP JELLY TIGHT*
1970 #32 *STIR IT UP AND SERVE IT*
1970 #30 *PEARL*
1970 #35 *WE CAN MAKE MUSIC*
1971 #19 *STAGGER LEE*

JULIE ROGERS

1965 #9 *THE WEDDING*

KENNY ROGERS & THE FIRST EDITION (*also* FIRST EDITION)

released as by THE FIRST EDITION:

1968 #5 *JUST DROPPED IN (TO SEE WHAT CONDITION MY CONDITION WAS IN)*
  (S) (3:19) Rhino 75754   Even More Nuggets.
  (S) (3:18) MCA 5895   15 Greatest Hits.
  (S) (3:18) MCA 31311   Greatest Hits.
  (S) (3:19) EMI 48047   Kenny Rogers: Ten Years Of Gold. *(rerecorded)*
  (S) (3:18) Pair 1238   Breakout.

1969 #15 *BUT YOU KNOW I LOVE YOU*
  (S) (3:01) MCA 5895   15 Greatest Hits.
  (S) (3:12) EMI 48047   Kenny Rogers: Ten Years Of Gold. *(rerecorded)*

released as by KENNY ROGERS & THE FIRST EDITION:

1969 #7 *RUBY, DON'T TAKE YOUR LOVE TO TOWN*
  (S) (2:56) MCA 5895   15 Greatest Hits.
  (S) (2:56) MCA 31311   Greatest Hits.
  (S) (2:50) Reprise 26711   Kenny Rogers 20 Great Years. *(rerecorded)*
  (S) (2:49) EMI 46106   Kenny Rogers Twenty Greatest Hits. *(rerecorded)*
  (S) (2:49) EMI 48047   Kenny Rogers: Ten Years Of Gold. *(rerecorded)*
  (S) (2:53) Pair 1238   Breakout.

1969 #14 *RUBEN JAMES*
  (S) (2:45) MCA 5895   15 Greatest Hits. *(truncated fade)*
  (S) (2:45) MCA 31311   Greatest Hits.
  (S) (2:37) EMI 46106   Kenny Rogers Twenty Greatest Hits. *(rerecorded)*
  (S) (2:37) EMI 48047   Kenny Rogers: Ten Years Of Gold. *(rerecorded)*
  (S) (2:44) Pair 1238   Breakout.

1970 #5 *SOMETHING'S BURNING*
  (S) (3:55) MCA 5895   15 Greatest Hits.
  (S) (3:55) MCA 31311   Greatest Hits.
  (S) (4:02) Reprise 26711   Kenny Rogers 20 Great Years. *(rerecorded)*
  (S) (4:17) EMI 46106   Kenny Rogers Twenty Greatest Hits. *(rerecorded)*
  (S) (4:16) EMI 48047   Kenny Rogers: Ten Years Of Gold. *(rerecorded)*
  (S) (3:48) Pair 1238   Breakout.

1970 #17 *TELL IT ALL BROTHER*
  (S) (3:20) MCA 5895   15 Greatest Hits.
  (S) (3:20) MCA 31311   Greatest Hits.
  (S) (3:22) Pair 1238   Breakout.

1970 #21 *HEED THE CALL*
  (S) (3:17) MCA 5895   15 Greatest Hits.
  (S) (3:17) MCA 31311   Greatest Hits.
  (S) (3:18) Pair 1238   Breakout.

TIMMIE "OH YEAH" ROGERS
1957 #30 *BACK TO SCHOOL AGAIN*

ROLLING STONES
1964 #27 *TELL ME (YOU'RE COMING BACK)*
- (M) (2:45) Abkco 1218 Singles Collection: The London Years. (*45 version*)
- (M) (3:46) Abkco 8001 Big Hits (High Tide And Green Grass). (*LP version*)
- (M) (3:46) Abkco 7375 England's Newest Hitmakers. (*LP version*)
- (M) (3:46) Abkco 6267 More Hot Rocks. (*LP version*)

1964 #25 *IT'S ALL OVER NOW*
- (M) (3:26) Abkco 1218 Singles Collection: The London Years.
- (M) (3:26) Abkco 8001 Big Hits (High Tide And Green Grass).
- (M) (3:25) Abkco 7402 12 x 5.
- (M) (3:26) Abkco 6267 More Hot Rocks.

1964 #6 *TIME IS ON MY SIDE*
- (M) (2:57) Abkco 1218 Singles Collection: The London Years. (*neither the U.S. 45 or LP version; this version first showed up on the vinyl LP "Big Hits (High Tide And Green Grass)"*)
- (M) (2:49) Abkco 8001 Big Hits (High Tide And Green Grass). (*45 and "12 x 5" LP version; not the version that appeared on the vinyl LP "Big Hits (High Tide And Green Grass)"*)
- (M) (2:51) Abkco 7402 12 x 5.
- (M) (2:57) Abkco 6667 Hot Rocks 1964-1971. (*same comments as for Abkco 1218*)

1965 #16 *HEART OF STONE*
- (M) (2:42) Abkco 1218 Singles Collection: The London Years. (*the first :01 is stereo, the rest of the song is mono*)
- (S) (2:45) Abkco 8001 Big Hits (High Tide And Green Grass).
- (S) (2:45) Abkco 7420 Now!
- (M) (2:42) Abkco 6667 Hot Rocks 1964-1971. (*the first :01 is stereo, the rest of the song is mono*)

1965 #10 *THE LAST TIME*
- (M) (3:38) Abkco 1218 Singles Collection: The London Years.
- (M) (3:39) Abkco 7429 Out Of Our Heads.
- (M) (3:39) Abkco 8001 Big Hits (High Tide And Green Grass).
- (M) (3:39) Abkco 6267 More Hot Rocks.

1965 #1 *(I CAN'T GET NO) SATISFACTION*
- (M) (3:44) Abkco 1218 Singles Collection: The London Years.
- (M) (3:42) Abkco 7429 Out Of Our Heads.
- (M) (3:42) Abkco 8001 Big Hits (High Tide And Green Grass).
- (M) (3:44) Abkco 6667 Hot Rocks 1964-1971.

1965 #1 *GET OFF MY CLOUD*
- (M) (2:54) Abkco 1218 Singles Collection: The London Years.
- (M) (2:56) Abkco 7451 December's Children.
- (M) (2:56) Abkco 8001 Big Hits (High Tide And Green Grass).
- (M) (2:54) Abkco 6667 Hot Rocks 1964-1971.

1966 #3 *AS TEARS GO BY*
- (M) (2:42) Abkco 1218 Singles Collection: The London Years.
- (M) (2:43) Abkco 7451 December's Children.
- (M) (2:42) Abkco 8001 Big Hits (High Tide And Green Grass).
- (M) (2:43) Abkco 6667 Hot Rocks 1964-1971.

1966 #1 *19TH NERVOUS BREAKDOWN*
- (M) (3:56) Abkco 1218 Singles Collection: The London Years.
- (M) (3:56) Abkco 8001 Big Hits (High Tide And Green Grass).
- (M) (3:56) Abkco 6667 Hot Rocks 1964-1971.

ROLLING STONES (Continued)

1966 #1 PAINT IT, BLACK
- (M) (3:44) Abkco 1218   Singles Collection: The London Years. (*:23 longer than 45 and LP*)
- (M) (3:45) Abkco 8003   Through The Past Darkly (Big Hits Vol. 2). (*:24 longer than 45 and LP*)
- (M) (3:44) Abkco 6667   Hot Rocks 1964-1971. (*:23 longer than 45 and LP*)
- (M) (3:46) Abkco 7476   Aftermath. (*:25 longer than 45 and LP*)

1966 #4 MOTHERS LITTLE HELPER
- (M) (2:45) Abkco 1218   Singles Collection: The London Years.
- (E) (2:45) Abkco 8003   Through The Past Darkly (Big Hits Vol. 2).
- (E) (2:45) Abkco 6667   Hot Rocks 1964-1971.
- (E) (2:45) Abkco 7509   Flowers.

1966 #4 HAVE YOU SEEN YOUR MOTHER, BABY, STANDING IN THE SHADOW?
- (E) (2:33) Abkco 1218   Singles Collection: The London Years.
- (E) (2:33) Abkco 8003   Through The Past Darkly (Big Hits Vol. 2).
- (E) (2:33) Abkco 6267   More Hot Rocks.
- (E) (2:33) Abkco 7509   Flowers.

1967 #1 RUBY TUESDAY
- (M) (3:11) Abkco 1218   Singles Collection: The London Years.
- (S) (3:15) Abkco 8003   Through The Past Darkly (Big Hits Vol. 2).
- (S) (3:15) Abkco 7499   Between The Buttons.
- (S) (3:15) Abkco 6667   Hot Rocks 1964-1971.
- (S) (3:15) Abkco 7509   Flowers.

1967 #28 LET'S SPEND THE NIGHT TOGETHER
(the actual LP time is (3:36) not (3:29) as stated on the record label)
- (M) (3:24) Abkco 1218   Singles Collection: The London Years.
- (S) (3:37) Abkco 8003   Through The Past Darkly (Big Hits Vol. 2).
- (E) (3:36) Abkco 7499   Between The Buttons.
- (S) (3:36) Abkco 6667   Hot Rocks 1964-1971.
- (S) (3:36) Abkco 7509   Flowers.

1967 #6 DANDELION
(the actual LP time is (3:30) not (3:56) as stated on the record label; the actual 45 time is (3:50) not (3:56) as stated on the record label)
- (M) (3:47) Abkco 1218   Singles Collection: The London Years. (*45 version*)
- (S) (3:30) Abkco 8003   Through The Past Darkly (Big Hits Vol. 2). (*LP version*)
- (S) (3:30) Abkco 6267   More Hot Rocks. (*LP version*)

1968 #10 SHE'S A RAINBOW
- (M) (4:08) Abkco 1218   Singles Collection: The London Years. (*45 version*)
- (S) (4:35) Abkco 8003   Through The Past Darkly (Big Hits Vol. 2). (*LP version*)
- (S) (4:35) Abkco 6267   More Hot Rocks. (*LP version*)
- (S) (5:18) Abkco 8002   Their Satanic Majesties Request. (*LP version; mistakenly includes :42 outro from the selection "SING ALL THIS TOGETHER (SEE WHAT HAPPENS)"*)

1968 #1 JUMPIN' JACK FLASH
- (S) (3:39) Abkco 1218   Singles Collection: The London Years.
- (M) (3:40) Abkco 8003   Through The Past Darkly (Big Hits Vol. 2).
- (S) (3:39) Abkco 6667   Hot Rocks 1964-1971.

ROLLING STONES (Continued)

1968 #30 STREET FIGHTING MAN
- (S) (3:15) Abkco 1218 Singles Collection: The London Years. (*very poor stereo separation*)
- (S) (3:16) Abkco 8003 Through The Past Darkly (Big Hits Vol. 2). (*very poor stereo separation*)
- (S) (3:15) Abkco 7539 Beggar's Banquet. (*very poor stereo separation*)
- (S) (3:14) Abkco 6667 Hot Rocks 1964-1971. (*very poor stereo separation*)

1969 #1 HONKY TONK WOMEN
- (M) (2:59) Abkco 1218 Singles Collection: The London Years.
- (M) (3:00) Abkco 8003 Through The Past Darkly (Big Hits Vol. 2). (*noise on introduction*)
- (M) (2:59) Abkco 6667 Hot Rocks 1964-1971.

1971 #2 BROWN SUGAR
- (S) (3:47) Atlantic 81908 Classic Rock 1966-1988. (*LP mix*)
- (S) (3:47) Atlantic 82306 Atlantic Rock & Roll Box Set. (*LP mix*)
- (S) (3:47) Abkco 1218 Singles Collection: The London Years. (*LP mix*)
- (S) (3:47) Abkco 6667 Hot Rocks 1964-1971. (*LP mix*)
- (S) (3:48) Columbia 40488 Sticky Fingers. (*LP mix*)
- (S) (3:47) Columbia 40505 Rewind. (*LP mix*)
- (S) (3:49) Columbia 40494 Made In The Shade. (*LP mix*)

1971 #18 WILD HORSES
(dj copies of this 45 ran (5:38) and (3:25); commercial copies were all (5:38))
- (S) (5:39) Abkco 1218 Singles Collection: The London Years.
- (S) (5:39) Abkco 6667 Hot Rocks 1964-1971.
- (S) (5:40) Columbia 40488 Sticky Fingers.
- (S) (5:41) Columbia 40494 Made In The Shade.

1972 #10 TUMBLING DICE
- (S) (3:42) Columbia 40489 Exile On Main Street.
- (S) (3:37) Columbia 40505 Rewind.
- (S) (3:44) Columbia 40494 Made In The Shade.

1972 #14 HAPPY
- (S) (3:01) Columbia 40489 Exile On Main Street.
- (S) (3:03) Columbia 40494 Made In The Shade.

1973 #34 YOU CAN'T ALWAYS GET WHAT YOU WANT
- (S) (4:49) Abkco 1218 Singles Collection: The London Years. (*45 version*)
- (S) (7:27) Abkco 8004 Let It Bleed. (*LP version*)
- (S) (7:29) Abkco 6667 Hot Rocks 1964-1971. (*LP version*)

1973 #1 ANGIE
- (S) (4:30) Columbia 40492 Goats Head Soup.
- (S) (4:30) Columbia 40505 Rewind.
- (S) (4:29) Columbia 40494 Made In The Shade.

RONALD & RUBY
1958 #2 LOLLIPOP

DON RONDO
1956 #12 TWO DIFFERENT WORLDS
1957 #6 WHITE SILVER SANDS

RONETTES
1963 #1 BE MY BABY
- (M) (2:38) RCA 6408 O.S.T. Dirty Dancing.
- (M) (2:39) Abkco 7118 Phil Spector/Back To Mono (1958-1969).

1964 #24 BABY, I LOVE YOU
- (M) (2:48) Abkco 7118 Phil Spector/Back To Mono (1958-1969).

RONETTES (Continued)
1964 #36 *DO I LOVE YOU?*
  (M) (2:49) Abkco 7118 Phil Spector/Back To Mono (1958-1969).
1964 #20 *WALKING IN THE RAIN*
  (M) (3:14) Abkco 7118 Phil Spector/Back To Mono (1958-1969).

RONNIE & THE HI-LITES
1962 #18 *I WISH THAT WE WERE MARRIED*
  (M) (2:50) Rhino 70589 Rockin' & Rollin' Wedding Songs Volume 2.

RONNY & THE DAYTONAS
1964 #5 *G.T.O.*
  (M) (2:26) JCI 3106 Surfin' Sixties.
  (M) (2:27) Dunhill Compact Classics 030 Beach Classics.

LINDA RONSTADT
1970 #26 *LONG LONG TIME*
  (S) (4:21) Asylum 106 Greatest Hits.

ROOFTOP SINGERS
1963 #1 *WALK RIGHT IN*
  (S) (2:32) Vanguard 17/18 Greatest Folksingers Of The 60's.
  (S) (2:33) Rhino 70995 One Hit Wonders Of The 60's Volume 1.
  (S) (2:33) Rhino 70264 Troubadours Of The Folk Era Volume 2.
  (M) (2:33) Vanguard 79457 Best Of.
1963 #20 *TOM CAT*
  (M) (2:25) Vanguard 79457 Best Of.

EDMUNDO ROS
1958 #15 *COLONEL BOGEY*

ANDY ROSE
1958 #28 *JUST YOUNG*

DAVID ROSE & HIS ORCHESTRA
1957 #33 *CALYPSO MELODY*
1958 #18 *SWINGING SHEPHERD BLUES*
1962 #1 *THE STRIPPER*
  (S) (1:54) Rhino 70995 One Hit Wonders Of The 60's Volume 1.

ROSE GARDEN
1967 #15 *NEXT PLANE TO LONDON*

ROSIE & THE ORIGINALS
1961 #6 *ANGEL BABY*

DIANA ROSS
1970 #10 *REACH OUT AND TOUCH (SOMEBODY'S HAND)*
  (S) (3:04) Motown 6140 The Composer Series: Ashford & Simpson.
  (S) (3:03) Motown 9097 The Most Played Oldies On America's Jukeboxes.
  (S) (2:58) Motown 6197 and 6049 Anthology.
  (S) (3:03) Motown 6072 Compact Command Performances.
  (S) (2:58) Motown 0869 Greatest Hits. *(truncated fade)*
  (S) (2:58) Motown 0960 All The Great Hits.
  (S) (3:03) Motown 8042 and 8142 Ain't No Mountain High
      Enough/Surrender.
  (S) (3:02) Motown 5135 Ain't No Mountain High Enough.
1970 #1 *AIN'T NO MOUNTAIN HIGH ENOUGH*
  (S) (3:29) Motown 6132 25 #1 Hits From 25 Years.
  (S) (3:29) Motown 6140 The Composer Series: Ashford & Simpson.

    (S) (3:55) Rhino 70658 Billboard's Top R&B Hits Of 1970. *(neither the 45 or LP version)*

    (S) (3:28) Motown 5344 Every Great Motown Song: The First 25 Years Volume 2. *(most selections on this cd have noise on the fade out)*

    (S) (3:28) Motown 8034 and 8134 Every Great Motown Song: The First 25 Years Volumes 1 & 2. *(most selections on this cd have noise on the fade out)*

    (S) (3:28) Motown 9060 Motown's Biggest Pop Hits.

    (S) (6:15) Motown 0937 20/20 Twenty No. 1 Hits From Twenty Years At Motown. *(LP version)*

    (S) (3:40) Motown 6197 and 6049 Anthology. *(neither the 45 or LP version)*

    (S) (6:16) Motown 6072 Compact Command Performances. *(LP version)*

    (S) (6:16) Motown 0869 Greatest Hits. *(LP version)*

    (S) (6:16) Motown 0960 All The Great Hits. *(LP version)*

    (S) (6:14) Motown 8042 and 8142 Ain't No Mountain High Enough/Surrender. *(LP version)*

    (S) (6:15) Motown 5135 Ain't No Mountain High Enough. *(LP version)*

1971 #8 REMEMBER ME
4(the 45 time is (3:16); the LP time is (3:29))

    (S) (3:28) Motown 9109 Motown Memories Volume 3.

    (S) (3:30) Motown 6140 The Composer Series: Ashford & Simpson.

    (S) (3:16) Motown 619 and 6049 Anthology.

    (S) (3:29) Motown 6072 Compact Command Performances.

    (S) (3:17) Motown 0869 Greatest Hits.

    (S) (3:16) Motown 0960 All The Great Hits.

    (S) (3:29) Motown 8042 and 8142 Ain't No Mountain High Enough/Surrender. *(truncated fade)*

    (S) (3:26) Motown 5423 Surrender.

1971 #19 REACH OUT I'LL BE THERE

    (S) (5:34) Motown 6197 and 6049 Anthology. *(LP version)*

    (S) (4:01) Motown 6072 Compact Command Performances. *(neither 45 or LP version)*

    (S) (5:27) Motown 8042 and 8142 Ain't No Mountain High Enough/Surrender. *(LP version)*

    (S) (5:25) Motown 5423 Surrender. *(LP version)*

1973 #30 GOOD MORNING HEARTACHE

    (S) (2:19) Motown 6197 and 6049 Anthology.

    (S) (2:20) Motown 6072 Compact Command Performances.

    (S) (2:19) Motown 0869 Greatest Hits.

1973 #1 TOUCH ME IN THE MORNING
(the 45 time is (3:51); the LP time is (3:25))

    (S) (3:26) Motown 6137 20 Greatest Songs In Motown History.

    (S) (3:25) Motown 6177 Endless Love.

    (S) (3:25) Motown 5385 Three Times A Lady: Great Motown Love Songs.

    (S) (3:25) Motown 9021 and 5309 25 Years Of Grammy Greats.

    (S) (3:25) Motown 5344 Every Great Motown Song: The First 25 Years Volume 2. *(most selections on this cd have noise on the fadeout)*

    (S) (3:25) Motown 5275 12 #1 Hits From The 70's.

    (S) (3:26) Motown 8034 and 8134 Every Great Motown Song: The First 25 Years Volumes 1 & 2. *(most selections on this cd have noise on the fade out)*

    (S) (3:47) Motown 6197 and 6049 Anthology.

    (S) (3:25) Motown 6072 Compact Command Performances.

    (S) (3:51) Motown 0869 Greatest Hits.

DIANA ROSS (Continued)
(S) (3:51) Motown 0960 All The Great Hits.
(S) (3:25) Motown 6105 All The Great Love Songs.
(S) (3:51) Motown 5163 Touch Me In The Morning.
(S) (3:26) Motown 8026 and 8126 Touch Me In The Morning/ Baby It's Me.

DIANA ROSS & MARVIN GAYE
1973 #14 *YOU'RE A SPECIAL PART OF ME*
(S) (3:36) Motown 9109 Motown Memories Volume 3.
(S) (3:37) Motown 6153 and 9053 Marvin Gaye & His Women.
(S) (4:36) Motown 6311 The Marvin Gaye Collection. (*previously unreleased extended version*)
(S) (3:36) Motown 6197 and 6049 Diana Ross Anthology.
(S) (3:36) Motown 9090 and 5124 Diana & Marvin.

JACK ROSS
1962 #35 *CINDERELLA*

JACKIE ROSS
1964 #11 *SELFISH ONE*
(S) (3:15) MCA 31205 Vintage Music Volume 8.
(S) (3:15) MCA 5805 Vintage Music Volumes 7 & 8.
(S) (3:15) Chess 31318 Best Of Chess Rhythm & Blues Volume 2.

SPENCER ROSS
1960 #15 *TRACY'S THEME*

ROUTERS
1962 #27 *LET'S GO (PONY)*
(S) (2:16) Warner Special Projects 27610 More Party Classics.
(S) (2:16) JCI 3106 Surfin' Sixties.

ROVER BOYS
1956 #6 *GRADUATION DAY*

BILLY JOE ROYAL
1965 #6 *DOWN IN THE BOONDOCKS*
(S) (2:32) Columbia 45018 Rock Classics Of The 60's.
(S) (2:32) Columbia 45063 Greatest Hits.

1965 #14 *I KNEW YOU WHEN*
(S) (2:30) Columbia 45063 Greatest Hits.

1966 #35 *I'VE GOT TO BE SOMEBODY*
(S) (3:01) Columbia 45063 Greatest Hits.

1969 #15 *CHERRY HILL PARK*
(S) (2:59) Columbia 45063 Greatest Hits. (*includes additional background vocals not found on the 45 or LP; :13 longer than 45 or LP*)
(S) (2:46) Rhino 70921 Super Hits Of The 70's Volume 1.
(S) (2:46) Rhino 72009 Super Hits Of The 70's Volumes 1-4 Box Set.

ROYALETTES
1965 #37 *IT'S GONNA TAKE A MIRACLE*

ROYAL GUARDSMEN
1967 #2 *SNOOPY VS. THE RED BARON*
1967 #15 *RETURN OF THE RED BARON*
1967 #10 *SNOOPY'S CHRISTMAS*
1969 #33 *BABY LET'S WAIT*
(M) (2:35) K-Tel 205 Battle Of The Bands Volume 3.

ROYAL SCOTS DRAGOON GUARDS
1972 #10 *AMAZING GRACE*
    (E) (3:18) RCA 52008 Amazing Grace.

ROYAL TEENS
1958 #3 *SHORT SHORTS*
    (M) (2:36) MCA 31201 Vintage Music Volume 4.
    (M) (2:36) MCA 5778 Vintage Music Volumes 3 & 4.
1959 #24 *BELIEVE ME*

ROYALTONES
1958 #31 *POOR BOY*

RUBY & THE ROMANTICS
1963 #1 *OUR DAY WILL COME*
    (S) (2:31) Rhino 70649 Billboard's Top R&B Hits Of 1963.
    (S) (2:31) MCA 31206 Vintage Music Volume 9.
    (S) (2:31) MCA 5806 Vintage Music Volumes 9 & 10.
1963 #20 *MY SUMMER LOVE*
1963 #34 *HEY THERE LONELY BOY*
1963 #40 *YOUNG WINGS CAN FLY*

DAVID RUFFIN
1969 #9 *MY WHOLE WORLD ENDED (THE MOMENT YOU LEFT ME)*
    (S) (3:26) Motown 6183 Hard To Find Motown Classics Volume 1.
    (S) (3:26) Motown 5211 At His Best.
    (S) (3:26) Motown 5108 Jimmy & David Ruffin Superstar Series Volume 8.

JIMMY RUFFIN
1966 #9 *WHAT BECOMES OF THE BROKEN HEARTED*
    (S) (2:57) Motown 6183 Hard To Find Motown Classics Volume 1.
    (S) (2:56) Motown 5454 A Collection Of 16 Big Hits Volume 7.
    (S) (2:57) Motown 5445 Sings Top Ten.
    (S) (2:57) Motown 5108 Jimmy & David Ruffin Superstar Series Volume 8.
1967 #17 *I'VE PASSED THIS WAY BEFORE*
    (S) (2:41) Motown 6183 Hard To Find Motown Classics Volume 1.
    (S) (2:41) Motown 5445 Sings Top Ten.
    (S) (2:41) Motown 5108 Jimmy & David Ruffin Superstar Series Volume 8.

RUGBYS
1969 #22 *YOU, I*

TODD RUNDGREN (*also* RUNT)
released as by RUNT:
1971 #21 *WE GOTTA GET YOU A WOMAN*
    (S) (3:06) Rhino 71491 Anthology (1968-1985).
    (S) (3:06) Rhino 70862 Runt.

released as by TODD RUNDGREN:
1972 #11 *I SAW THE LIGHT*
    (S) (2:57) Sandstone 33000 Reelin' In The Years Volume 1.
    (S) (2:57) Epic 48732 O.S.T. My Girl.
    (S) (2:57) Rhino 71491 Anthology (1968-1985).
    (S) (2:59) Rhino 71107 Something/Anything.

TODD RUNDGREN (Continued)
1973 #2 HELLO IT'S ME
    (S) (3:47) Priority 7997 Super Songs/70's Greatest Rock Hits Volume 8.
    (S) (3:49) Sandstone 33003 Reelin' In The Years Volume 4.
    (S) (3:49) Rhino 71491 Anthology (1968-1985).
    (S) (4:37) Rhino 71107 Something/Anything. *(LP version)*

RUNT (see TODD RUNDGREN)

MERRILEE RUSH & THE TURNABOUTS
1968 #3 ANGEL OF THE MORNING
    (M) (3:09) Rhino 70996 One Hit Wonders Of The 60's Volume 2.
1968 #40 THAT KIND OF WOMAN

BOBBY RUSSELL
1971 #34 SATURDAY MORNING CONFUSION
    (S) (3:04) Rhino 70926 Super Hits Of The 70's Volume 6.

LEON RUSSELL
1972 #10 TIGHT ROPE
    (S) (2:57) Priority 7997 Super Songs/70's Greatest Rock Hits Volume 8.
    (S) (2:59) Shelter/Dunhill Compact Classics 8006 Carney.
    (S) (2:58) Shelter/Dunhill compact Classics 8017 Best Of. *(noise on fadeout)*

CHARLIE RYAN & THE TIMBERLINE RIDERS
1960 #25 HOT ROD LINCOLN

BOBBY RYDELL
1959 #16 KISSIN' TIME
1959 #4 WE GOT LOVE
1960 #3 WILD ONE
1960 #6 SWINGIN' SCHOOL
1960 #17 DING-A-LING
1960 #4 VOLARE
1960 #12 SWAY
1961 #13 GOOD TIME BABY
1961 #21 THAT OLD BLACK MAGIC
1961 #17 THE FISH
1961 #22 I WANNA THANK YOU
1962 #17 I'VE GOT BONNIE
1962 #19 I'LL NEVER DANCE AGAIN
1962 #13 THE CHA-CHA-CHA
1963 #24 BUTTERFLY BABY
1963 #26 WILDWOOD DAYS
1964 #5 FORGET HIM

BOBBY RYDELL & CHUBBY CHECKER
1962 #38 JINGLE BELL ROCK

MITCH RYDER & THE DETROIT WHEELS
1966 #17 JENNY TAKE A RIDE!
    (S) (3:20) Dunhill Compact Classics 029 Toga Rock.
    (E) (3:20) JCI 3101 Rockin' Sixties.
    (S) (3:21) K-Tel 686 Battle Of The Bands Volume 4.
    (S) (3:21) Rhino 70941 Rev Up: The Best Of.

MITCH RYDER & THE DETROIT WHEELS (Continued)
1966 #16 *LITTLE LATIN LUPE LU*
      (S)   (3:06) Rhino 70941 Rev Up: The Best Of.
      (S)   (3:06) Pair 1277 Big Wheels.
1966 #4 *DEVIL WITH A BLUE DRESS ON & GOOD GOLLY MISS MOLLY*
      (S)   (3:04) Rhino 70906 American Bandstand Greatest Hits Collection. *(LP version)*
      (S)   (3:04) Rhino 75772 Son Of Frat Rock. *(LP version)*
      (S)   (3:03) JCI 3100 Dance Sixties. *(LP version)*
      (S)   (3:04) Dunhill Compact Classics 029 Toga Rock. *(LP version)*
      (S)   (3:28) Rhino 70941 Rev Up: The Best Of Mitch Ryder. *(very similar to the 45 version but includes some extra background vocals near the end and has a slightly longer fade)*
      (S)   (3:28) Pair 1277 Big Wheels. *(same comments as for Rhino 70941)*
1967 #4 *SOCK IT TO ME BABY!*
      (S)   (3:10) Rhino 70941 Rev Up: The Best Of. *(LP version)*
      (S)   (3:10) Rhino 70794 KFOG Presents M. Dung's Idiot Show. *(LP version)*
1967 #26 *TOO MANY FISH IN THE SEA & THREE LITTLE FISHES*
      (S)   (2:59) Rhino 70941 Rev Up: The Best Of.
      (S)   (2:59) Pair 1277 Big Wheels.

released as by MITCH RYDER:
1967 #39 *JOY*
      (S)   (3:07) Rhino 70941 Rev Up: The Best Of.
      (S)   (3:07) Pair 1277 Big Wheels.
1967 #22 *WHAT NOW MY LOVE*
      (S)   (3:58) Pair 1277 Big Wheels.

SSgt. BARRY SADLER
1966 #1 *THE BALLAD OF THE GREEN BERETS*
      (S)   (2:27) RCA 8475 Nipper's Greatest Hits Of The 60's Volume 2.
      (S)   (2:27) RCA 9902 Nipper's #1 Hits 1956-1986.
      (S)   (2:27) RCA 5802 Best Of The 60's.
1966 #18 *THE "A" TEAM*
SAFARIS
1960 #7 *IMAGE OF A GIRL*
SAILCAT
1972 #19 *MOTORCYCLE MAMA*
      (S)   (2:04) Rhino 70928 Super Hits Of The 70's Volume 8.
BUFFY SAINTE-MARIE
1972 #40 *MISTER CAN'T YOU SEE*

CRISPIAN ST. PETERS
1966 #4 *THE PIED PIPER*
KYU SAKAMOTO
1963 #1 *SUKIYAKI*
    (M) (3:03) Capitol 98665 When AM Was King. *(sounds like it was mastered from vinyl)*

SAM & DAVE
1966 #16 *HOLD ON! I'M COMIN'*
    (M) (2:34) Atlantic Group 88218 Complete Stax/Volt Singles.
    (M) (2:32) Atlantic 81297 Atlantic Rhythm & Blues Volume 5.
    (S) (2:28) JCI 3105 Soul Sixties.
    (S) (2:26) Stax 88005 Top Of The Stax.
    (M) (2:34) Warner Special Products 27602 20 Party Classics.
    (S) (2:29) Atlantic 82305 Atlantic Rhythm And Blues 1947-1974 Box Set.
    (S) (2:29) Atlantic 81279 Best Of.
    (S) (2:30) Atlantic 80255 Hold On I'm Comin'.
1967 #1 *SOUL MAN*
    (M) (2:37) Atlantic Group 88218 Complete Stax/Volt Singles.
    (M) (2:34) Atlantic 81298 Atlantic Rhythm & Blues Volume 6.
    (M) (2:34) Atlantic 81911 Golden Age Of Black Music (1960-1970).
    (S) (2:35) Warner Special Products 27601 Atlantic Soul Classics.
    (M) (2:36) Atlantic 82305 Atlantic Rhythm And Blues 1947-1974 Box Set.
    (M) (2:36) Atlantic 81279 Best Of.
    (S) (2:36) Rhino 70296 Soul Men.
1968 #8 *I THANK YOU*
    (M) (2:43) Atlantic Group 88218 Complete Stax/Volt Singles.
    (S) (2:52) Warner Special Products 27609 Memphis Soul Classics.
    (S) (2:51) Atlantic 81279 Best Of.
1968 #40 *YOU DON'T KNOW WHAT YOU MEAN TO ME*
    (S) (2:39) Atlantic 81279 Best Of.

SAM THE SHAM & THE PHARAOHS
1965 #2 *WOOLY BULLY*
    (S) (2:18) Warner Brothers 25613 O.S.T. Full Metal Jacket.
    (M) (2:18) Rhino 70626 Billboard's Top Rock & Roll Hits Of 1965.
    (M) (2:18) Rhino 72007 Billboard's Top Rock & Roll Hits 1962-1966 Box Set.
    (M) (2:18) Rhino 75778 Frat Rock.
    (S) (2:18) Mercury 816555 45's On CD Volume 2.
    (S) (2:18) Dunhill Compact Classics 029 Toga Rock.
    (S) (2:19) K-Tel 205 Battle Of The Bands Volume 3.
    (S) (2:19) Warner Special Products 27607 Highs Of The 60's.
    (S) (2:17) Priority 7909 Vietnam: Rockin' The Delta.
    (S) (2:19) Polydor 827917 Best Of.
1965 #28 *JU JU HAND*
    (M) (2:07) Polydor 827917 Best Of.
1965 #28 *RING DANG DOO*
    (M) (2:21) Rhino 70794 KFOG Presents M. Dung's Idiot Show.
    (S) (2:24) Polydor 827917 Best Of.
1966 #1 *LIL' RED RIDING HOOD*
    (M) (2:38) Dunhill Compact Classics 050 Monster Rock 'n' Roll Show.
    (M) (2:39) Polydor 827917 Best Of.
1966 #20 *THE HAIR ON MY CHINNY CHIN CHIN*
    (M) (2:35) Polydor 827917 Best Of.
1967 #31 *HOW DO YOU CATCH A GIRL*

SANDPEBBLES
1968 #36 *LOVE POWER*

SANDPIPERS
1966 #7   *GUANTANAMERA*
    (S)   (3:10) Priority 9461   Mellow 60's.
1966 #35 *LOUIE LOUIE*
    (S)   (2:47) Rhino 70605   Best Of Louie Louie. *(sounds like it was mastered from vinyl)*
1970 #13 *COME SATURDAY MORNING*
    (S)   (2:59) Rhino 70921   Super Hits Of The 70's Volume 1.
    (S)   (2:59) Rhino 72009   Super Hits Of The 70's Volumes 1-4 Box Set.

JODIE SANDS
1957 #19 *WITH ALL MY HEART*

TOMMY SANDS
1957 #2   *TEEN-AGE CRUSH*
1957 #25 *MY LOVE SONG*
1957 #31 *RING-A-DING-A-DING*
1957 #24 *GOIN' STEADY*

MONGO SANTAMARIA
1963 #9   *WATERMELON MAN*
    (S)   (3:12) Columbia 1060   Greatest Hits. *(rerecording)*

SANTANA
1969 #37 *JINGO*
    (S)   (4:19) Columbia 9781   Santana. *(LP version)*
1970 #7   *EVIL WAYS*
    (S)   (3:51) Columbia 45018   Rock Classics Of The 60's. *(LP version)*
    (S)   (3:55) Columbia 9781   Santana. *(LP version)*
1971 #4   *BLACK MAGIC WOMAN*
(the LP version is a medley of "BLACK MAGIC WOMAN" and "GYPSY QUEEN")
    (S)   (3:17) Rhino 70632   Billbord's Top Rock & Roll Hits Of 1971.
    (S)   (3:17) JCI 3302   Electric 70's.
    (S)   (5:20) Columbia 45048   Rock Classics Of The 70's. *(LP version)*
    (S)   (5:16) Columbia 30130   Abraxas. *(LP version; previous selection tracks over introduction)*
    (S)   (5:19) MFSL 552   Abraxas. *(LP version; previous selection tracks over introduction)*
1971 #10 *OYE COMO VA*
    (S)   (4:15) Columbia 30130   Abraxas. *(LP version)*
    (S)   (4:16) MFSL 552   Abraxas. *(LP version)*
1971 #10 *EVERYBODY'S EVERYTHING*
    (S)   (3:27) Columbia 30595   Santana.
1972 #17 *NO ONE TO DEPEND ON*
    (S)   (5:30) Columbia 30595   Santana. *(LP version; this song, the preceeding song and the following song are all segued together)*

SANTO & JOHNNY
1959 #2   *SLEEP WALK*
    (M)   (2:20) Rhino 70620   Billboard's Top Rock & Roll Hits Of 1959.
    (M)   (2:20) Rhino 72004   Billboard's Top Rock & Roll Hits 1957-1961 Box Set.
    (M)   (2:20) Geffen 24310   O.S.T. Mermaids.
    (M)   (2:20) Rhino 70561   Legends Of Guitar - Rock: The 50's Volume 2.

SANTO & JOHNNY (Continued)
1960 #22 *TEAR DROP*
1960 #39 *CARAVAN*
1960 #39 *TWISTIN' BELLS*
>   (M) (2:16) Rhino 70192 Christmas Classics. (*sounds like it was mastered from vinyl*)

SAPPHIRES
1964 #23 *WHO DO YOU LOVE*

LALO SCHIFRIN
1968 #39 *MISSION IMPOSSIBLE*

BOBBY SCOTT
1956 #10 *CHAIN GANG*

FREDDIE SCOTT
1963 #10 *HEY, GIRL*
>   (S) (3:06) Collectables 5413 Sings And Sings And Sings. (*truncated fade*)

1967 #29 *ARE YOU LONELY FOR ME*

JACK SCOTT
1958 #35 *LEROY*
>   (M) (2:07) Curb 77255 Greatest Hits.

1958 #7 *MY TRUE LOVE*
>   (M) (2:45) Curb 77354 50's Hits Volume 1.
>   (M) (2:44) Curb 77525 Greatest Hits Of Rock 'N' Roll Volume 2.
>   (M) (2:44) Curb 77255 Greatest Hits.

1958 #29 *WITH YOUR LOVE*
>   (M) (2:01) Curb 77255 Greatest Hits.

1959 #10 *GOODBYE BABY*
>   (M) (2:07) Elektra 60107 O.S.T. Diner.
>   (M) (2:07) Curb 77255 Greatest Hits.

1959 #25 *THE WAY I WALK*
>   (M) (2:40) Rhino 70742 Rock This Town: Rockabilly Hits Volume 2.
>   (M) (2:40) Curb 77255 Greatest Hits.

1960 #5 *WHAT IN THE WORLD'S COME OVER YOU*
>   (S) (2:42) Curb 77355 60's Hits Volume 1.
>   (S) (2:51) Capitol 93192 Capitol Collector's Series. (*includes :08 studio talk*)
>   (S) (2:42) Curb 77255 Greatest Hits.

1960 #4 *BURNING BRIDGES*
>   (S) (2:41) Capitol 93192 Capitol Collector's Series.
>   (S) (2:39) Curb 77255 Greatest Hits.

1960 #28 *IT ONLY HAPPENED YESTERDAY*
>   (S) (2:44) Capitol 93192 Capitol Collector's Series.

LINDA SCOTT
1961 #6 *I'VE TOLD EVERY LITTLE STAR*
1961 #10 *DON'T BET MONEY HONEY*
1961 #11 *I DON'T KNOW WHY*

PEGGY SCOTT & JO JO BENSON
1968 #22 *LOVER'S HOLIDAY*
1968 #27 *PICKIN' WILD MOUNTAIN BERRIES*

JOHNNY SEA
1966 #27 *DAY FOR DECISION*

SEALS & CROFTS
1972 #6 SUMMER BREEZE
    (S) (3:24) Warner Brothers 3109 Greatest Hits.
1973 #15 HUMMINGBIRD
    (dj copies of this 45 ran (3:30) and (4:35); commercial copies ran (4:35))
    (S) (4:36) Warner Brothers 3109 Greatest Hits.
1973 #8 DIAMOND GIRL
    (S) (4:12) Warner Brothers 3109 Greatest Hits. *(LP version)*
1973 #18 WE MAY NEVER PASS THIS WAY AGAIN
    (S) (4:15) Warner Brothers 3109 Greatest Hits.

SEARCHERS
1964 #12 NEEDLES AND PINS
    (S) (2:11) Rhino 70319 History Of British Rock Volume 1.
    (S) (2:11) Rhino 70319 History Of British Rock Box Set.
    (S) (2:11) Rhino 72008 History Of British Rock Volumes 1-4 Box Set.
    (S) (2:11) Rhino 75773 Greatest Hits.
1964 #13 DON'T THROW YOUR LOVE AWAY
    (S) (2:15) Rhino 70320 History Of British Rock Volume 2.
    (S) (2:15) Rhino 70319 History Of British Rock Box Set.
    (S) (2:15) Rhino 72008 History Of British Rock Volumes 1-4 Box Set.
    (S) (2:15) Rhino 75773 Greatest Hits.
1964 #36 SOME DAY WE'RE GONNA LOVE AGAIN
    (S) (1:57) Rhino 75773 Greatest Hits.
1964 #29 WHEN YOU WALK INTO THE ROOM
    (S) (2:20) Rhino 75773 Greatest Hits.
1965 #2 LOVE POTION NUMBER NINE
    (S) (2:04) Rhino 70321 History Of British Rock Volume 3.
    (S) (2:04) Rhino 70319 History Of British Rock Box Set.
    (S) (2:04) Rhino 72008 History Of British Rock Volumes 1-4 Box Set.
    (S) (2:04) Rhino 75773 Greatest Hits.
1965 #28 WHAT HAVE THEY DONE TO THE RAIN
    (S) (2:33) Rhino 75773 Greatest Hits.
1965 #18 BUMBLE BEE
    (S) (2:14) Rhino 75773 Greatest Hits.

SECRETS
1963 #28 THE BOY NEXT DOOR

NEIL SEDAKA
1959 #22 THE DIARY
    (M) (2:24) RCA 53465 Sings His Greatest Hits.
    (S) (2:12) RCA 8467 Nipper's Greatest Hits Of The 50's Volume 2.
    (S) (2:14) RCA 6876 All Time Greatest Hits.
    (S) (2:51) RCA 2406 All Time Greatest Hits Volume 2. *(alternate take; includes :06 studio talk)*
    (S) (2:15) Pair 1283 Neil Sedaka's Diary.
1959 #40 I GO APE
    (S) (2:31) RCA 2406 All Time Greatest Hits Volume 2.
    (S) (2:31) Pair 1283 Neil Sedaka's Diary.
1959 #5 OH! CAROL
    (S) (2:13) RCA 53465 Sings His Greatest Hits.
    (S) (2:14) RCA 8466 Nipper's Greatest Hits Of The 50's Volume 1.
    (S) (2:15) RCA 6876 All Time Greatest Hits.
    (S) (2:14) Special Music 2701 Oh! Carol And Other Hits.
    (S) (2:14) Pair 1283 Neil Sedaka's Diary.

NEIL SEDAKA (Continued)

1960 #6 STAIRWAY TO HEAVEN
    (E) (2:41) RCA 53465 Sings His Greatest Hits.
    (S) (2:40) RCA 6876 All Time Greatest Hits.

1960 #19 YOU MEAN EVERYTHING TO ME
    (S) (2:37) RCA 6876 All Time Greatest Hits.
    (S) (2:36) Pair 1283 Neil Sedaka's Diary.

1960 #31 RUN SAMSON RUN
    (S) (2:49) RCA 53465 Sings His Greatest Hits.
    (S) (2:51) RCA 6876 All Time Greatest Hits.

1961 #4 CALENDAR GIRL
    (S) (2:36) RCA 53465 Sings His Greatest Hits.
    (S) (2:37) RCA 6876 All Time Greatest Hits.
    (S) (2:36) Special Music 2701 Oh! Carol And Other Hits.
    (S) (2:35) Pair 1283 Neil Sedaka's Diary.

1961 #9 LITTLE DEVIL
    (S) (2:35) RCA 53465 Sings His Greatest Hits.
    (S) (2:42) RCA 6876 All Time Greatest Hits.
    (S) (2:41) Special Music 2701 Oh! Carol And Other Hits.
    (S) (2:41) Pair 1283 Neil Sedaka's Diary.

1961 #9 HAPPY BIRTHDAY SWEET SIXTEEN
    (S) (2:41) RCA 53465 Sings His Greatest Hits.
    (S) (2:34) RCA 6876 All Time Greatest Hits.

1962 #1 BREAKING UP IS HARD TO DO
    (S) (2:16) RCA 53465 Sings His Greatest Hits.
    (S) (2:14) Rhino 70623 Billboard's Top Rock & Roll Hits Of 1962.
    (S) (2:14) Rhino 72007 Billboard's Top Rock & Roll Hits Of 1962-1966 Box Set.
    (S) (2:17) RCA 9902 Nipper's #1 Hits 1956-1986.
    (S) (2:20) RCA 8474 Nipper's Greatest Hits Of The 60's Volume 1.
    (S) (2:15) RCA 6876 All Time Greatest Hits.
    (S) (2:15) Special Music 2701 Oh! Carol And Other Hits.

1962 #10 NEXT DOOR TO AN ANGEL
    (S) (2:24) RCA 53465 Sings His Greatest Hits.
    (S) (2:24) RCA 6876 All Time Greatest Hits.

1963 #23 ALICE IN WONDERLAND
    (S) (2:32) RCA 6876 All Time Greatest Hits.

1963 #35 LET'S GO STEADY AGAIN
    (S) (2:34) RCA 6876 All Time Greatest Hits.

SEEDS

1967 #40 PUSHIN' TOO HARD
    (E) (2:37) Warner Special Products 27607 Highs Of The 60's.
    (E) (2:35) Rhino 75892 Nuggets.
    (E) (2:37) Dunhill Compact Classics 029 Toga Rock.
    (E) (2:34) K-Tel 713 Battle Of The Bands.
    (E) (2:34) MCA 6467 O.S.T. Air America.
    (E) (2:35) GNP Crescendo 2023 The Seeds.

SEEKERS

1965 #4 I'LL NEVER FIND ANOTHER YOU
    (M) (2:41) Rhino 70321 History Of British Rock Volume 3.
    (M) (2:41) Rhino 70319 History Of British Rock Box Set.
    (M) (2:41) Rhino 72008 History Of British Rock Volumes 1-4 Box Set.
    (S) (2:39) Curb 77485 Best Of Today. *(rerecording)*
    (M) (2:41) Capitol 91846 Capitol Collectors Series.

SEEKERS (Continued)
1965 #21 *A WORLD OF OUR OWN*
        (S)   (2:42) Curb 77485 Best Of Today. *(rerecording)*
        (S)   (2:57) Capitol 91846 Capitol Collectors Series. *(includes :15 of studio talk)*

1967 #1 *GEORGY GIRL*
        (S)   (2:19) Rhino 70322 History Of British Rock Volume 4.
        (S)   (2:19) Rhino 70319 History Of British Rock Box Set.
        (S)   (2:19) Rhino 72008 History Of British Rock Volumes 1-4 Box Set.
        (S)   (2:28) Curb 77485 Best Of Today. *(rerecording)*
        (S)   (2:18) Capitol 91846 Capitol Collectors Series.
        (S)   (2:18) Capitol 98665 When AM Was King.

BOB SEGER SYSTEM
1969 #22 *RAMBLIN' GAMBLIN' MAN*

SENATOR BOBBY
1967 #14 *WILD THING*

SENSATIONS
1962 #3 *LET ME IN*
        (M) (3:05) Rhino 70648 Billboard's Top R&B Hits Of 1962.
        (M) (3:04) MCA 31203 Vintage Music Volume 6.
        (M) (3:04) MCA 5804 Vintage Music Volumes 5 & 6.
        (M) (3:02) JCI 3110 Sock Hoppin' Sixties.
        (M) (3:01) Garland 011 Footstompin' Oldies.
        (M) (3:02) Chess 31320 Best Of Chess Rock 'n' Roll Volume 2.

SERENDIPITY SINGERS
1964 #5 *DON'T LET THE RAIN COME DOWN (CROOKED LITTLE MAN)*
1964 #28 *BEANS IN MY EARS*

DAVID SEVILLE
1956 #34 *ARMEN'S THEME*
1958 #1 *WITCH DOCTOR*
        (M) (2:18) Rhino 70743 Dr. Demento 20th Anniversary Collection.
        (S)   (2:00) EMI 91684 Very Best Of The Chipmunks. *(rerecording)*

SHADES OF BLUE
1966 #13 *OH HOW HAPPY*

SHADOWS OF KNIGHT
1966 #7 *GLORIA*
        (M) (2:34) Warner Special Products 27607 Highs Of The 60's.
        (M) (2:34) JCI 3101 Rockin' Sixties.
        (S)   (2:34) Rhino 75754 Even More Nuggets.

1968 #39 *SHAKE*
        (E)   (2:26) Pair 1199 Best Of Bubblegum Music.
        (E)   (2:26) K-Tel 713 Battle Of The Bands.

SHANGRI-LAS
1964 #5 *REMEMBER (WALKIN' IN THE SAND)*
        (M) (2:16) Rhino 70988 Best Of The Girl Groups Volume 1.
        (M) (2:14) Atlantic 82152 O.S.T. Goodfellas. *(buzz noticeable on fade out)*
        (E)   (2:16) Motown 5322 and 9087 Girl Groups: The Story Of A Sound.

1964 #1 *LEADER OF THE PACK*
        (M) (2:51) Warner Special Products 27602 20 Party Classics.
        (M) (2:51) Rhino 70625 Billboard's Top Rock & Roll Hits Of 1964.
        (M) (2:51) Rhino 72007 Billboard's Top Rock & Roll Hits Of 1962-1966 Box Set.

SHANGRI-LAS (Continued)

    (M) (2:51) Rhino 70988 Best Of The Girl Groups Volume 1.
    (E) (2:48) Pair 1202 Best Of Buddah. *(mastered from vinyl)*
    (M) (2:50) JCI 3110 Sock Hoppin' Sixties.
    (E) (2:49) Motown 5322 and 9087 Girl Groups: The Story Of A Sound.

1965 #15 *GIVE HIM A GREAT BIG KISS*

    (M) (2:10) Rhino 70988 Best Of The Girl Groups Volume 1.
    (M) (2:09) Motown 5322 and 9087 Girl Groups: The Story Of A Sound.

1965 #33 *GIVE US YOUR BLESSINGS*

1965 #7 *I CAN NEVER GO HOME ANYMORE*

1966 #35 *LONG LIVE OUR LOVE*

DEL SHANNON

1961 #1 *RUNAWAY*

    (M) (2:19) Rhino 70622 Billboard's Top Rock & Roll Hits Of 1961.
    (M) (2:19) Rhino 72007 Billboard's Top Rock & Roll Hits Of 1962-1966 Box
                Set.
    (E) (2:17) JCI 3110 Sock Hoppin' Sixties.
    (M) (2:18) Rhino 70977 Greatest Hits.
    (S) (2:17) Rhino 70983 Little Town Flirt. *(alternate take)*
    (M) (2:20) Pair 1293 Runaway.

1961 #2 *HATS OFF TO LARRY*

    (M) (1:59) Rhino 70977 Greatest Hits.
    (S) (2:00) Rhino 70983 Little Town Flirt.
    (S) (2:00) Pair 1293 Runaway.
    (S) (2:00) Special Music 4823 At His Best.

1961 #38 *SO LONG BABY*

    (M) (1:58) Rhino 70977 Greatest Hits.
    (M) (1:59) Pair 1293 Runaway.
    (M) (1:59) Special Music 4823 At His Best.

1963 #11 *LITTLE TOWN FLIRT*

    (M) (2:47) Rhino 70977 Greatest Hits.
    (S) (2:47) Rhino 70983 Little Town Flirt.
    (S) (2:47) Pair 1293 Runaway.
    (S) (2:47) Special Music 4823 At His Best.

1964 #19 *HANDY MAN*

    (M) (2:11) Rhino 70977 Greatest Hits.
    (M) (2:08) Pair 1293 Runaway. *(truncated fade)*
    (M) (2:08) Special Music 4823 At His Best. *(truncated fade)*

1965 #8 *KEEP SEARCHIN' (WE'LL FOLLOW THE SUN)*

    (M) (2:10) Rhino 70977 Greatest Hits.
    (M) (2:08) Pair 1293 Runaway.
    (M) (2:08) Special Music 4823 At His Best.

1965 #33 *STRANGER IN TOWN*

    (M) (2:30) Rhino 70977 Greatest Hits.
    (M) (2:30) Pair 1293 Runaway.
    (M) (2:30) Special Music 4823 At His Best.

DEE DEE SHARP

1962 #1 *MASHED POTATO TIME*

1962 #9 *GRAVY (FOR MY MASHED POTATOES)*

1962 #9 *RIDE!*

1963 #12 *DO THE BIRD*

1963 #29 *WILD!*

SANDIE SHAW
1965 #35 *GIRL DON'T COME*

SHELLS
1961 #23 *BABY OH BABY*
          (M) (2:27) Collectables 2507 History Of Rock - The Doo Wop Era Part 1.

SHEP & THE LIMELITES
1961 #3 *DADDY'S HOME*
          (M) (2:48) Rhino 75763 Best Of Doo Wop Ballads.
          (M) (2:50) Rhino 70952 Best Of The Heartbeats.
          (M) (2:50) Collectables 8805 Heartbeats/Shep & The Limelites For Collectors Only.

SHEPHERD SISTERS
1957 #22 *ALONE (WHY MUST I BE ALONE)*

ALLAN SHERMAN
1963 #1 *HELLO MUDDAH, HELLO FADDUH! (A LETTER FROM CAMP)*
          (S) (2:47) Rhino 75768 Dr. Demento Presents.
          (S) (2:44) Rhino 70743 Dr. Demento 20th Anniversary Collection.
          (S) (2:50) Rhino 75771 My Son, The Greatest: Best Of.
1965 #25 *CRAZY DOWNTOWN*
          (S) (2:56) Rhino 75771 My Son, The Greatest: Best Of.

BOBBY SHERMAN
1969 #1 *LITTLE WOMAN*
          (S) (2:19) Restless 2520 Very Best Of.
1970 #11 *LA LA LA (IF I HAD YOU)*
          (S) (2:40) Restless 2520 Very Best Of.
1970 #7 *EASY COME, EASY GO*
          (S) (2:38) Restless 2520 Very Best Of.
1970 #23 *HEY, MISTER SUN*
          (S) (2:29) Restless 2520 Very Best Of.
1970 #3 *JULIE DO YOU LOVE ME*
          (S) (2:53) Rhino 70923 Super Hits Of The 70's Volume 3.
          (S) (2:53) Rhino 72009 Super Hits Of The 70's Volumes 1-4 Box Set.
          (S) (2:52) Restless 2520 Very Best Of.
1971 #10 *CRIED LIKE A BABY*
          (S) (3:17) Restless 2520 Very Best Of.
1971 #22 *THE DRUM*
          (S) (2:16) Restless 2520 Very Best Of.
1971 #38 *JENNIFER*

SHERRYS
1962 #40 *POP POP POP-PIE*

SHIELDS
1958 #11 *YOU CHEATED*
          (M) (2:25) MCA 5936 Vintage Music Volumes 11 & 12.
          (M) (2:25) MCA 31209 Vintage Music Volume 12.
          (M) (2:18) Original Sound 1960 Memories Of El Monte.

SHIRELLES
1958 #24 *I MET HIM ON A SUNDAY (RONDE-RONDE)*
          (M) (2:13) Rhino 70989 Best Of The Girl Groups Volume 2.
          (M) (2:12) MCA 5937 Vintage Music Volumes 13 & 14.
          (M) (2:12) MCA 31211 Vintage Music Volume 14.

SHIRELLES (Continued)

    (E)   (2:01) Special Music 4805 Greatest Hits. *(rerecording)*

    (E)   (2:40) Pair 1241 Dedicated To You. *(rerecording)*

1960 #20 *TONIGHT'S THE NIGHT*

    (S)   (1:59) Rhino 75891 Wonder Women.

    (S)   (2:00) Rhino 75897 Anthology.

    (S)   (1:59) Collectables 5247 Golden Classics.

    (S)   (1:55) Special Music 4805 Greatest Hits.

    (S)   (1:56) Pair 1241 Dedicated To You.

    (S)   (1:58) Capricorn 42003 The Scepter Records Story. *(includes :05 studio talk)*

1961 #1 *WILL YOU LOVE ME TOMORROW*

    (S)   (2:41) Rhino 70622 Billboard's Top Rock & Roll Hits Of 1961.

    (S)   (2:41) Rhino 72007 Billboard's Top Rock & Roll Hits Of 1962-1966 Box Set.

    (S)   (2:40) Rhino 70988 Best Of The Girl Groups Volume 1.

    (S)   (2:33) JCI 3102 Love Sixties.

    (S)   (2:40) RCA 6965 More Dirty Dancing.

    (S)   (2:36) Motown 5322 and 9087 Girl Groups: The Story Of A Sound.

    (S)   (2:40) Rhino 75897 Anthology.

    (S)   (2:41) Collectables 5247 Golden Classics.

    (S)   (2:39) Special Music 4805 Greatest Hits.

    (S)   (2:40) Pair 1241 Dedicated To You.

    (M)   (2:40) Capricorn 42003 The Scepter Records Story.

1961 #3 *DEDICATED TO THE ONE I LOVE*

    (M)   (2:04) Dunhill Compact Classics 031 Back Seat Jams.

    (M)   (2:03) Rhino 75897 Anthology.

    (M)   (2:03) Collectables 5247 Golden Classics.

    (M)   (2:01) Special Music 4805 Greatest Hits.

    (M)   (2:01) Pair 1241 Dedicated To You.

    (M)   (2:03) Capricorn 42003 The Scepter Records Story.

1961 #4 *MAMA SAID*

    (S)   (2:09) Rhino 75891 Wonder Women.

    (S)   (2:07) Garland 011 Footstompin' Oldies.

    (S)   (2:09) Rhino 75897 Anthology.

    (S)   (2:09) Collectables 5247 Golden Classics.

    (S)   (2:04) Special Music 4805 Greatest Hits.

    (S)   (2:05) Pair 1241 Dedicated To You.

    (S)   (2:21) Capricorn 42003 The Scepter Records Story. *(alternate take)*

1961 #22 *A THING OF THE PAST*

    (S)   (2:36) Rhino 75897 Anthology.

    (S)   (2:36) Collectables 5247 Golden Classics.

    (S)   (2:35) Pair 1241 Dedicated To You.

1961 #30 *WHAT A SWEET THING THAT WAS*

    (S)   (2:28) Rhino 75897 Anthology.

    (S)   (2:28) Collectables 5247 Golden Classics. *(truncated fade)*

1961 #26 *BIG JOHN*

    (S)   (2:20) Rhino 75897 Anthology.

    (*)   (****) Special Music 4805 Greatest Hits. *(the cd jacket states that "BIG JOHN" is track 11, when in reality track 11 is "THANK YOU BABY")*

    (M)   (2:24) Capricorn 42003 The Scepter Records Story. *(includes :05 studio talk)*

SHIRELLES (Continued)

1962 #8 BABY IT'S YOU

- (S) (2:37) Rhino 70988 Best Of The Girl Groups Volume 1. *(alternate take)*
- (S) (2:38) Atlantic 81885 O.S.T. Stealing Home. *(alternate take)*
- (M) (2:40) Warner Brothers 3359 O.S.T. The Wanderers.
- (S) (2:38) Rhino 75897 Anthology. *(alternate take)*
- (S) (2:37) Collectables 5247 Golden Classics. *(alternate take)*
- (S) (2:36) Special Music 4805 Greatest Hits. *(alternate take)*
- (S) (2:36) Pair 1241 Dedicated To You. *(alternate take)*
- (M) (2:41) Capricorn 42003 The Scepter Records Story.

1962 #1 SOLDIER BOY

- (S) (2:39) Rhino 70623 Billboard's Top Rock & Roll Hits Of 1962.
- (S) (2:39) Rhino 72007 Billboard's Top Rock & Roll Hits Of 1962-1966 Box Set.
- (S) (2:39) Rhino 75891 Wonder Women.
- (S) (2:39) Garland 012 Remember When.
- (M) (2:39) Warner Brothers 3359 O.S.T. The Wanderers.
- (S) (2:41) MCA 6340 O.S.T. Born On The Fourth Of July.
- (S) (2:39) Rhino 75897 Anthology.
- (M) (2:39) Collectables 5247 Golden Classics.
- (S) (2:38) Special Music 4805 Greatest Hits.
- (S) (2:38) Pair 1241 Dedicated To You.
- (S) (2:44) Capricorn 42003 The Scepter Records Story. *(includes :04 countoff)*

1962 #30 WELCOME HOME BABY

- (S) (2:31) Pair 1241 Dedicated To You.
- (M) (2:31) Capricorn 42003 The Scepter Records Story.

1963 #17 EVERYBODY LOVES A LOVER

- (S) (2:40) Rhino 75897 Anthology.
- (S) (2:39) Collectables 5247 Golden Classics.
- (S) (2:39) Special Music 4805 Greatest Hits.
- (S) (2:38) Pair 1241 Dedicated To You.

1963 #6 FOOLISH LITTLE GIRL

- (S) (2:18) Rhino 75897 Anthology.
- (S) (2:17) Collectables 5247 Golden Classics.
- (S) (2:14) Special Music 4805 Greatest Hits.
- (S) (2:15) Pair 1241 Dedicated To You.
- (S) (2:15) Capricorn 42003 The Scepter Records Story.

1963 #29 DON'T SAY GOODNIGHT AND MEAN GOODBYE

- (S) (2:41) Rhino 75897 Anthology.
- (S) (2:40) Collectables 5247 Golden Classics.
- (S) (2:40) Pair 1241 Dedicated To You.

SHIRLEY & LEE

1956 #24 LET THE GOOD TIMES ROLL

- (M) (2:22) Rhino 75766 Best Of New Orleans Rhythm & Blues Volume 2.
- (M) (2:22) Rhino 70642 Billboard's Top R&B Hits Of 1956.
- (E) (2:22) EMI 90614 Non-Stop Party Rock.
- (M) (2:22) Sire 26617 Music From The Film A Rage In Harlem.
- (M) (2:21) Atlantic 81677 O.S.T. Stand By Me.
- (M) (2:22) EMI 96268 24 Greatest Hits Of All Time.
- (M) (2:20) Curb 77323 All Time Greatest Hits Of Rock 'N' Roll.
- (M) (2:21) Atlantic 82155 O.S.T. Book Of Love.
- (M) (2:22) EMI 92775 Legendary Masters Series.

1956 #40 I FEEL GOOD

- (M) (2:17) EMI 92775 Legendary Masters Series.

SHOCKING BLUE
1970 #1 VENUS
- (M) (3:03) Rhino 70921 Super Hits Of The 70's Volume 1.
- (M) (3:03) Rhino 72009 Super Hits Of The 70's Volumes 1-4 Box Set.
- (M) (3:03) Rhino 70631 Billboard's Top Rock & Roll Hits Of 1970.
- (M) (3:03) Rhino 72005 Billboard's Top Rock & Roll Hits 1968-1972 Box Set.
- (M) (3:03) JCI 3101 Rockin' Sixties.
- (M) (2:59) JCI 3115 Groovin' Sixties.

1970 #30 MIGHTY JOE

TROY SHONDELL
1961 #5 THIS TIME

DINAH SHORE
1957 #39 CHANTEZ-CHANTEZ

BUNNY SIGLER
1967 #21 LET THE GOOD TIMES ROLL & FEEL SO GOOD

SILHOUETTES
1958 #1 GET A JOB
- (M) (2:44) Rhino 75764 Best Of Doo Wop Uptempo.
- (M) (2:44) Rhino 70619 Billboard's Top Rock & Roll Hits Of 1958.
- (M) (2:44) Rhino 72004 Billboard's Top Rock & Roll Hits 1957-1961 Box Set.
- (M) (2:45) JCI 3204 Heart & Soul Fifties.
- (M) (2:44) Atlantic 81677 O.S.T. Stand By Me. (*sounds like it was mastered from vinyl*)
- (M) (2:45) Arista 8605 16 Original Doo-Wop Classics.
- (M) (2:45) Collectables 2508 History Of Rock - The Doo Wop Era Part 2.

SILKIE
1965 #14 YOU'VE GOT TO HIDE YOUR LOVE AWAY
- (M) (2:11) Rhino 70324 History Of British Rock Volume 6.
- (M) (2:11) Rhino 70319 History Of British Rock Box Set.

HARRY SIMEONE CHORALE
1959 #10 THE LITTLE DRUMMER BOY
- (S) (3:18) Rhino 70636 Billboard's Greatest Christmas Hits. (*rerecording*)
- (S) (3:18) MCA 25988 Traditional Country Classics. (*rerecording*)
- (M) (3:02) Casablanca 822744 The Little Drummer Boy.
- (S) (3:09) Special Music 4601 The Little Drummer Boy. (*rerecording*)

1960 #26 THE LITTLE DRUMMER BOY
(see 1959 listings above)
1963 #38 THE LITTLE DRUMMER BOY
(see 1959 listings above)

JUMPIN GENE SIMMONS
1964 #11 HAUNTED HOUSE
- (M) (2:32) Rhino 71492 Elvira Presents Haunted Hits.
- (M) (2:32) Rhino 70535 Halloween Hits.

CARLY SIMON
1971 #9 THAT'S THE WAY I'VE ALWAYS HEARD IT SHOULD BE
- (S) (4:15) Elektra 109 Best Of.
- (S) (4:15) Elektra 74082 Carly Simon.

1972 #10 ANTICIPATION
- (S) (3:18) JCI 3304 Mellow Seventies.
- (S) (3:18) Elektra 109 Best Of.
- (S) (3:18) Elektra 75016 Anticipation.

CARLY SIMON (Continued)
1973 #1 **YOU'RE SO VAIN**
    (S) (4:17) Priority 8664 High Times/70's Greatest Rock Hits Volume 3.
    (S) (4:16) Elektra 109 Best Of.
    (S) (4:17) Elektra 75049 No Secrets.

1973 #10 **THE RIGHT THING TO DO**
    (S) (2:57) Elektra 109 Best Of.
    (S) (2:58) Elektra 75049 No Secrets.

JOE SIMON
1969 #13 **THE CHOKIN' KIND**

1970 #40 **MOON WALK (PART 1)**

1971 #30 **YOUR TIME TO CRY**

1972 #8 **DROWNING IN THE SEA OF LOVE**
    (S) (3:20) Rhino 70787 Soul Hits Of The 70's Volume 7.

1972 #10 **POWER OF LOVE**
    (S) (2:55) Rhino 70660 Billboard's Top R&B Hits Of 1972.
    (S) (2:55) Rhino 70788 Soul Hits Of The 70's Volume 8.

1973 #29 **STEP BY STEP**

1973 #14 **THEME FROM CLEOPATRA JONES**
    (S) (3:45) Rhino 70552 Soul Hits Of The 70's Volume 12.

PAUL SIMON
1972 #4 **MOTHER AND CHILD REUNION**
    (S) (3:03) Warner Brothers 25588 Paul Simon.
    (S) (2:48) Warner Brothers 25789 Negotiations And Love Songs (1971 - 1986). (:15 shorter than either the 45 or LP)
    (S) (2:50) Columbia 35042 Greatest Hits, Etc. (:13 shorter than either the 45 or LP)

1972 #7 **ME AND JULIO DOWN BY THE SCHOOLYARD**
    (S) (2:41) Warner Brothers 25588 Paul Simon.
    (S) (2:41) Warner Brothers 25789 Negotiations And Love Songs (1971 - 1986).
    (S) (2:42) Columbia 35042 Greatest Hits, Etc.

1973 #2 **KODACHROME**
    (S) (3:32) Warner Brothers 25589 There Goes Rhymin' Simon.
    (S) (3:30) Warner Brothers 25789 Negotiations And Love Songs (1971 - 1986).
    (S) (3:32) Columbia 35042 Greatest Hits, Etc.

1973 #1 **LOVES ME LIKE A ROCK**
(the actual 45 time is (3:28) not (3:32) as stated on the record label)
    (S) (3:32) Warner Brothers 25589 There Goes Rhymin' Simon. (LP version which includes a :04 intro)
    (S) (3:17) Warner Brothers 25789 Negotiations And Love Songs (1971 - 1986). (45 version which does not include an intro but :11 shorter than the 45)
    (S) (3:27) Columbia 35042 Greatest Hits, Etc. (45 version)

SIMON & GARFUNKEL
1966 #1 **THE SOUNDS OF SILENCE**
    (S) (3:03) Columbia 3180 O.S.T. The Graduate.
    (S) (3:07) Columbia 3180 O.S.T. The Graduate. (accoustic version peculiar to this soundtrack)
    (S) (3:03) Columbia 9049 Wednesday Morning 3 A.M. (original accoustic version but not the hit version)
    (S) (3:04) Columbia 9269 Sounds Of Silence.

    (S)   (3:03) Columbia 31350 Greatest Hits. *(applause from preceeding selection tracks into introduction)*
    (S)   (3:03) Columbia 45322 Collected Works. *(original accoustic version but not the hit version)*
    (S)   (3:04) Columbia 45322 Collected Works.

1966 #5 HOMEWARD BOUND
    (S)   (2:26) Columbia 9363 Parsley, Sage, Rosemary & Tyme.
    (S)   (2:42) Columbia 31350 Greatest Hits. *(live)*
    (S)   (2:26) Columbia 45322 Collected Works.

1966 #4 I AM A ROCK
    (S)   (2:49) Columbia 9269 Sounds Of Silence.
    (S)   (2:50) Columbia 31350 Greatest Hits.
    (S)   (2:49) Columbia 45322 Collected Works.

1966 #15 THE DANGLING CONVERSATION
    (S)   (2:35) Columbia 9363 Parsley, Sage, Rosemary & Tyme.
    (S)   (2:35) Columbia 45322 Collected Works.

1966 #17 A HAZY SHADE OF WINTER
    (S)   (2:17) Columbia 9529 Bookends. *(tracks into next selection)*
    (S)   (2:17) Columbia 45322 Collected Works. *(tracks into next selection)*

1967 #15 AT THE ZOO
    (S)   (2:21) Columbia 9529 Bookends.
    (S)   (2:21) Columbia 45322 Collected Works.

1967 #15 FAKIN' IT
    (S)   (3:14) Columbia 9529 Bookends.
    (S)   (3:14) Columbia 45322 Collected Works.

1968 #19 SCARBOROUGH FAIR
    (S)   (6:19) Columbia 3180 O.S.T. The Graduate. *(soundtrack version)*
    (S)   (3:07) Columbia 9363 Parsley, Sage, Rosemary & Tyme.
    (S)   (3:08) Columbia 31350 Greatest Hits.
    (S)   (3:07) Columbia 45322 Collected Works.

1968 #1 MRS. ROBINSON
    (S)   (1:12) Columbia 3180 O.S.T. The Graduate. *(soundtrack version 1)*
    (S)   (1:09) Columbia 3180 O.S.T. The Graduate. *(soundtrack version 2)*
    (S)   (3:59) Columbia 9529 Bookends.
    (S)   (3:50) Columbia 31350 Greatest Hits.
    (S)   (3:59) Columbia 45322 Collected Works.

1969 #4 THE BOXER
    (S)   (5:08) Columbia 9914 Bridge Over Troubled Water.
    (S)   (5:08) Columbia 31350 Greatest Hits.
    (S)   (5:07) Columbia 45322 Collected Works.

1970 #1 BRIDGE OVER TROUBLED WATER
    (S)   (4:51) Columbia 9914 Bridge Over Troubled Water.
    (S)   (4:51) Columbia 31350 Greatest Hits. *(applause from previous selection tracks over introduction)*
    (S)   (4:51) Columbia 45322 Collected Works.

1970 #1 CECILIA
    (S)   (2:54) Columbia 9914 Bridge Over Troubled Water. *(tracks into next selection)*
    (S)   (2:52) Columbia 31350 Greatest Hits.
    (S)   (2:54) Columbia 45322 Collected Works. *(tracks into next selection)*

1970 #11 EL CONDOR PASA
    (S)   (3:06) Columbia 9914 Bridge Over Troubled Water.
    (S)   (3:05) Columbia 31350 Greatest Hits.
    (S)   (3:05) Columbia 45322 Collected Works.

NINA SIMONE
1959 #15 *I LOVES YOU, PORGY*

FRANK SINATRA
1955 #2 *LEARNIN' THE BLUES*
    (M) (2:59) Capitol 94317 The Capitol Years.
    (M) (2:59) Capitol 92160 Capitol Collector's Series.
    (S) (2:29) Reprise 1016 A Man And His Music. *(rerecording; includes :04 introduction)*

1955 #4 *LOVE AND MARRIAGE*
    (M) (2:36) Capitol 94317 The Capitol Years.
    (M) (2:36) Capitol 92160 Capitol Collector's Series.
    (S) (2:12) Reprise 26501 Sinatra Reprise: The Very Good Years. *(rerecording)*
    (S) (1:29) Reprise 1016 A Man And His Music. *(rerecording)*
    (S) (2:12) Reprise 26340 The Reprise Collection. *(rerecording)*

1956 #8 *HEY! JEALOUS LOVER*
    (M) (2:20) Capitol 94317 The Capitol Years.
    (M) (2:39) Capitol 92160 Capitol Collector's Series. *(includes :19 studio talk)*

1957 #20 *CAN I STEAL A LITTLE LOVE*
    (M) (2:30) Capitol 92160 Capitol Collector's Series.

1958 #7 *ALL THE WAY*
    (M) (2:51) Capitol 94317 The Capitol Years.
    (M) (2:53) Capitol 91150 All The Way.
    (M) (2:53) Capitol 92160 Capitol Collector's Series.
    (S) (3:28) Reprise 1011 Academy Award Winners. *(rerecording)*
    (S) (3:54) Reprise 1016 A Man And His Music. *(rerecording; with spoken introduction)*

1958 #13 *WITCHCRAFT*
    (M) (2:51) Capitol 94317 The Capitol Years.
    (M) (2:51) Capitol 91150 All The Way.
    (M) (2:51) Capitol 92160 Capitol Collector's Series.
    (S) (2:42) Reprise 1016 A Man And His Music. *(rerecording; includes spoken introduction)*

1958 #29 *MR. SUCCESS*

1959 #22 *HIGH HOPES*
    (S) (2:40) Capitol 94317 The Capitol Years.
    (S) (2:41) Capitol 91150 All The Way.
    (S) (2:51) Capitol 92160 Capitol Collector's Series. *(includes :09 studio talk)*

1959 #27 *TALK TO ME*
    (S) (2:59) Capitol 91150 All The Way.

1960 #32 *OL' MAC DONALD*
    (S) (2:39) Capitol 91150 All The Way.

1962 #26 *POCKETFUL OF MIRACLES*

1964 #38 *SOFTLY, AS I LEAVE YOU*
    (S) (3:00) Reprise 1016 A Man And His Music. *((1:02) spoken introduction preceeds music; talk over the music introduction; edited)*
    (S) (2:51) Reprise 1013 Softly As I Leave You.
    (S) (2:50) Reprise 2274 Greatest Hits.

1965 #32 *SOMEWHERE IN YOUR HEART*
    (S) (2:27) Reprise 2274 Greatest Hits.

1966 #33 *IT WAS A VERY GOOD YEAR*
    (S) (4:25) Reprise 26501 Sinatra Reprise: The Very Good Years.
    (S) (4:25) Reprise 1014 September Of My Years.

FRANK SINATRA (Continued)

      (S) (4:25) Reprise 2274   Greatest Hits.
      (S) (4:25) Reprise 26340   The Reprise Collection.

1966 #1 STRANGERS IN THE NIGHT

      (S) (2:35) Reprise 26501   Sinatra Reprise: The Very Good Years.
      (S) (2:35) Reprise 1017   Strangers In The Night.
      (S) (2:35) Reprise 2274   Greatest Hits.
      (S) (2:35) Reprise 26340   The Reprise Collection.

1966 #26 SUMMER WIND

      (S) (2:54) Reprise 26501   Sinatra Reprise: The Very Good Years.
      (S) (2:54) Reprise 1017   Strangers In The Night.
      (S) (2:54) Reprise 2274   Greatest Hits.
      (S) (2:54) Reprise 26340   The Reprise Collection.

1966 #5 THAT'S LIFE

      (S) (3:06) Reprise 26501   Sinatra Reprise: The Very Good Years.
      (S) (3:06) Reprise 1020   That's Life.
      (S) (3:06) Reprise 2274   Greatest Hits.
      (S) (3:06) Reprise 26340   The Reprise Collection.

1967 #22 THE WORLD WE KNEW (OVER AND OVER)

      (S) (2:46) Reprise 1022   The World We Knew.
      (S) (2:46) Reprise 2274   Greatest Hits.

1969 #29 MY WAY

      (S) (4:35) Reprise 26501   Sinatra Reprise: The Very Good Years.
      (S) (4:35) Reprise 1029   My Way.
      (S) (4:31) Reprise 2275   Greatest Hits Volume 2.
      (S) (4:35) Reprise 26340   The Reprise Collection.

NANCY SINATRA

1966 #1 THESE BOOTS ARE MADE FOR WALKIN'

      (S) (2:39) Warner Brothers 25613   O.S.T. Full Metal Jacket.
      (S) (2:43) Rhino 70627   Billboard's Top Rock & Roll Hits Of 1966.
      (S) (2:43) Rhino 72007   Billboard's Top Rock & Roll Hits 1962-1966 Box Set.
      (S) (2:40) Priority 7909   Vietnam: Rockin' The Delta.
      (S) (2:43) Rhino 75885   The Hit Years.

1966 #13 HOW DOES THAT GRAB YOU DARLIN'?

      (S) (2:32) Rhino 75885   The Hit Years.

1967 #4 SUGAR TOWN

      (S) (2:23) Rhino 75885   The Hit Years.

1967 #23 LOVE EYES

      (S) (2:33) Rhino 75885   The Hit Years.

1967 #19 LIGHTNING'S GIRL

      (S) (2:53) Rhino 75885   The Hit Years.

NANCY & FRANK SINATRA

1967 #1 SOMETHIN' STUPID

      (S) (2:43) Reprise 1022   Frank Sinatra: The World We Knew.
      (S) (2:43) Reprise 2274   Frank Sinatra's Greatest Hits.
      (S) (2:40) Reprise 26340   Frank Sinatra: The Reprise Collection.
      (S) (2:39) Rhino 75885   The Hit Years.

NANCY SINATRA & LEE HAZLEWOOD

1967 #13 JACKSON

      (S) (2:45) Rhino 75885   The Hit Years.
      (S) (2:47) Rhino 70166   Fairytales And Fantasies:The Best Of.

NANCY SINATRA & LEE HAZLEWOOD (Continued)

1967 #40 *LADY BIRD*
      (S)   (3:00) Rhino 75885 The Hit Years.
      (S)   (3:01) Rhino 70166 Fairytales And Fantasies:The Best Of.

1968 #37 *SOME VELVET MORNING*
      (S)   (3:37) Rhino 75885 The Hit Years.
      (S)   (3:40) Rhino 70166 Fairytales And Fantasies:The Best Of.

SINGING NUN
1963 #1 *DOMINIQUE*

SIR DOUGLAS QUINTET
1965 #24 *SHE'S ABOUT A MOVER*

1969 #14 *MENDOCINO*
      (S)   (2:38) Mercury 834216 45's On CD Volume 3.
      (S)   (2:38) Mercury 846586 Best Of Doug Sahm & The Sir Douglas Quintet.

SIX TEENS
1956 #35 *A CASUAL LOOK*

SKIP & FLIP
1959 #12 *IT WAS I*

1960 #11 *CHERRY PIE*

SKYLARK
1973 #9 *WILDFLOWER*
      (S)   (4:07) Rhino 70930 Super Hits Of The 70's Volume 10.
      (S)   (4:06) EMI 90603 Rock Me Gently.

SKYLINERS
1959 #7 *SINCE I DON'T HAVE YOU*
      (M)   (2:38) Rhino 75763 Best Of Doo Wop Ballads.
      (M)   (2:35) Dunhill Compact Classics 031 Back Seat Jams.

1959 #31 *THIS I SWEAR*

1960 #24 *PENNIES FROM HEAVEN*

FELIX SLATKIN
1960 #38 *THEME FROM THE SUNDOWNERS*

PERCY SLEDGE
1966 #1 *WHEN A MAN LOVES A WOMAN*
      (M)   (2:49) Atlantic 81911 Golden Age Of Black Music (1960-1970).
      (M)   (2:49) Atlantic 81742 O.S.T. Platoon.
      (M)   (2:50) Atlantic 81297 Atlantic Rhythm & Blues Volume 5.
      (E)   (2:50) Warner Special Products 27601 Atlantic Soul Classics.
      (M)   (2:50) MCA 6214 Moonlighting - TV Soundtrack.
      (E)   (2:49) Priority 7909 Vietnam: Rockin' The Delta.
      (M)   (2:49) Motown 6094 More Songs From The Original Soundtrack Of The "Big Chill".
      (M)   (2:49) Atlantic 82305 Atlantic Rhythm And Blues 1947-1974 Box Set.
      (E)   (2:49) Atlantic 8210 Best Of.
      (M)   (2:50) Atlantic 80212 Ultimate Collection.
      (M)   (2:50) Rhino 70285 It Tears Me Up.

1966 #16 *WARM AND TENDER LOVE*
      (E)   (3:12) Atlantic 8210 Best Of.
      (M)   (3:18) Atlantic 80212 Ultimate Collection.
      (M)   (3:17) Rhino 70285 It Tears Me Up. *(truncated fade)*

PERCY SLEDGE (Continued)
1966 #14 *IT TEARS ME UP*
  (E) (2:45) Atlantic 8210 Best Of.
  (M) (2:46) Atlantic 80212 Ultimate Collection.
  (M) (2:46) Rhino 70285 It Tears Me Up.
1968 #13 *TAKE TIME TO KNOW HER*
  (S) (3:01) Atlantic 8210 Best Of.
  (S) (3:01) Atlantic 80212 Ultimate Collection.
  (S) (3:01) Rhino 70285 It Tears Me Up.

SLY & THE FAMILY STONE
1968 #8 *DANCE TO THE MUSIC*
  (M) (2:56) Rhino 75778 Frat Rock.
  (S) (2:58) Dunhill Compact Classics 043 Toga Rock II.
  (M) (2:57) Rhino 70536 San Francisco Nights.
  (S) (2:58) Epic 30325 Greatest Hits.
  (S) (2:58) Epic 37071 Anthology.
1969 #1 *EVERYDAY PEOPLE*
  (S) (2:19) Rhino 70655 Billboard's Top R&B Hits Of 1969.
  (S) (2:19) Rhino 72006 Billboard's Top R&B Hits 1965-1969 Box Set.
  (S) (2:20) Epic 30325 Greatest Hits.
  (S) (2:20) Epic 37071 Anthology.
  (S) (2:18) Epic 26456 Stand!
1969 #23 *STAND!*
  (S) (3:05) Epic 30325 Greatest Hits.
  (S) (3:05) Epic 37071 Anthology.
  (S) (3:05) Epic 26456 Stand!
1969 #6 *HOT FUN IN THE SUMMERTIME*
  (S) (3:02) Columbia/Legacy 46160 Rock Artifacts Volume 1. (*:25 longer
          than either the 45 or LP)*
  (M) (2:37) Rhino 70655 Billboard's Top R&B Hits Of 1969.
  (M) (2:37) Rhino 72006 Billboard's Top R&B Hits 1965-1969 Box Set.
  (M) (2:37) Rhino 70087 Summer & Sun.
  (E) (2:36) Epic 48732 O.S.T. My Girl.
  (E) (2:37) Epic 30325 Greatest Hits.
  (E) (2:37) Epic 37071 Anthology.
1970 #1 *THANK YOU (FALETTINME BE MICE ELF AGIN)*
  (E) (4:38) Epic 46940 O.S.T. Queenslogic.
  (E) (4:48) Epic 30325 Greatest Hits.
  (E) (4:48) Epic 37071 Anthology.
1970 #40 *EVERYBODY IS A STAR*
  (E) (3:00) Epic 30325 Greatest Hits.
  (E) (3:00) Epic 37071 Anthology.
1970 #40 *I WANT TO TAKE YOU HIGHER*
  (S) (5:22) Epic 30325 Greatest Hits. (*LP version)*
  (S) (5:22) Epic 37071 Anthology. (*LP version)*
  (S) (5:19) Epic 26456 Stand! (LP version)
1971 #1 *FAMILY AFFAIR*
  (S) (3:03) Rhino 70632 Billboard's Top Rock & Roll Hits Of 1971.
  (S) (3:03) Rhino 72005 Billboard's Top Rock & Roll Hits 1968-1972 Box
          Set.
  (S) (3:01) JCI 3304 Mellow Seventies.
  (S) (3:03) Epic 37071 Anthology.
  (S) (3:02) Epic 30986 There's A Riot Goin' On.

SLY & THE FAMILY STONE (Continued)
1972 #11 *RUNNIN' AWAY*
        (S) (2:53) Epic 37071 Anthology.
        (S) (2:53) Epic 30986 There's A Riot Goin' On.

1972 #25 *SMILIN'*
        (S) (2:51) Epic 37071 Anthology.
        (S) (2:51) Epic 30986 There's A Riot Goin' On.

1973 #15 *IF YOU WANT ME TO STAY*
        (S) (2:56) Epic 37071 Anthology.
        (S) (2:57) Epic 32134 Fresh.

MILLIE SMALL
1964 #4 *MY BOY LOLLIPOP*
        (M) (1:59) Island 90684 and 842901 The Island Story. *(cd jacket identifies the singer only as "MILLIE")*

1964 #33 *SWEET WILLIAM*

SMALL FACES
1968 #13 *ITCHYCOO PARK*
        (M) (2:44) Sony Music Special Products 47351 The Immediate Singles Collection Volume 1.
        (S) (2:48) Sony Music Special Products 47895 There Are But Four Small Faces.
        (S) (2:47) Pair 1287 Original British Rock Classics.
        (S) (2:47) Special Music 4941 More Of The Best Of British Rock.

SMITH
1969 #4 *BABY IT'S YOU*
        (S) (3:21) Rhino 70921 Super Hits Of The 70's Volume 1. *(LP version)*
        (S) (3:21) Rhino 72009 Super Hits Of The 70's Volumes 1-4 Box Set. *(LP version)*
        (S) (3:25) MCA 31274 Classic Rock Volume 2. *(LP version)*
        (S) (3:20) JCI 3101 Rockin' Sixties. *(LP version)*

1970 #26 *TAKE A LOOK AROUND*

HUEY "PIANO" SMITH & THE CLOWNS
1958 #12 *DON'T YOU JUST KNOW IT*
        (M) (2:27) Rhino 70794 KFOG Presents M. Dung's Idiot Show.
        (M) (2:30) Rhino 70587 New Orleans Party Classics.
        (M) (2:30) Ace 2021 Rock 'N Roll Revival.

HURRICANE SMITH
1973 #1 *OH BABE, WHAT WOULD YOU SAY?*
        (S) (3:26) Rhino 70930 Super Hits Of The 70's Volume 10.
        (S) (3:26) EMI 90603 Rock Me Gently.
        (S) (3:25) Capitol 98665 When AM Was King.

JIMMY SMITH
1962 #15 *WALK ON THE WILD SIDE (PART 1)*
        (S) (5:53) Verve 831374 Jimmy Smith: Compact Jazz. *(Parts 1 & 2)*

O.C. SMITH
1968 #3 *LITTLE GREEN APPLES*
        (S) (3:54) Columbia 45019 Pop Classics Of The 60's.

1969 #33 *DADDY'S LITTLE MAN*

RAY SMITH
1960 #25 *ROCKIN' LITTLE ANGEL*

SAMMI SMITH
1971 #9 *HELP ME MAKE IT THROUGH THE NIGHT*
    (S) (2:31) Rhino 70924 Super Hits Of The 70's Volume 4.
    (S) (2:31) Rhino 72009 Super Hits Of The 70's Volumes 1-4 Box Set.
    (S) (2:31) Sony Music Special Products 48621 Kris Kristofferson:
        Singer/Songwriter.

SOMETHIN' SMITH & THE REDHEADS
1955 #10 *IT'S A SIN TO TELL A LIE*

WHISTLING JACK SMITH
1967 #14 *I WAS KAISER BILL'S BATMAN*

JOANIE SOMMERS
1962 #11 *JOHNNY GET ANGRY*
    (S) (2:31) Rhino 70989 Best Of The Girl Groups Volume 2.

SONNY
1965 #11 *LAUGH AT ME*
    (M) (2:54) Rhino 70734 Songs Of Protest.
    (M) (2:51) Atco 91796 The Beat Goes On.

SONNY & CHER
1965 #1 *I GOT YOU BABE*
    (S) (3:08) Atlantic 81905 O.S.T. Buster. *(segues together with the preceeding selection)*
    (M) (3:10) Atco 91796 The Beat Goes On.
    (M) (2:15) Atco 91796 The Beat Goes On. *(this version is from the "Good Times" soundtrack and is not the hit version)*
1965 #10 *BABY DON'T GO*
    (E) (3:08) Warner Special Projects 27610 More Party Classics.
    (E) (3:08) JCI 3110 Sock Hoppin' Sixties.
    (M) (3:09) Atco 91796 The Beat Goes On.
1965 #31 *JUST YOU*
    (M) (4:04) Atco 91796 The Beat Goes On. *(LP version lyrics but :34 longer than the vinyl LP version)*
1965 #23 *BUT YOU'RE MINE*
    (M) (3:02) Atco 91796 The Beat Goes On.
1966 #18 *WHAT NOW MY LOVE*
    (M) (3:36) Atco 91796 The Beat Goes On.
1966 #17 *LITTLE MAN*
    (M) (3:19) Atco 91796 The Beat Goes On.
1967 #7 *THE BEAT GOES ON*
    (S) (3:26) Warner Special Products 27602 20 Party Classics.
    (S) (3:26) Atlantic 81909 Hit Singles 1958-1977.
    (S) (3:26) Atco 91796 The Beat Goes On.
1972 #6 *ALL I EVER NEED IS YOU*
1972 #6 *A COWBOYS WORK IS NEVER DONE*
1972 #30 *WHEN YOU SAY LOVE*

SOPWITH CAMEL
1967 #25 *HELLO HELLO*
    (S) (2:24) Pair 1202 Best Of Buddah.
    (M) (2:23) Rhino 70536 San Francisco Nights.

JIMMY SOUL
1962 #17 *TWISTIN' MATILDA*
    (M) (2:52) Rhino 70527 Best Of Jimmy Soul.

JIMMY SOUL (Continued)

1963 #1 *IF YOU WANNA BE HAPPY*
    (the 45 time is (2:08) and the LP time is (2:14))
       (M) (2:09) Rhino 75772 Son Of Frat Rock.
       (S) (2:10) Rhino 70995 One Hit Wonders Of The 60's Volume 1.
       (S) (2:10) Geffen 24310 O.S.T. Mermaids.
       (S) (2:19) Rhino 70527 Best Of Jimmy Soul.
       (S) (2:19) Rhino 70589 Rockin' & Rollin' Wedding Songs Volume 2.

SOUL CHILDREN

1972 #22 *HEARSAY*
       (S) (3:32) Rhino 70789 Soul Hits Of The 70's Volume 9.
       (S) (3:30) Stax 88008 Top Of The Stax Volume 2.
       (S) (3:34) Stax 4120 Chronicle.

SOUL SURVIVORS

1967 #7 *EXPRESSWAY TO YOUR HEART*
       (M) (2:20) Dunhill Compact Classics 029 Toga Rock.
       (M) (2:18) Rhino 70996 One Hit Wonders Of The 60's Volume 2.
       (E) (2:18) K-Tel 686 Battle Of The Bands Volume 4.

SOUNDS OF SUNSHINE

1971 #40 *LOVE MEANS (YOU NEVER HAVE TO SAY YOU'RE SORRY)*

SOUNDS ORCHESTRAL

1965 #9 *CAST YOUR FATE TO THE WIND*
       (S) (3:11) Rhino 70995 One Hit Wonders Of The 60's Volume 1.

JOE SOUTH

1969 #10 *GAMES PEOPLE PLAY*
       (S) (3:32) EMI 90603 Rock Me Gently.
       (S) (3:29) Rhino 70994 Best Of.
       (S) (3:31) Capitol 98665 When AM Was King.

1970 #12 *WALK A MILE IN MY SHOES*
       (S) (3:42) Rhino 70994 Best Of.

SPACEMEN

1959 #36 *THE CLOUDS*

SPANKY & OUR GANG

1967 #9 *SUNDAY WILL NEVER BE THE SAME*
       (S) (2:55) Mercury 834216 45's On CD Volume 3.
       (S) (2:56) Mercury 832584 Greatest Hits.

1967 #22 *MAKING EVERY MINUTE COUNT*
       (S) (2:32) Mercury 832584 Greatest Hits.

1967 #18 *LAZY DAY*
       (S) (3:04) Mercury 832584 Greatest Hits.

1968 #19 *SUNDAY MORNIN'*
       (S) (6:11) Mercury 832584 Greatest Hits. *(this version first appeared on the vinyl LP "Spanky's Greatest Hits")*

1968 #13 *LIKE TO GET TO KNOW YOU*
       (S) (3:17) Mercury 832584 Greatest Hits.

1968 #27 *GIVE A DAMN*
       (S) (3:34) Mercury 832584 Greatest Hits.

SPINNERS

1961 #39 *THAT'S WHAT GIRLS ARE MADE FOR*
       (E) (3:07) Motown 5450 A Collection Of 16 Big Hits Volume 3.
       (M) (3:06) Atlantic 82332 One Of A Kind Love Affair.

SPINNERS (Continued)
1970 #15 IT'S A SHAME
    (S) (3:11) Motown 6183 Hard To Find Motown Classics Volume 1.
    (S) (3:10) Rhino 70783 Soul Hits Of The 70's Volume 3.
    (S) (3:10) Motown 5199 and 9008 Best Of.
    (S) (3:10) Atlantic 82332 One Of A Kind Love Affair.
    (S) (3:10) Ripete 392183 Ocean Drive.

1972 #1 I'LL BE AROUND
    (S) (3:08) Atlantic 81299 Atlantic Rhythm & Blues Volume 7.
    (S) (3:09) Atlantic 81912 Golden Age Of Black Music (1970-1975).
    (S) (3:08) Atlantic 82305 Atlantic Rhythm And Blues 1947-1974 Box Set.
    (S) (3:08) Atlantic 81547 Best Of.
    (S) (3:09) Atlantic 82332 One Of A Kind Love Affair.

1973 #1 COULD IT BE I'M FALLING IN LOVE
    (S) (4:09) Atlantic 81299 Atlantic Rhythm & Blues Volume 7.
    (S) (4:10) Rhino 70906 American Bandstand Greatest Hits Collection.
    (S) (4:10) Atlantic 81912 Golden Age Of Black Music (1970-1975).
    (S) (4:09) Atlantic 82305 Atlantic Rhythm And Blues 1947-1974 Box Set.
            (truncated fade)
    (S) (4:09) Atlantic 81547 Best Of.
    (S) (4:31) Atlantic 82332 One Of A Kind Love Affair. *(includes previously unreleased :20 coda)*

1973 #8 ONE OF A KIND (LOVE AFFAIR)
    (S) (3:20) Atlantic 82305 Atlantic Rhythm And Blues 1947-1974 Box Set. *(censored version)*
    (S) (3:19) Atlantic 81547 Best Of. *(censored version)*
    (S) (3:30) Atlantic 82332 One Of A Kind Love Affair. *(uncensored version)*

1973 #24 GHETTO CHILD
    (S) (3:43) Atlantic 81547 Best Of.
    (S) (3:46) Atlantic 82332 One Of A Kind Love Affair. *(tracks into next selection)*

SPIRAL STARECASE
1969 #7 MORE TODAY THAN YESTERDAY
    (S) (2:55) Rhino 70921 Super Hits Of The 70's Volume 1. *(LP length)*
    (S) (2:55) Rhino 72009 Super Hits Of The 70's Volumes 1-4 Box Set. *(LP length)*
    (S) (2:48) Columbia 45019 Pop Classics Of The 60's. *(45 length)*
    (S) (2:54) Columbia/Legacy 46160 Rock Artifacts Volume 1. *(LP length)*
    (S) (2:54) Epic 48732 O.S.T. My Girl. *(LP length)*

SPIRIT
1969 #25 I GOT A LINE ON YOU
    (S) (2:39) JCI 3103 Electric Sixties.
    (S) (2:39) Epic 32271 Best Of.
    (S) (2:46) Epic/Legacy 47363 Time Circle. *(:07 longer than 45 or LP)*

SPOKESMEN
1965 #22 DAWN OF CORRECTION
    (S) (3:23) MCA 31206 Vintage Music Volume 9. *(dreadful sounding stereo with reverb added)*
    (S) (3:23) MCA 5806 Vintage Music Volumes 9 & 10. *(dreadful sounding stereo with reverb added)*

DUSTY SPRINGFIELD

1964 #14 *I ONLY WANT TO BE WITH YOU*
    (M) (2:35) Rhino 70323 History Of British Rock Volume 5.
    (M) (2:35) Rhino 70319 History Of British Rock Box Set.

1964 #4 *WISHIN' AND HOPIN'*
    (S) (2:52) Rhino 70324 History Of British Rock Volume 6.
    (S) (2:52) Rhino 70319 History Of British Rock Box Set.

1964 #31 *ALL CRIED OUT*

1966 #3 *YOU DON'T HAVE TO SAY YOU LOVE ME*
    (S) (2:47) Rhino 70325 History Of British Rock Volume 7.
    (S) (2:47) Rhino 70319 History Of British Rock Box Set.

1966 #21 *ALL I SEE IS YOU*

1967 #29 *I'LL TRY ANYTHING*

1967 #29 *THE LOOK OF LOVE*
    (S) (4:06) Varese 5265 O.S.T. Casino Royale. *(rerecording)*

1969 #12 *SON OF A PREACHER MAN*
    (S) (2:25) Rhino 71035 Dusty In Memphis.
    (S) (2:26) Atlantic 81909 Hit Singles 1958-1977.

1969 #22 *THE WINDMILLS OF YOUR MIND*
    (S) (3:49) Rhino 71035 Dusty In Memphis.

1970 #22 *A BRAND NEW ME*
    (S) (2:26) Rhino 71035 A Brand New Me.

RICK SPRINGFIELD

1972 #15 *SPEAK TO THE SKY*
    (S) (2:40) Rhino 70929 Super Hits Of The 70's Volume 9.

SPRINGFIELDS

1962 #23 *SILVER THREADS AND GOLDEN NEEDLES*
    (M) (2:12) Rhino 70264 Troubadours Of The Folk Era Volume 2.

JIM STAFFORD

1973 #31 *SWAMP WITCH*

JO STAFFORD

1955 #8 *SUDDENLY THERE'S A VALLEY*
1956 #33 *ON LONDON BRIDGE*
1957 #33 *WIND IN THE WILLOW*

TERRY STAFFORD

1964 #3 *SUSPICION*
    (M) (2:28) Rhino 70625 Billboard's Top Rock & Roll Hits Of 1964.
    (M) (2:28) Rhino 72007 Billboard's Top Rock & Roll Hits 1962-1966 Box Set.
    (M) (2:28) Garland 012 Remember When.

1964 #22 *I'LL TOUCH A STAR*

STAMPEDERS

1971 #7 *SWEET CITY WOMAN*
    (S) (3:25) Rhino 70926 Super Hits Of The 70's Volume 6. *(LP length)*

JOE STAMPLEY

1973 #33 *SOUL SONG*

STANDELLS

1966 #8 *DIRTY WATER*
    (M) (2:46) Rhino 75892 Nuggets.
    (M) (2:46) Dunhill Compact Classics 029 Toga Rock.

STANDELLS *(Continued)*
        (M) (2:57) Rhino 70732 Grandson Of Frat Rock. *(:10 longer the 45 or LP)*
        (M) (2:47) K-Tel 713 Battle Of The Bands.
        (M) (2:57) Rhino 70176 Best Of. *(:10 longer than the 45 or LP)*

STAPLE SINGERS
1971 #24 *HEAVY MAKES YOU HAPPY*
        (S) (3:05) Rhino 70784 Soul Hits Of The 70's Volume 4.
        (S) (3:05) Stax 60-007 Best Of.
1971 #10 *RESPECT YOURSELF*
        (S) (4:51) Stax 88005 Top Of The Stax. *(LP version)*
        (S) (3:30) Rhino 70786 Soul Hits Of The 70's Volume 6.
        (S) (3:31) Warner Special Products 27609 Memphis Soul Classics.
        (S) (4:53) Stax 60-007 Best Of. *(LP version)*
        (S) (4:52) Stax 4116 Be Altitude: Respect Yourself. *(LP version)*
1972 #1 *I'LL TAKE YOU THERE*
        (S) (3:14) Rhino 70660 Billboard's Top R&B Hits Of 1972.
        (S) (3:14) Rhino 70788 Soul Hits Of The 70's Volume 8.
        (S) (4:37) Stax 88005 Top Of The Stax. *(LP version)*
        (S) (4:44) Stax 60-007 Best Of. *(LP version)*
        (S) (4:44) Stax 4116 Be Altitude: Respect Yourself. *(LP version)*
1972 #36 *THIS WORLD*
        (S) (3:32) Stax 60-007 Best Of.
        (S) (3:37) Stax 4116 Be Altitude: Respect Yourself.
1973 #35 *OH LA DE DA*
        (S) (3:34) Stax 60-007 Best Of.
1973 #9 *IF YOU'RE READY (COME GO WITH ME)*
        (S) (3:22) Rhino 70551 Soul Hits Of The 70's Volume 11.
        (S) (3:21) Rhino 70661 Billboard's Top R&B Hits Of 1973.
        (S) (3:20) Stax 88008 Top Of The Stax Volume 2.
        (S) (4:27) Stax 60-007 Best Of. *(LP version)*
        (S) (4:26) Stax 4116 Be What You Are. *(LP version)*

CYRIL STAPLETON & HIS ORCHESTRA
1956 #36 *THE ITALIAN THEME*
1959 #5 *THE CHILDREN'S MARCHING SONG*

BUDDY STARCHER
1966 #40 *HISTORY REPEATS ITSELF*

EDWIN STARR
1965 #27 *AGENT DOUBLE-O-SOUL*
        (M) (2:39) Rhino 75757 Soul Shots Volume 3.
        (E) (2:38) Motown 6219 Hard To Find Motown Classics Volume 3.
1969 #6 *TWENTY-FIVE MILES*
        (S) (3:17) Motown 6183 Hard To Find Motown Classics Volume 1.
        (S) (3:18) Motown 8120 and 8020 25 Miles/War And Peace.
        (S) (3:18) Motown 5426 25 Miles.
        (S) (3:16) Motown 9071 Motown Dance Party Volume 1. *(all selections on this cd are segued together)*
        (S) (3:16) Motown 5103 Superstar Series Volume 3.
1970 #1 *WAR*
        (S) (3:21) Rhino 70734 Songs Of Protest.
        (S) (3:22) Rhino 70631 Billboard's Top Rock & Roll Hits Of 1970.
        (S) (3:22) Rhino 72005 Billboard's Top Rock & Roll Hits 1968-1972 Box Set.

EDWIN STARR (Continued)

    (S)   (3:21)   Dunhill Compact Classics 043   Toga Rock II.
    (S)   (3:21)   Motown 6183   Hard To Find Classics Volume 1.
    (S)   (3:21)   Rhino 70783   Soul Hits Of The 70's Volume 3.
    (S)   (3:17)   Priority 7909   Vietnam: Rockin' The Delta.
    (S)   (3:19)   Motown 9072   Motown Dance Party Volume 2. *(all selections on this cd are segued together)*
    (S)   (3:18)   Motown 5275   12 #1 Hits From The 70's.
    (S)   (3:21)   Motown 9060   Motown's Biggest Pop Hits.
    (S)   (3:19)   Motown 8120 and 8020   25 Miles/War And Peace.
    (S)   (3:19)   Motown 5170   War And Peace.
    (S)   (3:20)   Motown 5103   Superstar Series Volume 3.

1971 #24 STOP THE WAR NOW

KAY STARR

1956 #1 ROCK AND ROLL WALTZ

    (M)   (2:56)   RCA 8466   Nipper's Greatest Hits Of The 50's Volume 1.
    (M)   (2:55)   RCA 9902   Nipper's #1 Hits 1956-1986.
    (S)   (2:44)   Capitol 94080   Capitol Collector's Series. *(rerecording)*

1957 #36 JAMIE BOY

1957 #16 MY HEART REMINDS ME

RANDY STARR

1957 #33 AFTER SCHOOL

RINGO STARR

1971 #1 IT DON'T COME EASY

    (S)   (3:01)   Capitol 46663   Blast From Your Past.
    (S)   (3:00)   Capitol 95637   Ringo.

1972 #10 BACK OFF BOOGALOO

    (S)   (3:16)   Capitol 46663   Blast From Your Past.

1973 #1 PHOTOGRAPH

    (S)   (3:53)   Capitol 46663   Blast From Your Past.
    (S)   (3:55)   Capitol 95637   Ringo.

STATLER BROTHERS

1966 #8 FLOWERS ON THE WALL

    (S)   (2:18)   Rhino 70687   Billboard's Top Country Hits Of 1966.
    (S)   (2:18)   Columbia 45019   Pop Classics Of The 60's.
    (S)   (2:18)   Columbia 46031   Columbia Country Classics Volume 3.
    (S)   (2:18)   Columbia 31557   World Of.

CANDI STATON

1970 #21 STAND BY YOUR MAN

1972 #36 IN THE GHETTO

STATUS QUO

1968 #11 PICTURES OF MATCHSTICK MEN

    (M)   (3:08)   Rhino 70326   History Of British Rock Volume 8.
    (M)   (3:08)   Rhino 70319   History Of British Rock Box Set.

STEALERS WHEEL

1973 #3 STUCK IN THE MIDDLE WITH YOU

    (S)   (3:23)   Rhino 70930   Super Hits Of The 70's Volume 10.

1973 #33 EVERYONE'S AGREED THAT EVERYTHING WILL TURN OUT FINE

STEAM

1969 #3 NA NA HEY HEY KISS HIM GOODBYE
- (S) (4:08) Rhino 70921 Super Hits Of The 70's Volume 1. (*LP version*)
- (S) (4:08) Rhino 72009 Super Hits Of The 70's Volumes 1-4 Box Set. (*LP version*)
- (S) (4:03) Rhino 70630 Billboard's Top Rock & Roll Hits Of 1969. (*LP version*)
- (S) (4:03) Rhino 72005 Billboard's Top Rock & Roll Hits 1968-1972 Box Set. (*LP version*)
- (S) (4:05) Mercury 834216 45's On CD Volume 3. (*LP version*)
- (S) (4:05) Dunhill Compact Classics 029 Toga Rock. (*LP version*)
- (S) (4:09) K-Tel 205 Battle Of The Bands Volume 3. (*LP version*)

1970 #38 I'VE GOTTA MAKE YOU LOVE ME

STEELY DAN

1973 #7 DO IT AGAIN
- (S) (5:53) MCA 31273 Classic Rock Volume 1. (*LP version*)
- (S) (5:00) MCA 6467 O.S.T. Air America. (*neither the LP or 45 version*)
- (S) (5:53) MCA 31192 Can't Buy A Thrill. (*LP version*)
- (S) (5:55) MCA 5570 A Decade Of. (*LP version*)

1973 #7 REELING IN THE YEARS
- (S) (4:32) MCA 25240 Classic Rock Volume 3.
- (S) (4:33) MCA 31192 Can't Buy A Thrill.
- (S) (4:36) MCA 5570 A Decade Of.

1973 #30 SHOW BIZ KIDS
- (S) (5:47) MCA 31156 Countdown To Ecstasy. (*LP version*)

LOU STEIN

1957 #16 ALMOST PARADISE
1958 #31 GOT A MATCH?

STEPPENWOLF

1968 #2 BORN TO BE WILD
- (S) (3:28) Rhino 70629 Billboard's Top Rock & Roll Hits Of 1968.
- (S) (3:28) Rhino 72005 Billboard's Top Rock & Roll Hits 1968-1972 Box Set.
- (S) (3:37) MCA 31206 Vintage Music Volume 9. (*long version that has a cold ending and is missing a guitar overdub that should start at (3:12)*)
- (S) (3:37) MCA 5806 Vintage Music Volumes 9 & 10. (*same comments as for MCA 31206*)
- (S) (3:28) MCA 31273 Classic Rock Volume 1.
- (S) (3:28) MCA 37049 16 Greatest Hits.
- (S) (3:27) MCA 10389 Born To Be Wild/A Retrospective.
- (S) (3:28) MCA 31020 Steppenwolf.

1968 #2 MAGIC CARPET RIDE
- (S) (4:26) MCA 25240 Classic Rock Volume 3. (*LP version*)
- (S) (4:24) JCI 3103 Electric Sixties. (*LP version*)
- (S) (4:28) MCA 31207 Vintage Music Volume 10. (*LP version*)
- (S) (4:28) MCA 5806 Vintage Music Volumes 9 & 10. (*LP version*)
- (S) (4:26) MCA 37049 16 Greatest Hits. (*LP version*)
- (S) (4:19) MCA 10389 Born To Be Wild/A Retrospective. (*LP version*)
- (S) (4:27) MCA 31021 The Second. (*LP version*)

1969 #8 ROCK ME
- (S) (3:35) MCA 5937 Vintage Music Volumes 13 & 14.
- (S) (3:35) MCA 31210 Vintage Music Volume 13.
- (S) (3:39) MCA 37049 16 Greatest Hits.

STEPPENWOLF (Continued)
     (S) (3:40) MCA 10389 Born To Be Wild/A Retrospective.
     (S) (3:38) MCA 1668 At Your Birthday Party.
1969 #35 IT'S NEVER TOO LATE
     (S) (3:00) MCA 37049 16 Greatest Hits. *(45 version)*
     (S) (4:02) MCA 10389 Born To Be Wild/A Retrospective. *(LP version)*
     (S) (4:02) MCA 1668 At Your Birthday Party. *(LP version)*
1969 #16 MOVE OVER
     (S) (2:52) MCA 37049 16 Greatest Hits.
     (S) (2:51) MCA 10389 Born To Be Wild/A Retrospective.
     (S) (2:52) MCA 31328 Monster.
1970 #23 MONSTER
(the LP version of this song is a medley of "MONSTER", "SUICIDE" and "AMERICA")
     (S) (3:55) MCA 37049 16 Greatest Hits. *(45 version)*
     (S) (9:12) MCA 10389 Born To Be Wild/A Retrospective. *(LP version)*
     (S) (9:17) MCA 31328 Monster. *(LP version)*
1970 #21 HEY LAWDY MAMA
     (S) (2:54) MCA 37049 16 Greatest Hits.
     (S) (2:53) MCA 10389 Born To Be Wild/A Retrospective.
1971 #31 RIDE WITH ME
     (S) (3:22) MCA 37049 16 Greatest Hits.
     (S) (3:21) MCA 10389 Born To Be Wild/A Retrospective.
     (S) (3:24) MCA 31354 For Ladies Only.

STEREOS
1961 #25 I REALLY LOVE YOU
     (S) (2:16) Rhino 75764 Best Of Doo Wop Uptempo.

STEVE & EYDIE (STEVE LAWRENCE & EYDIE GORME)
1963 #28 I WANT TO STAY HERE

CAT STEVENS
1971 #18 WILD WORLD
     (S) (3:18) A&M 4519 Greatest Hits.
     (S) (3:17) A&M 4280 Tea For The Tillerman.
     (S) (3:18) MFSL 519 Tea For The Tillerman.
1971 #26 MOON SHADOW
     (S) (2:47) A&M 2522 Classics Volume 24.
     (S) (2:48) A&M 4519 Greatest Hits.
     (S) (2:48) A&M 4313 Teaser And The Firecat.
1971 #4 PEACE TRAIN
     (S) (4:00) A&M 2522 Classics Volume 24. *(LP length)*
     (S) (4:11) A&M 4519 Greatest Hits. *(:10 longer than LP length)*
     (S) (4:01) A&M 4313 Teaser And The Firecat. *(LP length)*
1972 #11 MORNING HAS BROKEN
     (S) (3:15) A&M 2522 Classics Volume 24.
     (S) (3:17) A&M 4519 Greatest Hits.
     (S) (3:16) A&M 4313 Teaser And The Firecat.
1973 #21 SITTING
     (S) (3:10) A&M 2522 Classics Volume 24.
     (S) (3:11) A&M 4519 Greatest Hits.
     (S) (3:10) A&M 4365 Catch Bull At Four.
1973 #25 THE HURT
     (S) (4:16) A&M 3285 Footsteps In The Dark/Greatest Hits Volume 2.
     (S) (4:17) A&M 4391 Foreigner.

CONNIE STEVENS
1960 #5 *SIXTEEN REASONS*

DODIE STEVENS
1959 #3 *PINK SHOE LACES*
    (S) (2:22) MCA 5939   Vintage Music Volumes 17 & 18. *(rerecording)*
    (S) (2:22) MCA 31215   Vintage Music Volume 18. *(rerecording)*

RAY STEVENS
1961 #38 *JEREMIAH PEABODY'S POLY UNSATURATED QUICK DISSOLVING FAST ACTING PLEASANT TASTING GREEN AND PURPLE PILLS*
    (S) (2:22) MCA 42062   Greatest Hits Volume 2.
    (S) (2:21) Special Music 838169   Ahab The Arab.

1962 #2 *AHAB, THE ARAB*
    (S) (3:48) Mercury 826448   Oldies Golden Million Sellers. *(LP version)*
    (S) (3:32) RCA 5153   Greatest Hits. *(live)*
    (S) (3:47) MCA 5918   Greatest Hits. *(live)*
    (S) (3:45) Curb 77312   His All-Time Greatest Comic Hits. *(live)*
    (S) (3:47) Special Music 838169   Ahab The Arab. *(LP version)*

1963 #37 *SANTA CLAUS IS WATCHING YOU*
    (M) (3:16) Rhino 70192   Christmas Classics.

1963 #19 *HARRY THE HAIRY APE*
    (S) (2:49) Special Music 838169   Ahab The Arab..

1968 #15 *MR. BUSINESSMAN*
    (S) (3:22) RCA 5153   Greatest Hits.
    (S) (3:21) MCA 42062   Greatest Hits Volume 2.
    (S) (3:21) Curb 77464   Greatest Hits.

1969 #7 *GITARZAN*
    (S) (3:10) Rhino 70743   Dr. Demento 20th Anniversary Collection.
    (S) (3:10) Rhino 70794   KFOG Presents M. Dung's Idiot Show.
    (S) (3:11) RCA 5153   Greatest Hits.
    (S) (3:13) MCA 5918   Greatest Hits.
    (S) (3:13) Curb 77312   His All-Time Greatest Comic Hits.

1969 #24 *ALONG CAME JONES*
    (S) (3:45) Rhino 70593   The Rock 'N' Roll Classics Of Leiber & Stoller.
    (S) (3:45) MCA 5918   Greatest Hits.
    (S) (3:45) Curb 77464   Greatest Hits.

1970 #1 *EVERYTHING IS BEAUTIFUL*
    (S) (3:29) Rhino 70922   Super Hits Of The 70's Volume 2.
    (S) (3:29) Rhino 72009   Super Hits Of The 70's Volumes 1-4 Box Set.
    (S) (3:31) RCA 5153   Greatest Hits.
    (S) (3:32) MCA 5918   Greatest Hits.
    (S) (3:32) Curb 77464   Greatest Hits.

1970 #38 *AMERICA COMMUNICATE WITH ME*

B.W. STEVENSON
1973 #7 *MY MARIA*
    (S) (2:24) RCA 8476   and 9684 Nipper's Greatest Hits Of The 70's.
    (S) (2:29) Rhino 70758   Super Hits Of The 70's Volume 11.

BILLY STEWART
1965 #24 *I DO LOVE YOU*
    (S) (2:58) Garland 012   Remember When. *(LP version)*
    (S) (2:58) Chess 31317   Best Of Chess Rhythm & Blues Volume 1. *(LP version)*
    (S) (2:58) MCA 31207   Vintage Music Volume 10. *(LP version)*
    (S) (2:58) MCA 5806   Vintage Music Volumes 9 & 10. *(LP version)*

BILLY STEWART (Continued)
<blockquote>

(M) (3:00) Chess 6027 One More Time. *(45 version)*

(S) (2:57) MCA 10288 Classic Soul. *(LP version)*
</blockquote>

1965 #21 *SITTING IN THE PARK*
<blockquote>

(S) (3:15) Chess 6027 One More Time.

(S) (3:15) Original Sound 1960 Memories Of El Monte.
</blockquote>

1966 #8 *SUMMERTIME*
<blockquote>

(S) (2:40) Rhino 70087 Summer & Sun.

(S) (2:40) Rhino 75774 Soul Shots.

(S) (4:54) Chess 6027 One More Time. *(alternate take)*

(S) (4:55) MCA 31205 Vintage Music Volume 8. *(alternate take)*

(S) (4:55) MCA 5805 Vintage Music Volumes 7 & 8. *(alternate take)*

(S) (4:55) Chess 31318 Best Of Chess Rhythm & Blues Volume 2. *(alternate take)*
</blockquote>

1966 #37 *SECRET LOVE*
<blockquote>

(S) (2:58) Chess 6027 One More Time.
</blockquote>

ROD STEWART

1971 #1 *MAGGIE MAY*
<blockquote>

(the actual 45 time is (5:11) not (5:15) as stated on the record label)

(S) (5:12) Rhino 70632 Billboard's Top Rock & Roll Hits Of 1971.

(S) (5:12) Rhino 72005 Billboard's Top Rock & Roll Hits 1968-1972 Box Set.

(S) (5:12) Warner Special Products 27614 Highs Of The 70's.

(S) (3:43) Priority 7997 Super Songs/70's Greatest Rock Hits Volume 8. *(highly edited)*

(S) (5:13) Sandstone 33001 Reelin' In The Years Volume 2.

(S) (5:12) Mercury 824882 Sing It Again Rod.

(S) (5:43) Mercury 822385 Every Picture Tells A Story. *(LP version)*

(S) (4:57) Warner Brothers 3373 Greatest Hits. *(:14 shorter than 45 length)*

(S) (5:44) Warner Brothers 25987 Storyteller. *(LP version)*

(S) (5:45) MFSL 532 Every Picture Tells A Story. *(LP version)*

(S) (5:43) Special Music 836739 You Wear It Well. *(LP version)*
</blockquote>

1972 #22 *(I KNOW) I'M LOSING YOU*
<blockquote>

(S) (3:40) Rhino 70327 History Of British Rock Volume 9.

(S) (3:40) Rhino 70319 History Of British Rock Box Set.

(S) (5:03) Mercury 824882 Sing It Again Rod. *(edit of LP version; preceeding selection, this song, and the following selection are all segued together)*

(S) (5:20) Mercury 822385 Every Picture Tells A Story. *(LP version)*

(S) (5:19) Warner Brothers 25987 Storyteller. *(LP version)*

(S) (5:20) MFSL 532 Every Picture Tells A Story. *(LP version)*

(S) (5:20) Special Music 836739 You Wear It Well. *(LP version)*
</blockquote>

1972 #38 *HANDBAGS AND GLADRAGS*
<blockquote>

(S) (4:21) Mercury 824882 Sing It Again Rod.

(S) (4:21) Warner Brothers 25987 Storyteller.

(S) (4:21) Mercury 830572 The Rod Stewart album.
</blockquote>

1972 #14 *YOU WEAR IT WELL*
<blockquote>

(S) (4:17) Warner Special Products 27616 Classic Rock.

(S) (4:20) Mercury 826263 Never A Dull Moment.

(S) (4:10) Mercury 824882 Sing It Again Rod. *(tracks into next selection)*

(S) (5:01) Warner Brothers 25987 Storyteller. *(includes :39 introduction)*

(S) (4:22) Special Music 836739 You Wear It Well.
</blockquote>

1972 #39 *ANGEL*
<blockquote>

(S) (4:02) Mercury 826263 Never A Dull Moment.

(S) (4:03) Warner Brothers 25987 Storyteller.
</blockquote>

ROD STEWART (Continued)
1973 #35 _TWISTING THE NIGHT AWAY_
    (S) (3:13) Mercury 826263 Never A Dull Moment.
    (S) (3:07) Mercury 824882 Sing It Again Rod. _(tracks into next selection)_
    (S) (3:13) Warner Brothers 25987 Storyteller.

SANDY STEWART
1963 #13 _MY COLORING BOOK_

STEPHEN STILLS
1971 #16 _LOVE THE ONE YOU'RE WITH_
    (S) (3:03) Atlantic 81909 Hit Singles 1958-1977.
    (S) (3:03) Priority 8664 High Times/70's Greatest Rock Hits Volume 3.
    (S) (3:04) Atlantic 82319 Crosby, Stills & Nash Box Set.
    (S) (3:04) Atlantic 7202 Stephen Stills.
    (S) (3:04) Capitol 96647 Hearts Of Gold - The Classic Rock Collection.
1971 #31 _SIT YOURSELF DOWN_
    (S) (3:04) Atlantic 7202 Stephen Stills.
1971 #38 _CHANGE PARTNERS_
    (S) (3:13) Atlantic 82319 Crosby, Stills & Nash Box Set. _(tracks into next selection)_
    (S) (3:14) Atlantic 7206 Stephen Stills 2.
1971 #31 _MARIANNE_
    (S) (2:27) Atlantic 7206 Stephen Stills 2.

GARY STITES
1959 #29 _LONELY FOR YOU_

MORRIS STOLOFF
1956 #1 _MOONGLOW AND THEME FROM "PICNIC"_
    (M) (2:48) MCA 5936 Vintage Music Volumes 11 & 12.
    (M) (2:48) MCA 31209 Vintage Music Volume 12.

KIRBY STONE FOUR
1958 #31 _BAUBLES, BANGLES AND BEADS_

STONE PONEYS
1968 #12 _DIFFERENT DRUM_
    (S) (2:35) JCI 3104 Mellow Sixties. _(45 version)_
    (S) (2:36) Asylum 106 Greatest Hits. _(45 version)_

PAUL STOOKEY
1971 #21 _WEDDING SONG (THERE IS LOVE)_

STORIES
1972 #26 _I'M COMING HOME_
1973 #1 _BROTHER LOUIE_
    (S) (3:54) Rhino 70930 Super Hits Of The 70's Volume 10.
    (S) (3:54) Rhino 70634 Billboard's Top Rock & Roll Hits Of 1973.
    (S) (3:54) Pair 1202 Best Of Buddah.
    (S) (3:53) Priority 7942 Hard Rockin' 70's.
    (S) (3:53) Pair 3303 About Us.
1973 #21 _MAMMY BLUE_

BILLY STORM
1959 #24 _I'VE COME OF AGE_

GALE STORM
1956 #2 _I HEAR YOU KNOCKING_
1956 #6 _TEEN AGE PRAYER_
1956 #2 _IVORY TOWER_
1957 #5 _DARK MOON_

STRANGELOVES
1965 #12 *I WANT CANDY*
     (M) (2:33) Dunhill Compact Classics 043 Toga Rock II. *(mastered from vinyl)*
     (M) (2:33) Rhino 70732 Grandson Of Frat Rock.
     (M) (2:33) Rhino 70291 Bo Diddley Beats.
1966 #21 *NIGHT TIME*

STRAWBERRY ALARM CLOCK
1967 #1 *INCENSE AND PEPPERMINTS*
     (M) (2:46) MCA 5940 Vintage Music Volumes 19 & 20.
     (M) (2:46) MCA 31217 Vintage Music Volume 20.
     (M) (2:46) MCA 31206 Vintage Music Volume 9.
     (M) (2:46) MCA 5806 Vintage Music Volumes 9 & 10.
     (M) (2:48) Rhino 75754 Even More Nuggets.
     (M) (2:47) Rhino 70628 Billboard's Top Rock & Roll Hits Of 1967.
     (M) (2:45) Priority 7909 Vietnam: Rockin' The Delta.
1968 #14 *TOMORROW*

STREET PEOPLE
1970 #36 *JENNIFER TOMKINS*

BARBRA STREISAND
1964 #5 *PEOPLE*
     (S) (3:39) Columbia 9968 Greatest Hits.
     (S) (5:00) Columbia 3220 O.S.T. Funny Girl. *(soundtrack version - not the hit version)*
     (S) (3:40) Columbia 9015 People.
     (S) (3:38) Columbia 44111 Just For The Record.
1966 #36 *SECOND HAND ROSE*
     (S) (2:08) Columbia 9968 Greatest Hits.
     (S) (2:09) Columbia 9209 My Name Is Barbra, Two.
1971 #7 *STONEY END*
     (S) (2:58) Columbia 35679 Greatest Hits Volume 2.
     (S) (2:57) Columbia 30378 Stoney End.
     (S) (2:57) Columbia 44111 Just For The Record.
1971 #40 *WHERE YOU LEAD*
     (S) (2:58) Columbia 30792 Barbra Joan Streisand.

STRING-A-LONGS
1961 #4 *WHEELS*

BARRETT STRONG
1960 #14 *MONEY (THAT'S WHAT I WANT)*
     (E) (2:34) Motown 5448 A Package Of 16 Big Hits.
     (M) (2:33) Rhino 75778 Frat Rock.
     (M) (2:35) Rhino 70646 Billboard's Top R&B Hits Of 1960.
     (M) (2:33) Motown 6184 Hard To Find Motown Classics Volume 2.
     (M) (2:33) Garland 011 Footstompin' Oldies.
     (M) (2:33) Dunhill Compact Classics 043 Toga Rock II.
     (M) (2:34) Motown 5448 A Package Of 16 Big Hits.

JUD STRUNK
1973 #10 *DAISY A DAY*
     (S) (2:47) Rhino 70758 Super Hits Of The 70's Volume 11.
     (S) (2:46) Curb 77443 Mike Curb Congregation Greatest Hits.

STYLISTICS

1971 #34 *STOP, LOOK, LISTEN (TO YOUR HEART)*

1972 #9 *YOU ARE EVERYTHING*
        (S) (2:54) Amherst 9743 Best Of.

1972 #3 *BETCHA BY GOLLY, WOW*
        (S) (3:15) Amherst 9743 Best Of.

1972 #18 *PEOPLE MAKE THE WORLD GO ROUND*
        (S) (3:28) Amherst 9743 Best Of.

1972 #9 *I'M STONE IN LOVE WITH YOU*
        (S) (3:17) Amherst 9743 Best Of.

1973 #10 *BREAK UP TO MAKE UP*
        (S) (3:57) Amherst 9743 Best Of.

1973 #16 *YOU'LL NEVER GET TO HEAVEN (IF YOU BREAK MY HEART)*
        (S) (3:36) Amherst 9745 Best Of Volume 2.

1973 #20 *ROCKIN' ROLL BABY*
        (S) (3:14) Amherst 9743 Best Of.

SUGAR BEARS

1972 #38 *YOU ARE THE ONE*

SUGARLOAF

1970 #5 *GREEN-EYED LADY*
        (S) (3:37) Rhino 70923 Super Hits Of The 70's Volume 3.
        (S) (3:37) Rhino 72009 Super Hits Of The 70's Volumes 1-4 Box Set.
        (S) (3:38) Rhino 70631 Billboard's Top Rock & Roll Hits Of 1970.
        (S) (3:38) Rhino 72005 Billboard's Top Rock & Roll Hits 1968-1972 Box Set.
        (S) (3:38) EMI 90603 Rock Me Gently.
        (S) (3:38) Curb 77356 70's Hits Volume 2.
        (S) (3:38) Priority 7066 #1 Groups/70's Greatest Rock Hits Volume 12.

1971 #40 *TONGUE IN CHEEK*

SUNNY & THE SUNGLOWS

1963 #9 *TALK TO ME*

SUNSHINE COMPANY

1967 #31 *HAPPY*

SUPREMES

released as by THE SUPREMES:

1964 #20 *WHEN THE LOVELIGHT STARTS SHINING THROUGH HIS EYES*
        (S) (2:35) Motown 5449 A Collection Of 16 Big Hits Volume 2.
        (S) (3:03) Motown 5270 Where Did Our Love Go. *(LP version)*
        (S) (2:38) Motown 6198 and 0794 Anthology.
        (S) (3:02) Motown 6193 25th Anniversary. *(LP version)*
        (S) (2:36) Motown 8029 and 8129 and 0237 Greatest Hits Volume 1/Greatest Hits Volume 2.
        (S) (2:36) Motown 5357 Greatest Hits Volume 1.
        (S) (3:02) Motown 8005 and 8105 Where Did Our Love Go/ I Hear A Symphony. *(LP version)*
        (S) (3:02) Motown 6073 Compact Command Performances. *(LP version)*
        (S) (2:37) Motown 5101 Superstar Series Volume 1.

1964 #1 *WHERE DID OUR LOVE GO*
        (S) (2:31) Motown 6159 The Good-Feeling Music Of The Big Chill Generation Volume 1. *(noisy intro)*
        (S) (2:31) Motown 6137 20 Greatest Songs In Motown History.

 (S) (2:32) Motown 6138 The Composer Series: Holland/Dozier/ Holland.
 (S) (2:29) Motown 5452 A Collection Of 16 Big Hits Volume 5.
 (S) (2:31) Rhino 70650 Billboard's Top R&B Hits Of 1964.
 (S) (2:31) Motown 9017 and 5248 16 #1 Hits From The Early 60's.
 (S) (2:31) Motown 9097 The Most Played Oldies On America's Jukeboxes.
 (S) (2:31) Motown 5343 Every Great Motown Song: The First 25 Years
           Volume 1. *(most selections on this cd have noise on the fade out)*
 (S) (2:31) Motown 8034 and 8134 Every Great Motown Song: The First 25
           Years Volumes 1 & 2. *(most selections on this cd have noise on the
           fade out)*
 (S) (2:31) Motown 9098 Radio's #1 Hits.
 (S) (2:31) Motown 9060 Motown's Biggest Pop Hits.
 (S) (2:31) Motown 5270 Where Did Our Love Go.
 (S) (2:30) Motown 5313 Great Songs And Performances That Inspired The
           Motown 25th Anniversary TV Special.
 (S) (2:29) Motown 6198 and 0794 Anthology.
 (S) (2:30) Motown 8005 and 8105 Where Did Our Love Go/ I Hear A
           Symphony.
 (S) (2:31) Motown 6193 25th Anniversary.
 (S) (2:30) Motown 8029 and 8129 and 0237 Greatest Hits Volume
           1/Greatest Hits Volume 2.
 (M) (2:31) Motown 9038 and 5498 Every Great #1 Hit.
 (S) (2:30) Motown 5357 Greatest Hits Volume 1.
 (S) (2:31) Motown 6073 Compact Command Performances.
 (S) (2:31) Motown 6192 You Can't Hurry Love: All The Great Love Songs
           Of The Past 25 Years.
 (S) (2:29) Motown 9071 Motown Dance Party Volume 1. *(all selections on
           this cd are segued together)*

1964 #1 BABY LOVE

 (S) (2:36) Motown 6132 25 #1 Hits From 25 Years.
 (S) (2:35) Motown 6161 The Good-Feeling Music Of The Big Chill
           Generation Volume 3.
 (S) (2:36) Motown 6138 The Composer Series: Holland/Dozier/ Holland.
 (S) (2:32) Motown 5451 A Collection Of 16 Big Hits Volume 4.
 (S) (2:35) Motown 6110 Motown Grammy R&B Performances Of The 60's
           & 70's.
 (S) (2:40) Rhino 70650 Billboard's Top R&B Hits Of 1964.
 (S) (2:35) Motown 9017 and 5248 16 #1 Hits From the Early 60's.
 (S) (2:35) Motown 9097 The Most Played Oldies On America's Jukeboxes.
 (S) (2:35) Motown 5343 Every Great Motown Song: The First 25 Years
           Volume 1. *(most selections on this cd have noise on the fade out)*
 (S) (2:35) Motown 8034 and 8134 Every Great Motown Song: The First 25
           Years Volumes 1 & 2. *(most selections on this cd have noise on the
           fade out)*
 (S) (2:35) Motown 9060 Motown's Biggest Pop Hits.
 (S) (2:35) Motown 5322 and 9087 Girl Groups: The Story Of A Sound.
 (S) (2:35) Motown 5270 Where Did Our Love Go.
 (S) (2:34) Motown 5313 Great Songs And Performances That Inspired The
           Motown 25th Anniversary TV Special.
 (S) (2:33) Motown 6198 and 0794 Anthology.
 (S) (2:35) Motown 8005 and 8105 Where Did Our Love Go/ I Hear A
           Symphony.
 (S) (2:35) Motown 6193 25th Anniversary.

THE SUPREMES (Continued)

    (S)   (2:34) Motown 8029 and 8129 and 0237 Greatest Hits Volume 1/Greatest Hits Volume 2.

    (M) (2:33) Motown 9038 and 5498 Every Great #1 Hit.

    (S)   (2:34) Motown 5357 Greatest Hits Volume 1.

    (S)   (2:35) Motown 6073 Compact Command Performances.

    (S)   (2:35) Motown 6192 You Can't Hurry Love: All The Great Love Songs Of The Past 25 Years.

1964 #1 COME SEE ABOUT ME

    (S)   (2:41) Motown 6159 The Good-Feeling Music Of The Big Chill Generation Volume 1.

    (S)   (2:42) Motown 6138 The Composer Series: Holland/Dozier/ Holland. *(fade truncated)*

    (S)   (2:35) Motown 5452 A Collection Of 16 Big Hits Volume 5.

    (S)   (2:40) Motown 9072 Motown Dance Party Volume 2. *(all selections on this cd are segued together)*

    (S)   (2:41) Motown 9017 and 5248 16 #1 Hits From the Early 60's.

    (S)   (2:41) Motown 9060 Motown's Biggest Pop Hits.

    (S)   (2:41) Motown 5322 and 9087 Girl Groups: The Story Of A Sound.

    (S)   (2:41) Motown 5270 Where Did Our Love Go.

    (S)   (2:41) Motown 5313 Great Songs And Performances That Inspired The Motown 25th Anniversary TV Special.

    (S)   (2:35) Motown 6198 and 0794 Anthology. *(hum noticeable on both the introduction and the fadeout)*

    (S)   (2:41) Motown 8005 and 8105 Where Did Our Love Go/ I Hear A Symphony.

    (S)   (2:41) Motown 6193 25th Anniversary.

    (S)   (2:35) Motown 8029 and 8129 and 0237 Greatest Hits Volume 1/Greatest Hits Volume 2.

    (M) (2:38) Motown 9038 and 5498 Every Great #1 Hit.

    (S)   (2:34) Motown 5357 Greatest Hits Volume 1.

    (S)   (2:42) Motown 6073 Compact Command Performances.

1965 #1 STOP! IN THE NAME OF LOVE

    (S)   (2:51) Motown 6160 The Good-Feeling Music Of The Big Chill Generation Volume 2.

    (S)   (2:51) Motown 6137 20 Greatest Songs In Motown History.

    (S)   (2:52) Motown 6138 The Composer Series: Holland/Dozier/ Holland.

    (S)   (2:51) Motown 5453 A Collection Of 16 Big Hits Volume 6.

    (S)   (2:51) Rhino 70651 Billboard's Top R&B Hits Of 1965.

    (S)   (2:51) Rhino 72006 Billboard's Top R&B Hits 1965-1969 Box Set.

    (S)   (2:49) Motown 9072 Motown Dance Party Volume 2. *(all selections on this cd are segued together)*

    (S)   (2:51) Motown 9017 and 5248 16 #1 Hits From The Early 60's.

    (S)   (2:51) Motown 9097 The Most Played Oldies On America's Jukeboxes.

    (S)   (2:51) Motown 9098 Radio's #1 Hits.

    (S)   (2:51) Motown 5322 and 9087 Girl Groups: The Story Of A Sound.

    (S)   (2:53) Motown 8051 and 8151 More Hits By The Supremes/ Sing Holland-Dozier-Holland.

    (S)   (2:51) Motown 5313 Great Songs And Performances That Inspired The Motown 25th Anniversary TV Special.

    (S)   (2:52) Motown 5440 More Hits By The Supremes.

    (S)   (2:49) Motown 619 and 0794 Anthology.

    (S)   (2:51) Motown 6193 25th Anniversary.

    (S)   (2:50) Motown 8029 and 8129 and 0237 Greatest Hits Volume 1/Greatest Hits Volume 2.

THE SUPREMES (Continued)

    (M) (2:49) Motown 9038 and 5498 Every Great #1 Hit.
    (S) (2:50) Motown 5357 Greatest Hits Volume 1.
    (S) (2:52) Motown 6073 Compact Command Performances.
    (S) (2:50) Motown 6192 You Can't Hurry Love: All The Great Love Songs Of The Past 25 Years.

1965 #1 BACK IN MY ARMS AGAIN

    (S) (2:51) Motown 6161 The Good-Feeling Music Of The Big Chill Generation Volume 3.
    (S) (2:49) Motown 5454 A Collection Of 16 Big Hits Volume 7.
    (S) (2:51) Motown 9017 and 5248 16 #1 Hits From The Early 60's.
    (S) (2:51) Motown 5322 and 9087 Girl Groups: The Story Of A Sound.
    (S) (2:51) Motown 8051 and 8151 More Hits By The Supremes/ Sing Holland-Dozier-Holland.
    (S) (2:50) Motown 5313 Great Songs And Performances That Inspired The Motown 25th Anniversary TV Special.
    (S) (2:51) Motown 5440 More Hits By The Supremes.
    (S) (2:50) Motown 6198 and 0794 Anthology.
    (S) (2:51) Motown 6193 25th Anniversary.
    (S) (2:50) Motown 8029 and 8129 and 0237 Greatest Hits Volume 1/Greatest Hits Volume 2.
    (M) (2:53) Motown 9038 and 5498 Every Great #1 Hit.
    (S) (2:50) Motown 5357 Greatest Hits Volume 1.
    (S) (2:52) Motown 6073 Compact Command Performances.

1965 #8 NOTHING BUT HEARTACHES

    (S) (2:57) Motown 8051 and 8151 More Hits By The Supremes/ Sing Holland-Dozier-Holland.
    (S) (2:55) Motown 5440 More Hits By The Supremes.
    (S) (2:54) Motown 6198 and 0794 Anthology.
    (S) (2:56) Motown 6193 25th Anniversary.
    (S) (2:55) Motown 8029 and 8129 and 0237 Greatest Hits Volume 1/Greatest Hits Volume 2.
    (S) (2:55) Motown 5357 Greatest Hits Volume 1.
    (S) (2:54) Motown 5101 Superstar Series Volume 1.

1965 #1 I HEAR A SYMPHONY

    (E) (2:41) Motown 6160 The Good-Feeling Music Of The Big Chill Generation Volume 2.
    (S) (2:36) Motown 5454 A Collection Of 16 Big Hits Volume 7.
    (M) (2:42) Motown 6138 The Composer Series: Holland/Dozier/ Holland.
    (E) (2:41) Motown 9017 and 5248 16 #1 Hits From The Early 60's.
    (E) (2:41) Motown 5313 Great Songs And Performances That Inspired The Motown 25th Anniversary TV Special.
    (S) (2:38) Motown 6198 and 0794 Anthology. *(hum noticeable on fadeout)*
    (E) (2:41) Motown 6193 25th Anniversary.
    (S) (2:37) Motown 8029 and 8129 and 0237 Greatest Hits Volume 1/Greatest Hits Volume 2.
    (M) (2:41) Motown 9038 and 5498 Every Great #1 Hit.
    (S) (2:37) Motown 5358 Greatest Hits Volume 2.
    (E) (2:41) Motown 9027 and 5147 I Hear A Symphony.
    (E) (2:41) Motown 8005 and 8105 Where Did Our Love Go/ I Hear A Symphony.
    (E) (2:42) Motown 6073 Compact Command Performances.

1966 #5 MY WORLD IS EMPTY WITHOUT YOU

    (S) (2:33) Motown 6138 The Composer Series: Holland/Dozier/ Holland.
    (S) (2:30) Motown 5455 A Collection Of 16 Big Hits Volume 8.

THE SUPREMES (Continued)

(S) (2:32) Motown 9095 and 5325 Motown Girl Groups: Top 10 With A Bullet!
(S) (2:32) Motown 6198 and 0794 Anthology. *(hum noticeable on fadeout)*
(S) (2:33) Motown 6193 25th Anniversary.
(S) (2:31) Motown 8029 and 8129 and 0237 Greatest Hits Volume 1/Greatest Hits Volume 2.
(S) (2:31) Motown 5358 Greatest Hits Volume 2.
(S) (2:33) Motown 9027 and 5147 I Hear A Symphony.
(E) (2:33) Motown 8005 and 8105 Where Did Our Love Go/ I Hear A Symphony.
(S) (2:33) Motown 6073 Compact Command Performances.

1966 #9 LOVE IS LIKE AN ITCHING IN MY HEART

(S) (2:54) Motown 9072 Motown Dance Party Volume 2. *(all selections on this cd are segued together)*
(S) (2:55) Motown 6198 and 0794 Anthology.
(S) (2:53) Motown 8021 and 8121 Love Child/Supremes A Go Go.
(S) (2:51) Motown 6193 25th Anniversary.
(S) (2:54) Motown 8029 and 8129 and 0237 Greatest Hits Volume 1/Greatest Hits Volume 2.
(S) (2:54) Motown 5358 Greatest Hits Volume 2.
(S) (2:53) Motown 5138 Supremes A Go Go.
(S) (2:52) Motown 6073 Compact Command Performances.

1966 #1 YOU CAN'T HURRY LOVE

(S) (2:45) Rhino 70627 Billboard's Top Rock & Roll Hits Of 1966.
(S) (2:45) Rhino 72007 Billboard's Top Rock & Roll Hits 1962-1966 Box Set.
(S) (2:46) Motown 6132 25 #1 Hits From 25 Years.
(S) (2:45) Motown 6161 The Good-Feeling Music Of The Big Chill Generation Volume 3.
(S) (2:44) Motown 6137 20 Greatest Songs In Motown History.
(S) (2:43) Motown 5455 A Collection Of 16 Big Hits Volume 8.
(S) (2:46) Motown 6138 The Composer Series: Holland/Dozier/ Holland.
(S) (2:44) Motown 9018 and 5249 16 #1 Hits From The Late 60's.
(S) (2:44) Motown 9098 Radio's #1 Hits.
(S) (2:44) Motown 5313 Great Songs And Performances That Inspired The Motown 25th Anniversary TV Special.
(S) (2:44) Motown 6198 and 0794 Anthology. *(hum noticeable on fadeout)*
(S) (2:45) Motown 8021 and 8121 Love Child/Supremes A Go Go.
(S) (2:44) Motown 6193 25th Anniversary.
(S) (2:44) Motown 8029 and 8129 and 0237 Greatest Hits Volume 1/Greatest Hits Volume 2.
(M) (2:44) Motown 9038 and 5498 Every Great #1 Hit.
(S) (2:44) Motown 5358 Greatest Hits Volume 2.
(S) (2:44) Motown 5138 Supremes A Go Go.
(S) (2:45) Motown 6073 Compact Command Performances.
(S) (2:44) Motown 6192 You Can't Hurry Love: All The Great Love Songs Of The Past 25 Years.
(S) (2:42) Motown 9071 Motown Dance Party Volume 1. *(all selections on this cd are segued together)*

1966 #1 YOU KEEP ME HANGIN' ON

(S) (2:41) Motown 6159 The Good-Feeling Music Of The Big Chill Generation Volume 1.
(S) (2:41) Motown 6137 20 Greatest Songs In Motown History.

(S) (2:39) Motown 5456   A Collection Of 16 Big Hits Volume 9.
(S) (2:42) Motown 6138   The Composer Series: Holland/Dozier/ Holland.
(S) (2:45) Rhino 70652   Billboard's Top R&B Hits Of 1966.
(S) (2:45) Rhino 72006   Billboard's Top R&B Hits 1965-1969 Box Set.
(S) (2:41) Motown 9018 and 5249   16 #1 Hits From The Late 60's.
(S) (2:41) Motown 5343   Every Great Motown Song: The First 25 Years Volume 1. *(most selections on this cd have noise on the fade out)*
(S) (2:41) Motown 8034 and 8134   Every Great Motown Song: The First 25 Years Volumes 1 & 2. *(most selections on this cd have noise on the fade out)*
(S) (2:40) Motown 8051 and 8151   More Hits By The Supremes/ Sing Holland-Dozier-Holland.
(S) (2:40) Motown 6198 and 0794   Anthology. *(hum noticeable on fadeout)*
(S) (2:41) Motown 6193   25th Anniversary. *(noisy fadeout)*
(S) (2:39) Motown 8029 and 8129 and 0237   Greatest Hits Volume 1/Greatest Hits Volume 2.
(M) (2:44) Motown 9038 and 5498   Every Great #1 Hit.
(S) (2:39) Motown 5358   Greatest Hits Volume 2.
(S) (2:41) Motown 5182   Sing Holland-Dozier-Holland.
(S) (2:41) Motown 6073   Compact Command Performances.
(S) (2:38) Motown 9071   Motown Dance Party Volume 1. *(all selections on this cd are segued together)*

1967 #1 *LOVE IS HERE AND NOW YOU'RE GONE*

(S) (2:45) Motown 6160   The Good-Feeling Music Of The Big Chill Generation Volume 2.
(S) (2:44) Motown 5456   A Collection Of 16 Big Hits Volume 9.
(S) (2:45) Rhino 70653   Billboard's Top R&B Hits Of 1967.
(S) (2:45) Rhino 72006   Billboard's Top R&B Hits 1965-1969 Box Set.
(S) (2:45) Motown 9018 and 5249   16 #1 Hits From The Late 60's.
(S) (2:46) Motown 8051 and 8151   More Hits By The Supremes/ Sing Holland-Dozier-Holland.
(S) (2:44) Motown 6198 and 0794   Anthology.
(S) (2:45) Motown 6193   25th Anniversary.
(S) (2:45) Motown 8029 and 8129 and 0237   Greatest Hits Volume 1/Greatest Hits Volume 2.
(S) (2:45) Motown 5203   Greatest Hits Volume 3. *(truncated fade)*
(M) (2:46) Motown 9038 and 5498   Every Great #1 Hit.
(S) (2:45) Motown 5358   Greatest Hits Volume 2.
(S) (2:46) Motown 5182   Sing Holland-Dozier-Holland.
(S) (2:45) Motown 6073   Compact Command Performances.
(S) (2:45) Motown 6192   You Can't Hurry Love: All The Great Love Songs Of The Past 25 Years.

1967 #1 *THE HAPPENING*

(S) (2:47) Motown 6161   The Good-Feeling Music Of The Big Chill Generation Volume 3.
(S) (2:45) Motown 5457   A Collection Of 16 Big Hits Volume 10.
(S) (2:47) Motown 9018 and 5249   16 #1 Hits From The Late 60's.
(S) (2:48) Motown 6198 and 0794   Anthology. *(hum noticeable on fadeout)*
(S) (2:47) Motown 6193   25th Anniversary.
(S) (2:48) Motown 8029 and 8129 and 0237   Greatest Hits Volume 1/Greatest Hits Volume 2.
(S) (2:48) Motown 5203   Greatest Hits Volume 3.
(M) (2:49) Motown 9038 and 5498   Every Great #1 Hit.
(S) (2:48) Motown 5358   Greatest Hits Volume 2.
(S) (2:46) Motown 5101   Superstar Series Volume 1. *(numerous dropouts)*

releases from this point on were credited to **DIANA ROSS & THE SUPREMES:**

1967 #2 *REFLECTIONS*
    (S) (2:50) Motown 6138 The Composer Series: Holland/Dozier/ Holland.
    (S) (2:13) SBK 93744 China Beach - Music & Memories. (*sound effects can be heard over the intro; edited*)
    (S) (2:49) Motown 9095 and 5325 Motown Girl Groups: Top 10 With A Bullet!
    (S) (2:49) Motown 5494 Reflections.
    (S) (2:48) Motown 6198 and 0794 Anthology.
    (S) (2:50) Motown 6193 25th Anniversary.
    (S) (2:50) Motown 5203 Greatest Hits Volume 3.
    (S) (2:49) Motown 6073 Compact Command Performances.

1967 #10 *IN AND OUT OF LOVE*
    (S) (2:38) Motown 5494 Reflections.
    (S) (2:37) Motown 6198 and 0794 Anthology.
    (S) (2:38) Motown 6193 25th Anniversary.
    (S) (2:39) Motown 5203 Greatest Hits Volume 3.

1968 #13 *FOREVER CAME TODAY*
    (S) (3:12) Motown 5494 Reflections.
    (S) (3:12) Motown 6198 and 0794 Anthology.
    (S) (3:11) Motown 6193 25th Anniversary.
    (S) (3:12) Motown 5203 Greatest Hits Volume 3.

1968 #22 *SOME THINGS YOU NEVER GET USED TO*
    (S) (2:24) Motown 6140 The Composer Series: Ashford & Simpson.
    (S) (2:22) Motown 6198 and 0794 Anthology.
    (S) (2:23) Motown 8021 and 8121 Love Child/Supremes A Go Go.
    (S) (2:23) Motown 6193 25th Anniversary.
    (S) (2:22) Motown 5245 Love Child.
    (S) (2:22) Motown 5203 Greatest Hits Volume 3.

1968 #1 *LOVE CHILD*
    (S) (2:55) Motown 6159 The Good-Feeling Music Of The Big Chill Generation Volume 1.
    (S) (2:55) Motown 6177 Endless Love.
    (S) (2:54) Rhino 70629 Billboard's Top Rock & Roll Hits Of 1968.
    (S) (2:54) Rhino 72005 Billboard's Top Rock & Roll Hits 1968-1972 Box Set.
    (S) (2:54) MCA 10063 Original Television Soundtrack "The Sounds Of Murphy Brown".
    (S) (2:56) Motown 5385 Three Times A Lady: Great Motown Love Songs.
    (S) (2:55) Motown 9018 and 5249 16 #1 Hits From The Late 60's.
    (S) (2:55) Motown 9060 Motown's Biggest Pop Hits.
    (S) (2:54) Motown 5313 Great Songs And Performances That Inspired The Motown 25th Anniversary TV Special.
    (S) (2:54) Motown 6198 and 0794 Anthology.
    (S) (2:54) Motown 8021 and 8121 Love Child/Supremes A Go Go.
    (S) (2:55) Motown 6193 25th Anniversary.
    (S) (2:54) Motown 5245 Love Child.
    (S) (2:54) Motown 5203 Greatest Hits Volume 3.
    (M) (2:54) Motown 9038 and 5498 Every Great #1 Hit.
    (S) (2:55) Motown 6073 Compact Command Performances.
    (S) (2:51) Motown 6192 You Can't Hurry Love: All The Great Love Songs Of The Past 25 Years.
    (S) (2:53) Motown 5101 Superstar Series Volume 1.

DIANA ROSS & THE SUPREMES (Continued)

1969 #8 *I'M LIVIN' IN SHAME*

    (S) (2:58) Motown 9095 and 5325 Motown Girl Groups: Top 10 With A Bullet!

    (S) (2:55) Motown 6198 and 0794 Anthology.

    (S) (2:58) Motown 6193 25th Anniversary.

    (S) (2:57) Motown 5203 Greatest Hits Volume 3.

    (S) (2:58) Motown 5305 Let The Sunshine In.

    (S) (2:58) Motown 8032 and 8132 Let The Sunshine In/ Cream Of The Crop.

    (S) (2:56) Motown 5101 Superstar Series Volume 1.

1969 #21 *THE COMPOSER*

    (S) (2:57) Motown 6198 and 0794 Anthology.

    (S) (2:56) Motown 6193 25th Anniversary.

    (S) (2:59) Motown 5203 Greatest Hits Volume 3.

    (S) (2:59) Motown 5305 Let The Sunshine In.

1969 #27 *NO MATTER WHAT SIGN YOU ARE*

    (E) (2:46) Motown 6198 and 0794 Anthology.

    (E) (2:45) Motown 6193 25th Anniversary.

    (E) (2:52) Motown 5203 Greatest Hits Volume 3.

    (E) (2:52) Motown 5305 Let The Sunshine In.

    (E) (2:52) Motown 8032 and 8132 Let The Sunshine In/ Cream Of The Crop.

1969 #1 *SOMEDAY WE'LL BE TOGETHER*

(the actual 45 time is (3:30) not (3:14) as stated on the record label)

    (S) (3:28) Motown 6160 The Good-Feeling Music Of The Big Chill Generation Volume 2.

    (S) (3:28) Motown 6177 Endless Love.

    (S) (3:29) Rhino 70655 Billboard's Top R&B Hits Of 1969.

    (S) (3:29) Rhino 72006 Billboard's Top R&B Hits 1965-1969 Box Set.

    (S) (3:28) Motown 9097 The Most Played Oldies On America's Jukeboxes.

    (S) (3:27) Motown 9018 and 5249 16 #1 Hits From The Late 60's.

    (S) (3:28) Motown 9098 Radio's #1 Hits. *(noisy fadeout)*

    (S) (3:28) Motown 5322 and 9087 Girl Groups: The Story Of A Sound.

    (S) (3:28) Motown 0937 20/20 Twenty No. 1 Hits From Twenty Years At Motown.

    (S) (3:28) Motown 5313 Great Songs And Performances That Inspired The Motown 25th Anniversary TV Special.

    (S) (3:25) Motown 6198 and 0794 Anthology.

    (S) (3:27) Motown 6193 25th Anniversary.

    (S) (3:30) Motown 5203 Greatest Hits Volume 3.

    (M) (3:19) Motown 9038 and 5498 Every Great #1 Hit. *(:10 shorter than either the 45 or LP)*

    (S) (3:31) Motown 5435 Cream Of The Crop.

    (S) (3:31) Motown 8032 and 8132 Let The Sunshine In/ Cream Of The Crop.

    (S) (3:29) Motown 6073 Compact Command Performances.

    (S) (3:27) Motown 5101 Superstar Series Volume 1.

releases from this point on were credited once again to THE SUPREMES:

1970 #9 *UP THE LADDER TO THE ROOF*

    (S) (3:10) Motown 9110 Motown Memories Volume 4. *(alternate take)*

    (M) (3:15) Motown 5487 Greatest Hits And Rare Classics.

    (S) (3:09) Motown 6198 and 0794 Anthology.

    (S) (3:10) Motown 5442 Right On.

    (S) (3:11) Motown 6073 Compact Command Performances.

THE SUPREMES (Continued)
1970 #14 *EVERYBODY'S GOT THE RIGHT TO LOVE*
      (M)   (2:33) Motown 5487 Greatest Hits And Rare Classics.
      (S)   (2:35) Motown 6198 and 0794 Anthology.
      (S)   (2:36) Motown 5442 Right On.

1970 #5 *STONED LOVE*
(the actual 45 time is (2:57) not (2:49) as stated on the record label)
      (S)   (4:06) Motown 9109 Motown Memories Volume 3. *(LP version)*
      (S)   (3:43) Rhino 70658 Billboard's Top R&B Hits Of 1970. *(45 lyrics with LP introduction)*
      (S)   (3:16) Motown 9072 Motown Dance Party Volume 2. *(all selections on this cd are segued together; LP lyrics but missing the spoken introduction)*
      (M)   (2:57) Motown 5487 Greatest Hits And Rare Classics. *(45 version)*
      (S)   (4:06) Motown 6198 and 0794 Anthology. *(LP version)*
      (S)   (4:07) Motown 6073 Compact Command Performances. *(LP version)*
      (S)   (4:06) Motown 6192 You Can't Hurry Love: All The Great Love Songs Of The Past 25 Years. *(LP version)*
      (S)   (4:07) Motown 5497 New Ways But Love Stays. *(LP version)*

1971 #10 *NATHAN JONES*
      (S)   (3:00) Motown 9095 and 5325 Motown Girl Groups: Top 10 With A Bullet!
      (M)   (3:02) Motown 5487 Greatest Hits And Rare Classics.
      (S)   (2:57) Motown 6198 and 0794 Anthology.
      (S)   (3:00) Motown 5447 Touch.
      (S)   (3:00) Motown 6073 Compact Command Performances.

1972 #16 *FLOY JOY*
      (S)   (2:30) Motown 9104 Motown Memories Volume 1.
      (M)   (2:45) Motown 5487 Greatest Hits And Rare Classics. *(LP length)*
      (M)   (2:30) Motown 6198 and 0794 Anthology.
      (S)   (2:49) Motown 5441 Floy Joy. *(LP length)*

1972 #37 *AUTOMATICALLY SUNSHINE*
      (M)   (3:02) Motown 5487 Greatest Hits And Rare Classics. *(previously unreleased extended version; truncated fade)*
      (S)   (2:35) Motown 6198 and 0794 Anthology.
      (S)   (2:37) Motown 5441 Floy Joy.

SUPREMES & FOUR TOPS
1971 #15 *RIVER DEEP - MOUNTAIN HIGH*
(the actual 45 time is (3:13) not (3:05) as stated on the record label)
      (S)   (4:47) Motown 6184 20 Hard To Find Motown Classics Volume 2. *(LP version)*
      (M)   (3:13) Motown 5491 Best Of The Supremes & Four Tops. *(45 version)*
      (S)   (4:50) Motown 5123 Magnificent 7. *(LP version)*
      (E)   (4:29) Motown 0809 and 6188 Four Tops Anthology. *(edit of LP version)*

SUPREMES & TEMPTATIONS
released as by DIANA ROSS AND THE SUPREMES & THE TEMPTATIONS:
1969 #1 *I'M GONNA MAKE YOU LOVE ME*
      (S)   (3:05) Motown 6160 The Good-Feeling Music Of The Big Chill Generation Volume 2.
      (S)   (3:05) Motown 9031 and 5214 Diana's Duets.
      (S)   (3:05) Motown 6198 and 0794 Supremes Anthology.
      (S)   (3:05) Motown 6193 Diana Ross & The Supremes 25th Anniversary.
      (S)   (3:05) Motown 5139 Join The Temptations.
      (S)   (3:05) Motown 8038 and 8138 Join The Temptations/ Together.
      (S)   (3:06) Motown 6073 Supremes Compact Command Performances.

DIANA ROSS AND THE SUPREMES & THE TEMPTATIONS (Continued)

(S) (3:05) Motown 0782 and 6189 Temptations Anthology.
(S) (3:05) Motown 6204 and 5389 Temptations 25th Anniversary.

1969 #21 *I'LL TRY SOMETHING NEW*

(S) (2:19) Motown 9031 and 5214 Diana's Duets.
(S) (2:19) Motown 5313 Diana Ross & The Supremes: Great Songs And Performances That Inspired The Motown 25th Anniversary TV Special.
(S) (2:17) Motown 6198 and 0794 Supremes Anthology.
(S) (2:19) Motown 5139 Join The Temptations.
(S) (2:19) Motown 8038 and 8138 Join The Temptations / Together.
(S) (2:19) Motown 6073 Supremes Compact Command Performances.

1969 #39 *THE WEIGHT*

(S) (3:00) Motown 8038 and 8138 Join The Temptations / Together.
(S) (3:00) Motown 5436 Together.

SURFARIS

1963 #5 *WIPE OUT*

(M) (2:36) Rhino 70089 Surfin' Hits. *(:19 longer than 45 or LP)*
(M) (2:37) Rhino 75778 Frat Rock. *(:20 longer than 45 or LP)*
(E) (2:37) RCA 6965 More Dirty Dancing. *(:20 longer than 45 or LP)*
(M) (2:37) MCA 31205 Vintage Music Volume 8. *(:20 longer than 45 or LP)*
(M) (2:37) MCA 5805 Vintage Music Volumes 7 & 8. *(:20 longer than 45 or LP)*
(M) (2:37) JCI 3106 Surfin' Sixties. *(:20 longer than 45 or LP)*
(M) (2:36) Rhino 70794 KFOG Presents M. Dung's Idiot Show. *(:19 longer than 45 or LP)*

1966 #9 *WIPEOUT*

(this song was a hit in 1963 and 1966; see 1963 listings)

SUTHERLAND BROTHERS & QUIVER

1973 #20 *(I DON'T WANT TO LOVE YOU BUT) YOU GOT ME ANYWAY*

BETTYE SWANN

1967 #20 *MAKE ME YOURS*

(E) (2:56) Collectables 5177 Make Me Yours. *(sounds like it was mastered from vinyl)*

1969 #40 *DON'T TOUCH ME*

SWEATHOG

1971 #28 *HALLELUJAH*

(S) (2:57) Rhino 70927 Super Hits Of The 70's Volume 7.
(S) (2:56) Columbia/Legacy 46160 Rock Artifacts Volume 1.

SWEET

1973 #3 *LITTLE WILLY*

SWEET INSPIRATIONS

1968 #20 *SWEET INSPIRATION*

(S) (2:52) Rhino 75757 Soul Shots Volume 3.
(S) (2:52) Stax 8565 Estelle, Myrna and Sylvia.
(M) (2:52) Rhino 70278 Rare Soul: Beach Music Classics Volume 2.

SWINGING BLUE JEANS

1964 #23 *HIPPY HIPPY SHAKE*

(S) (1:44) Rhino 70319 History Of British Rock Volume 1.
(S) (1:44) Rhino 70319 History Of British Rock Box Set.
(S) (1:44) Rhino 72008 History Of British Rock Volumes 1-4 Box Set.

SWINGIN' MEDALLIONS
1966 #18 *DOUBLE SHOT (OF MY BABY'S LOVE)*
    (S) (2:18) Warner Special Products 27607 Highs Of The 60's. (*"worst hangover" lyric; 45 and stereo LP version*)
    (M) (2:12) Rhino 75778 Frat Rock. (*"worst hangover" lyric; 45 and stereo LP version*)
    (S) (2:18) Mercury 816555 45's On CD Volume 2. (*"worst hangover" lyric; 45 and stereo LP version*)
    (S) (2:18) Dunhill Compact Classics 029 Toga Rock. (*"worst hangover" lyric; 45 and stereo LP version*)

FOSTER SYLVERS
1973 #14 *MISDEMEANOR*

SYLVIA
1973 #2 *PILLOW TALK*
    (M) (4:05) Rhino 70790 Soul Hits Of The 70's Volume 10.

SYNDICATE OF SOUND
1966 #8 *LITTLE GIRL*
    (S) (2:27) Warner Special Products 27602 20 Party Classics.
    (S) (2:25) Rhino 75892 Nuggets.
    (S) (2:25) K-Tel 839 Battle Of The Bands Volume 2.

T

TAMS
1964 #9 *WHAT KIND OF FOOL (DO YOU THINK I AM)*
    (M) (1:59) MCA 31207 Vintage Music Volume 10.
    (M) (1:59) MCA 5806 Vintage Music Volumes 9 & 10.
    (E) (1:59) Ripete 35190 15 Greatest Hits.
    (M) (1:59) Ripete 392183 Ocean Drive.

NORMA TANEGA
1966 #25 *WALKIN' MY CAT NAMED DOG*

TARRIERS
1957 #2 *THE BANANA BOAT SONG*
    (M) (2:58) Rhino 70264 Troubadours Of The Folk Era Volume 2. (*mastered from a very scratchy record*)

TAVARES
1973 #34 *CHECK IT OUT*
    (S) (3:17) Capitol 91640 Best Of.

GLORIA TAYLOR
1969 #38 *YOU GOT TO PAY THE PRICE*

JAMES TAYLOR

1970 #4 *FIRE AND RAIN*
(S) (3:19) Warner Special Products 27615 Storytellers: Singers & Songwriters.
(S) (3:21) Priority 8664 High Times/70's Greatest Rock Hits Volume 3.
(S) (3:20) Warner Brothers 1843 Sweet Baby James.
(S) (3:22) Warner Brothers 3113 Greatest Hits.

1971 #25 *COUNTRY ROAD*
(S) (3:20) Warner Brothers 1843 Sweet Baby James.
(S) (3:21) Warner Brothers 3113 Greatest Hits.

1971 #1 *YOU'VE GOT A FRIEND*
(S) (4:20) Warner Brothers 2561 Mud Slide Slim And The Blue Horizon.
(S) (4:27) Warner Brothers 3113 Greatest Hits.

1971 #16 *LONG AGO AND FAR AWAY*
(S) (2:19) Warner Brothers 2561 Mud Slide Slim And The Blue Horizon.

1973 #15 *DON'T LET ME BE LONELY TONIGHT*
(S) (2:34) Warner Brothers 3113 Greatest Hits.
(S) (2:33) Warner Brothers 25933 One Man Dog.

JOHNNIE TAYLOR

1968 #6 *WHO'S MAKING LOVE*
(S) (2:47) Rhino 75770 Soul Shots Volume 2.
(S) (2:46) JCI 3105 Soul Sixties.
(S) (2:47) Rhino 70654 Billboard's Top R&B Hits Of 1968.
(S) (2:47) Rhino 72006 Billboard's Top R&B Hits 1965-1969 Box Set.
(S) (2:46) Stax 88005 Top Of The Stax.
(S) (2:46) Warner Special Products 27609 Memphis Soul Classics.
(S) (2:46) Stax 60-006 Chronicle: The 20 Greatest Hits.
(S) (2:45) Stax 4115 Who's Making Love.

1969 #26 *TAKE CARE OF YOUR HOMEWORK*
(S) (2:38) Stax 60-006 Chronicle: The 20 Greatest Hits. *(noise on fadeout)*
(S) (2:37) Stax 4115 Who's Making Love. *(noise on fadeout)*

1969 #36 *TESTIFY (I WONNA)*
(S) (4:03) Stax 88008 Top Of The Stax Volume 2.
(S) (4:03) Stax 60-006 Chronicle: The 20 Greatest Hits.
(S) (4:03) Stax 8563 Johnnie Taylor Philosophy Continues.

1970 #32 *LOVE BONES*
(S) (4:03) Stax 60-006 Chronicle: The 20 Greatest Hits. *(LP version)*
(S) (4:04) Stax 8563 Johnnie Taylor Philosophy Continues. *(LP version)*

1970 #23 *STEAL AWAY*
(S) (3:26) Stax 8547 Stax Blues Brothers.
(S) (3:27) Stax 8559 Superblues Volume 2.
(S) (3:27) Stax 60-006 Chronicle: The 20 Greatest Hits.
(S) (7:48) Stax 8558 Little Bluebird. *(live)*

1970 #30 *I AM SOMEBODY (PART 2)*
(S) (3:22) Stax 60-006 Chronicle: The 20 Greatest Hits.

1971 #27 *JODY'S GOT YOUR GIRL AND GONE*
(S) (2:59) Stax 60-006 Chronicle: The 20 Greatest Hits.
(S) (5:47) Stax 8558 Little Bluebird. *(live)*

1973 #5 *I BELIEVE IN YOU (YOU BELIEVE IN ME)*
(S) (4:31) Stax 88008 Top Of The Stax Volume 2.
(S) (5:06) Stax 60-006 Chronicle: The 20 Greatest Hits. *(LP version)*

1973 #18 *CHEAPER TO KEEP HER*
(S) (2:46) Stax 88005 Top Of The Stax. *(edited)*
(S) (3:25) Stax 60-006 Chronicle: The 20 Greatest Hits. *(truncated fade)*

KO KO TAYLOR
1966 #36 *WANG DANG DOODLE*
(S) (2:59) Stax 8551 Superblues Volume 1.

LITTLE JOHNNY TAYLOR
1963 #19 *PART TIME LOVE*
(S) (3:47) Stax 8551 Superblues Volume 1.
(S) (3:50) Fantasy 4510 Greatest Hits.

R. DEAN TAYLOR
1970 #1 *INDIANA WANTS ME*
(there are two 45 versions of this song; one runs (3:01) and has no sirens on the intro, the other runs (3:05) and has sirens on the intro; the real LP time is (3:43) not (3:15) as stated on the record label)
(S) (3:39) Rhino 70923 Super Hits Of The 70's Volume 3. *(LP version)*
(S) (3:39) Rhino 72009 Super Hits Of The 70's Volumes 1-4 Box Set. *(LP version)*
(E) (3:45) Motown 6184 Hard To Find Motown Classics Volume 2. *(LP version)*

SAM "THE MAN" TAYLOR
1958 #35 *BIG GUITAR*

T-BONES
1966 #3 *NO MATTER WHAT SHAPE (YOUR STOMACH'S IN)*
(S) (2:15) Curb 77402 All-Time Great Instrumental Hits Volume 2.

TEDDY BEARS
1958 #1 *TO KNOW HIM IS TO LOVE HIM*
(M) (2:22) Rhino 70619 Billboard's Top Rock & Roll Hits Of 1958.
(M) (2:22) Rhino 72004 Billboard's Top Rock & Roll Hits 1957-1961 Box Set.
(M) (2:22) Abkco 7118 Phil Spector/Back To Mono (1958-1969).

TEE SET
1970 #6 *MA BELLE AMIE*
(S) (3:12) Rhino 70922 Super Hits Of The 70's Volume 2.
(S) (3:12) Rhino 72009 Super Hits Of The 70's Volumes 1-4 Box Set.
(S) (3:12) JCI 3115 Groovin' Sixties.

TEEGARDEN & VAN WINKLE
1970 #14 *GOD, LOVE AND ROCK & ROLL*

TEENAGERS (see FRANKIE LYMON & THE TEENAGERS)

NINO TEMPO & APRIL STEVENS
1963 #1 *DEEP PURPLE*
(S) (2:40) Atlantic 81909 Hit Singles 1958-1977.
1964 #11 *WHISPERING*
1964 #30 *STARDUST*
1966 #29 *ALL STRUNG OUT*

NINO TEMPO & 5TH AVE. SAX
1973 #40 *SISTER JAMES*

TEMPOS
1959 #22 *SEE YOU IN SEPTEMBER*
(M) (2:06) Essex 7053 A Hot Summer Night In '59.

TEMPTATIONS (New York group)
1960 #38 *BARBARA*

TEMPTATIONS (Detroit group)
1964 #10 *THE WAY YOU DO THE THINGS YOU DO*
- (S) (2:44) Motown 6139 The Composer Series: Smokey Robinson. (*LP length*)
- (S) (2:35) Motown 5450 A Collection Of 16 Big Hits Volume 3. (*45 length*)
- (S) (2:44) Rhino 70650 Billboard's Top R&B Hits Of 1964. (*excessive noise at 2:44; LP length*)
- (S) (2:42) Motown 0782 and 6189 Anthology. (*LP length*)
- (S) (2:42) Motown 5411 Greatest Hits. (*LP length*)
- (S) (2:42) Motown 8060 and 8160 Meet The Temptations/ Temptations Sing Smokey. (*LP length*)
- (S) (2:44) Motown 5205 Temptations Sing Smokey. (*LP length*)
- (S) (2:44) Motown 5140 Meet The Temptations. (*LP length*)
- (S) (2:42) Motown 9071 Motown Dance Party Volume 1. (*LP length; all selections on this cd are segued together*)

1964 #32 *I'LL BE IN TROUBLE*
- (S) (2:51) Motown 5451 A Collection Of 16 Big Hits Volume 4.
- (S) (2:54) Motown 0782 and 6189 Anthology.
- (S) (2:54) Motown 5411 Greatest Hits.

1964 #27 *GIRL (WHY YOU WANNA MAKE ME BLUE)*
- (S) (2:16) Motown 0782 and 6189 Anthology.
- (S) (2:17) Motown 6125 Compact Command Performances.
- (S) (2:16) Motown 5411 Greatest Hits.
- (S) (2:16) Motown 5374 The Temptin' Temptations.

1965 #2 *MY GIRL*
(the mono mix of this song is far superior to the stereo mixes which have problems with phase cancellation, thus wiping out portions of the background harmony)
- (S) (2:42) Motown 6132 25 #1 Hits From 25 Years. (*noisy intro*)
- (M) (2:55) Motown 6120 O.S.T. The Big Chill. (*:14 longer than either the LP or 45*)
- (E) (2:55) Motown 5452 A Collection Of 16 Big Hits Volume 5. (*:14 longer than either the 45 or LP*)
- (S) (2:42) Motown 6137 20 Greatest Songs In Motown History. (*noisy intro*)
- (S) (2:42) Motown 6159 The Good-Feeling Music Of The Big Chill Generation Volume 1.
- (S) (2:43) Motown 6139 The Composer Series: Smokey Robinson.
- (S) (2:42) Rhino 70651 Billboard's Top R&B Hits Of 1965.
- (S) (2:42) Rhino 72006 Billboard's Top R&B Hits 1965-1969 Box Set.
- (S) (2:41) Epic 48732 O.S.T. My Girl.
- (S) (2:41) MCA 6340 O.S.T. Born On The Fourth Of July.
- (S) (2:41) Motown 9017 and 5248 16 #1 Hits From The Early 60's.
- (S) (2:42) Motown 9097 The Most Played Oldies On America's Jukeboxes.
- (S) (2:42) Motown 5343 Every Great Motown Song: The First 25 Years Volume 1. (*most selections on this cd have noise on the fade out*)
- (S) (2:42) Motown 8034 and 8134 Every Great Motown Song: The First 25 Years Volumes 1 & 2. (*most selections on this cd have noise on the fade out*)
- (S) (2:41) Motown 0782 and 6189 Anthology.
- (S) (2:43) Motown 6125 Compact Command Performances.
- (S) (2:42) Motown 6204 and 5389 25th Anniversary.
- (S) (2:42) Motown 9033 and 5315 Great Songs And Performances That Inspired The Motown 25th Anniversary TV Special.
- (E) (2:55) Motown 5212 All The Million Sellers. (*:14 longer than either the 45 or LP*)

    (S) (2:42) Motown 5411 Greatest Hits.

    (S) (2:41) Motown 8060 and 8160 Meet The Temptations/ Temptations Sing Smokey.

    (S) (2:41) Motown 5205 Temptations Sing Smokey.

    (S) (2:41) Ripete 392183 Ocean Drive. *(truncated fade; noise on introduction)*

1965 #19 *IT'S GROWING*

    (S) (2:55) Motown 5452 A Collection Of 16 Big Hits Volume 5.

    (S) (2:56) Motown 0782 and 6189 Anthology.

    (S) (2:56) Motown 5411 Greatest Hits.

    (S) (2:55) Motown 8060 and 8160 Meet The Temptations/ Temptations Sing Smokey.

    (S) (2:55) Motown 5205 Temptations Sing Smokey.

1965 #18 *SINCE I LOST MY BABY*

    (E) (2:50) Motown 9105 Motown Memories Volume 2.

    (E) (2:50) Motown 0782 and 6189 Anthology.

    (E) (2:51) Motown 6125 Compact Command Performances.

    (E) (2:50) Motown 6204 and 5389 25th Anniversary. *(noisy fadeout)*

    (E) (2:50) Motown 5411 Greatest Hits.

    (E) (2:50) Motown 5374 The Temptin' Temptations.

1965 #18 *MY BABY*

    (S) (3:00) Motown 5453 A Collection Of 16 Big Hits Volume 6.

    (S) (3:00) Motown 0782 and 6189 Anthology.

    (S) (3:00) Motown 5411 Greatest Hits.

    (S) (3:00) Motown 5374 The Temptin' Temptations.

1966 #29 *GET READY*

    (S) (2:37) Motown 6160 The Good-Feeling Music Of The Big Chill Generation Volume 2.

    (S) (2:38) Motown 6139 The Composer Series: Smokey Robinson.

    (S) (2:35) MCA 10063 Original Television Soundtrack "The Sounds Of Murphy Brown".

    (S) (2:36) MCA 6467 O.S.T. Air America.

    (S) (2:36) Motown 9072 Motown Dance Party Volume 2. *(all selections on this cd are segued together)*

    (S) (2:38) Motown 9097 The Most Played Oldies On America's Jukeboxes.

    (S) (2:37) Motown 9018 and 5249 16 #1 Hits From The Late 60's.

    (S) (2:37) Motown 0782 and 6189 Anthology.

    (S) (2:37) Motown 6204 and 5389 25th Anniversary.

    (S) (2:38) Motown 9033 and 5315 Great Songs And Performances That Inspired The Motown 25th Anniversary TV Special.

    (S) (2:37) Motown 5411 Greatest Hits.

    (S) (2:37) Motown 5373 Gettin' Ready.

1966 #10 *AIN'T TOO PROUD TO BEG*

    (S) (2:31) Motown 6160 The Good-Feeling Music Of The Big Chill Generation Volume 2. *(noisy intro)*

    (S) (2:31) Motown 6120 O.S.T. The Big Chill.

    (S) (2:32) Motown 5454 A Collection Of 16 Big Hits Volume 7.

    (S) (2:32) Rhino 70652 Billboard's Top R&B Hits Of 1966.

    (S) (2:32) Rhino 72006 Billboard's Top R&B Hits 1965-1969 Box Set.

    (S) (2:31) Motown 9018 and 5249 16 #1 Hits From The Late 60's.

    (S) (2:31) Motown 0782 and 6189 Anthology.

    (S) (2:32) Motown 6125 Compact Command Performances.

    (S) (2:31) Motown 6204 and 5389 25th Anniversary.

    (S) (2:31) Motown 9033 and 5315 Great Songs And Performances That Inspired The Motown 25th Anniversary TV Special.

        (S) (2:31) Motown 5212 All The Million Sellers.
        (S) (2:31) Motown 5411 Greatest Hits.
        (S) (2:31) Motown 5373 Gettin' Ready.
        (S) (2:29) Motown 9071 Motown Dance Party Volume 1. *(all selections on this cd are segued together)*
        (S) (2:31) Ripete 392183 Ocean Drive.

1966 #5 BEAUTY IS ONLY SKIN DEEP
        (S) (2:21) Motown 6159 The Good-Feeling Music Of The Big Chill Generation Volume 1. *(noisy intro)*
        (S) (2:20) Motown 5455 A Collection Of 16 Big Hits Volume 8.
        (S) (2:21) Rhino 70652 Billboard's Top R&B Hits Of 1966.
        (S) (2:21) Rhino 72006 Billboard's Top R&B Hits 1965-1969 Box Set.
        (S) (2:21) Motown 0782 and 6189 Anthology.
        (S) (2:21) Motown 5411 Greatest Hits.

1966 #11 (I KNOW) I'M LOSING YOU
        (S) (2:25) Motown 6161 The Good-Feeling Music Of The Big Chill Generation Volume 3.
        (S) (2:25) Motown 5455 A Collection Of 16 Big Hits Volume 8.
        (S) (2:26) Motown 9018 and 5249 16 #1 Hits From The Late 60's.
        (S) (2:25) Motown 0782 and 6189 Anthology.
        (S) (2:26) Motown 6125 Compact Command Performances.
        (S) (2:26) Motown 9033 and 5315 Great Songs And Performances That Inspired The Motown 25th Anniversary TV Special.
        (S) (2:24) Motown 5412 Greatest Hits Volume 2.
        (S) (2:24) Motown 8137 and 8037 Live At The Copa/With A Lot O' Soul.
        (S) (2:25) Motown 5299 With A Lot O' Soul.

1967 #8 ALL I NEED
        (S) (3:05) Motown 5456 A Collection Of 16 Big Hits Volume 9.
        (S) (3:05) Motown 0782 and 6189 Anthology.
        (S) (3:06) Motown 8137 and 8037 Live At The Copa/With A Lot O' Soul.
        (S) (3:07) Motown 5299 With A Lot O' Soul.

1967 #7 YOU'RE MY EVERYTHING
        (S) (2:57) Motown 0782 and 6189 Anthology.
        (S) (2:57) Motown 6125 Compact Command Performances.
        (S) (2:57) Motown 5412 Greatest Hits Volume 2.
        (S) (2:56) Motown 8137 and 8037 Live At The Copa/With A Lot O' Soul.
        (S) (2:56) Motown 5299 With A Lot O' Soul.

1967 #11 (LONELINESS MADE ME REALIZE) IT'S YOU THAT I NEED
        (S) (2:34) Motown 5456 A Collection Of 16 Big Hits Volume 9.
        (S) (2:35) Motown 0782 and 6189 Anthology.
        (S) (2:34) Motown 5412 Greatest Hits Volume 2.
        (S) (2:33) Motown 8137 and 8037 Live At The Copa/With A Lot O' Soul.
        (S) (2:33) Motown 5299 With A Lot O' Soul.

1968 #2 I WISH IT WOULD RAIN
        (S) (2:45) Motown 6160 The Good-Feeling Music Of The Big Chill Generation Volume 2.
        (S) (2:45) Motown 5457 a Collection Of 16 Big Hits Volume 10.
        (S) (2:45) Rhino 70654 Billboard's Top R&B Hits Of 1968.
        (S) (2:45) Rhino 72006 Billboard's Top R&B Hits 1965-1969 Box Set.
        (S) (2:45) Motown 9018 and 5249 16 #1 Hits From The Late 60's.
        (S) (2:44) Motown 0782 and 6189 Anthology.
        (S) (2:47) Motown 6125 Compact Command Performances.
        (S) (2:47) Motown 9033 and 5315 Great Songs And Performances That Inspired The Motown 25th Anniversary TV Special.

TEMPTATIONS (Continued)

    (S) (2:48) Motown 5212 All The Million Sellers.
    (S) (2:45) Motown 5412 Greatest Hits Volume 2.
    (S) (2:41) Motown 5276 I Wish It Would Rain.

1968 #10 *I COULD NEVER LOVE ANOTHER (AFTER LOVING YOU)*

    (S) (3:32) Motown 9109 Motown Memories Volume 3.
    (S) (3:32) Motown 6161 The Good-Time Feeling Of The Big Chill Generation Volume 3.
    (S) (3:32) Motown 0782 and 6189 Anthology.
    (S) (3:33) Motown 6125 Compact Command Performances.
    (S) (3:29) Motown 6192 You Can't Hurry Love: All The Great Love Songs Of The Past 25 Years.
    (S) (3:32) Motown 9033 and 5315 Great Songs And Performances That Inspired The Motown 25th Anniversary TV Special.
    (S) (3:32) Motown 5412 Greatest Hits Volume 2.
    (S) (3:34) Motown 5276 I Wish It Would Rain.

1968 #23 *PLEASE RETURN YOUR LOVE TO ME*

    (S) (2:19) Motown 9105 Motown Memories Volume 2.
    (S) (2:21) Motown 0782 and 6189 Anthology.
    (S) (2:21) Motown 5412 Greatest Hits Volume 2.
    (S) (2:22) Motown 5276 I Wish It Would Rain.

1969 #8 *CLOUD NINE*

    (S) (3:30) Motown 6110 Motown Grammy R&B Performances Of The 60's & 70's.
    (S) (3:29) Rhino 70654 Billboard's Top R&B Hits Of 1968.
    (S) (3:29) Rhino 72006 Billboard's Top R&B Hits 1965-1969 Box Set.
    (S) (3:29) Motown 9021 and 5309 25 Years Of Grammy Greats.
    (S) (3:29) Motown 0782 and 6189 Anthology.
    (S) (3:30) Motown 6125 Compact Command Performances.
    (S) (4:15) Motown 6204 and 5389 25th Anniversary. *(live)*
    (S) (3:29) Motown 9033 and 5315 Great Songs And Performances That Inspired The Motown 25th Anniversary TV Special.
    (S) (3:28) Motown 5212 All The Million Sellers.
    (S) (3:29) Motown 5412 Greatest Hits Volume 2.
    (S) (3:29) Motown 9096 and 5159 Cloud Nine.
    (S) (3:29) Motown 8016 and 8116 Cloud Nine/Puzzle People.

1969 #8 *RUN AWAY CHILD, RUNNING WILD*

(the actual 45 time is (4:43) not (4:30) as stated on the record label)

    (S) (4:52) Motown 6161 The Good-Feeling Music Of The Big Chill Generation Volume 3.
    (S) (4:36) Motown 0782 and 6189 Anthology.
    (S) (4:52) Motown 6125 Compact Command Performances.
    (S) (4:52) Motown 9033 and 5315 Great Songs And Performances That Inspired The Motown 25th Anniversary TV Special.
    (S) (4:49) Motown 5212 All The Million Sellers.
    (S) (4:52) Motown 5412 Greatest Hits Volume 2.
    (S) (9:33) Motown 9096 and 5159 Cloud Nine. *(LP version)*
    (S) (4:36) Motown 8016 and 8116 Cloud Nine/Puzzle People.

1969 #20 *DON'T LET THE JONESES GET YOU DOWN*

(the actual 45 time is (4:37) not (4:15) as stated on the record label)

    (S) (4:43) Motown 0782 and 6189 Anthology.
    (S) (4:43) Motown 5412 Greatest Hits Volume 2.
    (S) (4:43) Motown 8016 and 8116 Cloud Nine/Puzzle People.
    (S) (4:43) Motown 5172 Puzzle People.

1969 #3   *I CAN'T GET NEXT TO YOU*

     (S)   (2:52) Rhino 70630 Billboard's Top Rock & Roll Hits Of 1969.

     (S)   (2:52) Rhino 72005 Billboard's Top Rock & Roll Hits 1968-1972 Box Set.

     (S)   (2:51) Motown 6161 The Good-Feeling Music Of The Big Chill Generation Volume 3.

     (S)   (2:50) Motown 9072 Motown Dance Party Volume 2. *(all selections on this cd are segued together)*

     (S)   (2:51) Motown 9018 and 5249 16 #1 Hits From The Late 60's.

     (S)   (2:52) Motown 9060 Motown's Biggest Pop Hits.

     (S)   (2:51) Motown 0782 and 6189 Anthology.

     (S)   (2:52) Motown 6125 Compact Command Performances.

     (S)   (2:12) Motown 6204 and 5389 25th Anniversary. *(live)*

     (S)   (2:51) Motown 9033 and 5315 Great Songs And Performances That Inspired The Motown 25th Anniversary TV Special.

     (S)   (2:51) Motown 5212 All The Million Sellers.

     (S)   (2:51) Motown 5412 Greatest Hits Volume 2.

     (S)   (2:51) Motown 8016 and 8116 Cloud Nine/Puzzle People.

     (S)   (2:51) Motown 5172 Puzzle People.

1970 #4   *PSYCHEDELIC SHACK*

     (S)   (3:50) Motown 0782 and 6189 Anthology.

     (S)   (3:50) Motown 6125 Compact Command Performances.

     (E)   (3:48) Motown 5212 All The Million Sellers.

     (S)   (3:50) Motown 5412 Greatest Hits Volume 2.

     (S)   (3:50) Motown 8022 and 8122 All Directions/Psychedelic Shack.

     (S)   (3:49) Motown 5164 Psychedelic Shack.

1970 #1   *BALL OF CONFUSION (THAT'S WHAT THE WORLD IS TODAY)*

     (S)   (4:04) Rhino 70734 Songs Of Protest.

     (S)   (4:04) Rhino 70658 Billboard's Top R&B Hits Of 1970.

     (S)   (4:04) Motown 0782 and 6189 Anthology.

     (S)   (4:04) Motown 6125 Compact Command Performances.

     (S)   (4:04) Motown 9033 and 5315 Great Songs And Performances That Inspired The Motown 25th Anniversary TV Special.

     (S)   (4:04) Motown 5212 All The Million Sellers.

     (S)   (4:03) Motown 5412 Greatest Hits Volume 2.

1970 #30   *UNGENA ZA ULIMWENGU (UNITE THE WORLD)*

     (the actual 45 time is (4:14) not (3:45) as stated on the record label)

     (S)   (4:28) Motown 5474 Sky's The Limit. *(LP length)*

1971 #1   *JUST MY IMAGINATION (RUNNING AWAY WITH ME)*

     (S)   (3:48) Motown 6132 25 #1 Hits From 25 Years.

     (S)   (3:47) Motown 6137 20 Greatest Songs In Motown History.

     (S)   (3:52) Rhino 70659 Billboard's Top R&B Hits Of 1971.

     (S)   (3:46) Motown 5344 Every Great Motown Song: The First 25 Years Volume 2. *(most selections on this cd have noise on the fade out)*

     (S)   (3:46) Motown 5275 12 #1 Hits From The 70's.

     (S)   (3:47) Motown 8034 and 8134 Every Great Motown Song: The First 25 Years Volumes 1 & 2. *(most selections on this cd have noise on the fade out)*

     (S)   (3:46) Motown 9060 Motown's Biggest Pop Hits. *(buzz noticeable on fadeout)*

     (S)   (3:46) Motown 0782 and 6189 Anthology.

     (S)   (3:47) Motown 6125 Compact Command Performances.

     (S)   (3:46) Motown 6204 and 5389 25th Anniversary.

TEMPTATIONS (Continued)

        (S)   (3:45) Motown 5212 All The Million Sellers.

        (S)   (3:46) Motown 5474 Sky's The Limit.

1971 #40 IT'S SUMMER

        (S)   (2:54) Motown 5480 Solid Rock.

        (S)   (2:34) Motown 8022 and 8122 All Directions/Psychedelic Shack. *("Psychedelic Shack" LP version and not the hit version)*

        (S)   (2:34) Motown 5164 Psychedelic Shack. *("Psychedelic Shack" LP version and not the hit version)*

1971 #13 SUPERSTAR (REMEMBER HOW YOU GOT WHERE YOU ARE)

        (S)   (2:50) Motown 0782 and 6189 Anthology.

        (S)   (2:51) Motown 6125 Compact Command Performances.

        (S)   (2:52) Motown 5480 Solid Rock.

1972 #28 TAKE A LOOK AROUND

        (S)   (2:42) Motown 5480 Solid Rock.

1972 #1 PAPA WAS A ROLLING STONE

        (M) (6:52) Rhino 70633 Billboard's Top Rock & Roll Hits Of 1972.

        (M) (6:52) Rhino 72005 Billboard's Top Rock & Roll Hits 1968-1972 Box Set.

        (E) (6:54) Motown 6110 Motown Grammy R&B Performances Of The 60's & 70's.

        (E) (6:53) Motown 6132 25 #1 Hits From 25 Years.

        (E) (6:52) Motown 9021 and 5309 25 Years Of Grammy Greats.

        (E) (6:52) Motown 0937 20/20 Twenty No. 1 Hits From Twenty Years At Motown.

        (E) (6:51) Motown 0782 and 6189 Anthology.

        (E) (6:53) Motown 6125 Compact Command Performances. *(tracks into next selection)*

        (S)   (7:23) Motown 6204 and 5389 25th Anniversary. *(live)*

        (E) (6:54) Motown 9033 and 5315 Great Songs And Performances That Inspired The Motown 25th Anniversary TV Special.

        (E) (6:55) Motown 5212 All The Million Sellers.

        (S) (11:43) Motown 8022 and 8122 All Directions/Psychedelic Shack. *(LP version)*

        (S) (11:44) Motown 5172 All Directions. *(LP version)*

1973 #9 MASTERPIECE

(the actual 45 time is (4:26) not (5:30) as stated on the record label)

        (S)   (4:22) Rhino 70661 Billboard's Top R&B Hits Of 1973.

        (S)   (4:19) Motown 0782 and 6189 Anthology.

        (S) (13:48) Motown 5144 Masterpiece. *(LP version)*

1973 #33 THE PLASTIC MAN

        (S)   (5:52) Motown 5144 Masterpiece. *(LP version)*

1973 #27 HEY GIRL (I LIKE YOUR STYLE)

        (S)   (2:38) Motown 6125 Compact Command Performances. *(this is not "HEY GIRL (I LIKE YOUR STYLE)" as the jacket indicates but another song simply titled "HEY GIRL")*

        (S)   (3:05) Motown 6204 and 5389 25th Anniversary. *(this is not "HEY GIRL (I LIKE YOUR STYLE)" as the jacket indicates but another song simply titled "HEY GIRL")*

        (S)   (4:35) Motown 5144 Masterpiece. *(LP version)*

TEMPTATIONS & DIANA ROSS AND THE SUPREMES

1969 #1 I'M GONNA MAKE YOU LOVE ME

        (S)   (3:05) Motown 6160 The Good-Feeling Music Of The Big Chill Generation Volume 2.

        (S)   (3:05) Motown 9031 and 5214 Diana's Duets.

TEMPTATIONS & DIANA ROSS AND THE SUPREMES (Continued)

      (S) (3:05) Motown 6198 and 0794 Supremes Anthology.
      (S) (3:05) Motown 6193 Diana Ross & The Suprmes 25th Anniversary.
      (S) (3:05) Motown 5139 Join The Temptations.
      (S) (3:05) Motown 8038 and 8138 Join The Temptations/ Together.
      (S) (3:06) Motown 6073 Supremes Compact Command Performances.
      (S) (3:05) Motown 0782 and 6189 Temptations Anthology.
      (S) (3:05) Motown 6204 and 5389 Temptations 25th Anniversary.

1969 #21 I'LL TRY SOMETHING NEW

      (S) (2:19) Motown 9031 and 5214 Diana's Duets.
      (S) (2:19) Motown 5313 Diana Ross & The Supremes: Great Songs And Performances That Inspired The Motown 25th Anniversary TV Special.
      (S) (2:17) Motown 6198 and 0794 Supremes Anthology.
      (S) (2:19) Motown 5139 Join The Temptations.
      (S) (2:19) Motown 8038 and 8138 Join The Temptations/ Together.
      (S) (2:19) Motown 6073 Supremes Compact Command Performances.

1969 #39 THE WEIGHT

      (S) (3:00) Motown 8038 and 8138 Join The Temptations/ Together.
      (S) (3:00) Motown 5436 Together.

TEN YEARS AFTER

1971 #28 I'D LOVE TO CHANGE THE WORLD

      (S) (3:42) Dunhill Compact Classics 045 Golden Age Of Underground Radio. (LP version)
      (S) (3:41) Priority 7942 Hard Rockin' 70's. (LP version)
      (S) (3:43) Rhino 70272 Metal Age: The Roots Of Metal. (LP version)

JOE TEX

1965 #6 HOLD WHAT YOU'VE GOT

      (M) (3:04) Atlantic 81297 Atlantic Rhythm & Blues Volume 5.
      (M) (3:04) Atlantic 82305 Atlantic Rhythm And Blues 1947-1974 Box Set.
      (M) (3:07) Rhino 70191 Best Of.
      (M) (3:07) Curb 77520 Greatest Hits.

1965 #18 I WANT TO (DO EVERYTHING FOR YOU)

      (M) (2:08) Atlantic 82305 Atlantic Rhythm And Blues 1947-1974 Box Set.
      (M) (2:08) Rhino 70191 Best Of.
      (M) (2:07) Curb 77520 Greatest Hits.

1966 #20 A SWEET WOMAN LIKE YOU

      (M) (2:36) Rhino 70652 Billboard's Top R&B Hits Of 1966.
      (M) (2:36) Rhino 72006 Billboard's Top R&B Hits 1965-1969 Box Set.
      (M) (2:35) Atlantic 82305 Atlantic Rhythm And Blues 1947-1974 Box Set.
      (M) (2:36) Rhino 70191 Best Of.
      (M) (2:35) Curb 77520 Greatest Hits.

1967 #29 PAPA WAS TOO

      (S) (2:56) Rhino 70191 Best Of.
      (S) (2:54) Curb 77520 Greatest Hits.

1968 #9 SKINNY LEGS AND ALL

      (M) (3:09) Atlantic 81298 Atlantic Rhythm & Blues Volume 6.
      (S) (3:05) Rhino 70653 Billboard's Top R&B Hits Of 1967.
      (S) (3:05) Rhino 72006 Billboard's Top R&B Hits 1965-1969 Box Set.
      (S) (3:09) Atlantic 82305 Atlantic Rhythm And Blues 1947-1974 Box Set.
      (S) (3:04) Rhino 70191 Best Of.
      (S) (3:04) Curb 77520 Greatest Hits.

JOE TEX (Continued)
1968 #26 MEN ARE GETTIN' SCARCE
1969 #39 BUYING A BOOK
    (S) (3:25) Rhino 70191 Best Of.

1972 #3 I GOTCHA
    (S) (2:27) Rhino 70788 Soul Hits Of The 70's Volume 8.
    (S) (2:26) Rhino 70660 Billboard's Top R&B Hits Of 1972.
    (S) (2:27) Rhino 70191 Best Of.
    (S) (2:26) Curb 77520 Greatest Hits.

THEE PROPHETS
1969 #39 PLAYGIRL
    (S) (2:06) Ripete 392183 Ocean Drive.

THEM
1965 #18 HERE COMES THE NIGHT
    (S) (2:46) Rhino 70324 History Of British Rock Volume 6.
    (S) (2:46) Rhino 70319 History Of British Rock Box Set.
    (S) (2:45) Mercury 841970 Best Of Van Morrison.
    (S) (2:46) London 810165 Them Featuring Van Morrison.

1965 #29 MYSTIC EYES
    (S) (2:41) Rhino 70324 History Of British Rock Volume 6.
    (S) (2:41) Rhino 70319 History Of British Rock Box Set.
    (S) (2:41) London 810165 Them Featuring Van Morrison.
    (S) (2:40) London 820563 Them.

THINK
1972 #29 ONCE YOU UNDERSTAND

B.J. THOMAS
1966 #9 I'M SO LONESOME I COULD CRY
    (M) (3:08) Rhino 70752 Greatest Hits.
    (M) (3:06) Deluxe 1014 16 Greatest Hits.
    (M) (3:08) Collectables 5099 His Golden Classics.
    (M) (3:07) Curb 77452 Greatest Hits.
    (M) (3:07) Capricorn 42003 The Scepter Records Story.

1966 #15 MAMA
    (the actual LP time is (2:56) not (2:47) as the record label states)
    (S) (2:55) Rhino 70752 Greatest Hits. *(LP length)*
    (S) (2:53) Deluxe 1014 16 Greatest Hits. *(LP length)*
    (S) (2:55) Collectables 5099 His Golden Classics. *(LP length)*
    (S) (2:45) Capricorn 42003 The Scepter Records Story. *(45 length)*

1966 #33 BILLY AND SUE
    (S) (3:11) Rhino 70752 Greatest Hits.
    (S) (3:11) Curb 77452 Greatest Hits.

1968 #31 THE EYES OF A NEW YORK WOMAN
    (S) (3:00) Rhino 70752 Greatest Hits.
    (S) (3:00) Deluxe 1014 16 Greatest Hits.
    (S) (3:00) Collectables 5099 His Golden Classics.
    (S) (3:01) Curb 77452 Greatest Hits.
    (S) (2:59) Capricorn 42003 The Scepter Records Story.

1969 #5 HOOKED ON A FEELING
    (S) (2:44) Rhino 70752 Greatest Hits. *(LP version)*
    (S) (2:44) Deluxe 1014 16 Greatest Hits. *(LP version)*
    (S) (2:44) Collectables 5099 His Golden Classics. *(LP version)*
    (S) (2:44) Curb 77452 Greatest Hits. *(LP version)*
    (S) (2:45) Capricorn 42003 The Scepter Records Story. *(LP version)*

B.J. THOMAS (Continued)

1969 #28 *IT'S ONLY LOVE*
    (S) (2:53) Collectables 5099 His Golden Classics.

1970 #1 *RAINDROPS KEEP FALLIN' ON MY HEAD*
    (S) (2:57) Priority 8669 #1 Hits/70's Greatest Rock Hits Volume 9.
    (S) (2:59) Rhino 70752 Greatest Hits.
    (S) (3:01) Deluxe 1014 16 Greatest Hits.
    (S) (2:59) Collectables 5099 His Golden Classics.
    (S) (3:00) Curb 77452 Greatest Hits.
    (S) (3:00) Capricorn 42003 The Scepter Records Story.
    (S) (2:57) A&M 3159 O.S.T. Butch Cassidy & The Sundance Kid.

1970 #21 *EVERYBODY'S OUT OF TOWN*
    (S) (2:40) Rhino 70752 Greatest Hits.
    (S) (2:40) Collectables 5099 His Golden Classics.
    (S) (2:42) Capricorn 42003 The Scepter Records Story.

1970 #11 *I JUST CAN'T HELP BELIEVING*
    (S) (2:54) Rhino 70752 Greatest Hits.
    (S) (2:56) Deluxe 1014 16 Greatest Hits.
    (S) (2:54) Collectables 5099 His Golden Classics.
    (S) (2:56) Curb 77452 Greatest Hits.
    (S) (2:55) Capricorn 42003 The Scepter Records Story.

1971 #30 *MOST OF ALL*
    (S) (2:51) Rhino 70752 Greatest Hits.
    (S) (2:52) Deluxe 1014 16 Greatest Hits.
    (S) (2:52) Collectables 5099 His Golden Classics.

1971 #14 *NO LOVE AT ALL*
    (S) (2:51) Rhino 70752 Greatest Hits.
    (S) (2:52) Deluxe 1014 16 Greatest Hits.
    (S) (2:51) Collectables 5099 His Golden Classics.
    (S) (2:52) Capricorn 42003 The Scepter Records Story. *(truncated fade)*

1971 #39 *MIGHTY CLOUDS OF JOY*
    (S) (3:13) Rhino 70752 Greatest Hits.
    (S) (3:14) Deluxe 1014 16 Greatest Hits.
    (S) (3:13) Collectables 5099 His Golden Classics.

1972 #12 *ROCK AND ROLL LULLABY*
    (S) (4:11) Rhino 70752 Greatest Hits.
    (S) (4:08) Deluxe 1014 16 Greatest Hits.
    (S) (4:11) Collectables 5099 His Golden Classics.
    (S) (4:08) Curb 77452 Greatest Hits.
    (S) (4:10) Capricorn 42003 The Scepter Records Story.

CARLA THOMAS

1961 #9 *GEE WHIZ*
    (M) (2:18) Atlantic Group 88218 Complete Stax/Volt Singles.
    (M) (2:17) Atlantic 81296 Atlantic Rhythm & Blues Volume 4. *(some vocal distortion)*
    (M) (2:18) Atlantic 82305 Atlantic Rhythm And Blues 1947-1974 Box Set.

1966 #16 *B-A-B-Y*
    (M) (2:53) Atlantic Group 88218 Complete Stax/Volt Singles.
    (E) (2:46) Stax 88005 Top Of The Stax.
    (E) (2:47) Warner Special Products 27609 Memphis Soul Classics.
    (E) (2:46) JCI 3105 Soul Sixties.
    (M) (2:52) Atlantic 82340 Carla.

CARLA THOMAS & OTIS REDDING
released as by OTIS & CARLA:
1967 #19 TRAMP
    (M) (2:59) Atlantic Group 88218 Complete Stax/Volt Singles.
    (S) (2:59) Atlantic 82256 King & Queen.
    (S) (2:59) Atlantic 81762 Otis Redding Story.
    (S) (2:59) Atco 80254 The Dock Of The Bay.
    (S) (2:57) Warner Special Products 27608 Ultimate Otis Redding.
    (S) (2:59) Atlantic 82305 Atlantic Rhythm And Blues 1947-1974 Box Set.

IAN THOMAS
1973 #27 PAINTED LADIES

IRMA THOMAS
1964 #17 WISH SOMEONE WOULD CARE
    (M) (2:19) Rhino 75765 Best Of New Orleans Rhythm & Blues Volume 1.
    (S) (2:18) Stax 8551 Superblues Volume 1.
    (S) (2:27) EMI 97988 Time Is On My Side - The Best Of.

JON THOMAS
1960 #27 HEARTBREAK (IT'S HURTIN' ME)

RUFUS THOMAS
1963 #10 WALKING THE DOG
    (M) (2:33) Atlantic Group 88218 Complete Stax/Volt Singles.
    (M) (2:29) Warner Special Products 27602 20 Party Classics.
    (M) (2:28) Warner Special Products 27609 Memphis Soul Classics.
    (M) (2:28) Atlantic 81297 Atlantic Rhythm & Blues Volume 5.
    (M) (2:33) Atlantic 82305 Atlantic Rhythm And Blues 1947-1974 Box Set.
    (M) (2:31) Atlantic 82254 Walking The Dog.
    (M) (2:24) Stax 8569 Can't Get Away From The Dog. *(alternate take)*
1964 #37 CAN YOUR MONKEY DO THE DOG
    (M) (1:53) Atlantic 82254 Walking The Dog. *(LP version)*
    (M) (2:25) Atlantic Group 88218 Complete Stax/Volt Singles. *(45 version)*
    (M) (2:02) Stax 8569 Can't Get Away From The Dog. *(alternate take)*
1971 #20 (DO THE) PUSH AND PULL (PART 1)
    (S) (3:17) Stax 88005 Top Of The Stax.
    (S) (2:17) Stax 4124 Rufus & Carla Thomas Chronicle. *(edit)*
1971 #31 THE BREAKDOWN (PART 1)
    (S) (3:17) Stax 88008 Top Of The Stax Volume 2.
    (S) (3:17) Stax 4124 Rufus & Carla Thomas Chronicle.

TIMMY THOMAS
1973 #2 WHY CAN'T WE LIVE TOGETHER
    (M) (3:53) Rhino 70661 Billboard's Top R&B Hits Of 1973. *(LP version)*
    (M) (3:53) Rhino 71003 Best Of TK Records. *(LP version)*
    (M) (3:53) Rhino 70790 Soul Hits Of The 70's Volume 10. *(LP version)*

SUE THOMPSON
1961 #5 SAD MOVIES (MAKE ME CRY)
    (S) (3:15) Curb 77462 Greatest Hits.
1962 #4 NORMAN
    (S) (2:17) Curb 77462 Greatest Hits.
1962 #37 TWO OF A KIND
    (S) (2:47) Curb 77462 Greatest Hits.
1962 #31 HAVE A GOOD TIME
    (S) (3:12) Curb 77462 Greatest Hits.

SUE THOMPSON (Continued)
1962 #22 JAMES (HOLD THE LADDER STEADY)
    (S) (2:12) Curb 77462 Greatest Hits.
1965 #18 PAPER TIGER
    (S) (2:25) Curb 77462 Greatest Hits.

THREE DEGREES
1970 #24 MAYBE
    (S) (3:37) Rhino 70782 Soul Hits Of The 70's Volume 2.

THREE DOG NIGHT
1969 #22 TRY A LITTLE TENDERNESS
    (S) (4:09) MCA 6018 Best Of.
    (S) (4:05) MCA 31045 Three Dog Night.

1969 #2 ONE
    (S) (3:00) MCA 31206 Vintage Music Volume 9.
    (S) (3:00) MCA 5806 Vintage Music Volumes 9 & 10.
    (S) (3:03) MCA 6018 Best Of.
    (S) (3:02) MCA 1466 Joy To The World: Their Greatest Hits.
    (S) (3:04) MCA 31045 Three Dog Night.

1969 #3 EASY TO BE HARD
    (S) (3:11) MCA 5936 Vintage Music Volumes 11 & 12.
    (S) (3:11) MCA 31209 Vintage Music Volume 12.
    (S) (3:10) MCA 6018 Best Of.
    (S) (3:11) MCA 31046 Suitable For Framing.

1969 #8 ELI'S COMING
    (S) (2:40) MCA 31207 Vintage Music Volume 10.
    (S) (2:40) MCA 5806 Vintage Music Volumes 9 & 10.
    (S) (2:40) MCA 6018 Best Of.
    (S) (2:40) MCA 31046 Suitable For Framing.

1970 #12 CELEBRATE
    (S) (3:13) MCA 6018 Best Of.
    (S) (3:13) MCA 31046 Suitable For Framing.

1970 #1 MAMA TOLD ME (NOT TO COME)
    (S) (3:17) Rhino 70631 Billboard's Top Rock & Roll Hits Of 1970.
    (S) (3:17) Rhino 72005 Billboard's Top Rock & Roll Hits 1968-1972 Box Set.
    (S) (3:17) Motown 6161 The Good-Feeling Music Of The Big Chill Generation Volume 3.
    (S) (3:17) Dunhill Compact Classics 043 Toga Rock II.
    (S) (3:17) MCA 31274 Classic Rock Volume 2.
    (S) (3:17) MCA 5940 Vintage Music Volumes 19 & 20.
    (S) (3:17) MCA 31216 Vintage Music Volume 19.
    (S) (3:16) MCA 6018 Best Of.
    (S) (3:17) MCA 31047 It Ain't Easy.
    (S) (3:16) Priority 7066 #1 Groups/70's Greatest Rock Hits Volume 12.

1970 #9 OUT IN THE COUNTRY
    (S) (3:07) MCA 6018 Best Of.
    (S) (3:07) MCA 31047 It Ain't Easy.

1970 #13 ONE MAN BAND
    (S) (2:49) MCA 6018 Best Of.
    (S) (2:50) MCA 1466 Joy To The World: Their Greatest Hits.
    (S) (2:51) MCA 31355 Naturally.

THREE DOG NIGHT *(Continued)*
1971 #1 *JOY TO THE WORLD*
- (M) (3:16) Rhino 70632 Billboard's Top Rock & Roll Hits Of 1971. *(45 version)*
- (M) (3:16) Rhino 72005 Billboard's Top Rock & Roll Hits 1968-1972 Box Set. *(45 version)*
- (S) (3:36) Motown 6160 The Good-Feeling Music Of The Big Chill Generation Volume 2. *(LP version)*
- (S) (3:34) Motown 6120 O.S.T. The Big Chill. *(LP version)*
- (S) (3:33) MCA 6018 Best Of. *(LP version)*
- (S) (3:36) MCA 1466 Joy To The World: Their Greatest Hits. *(LP version)*
- (S) (3:39) MCA 31355 Naturally. *(LP version)*

1971 #8 *LIAR*
- (S) (3:02) MCA 6018 Best Of. *(45 version)*
- (S) (3:02) MCA 1466 Joy To The World: Their Greatest Hits. *(45 version)*
- (S) (3:52) MCA 31355 Naturally. *(LP version)*

1971 #4 *AN OLD FASHIONED LOVE SONG*
(the actual 45 time is (3:42) not (3:21) as stated on the record label)
- (S) (3:23) MCA 6018 Best Of. *(LP version)*
- (S) (3:22) MCA 1466 Joy To The World: Their Greatest Hits. *(LP version)*
- (S) (3:23) MCA 31329 Harmony. *(LP version)*

1972 #5 *NEVER BEEN TO SPAIN*
- (S) (3:42) MCA 6018 Best Of.
- (S) (3:43) MCA 1466 Joy To The World: Their Greatest Hits.
- (S) (3:44) MCA 31329 Harmony.

1972 #10 *THE FAMILY OF MAN*
- (S) (3:08) MCA 6018 Best Of.
- (S) (3:09) MCA 1466 Joy To The World: Their Greatest Hits.
- (S) (3:33) MCA 31329 Harmony. *(LP length)*

1972 #1 *BLACK & WHITE*
- (S) (3:47) Rhino 70633 Billboard's Top Rock & Roll Hits Of 1972. *(LP version)*
- (S) (3:47) Rhino 72005 Billboard's Top Rock & Roll Hits 1968-1972 Box Set. *(LP version)*
- (S) (3:44) MCA 6018 Best Of. *(LP version)*
- (S) (3:47) MCA 1466 Joy To The World: Their Greatest Hits. *(LP version)*
- (S) (3:47) MCA 31399 Seven Separate Fools. *(LP version)*

1973 #18 *PIECES OF APRIL*
- (S) (4:10) MCA 6018 Best Of.
- (S) (4:10) MCA 31399 Seven Separate Fools.

1973 #1 *SHAMBALA*
- (E) (3:22) MCA 6018 Best Of.
- (E) (3:23) MCA 1466 Joy To The World: Their Greatest Hits.
- (E) (3:23) MCA 31366 Cyan.

1973 #12 *LET ME SERENADE YOU*
- (S) (3:02) MCA 6018 Best Of.
- (S) (3:03) MCA 1466 Joy To The World: Their Greatest Hits.
- (S) (3:15) MCA 31366 Cyan. *(LP length)*

JOHNNY THUNDER
1963 #9 *LOOP DE LOOP*

JOHNNY TILLOTSON
1960 #31 *WHY DO I LOVE YOU SO*
1960 #2 *POETRY IN MOTION*
- (S) (2:30) Rhino 75893 Jukebox Classics Volume 1.

JOHNNY TILLOTSON (Continued)

1961 #12 *WITHOUT YOU*

1962 #5 *IT KEEPS RIGHT ON A HURTIN'*
      (S) (2:51) Rhino 75894 Jukebox Classics Volume 2.

1962 #14 *SEND ME THE PILLOW YOU DREAM ON*

1962 #29 *I CAN'T HELP IT (IF I'M STILL IN LOVE WITH YOU)*

1963 #23 *OUT OF MY MIND*

1963 #18 *YOU CAN NEVER STOP ME LOVING YOU*

1964 #7 *TALK BACK TREMBLING LIPS*

1964 #38 *WORRIED GUY*

1964 #29 *SHE UNDERSTANDS ME*

1965 #32 *HEARTACHES BY THE NUMBER*

TIN TIN

1971 #16 *TOAST AND MARMALADE FOR TEA*

TINY TIM

1968 #19 *TIP-TOE THRU' THE TULIPS WITH ME*

ART & DOTTY TODD

1958 #7 *CHANSON D'AMOUR (SONG OF LOVE)*

NICK TODD

1958 #28 *PLAYTHING*

TOKENS

1961 #15 *TONIGHT I FELL IN LOVE*

1961 #1 *THE LION SLEEPS TONIGHT*
      (S) (2:39) Rhino 70622 Billboard's Top Rock & Roll Hits Of 1961.
      (S) (2:39) Rhino 72004 Billboard's Top Rock & Roll Hits 1957-1961 Box Set.
      (S) (2:39) RCA 8474 Nipper's Greatest Hits Of The 60's Volume 1.
      (S) (2:39) RCA 9902 Nipper's #1 Hits 1956-1986.

1966 #40 *I HEAR TRUMPETS BLOW*

1967 #25 *PORTRAIT OF MY LOVE*

OSCAR TONEY JR.

1967 #28 *FOR YOUR PRECIOUS LOVE*

TORNADOES

1962 #1 *TELSTAR*
      (M) (3:17) Rhino 70323 History Of British Rock Volume 5.
      (M) (3:17) Rhino 70319 History Of British Rock Box Set.

MITCHELL TOROK

1957 #14 *PLEDGE OF LOVE*

1959 #30 *CARIBBEAN*

TOWER OF POWER

1972 #22 *YOU'RE STILL A YOUNG MAN*
      (S) (3:36) Original Sound 1960 Memories Of El Monte.

1973 #19 *SO VERY HARD TO GO*
      (S) (3:38) Warner Brothers 2681 Tower Of Power.

ED TOWNSEND

1958 #14 *FOR YOUR LOVE*
      (M) (2:48) Capitol 98138 Spring Break Volume 1.

TOYS
1965 #1 *A LOVER'S CONCERTO*
(M) (2:34) JCI 3102 Love Sixties.
(M) (2:39) Rhino 70989 Best Of The Girl Groups Volume 2.
1966 #22 *ATTACK*

TRADEWINDS
1965 #38 *NEW YORK'S A LONELY TOWN*
(M) (2:16) Rhino 70089 Surfin' Hits.
(M) (2:13) Dunhill Compact Classics 030 Beach Classics.

TRASHMEN
1964 #4 *SURFIN' BIRD*
(M) (2:21) Rhino 70089 Surfin' Hits.
(M) (2:20) Dunhill Compact Classics 030 Beach Classics.
(M) (2:21) Rhino 70732 Grandson Of Frat Rock.
(M) (2:21) Rhino 70743 Dr. Demento 20th Anniversary Collection.
(E) (2:14) Warner Brothers 25613 O.S.T. Full Metal Jacket.
(M) (2:19) Rhino 70794 KFOG Presents M. Dung's Idiot Show.
(M) (2:20) Curb 77356 70's Hits Volume 2.
(M) (2:20) Capitol 96861 Monster Summer Hits - Wild Surf.
(M) (2:20) Sundazed 11011 Tube City! The Best Of.
1964 #31 *BIRD DANCE BEAT*
(M) (2:07) Sundazed 11011 Tube City! The Best Of.

TRAVIS & BOB
1959 #11 *TELL HIM NO*

TREMELOES
1967 #11 *HERE COMES MY BABY*
(M) (2:45) Rhino 70324 History Of British Rock Volume 6.
(M) (2:45) Rhino 70319 History Of British Rock Box Set.
(M) (2:45) Rhino 70528 Best Of.
1967 #9 *SILENCE IS GOLDEN*
(M) (3:07) Columbia/Legacy 46984 Rock Artifacts Volume 4.
(M) (3:06) Rhino 70325 History Of British Rock Volume 7.
(M) (3:06) Rhino 70319 History Of British Rock Box Set.
(M) (3:07) Rhino 70528 Best Of.
1968 #40 *SUDDENLY YOU LOVE ME*
(M) (2:44) Rhino 70528 Best Of.

T. REX
1972 #12 *BANG A GONG (GET IT ON)*
(S) (4:23) Reprise 6466 Electric Warrior.

TROGGS
1966 #1 *WILD THING*
(M) (2:34) Warner Special Projects 27610 More Party Classics.
(M) (2:34) Rhino 70321 History Of British Rock Volume 3.
(M) (2:34) Rhino 70319 History Of British Rock Box Set.
(M) (2:34) Rhino 72008 History Of British Rock Volumes 1-4 Box Set.
(M) (2:34) Rhino 75892 Nuggets.
(M) (2:33) Rhino 75778 Frat Rock.
(M) (2:34) Rhino 70627 Billboard's Top Rock & Roll Hits Of 1966.
(M) (2:34) Rhino 72007 Billboard's Top Rock & Roll Hits 1962-1966 Box Set.
(M) (2:34) Rhino 70243 Greatest Movie Rock Hits.
(M) (2:33) Mercury 816555 45's On CD Volume 2.
(M) (2:33) Rhino 70794 KFOG Presents M. Dung's Idiot Show.

TROGGS (Continued)
1966 #38 *I CAN'T CONTROL MYSELF*
1968 #12 *LOVE IS ALL AROUND*
    (M) (2:54) Mercury 834216 45's On CD Volume 3.
    (M) (2:59) Rhino 70326 History Of British Rock Volume 8.
    (M) (2:59) Rhino 70319 History Of British Rock Box Set.

DORIS TROY
1963 #9 *JUST ONE LOOK*
    (E) (2:22) Warner Special Prouducts 27601 Atlantic Soul Classics.
    (E) (2:27) JCI 3105 Soul Sixties.
    (M) (2:28) Atlantic 81297 Atlantic Rhythm & Blues Volume 5.
    (M) (2:26) Geffen 24310 O.S.T. Mermaids.
    (M) (2:28) Atlantic 82305 Atlantic Rhythm And Blues 1947-1974 Box Set.

TOMMY TUCKER
1964 #10 *HI-HEEL SNEAKERS*
    (M) (2:49) Rhino 75758 Soul Shots Volume 4.
    (M) (2:48) MCA 31204 Vintage Music Volume 7.
    (M) (2:48) MCA 5805 Vintage Music Volumes 7 & 8.
    (M) (2:48) Garland 011 Footstompin' Oldies.
    (M) (2:48) Chess 31320 Best Of Chess Rock 'n' Roll Volume 2.

TUNE ROCKERS
1958 #40 *THE GREEN MOSQUITO*
    (M) (2:18) Curb 77402 All Time Greatest Instrumental Hits Volume 2.

TUNE WEAVERS
1957 #7 *HAPPY, HAPPY BIRTHDAY BABY*
    (M) (2:17) MCA 31200 Vintage Music Volume 3.
    (M) (2:17) MCA 5778 Vintage Music Volumes 3 & 4.
    (M) (2:16) Garland 012 Remember When.
    (M) (2:16) Chess 31320 Best Of Chess Rock 'n' Roll Volume 2.

IKE & TINA TURNER
1960 #19 *A FOOL IN LOVE*
    (M) (2:50) EMI 95846 Proud Mary/Best Of.
    (M) (2:49) Curb 77332 Greatest Hits.
    (M) (2:49) EMI 46599 Best Of.
1961 #21 *IT'S GONNA WORK OUT FINE*
    (M) (3:02) Garland 011 Footstompin' Oldies.
    (M) (3:00) EMI 95846 Proud Mary/Best Of.
    (M) (3:01) Curb 77323 All Time Greatest Hits Of Rock 'N' Roll.
    (M) (3:02) Stax 8551 Superblues Volume 1.
    (M) (3:02) Curb 77332 Greatest Hits.
    (M) (3:02) EMI 46599 Best Of.
    (M) (3:03) Special Music 4826 So Fine!
    (M) (3:03) Pair 1292 Workin' It Out.
    (S) (2:26) Saja 91228 Greatest Hits Volume 3. *(rerecording)*
1962 #23 *POOR FOOL*
    (M) (2:31) EMI 95846 Proud Mary/Best Of.
    (E) (2:32) Curb 77332 Greatest Hits.
    (M) (2:32) Special Music 4826 So Fine!
    (M) (2:32) Pair 1292 Workin' It Out.
1971 #5 *PROUD MARY*
    (S) (3:27) Rhino 70784 Soul Hits Of The 70's Volume 4. *(:12 longer than 45 version)*
    (S) (4:55) EMI 95846 Proud Mary/Best Of. *(LP version)*

IKE & TINA TURNER (Continued)
    (S) (4:54) EMI 96268 24 Greatest Hits Of All Time. *(LP version)*
    (S) (3:15) JCI 3100 Dance Sixties. *(45 version)*
    (S) (4:55) Curb 77356 70's Hits Volume 2. *(LP version)*
    (S) (4:55) Curb 77332 Greatest Hits. *(LP version)*
    (S) (4:55) EMI 46599 Best Of. *(LP version)*
    (S) (2:38) Saja 91223 Greatest Hits Volume 1. *(rerecording)*

1971 #37 OOH POO PAH DOO
    (S) (3:34) EMI 95846 Proud Mary/Best Of. *(LP version)*

1973 #26 NUTBUSH CITY LIMITS
    (S) (2:56) EMI 95846 Proud Mary/Best Of.
    (S) (2:55) Curb 77332 Greatest Hits.
    (S) (2:56) EMI 46599 Best Of.

JESSE LEE TURNER
1959 #18 THE LITTLE SPACE GIRL

SAMMY TURNER
1959 #4 LAVENDER-BLUE
1959 #17 ALWAYS
1960 #34 PARADISE

SPYDER TURNER
1967 #11 STAND BY ME

TURTLES
1965 #8 IT AIN'T ME BABE
    (S) (2:06) Rhino 5160 20 Greatest Hits.

1965 #26 LET ME BE
    (M) (2:21) Rhino 70734 Songs Of Protest.
    (S) (2:22) Rhino 5160 20 Greatest Hits.

1966 #17 YOU BABY
    (S) (2:15) K-Tel 839 Battle Of The Bands Volume 2.
    (S) (2:16) Rhino 5160 20 Greatest Hits.

1967 #1 HAPPY TOGETHER
    (S) (2:53) Rhino 70628 Billboard's Top Rock & Roll Hits Of 1967.
    (S) (2:53) Rhino 5160 20 Greatest Hits.

1967 #2 SHE'D RATHER BE WITH ME
    (S) (2:14) JCI 3104 Mellow Sixties.
    (S) (2:19) K-Tel 205 Battle Of The Bands Volume 3.
    (S) (2:18) Rhino 5160 20 Greatest Hits.

1967 #12 YOU KNOW WHAT I MEAN
    (S) (1:59) Rhino 5160 20 Greatest Hits.

1967 #15 SHE'S MY GIRL
    (E) (2:31) Rhino 5160 20 Greatest Hits.

1968 #32 SOUND ASLEEP
    (M) (2:25) Rhino 5160 20 Greatest Hits. *(truncated fade)*

1968 #40 THE STORY OF ROCK AND ROLL
    (S) (2:36) Rhino 5160 20 Greatest Hits.

1968 #5 ELENORE
    (S) (2:29) Rhino 5160 20 Greatest Hits.
    (S) (2:29) Essex 7052 All Time Rock Classics.

1969 #4 YOU SHOWED ME
    (S) (3:13) Rhino 5160 20 Greatest Hits.

CONWAY TWITTY

1958 #1 *IT'S ONLY MAKE BELIEVE*

    (S) (2:11) Rhino 70619 Billboard's Top Rock & Roll Hits Of 1958.

    (S) (2:11) Rhino 72004 Billboard's Top Rock & Roll Hits 1957-1961 Box Set.

    (S) (2:11) JCI 3203 Lovin' Fifties.

    (S) (2:11) Mercury 849574 Best Of Volume 1: Rockin' Years.

    (S) (2:19) Curb 77365 Greatest Hits. *(rerecording)*

    (S) (2:11) Special Music 837668 It's Only Make Believe.

    (S) (2:19) MCA 31240 Greatest Hits Volume 2. *(rerecording)*

1959 #30 *THE STORY OF MY LOVE*

    (S) (2:15) Special Music 837668 It's Only Make Believe.

1959 #30 *MONA LISA*

    (S) (2:24) Mercury 849574 Best Of Volume 1: Rockin' Years.

1959 #7 *DANNY BOY*

    (M) (2:44) Rhino 70742 Rock This Town: Rockabilly Hits Volume 2.

    (S) (2:44) Mercury 849574 Best Of Volume 1: Rockin' Years.

    (S) (2:43) Special Music 837668 It's Only Make Believe.

1960 #8 *LONELY BLUE BOY*

    (S) (2:13) Mercury 832041 45's On CD Volume 1.

    (S) (2:12) Mercury 849574 Best Of Volume 1: Rockin' Years.

    (S) (2:12) Curb 77365 Greatest Hits.

    (S) (2:12) Special Music 837668 It's Only Make Believe.

1960 #19 *WHAT AM I LIVING FOR*

    (S) (2:35) Mercury 849574 Best Of Volume 1: Rockin' Years.

    (S) (2:33) Curb 77365 Greatest Hits.

1960 #33 *IS A BLUE BIRD BLUE*

    (S) (2:34) Mercury 849574 Best Of Volume 1: Rockin' Years.

1961 #31 *C'EST SI BON (IT'S SO GOOD)*

    (S) (2:15) Mercury 849574 Best Of Volume 1: Rockin' Years.

1973 #18 *YOU'VE NEVER BEEN THIS FAR BEFORE*

    (S) (2:59) Curb 77365 Greatest Hits.

    (S) (2:58) MCA 31240 Greatest Hits Volume 2.

    (S) (2:58) MCA 5976 20 Greatest Hits.

TYMES

1963 #2 *SO MUCH IN LOVE*

1963 #10 *WONDERFUL! WONDERFUL!*

1964 #14 *SOMEWHERE*

U

UNDERGROUND SUNSHINE
1969 #19 *BIRTHDAY*

UNDISPUTED TRUTH
1971 #1 *SMILING FACES SOMETIMES*
    (S) (3:14) Motown 6184   Hard To Find Motown Classics Volume 2.
    (S) (3:14) Rhino 70785   Soul Hits Of The 70's Volume 5.
    (M) (3:17) Motown 5489   Best Of.

UNIFICS
1968 #20 *COURT OF LOVE*

UNION GAP (see GARY PUCKETT & THE UNION GAP)

UNIT FOUR PLUS TWO
1965 #12 *CONCRETE AND CLAY*
    (M) (2:16) Rhino 70324   History Of British Rock Volume 6.
    (M) (2:16) Rhino 70319   History Of British Rock Box Set.

PHIL UPCHURCH COMBO
1961 #19 *YOU CAN'T SIT DOWN (PART 2)*

URIAH HEEP
1972 #32 *EASY LIVIN'*
    (S) (2:35) Rhino 70986   Heavy Metal Memories
    (S) (2:35) JCI 3302   Electric Seventies.
    (S) (2:35) Mercury 822476   Best Of.
    (S) (2:35) Mercury 812297   Demons And Wizards.

V

JERRY VALE
1956 #13 YOU DON'T KNOW ME
      (M) (2:31) Columbia 40216 17 Most Requested Songs.
1957 #29 PRETEND YOU DON'T SEE HER
      (E) (2:41) Columbia 40216 17 Most Requested Songs.
1965 #29 HAVE YOU LOOKED INTO YOUR HEART
      (S) (2:21) Columbia 40216 17 Most Requested Songs.
1965 #35 FOR MAMA

RITCHIE VALENS
1959 #2 DONNA
      (M) (2:23) Dunhill Compact Classics 031 Back Seat Jams.
      (M) (2:20) Rhino 70178 Best Of.
1959 #49 LA BAMBA
      (even though this song only reached #49 on the Cash Box charts, it is included in this book because of the song's lasting historical value)
      (M) (2:02) Rhino 70243 Greatest Movie Rock Hits.
      (M) (2:02) Rhino 75772 Son Of Frat Rock.
      (M) (2:04) Rhino 70617 Best Of La Bamba.
      (M) (2:02) Capitol 48993 Spuds Mackenzie's Party Faves.
      (M) (2:01) Rhino 70178 Best Of.
      (M) (2:01) Essex 7052 All Time Rock Classics.

CATERINA VALENTE
1955 #8 THE BREEZE AND I

MARK VALENTINO
1962 #30 THE PUSH AND KICK

JOE VALINO
1956 #15 GARDEN OF EDEN

VALJEAN
1962 #32 THEME FROM BEN CASEY

FRANKIE VALLI
1966 #40 (YOU'RE GONNA) HURT YOURSELF
      (S) (2:30) Rhino 72998 Four Seasons 25th Anniversary Collection.
1967 #1 CAN'T TAKE MY EYES OFF YOU
      (S) (3:20) Rhino 72998 Four Seasons 25th Anniversary Collection.
      (S) (3:20) Rhino 71490 Four Seasons Anthology.
      (S) (3:20) Rhino 70595 Four Seasons Greatest Hits Volume 2.
1967 #21 I MAKE A FOOL OF MYSELF
      (M) (3:38) Rhino 72998 Four Seasons 25th Anniversary Collection.
1968 #17 TO GIVE (THE REASON I LIVE)
      (S) (3:21) Rhino 72998 Four Seasons 25th Anniversary Collection.
1969 #28 THE GIRL I'LL NEVER KNOW (ANGELS NEVER FLY THIS LOW)
      (S) (3:39) Rhino 72998 Four Seasons 25th Anniversary Collection.

JUNE VALLI
1959 #19 *THE WEDDING*
1960 #24 *APPLE GREEN*
LEROY VAN DYKE
1956 #22 *THE AUCTIONEER*
1961 #3 *WALK ON BY*
    (S) (2:19) Rhino 70682 Billboard's Top Country Hits Of 1961.
1962 #33 *IF A WOMAN ANSWERS (HANG UP THE PHONE)*
VANILLA FUDGE
1968 #7 *YOU KEEP ME HANGIN' ON*
    (the true LP version of this song is a medley of "ILLUSIONS OF MY CHILDHOOD PART 1", "YOU KEEP ME HANGIN' ON" and "ILLUSIONS OF MY CHILDHOOD PART 2")
    (M) (2:57) Warner Special Products 27607 Highs Of The 60's. *(45 version)*
    (M) (7:24) JCI 3103 Electric Sixties (LP version).
    (M) (7:25) Atlantic 81908 Classic Rock 1966-1988. *(LP version)*
    (M) (7:25) Atlantic 82306 Atlantic Rock & Roll Box Set. *(LP version)*
    (M) (7:25) Atco 33224 Vanilla Fudge. *(LP version)*
    (M) (7:23) Atco 90006 Best Of. *(this cd breaks down the medley into three distinct tracks which are still segued together just like the vinyl LP)*

VANITY FARE
1970 #10 *EARLY IN THE MORNING*
    (the LP length is (2:42) and the 45 length is (2:48))
    (S) (2:42) Rhino 70921 Super Hits Of The 70's Volume 1. *(LP mix)*
    (S) (2:42) Rhino 72009 Super Hits Of The 70's Volumes 1-4 Box Set. *(LP mix)*
1970 #4 *HITCHIN' A RIDE*
    (M) (3:04) Rhino 70922 Super Hits Of The 70's Volume 2. *(LP length)*
    (M) (3:04) Rhino 72009 Super Hits Of The 70's Volumes 1-4 Box Set. *(LP length)*

MARIANNE VASEL & ERICH STORZ
1958 #40 *THE LITTLE TRAIN (DIE KLEINE BIMMELBAHN)*
SARAH VAUGHAN
1955 #7 *MAKE YOURSELF COMFORTABLE*
    (M) (2:38) Mercury 824891 Golden Hits.
    (M) (2:38) Mercury 826320 Complete On Mercury Volume 1.
1955 #5 *HOW IMPORTANT CAN IT BE?*
    (M) (2:26) Mercury 824891 Golden Hits.
    (M) (2:27) Mercury 826320 Complete On Mercury Volume 1.
1955 #5 *WHATEVER LOLA WANTS*
    (M) (2:35) Mercury 824891 Golden Hits.
    (M) (2:35) Mercury 826320 Complete On Mercury Volume 1.
1956 #15 *THE BANANA BOAT SONG*
    (M) (2:20) Mercury 824891 Golden Hits.
    (M) (2:20) Mercury 826327 Complete On Mercury Volume 2.
1957 #36 *PASSING STRANGERS*
    (S) (2:37) Mercury 824891 Golden Hits.
    (S) (2:37) Mercury 826327 Complete On Mercury Volume 2.
1959 #6 *BROKEN-HEARTED MELODY*
    (S) (2:22) Mercury 824891 Golden Hits.
    (S) (2:23) Mercury 826333 Complete On Mercury Volume 3.
    (S) (2:21) Essex 7053 A Hot Summer Night In '59.
1959 #32 *SMOOTH OPERATOR*
    (S) (2:18) Rhino 75757 Soul Shots Volume 3.

SARAH VAUGHAN (Continued)
        (S) (2:19) Mercury 824891 Golden Hits. *(truncated fade)*
        (S) (2:19) Mercury 826333 Complete On Mercury Volume 3.

BILLY VAUGHN
1955 #1 *MELODY OF LOVE*
        (E) (2:59) Curb 77345 Greatest Hits.

1955 #5 *THE SHIFTING WHISPERING SANDS (PARTS 1 & 2)*
        (S) (2:57) Curb 77345 Greatest Hits. *(Part 1; extra instrumentation and*
                             background vocals added to the original mono recording to get stereo)
        (S) (2:52) Curb 77345 Greatest Hits. *(Part 2; extra instrumentation and*
                             background vocals added to the original mono recording to get stereo)

1956 #16 *WHEN THE LILACS BLOOM AGAIN*
        (M) (2:06) Curb 77345 Greatest Hits.

1957 #25 *RAUNCHY*
        (M) (2:12) Curb 77345 Greatest Hits. *(truncated fade)*

1958 #4 *SAIL ALONG SILVERY MOON*
        (E) (2:07) Curb 77345 Greatest Hits.
        (S) (1:59) Ranwood 7025 22 Of His Greatest Hits. *(rerecording)*

1958 #30 *TUMBLING TUMBLEWEEDS*
        (M) (1:59) Curb 77345 Greatest Hits.

1958 #27 *LA PALOMA*
1958 #36 *CIMARRON (ROLL ON)*
1959 #33 *BLUE HAWAII*
        (S) (2:01) Curb 77345 Greatest Hits.
        (S) (1:51) Ranwood 7025 22 Of His Greatest Hits. *(rerecording)*

1960 #13 *LOOK FOR A STAR*
1960 #38 *THE SUNDOWNERS*
1962 #11 *A SWINGIN' SAFARI*
        (M) (2:14) MCA 5937 Vintage Music Volumes 13 & 14.
        (M) (2:14) MCA 31211 Vintage Music Volume 14.
        (S) (2:12) Curb 77345 Greatest Hits.

BOBBY VEE
released as by BOBBY VEE:
1960 #4 *DEVIL OR ANGEL*
        (S) (2:17) EMI 48412 Best Of.
        (S) (2:18) EMI 92774 Legendary Masters Series.

1961 #6 *RUBBER BALL*
        (S) (2:17) EMI 48412 Best Of.
        (S) (2:30) EMI 92774 Legendary Masters Series. *(:13 longer than either the*
                             45 or LP)

1961 #32 *STAYIN' IN*
        (S) (2:02) EMI 92774 Legendary Masters Series.

1961 #1 *TAKE GOOD CARE OF MY BABY*
        (S) (2:27) EMI 96268 24 Greatest Hits Of All Time.
        (S) (2:36) Rhino 70622 Billboard's Top Rock & Roll Hits Of 1961. *(:10*
                             longer than the 45 length)
        (S) (2:36) Rhino 72004 Billboard's Top Rock & Roll Hits 1957 - 1961 Box
                             Set. *(:10 longer than the 45 length)*
        (S) (2:27) EMI 48412 Best Of.
        (S) (2:38) EMI 92774 Legendary Masters Series. *(:12 longer than the 45*
                             length)

1961 #4 *RUN TO HIM*
        (S) (2:13) EMI 92774 Legendary Masters Series. *(includes :04 countoff)*

BOBBY VEE (Continued)
1962 #18 PLEASE DON'T ASK ABOUT BARBARA
- (S) (2:01) EMI 48412 Best Of.
- (S) (2:03) EMI 92774 Legendary Masters Series.

1962 #20 SHARING YOU
- (S) (2:01) EMI 92774 Legendary Masters Series.

1962 #32 PUNISH HER
- (S) (1:52) EMI 48412 Best Of.
- (S) (1:59) EMI 92774 Legendary Masters Series.

1963 #4 THE NIGHT HAS A THOUSAND EYES
- (S) (2:33) Curb 77355 60's Hits Volume 1.
- (S) (2:34) EMI 48412 Best Of.
- (S) (2:40) EMI 92774 Legendary Masters Series. *(includes :06 countoff)*

1963 #15 CHARMS
- (S) (2:21) EMI 92774 Legendary Masters Series.

1963 #36 BE TRUE TO YOURSELF
- (S) (2:03) EMI 92774 Legendary Masters Series. *(truncated fade)*

released as by BOBBY VEE & THE STRANGERS:
1967 #3 COME BACK WHEN YOU GROW UP
- (S) (2:14) EMI 48412 Best Of.
- (S) (2:52) EMI 92774 Legendary Masters Series. *(includes :04 countoff; previously unreleased :07 introduction; :24 longer ending than either the 45 or LP)*

1967 #27 BEAUTIFUL PEOPLE
- (S) (2:16) EMI 48412 Best Of.
- (S) (2:18) EMI 92774 Legendary Masters Series.

1968 #38 MAYBE JUST TODAY
- (S) (2:07) EMI 92774 Legendary Masters Series.

released as by BOBBY VEE:
1968 #17 MY GIRL/HEY GIRL (MEDLEY)
- (S) (2:32) EMI 92774 Legendary Masters Series. *(truncated fade)*

VELVETS
1961 #18 TONIGHT (COULD BE THE NIGHT)

VENTURES
1960 #3 WALK — DON'T RUN
- (S) (2:03) Rhino 70621 Billboard's Top Rock & Roll Hits Of 1960.
- (S) (2:03) Rhino 72004 Billboard's Top Rock & Roll Hits 1957-1961 Box Set.
- (M) (2:04) Curb 77402 All-Time Great Instrumental Hits Volume 2.
- (S) (2:02) EMI 96268 24 Greatest Hits Of All Time.
- (E) (2:04) EMI 90614 Non Stop Party Rock.
- (S) (2:02) EMI 93451 Walk Don't Run - The Best Of.
- (E) (2:03) Curb 77376 Greatest Hits.
- (E) (2:03) EMI 46600 Best Of.

1960 #18 PERFIDIA
- (S) (2:03) EMI 93451 Walk Don't Run - The Best Of.
- (S) (2:03) Curb 77376 Greatest Hits.
- (S) (2:03) EMI 46600 Best Of.

1964 #9 WALK — DON'T RUN '64
- (S) (2:28) EMI 93451 Walk Don't Run - The Best Of. *(includes :03 countoff; 3 extra drum beats at (2:21)- (2:22) not found on either the 45 or LP)*

VENTURES (Continued)
1969 #6 HAWAII FIVE-O
    (S) (1:50) Curb 77402 All-Time Great Instrumental Hits Volume 2.
    (S) (1:51) EMI 90604 Beach Party Blasts.
    (S) (1:51) Capitol 96861 Monster Summer Hits - Wild Surf.
    (S) (1:51) EMI 93451 Walk Don't Run - The Best Of.
    (S) (1:50) Curb 77376 Greatest Hits.
    (S) (1:50) EMI 46600 Best Of.

VIK VENUS
1969 #23 MOONLIGHT

BILLY VERA
1968 #25 WITH PEN IN HAND

LARRY VERNE
1960 #3 MR. CUSTER

VIBRATIONS
1961 #29 THE WATUSI
    (M) (2:34) MCA 5939 Vintage Music Volumes 17 & 18.
    (M) (2:34) MCA 31215 Vintage Music Volume 18.
    (M) (2:37) Chess 31317 Best Of Chess Rhythm & Blues Volume 1.
1964 #29 MY GIRL SLOOPY

VILLAGE STOMPERS
1963 #2 WASHINGTON SQUARE

GENE VINCENT & HIS BLUE CAPS
1956 #5 BE-BOP-A-LULA
    (M) (2:34) Rhino 70599 Billboard's Top Rock & Roll Hits Of 1956.
    (M) (2:33) Rhino 70906 American Bandstand Greatest Hits Collection.
    (M) (2:34) JCI 3202 Rockin' Fifties.
    (E) (2:34) EMI 90614 Non Stop Party Rock.
    (M) (2:33) Curb 77323 All Time Greatest Hits Of Rock 'N' Roll.
    (M) (2:34) Capitol 98138 Spring Break Volume 1.
    (M) (2:33) Capitol 94074 Capitol Collector's Series.
    (M) (2:34) Capitol 91151 Greatest.
1957 #12 LOTTA LOVIN'
    (M) (2:09) Rhino 70741 Rock This Town: Rockabilly Hits Volume 1.
    (M) (2:09) Capitol 98139 Spring Break Volume 2.
    (M) (2:09) Capitol 94074 Capitol Collector's Series.
    (M) (2:09) Capitol 91151 Greatest.
1957 #36 DANCE TO THE BOP
    (M) (2:13) Capitol 94074 Capitol Collector's Series.

BOBBY VINTON
1962 #1 ROSES ARE RED (MY LOVE)
    (S) (2:36) Epic 26098 Greatest Hits.
    (S) (2:35) Curb 77253 Greatest Hits.
    (S) (2:37) Epic/Legacy 47855 16 Most Requested Songs.
    (S) (3:45) Curb 77412 His Greatest Songs Today. *(rerecorded)*
1962 #18 RAIN RAIN GO AWAY
    (S) (2:54) Epic 26098 Greatest Hits.
1962 #39 I LOVE YOU THE WAY YOU ARE
    (S) (2:53) Epic 26098 Greatest Hits.
1963 #37 TROUBLE IS MY MIDDLE NAME
    (S) (2:25) Epic 26098 Greatest Hits.

BOBBY VINTON (Continued)

1963 #33 *LET'S KISS AND MAKE UP*
  (S) (2:26) Epic 26098 Greatest Hits.

1963 #20 *OVER THE MOUNTAIN (ACROSS THE SEA)*
  (S) (2:25) Epic 26098 Greatest Hits.
  (S) (2:24) Epic/Legacy 47855 16 Most Requested Songs.

1963 #3 *BLUE ON BLUE*
  (S) (2:21) Epic 26098 Greatest Hits.
  (S) (3:09) Curb 77253 Greatest Hits. *(rerecorded)*
  (S) (2:29) Epic/Legacy 47855 16 Most Requested Songs.
  (S) (3:09) Curb 77412 His Greatest Songs Today. *(rerecorded)*

1963 #1 *BLUE VELVET*
  (S) (2:45) Curb 77532 Your Favorite Songs.
  (S) (2:47) Epic 26098 Greatest Hits.
  (S) (2:46) Curb 77253 Greatest Hits.
  (S) (2:47) Epic/Legacy 47855 16 Most Requested Songs.
  (S) (4:25) Curb 77412 His Greatest Songs Today. *(rerecorded)*

1964 #1 *THERE I'VE SAID IT AGAIN*
  (S) (2:19) Epic 26098 Greatest Hits.
  (S) (2:20) Epic/Legacy 47855 16 Most Requested Songs.

1964 #8 *MY HEART BELONGS TO ONLY YOU*
  (S) (2:40) Epic 26098 Greatest Hits.
  (S) (2:41) Epic/Legacy 47855 16 Most Requested Songs.

1964 #11 *TELL ME WHY*
  (S) (2:36) Epic 26098 Greatest Hits.
  (S) (2:35) Epic/Legacy 47855 16 Most Requested Songs.

1964 #14 *CLINGING VINE*
  (S) (2:27) Epic 26187 More Of Bobby's Greatest Hits.

1964 #2 *MR. LONELY*
  (S) (2:39) Epic 26098 Greatest Hits.
  (S) (2:38) Curb 77253 Greatest Hits.
  (S) (2:39) Epic/Legacy 47855 16 Most Requested Songs.
  (S) (2:41) Curb 77412 His Greatest Songs Today. *(rerecorded)*

1965 #14 *LONG LONELY NIGHTS*
  (S) (2:26) Epic 26187 More Of Bobby's Greatest Hits.

1965 #20 *L-O-N-E-L-Y*
  (S) (2:23) Epic 26187 More Of Bobby's Greatest Hits.
  (S) (2:23) Epic/Legacy 47855 16 Most Requested Songs.

1965 #34 *WHAT COLOR (IS A MAN)*
  (S) (1:55) Epic 26187 More Of Bobby's Greatest Hits.

1966 #21 *SATIN PILLOWS*
  (S) (2:25) Epic 26187 More Of Bobby's Greatest Hits.

1966 #32 *DUM-DE-DA*
  (S) (2:05) Epic 26187 More Of Bobby's Greatest Hits.

1967 #8 *COMING HOME SOLDIER*
  (S) (2:28) Epic/Legacy 47855 16 Most Requested Songs.

1967 #5 *PLEASE LOVE ME FOREVER*
  (S) (2:34) Epic/Legacy 47855 16 Most Requested Songs.

1968 #14 *JUST AS MUCH AS EVER*
  (S) (2:20) Epic/Legacy 47855 16 Most Requested Songs.

1968 #26 *TAKE GOOD CARE OF MY BABY*
  (S) (2:45) Epic/Legacy 47855 16 Most Requested Songs.

BOBBY VINTON (Continued)

1968 #17 HALFWAY TO PARADISE
      (S) (2:39) Epic/Legacy 47855 16 Most Requested Songs.

1969 #4 I LOVE HOW YOU LOVE ME
      (S) (2:29) Epic/Legacy 47855 16 Most Requested Songs.

1969 #22 TO KNOW YOU IS TO LOVE YOU
      (S) (2:20) Epic/Legacy 47855 16 Most Requested Songs.

1969 #24 THE DAYS OF SAND AND SHOVELS

1970 #34 MY ELUSIVE DREAMS

1972 #18 EVERY DAY OF MY LIFE

1972 #14 SEALED WITH A KISS
      (S) (2:42) Curb 77253 Greatest Hits. *(rerecording)*

VIRTUES

1959 #5 GUITAR BOOGIE SHUFFLE
      (E) (2:32) Rhino 70719 Legends Of Guitar - Rock; The 50's.
      (E) (2:31) Virtue 1991 Frank Virtue & The Virtues.

VISCOUNTS

1960 #28 HARLEM NOCTURNE

VOGUES

1965 #7 YOU'RE THE ONE
      (E) (2:21) Rhino 70245 Greatest Hits.

1966 #3 FIVE O'CLOCK WORLD
      (S) (2:18) Warner Special Projects 27610 More Party Classics.
      (instrumentation added to obtain stereo)
      (S) (2:18) A&M 3913 O.S.T. Good Morning Vietnam. *(instrumentation added to obtain stereo)*
      (E) (2:06) Rhino 70243 Greatest Movie Rock Hits.
      (E) (2:06) Rhino 70245 Greatest Hits.

1966 #20 MAGIC TOWN
      (E) (3:10) Rhino 70245 Greatest Hits.

1966 #36 THE LAND OF MILK AND HONEY
      (E) (2:43) Rhino 70245 Greatest Hits.

1968 #4 TURN AROUND, LOOK AT ME
      (S) (2:44) Rhino 70245 Greatest Hits.

1968 #6 MY SPECIAL ANGEL
      (S) (2:57) Rhino 70245 Greatest Hits.

1968 #16 TILL
      (S) (2:19) Rhino 70245 Greatest Hits.

1969 #33 WIMAN HELPING MAN
      (S) (3:10) Rhino 70245 Greatest Hits.

1969 #30 EARTH ANGEL
      (S) (2:33) Rhino 70245 Greatest Hits.

VOLUMES

1962 #20 I LOVE YOU
      (M) (2:35) Rhino 75764 Best Of Doo Wop Uptempo.
      (M) (2:34) Collectables 5032 I Love You/Golden Classics. *(truncated fade)*

VOXPOPPERS

1958 #17 WISHING FOR YOUR LOVE

ADAM WADE
1961 #10 *TAKE GOOD CARE OF HER*
1961 #10 *THE WRITING ON THE WALL*
1961 #19 *AS IF I DIDN'T KNOW*

WADSWORTH MANSION
1971 #5 *SWEET MARY*
　　　　(M) (2:39) Rhino 70924 Super Hits Of The 70's Volume 4. *(45 version)*
　　　　(M) (2:39) Rhino 72009 Super Hits Of The 70's Volumes 1-4 Box Set. *(45 version)*

WAIKIKIS
1965 #34 *HAWAII TATTOO*

LOUDON WAINWRIGHT III
1973 #12 *DEAD SKUNK*
　　　　(S) (3:05) Rhino 70930 Super Hits Of The 70's Volume 10.
　　　　(S) (3:03) Priority 8670 Hitchin' A Ride/70's Greatest Rock Hits Volume 10.
　　　　(S) (3:06) Columbia 31462 Album III.

JR. WALKER & THE ALL STARS
1965 #4 *SHOTGUN*
　　　　(S) (3:01) Motown 6160 The Good-Feeling Music Of The Big Chill Generation Volume 2.
　　　　(S) (3:00) Motown 5452 A Collection Of 16 Big Hits Volume 5.
　　　　(S) (3:01) Rhino 70651 Billboard's Top R&B Hits Of 1965.
　　　　(S) (3:01) Rhino 72006 Billboard's Top R&B Hits 1965-1969 Box Set.
　　　　(S) (3:01) Motown 9017 and 5248 16 #1 Hits From The Early 60's.
　　　　(S) (3:00) Motown 9012 and 5208 Greatest Hits.
　　　　(S) (3:00) Motown 6203 Compact Command Performances.
　　　　(S) (3:00) Motown 5297 All The Great Hits.
　　　　(S) (3:00) Motown 5141 Shotgun.
　　　　(S) (3:00) Motown 8023 and 8123 Shotgun/Road Runner.
　　　　(S) (2:59) Motown 9071 Motown Dance Party Volume 1. *(all selections on this cd are segued together)*
1965 #35 *DO THE BOOMERANG*
　　　　(S) (2:20) Motown 6203 Compact Command Performances.
　　　　(S) (2:20) Motown 5141 Shotgun.
　　　　(S) (2:20) Motown 8023 and 8123 Shotgun/Road Runner.
1965 #33 *SHAKE AND FINGERPOP*
　　　　(S) (2:41) Motown 5453 A Collection Of 16 Big Hits Volume 6.
　　　　(S) (2:40) Motown 9012 and 5208 Greatest Hits.
　　　　(S) (2:40) Motown 6203 Compact Command Performances.
　　　　(S) (2:40) Motown 5297 All The Great Hits.
　　　　(S) (2:42) Motown 5141 Shotgun.
　　　　(S) (2:42) Motown 8023 and 8123 Shotgun/Road Runner.
1965 #37 *CLEO'S BACK*
　　　　(S) (2:30) Motown 5141 Shotgun.
　　　　(S) (2:30) Motown 8023 and 8123 Shotgun/Road Runner.

JR. WALKER & THE ALL STARS (Continued)

1966 #21 (I'M A) ROADRUNNER
    (S) (2:40) Motown 5455 A Collection Of 16 Big Hits Volume 8. (S)
        (2:39) Motown 9072 Motown Dance Party Volume 2. (all selections on this cd are segued together)
    (S) (2:47) Motown 5427 Road Runner. (both the 45 and LP time is (2:47))
    (S) (2:41) Motown 9012 and 5208 Greatest Hits.
    (S) (2:41) Motown 6203 Compact Command Performances.
    (S) (2:46) Motown 8023 and 8123 Shotgun/Road Runner.

1966 #21 HOW SWEET IT IS (TO BE LOVED BY YOU)
    (S) (2:57) Motown 5454 A Collection Of 16 Big Hits Volume 7.
    (S) (2:57) Motown 9098 Radio's #1 Hits.
    (S) (2:58) Motown 5460 Gotta Hold On To This Feeling.
    (S) (3:01) Motown 5427 Road Runner.
    (S) (2:57) Motown 9012 and 5208 Greatest Hits.
    (S) (2:58) Motown 6203 Compact Command Performances.
    (S) (2:57) Motown 5297 All The Great Hits.
    (S) (3:01) Motown 8023 and 8123 Shotgun/Road Runner.
    (S) (2:58) Ripete 392183 Ocean Drive.

1966 #32 MONEY (THAT'S WHAT I WANT) (PART 1)
    (S) (4:31) Motown 5427 Road Runner. (Parts 1 & 2)
    (S) (2:06) Motown 9012 and 5208 Greatest Hits.
    (S) (2:05) Motown 6203 Compact Command Performances.
    (S) (4:31) Motown 8023 and 8123 Shotgun/Road Runner. (Parts 1 & 2)

1967 #35 PUCKER UP BUTTERCUP
    (S) (3:13) Motown 5454 A Collection Of 16 Big Hits Volume 7.
    (S) (3:13) Motown 5427 Road Runner.
    (S) (3:17) Motown 9012 and 5208 Greatest Hits.
    (S) (3:17) Motown 6203 Compact Command Performances.
    (S) (3:13) Motown 8023 and 8123 Shotgun/Road Runner.

1968 #27 COME SEE ABOUT ME
    (S) (2:59) Motown 5456 A Collection Of 16 Big Hits Volume 9.
    (S) (2:58) Motown 9012 and 5208 Greatest Hits.
    (S) (2:58) Motown 6203 Compact Command Performances.

1968 #28 HIP CITY (PART 2)
    (S) (2:55) Motown 9012 and 5208 Greatest Hits.
    (S) (2:55) Motown 6203 Compact Command Performances.
    (S) (2:48) Motown 5297 All The Great Hits.

1969 #5 WHAT DOES IT TAKE (TO WIN YOUR LOVE)
    (S) (2:23) Motown 9104 Motown Memories Volume 1.
    (S) (2:26) Motown 6160 The Good-Feeling Music Of The Big Chill Generation Volume 2.
    (S) (2:26) Motown 6110 Motown Grammy R&B Performances Of The 60's & 70's.
    (S) (2:26) Rhino 70655 Billboard's Top R&B Hits Of 1969.
    (S) (2:26) Rhino 72006 Billboard's Top R&B Hits 1965-1969 Box Set.
    (S) (2:26) Motown 5460 Gotta Hold On To This Feeling.
    (S) (2:23) Motown 9012 and 5208 Greatest Hits.
    (S) (2:23) Motown 6203 Compact Command Performances.
    (S) (2:23) Motown 5297 All The Great Hits.
    (S) (2:25) Ripete 392183 Ocean Drive.

1969 #27 THESE EYES
    (S) (3:33) Motown 9105 Motown Memories Volume 2.
    (S) (3:34) Motown 5460 Gotta Hold On To This Feeling.
    (S) (3:33) Motown 6203 Compact Command Performances.
    (S) (3:33) Motown 5297 All The Great Hits.

JR. WALKER & THE ALL STARS (Continued)
1970 #14 GOTTA HOLD ON TO THIS FEELING
    (S) (3:35) Rhino 70658 Billboard's Top R&B Hits Of 1970.
    (S) (3:32) Motown 5460 Gotta Hold On To This Feeling.
    (S) (3:31) Motown 6203 Compact Command Performances.
    (S) (3:30) Motown 5297 All The Great Hits.
1970 #25 DO YOU SEE MY LOVE (FOR YOU GROWING)
    (S) (3:25) Motown 6203 Compact Command Performances.
    (S) (3:25) Motown 5297 All The Great Hits.

WALKER BROTHERS
1965 #23 MAKE IT EASY ON YOURSELF
    (S) (3:11) Rhino 70324 History Of British Rock Volume 6.
    (S) (3:11) Rhino 70319 History Of British Rock Box Set.
1966 #14 THE SUN AIN'T GONNA SHINE ANYMORE
    (S) (3:00) Mercury 816555 45's On CD Volume 2.
    (M) (3:04) JCI 3102 Love Sixties.
    (S) (3:00) Rhino 70325 History Of British Rock Volume 7.
    (S) (3:00) Rhino 70319 History Of British Rock Box Set.

JERRY WALLACE
1958 #19 HOW THE TIME FLIES
    (M) (2:25) Curb 77262 Greatest Hits.
1959 #5 PRIMROSE LANE
    (E) (2:16) Curb 77262 Greatest Hits. *(much faster than the original recording speed)*
1961 #20 THERE SHE GOES
    (S) (2:29) Curb 77262 Greatest Hits. *(rerecording)*
1963 #20 SHUTTERS AND BOARDS
    (S) (2:43) Curb 77262 Greatest Hits. *(much faster than the original recording speed)*
1964 #19 IN THE MISTY MOONLIGHT
    (S) (2:48) Curb 77262 Greatest Hits. *(much faster than the original recording speed)*
1972 #39 IF YOU LEAVE ME TONIGHT I'LL CRY
    (S) (2:33) Curb 77262 Greatest Hits. *(much faster than the original recording speed)*

JOE WALSH
1973 #13 ROCKY MOUNTAIN WAY
    (S) (3:48) Rhino 70986 Heavy Metal Memories. *(neither the 45 or LP version)*
    (S) (5:15) MCA 31273 Classic Rock Volume 1. *(LP version)*
    (S) (3:39) Warner Special Products 27616 Classic Rock. *(45 version)*
    (S) (5:12) Priority 8662 Hard 'N Heavy/70's Greatest Rock Hits Volume 1. *(LP version)*
    (S) (5:13) Sandstone 33002 Reelin' In The Years Volume 3. *(LP version)*
    (S) (5:14) MCA 1601 Best Of. *(LP version)*
    (S) (5:14) MCA 31121 The Smoker You Drink, The Player You Get. *(LP version)*

WALTER WANDERLY
1966 #30 SUMMER SAMBA (SO NICE)
    (S) (3:03) Verve 833289 Best Of Bossa Nova.

WAR

1971 #28 ALL DAY MUSIC
(dj copies of this song ran (2:34) while commercial copies ran (3:59))
   (S) (2:34) Priority 9467 Best Of.
   (S) (2:34) Rhino 70072 Best Of.

1972 #12 SLIPPIN' INTO DARKNESS
(the actual time of the commercial 45 was (4:15) not (3:59) as stated on the record label; dj copies ran (3:45))
   (S) (3:45) Priority 9467 Best Of.
   (S) (3:45) Rhino 70072 Best Of.

1973 #9 THE WORLD IS A GHETTO
   (S) (4:05) Rhino 70790 Soul Hits Of The 70's Volume 10.

1973 #2 THE CISCO KID
(dj copies of this 45 ran (3:50); commercial copies ran (4:35))
   (S) (3:51) Priority 9467 Best Of.
   (S) (3:50) Rhino 70072 Best Of.

1973 #7 GYPSY MAN

BILLY WARD & HIS DOMINOES

1956 #24 ST. THERESE OF THE ROSES
1957 #13 STAR DUST
   (M) (3:10) Atlantic 82152 O.S.T. Goodfellas.

1957 #28 DEEP PURPLE

DALE WARD

1964 #29 A LETTER FROM SHERRY
   (M) (2:19) MCA 5940 Vintage Music Volumes 19 & 20.
   (M) (2:19) MCA 31216 Vintage Music Volume 19.

ROBIN WARD

1963 #15 WONDERFUL SUMMER
   (S) (2:25) MCA 5936 Vintage Music Volumes 11 & 12.
   (S) (2:25) MCA 31208 Vintage Music Volume 11.
   (S) (2:25) Rhino 70989 Best Of The Girl Groups Volume 2.

DIONNE WARWICK

1963 #17 DON'T MAKE ME OVER
   (S) (2:45) Rhino 75891 Wonder Women.
   (S) (2:45) Rhino 75898 Anthology 1962 - 1969.
   (S) (3:21) Rhino 71100 Collection - Her Greatest Hits. (*previously unreleased version*)
   (S) (2:44) Pair 1243 At Her Very Best.
   (S) (2:53) Capricorn 42003 The Scepter Records Story. (*includes :08 studio talk*)

1964 #8 ANYONE WHO HAD A HEART
   (S) (2:59) Rhino 75898 Anthology 1962 - 1969. (*mastered from vinyl*)
   (S) (3:07) Rhino 71100 Collection - Her Greatest Hits.
   (S) (2:58) Pair 1243 At Her Very Best.
   (S) (2:58) Capricorn 42003 The Scepter Records Story.

1964 #6 WALK ON BY
   (S) (2:51) JCI 3102 Love Sixties.
   (S) (2:51) Rhino 75898 Anthology 1962 - 1969.
   (S) (2:54) Rhino 71100 Collection - Her Greatest Hits.
   (S) (2:51) Pair 1243 At Her Very Best.
   (S) (3:00) Capricorn 42003 The Scepter Records Story. (*includes :05 countoff*)

DIONNE WARWICK (Continued)

1964 #28 YOU'LL NEVER GET TO HEAVEN (IF YOU BREAK MY HEART)
- (S) (3:06) Rhino 75898 Anthology 1962 - 1969.
- (S) (3:07) Rhino 71100 Collection - Her Greatest Hits.
- (S) (3:05) Pair 1243 At Her Very Best.

1964 #21 REACH OUT FOR ME
- (S) (2:47) Rhino 75898 Anthology 1962 - 1969.
- (S) (2:50) Rhino 71100 Collection - Her Greatest Hits.
- (S) (2:46) Pair 1243 At Her Very Best.

1966 #36 ARE YOU THERE (WITH ANOTHER GIRL)
- (S) (2:49) Rhino 75898 Anthology 1962 - 1969.
- (S) (2:48) Rhino 71100 Collection - Her Greatest Hits.
- (S) (2:49) Pair 1243 At Her Very Best.

1966 #9 MESSAGE TO MICHAEL
- (M) (3:04) Rhino 75898 Anthology 1962 - 1969.
- (S) (3:05) Rhino 71100 Collection - Her Greatest Hits.
- (M) (3:04) Pair 1243 At Her Very Best.

1966 #31 TRAINS AND BOATS AND PLANES
- (S) (2:46) Rhino 75898 Anthology 1962 - 1969. (*truncated fade*)
- (S) (2:46) Rhino 71100 Collection - Her Greatest Hits.
- (S) (2:43) Pair 1243 At Her Very Best.

1966 #24 I JUST DON'T KNOW WHAT TO DO WITH MYSELF
- (S) (2:44) Rhino 71100 Collection - Her Greatest Hits.
- (S) (2:43) Pair 1243 At Her Very Best.

1967 #15 ALFIE
- (S) (2:43) Rhino 75898 Anthology 1962 - 1969.
- (S) (2:43) Rhino 71100 Collection - Her Greatest Hits.
- (S) (2:43) Pair 1243 At Her Very Best.

1967 #40 THE WINDOWS OF THE WORLD
- (S) (3:16) Rhino 75898 Anthology 1962 - 1969.
- (S) (3:16) Rhino 71100 Collection - Her Greatest Hits.
- (S) (3:16) Pair 1243 At Her Very Best.

1967 #5 I SAY A LITTLE PRAYER
- (S) (3:06) Rhino 75898 Anthology 1962 - 1969.
- (S) (3:04) Rhino 71100 Collection - Her Greatest Hits.
- (S) (3:06) Pair 1243 At Her Very Best.
- (S) (3:17) Capricorn 42003 The Scepter Records Story. (*includes :15 of studio talk*)

1968 #3 (THEME FROM) VALLEY OF THE DOLLS
- (S) (3:36) Rhino 75898 Anthology 1962 - 1969.
- (S) (3:36) Rhino 71100 Collection - Her Greatest Hits.
- (S) (3:32) Capricorn 42003 The Scepter Records Story.

1968 #10 DO YOU KNOW THE WAY TO SAN JOSE
- (S) (2:56) Rhino 75898 Anthology 1962 - 1969.
- (S) (2:55) Rhino 71100 Collection - Her Greatest Hits.
- (S) (2:55) Pair 1243 At Her Very Best.

1968 #22 WHO IS GONNA LOVE ME?
- (S) (3:10) Rhino 70329 Hidden Gems.
- (M) (3:07) Pair 1243 At Her Very Best.

1968 #15 PROMISES, PROMISES
- (S) (2:58) Rhino 75898 Anthology 1962 - 1969.
- (S) (2:56) Rhino 71100 Collection - Her Greatest Hits.

1969 #9 THIS GIRL'S IN LOVE WITH YOU
- (S) (5:20) Rhino 70329 Hidden Gems. (*previously unreleased version*)
- (M) (4:12) Pair 1243 At Her Very Best.

383

DIONNE WARWICK (Continued)

1969 #37 *THE APRIL FOOLS*
    (S) (3:15) Rhino 71100 Collection - Her Greatest Hits.

1969 #14 *YOU'VE LOST THAT LOVIN' FEELING*
    (S) (4:14) Pair 1243 At Her Very Best.

1970 #6 *I'LL NEVER FALL IN LOVE AGAIN*
    (S) (2:52) Rhino 75898 Anthology 1962 - 1969.
    (S) (3:00) Rhino 71100 Collection - Her Greatest Hits.
    (S) (2:51) Pair 1243 At Her Very Best.
    (S) (2:52) Capricorn 42003 The Scepter Records Story.

1970 #26 *LET ME GO TO HIM*
    (S) (3:50) Rhino 70329 Hidden Gems.

1970 #31 *PAPER MACHE*

1970 #25 *MAKE IT EASY ON YOURSELF*
    (M) (2:40) Rhino 70329 Hidden Gems. *(studio recording; the hit version was live)*
    (S) (2:58) Pair 1243 At Her Very Best. *(studio recording; the hit version was live)*

DINAH WASHINGTON

1959 #4 *WHAT A DIFFERENCE A DAY MAKES*
    (S) (2:28) Mercury 818815 What A Difference A Day Makes.
    (S) (2:27) Mercury 838956 Complete Dinah Washington On Mercury Volume 6.
    (S) (2:28) Mercury 830700 Compact Jazz.

1959 #2 *UNFORGETTABLE*
    (S) (2:41) Mercury 838956 Complete Dinah Washington On Mercury Volume 6.
    (S) (2:41) Mercury 510602 Unforgettable.
    (S) (2:40) Mercury 830700 Compact Jazz.

1960 #23 *THIS BITTER EARTH*
    (S) (2:25) Mercury 838956 Complete Dinah Washington On Mercury Volume 6.
    (S) (2:26) Mercury 510602 Unforgettable.
    (S) (2:25) Mercury 830700 Compact Jazz.

1960 #18 *LOVE WALKED IN*
    (S) (2:08) Mercury 838956 Complete Dinah Washington On Mercury Volume 6.

1961 #19 *SEPTEMBER IN THE RAIN*
    (S) (2:06) Mercury 838956 Complete Dinah Washington On Mercury Volume 6.

1962 #38 *WHERE ARE YOU*

DINAH WASHINGTON & BROOK BENTON

1960 #2 *BABY (YOU GOT WHAT IT TAKES)*
    (S) (2:44) Mercury 816555 45's On CD Volume 2.
    (S) (2:44) Mercury 836755 Forty Greatest Hits.
    (S) (2:43) Rhino 70646 Billboard's Top R&B Hits Of 1960.
    (S) (2:44) Mercury 838956 Complete Dinah Washington On Mercury Volume 6.

1960 #5 *A ROCKIN' GOOD WAY (TO MESS AROUND AND FALL IN LOVE)*
    (S) (2:25) Rhino 70646 Billboard's Top R&B Hits Of 1960.
    (S) (2:25) Mercury 836755 Forty Greatest Hits.
    (S) (2:25) Curb 77445 Best Of Brook Benton.
    (S) (2:25) Mercury 838956 Complete Dinah Washington On Mercury Volume 6.

WATTS 103RD STREET RHYTHM BAND *(see CHARLES WRIGHT & THE WATTS 103RD STREET BAND)*

THOMAS WAYNE
1959 #7 *TRAGEDY*

WE FIVE
1965 #2 *YOU WERE ON MY MIND*
    (E) (2:34) Priority 9461   Mellow 60's.
    (M) (2:36) Rhino 70536   San Francisco Nights.
    (S) (2:32) Rhino 70995   One Hit Wonders Of The 60's Volume 1. *(missing some overdubs)*
1965 #31 *LET'S GET TOGETHER*

JOAN WEBER
1955 #1 *LET ME GO LOVER*
    (M) (2:22) Columbia 45110   16 Most Requested Songs Of The 50's Volume 1.
    (M) (2:22) Columbia 45017   Radio Classics Of The 50's.

ERIC WEISSBERG & STEVE MANDELL
1973 #1 *DUELING BANJOS*
    (S) (2:16) Rhino 70758   Super Hits Of The 70's Volume 11. *(neither the LP or 45 version; hiss on introduction)*
    (S) (3:14) Warner Brothers 2683   O.S.T. Deliverance. *(LP version)*

LENNY WELCH
1963 #4 *SINCE I FELL FOR YOU*
    (S) (2:53) Rhino 75893   Jukebox Classics Volume 1.
    (S) (2:51) Columbia 45019   Pop Classics Of The 60's.
1964 #27 *EBB TIDE*
1970 #32 *BREAKING UP IS HARD TO DO*

LAWRENCE WELK
1956 #18 *WHEN THE WHITE LILACS BLOOM AGAIN*
1957 #29 *CINCO ROBLES*
1961 #1 *CALCUTTA*
    (S) (2:13) Ranwood 8226   18 Greatest Hits.
    (S) (2:12) Ranwood 1004   A Musical Anthology.
1961 #28 *THEME FROM MY THREE SONS*

MARY WELLS
1962 #4 *THE ONE WHO REALLY LOVES YOU*
    (S) (2:26) Motown 9105   Motown Memories Volume 2.
    (S) (2:28) Motown 5448   A Package Of 16 Big Hits.
    (S) (2:26) Motown 9095 and 5325   Motown Girl Groups: Top 10 With A Bullet! (buzz noticeable on fadeout)
    (S) (2:27) Motown 6171   Compact Command Performances.
    (S) (2:27) Motown 9016 and 5233   Greatest Hits.
    (S) (2:26) Motown 5420   The One Who Really Loves You.
1962 #9 *YOU BEAT ME TO THE PUNCH*
    (S) (2:43) Motown 6160   The Good-Feeling Music Of The Big Chill Generation Volume 2.
    (S) (2:46) Motown 5448   A Package Of 16 Big Hits.
    (S) (2:44) Rhino 70648   Billboard's Top R&B Hits Of 1962.
    (S) (2:43) Motown 6171   Compact Command Performances.
    (S) (2:43) Motown 9016 and 5233   Greatest Hits.
    (S) (2:43) Motown 5420   The One Who Really Loves You.
    (S) (2:43) Pair 1270   Original Motown Classics.

MARY WELLS (Continued)
1963 #10 *TWO LOVERS*
      (S)   (2:45) Motown 6161 The Good-Feeling Music Of The Big Chill Generation Volume 3.

      (S)   (2:41) Motown 5451 A Collection Of 16 Big Hits Volume 4.

      (S)   (2:45) Rhino 70649 Billboard's Top R&B Hits Of 1963.

      (S)   (2:45) Motown 9095 and 5325 Motown Girl Groups: Top 10 With A Bullet!

      (S)   (2:45) Motown 6171 Compact Command Performances.

      (S)   (2:45) Motown 9016 and 5233 Greatest Hits.

      (S)   (2:46) Motown 5221 Two Lovers.

      (S)   (2:45) Motown 8024 and 8124 Two Lovers/My Guy.

1963 #27 *LAUGHING BOY*
      (S)   (2:48) Motown 6171 Compact Command Performances.

      (S)   (2:48) Motown 9016 and 5233 Greatest Hits.

      (S)   (2:49) Motown 5221 Two Lovers.

      (S)   (2:48) Motown 8024 and 8124 Two Lovers/My Guy.

      (S)   (2:49) Pair 1270 Original Motown Classics.

1963 #22 *YOU LOST THE SWEETEST BOY*
      (S)   (2:26) Motown 5449 A Collection Of 16 Big Hits Volume 2.

      (S)   (2:26) Motown 6171 Compact Command Performances.

      (S)   (2:26) Motown 9016 and 5233 Greatest Hits.

      (S)   (2:26) Pair 1270 Original Motown Classics.

1964 #1 *MY GUY*
(the 45 length is (2:45); the LP length is (2:52))

      (S)   (2:51) Motown 6159 The Good-Feeling Music Of The Big Chill Generation Volume 1.

      (S)   (2:49) Motown 5451 A Collection Of 16 Big Hits Volume 4.

      (S)   (2:51) Motown 6139 The Composer Series: Smokey Robinson.

      (S)   (2:43) Rhino 70650 Billboard's Top R&B Hits Of 1964.

      (S)   (2:48) Motown 9072 Motown Dance Party Volume 2. *(all selections on this cd are segued together)*

      (S)   (2:50) Motown 9017 and 5248 16 #1 Hits From The Early 60's.

      (S)   (2:50) Motown 9097 The Most Played Oldies On America's Jukeboxes.

      (S)   (2:50) Motown 5322 and 9087 Girl Groups: The Story Of A Sound.

      (S)   (2:51) Motown 6171 Compact Command Performances.

      (S)   (2:51) Motown 9016 and 5233 Greatest Hits.

      (S)   (2:51) Motown 8024 and 8124 Two Lovers/My Guy.

      (S)   (2:51) Motown 5167 My Guy.

      (S)   (2:51) Ripete 392183 Ocean Drive.

      (S)   (2:51) Pair 1270 Original Motown Classics.

MARY WELLS & MARVIN GAYE
1964 #27 *ONCE UPON A TIME*
      (S)   (2:29) Motown 0791 and 6199 Marvin Gaye Anthology.

      (S)   (2:29) Motown 6153 and 9053 Marvin Gaye & His Women.

      (M) (2:29) Motown 6311 The Marvin Gaye Collection.

      (S)   (2:27) Motown 5451 A Collection Of 16 Big Hits Volume 4.

      (S)   (2:30) Motown 5246 Marvin Gaye And His Girls.

      (S)   (2:28) Motown 5260 Marvin Gaye & Mary Wells Together.

1964 #25 *WHAT'S THE MATTER WITH YOU BABY*
      (S)   (2:21) Motown 5451 A Collection Of 16 Big Hits Volume 4.

      (S)   (2:25) Motown 0791 and 6199 Marvin Gaye Anthology.

      (S)   (2:26) Motown 6153 and 9053 Marvin Gaye & His Women.

      (M) (2:21) Motown 6311 The Marvin Gaye Collection.

      (S)   (2:24) Motown 5246 Marvin Gaye And His Girls.

      (S)   (2:21) Motown 5260 Marvin Gaye & Mary Wells Together.

FRED WESLEY & THE JB'S
1973 #21 *DOING IT TO DEATH*
        (M)   (5:07)   Rhino 70661   Billboard's Top R&B Hits 1973.
        (E)   (5:07)   Rhino 70551   Soul Hits Of The 70's Volume 11.
        (M)   (5:21)   Polydor 825714   CD Of JB. *(includes :24 introduction)*
        (M)   (5:14)   Polydor 849109   Star Time.

NANCY WHISKEY
1957 #18 *FREIGHT TRAIN*

IAN WHITCOMB
1965 #10 *YOU TURN ME ON (TURN ON SONG)*
        (M)   (2:42)   Rhino 70322   History Of British Rock Volume 4.
        (M)   (2:42)   Rhino 70319   History Of British Rock Box Set.
        (M)   (2:42)   Rhino 72008   History Of British Rock Volumes 1-4 Box Set.

BARRY WHITE
1973 #4 *I'M GONNA LOVE YOU JUST A LITTLE MORE BABY*
        (S)   (4:08)   Rhino 70551   Soul Hits Of The 70's Volume 11.
        (S)   (4:10)   Casablanca 822782   Greatest Hits.
1973 #38 *I'VE GOT SO MUCH TO GIVE*
        (S)   (3:06)   Casablanca 822782   Greatest Hits.

TONY JOE WHITE
1969 #9 *POLK SALAD ANNIE*
        (S)   (3:42)   JCI 3101   Rockin' Sixties.

WHITE PLAINS
1970 #10 *MY BABY LOVES LOVIN'*
(the actual 45 time is (2:49) not (2:28) as stated on the record label; the LP length is (3:04))
        (S)   (2:57)   Rhino 70922   Super Hits Of The 70's Volume 2.
        (S)   (2:57)   Rhino 72009   Super Hits Of The 70's Volumes 1-4 Box Set.

WHO
1967 #13 *HAPPY JACK*
        (E)   (2:11)   MCA 31331   A Quick One (Happy Jack).
        (M)   (2:12)   MCA 37001   Meaty Beaty Big And Bouncy.
        (M)   (2:08)   MCA 1496   Greatest Hits.
        (M)   (2:11)   MCA 8031   Who's Better, Who's Best.
        (S)   (2:11)   MCA 6899   The Kids Are Alright. *(live)*
1967 #8 *I CAN SEE FOR MILES*
        (M)   (4:01)   MCA 12001   Hooligans.
        (S)   (4:05)   MCA 31332   Sell Out. *(most selections on this cd are segued together)*
        (S)   (4:05)   MCA 37001   Meaty Beaty Big And Bouncy.
        (S)   (4:06)   MCA 8031   Who's Better, Who's Best.
        (S)   (4:16)   MCA 6899   The Kids Are Alright.
1968 #38 *CALL ME LIGHTNING*
        (E)   (2:23)   MCA 31333   Magic Bus.
1968 #10 *MAGIC BUS*
        (S)   (3:17)   MCA 31333   Magic Bus.
        (S)   (3:19)   MCA 37001   Meaty Beaty Big And Bouncy.
        (M)   (3:20)   MCA 1496   Greatest Hits.
        (S)   (3:17)   MCA 8031   Who's Better, Who's Best.
        (E)   (3:21)   MCA 6899   The Kids Are Alright.
1969 #15 *PINBALL WIZARD*
        (S)   (2:59)   MCA 12001   Hooligans.
        (S)   (2:58)   MCA 37001   Meaty Beaty Big And Bouncy.

     (M) (2:59) MCA 1496 Greatest Hits.
     (S) (3:00) MCA 2-10005 Tommy.
     (S) (2:59) MCA 8031 Who's Better, Who's Best.
     (S) (2:47) MCA 6899 The Kids Are Alright. *(live)*
     (S) (3:00) MFSL 533 Tommy.

1969 #30 *I'M FREE*

     (S) (2:38) MCA 2-10005 Tommy.
     (S) (2:38) MCA 8031 Who's Better, Who's Best.
     (S) (2:38) MFSL 533 Tommy.

1970 #30 *THE SEEKER*

     (S) (3:11) MCA 37001 Meaty Beaty Big And Bouncy.
     (S) (3:10) MCA 1496 Greatest Hits.

1970 #14 *SUMMERTIME BLUES*

     (S) (3:22) MCA 12001 Hooligans. *(45 version)*
     (S) (3:29) MCA 37000 Live At Leeds. *(LP version)*

1970 #8 *SEE ME, FEEL ME*

     (S) (3:30) MCA 8031 Who's Better, Who's Best. *(:10 longer than the 45 version)*
     (S) (7:00) MCA 2-10005 Tommy. *(this track is only part of the selection known as "WE'RE NOT GONNA TAKE IT"; starts at (3:28) and ends at (7:00), about :12 longer than the 45 version)*
     (S) (7:04) MFSL 533 Tommy. *(this track is only part of the selection known as "WE'RE NOT GONNA TAKE IT"; starts at (3:28) and ends at (7:04), about :16 longer than the 45 version)*
     (S) (5:25) MCA 6899 The Kids Are Alright. *(live)*

1971 #9 *WON'T GET FOOLED AGAIN*

     (S) (8:30) MCA 1496 Greatest Hits. *(LP version)*
     (S) (8:29) MCA 37217 Who's Next. *(LP version)*
     (S) (3:36) MCA 8031 Who's Better, Who's Best. *(45 version)*
     (S) (9:48) MCA 6899 The Kids Are Alright. *(live)*

1971 #24 *BEHIND BLUE EYES*

     (S) (3:38) MCA 12001 Hooligans.
     (S) (3:40) MCA 37217 Who's Next.

1972 #28 *JOIN TOGETHER*

     (S) (4:20) MCA 12001 Hooligans.
     (S) (4:18) MCA 8031 Who's Better, Who's Best.

1973 #33 *THE RELAY*

     (S) (3:27) MCA 12001 Hooligans. *(highly edited; :25 shorter than the 45)*
     (S) (3:44) MCA 1496 Greatest Hits. *(:08 shorter than the 45)*

HARLOW WILCOX & THE OAKIES

1969 #25 *GROOVY GRUBWORM*

ANDY WILLIAMS

1956 #2 *CANADIAN SUNSET*

     (M) (2:36) Columbia 40213 16 Most Requested Songs.
     (M) (2:35) Curb 77439 Best Of.

1956 #35 *BABY DOLL*

1957 #3 *BUTTERFLY*

     (M) (2:19) Curb 77439 Best Of.

1957 #10 *I LIKE YOUR KIND OF LOVE*

     (M) (2:27) Curb 77439 Best Of.

1957 #20 *LIPS OF WINE*

ANDY WILLIAMS (Continued)
1958 #7 *ARE YOU SINCERE*
    (S) (2:44) Curb 77439 Best Of.

1958 #33 *PROMISE ME, LOVE*

1959 #6 *THE HAWAIIAN WEDDING SONG*
    (E) (2:26) Curb 77532 Your Favorite Songs.
    (S) (2:24) Columbia 40213 16 Most Requested Songs.
    (S) (2:25) Columbia 9979 Greatest Hits.
    (M) (2:26) Curb 77439 Best Of.

1959 #7 *LONELY STREET*
    (S) (2:44) Columbia 32384 Greatest Hits Volume 2. *(LP version)*
    (E) (2:42) Curb 77439 Best Of. *(LP version)*

1960 #9 *THE VILLAGE OF ST. BERNADETTE*
    (S) (3:19) Columbia 32384 Greatest Hits Volume 2.
    (S) (3:19) Curb 77439 Best Of.

1961 #25 *THE BILBAO SONG*
    (M) (2:11) Curb 77439 Best Of.

1962 #10 *STRANGER ON THE SHORE*

1963 #1 *CAN'T GET USED TO LOSING YOU*
    (S) (2:20) Columbia 40213 16 Most Requested Songs.
    (S) (2:20) Columbia 9979 Greatest Hits.

1963 #29 *DAYS OF WINE AND ROSES*
    (S) (2:44) Columbia 40213 16 Most Requested Songs.
    (S) (2:44) Columbia 9979 Greatest Hits.

1963 #17 *HOPELESS*

1964 #13 *A FOOL NEVER LEARNS*

1964 #27 *WRONG FOR EACH OTHER*

1964 #40 *ON THE STREET WHERE YOU LIVE*

1965 #15 *DEAR HEART*
    (S) (2:53) Columbia 40213 16 Most Requested Songs.
    (S) (2:52) Columbia 9979 Greatest Hits.

1965 #34 *AND ROSES AND ROSES*

1965 #35 *AIN'T IT TRUE*

1969 #26 *HAPPY HEART*
    (S) (3:11) Columbia 9979 Greatest Hits.

1971 #10 *(WHERE DO I BEGIN) LOVE STORY*
    (S) (3:08) Columbia 30497 Love Story.
    (S) (3:11) Columbia 32384 Greatest Hits Volume 2.

1972 #24 *LOVE THEME FROM "THE GODFATHER" (SPEAK SOFTLY LOVE)*
    (S) (3:00) Columbia 32384 Greatest Hits Volume 2.

BILLY WILLIAMS
1957 #2 *I'M GONNA SIT RIGHT DOWN AND WRITE MYSELF A LETTER*
1959 #27 *NOLA*

DANNY WILLIAMS
1964 #10 *WHITE ON WHITE*

LARRY WILLIAMS
1957 #12 *SHORT FAT FANNIE*
    (M) (2:23) Specialty 2109 Here's Larry Williams.
    (M) (2:23) Specialty 7002 Bad Boy. *(echo added)*

LARRY WILLIAMS (Continued)
1957 #17 *BONY MORONIE*
    (M) (3:05) Rhino 75894 Jukebox Classics Volume 2.
    (M) (3:01) JCI 3202 Rockin' Fifties.
    (M) (3:04) Specialty 2109 Here's Larry Williams.
    (M) (3:06) Specialty 7002 Bad Boy.

MASON WILLIAMS
1968 #1 *CLASSICAL GAS*
    (S) (3:02) Warner Brothers 1729 Phonograph Record.
    (S) (2:36) Vanguard 137/38 Music 1968-1971. *(rerecording)*

MAURICE WILLIAMS & ZODIACS
1960 #4 *STAY*
    (M) (1:34) Warner Special Products 27602 20 Party Classics. Classics.
    (M) (1:38) Rhino 70621 Billboard's Top Rock & Roll Hits Of 1960.
    (M) (1:38) Rhino 72004 Billboard's Top Rock & Roll Hits 1957-1961 Box Set.
    (M) (1:34) RCA 6408 O.S.T. Dirty Dancing.
    (M) (1:33) Dunhill Compact Classics 033 Beachbeat Shaggin'.
    (M) (1:38) Arista 8605 16 Original Doo-Wop Classics.
    (M) (1:35) Relic 7004 Best Of.

OTIS WILLIAMS & HIS CHARMS
1956 #2 *IVORY TOWER*

ROGER WILLIAMS
1955 #1 *AUTUMN LEAVES*
    (S) (2:55) Curb 77403 All-Time Great Instrumental Hits Volume 1. *(rerecording)*
    (S) (2:55) Curb 77267 Greatest Hits. *(rerecording)*
    (E) (2:59) MCA 63 Greatest Hits.
    (S) (2:55) MFSL 868 Collection. *(rerecording)*
1956 #34 *TUMBLING TUMBLEWEEDS*
1957 #16 *ALMOST PARADISE*
    (S) (2:30) MCA 63 Greatest Hits. *(rerecording)*
1957 #24 *TILL*
1958 #32 *ARRIVEDERCI, ROMA*
1958 #31 *YOUNG AND WARM AND WONDERFUL*
1958 #12 *NEAR YOU*
    (S) (2:44) MCA 63 Greatest Hits.
1958 #25 *THE WORLD OUTSIDE*
1962 #40 *MARIA*
1966 #7 *BORN FREE*
    (S) (2:15) Curb 77403 All-Time Great Instrumental Hits Volume 1. *(rerecording)*
    (S) (2:15) Curb 77267 Greatest Hits. *(rerecording)*
    (S) (2:16) MFSL 868 Collection. *(rerecording)*

ROGER WILLIAMS & JANE MORGAN
1956 #22 *TWO DIFFERENT WORLDS*

CHUCK WILLIS
1957 #32 *C.C. RIDER*
    (M) (2:33) JCI 3202 Rockin' Fifties.
    (M) (2:32) Atlantic 81295 Atlantic Rhythm & Blues Volume 3.
    (M) (2:33) Atlantic 82305 Atlantic Rhythm And Blues 1947-1974 Box Set.

CHUCK WILLIS *(Continued)*
1958 #9 *WHAT AM I LIVING FOR*
(M) (2:25) Atlantic 81295 Atlantic Rhythm & Blues Volume 3.
(M) (2:25) Atlantic 82305 Atlantic Rhythm And Blues 1947-1974 Box Set.

AL WILSON
1968 #32 *THE SNAKE*

BRIAN WILSON
1966 #28 *CAROLINE NO*
(M) (2:16) Capitol 46324 Made In The U.S.A. *(45 version)*
(M) (2:49) Capitol 48421 Pet Sounds. *(LP version)*
(M) (2:15) Capitol 96796 Absolute Best Volume 2. *(45 version)*

JACKIE WILSON
1957 #35 *REET PETITE (THE FINEST GIRL YOU EVER WANT TO MEET)*
(E) (2:42) Columbia 40866 Reet Petite.
(E) (2:42) Epic 38623 Jackie Wilson Story.
(M) (2:40) Rhino 70775 Mr. Excitement!

1958 #37 *TO BE LOVED*
(E) (2:26) Columbia 40866 Reet Petite.
(E) (2:26) Epic 38623 Jackie Wilson Story.
(M) (2:27) Rhino 70775 Mr. Excitement!

1959 #6 *LONELY TEARDROPS*
(E) (2:39) Columbia 40866 Reet Petite.
(S) (2:30) Rhino 70906 American Bandstand Greatest Hits Collection.
(S) (2:30) Rhino 70644 Billboard's Top R&B Hits Of 1958.
(E) (2:39) Epic 38623 Jackie Wilson Story. *(truncated fade)*
(M) (2:41) Rhino 70775 Mr. Excitement! (truncated fade)

1959 #13 *THAT'S WHY (I LOVE YOU SO)*
(S) (2:00) Rhino 70645 Billboard's Top R&B Hits Of 1959.
(S) (2:03) Columbia 40866 Reet Petite.
(S) (2:03) Epic 38623 Jackie Wilson Story.
(S) (2:04) Rhino 70775 Mr. Excitement!

1959 #20 *I'LL BE SATISFIED*
(S) (2:08) Columbia 40866 Reet Petite.
(E) (2:06) Epic 38623 Jackie Wilson Story.
(S) (2:09) Rhino 70775 Mr. Excitement!

1959 #35 *YOU BETTER KNOW IT*
(S) (2:00) Columbia 40866 Reet Petite.
(S) (1:59) Epic 38623 Jackie Wilson Story. *(truncated fade)*
(S) (1:59) Rhino 70775 Mr. Excitement!

1960 #33 *TALK THAT TALK*
(E) (2:13) Columbia 40866 Reet Petite.
(E) (2:13) Epic 38623 Jackie Wilson Story.
(S) (2:13) Rhino 70775 Mr. Excitement!

1960 #3 *NIGHT*
(S) (2:45) Epic 38623 Jackie Wilson Story.
(S) (2:47) Rhino 70775 Mr. Excitement!

1960 #17 *DOGGIN' AROUND*
(S) (2:48) Rhino 70646 Billboard's Top R&B Hits Of 1960.
(S) (2:49) Columbia 40866 Reet Petite.
(E) (2:50) Epic 38623 Jackie Wilson Story.
(S) (2:52) Rhino 70775 Mr. Excitement!

JACKIE WILSON (Continued)

1960 #8 (YOU WERE MADE FOR) ALL MY LOVE
    (S) (2:03) Rhino 70775 Mr. Excitement!

1960 #12 A WOMAN, A LOVER, A FRIEND
    (S) (2:31) Epic 38623 Jackie Wilson Story.
    (S) (2:34) Rhino 70775 Mr. Excitement!

1960 #10 ALONE AT LAST
    (S) (3:00) Rhino 70775 Mr. Excitement!

1960 #23 AM I THE MAN
    (S) (2:31) Epic 38623 Jackie Wilson Story.
    (S) (2:34) Rhino 70775 Mr. Excitement!

1961 #15 MY EMPTY ARMS
    (S) (2:49) Rhino 70775 Mr. Excitement!

1961 #40 THE TEAR OF THE YEAR
    (E) (2:35) Epic 38623 Jackie Wilson Story.
    (S) (2:35) Rhino 70775 Mr. Excitement!

1961 #23 PLEASE TELL ME WHY
    (E) (1:58) Epic 38623 Jackie Wilson Story.
    (S) (1:59) Rhino 70775 Mr. Excitement!

1961 #30 I'M COMIN' ON BACK TO YOU
    (E) (2:12) Epic 38623 Jackie Wilson Story.
    (S) (2:20) Rhino 70775 Mr. Excitement!

1962 #24 THE GREATEST HURT
    (S) (3:09) Rhino 70775 Mr. Excitement!

1963 #4 BABY WORKOUT
    (S) (2:58) Rhino 70649 Billboard's Top R&B Hits Of 1963.
    (S) (2:57) Columbia 40866 Reet Petite.
    (S) (2:57) Epic 38623 Jackie Wilson Story.
    (S) (3:00) Rhino 70775 Mr. Excitement!

1963 #40 SHAKE! SHAKE! SHAKE!
    (S) (2:06) Rhino 70775 Mr. Excitement!

1966 #19 WHISPERS (GETTIN' LOUDER)
    (E) (2:16) Columbia 40866 Reet Petite.
    (S) (2:16) Epic 38623 Jackie Wilson Story.
    (S) (2:24) Rhino 70775 Mr. Excitement!

1967 #6 (YOUR LOVE KEEPS LIFTING ME) HIGHER & HIGHER
    (E) (2:58) JCI 3100 Dance Sixties.
    (S) (2:57) Rhino 70243 Greatest Movie Rock Hits.
    (S) (2:56) Rhino 70653 Billboard's Top R&B Hits Of 1967.
    (S) (2:56) Rhino 72006 Billboard's Top R&B Hits 1965-1969 Box Set.
    (S) (2:56) Columbia 40866 Reet Petite.
    (S) (2:55) Epic 38623 Jackie Wilson Story.
    (S) (2:57) Rhino 70775 Mr. Excitement!

1967 #36 SINCE YOU SHOWED ME HOW TO BE HAPPY
    (S) (2:48) Rhino 70775 Mr. Excitement!

JACKIE WILSON & LINDA HOPKINS

1963 #36 SHAKE A HAND
    (S) (3:04) Rhino 70775 Mr. Excitement!

J. FRANK WILSON & THE CAVALIERS

1964 #1 LAST KISS
    (M) (2:25) Rhino 70625 Billboard's Top Rock & Roll Hits Of 1964.
    (M) (2:25) Rhino 72007 Billboard's Top Rock & Roll Hits 1962-1966 Box Set.
    (M) (2:24) Rhino 70995 One Hit Wonders Of The 60's Volume 1.

392

NANCY WILSON
1964 #12 *(YOU DON'T KNOW) HOW GLAD I AM*
WIND
1969 #18 *MAKE BELIEVE*
KAI WINDING
1963 #8 *MORE*
    (S) (2:01) Rhino 70995 One Hit Wonders Of The 60's Volume 1.
WINGS (see PAUL McCARTNEY)
WINSTONS
1969 #8 *COLOR HIM FATHER*
    (S) (3:04) Rhino 70781 Soul Hits Of The 70's Volume 1.
EDGAR WINTER GROUP
1973 #1 *FRANKENSTEIN*
    (S) (3:25) Rhino 70929 Super Hits Of The 70's Volume 9. *(45 version)*
    (S) (3:25) Rhino 70634 Billboard's Top Rock & Roll Hits Of 1973. *(45 version)*
    (S) (4:43) JCI 3302 Electric Seventies (LP version)
    (S) (4:44) Rhino 70895 Collection. *(LP version)*
    (S) (4:43) Epic 31584 They Only Come Out At Night. *(LP version)*
    (S) (4:44) Priority 7055 Heavy Hitters/70's Greatest Rock Hits Volume 11. *(LP version)*
1973 #10 *FREE RIDE*
    (S) (3:04) Rhino 70895 Collection. *(45 version)*
    (S) (3:06) Priority 8662 Hard 'N Heavy/70's Greatest Rock Hits Volume 1. *(LP version)*
    (S) (3:06) Epic 31584 They Only Come Out At Night. *(LP version)*
HUGO WINTERHALTER
1956 #2 *CANADIAN SUNSET*
    (M) (2:52) RCA 8467 Nipper's Greatest Hits Of The 50's Volume 2.
BILL WITHERS
1971 #4 *AIN'T NO SUNSHINE*
    (S) (2:03) Rhino 70786 Soul Hits Of The 70's Volume 6.
    (S) (2:03) Columbia 37199 Greatest Hits.
1971 #31 *GRANDMA'S HANDS*
    (S) (1:59) Columbia 37199 Greatest Hits.
1972 #1 *LEAN ON ME*
    (S) (3:46) Rhino 70660 Billboard's Top R&B Hits Of 1972. *(45 length)*
    (S) (3:54) Rhino 70788 Soul Hits Of The 70's Volume 8. *(edit of LP length)*
    (S) (4:16) Columbia 37199 Greatest Hits. *(LP length)*
1972 #5 *USE ME*
    (S) (3:44) Rhino 70789 Soul Hits Of The 70's Volume 9.
    (S) (3:40) Columbia 37199 Greatest Hits.
1973 #26 *KISSING MY LOVE*
CHARLES WOLCOTT
1960 #27 *RUBY DUBY DU*
BOBBY WOMACK
1972 #22 *THAT'S THE WAY I FEEL ABOUT CHA*
    (S) (3:14) Rhino 70787 Soul Hits Of The 70's Volume 7.
1972 #32 *WOMAN'S GOTTA HAVE IT*
1973 #25 *HAIRY HIPPIE*
1973 #30 *NOBODY WANTS YOU WHEN YOU'RE DOWN AND OUT*

STEVIE WONDER

1963 #1 *FINGERTIPS (PART 2)*
(the actual LP time is (6:40) not (7:00) as stated on the record label)

    (E)   (3:10) Motown 6159 The Good-Feeling Music Of The Big Chill Generation Volume 1.

    (E)   (3:10) Rhino 70624 Billboard's Top Rock & Roll Hits Of 1963.

    (E)   (3:10) Rhino 72007 Billboard's Top Rock & Roll Hits 1962-1966 Box Set.

    (E)   (3:10) Motown 6159 The Good Feeling Music Of The Big Chill Generation Volume 1.

    (E)   (3:10) Motown 5449 A Collection Of 16 Big Hits Volume 2.

    (E)   (3:10) Motown 9017 and 5248 16 #1 Hits From The Early 60's.

    (E)   (3:10) Motown 9060 Motown's Biggest Pop Hits.

    (E)   (3:09) Motown 0282 Greatest Hits.

    (M) (6:37) Motown 5131 The 12 Year Old Genius. *(LP version which is Parts 1 & 2)*

1963 #34 *WORKOUT STEVIE, WORKOUT*

    (S)   (2:38) Motown 0282 Greatest Hits.

1964 #32 *HEY HARMONICA MAN*

    (S)   (2:36) Motown 5450 A Collection Of 16 Big Hits Volume 3.

    (S)   (2:36) Motown 0282 Greatest Hits.

1966 #3 *UPTIGHT (EVERYTHING'S ALRIGHT)*

    (S)   (2:53) Motown 6160 The Good Feeling Music Of The Big Chill Generation Volume 2.

    (S)   (2:51) Motown 5453 A Collection Of 16 Big Hits Volume 6.

    (S)   (2:53) Motown 9018 and 5249 16 #1 Hits From The Late 60's.

    (S)   (2:52) Motown 9071 Motown Dance Party Volume 1. *(all selections on this cd are segued together)*

    (S)   (2:52) Motown 0282 Greatest Hits.

    (S)   (2:53) Motown 8025 and 8125 For Once In My Life/Uptight.

    (S)   (2:53) Motown 5183 Uptight.

1966 #20 *NOTHING'S TOO GOOD FOR MY BABY*

    (S)   (2:37) Motown 6144 and 9050 Love Songs: 20 Classic Hits.

    (S)   (2:42) Motown 0282 Greatest Hits. *(truncated fade)*

    (S)   (2:37) Motown 8025 and 8125 For Once In My Life/Uptight.

    (S)   (2:37) Motown 5183 Uptight.

1966 #11 *BLOWIN' IN THE WIND*

    (S)   (3:44) Motown 6159 The Good-Feeling Music Of The Big Chill Generation Volume 1. *(LP version)*

    (S)   (3:44) Motown 6144 and 9050 Love Songs: 20 Classic Hits. *(LP version)*

    (S)   (3:03) Motown 0282 Greatest Hits. *(45 version)*

    (S)   (3:44) Motown 8025 and 8125 For Once In My Life/Uptight. *(LP version)*

    (S)   (3:43) Motown 5183 Uptight. *(LP version)*

1966 #10 *A PLACE IN THE SUN*

    (S)   (2:49) Motown 5454 A Collection Of 16 Big Hits Volume 7.

    (S)   (2:48) Motown 6144 and 9050 Love Songs: 20 Classic Hits.

    (S)   (2:50) Motown 0282 Greatest Hits.

    (S)   (2:51) Motown 8053 and 8153 I Was Made To Love Her/ Down To Earth.

    (S)   (2:49) Motown 5166 Down To Earth.

1967 #2 *I WAS MADE TO LOVE HER*

    (S)   (2:34) Motown 6161 The Good-Feeling Music Of The Big Chill Generation Volume 3.

    (S)   (2:34) Motown 5456 A Collection Of 16 Big Hits Volume 9.

STEVIE WONDER (Continued)

- (S) (2:35) Motown 6177 Endless Love.
- (S) (2:35) Motown 9018 and 5249 16 #1 Hits From The Late 60's.
- (S) (2:34) Motown 6192 You Can't Hurry Love: All The Great Love Songs Of The Past 25 Years.
- (S) (2:35) Motown 6144 and 9050 Love Songs: 20 Classic Hits.
- (S) (2:34) Motown 0282 Greatest Hits.
- (S) (2:36) Motown 5273 I Was Made To Love Her.
- (S) (2:36) Motown 8053 and 8153 I Was Made To Love Her/ Down To Earth.

1967 #10 I'M WONDERING

- (S) (2:51) Motown 5457 A Collection Of 16 Big Hits Volume 10.
- (S) (2:53) Motown 6144 and 9050 Love Songs: 20 Classic Hits.
- (S) (2:52) Motown 0282 Greatest Hits.

1968 #7 SHOO-BE-DOO-BE-DOO-DA-DAY

- (S) (2:44) Motown 6159 The Good-Feeling Music Of The Big Chill Generation Volume 1.
- (S) (2:44) Motown 6144 and 9050 Love Songs: 20 Classic Hits.
- (S) (2:45) Motown 0313 Greatest Hits Volume 2.
- (S) (2:44) Motown 8025 and 8125 For Once In My Life/Uptight.
- (S) (2:44) Motown 9032 and 5234 For Once In My Life.

1968 #28 YOU MET YOUR MATCH

- (S) (2:36) Motown 0313 Greatest Hits Volume 2.
- (S) (2:37) Motown 8025 and 8125 For Once In My Life/Uptight.
- (S) (2:37) Motown 9032 and 5234 For Once In My Life.

1968 #1 FOR ONCE IN MY LIFE

- (S) (2:48) Motown 6159 The Good-Feeling Music Of The Big Chill Generation Volume 1. (truncated fade)
- (S) (2:48) Motown 6137 20 Greatest Songs In Motown History.
- (S) (2:48) Motown 6110 Motown Grammy R&B Performances Of The 60's & 70's.
- (S) (2:48) Motown 6144 and 9050 Love Songs: 20 Classic Hits. (truncated fade)
- (S) (2:46) Motown 0313 Greatest Hits Volume 2.
- (S) (2:48) Motown 8025 and 8125 For Once In My Life/Uptight.
- (S) (2:47) Motown 9032 and 5234 For Once In My Life.

1969 #3 MY CHERIE AMOUR

- (S) (2:50) Motown 5324 and 9035 Top Ten With A Bullet: Motown Love Songs.
- (S) (2:50) Motown 9098 Radio's #1 Hits.
- (S) (2:50) Motown 6144 and 9050 Love Songs: 20 Classic Hits.
- (S) (2:50) Motown 0313 Greatest Hits Volume 2.
- (S) (2:52) Motown 9083 and 5179 My Cherie Amour.
- (S) (2:52) Motown 8006 and 8106 My Cherie Amour/Signed, Sealed And Delivered.

1969 #9 YESTER-ME, YESTER-YOU, YESTERDAY

- (S) (3:03) Motown 6144 and 9050 Love Songs: 20 Classic Hits.
- (S) (3:00) Motown 0313 Greatest Hits Volume 2.
- (S) (3:05) Motown 9083 and 5179 My Cherie Amour.
- (S) (3:04) Motown 8006 and 8106 My Cherie Amour/Signed, Sealed And Delivered.

1970 #22 NEVER HAD A DREAM COME TRUE

- (S) (3:10) Motown 6144 and 9050 Love Songs: 20 Classic Hits.
- (S) (3:11) Motown 0313 Greatest Hits Volume 2.

STEVIE WONDER (Continued)

(S) (3:12) Motown 8006 and 8106 My Cherie Amour/Signed, Sealed And Delivered. *(noisy fadeout)*

(S) (3:12) Motown 9029 and 5176 Signed, Sealed And Delivered. *(noisy fadeout)*

1970 #1 SIGNED, SEALED, DELIVERED I'M YOURS

(S) (2:39) Motown 6110 Motown Grammy R&B Performances Of the 60's & 70's.

(S) (2:38) Motown 0937 20/20 Twenty No. 1 Hits From Twenty Years At Motown.

(S) (2:39) Motown 6144 and 9050 Love Songs: 20 Classic Hits.

(S) (2:37) Motown 0313 Greatest Hits Volume 2.

(S) (2:38) Motown 8006 and 8106 My Cherie Amour/Signed, Sealed And Delivered.

(S) (2:38) Motown 9029 and 5176 Signed, Sealed And Delivered.

1970 #9 HEAVEN HELP US ALL

(S) (3:12) Motown 6144 and 9050 Love Songs: 20 Classic Hits.

(S) (3:10) Motown 0313 Greatest Hits Volume 2.

(S) (3:12) Motown 8006 and 8106 My Cherie Amour/Signed, Sealed And Delivered.

(S) (3:12) Motown 9029 and 5176 Signed, Sealed And Delivered.

1971 #9 WE CAN WORK IT OUT

(S) (3:16) Motown 6144 and 9050 Love Songs: 20 Classic Hits.

(S) (3:11) Motown 0313 Greatest Hits Volume 2.

(S) (3:17) Motown 8006 and 8106 My Cherie Amour/Signed, Sealed And Delivered.

(S) (3:17) Motown 9029 and 5176 Signed, Sealed And Delivered.

1971 #9 IF YOU REALLY LOVE ME

(S) (2:55) Motown 9105 Motown Memories Volume 2.

(S) (2:56) Motown 5324 and 9035 Top Ten With A Bullet: Motown Love Songs.

(S) (2:56) Motown 6144 and 9050 Love Songs: 20 Classic Hits.

(S) (2:56) Motown 0313 Greatest Hits Volume 2.

(S) (3:00) Motown 5247 Where I'm Coming From.

1972 #32 SUPERWOMAN (WHERE WERE YOU WHEN I NEEDED YOU)

(S) (7:58) Motown 6175 and 6002 Original Musiquarium Volume 1. *(all selections on this cd are segued together; LP version)*

(S) (8:08) Motown 9076 and 0314 Music Of My Mind. *(LP version)*

1973 #1 SUPERSTITION

(S) (4:26) Motown 6132 25 #1 Hits From 25 Years.

(S) (4:24) MCA 10063 Original Television Soundtrack "The Sounds Of Murphy Brown".

(S) (4:23) Motown 9072 Motown Dance Party Volume 2. *(all selections on this cd are segued together)*

(S) (4:24) Motown 0937 20/20 Twenty No. 1 Hits From Twenty Years At Motown.

(S) (4:26) Motown 6175 and 6002 Original Musiquarium Volume 1. *(all selections on this cd are segued together)*

(S) (4:25) Motown 6151 and 0319 Talking Book. *(tracks into next selection)*

1973 #1 YOU ARE THE SUNSHINE OF MY LIFE

(the actial 45 and LP time is (3:00) not (2:45) as stated on the record label)

(S) (2:51) Motown 6132 25 #1 Hits From 25 Years.

(S) (2:57) Motown 0937 20/20 Twenty No. 1 Hits From Twenty Years At Motown.

STEVIE WONDER (Continued)

    (S)   (2:50) Motown 6175 and 6002 Original Musiquarium Volume 1. *(all selections on this cd are segued together)*

    (S)   (2:58) Motown 6151 and 0319 Talking Book.

1973 #1 HIGHER GROUND

    (S)   (3:47) Motown 6176 and 6002 Original Musiquarium Volume 2. *(all selections on this cd are segued together)*

    (S)   (3:42) Motown 6152 and 0326 Innervisions. *(tracks into next selection)*

    (S)   (3:42) MFSL 554 Innervisions. *(tracks into next selection)*

WONDER WHO?

1965 #10 DON'T THINK TWICE

    (S)   (2:57) Rhino 72998 Four Seasons 25th Anniversary Collection.

    (S)   (2:57) Rhino 70248 Four Seasons Sing Hits Of Bacharach/David/Dylan.

    (S)   (2:57) Rhino 71490 Four Seasons Anthology.

    (S)   (2:57) Rhino 70594 Four Seasons Greatest Hits Volume 1.

BRENTON WOOD

1967 #7 GIMME LITTLE SIGN

    (M)   (2:21) Warner Special Products 27602 20 Party Classics. *(hum noticeable on introduction)*

    (M)   (2:16) Rhino 75757 Soul Shots Volume 3.

    (M)   (2:19) JCI 3105 Soul Sixties.

    (S)   (2:19) Original Sound 8886 18 Best.

SHEB WOOLEY

1958 #1 THE PURPLE PEOPLE EATER

    (M)   (2:12) Rhino 71492 Elvira Presents Haunted Hits.

    (M)   (2:11) Rhino 75768 Dr. Demento Presents.

    (M)   (2:12) Rhino 70743 Dr. Demento 20th Anniversary Collection.

    (M)   (2:12) Rhino 70535 Halloween Hits.

    (M)   (2:12) Mercury 832041 45's On CD Volume 1.

    (M)   (2:12) Dunhill 050 Monster Rock 'n Roll Show.

LINK WRAY & HIS RAY MEN

1958 #18 RUMBLE

    (M)   (2:24) Rhino 70719 Legends Of Guitar - Rock; The 50's.

1959 #34 RAW-HIDE

    (E)   (2:04) CBS Special Products 37618 Rockabilly Stars Volume 1.

    (M)   (2:05) Epic/Legacy 47904 Walkin' With Link.

BETTY WRIGHT

1972 #4 CLEAN UP WOMAN

    (S)   (2:44) Rhino 70787 Soul Hits Of The 70's Volume 7.

    (S)   (2:43) Rhino 70659 Billboard's Top R&B Hits Of 1971.

    (S)   (2:46) Atlantic 81299 Atlantic Rhythm & Blues Volume 7.

    (S)   (2:45) Atlantic 82305 Atlantic Rhythm And Blues 1947-1974 Box Set.

CHARLES WRIGHT & THE WATTS 103RD STREET BAND

released as by THE WATTS 103RD STREET BAND:

1969 #14 DO YOUR THING

    (M)   (2:54) JCI 3105 Soul Sixties.

released as by CHARLES WRIGHT & THE WATTS 103RD STREET BAND:

1970 #16 LOVE LAND

    (S)   (3:03) Rhino 70782 Soul Hits Of The 70's Volume 2.

1970 #17 EXPRESS YOURSELF

    (S)   (3:50) Rhino 70783 Soul Hits Of The 70's Volume 3.

TAMMY WYNETTE

1969 #23 *STAND BY YOUR MAN*
    (S) (2:37) Rhino 70689 Billboard's Top Country Hits Of 1968.
    (S) (2:38) Columbia 46032 Columbia Country Classics Volume 4.
    (S) (2:38) Epic 38312 Biggest Hits.
    (S) (2:38) Epic 26846 Greatest Hits.
    (S) (2:38) Epic 40625 Anniversary: 20 Years Of Hits.

GLENN YARBROUGH

1965 #13 *BABY THE RAIN MUST FALL*
    (S) (2:19) RCA 8474 Nipper's Greatest Hits Of The 50's Volume 1.

YARDBIRDS

1965 #6 *FOR YOUR LOVE*
    (M) (2:28) Rhino 70319 History Of British Rock Volume 1.
    (M) (2:28) Rhino 70319 History Of British Rock Box Set.
    (M) (2:28) Rhino 72008 History Of British Rock Volumes 1-4 Box Set.
    (M) (2:28) Sony Music Special Products 48655 Volume 1: Smokestack Lightning.
    (M) (2:28) Rhino 75895 Greatest Hits Volume 1.

1965 #12 *HEART FULL OF SOUL*
    (M) (2:27) Rhino 70320 History Of British Rock Volume 2.
    (M) (2:27) Rhino 70319 History Of British Rock Box Set.
    (M) (2:27) Rhino 72008 History Of British Rock Volumes 1-4 Box Set.
    (M) (2:27) Epic/Legacy 48661 Jeff Beck: Beckology.
    (M) (2:27) Sony Music Special Products 48655 Volume 1: Smokestack Lightning.
    (M) (2:27) Sony Music Special Products 48658 Volume 2: Blues, Backtracks And Shapes Of Things.
    (M) (2:27) Rhino 75895 Greatest Hits Volume 1.

1965 #25 *I'M A MAN*
    (M) (2:36) Rhino 70321 History Of British Rock Volume 3.
    (M) (2:36) Rhino 70319 History Of British Rock Box Set.
    (M) (2:36) Rhino 72008 History Of British Rock Volumes 1-4 Box Set.
    (M) (2:35) Warner Special Products 27607 Highs Of The 60's.
    (M) (2:35) Epic/Legacy 48661 Jeff Beck: Beckology.
    (M) (2:35) Sony Music Special Products 48655 Volume 1: Smokestack Lightning.
    (M) (2:36) Rhino 75895 Greatest Hits Volume 1.

1966 #10 *SHAPES OF THINGS*
    (M) (2:25) Rhino 70322 History Of British Rock Volume 4.
    (M) (2:25) Rhino 70319 History Of British Rock Box Set.
    (M) (2:25) Rhino 72008 History Of British Rock Volumes 1-4 Box Set.
    (M) (2:23) JCI 3103 Electric Sixties.

YARDBIRDS (Continued)
    (M) (2:23) Epic/Legacy 48661 Jeff Beck: Beckology.
    (M) (2:24) Sony Music Special Products 48658 Volume 2: Blues, Backtracks
    And Shapes Of Things.
    (M) (2:35) Rhino 75895 Greatest Hits Volume 1. *(includes :10 studio talk)*
1966 #12 *OVER UNDER SIDEWAYS DOWN*
    (E) (2:20) Epic/Legacy 48661 Jeff Beck: Beckology.
1967 #34 *HAPPENINGS TEN YEARS TIME AGO*
    (M) (2:54) Epic/Legacy 48661 Jeff Beck: Beckology.

YES
1971 #29 *YOUR MOVE*
(the LP version of this song is a medley of "I"VE SEEN ALL GOOD PEOPLE", "YOUR MOVE" and "ALL GOOD PEOPLE")
    (S) (6:52) Atlantic 81908 Classic Rock 1966-1988. *(LP version)*
    (S) (6:51) Atlantic 82306 Atlantic Rock & Roll Box Set. *(LP version)*
    (S) (7:09) Atlantic 100-2 Yessongs. *(live)*
    (S) (6:53) Atlantic 19131 Yes Album. *(LP version)*
    (S) (6:53) Atco 91644 Yes Years. *(LP version)*
1972 #10 *ROUNDABOUT*
    (S) (8:32) Atlantic 100-2 Yessongs. *(live)*
    (S) (8:29) Atlantic 19132 Fragile. *(LP version)*
    (S) (8:30) Atco 91644 Yes Years. *(LP version)*
1972 #32 *AND YOU AND I (PART 1)*
    (S) (9:36) Atlantic 100-2 Yessongs. *(live)*
    (S) (10:04) Atlantic 19133 Close To The Bone. *(LP version)*

BARRY YOUNG
1966 #21 *ONE HAS MY NAME (THE OTHER HAS MY HEART)*

FARON YOUNG
1961 #10 *HELLO WALLS*
    (S) (2:21) Rhino 70682 Billboard's Top Country Hits Of 1961.
    (M) (2:22) Curb 77343 60's Hits - Country Volume 1.
    (M) (2:22) Curb 77334 All-Time Greatest Hits.

KATHY YOUNG
1960 #4 *A THOUSAND STARS*
1961 #30 *HAPPY BIRTHDAY BLUES*

NEIL YOUNG
1970 #20 *ONLY LOVE CAN BREAK YOUR HEART*
    (S) (3:07) Reprise 2283 After The Gold Rush.
1972 #1 *HEART OF GOLD*
    (S) (3:06) Reprise 2277 Harvest.
    (S) (3:06) Reprise 2257 Decade.
1972 #26 *OLD MAN*
    (S) (3:21) Reprise 2277 Harvest.
    (S) (3:21) Reprise 2257 Decade.

VICTOR YOUNG & HIS ORCHESTRA
1957 #6 *AROUND THE WORLD IN 80 DAYS*
    (S) (3:02) MCA 31134 Music From Around The World In 80 Days.

YOUNGBLOODS
1969 #4 *GET TOGETHER*
(commercial copies of this 45 ran (4:37) while dj copies ran (4:37) and (3:24))
    (S) (4:15) Polydor 837362 O.S.T. 1969. *(rerecording of this song by Jesse Colin Young, former lead singer of the Youngbloods)*
    (S) (4:37) Rhino 70630 Billboard's Top Rock & Roll Hits Of 1969.

YOUNGBLOODS (Continued)

      (S) (4:37) Rhino 72005 Billboard's Top Rock & Roll Hits 1968-1972 Box Set.
      (M) (4:38) Rhino 70536 San Francisco Nights.
      (S) (4:33) Dunhill 045 Golden Age Of Underground Radio.
      (S) (4:36) RCA 8475 Nipper's Greatest Hits Of The 60's Volume 2.
      (S) (4:36) RCA 3280 Best Of.

YOUNG-HOLT UNLIMITED
1969 #4 *SOULFUL STRUT*

YOUNG RASCALS (see RASCALS)

TIMI YURO
1961 #4 *HURT*
1962 #15 *WHAT'S A MATTER BABY (IS IT HURTING YOU)*
1963 #23 *MAKE THE WORLD GO AWAY*

FLORIAN ZABACH
1956 #16 *WHEN THE WHITE LILACS BLOOM AGAIN*

HELMUT ZACHARIAS & HIS MAGIC VIOLINS
1956 #16 *WHEN THE WHITE LILACS BLOOM AGAIN*

JOHN ZACHERLE
1958 #16 *DINNER WITH DRAC (PART 1)*

ZAGER & EVANS
1969 #1 *IN THE YEAR 2525 (EXORDIUM AND TERMINUS)*

      (S) (3:15) RCA 8475 Nipper's Greatest Hits Of The 60's Volume 2.
      (S) (3:14) RCA 9902 Nipper's #1 Hits 1956-1986.

SI ZENTNER
1961 #29 *UP A LAZY RIVER*

      (S) (2:04) Curb 77403 All-Time Great Instrumental Hits Volume 2.

ZOMBIES
1964 #1 *SHE'S NOT THERE*

      (M) (2:22) Rhino 70906 American Bandstand Greatest Hits Collection. (*45 version*)
      (M) (2:22) Rhino 70319 History Of British Rock Volume 1. (*45 version*)
      (M) (2:22) Rhino 70319 History Of British Rock Box Set. (*45 version*)
      (M) (2:22) Rhino 72008 History Of British Rock Volumes 1-4 Box Set. (*45 version*)
      (M) (2:22) Rhino 70625 Billboard's Top Rock & Roll Hits Of 1964. (*45 version*)

ZOMBIES (Continued)

    (M) (2:22) Rhino 72007 Billboard's Top Rock & Roll Hits 1962-1966 Box Set. *(45 version)*

    (M) (2:22) Dunhill 052 Greatest Hits. *(45 version)*

1965 #6 TELL HER NO

    (S) (2:04) Rhino 70320 History Of British Rock Volume 2. *(remix of the single version)*

    (S) (2:04) Rhino 70319 History Of British Rock Box Set. *(remix of the single version)*

    (S) (2:04) Rhino 72008 History Of British Rock Volumes 1-4 Box Set. *(remix of the single version)*

    (S) (2:05) Dunhill 052 Greatest Hits.

1969 #1 TIME OF THE SEASON

    (S) (3:31) Rhino 70630 Billboard's Top Rock & Roll Hits Of 1969.

    (S) (3:31) Rhino 72005 Billboard's Top Rock & Roll Hits 1968-1972 Box Set.

    (S) (3:30) Polydor 837362 O.S.T. 1969.

    (S) (3:29) Dunhill 052 Zombies Greatest Hits.

    (S) (3:31) Rhino 70186 Odessey And Oracle.

FINDING YOUR WAY AROUND THE *SONG TITLE SECTION*

This section contains the top 40 hits listed by song title. Below is a breakdown of what you'll find on these pages.

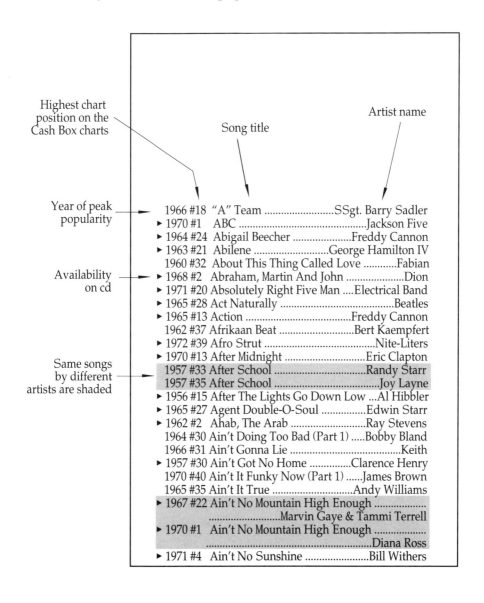

Highest chart position on the Cash Box charts

Song title

Artist name

Year of peak popularity

Availability on cd

Same songs by different artists are shaded

1966 #18 "A" Team ....SSgt. Barry Sadler
► 1970 #1 ABC ....Jackson Five
► 1964 #24 Abigail Beecher ....Freddy Cannon
► 1963 #21 Abilene ....George Hamilton IV
1960 #32 About This Thing Called Love ....Fabian
► 1968 #2 Abraham, Martin And John ....Dion
► 1971 #20 Absolutely Right Five Man ....Electrical Band
► 1965 #28 Act Naturally ....Beatles
► 1965 #13 Action ....Freddy Cannon
1962 #37 Afrikaan Beat ....Bert Kaempfert
► 1972 #39 Afro Strut ....Nite-Liters
► 1970 #13 After Midnight ....Eric Clapton
1957 #33 After School ....Randy Starr
1957 #35 After School ....Joy Layne
► 1956 #15 After The Lights Go Down Low ...Al Hibbler
► 1965 #27 Agent Double-O-Soul ....Edwin Starr
► 1962 #2 Ahab, The Arab ....Ray Stevens
1964 #30 Ain't Doing Too Bad (Part 1) .....Bobby Bland
1966 #31 Ain't Gonna Lie ....Keith
► 1957 #30 Ain't Got No Home ....Clarence Henry
1970 #40 Ain't It Funky Now (Part 1) ......James Brown
1965 #35 Ain't It True ....Andy Williams
► 1967 #22 Ain't No Mountain High Enough ....
.........................Marvin Gaye & Tammi Terrell
► 1970 #1 Ain't No Mountain High Enough ....
....Diana Ross
► 1971 #4 Ain't No Sunshine ....Bill Withers

▸ 1959 #11 Along Came Jones ....Coasters
▸ 1969 #24 Along Came Jones ....Ray Stevens
▸ 1966 #9 Along Comes Mary......................Association
▸ 1973 #4 Also Sprach Zarathustra ....Deodato
▸ 1959 #3 Alvin's Harmonica ....Chipmunks
  1960 #32 Alvin's Orchestra ....Chipmunks
  1959 #17 Always ....Sammy Turner
  1970 #22 Always Something There To Remind Me .....
           ....R.B. Greaves
▸ 1968 #35 Always Together ....Dells
▸ 1960 #29 Am I Losing You...........................Jim Reeves
▸ 1972 #31 Am I Losing You ....Partridge Family
▸ 1960 #19 Am I That Easy To Forget ....
           ....Debbie Reynolds
▸ 1968 #24 Am I That Easy To Forget ....
           ....Engelbert Humperdinck
▸ 1960 #23 Am I The Man ....Jackie Wilson
▸ 1971 #13 Amazing Grace..........................Judy Collins
▸ 1972 #10 Amazing Grace..
           ....Royal Scots Dragoon Guards
  1968 #36 Ame Caline (Soul Coaxing)........................
           ....Raymond Lefevre & His Orchestra
▸ 1964 #8 Amen..Impressions
▸ 1968 #37 Amen..Otis Redding
  1970 #38 America Communicate With Me.................
           ....Ray Stevens
▸ 1972 #28 American City Suite.........Cashman & West
▸ 1972 #1 American Pie (Parts 1 & 2)........Don McLean
▸ 1970 #1 American Woman ....Guess Who
▸ 1959 #5 Among My Souvenirs...........Connie Francis
▸ 1961 #19 Amor ....Ben E. King
▸ 1971 #8 Amos Moses...........................Jerry Reed
▸ 1957 #25 An Affair To Remember ....Vic Damone
▸ 1971 #4 An Old Fashioned Love Song ....
           ....Three Dog Night
  1967 #6 An Open Letter To My Teenage Son.............
           ....Victor Lundberg
  1956 #25 Anastasia ....Pat Boone
▸ 1968 #29 And Get Away ....Esquires
▸ 1964 #14 And I Love Her ....Beatles
▸ 1973 #18 And I Love You So ....Perry Como
  1965 #34 And Roses And Roses...........Andy Williams
  1957 #15 And That Reminds Me ....Della Reese
▸ 1969 #33 And That Reminds Me.............Four Seasons
  1970 #37 And The Grass Won't Pay No Mind.............
           ....Mark Lindsay
▸ 1969 #1 And When I Die.........Blood, Sweat & Tears
▸ 1972 #32 And You And I (Part 1)...........................Yes
▸ 1972 #39 Angel ....Rod Stewart
▸ 1973 #16 Angel ....Aretha Franklin
  1961 #6 Angel Baby.................Rosie & The Originals
▸ 1958 #38 Angel Baby ....Dean Martin
▸ 1968 #3 Angel Of The Morning...............................
           ....Merilee Rush & The Turnabouts
  1961 #26 Angel On My Shoulder ....Shelby Flint
  1958 #28 Angel Smile.............................Nat King Cole
  1964 #38 Angelito ....Rene & Rene
▸ 1959 #15 Angels Listened In ....Crests
▸ 1973 #1 Angie ....Rolling Stones
▸ 1964 #40 Another Cup Of Coffee...........Brook Benton
▸ 1971 #6 Another Day ....Paul McCartney
▸ 1963 #14 Another Saturday Night............Sam Cooke
▸ 1960 #17 Another Sleepless Night ......Jimmy Clanton
  1958 #38 Another Time, Another Place ....Patti Page
  1971 #40 Another Time, Another Place ....
           ....Engelbert Humperdinck
▸ 1972 #10 Anticipation ....Carly Simon

▸ 1962 #12 Any Day Now (My Wild Beautiful Bird) ....
           ....Chuck Jackson
  1964 #9 Any Way You Want It ....Dave Clark Five
▸ 1961 #23 Anybody But Me.........................Brenda Lee
  1960 #24 Anymore ....Teresa Brewer
▸ 1964 #8 Anyone Who Had A Heart..........................
           ....Dionne Warwick
  1961 #4 Apache ....Jorgen Ingmann
  1956 #37 Ape Call..............................Nervous Norvus
▸ 1971 #39 Apeman.......................................Kinks
  1960 #24 Apple Green ....June Valli
▸ 1967 #4 Apples, Peaches, Pumpkin Pie.....................
           ....Jay & The Techniques
▸ 1969 #37 April Fools ....Dionne Warwick
▸ 1957 #3 April Love ....Pat Boone
▸ 1969 #1 Aquarius/Let The Sunshine In ....
           ....Fifth Dimension
▸ 1969 #33 Are You Happy...........................Jerry Butler
  1967 #29 Are You Lonely For Me ....Freddie Scott
▸ 1960 #1 Are You Lonesome Tonight? ...Elvis Presley
▸ 1973 #14 Are You Man Enough...................Four Tops
▸ 1970 #12 Are You Ready? ....Pacific Gas & Electric
▸ 1958 #14 Are You Really Mine............Jimmie Rodgers
▸ 1958 #7 Are You Sincere....................Andy Williams
▸ 1966 #36 Are You There (With Another Girl) ....
           ....Dionne Warwick
▸ 1970 #9 Arizona ....Mark Lindsay
▸ 1973 #19 Armed And Extremely Dangerous..............
           ....First Choice
  1956 #34 Armen's Theme ....David Seville
▸ 1957 #6 Around The World ....
           ....Mantovani & His Orchestra
▸ 1957 #6 Around The World In 80 Days ....
           ....Victor Young & His Orchestra
▸ 1958 #32 Arrivederci Roma ....Mario Lanza
  1958 #32 Arrivederci, Roma ....Roger Williams
▸ 1960 #19 Artificial Flowers ....Bobby Darin
  1961 #19 As If I Didn't Know ....Adam Wade
▸ 1965 #30 As Tears Go By ....Marianne Faithful
▸ 1966 #3 As Tears Go By ....Rolling Stones
▸ 1970 #30 As The Years Go By.................Mashmakhan
▸ 1964 #11 As Usual ....Brenda Lee
  1961 #14 Asia Minor ....Kokomo
▸ 1964 #10 Ask Me ....Elvis Presley
  1972 #19 Ask Me What You Want ....Millie Jackson
▸ 1965 #26 Ask The Lonely ....Four Tops
▸ 1961 #19 Astronaut, The (Parts 1 & 2).....Jose Jimenez
▸ 1961 #30 At Last...Etta James
▸ 1955 #8 At My Front Door ....El Dorados
  1955 #8 At My Front Door (Crazy Little Mama) ....
           ....Pat Boone
▸ 1962 #40 At The Club ....Ray Charles
▸ 1958 #1 At The Hop.................Danny & The Juniors
  1966 #13 At The Scene....................Dave Clark Five
▸ 1967 #15 At The Zoo.....................Simon & Garfunkel
▸ 1969 #9 Atlantis ....Donovan
  1966 #22 Attack ....Toys
▸ 1973 #11 Aubrey...Bread
  1956 #22 Auctioneer, The...................Leroy Van Dyke
▸ 1972 #37 Automatically Sunshine................Supremes
▸ 1955 #1 Autumn Leaves ....Roger Williams
▸ 1968 #14 Autumn Of My Life...........Bobby Goldsboro

405

B

▸ 1966	#16	B-A-B-Y ....Carla Thomas
▸ 1969	#9	Baby, Baby Don't Cry ....Miracles
1961	#15	Baby Blue ....Echoes
1972	#9	Baby Blue ....Badfinger
1968	#26	Baby Come Back ....Equals
1956	#35	Baby Doll..............................Andy Williams
▸ 1972	#1	Baby Don't Get Hooked On Me.....Mac Davis
▸ 1965	#10	Baby Don't Go ....Sonny & Cher
▸ 1964	#27	Baby Don't You Do It................Marvin Gaye
▸ 1963	#40	Baby Don't You Weep ....
		................Garnet Mimms & The Enchanters
▸ 1962	#38	Baby Face ....Bobby Darin
▸ 1970	#25	Baby Hold On..........................Grass Roots
▸ 1967	#3	Baby I Love You...................Aretha Franklin
1969	#6	Baby, I Love You ....Andy Kim
▸ 1964	#24	Baby, I Love You ....Ronettes
▸ 1967	#6	Baby I Need Your Lovin' ....Johnny Rivers
▸ 1964	#15	Baby I Need Your Loving.............Four Tops
▸ 1971	#3	Baby I'm A Want You ....Bread
▸ 1969	#16	Baby I'm For Real ....Originals
▸ 1965	#10	Baby, I'm Yours...............Barbara Lewis
1973	#36	Baby I've Been Missing You ....Independents
▸ 1962	#8	Baby It's You ....Shirelles
▸ 1969	#4	Baby It's You...Smith
▸ 1971	#19	Baby Let Me Kiss You ....King Floyd
1972	#19	Baby Let Me Take You (In My Arms).............
		....Detroit Emeralds
▸ 1969	#33	Baby Let's Wait ....Royal Guardsmen
▸ 1964	#1	Baby Love ....Supremes
▸ 1968	#8	Baby, Now That I've Found You ....
		....Foundations
▸ 1961	#23	Baby Oh Baby ....Shells
▸ 1966	#13	Baby Scratch My Back ....Slim Harpo
1961	#10	Baby Sittin' Boogie ....Buzz Clifford
1970	#19	Baby Take Me In Your Arms...........Jefferson
▸ 1959	#7	Baby Talk.............................Jan & Dean
▸ 1965	#13	Baby The Rain Must Fall....Glenn Yarbrough
▸ 1963	#4	Baby Workout..........................Jackie Wilson
▸ 1960	#2	Baby (You Got What It Takes).....................
		............Dinah Washington & Brook Benton
▸ 1965	#1	Back In My Arms Again.................Supremes
▸ 1972	#10	Back Off Boogaloo.......................Ringo Starr
1957	#30	Back To School Again..................................
		............................Timmie "Oh Yeah" Rogers
1973	#25	Back When My Hair Was Short ....
		....Gunhill Road
1969	#12	Backfield In Motion ....Mel & Tim
▸ 1972	#1	Backstabbers...O'Jays
1966	#24	Backstage ....Gene Pitney
▸ 1973	#1	Bad, Bad Leroy Brown..................Jim Croce
1957	#24	Bad Boy ....Jive Bombers

▸ 1969	#2	Bad Moon Rising.................................
		.......................Creedence Clearwater Revival
▸ 1964	#10	Bad To Me ....
		..................Billy J Kramer With The Dakotas
1957	#36	Bahama Mama.................................Four Aces
▸ 1970	#1	Ball Of Confusion (That's What The World
		Is Today)..................................Temptations
▸ 1969	#11	Ball Of Fire ....
		..................Tommy James & The Shondells
▸ 1958	#28	Ballad Of A Teenage Queen .....Johnny Cash
▸ 1968	#6	Ballad Of Bonnie And Clyde.........................
		....Georgie Fame
1955	#1	Ballad Of Davy Crockett...............Bill Hayes
▸ 1969	#10	Ballad Of John And Yoko...................Beatles
1960	#35	Ballad Of The Alamo ....Bud & Travis
▸ 1960	#33	Ballad Of The Alamo ....Marty Robbins
▸ 1966	#1	Ballad Of The Green Berets ....
		....SSgt. Barry Sadler
▸ 1967	#24	Ballad Of You & Me & Pooneil ....
		....Jefferson Airplane
▸ 1957	#29	Ballerina ....Nat King Cole
▸ 1957	#30	Banana Boat (Day-O)...............Stan Freberg
▸ 1957	#4	Banana Boat (Day-O)...........Harry Belafonte
1956	#15	Banana Boat Song ....Fontane Sisters
1957	#5	Banana Boat Song ....Steve Lawrence
▸ 1956	#15	Banana Boat Song.................Sarah Vaughan
▸ 1957	#2	Banana Boat Song....................Tarriers
1966	#37	Band Of Gold..............................Mel Carter
▸ 1956	#5	Band Of Gold...........................Don Cherry
▸ 1970	#2	Band Of Gold.........................Freda Payne
▸ 1967	#32	Banda, A ....
		..................Herb Alpert & The Tijuana Brass
▸ 1972	#12	Bang A Gong (Get It On) ....T. Rex
▸ 1966	#2	Bang Bang (My Baby Shot Me Down)............
		....Cher
1968	#9	Bang-Shang-A-Lang......................Archies
▸ 1971	#20	Bangla-Desh.................George Harrison
1960	#38	Barbara ....Temptations
▸ 1961	#13	Barbara Ann ....Regents
▸ 1966	#1	Barbara Ann ....Beach Boys
▸ 1966	#11	Barefootin' ....Robert Parker
▸ 1973	#13	Basketball Jones Featuring Tyrone
		Shoelaces ....Cheech & Chong
▸ 1966	#14	Batman Theme................................Marketts
▸ 1966	#32	Batman Theme................................Neal Hefti
1971	#26	Battle Hymn Of Lt. Calley ....
		............C Company featuring Terry Nelson
1959	#11	Battle Hymn Of The Republic......................
		..................Mormon Tabernacle Choir
▸ 1959	#16	Battle Of Kookamonga ....Homer & Jethro
▸ 1959	#1	Battle Of New Orleans ....Johnny Horton
1958	#31	Baubles, Bangles And Beads ....
		....Kirby Stone Four
▸ 1973	#19	Be..Neil Diamond
▸ 1964	#23	Be Anything (But Be Mine)..........................
		....Connie Francis
▸ 1956	#5	Be-Bop-A-Lula ....
		..................Gene Vincent & His Blue Caps
▸ 1957	#6	Be-Bop Baby ....Rick Nelson
1963	#30	Be Careful Of Stones That You Throw.........
		....Dion
1970	#12	Be My Baby ....Andy Kim
▸ 1963	#1	Be My Baby ....Ronettes
▸ 1959	#8	Be My Guest ....Fats Domino
▸ 1972	#36	Be My Lover ....Alice Cooper
▸ 1963	#8	Be True To Your School ....Beach Boys

▸ 1963	#36	Be True To Yourself ....Bobby Vee
1964	#28	Beans In My Ears ....Serendipity Singers
▸ 1967	#7	Beat Goes On...........................Sonny & Cher
1960	#10	Beatnik Fly...........Johnny & The Hurricanes
▸ 1968	#3	Beautiful Morning..............................Rascals
1967	#35	Beautiful People ....Kenny O'Dell
▸ 1967	#27	Beautiful People ....Bobby Vee
▸ 1972	#16	Beautiful Sunday ....Daniel Boone
▸ 1966	#5	Beauty Is Only Skin Deep........Temptations
1964	#7	Because ....Dave Clark Five
▸ 1960	#3	Because They're Young............Duane Eddy
1959	#30	Because You're Young........Jimmie Rodgers
▸ 1962	#18	Beechwood 4-5789 ....Marvelettes
▸ 1973	#20	Been To Canaan ....Carole King
▸ 1958	#4	Beep Beep..Playmates
▸ 1965	#15	Before And After ....Chad & Jeremy
1967	#23	Beg, Borrow And Steal ....Ohio Express
▸ 1967	#12	Beggin'..................................Four Seasons
▸ 1971	#11	Beginnings ....Chicago
▸ 1971	#24	Behind Blue Eyes..Who
▸ 1973	#17	Behind Closed Doors.................Charlie Rich
▸ 1973	#24	Believe In Humanity ....Carole King
1959	#24	Believe Me ....Royal Teens
▸ 1958	#12	Believe What You Say ....Rick Nelson
▸ 1969	#20	Bella Linda ....Grass Roots
▸ 1970	#18	Bells, The ....Originals
1958	#28	Belonging To Someone.................Patti Page
▸ 1972	#2	Ben....................................Michael Jackson
▸ 1968	#3	Bend Me Shape Me ....American Breed
▸ 1967	#8	Bernadette ....Four Tops
1957	#20	Bernadine ....Pat Boone
▸ 1968	#37	Best Of Both Worlds...............................Lulu
▸ 1972	#3	Betcha By Golly, Wow ....Stylistics
▸ 1958	#31	Betty Lou Got A New Pair Of Shoes ....
		....Bobby Freeman
▸ 1960	#7	Beyond The Sea ....Bobby Darin
1955	#10	Bible Tells Me So ....Don Cornell
1955	#10	Bible Tells Me So ....Nick Noble
▸ 1961	#1	Big Bad John ....Jimmy Dean
▸ 1958	#39	Big Bopper's Wedding ....Big Bopper
▸ 1960	#20	Big Boy Pete ....Olympics
▸ 1973	#12	Big City Miss Ruth Ann ....Gallery
1961	#28	Big Cold Wind ....Pat Boone
▸ 1962	#1	Big Girls Don't Cry ....Four Seasons
1958	#32	Big Guitar.................Owen Bradley Quintet
1958	#35	Big Guitar ....Sam "The Man" Taylor
▸ 1959	#2	Big Hunk O' Love ....Elvis Presley
1960	#2	Big Hurt ....Miss Toni Fisher
▸ 1960	#26	Big Iron ....Marty Robbins
▸ 1961	#26	Big John..Shirelles
▸ 1958	#5	Big Man...Four Preps
▸ 1964	#14	Big Man In Town ....Four Seasons
1970	#24	Big Yellow Taxi ....Neighborhood
▸ 1961	#25	Bilbao Song ....Andy Williams
▸ 1973	#36	Billion Dollar Babies.................Alice Cooper
1958	#14	Billy...Kathy Linden
▸ 1966	#33	Billy And Sue .............................B.J. Thomas
▸ 1958	#11	Bimbombey ....Jimmie Rodgers
1964	#31	Bird Dance Beat ....Trashmen
▸ 1958	#2	Bird Dog ....Everly Brothers
1963	#14	Birdland...............................Chubby Checker
1965	#2	Birds And The Bees ....Jewel Akens
▸ 1971	#23	Birds Of A Feather ....
		..............................Paul Revere & The Raiders
1969	#19	Birthday ....Underground Sunshine
1964	#4	Bits And Pieces ....Dave Clark Five
▸ 1973	#30	Bitter Bad....................................Melanie

▸ 1972	#1	Black & White.....................Three Dog Night
▸ 1972	#9	Black Dog ....Led Zeppelin
▸ 1966	#3	Black Is Black................................Los Bravos
▸ 1971	#4	Black Magic Woman........................Santana
▸ 1969	#16	Black Pearl ....
		........Sonny Charles & The Checkmates, Ltd.
▸ 1957	#19	Black Slacks ....
		...................Joe Bennett & The Sparkletones
1959	#36	Blah, Blah, Blah ....Nick Paone
1963	#6	Blame It On The Bossa Nova......................
		....Eydie Gorme
1961	#17	Bless You ....Tony Orlando
▸ 1969	#40	Blessed Is The Rain ....Brooklyn Bridge
▸ 1958	#39	Blob, The ....Five Blobs
▸ 1955	#3	Blossom Fell............................Nat King Cole
▸ 1963	#2	Blowin' In The Wind ....Peter, Paul & Mary
▸ 1966	#11	Blowin' In The Wind ....Stevie Wonder
1970	#14	Blowing Away ....Fifth Dimension
▸ 1960	#13	Blue Angel ....Roy Orbison
▸ 1967	#37	Blue Autumn ....Bobby Goldsboro
▸ 1963	#21	Blue Bayou ....Roy Orbison
▸ 1958	#38	Blue Blue Day ....Don Gibson
▸ 1959	#33	Blue Hawaii ....Billy Vaughn
▸ 1957	#8	Blue Monday ....Fats Domino
▸ 1971	#23	Blue Money ....Van Morrison
▸ 1961	#1	Blue Moon ....Marcels
▸ 1963	#3	Blue On Blue ....Bobby Vinton
▸ 1956	#2	Blue Suede Shoes....................Carl Perkins
▸ 1973	#27	Blue Suede Shoes....................Johnny Rivers
1960	#17	Blue Tango....................Bill Black's Combo
▸ 1963	#1	Blue Velvet ....Bobby Vinton
▸ 1964	#16	Blue Winter....................Connie Francis
▸ 1956	#4	Blueberry Hill ....Fats Domino
▸ 1958	#39	Bluebirds Over The Mountain ....
		....Ersel Hickey
▸ 1967	#33	Blues Theme.......Davie Allan & The Arrows
1959	#7	Bobby Sox To Stockings......Frankie Avalon
1962	#2	Bobby's Girl ....Marcie Blane
▸ 1961	#2	Boll Weevil Song ....Brook Benton
1957	#28	Bon Voyage ....Janice Harper
▸ 1961	#27	Bonanza ....Al Caiola
1959	#16	Bongo Rock ....Preston Epps
1962	#30	Bongo Stomp ....Little Joey & The Flips
▸ 1960	#20	Bonnie Came Back ....Duane Eddy
▸ 1957	#17	Bony Moronie ....Larry Williams
▸ 1973	#40	Boo, Boo, Don't 'Cha Be Blue ....
		....Tommy James
1967	#9	Boogaloo Down Broadway ....
		....Fantastic Johnny C
▸ 1973	#6	Boogie Woogie Bugle Boy ....Bette Midler
▸ 1958	#7	Book Of Love ....Monotones
▸ 1965	#35	Boom Boom ....Animals)
1971	#24	Booty Butt ....Ray Charles
1970	#23	Border Song (Holy Moses)......................
		....Aretha Franklin
1966	#12	Born A Woman ....Sandy Posey
1968	#36	Born Free ....Hesitations
▸ 1966	#7	Born Free ....Roger Williams
▸ 1968	#2	Born To Be Wild.......................Steppenwolf
▸ 1956	#8	Born To Be With You ....Chordettes
▸ 1962	#39	Born To Lose ....Ray Charles
▸ 1971	#18	Born To Wander.......................Rare Earth
▸ 1958	#10	Born Too Late ....Poni Tails
1963	#30	Boss Guitar ....Duane Eddy
▸ 1963	#8	Bossa Nova Baby....................Elvis Presley
▸ 1968	#8	Both Sides Now ....Judy Collins
▸ 1968	#9	Bottle Of Wine ....Fireballs

407

409

▸ 1971 #36 D.O.A...Bloodrock
▸ 1968 #10 D.W. Washburn.................................Monkees
▸ 1973 #16 D'Yer Mak'er ....Led Zeppelin
▸ 1963 #4 Da Doo Ron Ron................................Crystals
▸ 1973 #15 Daddy Could Swear, I Declare......................
..............................Gladys Knight & The Pips
▸ 1972 #1 Daddy Don't You Walk So Fast ....
....Wayne Newton
▸ 1961 #3 Daddy's Home...........Shep & The Limelites
▸ 1973 #7 Daddy's Home.................Jermaine Jackson
1969 #33 Daddy's Little Man......................O.C. Smith
1956 #10 Daddy-O....................................Bonnie Lou
1956 #10 Daddy-O................................Fontane Sisters
▸ 1973 #10 Daisy A Day.............................Jud Strunk
1972 #39 Daisy Mae...
..................Hamilton, Joe Frank, & Reynolds
1964 #15 Daisy Petal Pickin'.................................
........................Jimmy Gilmer & The Fireballs
▸ 1961 #25 Dance By The Light Of The Moon................
....Olympics
▸ 1964 #10 Dance Dance Dance....................Beach Boys
1958 #27 Dance Everyone Dance ....Betty Madigan
▸ 1961 #12 Dance On Little Girl......................Paul Anka
1961 #16 Dance The Mess Around ....Chubby Checker
▸ 1957 #36 Dance To The Bop ....
..................Gene Vincent & His Blue Caps
▸ 1968 #8 Dance To The Music ....
..............................Sly & The Family Stone
▸ 1959 #10 Dance With Me ....Drifters
1955 #3 Dance With Me Henry (Wallflower).............
....Georgia Gibbs
▸ 1962 #11 (Dance With The) Guitar Man.....................
....Duane Eddy
1962 #14 Dancin' Party ....Chubby Checker
▸ 1968 #36 Dancing Bear ....Mama's & Papa's
1973 #10 Dancing In The Moonlight ....King Harvest
▸ 1964 #4 Dancing In The Street.............................
..............................Martha & The Vandellas
▸ 1967 #6 Dandelion..............................Rolling Stones
▸ 1966 #8 Dandy ....Herman's Hermits
▸ 1964 #7 Dang Me............................Roger Miller
▸ 1966 #15 Dangling Conversation ....
..............................Simon & Garfunkel
▸ 1973 #2 Daniel......................................Elton John
▸ 1963 #12 Danke Shoen ....Wayne Newton
▸ 1959 #7 Danny Boy...........................Conway Twitty
▸ 1973 #6 Danny's Song...........................Anne Murray
1957 #5 Dark Moon ....Bonnie Guitar
1957 #5 Dark Moon ....Gale Storm
▸ 1968 #10 Darlin'.....................................Beach Boys
▸ 1967 #15 Darling Be Home Soon ......Lovin' Spoonful
▸ 1955 #7 Darling Je Vous Aime Beaucoup ....
....Nat King Cole

1960 #35 Darling Lorraine ....Knockouts
1970 #10 Daughter Of Darkness.................Tom Jones
▸ 1964 #3 Dawn (Go Away).....................Four Seasons
▸ 1965 #22 Dawn Of Correction ....Spokesmen
1972 #3 Day After Day ....Badfinger
▸ 1972 #9 Day By Day ....Godspell
1966 #27 Day For Decision ....Johnny Sea
▸ 1972 #15 Day I Found Myself.....................Honeycone
▸ 1969 #20 Day Is Done ....Peter, Paul & Mary
1958 #17 Day The Rains Came ....
...............Raymond Lefevre & His Orchestra
▸ 1958 #17 Day The Rains Came ....Jane Morgan
▸ 1966 #10 Day Tripper ....Beatles
▸ 1966 #1 Daydream ....Lovin' Spoonful
▸ 1967 #1 Daydream Believer ....Monkees
▸ 1972 #5 Daydreaming ....Aretha Franklin
1969 #24 Days Of Sand And Shovels ...Bobby Vinton
▸ 1963 #29 Days Of Wine And Roses.....Andy Williams
▸ 1963 #29 Days Of Wine And Roses .....Henry Mancini
▸ 1967 #31 Dead End Street ....Lou Rawls
▸ 1964 #9 Dead Man's Curve......................Jan & Dean
▸ 1973 #12 Dead Skunk ....Loudon Wainwright III
1965 #15 Dear Heart.................................Jack Jones
▸ 1965 #15 Dear Heart...........................Andy Williams
▸ 1962 #21 Dear Ivan...................................Jimmy Dean
▸ 1962 #6 Dear Lady Twist................Gary U.S. Bonds
▸ 1962 #14 Dear Lonely Hearts ....Nat King Cole
1962 #11 Dear One.............................Larry Finnegan
▸ 1957 #39 Dearest...................................Mickey & Sylvia
▸ 1964 #33 Death Of An Angel......................Kingsmen
1959 #4 Deck Of Cards....................Wink Martindale
1958 #11 Dede Dinah ....Frankie Avalon
▸ 1961 #3 Dedicated To The One I Love ....Shirelles
▸ 1967 #2 Dedicated To The One I Love ....
..............................Mama's & Papa's
1957 #28 Deep Purple .....Billy Ward & His Dominoes
▸ 1963 #1 Deep Purple...Nino Tempo & April Stevens
▸ 1970 #21 Deeper & Deeper ....Freda Payne
1960 #17 Deleware ....Perry Como
▸ 1958 #36 Delicious ....Jim Backus & Friend
▸ 1968 #20 Delilah ....Tom Jones
▸ 1973 #1 Delta Dawn...........................Helen Reddy
▸ 1963 #13 Denise....................Randy & The Rainbows
▸ 1962 #11 Desafinado ....Stan Getz & Charlie Byrd
▸ 1963 #36 Desert Pete...........................Kingston Trio
1971 #11 Desiderata ....Les Crane
▸ 1963 #13 Detroit City.............................Bobby Bare
▸ 1967 #22 Detroit City.............................Tom Jones
1960 #18 Devil Or Angel ....Hollywood Flames
▸ 1960 #4 Devil Or Angel ....Bobby Vee
▸ 1966 #4 Devil With A Blue Dress On & Good Golly
Miss Molly...
...............Mitch Ryder & The Detroit Wheels
▸ 1962 #16 Devil Woman ....Marty Robbins
▸ 1958 #11 Devoted To You ....Everly Brothers
▸ 1972 #17 Dialogue (Part 1 & 2)........................Chicago
▸ 1973 #8 Diamond Girl ....Seals & Crofts
▸ 1960 #17 Diamonds And Pearls ....Paradons
▸ 1957 #2 Diana ....Paul Anka
▸ 1964 #10 Diane ....Bachelors
▸ 1972 #15 Diary ....Bread
▸ 1959 #22 Diary, The..........................Neil Sedaka
▸ 1966 #4 Did You Ever Have To Make Up Your Mind?
....Lovin' Spoonful
1969 #30 Did You See Her Eyes....................Illusion

1960 #19 Don't Throw Away All Those Teardrops .....
....Frankie Avalon
▸ 1964 #13 Don't Throw Your Love Away .....Searchers
1969 #40 Don't Touch Me ....Bettye Swann
1970 #40 Don't Try To Lay No Boogie Woogie On
The "King Of Rock & Roll" ....Crow
▸ 1971 #39 Don't Wanna Live Inside Myself.....Bee Gees
▸ 1961 #3 Don't Worry ....Marty Robbins
▸ 1964 #26 Don't Worry Baby......................Beach Boys
▸ 1971 #24 (Don't Worry) If There's A Hell Below
We're All Going To Go ....Curtis Mayfield
▸ 1967 #6 Don't You Care ....Buckinghams
▸ 1958 #12 Don't You Just Know It.................................
.............Huey "Piano" Smith & The Clowns
▸ 1959 #1 Don't You Know.........................Della Reese
▸ 1959 #2 Donna ....Ritchie Valens
▸ 1963 #6 Donna The Prima Donna......................Dion
1964 #8 Door Is Still Open To My Heart ....
....Dean Martin
▸ 1971 #27 Double Barrel ....Dave & Ansil Collins
▸ 1971 #9 Double Lovin'................................Osmonds
▸ 1966 #18 Double Shot (Of My Baby's Love) ....
................................Swingin' Medallions
▸ 1968 #25 Down At Lulu's.......................Ohio Express
1963 #13 (Down At) Papa Joe's ....Dixiebelles
▸ 1972 #3 Down By The Lazy River ....Osmonds
▸ 1960 #15 Down By The Station ....Four Preps
▸ 1965 #6 Down In The Boondocks ......Billy Joe Royal
▸ 1969 #10 Down On The Corner ....
......................Creedence Clearwater Revival
▸ 1958 #24 Down The Aisle Of Love ....Quin-Tones
1963 #39 Down The Aisle (Wedding Song)...................
....................Patti La Belle & The Blue Belles
1960 #31 Down Yonder......Johnny & The Hurricanes
▸ 1965 #1 Downtown ....Petula Clark
▸ 1963 #10 Drag City................................Jan & Dean
▸ 1971 #2 Draggin' The Line ....Tommy James
▸ 1968 #10 Dream A Little Dream Of Me.....Mama Cass
▸ 1962 #9 Dream Baby (How Long Must I Dream).......
....Roy Orbison
▸ 1971 #24 Dream Baby (How Long Must I Dream).......
....Glen Campbell
▸ 1959 #3 Dream Lover ....Bobby Darin
▸ 1965 #29 Dream On Little Dreamer ....Perry Como
▸ 1960 #8 Dreamin'...............................Johnny Burnette
▸ 1968 #38 Dreams Of The Everyday Housewife ....
....Glen Campbell
▸ 1973 #19 Dreidel ....Don McLean
▸ 1973 #8 Drift Away...................................Dobie Gray
1973 #25 Drinking Wine Spo-Dee-O'Dee ....
....Jerry Lee Lewis
▸ 1963 #5 Drip Drop ....Dion
1963 #34 Drownin' My Sorrows ....Connie Francis
▸ 1972 #8 Drowning In The Sea Of Love .....Joe Simon
▸ 1971 #22 Drum, The ....Bobby Sherman
1967 #22 Dry Your Eyes ....Brenda & The Tabulations
▸ 1966 #13 Duck, The ....Jackie Lee
▸ 1973 #1 Dueling Banjos...
................................Eric Weissberg & Steve Mandell
▸ 1962 #1 Duke Of Earl.......................Gene Chandler
▸ 1966 #32 Dum-De-Da.............................Bobby Vinton
▸ 1961 #4 Dum Dum ....Brenda Lee
▸ 1956 #9 Dungaree Doll ....Eddie Fisher
1960 #36 Dutchman's Gold................Walter Brennan

1958 #25 Early In The Morning ....Buddy Holly
▸ 1958 #25 Early In The Morning ....Rinky Dinks
▸ 1970 #10 Early In The Morning.................Vanity Fare
1955 #3 Earth Angel ....Crew-Cuts
▸ 1969 #30 Earth Angel ....Vogues
▸ 1955 #3 Earth Angel (Will You Be Mine).....Penguins
1956 #31 Earthbound ....Sammy Davis Jr.
▸ 1963 #1 Easier Said Than Done......................Essex
1967 #15 East West ....Herman's Hermits
▸ 1970 #7 Easy Come, Easy Go ....Bobby Sherman
▸ 1972 #32 Easy Livin' ....Uriah Heep
1971 #12 Easy Loving ....Freddie Hart
▸ 1969 #3 Easy To Be Hard ....Three Dog Night
1964 #27 Ebb Tide...................................Lenny Welch
▸ 1960 #38 Ebb Tide...................................Platters
▸ 1966 #4 Ebb Tide ....Righteous Brothers
▸ 1961 #8 Ebony Eyes..........................Everly Brothers
▸ 1969 #33 Echo Park ....Keith Barbour
1973 #10 Ecstasy ....Ohio Players
▸ 1965 #1 Eight Days A Week............................Beatles
▸ 1966 #12 Eight Miles High ....Byrds
▸ 1971 #21 Eighteen ....Alice Cooper
▸ 1963 #12 18 Yellow Roses ....Bobby Darin
1965 #39 81, The..........................Candy & The Kisses
▸ 1970 #11 El Condor Pasa ....Simon & Garfunkel
▸ 1960 #2 El Paso...................................Marty Robbins
1958 #21 El Rancho Rock ....Champs
1963 #18 El Watusi...............................Ray Barretto
▸ 1966 #12 Eleanor Rigby ....Beatles
▸ 1968 #39 Eleanor Rigby ....Ray Charles
▸ 1969 #23 Eleanor Rigby ....Aretha Franklin
▸ 1972 #18 Elected.....................................Alice Cooper
▸ 1968 #5 Elenore ....Turtles
▸ 1969 #8 Eli's Coming ....Three Dog Night
1966 #7 Elusive Butterfly ....Bob Lind
▸ 1961 #6 Emotions ....Brenda Lee
▸ 1957 #17 Empty Arms ....Ivory Joe Hunter
▸ 1957 #17 Empty Arms..........................Teresa Brewer
▸ 1959 #12 Enchanted ....Platters
1958 #12 Enchanted Island ....Four Lads
▸ 1959 #16 Enchanted Sea ....Islanders
▸ 1959 #39 Enchanted Sea ....Martin Denny
1958 #10 End, The..................................Earl Grant
▸ 1968 #11 End Of Our Road ....
................................Gladys Knight & The Pips
▸ 1970 #28 End Of Our Road ....Marvin Gaye
▸ 1963 #2 End Of The World ....Skeeter Davis
1956 #36 Endless ....McGuire Sisters
1958 #10 Endless Sleep ....Jody Reynolds
▸ 1959 #11 Endlessly..................................Brook Benton
▸ 1965 #9 Engine Engine #9 ....Roger Miller
▸ 1970 #14 Engine Number 9....................Wilson Pickett

413

415

1956	#15	Garden Of Eden..............................Joe Valino
▸ 1972	#3	Garden Party ....Rick Nelson
1958	#25	Gee, But It's Lonely......................Pat Boone
1960	#37	Gee Whiz ....Bobby Day
1961	#33	Gee Whiz ....Innocents
▸ 1961	#9	Gee Whiz ....Carla Thomas
1972	#30	George Jackson ....Bob Dylan
▸ 1960	#3	Georgia On My Mind ....Ray Charles
▸ 1967	#1	Georgy Girl ....Seekers
▸ 1958	#1	Get A Job ....Silhouettes
▸ 1969	#1	Get Back ....Beatles
▸ 1973	#4	Get Down ....Gilbert O'Sullivan
▸ 1971	#22	Get It On ....Chase
▸ 1973	#24	Get It Together ....Jackson Five
▸ 1967	#29	Get It Together (Part 1) ....James Brown
▸ 1965	#1	Get Off My Cloud ....Rolling Stones
▸ 1972	#10	Get On The Good Foot (Part 1) ....
		....James Brown
▸ 1967	#20	Get On Up.....................................Esquires
▸ 1968	#38	Get Out Now ....
		................Tommy James & The Shondells
1966	#38	Get Out Of My Life, Woman........Lee Dorsey
▸ 1966	#29	Get Ready.................................Temptations
▸ 1970	#2	Get Ready.................................Rare Earth
1965	#31	Get Together ....We Five
▸ 1969	#4	Get Together ....Youngbloods
▸ 1971	#35	Get Up, Get Into It, Get Involved ....
		....James Brown
▸ 1970	#17	Get Up (I Feel Like Being A) Sex Machine
		(Part 1) ....James Brown
▸ 1967	#14	Gettin' Together ....
		................Tommy James & The Shondells
▸ 1973	#24	Ghetto Child ....Spinners
1961	#25	(Ghost) Riders In The Sky ....Ramrods
1956	#35	Ghost Town ....Don Cherry
1959	#32	Gidget ....James Darren
▸ 1970	#7	Gimme Dat Ding ....Pipkins
▸ 1969	#6	Gimme Gimme Good Lovin' ....
		......................................Crazy Elephant
▸ 1967	#7	Gimme Little Sign ....Brenton Wood
▸ 1967	#5	Gimme Some Lovin' ....
		................................Spencer Davis Group
▸ 1962	#8	Gina ....Johnny Mathis
1958	#17	Ginger Bread ....Frankie Avalon
1962	#28	Ginny Come Lately.................Brian Hyland
▸ 1965	#27	Girl Come Running ....Four Seasons
1965	#35	Girl Don't Come ....Sandie Shaw
▸ 1964	#5	Girl From Ipanema ....
		........................Stan Getz & Astrud Gilberto
▸ 1969	#28	Girl I'll Never Know (Angels Never Fly This
		Low) ....Frankie Valli
▸ 1966	#24	Girl In Love....................................Outsiders
▸ 1967	#8	Girl Like You ....Rascals
1961	#27	Girl Of My Best Friend ....Ral Donner
1959	#31	Girl On Page 44 ....Four Lads
1968	#5	Girl Watcher ....O'Kaysions
▸ 1964	#27	Girl (Why You Wanna Make Me Blue)..........
		....Temptations
1957	#22	Girl With The Golden Braids.....Perry Como
▸ 1967	#9	Girl, You'll Be A Woman Soon...............
		....Neil Diamond
1962	#20	(Girls, Girls, Girls) Made To Love ....
		....Eddie Hodges
▸ 1967	#35	Girls In Love.....Gary Lewis & The Playboys
▸ 1969	#7	Gitarzan..................................Ray Stevens
▸ 1968	#27	Give A Damn..............Spanky & Our Gang
▸ 1965	#15	Give Him A Great Big Kiss ....Shangri-Las

1972	#38	Give Ireland Back To The Irish ....
		....Paul McCartney
▸ 1973	#15	Give It To Me ....J. Geils Band
▸ 1969	#24	Give It Up Or Turn It A Loose ....
		....James Brown
▸ 1970	#9	Give Me Just A Little More Time ....
		..............................Chairmen Of The Board
▸ 1973	#1	Give Me Love (Give Me Peace On Earth)......
		....George Harrison
1973	#18	Give Me Your Love.................Barbara Mason
▸ 1969	#11	Give Peace A Chance...............John Lennon
1956	#30	Give Us This Day ....Joni James
1965	#33	Give Us Your Blessings............Shangri-Las
▸ 1973	#20	Give Your Baby A Standing Ovation...........
		....Dells
1964	#5	Glad All Over.....................Dave Clark Five
▸ 1967	#23	Glad To Be Unhappy.........Mama's & Papa's
1956	#18	Glendora ....Perry Como
▸ 1966	#7	Gloria............................Shadows Of Knight
▸ 1972	#22	Glory Bound ....Grass Roots
▸ 1966	#30	Go Ahead And Cry........Righteous Brothers
▸ 1972	#4	Go All The Way........................Raspberries
1963	#1	Go Away Little Girl ....Steve Lawrence
1966	#13	Go Away Little Girl ....Happenings
▸ 1971	#1	Go Away Little Girl ....Donny Osmond
▸ 1970	#30	Go Back.............................Crabby Appleton
▸ 1971	#21	Go Down Gamblin'....Blood, Sweat & Tears
▸ 1960	#7	Go, Jimmy, Go ....Jimmy Clanton
▸ 1965	#6	Go Now!.................................Moody Blues
1962	#35	Go On Home ....Patti Page
1967	#16	Go Where You Wanna Go ....
		....Fifth Dimension
▸ 1959	#36	God Bless America.................Connie Francis
1961	#31	God, Country And My Baby ....
		....Johnny Burnette
1970	#14	God, Love And Rock & Roll........................
		...............................Teegarden & Van Winkle
▸ 1966	#38	God Only Knows ....Beach Boys
▸ 1973	#21	Goin' Home ....Osmonds
▸ 1964	#5	Goin' Out Of My Head ....
		...................Little Anthony & The Imperials
▸ 1968	#7	Goin' Out Of My Head/Can't Take My Eyes
		Off You ....Lettermen
1957	#24	Goin' Steady ....Tommy Sands
▸ 1964	#30	Going Going Gone...................Brook Benton
▸ 1969	#23	Going In Circles ....Friends Of Distinction
▸ 1966	#10	Going To A Go-Go......................Miracles
▸ 1969	#9	Going Up The Country............Canned Heat
▸ 1965	#7	Goldfinger..............................Shirley Bassey
1972	#26	Gone......................................Joey Heatherton
▸ 1957	#6	Gone...Ferlin Husky
▸ 1964	#33	Gone, Gone, Gone................Everly Brothers
1957	#24	Gonna Find Me A Bluebird ....
		....Marvin Rainwater
1956	#13	Gonna Get Along Without You Now ....
		...............................Patience & Prudence
1964	#35	Gonna Get Along Without You Now ....
		....Skeeter Davis
1964	#35	Gonna Get Along Without You Now ....
		....Tracey Dey
1960	#27	Gonzo...................................James Booker
▸ 1969	#28	Goo Goo Barabajagal ....
		..........................Donovan & The Jeff Beck Group
▸ 1958	#18	Good Golly Miss Molly ....Little Richard
▸ 1963	#25	Good Life ....Tony Bennett
▸ 1966	#1	Good Lovin' ....Rascals
▸ 1962	#1	Good Luck Charm ....Elvis Presley

417

▸ 1967	#34	Happenings Ten Years Time Ago	
		....Yardbirds	
▸ 1972	#8	Happiest Girl In The Whole U.S.A.	
		....Donna Fargo	
1956	#30	Happiness Street ....Georgia Gibbs	
1956	#30	Happiness Street (Corner Sunshine Square)	
		....Tony Bennett	
1967	#31	Happy ....Sunshine Company	
▸ 1972	#14	Happy..............................Rolling Stones	
1959	#34	Happy Anniversary....................Four Lads	
1959	#34	Happy Anniversary..................Jane Morgan	
1961	#30	Happy Birthday Blues.............Kathy Young	
▸ 1961	#9	Happy Birthday Sweet Sixteen.....................	
		....Neil Sedaka	
▸ 1961	#39	Happy Days.............................Marv Johnson	
1960	#11	Happy-Go-Lucky-Me...................Paul Evans	
▸ 1957	#7	Happy, Happy Birthday Baby	
		....Tune Weavers	
▸ 1969	#26	Happy Heart...........................Andy Williams	
▸ 1967	#13	Happy Jack ....Who	
▸ 1959	#1	Happy Organ ....Dave "Baby" Cortez	
1960	#31	Happy Reindeer	
		................................Dancer, Prancer & Nervous	
▸ 1968	#24	Happy Song (Dum-Dum)........Otis Redding	
1966	#30	Happy Summer Days.............Ronnie Dove	
▸ 1967	#1	Happy Together...............................Turtles	
1956	#8	Happy Whistler ....Don Robertson	
▸ 1972	#36	Happy Xmas (War Is Over) ......John Lennon	
▸ 1960	#7	Harbor Lights......................................Platters	
▸ 1964	#1	Hard Day's Night.......................Beatles	
▸ 1966	#29	Hard Day's Night ....Ramsey Lewis Trio	
▸ 1958	#3	Hard Headed Woman...............Elvis Presley	
1955	#3	Hard To Get ....Gisele MacKenzie	
1957	#28	Harem Dance............Armenian Jazz Sextet	
1960	#28	Harlem Nocturne ....Viscounts	
▸ 1964	#36	Harlem Shuffle...........................Bob & Earl	
▸ 1968	#1	Harper Valley P.T.A. ....Jeannie C. Riley	
▸ 1963	#19	Harry The Hairy Ape ....Ray Stevens	
▸ 1961	#2	Hats Off To Larry ....Del Shannon	
▸ 1964	#11	Haunted House ....Jumpin Gene Simmons	
▸ 1962	#31	Have A Good Time ....Sue Thompson	
▸ 1964	#4	Have I The Right.....................Honeycombs	
▸ 1957	#21	Have I Told You That I Love You	
		....Rick Nelson	
▸ 1971	#3	Have You Ever Seen The Rain	
		..................Creedence Clearwater Revival	
▸ 1963	#19	Have You Heard ....Duprees	
▸ 1965	#29	Have You Looked Into Your Heart...............	
		....Jerry Vale	
▸ 1971	#5	Have You Seen Her ....Chi-Lites	
▸ 1966	#4	Have You Seen Your Mother, Baby,	
		Standing In The Shadow? ....Rolling Stones	
▸ 1962	#16	Having A Party...........................Sam Cooke	
▸ 1969	#6	Hawaii Five-O ....Ventures	
1965	#34	Hawaii Tattoo ....Waikikis	
▸ 1959	#6	Hawaiian Wedding Song.....Andy Williams	
▸ 1966	#17	Hazy Shade Of Winter.................................	
		................................Simon & Garfunkel	
1955	#4	He ....Al Hibbler	
▸ 1955	#4	He ....McGuire Sisters	
▸ 1966	#15	He ....Righteous Brothers	
▸ 1970	#17	He Ain't Heavy, He's My Brother	
		....Neil Diamond	
▸ 1970	#8	He Ain't Heavy, He's My Brother .....Hollies	
▸ 1960	#3	He Will Break Your Heart..........Jerry Butler	
▸ 1960	#2	He'll Have To Go.....................Jim Reeves	
▸ 1960	#5	He'll Have To Stay...................Jeanne Black	

▸ 1962	#2	He's A Rebel....................................Crystals	
▸ 1958	#1	He's Got The Whole World (In His Hands)	
		....Laurie London	
▸ 1957	#31	He's Mine ....Platters	
▸ 1961	#22	(He's My) Dreamboat ....Connie Francis	
▸ 1963	#1	He's So Fine ....Chiffons	
▸ 1963	#14	He's Sure The Boy I Love ....Crystals	
▸ 1972	#22	Hearsay ....Soul Children	
1955	#10	Heart ....Four Aces	
▸ 1955	#10	Heart...............................Eddie Fisher	
▸ 1961	#16	Heart And Soul ....Cleftones	
▸ 1961	#16	Heart And Soul........................Jan & Dean	
▸ 1965	#12	Heart Full Of Soul ....Yardbirds	
▸ 1962	#21	Heart In Hand ....Brenda Lee	
▸ 1972	#1	Heart Of Gold ....Neil Young	
▸ 1965	#16	Heart Of Stone ....Rolling Stones	
▸ 1961	#16	Heartaches....................................Marcels	
1959	#1	Heartaches By The Number......Guy Mitchell	
1965	#32	Heartaches By The Number	
		................................Johnny Tillotson	
▸ 1973	#1	Heartbeat - It's A Lovebeat........................	
		................................De Franco Family	
▸ 1956	#1	Heartbreak Hotel ....Elvis Presley	
1960	#27	Heartbreak (It's Hurtin' Me) ......Jon Thomas	
1960	#27	Heartbreak (It's Hurtin' Me)	
		................................Little Willie John	
▸ 1972	#26	Heartbroken Bopper ....Guess Who	
1961	#17	Hearts Of Stone ....Bill Black's Combo	
▸ 1955	#1	Hearts Of Stone ....Fontane Sisters	
▸ 1973	#33	Hearts Of Stone............Blue Ridge Rangers	
▸ 1963	#4	Heat Wave ....Martha & The Vandellas	
1969	#14	Heather Honey ....Tommy Roe	
▸ 1969	#17	Heaven ....Rascals	
▸ 1970	#9	Heaven Help Us All ....Stevie Wonder	
▸ 1969	#13	Heaven Knows ....Grass Roots	
▸ 1971	#24	Heavy Makes You Happy......Staple Singers	
▸ 1970	#21	Heed The Call	
		................Kenny Rogers & The First Edition	
▸ 1964	#1	Hello Dolly ....Louis Armstrong	
▸ 1967	#1	Hello Goodbye............................Beatles	
▸ 1963	#33	Hello Heartache, Goodbye Love	
		................................Little Peggy March	
▸ 1967	#25	Hello Hello ....Sopwith Camel	
▸ 1973	#25	Hello Hurray ....Alice Cooper	
▸ 1968	#1	Hello I Love You ....Doors	
▸ 1973	#2	Hello It's Me........................Todd Rundgren	
▸ 1961	#9	Hello Mary Lou ....Rick Nelson	
▸ 1963	#1	Hello Muddah, Hello Fadduh! (A Letter	
		From Camp) ....Allan Sherman	
▸ 1963	#4	Hello Stranger ....Barbara Lewis	
▸ 1961	#10	Hello Walls ....Faron Young	
1960	#24	Hello Young Lovers....................Paul Anka	
▸ 1965	#1	Help ....Beatles	
▸ 1966	#40	Help Me Girl ....Outsiders	
▸ 1967	#33	Help Me Girl ....Animals	
▸ 1971	#9	Help Me Make It Through The Night	
		................................Sammi Smith	
▸ 1972	#37	Help Me Make It Through The Night	
		................Gladys Knight & The Pips	
▸ 1965	#1	Help Me Rhonda...................Beach Boys	
▸ 1968	#31	Help Yourself.............................Tom Jones	
▸ 1958	#38	Helpless...Platters	
1962	#9	Her Royal Majesty ....James Darren	
▸ 1967	#11	Here Comes My Baby ....Tremeloes	
▸ 1959	#24	Here Comes Summer ....Jerry Keller	

▸ 1971	#8	Here Comes That Rainy Day Feeling Again ....Fortunes
1968	#23	Here Comes The Judge ....Pigmeat Markham
▸ 1968	#10	Here Comes The Judge.............Shorty Long
▸ 1965	#18	Here Comes The Night ....Them
▸ 1971	#15	Here Comes The Sun ....Richie Havens
▸ 1973	#10	Here I Am (Come And Take Me) ....Al Green
1965	#37	Here It Comes Again ....Fortunes
▸ 1967	#18	Here We Go Again ....Ray Charles
▸ 1967	#8	Heroes And Villains ....Beach Boys
▸ 1962	#1	Hey! Baby...........................Bruce Channel
▸ 1969	#32	Hey! Baby..........................Jose Feliciano
▸ 1967	#5	Hey Baby (They're Playing Our Song)......... ....Buckinghams
▸ 1972	#24	Hey Big Brother ....Rare Earth
1964	#18	Hey, Bobba Needle ....Chubby Checker
▸ 1972	#9	Hey Girl ....Donny Osmond
▸ 1963	#10	Hey, Girl ....Freddie Scott
▸ 1973	#27	Hey Girl (I Like Your Style)......Tempations
▸ 1964	#32	Hey Harmonica Man.............Stevie Wonder
▸ 1956	#8	Hey! Jealous Lover ....Frank Sinatra
▸ 1969	#40	Hey Joe...............................Wilson Pickett
▸ 1968	#1	Hey Jude ....Beatles
▸ 1969	#20	Hey Jude ....Wilson Pickett
▸ 1970	#21	Hey Lawdy Mama....................Steppenwolf
1967	#35	Hey, Leroy, Your Mama's Callin' You ....Jimmy Castor Bunch
▸ 1962	#37	Hey Let's Twist.. ....Joey Dee & The Starlighters
▸ 1964	#4	Hey Little Cobra ....Rip Chords
▸ 1959	#20	Hey Little Girl.............................Dee Clark
▸ 1963	#17	Hey Little Girl..........................Major Lance
1960	#40	Hey Little One ....Dorsey Burnette
▸ 1970	#23	Hey, Mister Sun ....Bobby Sherman
▸ 1963	#1	Hey Paula ....Paul & Paula
1963	#34	Hey There Lonely Boy.................................... ....Ruby & The Romantics
▸ 1970	#2	Hey There Lonely Girl ....Eddie Holman
▸ 1968	#24	Hey, Western Union Man ....Jerry Butler
▸ 1970	#9	Hi-De-Ho ....Blood, Sweat & Tears
▸ 1964	#10	Hi-Heel Sneakers ....Tommy Tucker
▸ 1968	#13	Hi-Heel Sneakers....................Jose Feliciano
▸ 1973	#6	Hi Hi Hi ....Paul McCartney
1962	#39	Hide & Go Seek (Part 1).............Bunker Hill
▸ 1962	#26	Hide 'Nor Hair ....Ray Charles
1958	#19	Hideaway ....Four Esquires
▸ 1959	#22	High Hopes ....Frank Sinatra
▸ 1958	#20	High School Confidential ....Jerry Lee Lewis
1959	#30	High School U.S.A. ....Tommy Facenda
1958	#21	High Sign ....Diamonds
▸ 1971	#29	High Time We Went....................Joe Cocker
▸ 1973	#1	Higher Ground................Stevie Wonder
▸ 1967	#5	Him Or Me - What's It Gonna Be? ....Paul Revere & The Raiders
▸ 1968	#28	Hip City (Part 2) ....Jr. Walker & The All Stars
▸ 1967	#36	Hip Hug-Her..........Booker T & The MG's
▸ 1964	#23	Hippy Hippy Shake ....Swinging Blue Jeans
1966	#40	History Repeats Itself..........Buddy Starcher
▸ 1962	#36	Hit Record..............................Brook Benton
▸ 1961	#1	Hit The Road Jack.....................Ray Charles
1968	#37	Hitch It To The Horse .....Fantastic Johnny C
▸ 1970	#4	Hitchin' A Ride ....Vanity Fare
▸ 1973	#4	Hocus Pocus ....Focus
▸ 1972	#15	Hold Her Tight ....Osmonds
▸ 1965	#12	Hold Me, Thrill Me, Kiss Me ....Mel Carter

1968	#7	Hold Me Tight............................Johnny Nash
1970	#29	Hold On...Rascals
▸ 1966	#16	Hold On! I'm Comin'.................Sam & Dave
▸ 1965	#6	Hold What You've Got ....Joe Tex
▸ 1972	#5	Hold Your Head Up.........................Argent
1965	#29	Hole In The Wall ....Packers
▸ 1967	#12	Holiday ....Bee Gees
▸ 1969	#4	Holly Holy ....Neil Diamond
▸ 1961	#26	Hollywood...............................Connie Francis
1966	#29	Holy Cow ....Lee Dorsey
▸ 1967	#35	Homburg..............................Procol Harum
1965	#31	Home Of The Brave......................Jody Miller
▸ 1966	#5	Homeward Bound........Simon & Garfunkel
1960	#37	Honest I Do..................................Innocents
▸ 1968	#1	Honey...............................Bobby Goldsboro
▸ 1967	#12	Honey Chile ....Martha & The Vandellas
▸ 1970	#11	Honey Come Back.............Glen Campbell
1955	#5	Honey-Babe ....Art Mooney
▸ 1957	#1	Honeycomb ....Jimmie Rodgers
▸ 1972	#18	Honky Cat.......................................Elton John
1972	#38	Honky Tonk (Part 1)................James Brown
1956	#2	Honky Tonk (Part 1 & 2).........Bill Doggett
▸ 1969	#1	Honky Tonk Women ....Rolling Stones
▸ 1963	#10	Honolulu Lulu.......................Jan & Dean
1961	#14	Hoochi Coochi Coo.................................... ....Hank Ballard & The Midnighters
1964	#16	Hooka Tooka.............Chubby Checker
▸ 1969	#5	Hooked On A Feeling ................B.J. Thomas
1958	#37	Hoola Hoop Song ....Georgia Gibbs
1966	#6	Hooray For Hazel.....................Tommy Roe
1963	#39	Hootenanny ....Glencoves
1963	#17	Hopeless ....Andy Williams
▸ 1968	#4	Horse, The.............Cliff Nobles & Company
▸ 1972	#1	Horse With No Name ....America
▸ 1956	#1	Hot Diggity (Dog Ziggity Boom)................... ....Perry Como
▸ 1969	#6	Hot Fun In The Summertime ....Sly & The Family Stone
▸ 1971	#10	Hot Pants (She Got To Use What She Got, To Get What She Wants).........James Brown
▸ 1963	#13	Hot Pastrami..................................Dartells
▸ 1963	#40	Hot Pastrami With Mashed Potatoes (Part 1).. ....Joey Dee & The Starlighters
1960	#25	Hot Rod Lincoln.. ....Charlie Ryan & The Timberline Riders
1960	#25	Hot Rod Lincoln.....................Johnny Bond
▸ 1972	#7	Hot Rod Lincoln...........Commander Cody
▸ 1969	#16	Hot Smoke & Sasafrass ....Bubble Puppy
▸ 1963	#6	Hotel Happiness ....Brook Benton
▸ 1956	#1	Hound Dog ....Elvis Presley
1960	#11	Hound Dog Man..............................Fabian
▸ 1971	#38	House At Pooh Corner ....Nitty Gritty Dirt Band
1970	#6	House Of The Rising Sun ....Frijid Pink
▸ 1964	#1	House Of The Rising Sun................Animals
▸ 1968	#9	House That Jack Built ....Aretha Franklin
1956	#20	House With Love In It...................Four Lads
1965	#24	Houston ....Dean Martin
1960	#31	How About That ....Dee Clark
1972	#15	How Can I Be Sure................David Cassidy
▸ 1967	#2	How Can I Be Sure ....Rascals
▸ 1970	#27	How Can I Forget ....Marvin Gaye
▸ 1973	#20	How Can I Tell Her ....Lobo
▸ 1971	#1	How Can You Mend A Broken Heart ....Bee Gees
1967	#31	How Do You Catch A Girl................................ ....Sam The Sham & The Pharaohs

421

424

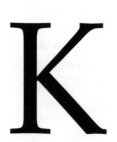
K

428

▶ 1961 #26	Lover's Island	Blue Jays
▶ 1959 #10	Lover's Question	Clyde McPhatter
▶ 1969 #38	Lover's Question	Otis Redding
▶ 1962 #34	Lovers By Night, Strangers By Day	Fleetwoods
▶ 1962 #5	Lovers Who Wander	Dion
▶ 1973 #1	Loves Me Like A Rock	Paul Simon
1965 #36	Lovin' Place	Gale Garnett
▶ 1969 #35	Lovin' Things	Grass Roots
1973 #36	Loving Arms	Dobie Gray
▶ 1971 #33	Loving Her Was Easier (Than Anything I'll Ever Do Again)	Kris Kristofferson
▶ 1957 #21	Loving You	Elvis Presley
▶ 1972 #31	Loving You Just Crossed My Mind	Sam Neely
▶ 1971 #25	Lowdown	Chicago
▶ 1957 #22	Lucille	Little Richard
1960 #32	Lucky Devil	Carl Dobkins Jr.
1959 #27	Lucky Ladybug	Billy & Lillie
▶ 1957 #26	Lucky Lips	Ruth Brown
▶ 1970 #17	Lucretia Mac Evil	Blood, Sweat & Tears
1961 #40	Lullaby Of Love	Frank Gari

M

▶ 1959 #17	M.T.A.	Kingston Trio
▶ 1970 #6	Ma Belle Amie	Tee Set
1968 #2	Mac Arthur Park	Richard Harris
▶ 1971 #36	Mac Arthur Park (Part 2)	Four Tops
▶ 1959 #1	Mack The Knife	Bobby Darin
1956 #7	Mack The Knife	Dick Hyman Trio
▶ 1960 #31	Mack The Knife	Ella Fitzgerald
1960 #14	Madison, The	Al Brown's Tunetoppers
▶ 1960 #25	Madison Time (Part 1)	Ray Bryant Combo
▶ 1971 #1	Maggie May	Rod Stewart
▶ 1968 #10	Magic Bus	Who
▶ 1968 #2	Magic Carpet Ride	Steppenwolf
▶ 1958 #21	Magic Moments	Perry Como
▶ 1966 #20	Magic Town	Vogues
▶ 1961 #24	Magnificent Seven	Al Caiola
1960 #3	Main Theme From Exodus	Mantovani & His Orchestra
1969 #18	Make Believe	Wind
▶ 1962 #24	Make It Easy On Yourself	Jerry Butler
▶ 1965 #23	Make It Easy On Yourself	Walker Brothers
▶ 1970 #25	Make It Easy On Yourself	Dionne Warwick
▶ 1971 #20	Make It Funky (Part 1)	James Brown
▶ 1970 #1	Make It With You	Bread
▶ 1958 #31	Make Me A Miracle	Jimmie Rodgers
▶ 1970 #11	Make Me Smile	Chicago
▶ 1972 #22	Make Me The Woman That You Go Home To	Gladys Knight & The Pips
▶ 1965 #19	Make Me Your Baby	Barbara Lewis
▶ 1967 #20	Make Me Yours	Bettye Swann
1963 #23	Make The World Go Away	Timi Yuro
▶ 1966 #12	Make The World Go Away	Eddy Arnold
▶ 1969 #25	Make Your Own Kind Of Music	Mama Cass
▶ 1955 #7	Make Yourself Comfortable	Sarah Vaughan
▶ 1959 #17	Makin' Love	Floyd Robinson
▶ 1965 #39	Makin' Whoopee	Ray Charles
▶ 1967 #22	Making Every Minute Count	Spanky & Our Gang
▶ 1960 #7	Mama	Connie Francis
▶ 1966 #15	Mama	B.J. Thomas
▶ 1963 #14	Mama Didn't Lie	Jan Bradley
▶ 1956 #14	Mama From The Train	Patti Page
▶ 1957 #9	Mama Look At Bubu	Harry Belafonte
▶ 1961 #4	Mama Said	Shirelles
1962 #31	Mama Sang A Song	Stan Kenton
1962 #31	Mama Sang A Song	Walter Brennan
▶ 1962 #31	Mama Sang A Song	Bill Anderson
1956 #31	Mama, Teach Me To Dance	Eydie Gorme
▶ 1970 #1	Mama Told Me (Not To Come)	Three Dog Night
▶ 1971 #1	Mama's Pearl	Jackson Five
▶ 1966 #17	Mame	Herb Alpert & The Tijuana Brass
1973 #21	Mammy Blue	Stories
1972 #40	Man Sized Job	Denise La Salle
▶ 1962 #8	(Man Who Shot) Liberty Valance	Gene Pitney
▶ 1968 #18	Man Without Love	Engelbert Humperdinck
1957 #23	Mangos	Rosemary Clooney
1959 #14	Manhattan Spiritual	Reg Owen & His Orchestra
▶ 1960 #9	Many Tears Ago	Connie Francis
1958 #22	March From The River Kwai And Colonel Bogey	Art Mooney
▶ 1958 #15	March From The River Kwai And Colonel Bogey	Mitch Miller
1958 #15	March From The River Kwai And Colonel Bogey	Edmundo Ros
▶ 1959 #32	Margie	Fats Domino
1962 #40	Maria	Roger Williams
▶ 1963 #7	Maria Elena	Los Indios Tabajaras
1957 #2	Marianne	Hilltoppers
▶ 1957 #2	Marianne	Terry Gilkyson & The Easy Riders
▶ 1971 #31	Marianne	Stephen Stills
▶ 1965 #16	Marie	Bachelors
▶ 1961 #21	(Marie's The Name) His Latest Flame	Elvis Presley
1959 #12	Marina	Rocco Granata
1959 #12	Marina	Willy Alberti
▶ 1963 #35	Marlena	Four Seasons
▶ 1969 #19	Marrakesh Express	Crosby, Stills & Nash
▶ 1963 #13	Martian Hop	Ran-Dells
1962 #39	Mary Ann Regrets	Burl Ives
▶ 1967 #27	Mary In The Morning	Al Martino
▶ 1959 #24	Mary Lou	Ronnie Hawkins & The Hawks
▶ 1957 #25	Mary's Boy Child	Harry Belafonte
1962 #1	Mashed Potato Time	Dee Dee Sharp
1968 #10	Master Jack	Four Jacks And A Jill
1973 #36	Master Of Eyes (The Deepness Of Your Eyes)	Aretha Franklin
▶ 1973 #9	Masterpiece	Temptations
▶ 1964 #21	Matador, The	Major Lance
▶ 1964 #17	Matchbox	Beatles

► 1969	#35	May I ....Bill Deal & The Rhondels
► 1965	#28	May The Bird Of Paradise Fly Up Your Nose ....Little Jimmy Dickens
► 1959	#21	May You Always ....McGuire Sisters
► 1958	#19	Maybe...Chantels
► 1970	#24	Maybe.......................................Three Degrees
► 1958	#11	Maybe Baby ....Buddy Holly
► 1964	#10	Maybe I Know ....Lesley Gore
► 1968	#38	Maybe Just Today ....Bobby Vee
► 1971	#16	Maybe Tomorrow ....Jackson Five
► 1955	#5	Maybellene ....Chuck Berry
► 1964	#11	Maybelline ....Johnny Rivers
► 1971	#1	Me And Bobby Mc Gee..................Janis Joplin
► 1972	#7	Me And Julio Down By The Schoolyard ....Paul Simon
► 1972	#1	Me And Mrs. Jones..........................Billy Paul
► 1971	#27	Me And My Arrow ....Nilsson
► 1971	#8	Me And You And A Dog Named Boo....... ....Lobo
► 1963	#7	Mean Woman Blues...................Roy Orbison
► 1963	#13	Mecca...Gene Pitney
1969	#21	Medicine Man (Part 1)......Buchanan Brothers
► 1966	#3	Mellow Yellow ....Donovan
► 1957	#7	Melodie D'Amour ....Ames Brothers
1955	#1	Melody Of Love ....David Carroll
1955	#1	Melody Of Love ....Four Aces
► 1955	#1	Melody Of Love ....Billy Vaughn
► 1969	#24	Memories.....................................Elvis Presley
► 1956	#1	Memories Are Made Of This.......Dean Martin
► 1963	#5	Memphis ....Lonnie Mack
► 1964	#2	Memphis ....Johnny Rivers
► 1967	#39	Memphis Soul Stew...................King Curtis
1968	#26	Men Are Gettin' Scarce.........................Joe Tex
1966	#7	Men In My Little Girl's Life.......Mike Douglas
► 1969	#14	Mendocino ....Sir Douglas Quintet
► 1969	#26	Mercy.......................................Ohio Express
► 1964	#26	Mercy, Mercy ....Don Covay & The Goodtimers
► 1971	#4	Mercy Mercy Me (The Ecology) ....Marvin Gaye
► 1967	#18	Mercy, Mercy, Mercy.....Cannonball Adderly
► 1967	#5	Mercy, Mercy, Mercy ....Buckinghams
1973	#39	Message, The ....Cymande
► 1966	#9	Message To Michael...........Dionne Warwick
1958	#26	Mexican Hat Rock ....Applejacks
1961	#6	Mexico ....Bob Moore
► 1961	#1	Michael.................................Highwaymen
1966	#18	Michelle ....David & Jonathan
► 1963	#9	Mickey's Monkey ....Miracles
1969	#38	Midnight ....Classics IV
► 1968	#5	Midnight Confessions................Grass Roots
► 1970	#10	Midnight Cowboy ....Ferrante & Teicher
1959	#32	Midnight Flyer.........................Nat King Cole
1962	#2	Midnight In Moskow ....Kenny Ball
► 1964	#10	Midnight Mary ....Joey Powers
► 1972	#31	Midnight Rider ....Joe Cocker
► 1965	#37	Midnight Special ....Johnny Rivers
► 1959	#35	Midnight Stroll...................................Revels
► 1973	#1	Midnight Train To Georgia ....Gladys Knight & The Pips
1960	#16	Midnite Special.........................Paul Evans
► 1971	#39	Mighty Clouds Of Joy ................B.J. Thomas
1970	#30	Mighty Joe................................Shocking Blue
1968	#4	Mighty Quinn (Quinn The Eskimo)............. ....Manfred Mann
1960	#6	Million To One ....Jimmy Charles
► 1973	#28	Million To One..........................Donny Osmond
1964	#39	Milord...Bobby Darin
► 1969	#19	Mind, Body And Soul..........Flaming Ember
► 1973	#10	Mind Games...............................John Lennon
1969	#34	Minotaur, The ....Dick Hyman & His Electric Eclectics
► 1969	#38	Minute Of Your Time ....Tom Jones
1956	#24	Miracle Of Love....................Eileen Rodgers
1956	#37	Miracle Of Love......................Ginny Gibson
► 1967	#10	Mirage ....Tommy James & The Shondells
1973	#14	Misdemeanor ....Foster Sylvers
1963	#40	Misery ....Dynamics
1970	#31	Miss America ....Mark Lindsay
1961	#27	Missing You...............................Ray Peterson
1960	#13	Mission Bell ....Donnie Brooks
1968	#39	Mission Impossible...................Lalo Schifrin
► 1970	#37	Mississippi...............................John Phillips
► 1970	#24	Mississippi Queen ....Mountain
1972	#40	Mister Can't You See ....Buffy Sainte-Marie
1963	#21	Misty ....Lloyd Price
1966	#32	Misty ....Richard "Groove" Holmes
► 1959	#14	Misty ....Johnny Mathis
1964	#28	Mixed-Up, Shook-Up, Girl........................... ....Patty & The Emblems
► 1963	#7	Mockingbird ....Inez Foxx
► 1961	#36	Model Girl...........................Johnny Maestro
1965	#18	Mohair Sam ....Charlie Rich
► 1955	#2	Moments To Remember ....Four Lads
► 1959	#30	Mona Lisa ....Carl Mann
► 1959	#30	Mona Lisa ....Conway Twitty
► 1966	#1	Monday Monday ....Mama's & Papa's
► 1964	#17	Money...Kingsmen
► 1966	#32	Money (That's What I Want) (Part 1) ....Jr. Walker & The All Stars
► 1960	#14	Money (That's What I Want)......................... ....Barrett Strong
► 1968	#40	Money...............................Lovin' Spoonful
► 1973	#10	Money...Pink Floyd
► 1963	#7	Monkey Time.............................Major Lance
► 1970	#23	Monster ....Steppenwolf
► 1962	#1	Monster Mash ....Bobby "Boris" Pickett
► 1962	#29	Monster's Holiday ......Bobby "Boris" Pickett
► 1970	#6	Montego Bay ....Bobby Bloom
► 1968	#10	Monterey ....Animals
► 1968	#3	Mony Mony ....Tommy James & The Shondells
► 1961	#2	Moody River ....Pat Boone
► 1969	#22	Moody Woman ....Jerry Butler
► 1961	#5	Moon River ....Henry Mancini
► 1961	#5	Moon River ....Jerry Butler
► 1971	#26	Moon Shadow ....Cat Stevens
1958	#24	Moon Talk.....................................Perry Como
1970	#40	Moon Walk (Part 1) ....Joe Simon
1956	#1	Moonglow And Theme From "Picnic" ....George Cates & His Orchestra
► 1956	#1	Moonglow And Theme From "Picnic" ....Morris Stoloff
1969	#23	Moonlight ....Vik Venus
► 1957	#6	Moonlight Gambler..................Frankie Laine
1956	#33	Moonlight Love ....Perry Como
1956	#9	More ....Perry Como
► 1963	#18	More..Vic Dana
► 1963	#8	More..Kai Winding
► 1966	#19	More I See You ....Chris Montez
► 1967	#19	More Love ....Miracles
► 1961	#18	More Money For You And Me.......Four Preps
► 1969	#7	More Today Than Yesterday....................... ....Spiral Starecase

431

433

P

435

S

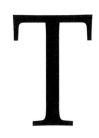

▸ 1972	#30	Talking Loud And Saying Nothing (Part 1) ....James Brown	
1959	#18	Tall Paul ....Annette	
▸ 1959	#6	Tallahassee Lassie ....Freddy Cannon	
1957	#10	Tammy ....Richard Hayman	
▸ 1957	#1	Tammy ....Debbie Reynolds	
▸ 1957	#10	Tammy ....Ames Brothers	
▸ 1971	#39	Tarkio Road ....Brewer & Shipley	
▸ 1965	#1	Taste Of Honey....................................	
		.................Herb Alpert & The Tijuana Brass	
1972	#13	Taurus	
		....Dennis Coffey & The Detroit Guitar Band	
▸ 1972	#20	Taxi..............................Harry Chapin	
1958	#2	Tea For Two Cha Cha Cha	
		...........................Tommy Dorsey Orchestra	
1955	#2	Teach Me Tonight ....De Castro Sisters	
1962	#31	Teach Me Tonight.................George Maharis	
▸ 1970	#16	Teach Your Children	
		.......................Crosby, Stills, Nash & Young	
▸ 1958	#20	Teacher, Teacher ....Johnny Mathis	
▸ 1958	#36	Teacher's Pet ....Doris Day	
▸ 1961	#24	Tear, A ....Gene McDaniels	
1960	#22	Tear Drop.............................Santo & Johnny	
▸ 1969	#37	Tear Drop City ....Monkees	
▸ 1957	#25	Tear Drops.........Lee Andrews & The Hearts	
▸ 1956	#6	Tear Fell...............................Teresa Brewer	
▸ 1961	#40	Tear Of The Year ....Jackie Wilson	
1957	#40	Teardrops In My Heart...........Teresa Brewer	
▸ 1964	#18	Tears And Roses ....Al Martino	
▸ 1970	#1	Tears Of A Clown ....Miracles	
▸ 1958	#7	Tears On My Pillow	
		.................Little Anthony & The Imperials	
1959	#33	Teasin'..................................Pyramids	
▸ 1960	#31	Teddy ....Connie Francis	
1973	#32	Teddy Bear Song.............Barbara Fairchild	
1957	#2	Teen-Age Crush.....................Tommy Sands	
▸ 1962	#9	Teen Age Idol ....Rick Nelson	
1956	#6	Teen Age Prayer ....Gale Storm	
1956	#6	Teen Age Prayer ....Gloria Mann	
▸ 1960	#1	Teen Angel...........................Mark Dinning	
1959	#4	Teen Beat...........................Sandy Nelson	
1964	#37	Teen Beat '65 ....Sandy Nelson	
1960	#40	Teenage Sonata ....Sam Cooke	
▸ 1959	#6	Teenager In Love ....Dion & The Belmonts	
▸ 1957	#8	Teenager's Romance ....Rick Nelson	
▸ 1969	#33	Tell All The People..............................Doors	
▸ 1965	#6	Tell Her No.............................Zombies	
▸ 1963	#5	Tell Him ....Exciters	
1959	#11	Tell Him No.............................Travis & Bob	
▸ 1970	#17	Tell It All Brother	
		.................Kenny Rogers & The First Edition	
▸ 1967	#3	Tell It Like It Is ....Aaron Neville	
▸ 1964	#31	Tell It On The Mountain	
		.................................Peter, Paul & Mary	
▸ 1967	#12	Tell It To The Rain ....Four Seasons	
▸ 1960	#5	Tell Laura I Love Her ....Ray Peterson	
▸ 1968	#27	Tell Mama ....Etta James	
1962	#23	Tell Me ....Dick & Deedee	
1967	#31	Tell Me To My Face.........................Keith	
▸ 1961	#22	Tell Me Why...........................Belmonts	
▸ 1964	#11	Tell Me Why...........................Bobby Vinton	
▸ 1966	#20	Tell Me Why ....Elvis Presley	
▸ 1964	#27	Tell Me (You're Coming Back)	
		.................................Rolling Stones	
▸ 1962	#1	Telstar...............................Tornadoes	
▸ 1961	#20	Temptation...........................Everly Brothers	
▸ 1971	#16	Temptation Eyes ....Grass Roots	

▸ 1958	#39	Ten Commandments Of Love ....Moonglows	
▸ 1960	#27	Tender Love And Care (T.L.C.)	
		.................................Jimmie Rodgers	
1965	#34	10 Little Bottles.........................Johnny Bond	
1970	#14	Tennessee Birdwalk	
		.................Jack Blanchard & Misty Morgan	
1964	#38	Tennessee Waltz.........................Sam Cooke	
▸ 1958	#1	Tequila ....Champs	
▸ 1969	#36	Testify (I Wonna) ....Johnnie Taylor	
▸ 1967	#13	Thank The Lord For The Night Time	
		.................................Neil Diamond	
▸ 1970	#1	Thank You (Falettinme Be Mice Elf Agin)	
		.................Sly & The Family Stone	
▸ 1964	#38	Thank You Girl ....Beatles	
▸ 1959	#10	Thank You Pretty Baby...........Brook Benton	
▸ 1965	#34	Thanks A Lot ....Brenda Lee	
1968	#40	That Kind Of Woman	
		.................Merilee Rush & The Turnabouts	
▸ 1973	#6	That Lady (Part 1)..................Isley Brothers	
▸ 1964	#20	That Lucky Old Sun ....Ray Charles	
1961	#21	That Old Black Magic...............Bobby Rydell	
▸ 1958	#13	That Old Black Magic	
		.................Louis Prima & Keely Smith	
1970	#40	That Same Old Feeling.........Pickettywitch	
1962	#39	That Stranger Used To Be My Girl	
		.................................Trade Martin	
▸ 1963	#15	That Sunday, That Summer	
		.................................Nat King Cole	
▸ 1957	#3	That'll Be The Day ....Buddy Holly	
1955	#3	That's All I Want From You	
		.................................Jaye P. Morgan	
1956	#17	That's All There Is To That ....Nat King Cole	
▸ 1960	#11	That's All You Gotta Do ....Brenda Lee	
1961	#28	That's It-I Quit-I'm Movin' On ...Sam Cooke	
▸ 1966	#5	That's Life ....Frank Sinatra	
▸ 1962	#15	That's Old Fashioned (That's The Way Love Should Be) ....Everly Brothers	
▸ 1964	#14	That's The Way Boys Are ....Lesley Gore	
▸ 1972	#22	That's The Way I Feel About Cha ....Bobby Womack	
▸ 1971	#9	That's The Way I've Always Heard It Should Be ....Carly Simon	
1963	#30	That's The Way Love Is...........Bobby Bland	
▸ 1969	#10	That's The Way Love Is.............Marvin Gaye	
▸ 1961	#39	That's What Girls Are Made For .....Spinners	
▸ 1964	#37	That's What Love Is Made Of...........Miracles	
1970	#20	That's Where I Went Wrong ....Poppy Family	
▸ 1959	#13	That's Why (I Love You So)...Jackie Wilson	
▸ 1961	#38	Them That Got ....Ray Charles	
▸ 1960	#1	Theme From A Summer Place ....Percy Faith & His Orchestra	
▸ 1965	#17	Theme From A Summer Place ....Lettermen	
1962	#32	Theme From Ben Casey ....Valjean	
▸ 1973	#14	Theme From Cleopatra Jones ....Joe Simon	
▸ 1961	#37	Theme From Dixie ....Duane Eddy	
1962	#13	Theme From Dr. Kildare (Three Stars Will Shine Tonight) ....Richard Chamberlain	
▸ 1971	#10	Theme From Love Story ......Andy Williams	
1971	#36	Theme From Love Story ....Francis Lai & His Orchestra	
▸ 1971	#11	Theme From Love Story........Henry Mancini	
1961	#28	Theme From My Three Sons ....Lawrence Welk	
▸ 1971	#1	Theme From Shaft..................Isaac Hayes	

446

451